The Guns of Independence

The Siege of Yorktown, 1781

Also by Jerome A. Greene

Yellowstone Command: Colonel Nelson A. Miles
and the Great Sioux War, 1876-1877 (Lincoln, 1991)

Battles and Skirmishes of the Great Sioux War,
1876-1877: The Military View (Norman, 1993)

Nez Perce Summer, 1877: The U.S. Army and
the Nee-Me-Poo Crisis (Helena, 2000)

Morning Star Dawn: The Powder River Expedition
and the Northern Cheyennes, 1876 (Norman, 2003)

Washita: The U.S. Army and the
Southern Cheyennes, 1867-1869 (Norman, 2004)

Finding Sand Creek: History, Archeology,
and the 1864 Massacre Site (Norman, 2004)

Jerome A. Greene

The Guns of Independence

The Siege of Yorktown, 1781

Savas Beatie
New York

SPELLMOUNT
Staplehurst, UK

Cataloging-in-Publication Data is available from the Library of Congress.

Published in the United Sates by Savas Beatie in 2005
First edition, first printing
ISBN 1-932714-05-7

SB

Savas Beatie LLC
521 Fifth Avenue, Suite 3400
New York, NY 10175
Phone: 610-853-9131
sales@savasbeatie.com
www.savasbeatie.com

―――――――――――――

British Library Cataloguing in Publication Data:
A catalogue record for this book is available
from the British Library

Also published in the UK in 2005
ISBN 1-86227-312-X

Spellmount Limited
The Village Centre
Staplehurst
Kent TN12 0BJ

Tel: 01580 893730
Fax: 01580 893731
E-mail: enquiries@spellmount.com
Website: www.spellmount.com

Printed in the United States of America.

To the memory of Thor Borressen

French artist Louis Eugene Lami's celebrated painting of
the attack on Redoubt 10, October 14, 1781.

Contents

Contents (continued)

Contents (continued)

Maps and Photographs

Maps and photographs are located throughout
for the convenience of the reader. A modern photographic
gallery can be found in Appendix 1.

Preface

*T*he Siege of Yorktown in 1781 by the combined armies of George Washington and Comte de Rochambeau resulted in the surrender of Lord Cornwallis and his British army. It was the pivotal event in American history, for its successful conclusion virtually assured the formulation and perpetuation of American democratic institutions from which all subsequent events followed. This study, which I believe to be the first modern in-depth treatment of this remarkable siege, affords a close look at the means by which the outcome was effected through the collaboration of American forces with those of France, from which nation the response to American entreaties for help, while expedient in the realm of international politics, proved nonetheless opportune and entirely appropriate. Without the aid of Rochambeau and his cadre of officers and 6,000 French soldiers who arrived in America in July of 1780, and the timely operations of the fleet of Admiral de Grasse, the American experiment would likely have failed, its leaders captured and hanged, and British government reasserted.

The core of the book you are now reading was originally completed to assist interpretation and management at Colonial National Historical Park, Virginia, during the observance of the American Bicentennial, 1975-83. A limited number of copies were spiral bound for private use under the title *The Allies at Yorktown: A Bicentennial History of the Siege of 1781*. In many ways it represents a synthesis of the voluminous body of materials, published and unpublished, bearing on the Yorktown Campaign. Throughout, I have attempted to produce a comprehensive account of this singular event, emphasizing the participation of the French and American forces from the time of their initial investment of Cornwallis's command, through the construction and occupation of their defenses during the course of the siege, to the British surrender and its aftermath. Although the study was originally considered an "in-house" publication for the use of National Park Service personnel alone, it has been recognized and studied by a small cadre of historians who have been aware of it since its completion.

In 2003, I was contacted by Theodore Savas of Savas Beatie LLC, who asked to see a copy of the study. Ted liked what he read and encouraged me to reformat and update the material for trade publication, long believing there was a glaring gap in literature surrounding the historic events at Yorktown. With the support of colleagues at Colonial National Historical Park, I incorporated his suggestions into this revised edition of the Bicentennial work, thus making it available for the first time to the general public. I must thank Ted and the staff at Savas Beatie LLC for their commitment and industry in producing this book. Royalties from sales will go to support the programs of Colonial National Historical Park.

There are also many other people and institutions I must thank. Almost certainly I have overlooked someone, and I apologize if I have done so.

Dr. Robert Selig graciously agreed to provide a Foreword and to read through a draft of the manuscript. Moreover, his suggestions helped eliminate many embarassing errors (especially having to do with foreign names and ranks). Dr. Selig has produced a fine body of work on the American Revolution and many other topics, and his help is deeply appreciated.

I wish to also thank the following people who assisted in the completion of the initial study in 1974-75. In the Historic Preservation Division, National Park Service, Denver Service Center, Colorado, the late Erwin N. Thompson, Historian (I have relied upon Thompson's own study of the British defenses at Yorktown to help revise my work); John F. Luzader, Chief, Division of Historic Preservation; James D. Mote, Historian; Linda W. Greene, Editor; Robert H. Todd, Cartographer; and typists Helen C. Athearn and Sharon Spera. At Colonial National Historical Park, I thank James R. Sullivan, Superintendent; James N.

Haskett, Park Historian; James Gott, Historian; and Laura J. Feller, Park Technician. At the Department of Anthropology, College of William and Mary, Williamsburg, Virginia, I thank Norman F. Barka, Arthur W. Barnes, and Edward Ayres. And at the Colonial Williamsburg Foundation, I acknowledge the assistance of Edward M. Riley, Director, and Archivists Nancy Merz and Linda Rowe.

This study required a visit to the William L. Clements Library at the University of Michigan. I appreciate the assistance there of Director Howard H. Peckham and his staff, in particular John Dann, Curator of Manuscripts; Douglas W. Marshall, Curator of Maps; and Arlene Kleeb, Assistant Manuscript Curator. I must also acknowledge the help of Gertrude A. Fisher, Massachusetts Historical Society; John L. Lochhead, The Mariners Museum, Newport News, Virginia; Edward B. Russell and John M. Dervan, U.S. Army Engineers Museum, Fort Belvoir, Virginia; John S. Aubrey, The Newberry Library, Chicago; Joseph P. Tustin, Tuckerton, New Jersey; Mary A. Thompson, and Paul Mellon Collection, Upperville, Virginia.

I must also thank the staffs of the following repositories: Princeton University Library, Princeton, New Jersey; John Carter Brown Library, Providence, Rhode Island; Library of Virginia, Richmond; Maryland Historical Society, Baltimore; Map Collection, Library of Congress, Washington, D.C.; Cartographic Archives Division, National Archives, Washington, D.C.; The New-York Historical Society, New York City; New York Public Library, New York City; The Pierpont Morgan Library, New York City; Fordham University Library, Bronx, New York; Morristown National Historical Park Library, Morristown, New Jersey; Historical Society of Pennsylvania, Philadelphia; University of Colorado Libraries, Boulder; the Denver Public Library; and Andrea Ashby, Independence National Historical Park, Philadelphia.

I am deeply indebted to the present management and staff at Colonial National Historical Park, Yorktown, Virginia. Without their cooperation, this new edition for public circulation would not have been possible: Karen G. Rehm, Chief Historian; Diane K. Depew, Supervisory Park Ranger; Jane M. Sundberg, Cultural Resource Management Specialist; David F. Riggs, Museum Curator, who answered email after email and oversaw a sea of loose ends; Michael D. Litterst, Public Affairs Officer; and Park Rangers Christopher S. Bryce, who snapped many of the wonderful photos inside this book while dodging rain storms and lawn mowers, and Matthew G. Fraas, who always answered questions in a timely fashion. I wish to also thank L. Clifford Soubier, Charles Town, West Virginia, for many favors tied to this work, and Gregory J. W. Urwin, Department of History, Temple University, for his loan of materials.

I also wish to thank both Ted Savas and Michael Varhola for their assistance with the revised text; Lee Merideth for his indexing talents; Leslie Andrich for her help in obtaining an image of Lauzun, and Karen Sabin for copyediting the final draft.

Finally, I would like to acknowledge the service rendered this study by the late Thor Borressen, who for many years during the 1930s and 1940s served as historian and technical aide at Colonial National Historical Park, and whose interest and productivity in studying the Siege of Yorktown has benefited my own work. This book is dedicated to Borressen's memory.

Jerome A. Greene
Arvada, Colorado

Foreword

*O*n October 19, 1781, he had handed over his sword and the garrison at Yorktown to General Benjamin Lincoln. The following day, a despondent General Charles O'Hara informed Augustus Henry Fitzroy, third Duke of Grafton and holder of the Lord Privy Seal in the administration of Lord North, of the surrender of Lord Cornwallis and his army:

> The Public account will inform you of the surrender of the Posts of York and Gloucester; with their Garrisons, to the combined Forces of France and America. Our Ministers will I hope be now persuaded that America is irretrievably lost, an event I have repeatedly told your Grace would certainly happen. The French talk of attacking Charles Town, altho' they must be too well acquainted with this Country to conceive any further Conquests necessary—America is theirs—.

Not only was America now French, for that is what O'Hara's "theirs" implies, but British fortunes appeared bleak all over the Western hemisphere:

> I think it very likely that Messr. Rochambeau, with the French Garrison of Rhode Island that were employ'd in the reduction of this Place, will sail with Messr. D'Grass to the West Indies, and take

our few remaining Windward and Leeward West India Island
Possessions; Or possibly to assist Spain in the Reduction of Jamaica.

For Charles O'Hara, the illegitimate son of James O'Hara, second
Lord Tyrawley, the end of British power in the New World was close at
hand. With the army "dispersed with very few Officers all over the
Continent," and the Royal Navy about to "sink into the most contemptible
State," the remaining British possessions were about to fall into French
and Spanish hands like dominoes. The conquests of 75 years of successful
warfare around the globe would soon be lost. Gone would be the spoils of
Queen Anne's War (also known as the War of the Spanish Succession)
brought about by the Peace of Utrecht of 1715; the gains of the War of the
Austrian Succession (known as King George's War in the colonies) that
the Peace of Aachen had confirmed in 1748; and the vast territorial
acquisitions of the triumphal Seven Years' War (the French and Indian
War) concluded by the Peace of Paris in 1763.

General George Washington would have been surprised at the lament
in O'Hara's missive. As far as Washington was concerned, Cornwallis's
surrender was merely "an interesting event that may be productive of
much good if properly improved." Few, if any, of the American and
French soldiers present at Yorktown, from the Commander in Chief to the
lowliest private, considered the war to be won outright with the surrender
of Cornwallis. The troops taken prisoner at Yorktown constituted only
about one-quarter of the British land forces operating on the American
mainland. Perhaps more important to the Allied cause was the impending
departure of the fleets of de Grasse and Barras. Their absence would erase
the temporary naval superiority that had made the victory at Yorktown
possible. Before the Royal Navy could again control North American
waters, Washington hoped to make the Yorktown victory "productive"
with an attack on Charleston or Savannah, or even New York, the biggest
prize of them all. Although he urged Admiral de Grasse and the comte de
Rochambeau to adopt his plan, de Grasse—who had already stayed longer
in American waters than he had originally planned—would have none of
it. In early November 1781, the French fleet sailed out of Chesapeake Bay,
never to return.

Despite O'Hara's dire predictions, all was not lost. The ministry of
Lord North in London realized the colonies were beyond retrieving and
would be independent. On the North American mainland, the tides of war

could not be changed. But North and his royal master King George III were determined to stem the tide of war in the West Indies, at Gibraltar, in Africa, in India, and wherever else the will of Parliament was still law. Despite the devastating loss at Yorktown, Britain still had the means with which to wage a powerful global defense: her navy. Within this global context, the naval Battle of the Capes of September 5, 1781—which had sealed Cornwallis's fate—turned out to be a blessing in disguise. If Admiral Graves had been able to slip or fight his way into the Chesapeake Bay with his 19 ships of the line, he would also have been caught in the trap that had netted Cornwallis. Once Admiral de Barras had joined his forces to those of de Grasse, the French fleet numbered more than 30 ships of the line—almost twice the force under Graves' command. But the British Navy emerged from the siege of Yorktown intact, allowing Admiral Sir George Bridges Rodney to score a decisive victory over de Grasse in the Battle of the Saintes on April 12, 1782.

What had begun as a rebellion—a family quarrel of sorts—at Lexington and Concord in 1775 had become a world war with the involvement of France, first clandestinely in 1776, and then openly with the signing of the treaties of Amity and Friendship and of Military Alliance in February 1778. At Yorktown in 1781, France's crucial aid had solved the family quarrel. The United States was anxious to make peace. France, as O'Hara and the British ministry rightly feared, was not quite ready to come to terms with Britain. For Louis XVI and the comte de Vergennes, his Foreign Minister, the war on the American mainland was never more than a secondary theater of operations. As far as Versailles was concerned, the war was not being fought over Britain's American colonies or for large territorial gains in the New World. The goal of the war France was waging across the globe with Britain was not the dismemberment of the British Empire, as O'Hara feared, or even the humiliation of a fellow monarch in London. Rather, it was to redress the balance of power in Europe and around the world that had been so rudely upset by Britain in 1763.

Within the global balance of power of 1781, the Caribbean islands, first and foremost Jamaica, were incomparably more valuable to the British crown than the American mainland. While France in its alliance with Spain continued to outnumber the British in the Caribbean, the Battle of the Saintes ensured that, for the time being, Jamaica would remain in King George's realm. Despite the outstanding efforts and daring seamanship of Admiral Pierre-André de Suffren de Saint-Tropez, India— the primary source of much of Britain's wealth in the nineteenth century— remained British as well. When peace finally arrived in 1783, Britain could congratulate herself for only losing those parts of her Empire that were most closely connected to her in language, culture, and traditions, and whose economy was closely intertwined with her own. Few observers shared the intuition of the Count de Aranda, Spanish Ambassador to France, about the historic world consequences of the events that had taken place in North America. Reflecting upon the Peace of Paris that gave the colonies their independence, he wrote to Louis XVI in 1783, that in America, "[a] federal republic is born a pygmy but a day will come when it will be a giant, a colossus, formidable for this country."

Since its birth at Yorktown, this "colossus" has indeed become formidable, not only for France and Spain but for the world as a whole. It is nigh impossible to overestimate the world-historical consequences of the events that took place at Yorktown in 1781. Yet, more than 120 years have passed since Henry P. Johnston's *Yorktown Campaign* was first published in 1881. Seventy years have gone by since Colonel H. L. Landers' *Virginia Campaign* rolled off the press in 1931. It has been more than four decades since Thomas Fleming's *Beat the Last Drum* (1963) and nearly that long since Burke Davis' *Campaign that Won America* (1970) were made available. The fact that all of these titles, except Landers' government-sponsored study, are still in print is ample evidence of the need for an updated study reexamining one of the most consequential sieges and victories in military history.

Coming as it does on the eve of the 225th anniversary of this momentous victory in October 2006, Jerome A. Greene's *The Guns of Independence: The Siege of Yorktown, 1781* meets that need admirably. Drawing upon decades of historical research that began almost 30 years ago with a historic resource study and historic structure report for the Colonial National Historical Park at Yorktown in 1976, Greene's study sheds new light on those crucial weeks of October 1781.

An expert at explaining the minutiae of the siege in a clear and understandable manner, Greene paints a vivid picture of the culmination of the campaign of 1781. Drawing upon the accounts of eyewitnesses and contemporaries from all sides of the battle—American, British, French, and German alike—the book is a highly readable account of the battle that, for all practical purposes, ended the Revolutionary War. Greene's wide range of primary sources is complemented by his in-depth knowledge of the secondary literature necessary to produce this outstanding work of scholarship.

But *The Guns of Independence* is much more than another (albeit highly necessary) historical account of the siege. In providing minute detail about the technicalities and procedures of a siege, the book addresses issues and answers questions nearly every other book leaves unanswered. Finally, it is also a veritable guide to the battlefield that almost begs the reader to go to Yorktown and survey the battlefield with the book in hand. Greene provides readers with the tool they need to walk in the footsteps of General Washington, of the marquis de Lafayette, the comte de Rochambeau, and of Lord Cornwallis; to stand where Colonels the marquis de Montmorency-Laval, Christian de Deux-Ponts, Elias Dayton, and Goose Van Schaick had stood; to storm Redoubts No. 9 and No. 10 with Alexander Hamilton, Jeremiah Olney, and William de Deux-Ponts; to encounter Duncan McPherson and von Seybothen; to meet Johann Ewald, Banistre Tarleton, the *duc* de Lauzun, and George Weedon; and finally, to dig trenches where Privates Joseph Plumb Martin, Georg Daniel Flohr, and thousands of other men—American, French, or British—had dug their trenches, fought, were wounded, celebrated victory, lamented defeat, or were buried more than two centuries ago. To read Greene's book is to look out over the Chesapeake Bay and imagine the veritable forest of masts that once rose from the decks of the French fleet that held Lord Cornwallis and his army captive and without which, the victory at Yorktown would not, could not, have been won.

Jerry Greene and his publisher are to be congratulated on a fine book that will be required reading for anyone interested in the siege of Yorktown and the victory that won America her independence.

Robert A. Selig, Ph.D.
Holland, MI

Chapter 1

The Campaign of the Allies

t about 3:00 p.m. on Friday, October 19, 1781, a large British army commanded by Lieutenant General Charles Cornwallis marched forth from heavily damaged works at Yorktown, Virginia, and formally surrendered to a combined French and American force under the supreme command of General George Washington. Pleading illness, the British general did not personally accompany his troops. A short distance away across the York River, a similar ceremony marked the capitulation of the British-held garrison at Gloucester Point.

The solemn pageantry of that autumn day bore significant implications. The impact of the victory of the Allied armies over Cornwallis represented the culmination of good fortune and a coordinated military-naval strategy that permitted the final tactical success. In its broader sense, Yorktown signified the ultimate accomplishment of American arms during the long and arduous revolutionary struggle, and virtually assured Great Britain's recognition of independence for her former colonies.

Victory at Yorktown revitalized American morale and afforded a striking contrast to the harrowing times experienced by Washington's army scarcely a year earlier. By mid-1780, American battlefield defeats had become common occurrences and raised serious doubts about the survival of the new nation. Grievous military setbacks in the South and Major General Benedict Arnold's treason in September 1780 had dealt a severe psychological blow to the Patriot cause.[1]

Problems organizing and maintaining an effective army had proved especially vexatious for Washington. While the timely arrival in July 1780 of almost 6,000 French regulars under General Jean Baptiste Donatien de Vimeur, comte de Rochambeau, had greatly augmented Washington's dwindling force, by late that year enlistments in the Continental Army had declined substantially. This occurred primarily because of difficulties in paying and provisioning the troops, and because of competition from the various states, which offered more lucrative inducements for enlistment in their militias. In mid-1778, Continental Army strength stood at nearly 17,000 men; just two years later, the patriots could field only some 8,000 effectives, a force supplemented by numerous provincial units.

By that time, however, a major army reorganization was underway with special consideration being given to the problems of subsistence, supply, and payment of troops. The fortunes of the American Army were decidedly on the rise when the calendar turned to 1781, despite some short-lived mutinies within the ranks and the fact that recruiting for the Continental force continued to decline during the new year's early months (the period from January to May produced only 2,574 enlistees).[2]

The strengthening American army was confronted with a shift in British strategy—particularly as it affected the Southern colonies. By 1780, inactivity in the North made a concerted British effort in the South more tenable than ever before. General Henry Clinton, the commander of the British forces in North America, had long harbored designs against the South, including Virginia.

The son of a prominent admiral whose brother was the Earl of Lincoln, Henry Clinton was born in Newfoundland, Canada, in 1738. He spent his early years in New York, where his father served as Royal Governor from 1741-1751. He returned to England as a young teen and was commissioned into the British Army. He distinguished himself in battle in Germany in 1760 during the Seven Years' War. Eventually elevated to the rank of colonel, Clinton served as an aide-de-camp to Prince Karl Wilhelm Ferdinand of Brunswick. Clinton seemed destined for prominent public service and his star was clearly in the ascendant. He was appointed groom of the bedchamber for the Duke of Gloucester (the

Sir Henry Clinton

National Park Service
Colonial National Historical Park
Yorktown Collection

King's brother) and attended the Duke of Newcastle, who saw to it that the young Clinton was elected to Parliament. Although surrounded by a royal web of relationships and obviously well liked, financial woes dogged Clinton. Unlike so many of his social class, he wed for love rather than money, taking Harriet Carter as his bride in early 1767. The marriage did nothing to improve his financial condition but did produce five children. Clinton's life changed thereafter, though not for the better. Just five years after their marriage, Harriet died. He felt her loss keenly and may have suffered a depression as a result of her passing. Barely able to function, he did not take his seat in Parliament. He retired from public life, his star nearly extinguished.

By the time the American Revolution began, Clinton was back in service and promoted to major general. In 1775, he was ordered to join the young effort in North America. When General Thomas Gage was recalled after the disastrous Bunker Hill outing, Clinton was elevated to second-in-command under Sir William Howe. His solid performance at the Battle of Long Island in 1776 eventually led to a knighthood the following year, but by this time Clinton was exhibiting disagreeable personality traits that did not endear him to his subordinates or to Howe. His quick temper and often child-like insistence on having his way alienated his fellow officers and did not instill faith in his abilities as a leader of men. As the Revolution entered its middle phase, Clinton adopted a mantle of excessive caution and obvious self-doubt that contrasted poorly with his highly visible performance during the war's early months.

As early as 1779, Clinton hoped to establish at least one base in the Chesapeake Bay from which he could command the region and also launch a drive against Pennsylvania. A British raid in the area in 1779 succeeded in temporarily arousing Loyalist sentiment, and Clinton, headquartered in New York City, hoped to capitalize on the situation. British civil and military leaders believed that by paralyzing Virginia, the colonies would be severed and more easily defeated.[3] Armed with a plan for subduing and ending the vexing rebellion, the British home government looked to Clinton's army and the superior British Navy for its successful execution.

Contrary to popular accounts, Clinton and his chief subordinate, General Cornwallis, did not hold opposing views on the question of taking Virginia. Whatever differences they may have held concerned degree and procedure. Both men realized Virginia's potential contribution to a British victory, but Clinton adhered to a conservative philosophy as the best means of reducing the state. Further, his position at New York seemed under threat of imminent attack early in 1781, and he was reluctant to divert his energies. At the same time, Clinton probably envisioned greater consequences from controlling the Chesapeake than did Cornwallis, for his initial raiding policy had been designed to control Virginia's waterways and establish a base in the Chesapeake vicinity.[4] To Cornwallis, however, such matters were fleeting and incidental. He advocated a more aggressive means of controlling Virginia, and argued that it should become the major theater for British offensive operations.[5] On the question of ultimate control over the province, Clinton and Cornwallis were in essential agreement.

Their relationship was complicated, however, because Cornwallis had managed to interest Colonial Secretary Lord George Germain in his views and had pressed for immediate military attention in the South. Germain's intrusion into the matter offended Clinton, although his own negativism and lack of imaginative policy doubtless figured into London's growing alignment with Cornwallis's aggressive views. The issue drove a wedge between the two men which, compounded by geographical separation and communication problems, practically ensured misunderstandings and a breakdown in cooperation.[6] Despite the gulf between them, however, Clinton had complete confidence in his junior officer's military judgment. This fact, coupled with Clinton's own passivity and preoccupation with defensive arrangements, influenced the final shift of British strategy from the Northern colonies to those in the South.[7]

That Clinton did not share Cornwallis's immediate enthusiasm for the control of Virginia is certain. By 1781, his own interest for prosecuting the war in the South lay in recruiting to the King's cause the sizable Loyalist population in the Carolinas, Maryland, Delaware, and southeastern Pennsylvania.[8] Clinton's Southern strategy was only partially successful. After a month-long siege by Clinton and Cornwallis, Charleston, South Carolina, succumbed to the British on May 12, 1780. In June, Clinton proclaimed the state once again under British control, a premature exclamation at best. Clinton's subsequent strategy was to secure South Carolina while rallying the Loyalists of that province in order to further solidify his gains.[9]

Left largely to his own designs after Clinton departed for New York, Cornwallis proposed to invade North Carolina and make that state a protective barrier for the conquered provinces below it. Clinton, albeit reluctantly, agreed to this course. He also agreed to launch a campaign in the Chesapeake to distract American forces in Virginia and keep them from joining a move to reconquer the southernmost colonies.[10]

Initially, the British plan appeared a success. On August 16, 1780, Cornwallis defeated the Americans under Major General Horatio Gates in one of the most decisive routs of the war at Camden, South Carolina. The victory scattered and demoralized the enemy. As far as the British were concerned, the stunning victory spelled an end to major conflict in the Deep South. Cornwallis was now free to turn his attention northward.

Such a view proved illusory. British hopes for an easy theater victory were shattered with the sudden American success at Kings Mountain, South Carolina, on October 7, 1780. The battle helped rejuvenate American morale and the determination to fight on. Shortly thereafter, Major General Nathanael Greene replaced the defeated Gates as the American commander in the South. Greene revitalized the army and improved its training, supply situation, and morale. Within a short time, he restored the army to fighting condition. Greene's fresh army stood directly in the path of British success in the South. In a move that surprised many, the Americans went on the offensive and launched a series of harassing attacks against Cornwallis's army. Anticipating the wane of Tory support in the wake of the debacle at Kings Mountain, Cornwallis was left to fend for himself.[11] Harassed by state militia, he prudently retreated to Winnsboro, South Carolina, to await reinforcements from Clinton.

In order to assist his subordinate, Clinton diverted 2,500 men scheduled to establish a base in Virginia to support Cornwallis. With these reinforcements, Cornwallis moved out again to invade North Carolina and confront Greene.[12] To impede the Americans, Cornwallis divided his command into three wings. One was sent to Camden to temporarily divert Greene's attention. Another was dispatched under his cavalry corps commander, Lieutenant Colonel Banastre Tarleton, to seek out Brigadier General Daniel Morgan's army in the Carolina back country. Cornwallis led the balance of his command north to engage and capture any of Morgan's troops who managed to escape Tarleton.[13]

On January 17, 1781, Tarleton's British Legion cornered Morgan at Cowpens, west of Kings Mountain near the North Carolina border. A shrewd tactician and capable commander, Morgan deployed his men skillfully in an effort to use the enemy's aggressive tactics to his own advantage. He sucked his opponent into a trap and then took the initiative, driving Tarleton's soldiers back in utter confusion. The British lost more than 80% of their effective force (nearly 950 men from all causes), while Morgan suffered a scant 72 casualties. The dramatic American victory instilled more confidence among the troops that they could fight pitched battles against the British.

After Cowpens, Morgan made a determined effort to rejoin Greene, who Cornwallis was following northward into North Carolina. Greene, too, was using Cornwallis's aggressive nature against him, wearing down his army as it chased after him deep into North Carolina. Angered by his inability to come to grips with the pesky general, Cornwallis burned his extra provisions and equipment to allow his soldiers to march faster and lighter in their pursuit of the Americans. The British general dogged Greene for days all the way to the Dan River, where Greene tricked Cornwallis and crossed safely into Virginia. By now, Cornwallis's army was hungry, tired, and exposed to the elements. He had driven the Americans out of the state, but Cornwallis had gained little in the effort except the weakening of his own army.

With Greene out of reach, Cornwallis turned south toward Hillsboro. Greene, however, was not about to let him go peacefully. With his militia enlistments about to expire, and reinforced with some 600 Continental Regulars, Greene crossed back into North Carolina on February 21 and began his own bold pursuit of the retreating Cornwallis. Unable to pass up an opportunity for battle, Cornwallis turned and met him.

On March 5, 1781, Greene took up a position at Guilford Court House and Cornwallis attacked him there. The hard-fought encounter ended in a costly victory for Cornwallis. Although he won the field late in the day, nearly a quarter of his 3,000 men had been killed or wounded in the attempt. Physically staggered by the exhausting chase of Greene and the Guilford Court House combat, the depleted British army retreated to the seacoast at Wilmington to recuperate and refit. Cornwallis was not ready for either another try at Greene or a return to South Carolina.[14]

Confident in the ability of remaining British troops to hold Charleston and Camden and still contend with Greene, Cornwallis turned his eyes toward Virginia. To his way of thinking, its capture and control was the only way to effectively contain and eventually defeat the Americans.[15] At the Wilmington depot, Cornwallis outfitted his tired soldiers for what was to be the final campaign of the war.

The presence in Virginia of 3,800 British soldiers under Generals Benedict Arnold and William Phillips beckoned Cornwallis northward. These troops had been sent by Clinton—who still adhered to his raiding policy—to foment discord among the inhabitants and divert attention from British operations in the Carolinas.[16] Early in 1781, Arnold had caused considerable damage at Richmond, Virginia, and had withdrawn to Portsmouth on Chesapeake Bay.[17]

In response, George Washington sent 1,200 troops to Virginia with the young French nobleman Marie Jean Paul Roch Yves Gilbert Motier, Marquis de Lafayette. His orders were to harass Arnold. The plan went awry when a supporting French naval squadron sailed from Newport, Rhode Island, to prevent Arnold's escape by water, but was forced back by a superior British fleet. The Battle of the Chesapeake prevented Lafayette's men from utilizing the bay to move from Annapolis. In response to the American buildup, Clinton dispatched 2,600 more troops under Phillips to aid the embattled Arnold. That April, Cornwallis wrote to Clinton to inform him of his intention to enter Virginia. That province, maintained Cornwallis, should now become "The Seat of War," even if

New York must be abandoned. Cornwallis clearly misconstrued the presence of Arnold and Phillips, for Clinton had never envisioned the Chesapeake as a major theater of operations while the focus of British power continued in the Carolinas.[18]

A shift in British military policy occurred with Cornwallis's march into Virginia on April 25, 1781. New York and the Carolinas became secondary considerations, just as Cornwallis intended; the course of events had swept Clinton's overall strategy off the table. From April on, Virginia's tidewater region loomed paramount in British strategy— whether Clinton approved or not.[19] On May 20, Cornwallis joined Phillips's command at Petersburg, Virginia, where he learned the general had died from fever only one week earlier. Cornwallis assumed command from Arnold, thereby increasing his army to about 7,000 British and Hessian soldiers. Arnold returned to New York.[20]

Fully committed to his Virginia strategy, Cornwallis proceeded to consolidate his position. He had acted forthrightly, he believed, albeit without the permission of his superior. As he later put it, "I was most firmly persuaded, that, until Virginia was reduced, we could not hold the more southern provinces and that after its reduction, they would fall without much difficulty."[21]

Clinton disagreed, fearing that even a temporary loss of sea power would cause grave setbacks. "Operations in the Chesapeake are attended with great risk unless we are sure of a permanent superiority at sea," he observed. "I tremble for the fatal consequences that may ensue."[22] As much as he feared a strong French Navy in the Chesapeake, Clinton additionally worried about the prospects of a summer campaign in that fever-ridden zone.[23] Unfortunately for Clinton and the British cause, Cornwallis's intrigue with Germain had borne fruit. Germain wrote Clinton in early June: "I am well pleased to find Lord Cornwallis's opinion entirely coincides with mine of the great importance of pushing the war on the side of Virginia with all the force that can be spared, until that province is reduced."[24]

Cornwallis had contemplated the manner of reducing Virginia. He hoped Clinton would join him with troops from New York. Starting at the Chesapeake, the army would ascend the navigable rivers, dominate town and countryside, and reassert British control. If any American forces were encountered, they would be defeated by the sizable British Army. Cornwallis's scheme also called for aid from the considerable Loyalist population he believed existed in the state.[25] By mounting a campaign in the most prominently rebellious province of any outside New England—and the most populous—Cornwallis hoped to strike a military blow against an active center of political opposition to British rule.[26]

Once in command in Virginia, Cornwallis was forced to contend with Lafayette and his 2,000 American soldiers. The zealous French nobleman and experienced soldier—who was but nineteen years old in 1777 when he volunteered his services without pay to the American

Independence National Historical Park

Marie Jean Paul Roch Yves Gilbert Motier, Marquis de Lafayette cause—had received a commission of major general from the Continental Congress. His distinguished service in Pennsylvania and New Jersey thereafter had won Washington's utmost confidence and taken him to Virginia in 1780. In late April 1781, Lafayette arrived at Richmond to protect the new state capital from British incursions. Cornwallis decided his first course of action was to send selected units to protect the British station at Portsmouth. Thereafter, he marched his remaining 5,300 men north toward Richmond to expel Lafayette and to destroy American supplies.[27]

Lafayette fully realized he was too weak to make a stand at the capital, and that his prime role while awaiting reinforcements was "that of a terrier baiting a bull." The Frenchman thus retreated generally northward, keeping one step ahead of Cornwallis's command, alternately threatening and withdrawing from his front. Throughout, he was careful to keep his troops situated between the British and the American capital at Philadelphia.[28] Eventually, Lafayette's command was bolstered by the arrival of militia from western Virginia and, on June 25, by about 800 Pennsylvania Continentals sent by Washington under the command of Brigadier General Anthony Wayne. A detachment under Major General Frederick William Augustus, Baron Von Steuben, further augmented Lafayette's command, which now totaled nearly 4,000 soldiers.[29]

Swift increases in Lafayette's strength coincided with a renewal of difficulties between Cornwallis and Clinton. The senior British commander ordered Cornwallis to move out from the interior to the Virginia coast and take up a defensive position at either Yorktown or Williamsburg on the peninsula between the James and York rivers. Once there, he was to dispatch the majority of his troops north via transport ship to help repel an expected siege against New York.[30] The news ended Cornwallis's dream of a grand offensive in Virginia. Dismayed, he endeavored to resurrect Clinton's earlier design of holding a naval station and launching periodic forays into the state. With the Portsmouth base now exposed in the face of the American buildup, the British general returned to Richmond while Tarleton made a dash on Charlottesville. Tarleton's thrust disrupted the state legislature, which was in session, and almost captured Governor Thomas Jefferson. Cornwallis also sent the "Queen's Rangers" under Lieutenant Colonel John Graves Simcoe to intimidate von Steuben's troops on the upper James River. Lafayette, however, continued to pursue and harass Cornwallis's retreating main army.[31]

From Richmond, Cornwallis continued moving down the peninsula, alarmed by the growing American numbers and dismayed by the prospect of suffering through a summer of suffocating tidewater humidity. He planned to rest his tired soldiers while simultaneously consolidating the British position on the Chesapeake. On June 26, Simcoe fought a segment of Pennsylvania troops a short distance from Williamsburg at Spencer's Ordinary, where Cornwallis soon halted his main command and dispatched patrols along the York and James rivers. Lafayette's soldiers cautiously hovered nearby.[32]

Four days later, Cornwallis reconnoitered Yorktown amid a wild bombardment from American artillery across the York River at Gloucester Point.[33] Yorktown, thought Cornwallis, was unsuitable for a naval station, and he feared its susceptibility to French attack. As a result, he returned to Williamsburg. Another four days passed. On the anniversary of the American proclamation of independence, Cornwallis moved his command from Williamsburg toward Jamestown Island. He planned to ford the James at that place, march for Portsmouth, and embark from there the reinforcements Clinton requested for New York.

When Lafayette realized his opponent would be vulnerable as he crossed the river, he moved to attack Cornwallis near Jamestown in what became known as the Battle of Green Spring. Cornwallis, himself a shrewd and aggressive tactician, anticipated the effort and tricked Lafayette into believing that only a small rear guard and some of his baggage wagons had not crossed the James. Endeavoring to keep contact with Cornwallis, Lafayette dispatched General Wayne with about 500 men as advance guard (later reinforced to 900 men). By the time Lafayette discovered Cornwallis had not crossed and was setting a trap, it was too late to notify Wayne, whose men called him "Mad Anthony" because of his audacity in battle. A brisk engagement ensued that cost the Americans about 140 killed, wounded, and missing. Lafayette and Wayne calmly executed an organized retreat in the face of a superior enemy and escaped from what could have been a significant defeat.[34]

Unruffled by the sharp but insignificant setback, Lafayette continued to embarrass British intentions, his ubiquitous soldiers especially hampering Cornwallis's foraging parties. The Americans followed Cornwallis across the James and along the south side of the river toward

Portsmouth, a move that also effectively checked Tarleton's plundering legion. When the British reached the Portsmouth station, the young Frenchman stopped and evaluated his next move.[35]

Cornwallis's withdrawal across the James to Portsmouth virtually freed the peninsula of British troops, a situation that seemed compatible with Clinton's desire to de-emphasize active operations in Virginia.[36] By July 17, the troops destined for Clinton in New York were prepared to sail, but a message from him suspended the embarkation. Cornwallis was instructed to keep his troops together pending further instructions, which arrived July 21. Completely reversing his policy in view of remonstrations from Germain and his anxiety over Washington's movements toward New York, Clinton stressed the importance of holding the peninsula to protect British ships anchored in the Chesapeake. Because Portsmouth—the principal protective station for the British Navy in the region—was now deemed unhealthy, Clinton urged Cornwallis to fortify Old Point Comfort, the station situated at the extreme tip of the peninsula guarding Hampton Roads and the entrance to the James. Clinton cancelled his urgent request for troops and directed Cornwallis to use whatever resources were at his disposal to garrison Old Point Comfort. Once that base was secure, the remaining soldiers might then be forwarded to New York. As additional protection, Cornwallis was instructed to take and hold Yorktown if he believed it would increase the security of his position.[37]

An examination by the Royal Engineers quickly demonstrated that Old Point Comfort would be difficult to fortify. It was impossible to secure the mouth of the James by occupying that place. Moreover, works erected there could easily be attacked and destroyed by an enemy fleet.[38] The need for a deep-water station that could accommodate British warships, as well as enable an effective defense, drew Cornwallis's eyes like a magnet once again toward Yorktown. Accordingly, in late July he wrote Clinton of his intention "to seize and fortify York and Gloucester Point, being the only harbour in which we can hope to be able to give effectual protection to line of battle ships."[39] The river at Yorktown lent itself admirably to the purposes of a British naval rendezvous point. At Yorktown, the channel of the stream narrowed to little more than one-half mile because Gloucester Point jutted southward from the northern shore, with the river widening again above the peninsula. The waterway could therefore be commanded easily by guns mounted at

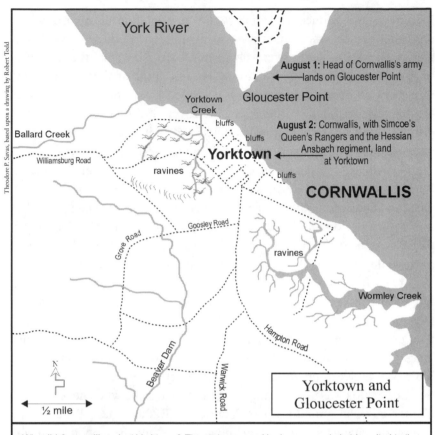

Theodore P. Savas, based upon a drawing by Robert Todd

York River

August 1: Head of Cornwallis's army lands on Gloucester Point

Gloucester Point

Yorktown Creek

bluffs

August 2: Cornwallis, with Simcoe's Queen's Rangers and the Hessian Ansbach regiment, land at Yorktown

Ballard Creek

bluffs

Yorktown

Williamsburg Road

ravines

bluffs

CORNWALLIS

Goosley Road

Grove Road

ravines

Wormley Creek

Hampton Road

N

½ mile

Beaver Dam

Warwick Road

Yorktown and Gloucester Point

Why did Cornwallis select Yorktown? The waterway and harbor were admirably suited to the purposes of a British naval rendezvous point, and artillery mounted at Yorktown and Gloucester Point could easily command the river. The elevation above the water made a successful enemy naval assault on Yorktown nearly impossible, and the terrain south of Yorktown, cut by numerous ravines and creeks, could easily be defended by an army deployed in a semicircle. However, this same area also consisted of rising ground, which meant that an outer defensive position was absolutely mandatory in order to hold any inner main works around the town proper for any length of time. Cornwallis had no intention of preparing for a proper siege when he fortified Yorktown.

Yorktown and Gloucester Point, while its elevation above the water precluded a successful enemy naval assault on Yorktown. With the narrow channel of the York closely guarded, British warships might float upstream unmolested.[40] In addition, the terrain south of Yorktown, cut by numerous ravines, could easily be defended by an army deployed in semicircular fashion.[41] Conversely, however, the rising nature of the ground south of the village constituted a disadvantage by making an outer defensive position mandatory in order to preserve the inner one.[42]

On August 1 the head of Cornwallis's army arrived at Gloucester Point.[43] The next day, Cornwallis with two regiments—the Corps of Queen's Rangers and the Hessian Ansbach-Bayreuth Regiment—landed at Yorktown. Cornwallis surveyed the area and began implementing a plan to defend it. Tarleton and his command (about 190 men), meanwhile, crossed Hampton Roads in small boats and reached Yorktown five days later on August 7. The final detachment of troops, left behind to level the works at Portsmouth, arrived under Brigadier General Charles O'Hara on August 22.[44] On that day, Cornwallis wrote Clinton: "The engineer has finished his survey and examination of this place, and has proposed his plan for fortifying it, which appearing judicious, I have approved of and directed [it] to be executed."[45]

Cornwallis was not preparing to withstand a siege when he relayed to Clinton his plans for fortifying Yorktown. Rather, the village would assume the character of a military bulwark to defend the navy from attack by land or sea by the French or Americans. Furthermore, Gloucester, located off the peninsula, was not expected to become the object of an Allied attack, and arrangements there were directed toward the establishment of an effective blockade against enemy vessels and toward facilitating forage operations by British troops. In event of emergency, Gloucester Point might also provide a means of escape from Yorktown.[46]

By late August the Yorktown and Gloucester area fairly bustled with activity. At Yorktown, the beach became a tented encampment for troops and for sailors recruited to help erect fortifications and move cannon and equipment from the ships. Operations of the British Army dominated the entire waterfront as Cornwallis's men occupied homes, stores, wharves, and warehouses.[47] In correspondence with Clinton, the British general estimated it would take six weeks to adequately fortify the site. Lacking men and entrenching tools, he wrote on August 27 that his defense "will be a work of great time and labour, and after all, I fear, [will] not be very strong."[48]

As Cornwallis uneasily entrenched his army, his every action was observed by Lafayette's soldiers. When the earl had departed Portsmouth, Lafayette, suspecting a British attempt on Baltimore, had hastened up the peninsula to Fredericksburg. Then, when Cornwallis took up a position at Yorktown, the Frenchman stationed himself near West Point, where the Pamunkey and Mattaponi rivers met to form the York. Meanwhile, Wayne camped below the James, expecting shortly to move south to cooperate with Greene in the Carolinas. In late August, Wayne's orders were abruptly rescinded because of a change in Allied strategy that evolved far to the north.[49]

A Move South

Since June, Washington had been alerted to Cornwallis's presence in Virginia. His own immediate objective was Clinton's army, which occupied defenses around New York. The movement of French troops under General Rochambeau toward the Hudson early that summer had alarmed Clinton and led him to suspect a major offensive against him was imminent. That, in turn, was when Clinton had urgently applied to Cornwallis for reinforcements. Clinton repealed his request only after it became obvious the French Navy posed a significant danger to the British in the area of Chesapeake Bay.[50]

The threat was indeed a real one, comprised of a fleet of warships commanded by Admiral Francois Joseph Paul, comte de Grasse-Tilly. Sailing in March from France with 20 ships of the line, three frigates, and scores of transports, de Grasse reached Martinique by the end of April. By late July he was in Haiti, where he received dispatches from Rochambeau outlining Allied needs in the way of naval support. Given the alternative of aiding operations at New York or in the Chesapeake, de Grasse—at the private urging of Rochambeau and under pressure from his own officers—declined to participate in the campaign against New York. By way of explanation, he cited the presence of sandbars in the harbor as obstacles to his success. Furthermore, the shorter distance to the Chesapeake and the easier navigation once in those waters influenced his decision, for de Grasse informed Rochambeau that his participation would necessarily be limited to the period between mid-July and mid-October, when he would be needed once again to resume his defensive posture around the French West Indian possessions.[51]

After sending word of his objective to Rochambeau, de Grasse set sail on August 5 with twenty ships for the Chesapeake, expecting to arrive there by September 1. The British Navy, which had let him leave France without interference, remained ignorant of his destination. Cognizant of the Allies' need for troops and money, de Grasse managed a loan of £15,000 from the Spanish governor of Havana and brought with his fleet the 3,000-man French garrison of Santo Domingo.[52]

De Grasse successfully eluded the British Admiral George Brydges Rodney, who was stationed in the Indies to prevent French naval assistance from reaching the rebellious colonies. When he learned of de Grasse's departure Rodney directed Admiral Samuel Hood and fourteen ships of the line to sail for the American coast to prevent the French from reaching America. De Grasse predicted this response and instead of taking the direct route east of the Bahamas, steered through the Old Bahama Channel, skirted Cuba, and pressed on with the Gulf Stream between the Bahamas and the Florida peninsula. Rodney subsequently dispatched six more warships from Jamaica to join Hood, but their commander disobeyed instructions and stayed behind. Rodney himself fell ill and in mid-August sailed home to England.[53]

On August 14, Washington learned of de Grasse's decision to cruise for the Chesapeake with 3,000 French troops. Earlier that month, Washington had marched down the Hudson and had been joined by Rochambeau's troops from Newport. Most of Washington's force now stood poised before New York. But the news from de Grasse suddenly dashed Allied prospects for an assault on that city, a design originally intended to chastise Clinton and prompt him to bring reinforcements north from Virginia and relieve British pressure on Lafayette.[54] Word of de Grasse's destination caused Washington to change his objective. Cornwallis, now in Virginia, offered an alternative goal for the Allies. The possibility of eluding Clinton, concentrating his force, and cornering Cornwallis far to the south intrigued the often audacious Washington.

On August 17, he and Rochambeau sent a message to de Grasse informing him of their new destination.[55] The enterprise necessarily entailed much uncertainty. For one thing, Washington feared that a British fleet from New York or the West Indies might seal off the

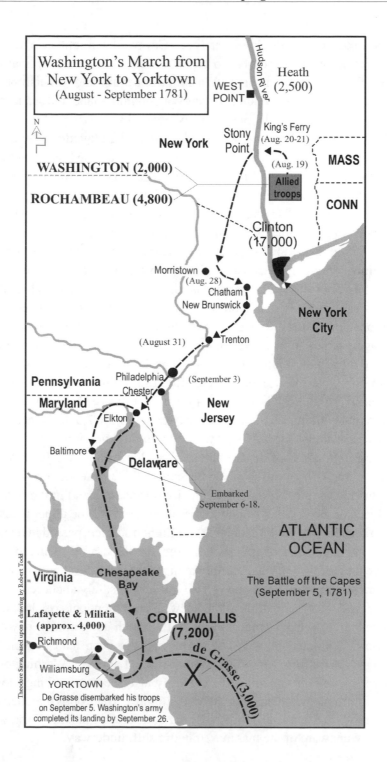

Washington's March from
New York to Yorktown
(August - September 1781)

N

Hudson River

Heath
(2,500)

WEST
POINT

New York

Stony
Point

King's Ferry
(Aug. 20-21)

WASHINGTON (2,000)

(Aug. 19)

MASS

Allied
troops

ROCHAMBEAU (4,800)

CONN

Clinton
(17,000)

Morristown
(Aug. 28)

Chatham

New Brunswick

**New York
City**

(August 31)   Trenton

Philadelphia
Chester   (September 3)

Pennsylvania

Maryland

Elkton

**New
Jersey**

Baltimore

Delaware

Embarked
September 6-18.

**ATLANTIC
OCEAN**

Theodore Savas, based upon a drawing by Robert Todd

Virginia

Chesapeake
Bay

The Battle off the Capes
(September 5, 1781)

**Lafayette & Militia
(approx. 4,000)**

Richmond

**CORNWALLIS
(7,200)**

de Grasse (3,000)

Williamsburg

YORKTOWN

De Grasse disembarked his troops
on September 5. Washington's army
completed its landing by September 26.

Chesapeake before de Grasse arrived. Cornwallis might also divine Allied intentions and escape into North Carolina. There also remained the risk that Clinton might detect Washington's move and and disrupt his strategy.[56] Close cooperation between Washington's land and sea forces would be mandatory if the plan had any hope of success.

Therefore, the Virginia commander ordered Lafayette to hold the British in Virginia at all costs. Comte Louis de Barras, the French admiral in command of the squadron at Newport, Rhode Island, was ordered to sail south with Rochambeau's siege artillery as well as most of the American artillery. De Barras would also aid de Grasse against any incursions of the British Navy into the Chesapeake.[57]

Washington, meanwhile, took extreme measures to convince Clinton of an impending move against him in New York in order to deceive him as to his true objective. The secret was conveyed to only a few of his most trusted subordinates; he contrived fictitious correspondence, and summoned provisions, forage, bake ovens, and boats—all indicative of a drive against New York.[58] Washington also assigned a diversionary army of 2,000 men under Major General William Heath to protect West Point and to complete the deception perpetrated on Clinton. Rochambeau's men began crossing the Hudson on August 18, followed by the American artillery; the infantry crossed the next day. Some 7,000 French and American men had slipped away without Clinton knowing it.[59]

Washington's confidence increased as his troops left New York behind them. At Trenton, however, he learned there were too few ships to carry his men south. Never one to let circumstances stand in the way of his objective, he decided simply to march his men for the upper reaches of Chesapeake Bay. At Philadelphia, the French soldiers passed in review before members of Congress, whom the French warmly saluted (the Americans marched through the city at night). At Chester, Pennsylvania, Washington received happy news: de Grasse was safely anchored in the Chesapeake. Robert Morris, the new Superintendent of Finance, arranged a loan from Rochambeau with which to partially pay the American Continentals, many of whom had not been paid in months. Through the efforts of Morris and John Laurens, Washington's trustworthy and outstanding aide, the army also secured clothing, flour, meat, salt, rum, and other sorely needed supplies. The troops marched on to Wilmington, Delaware. Clinton, sitting comfortably in New York, was blissfully unaware of the massive strategic shift underway.[60]

The Battle of the Capes and its Aftermath

Admiral de Grasse with his 28 ships of the line had reached the Virginia Capes on August 26. The journey from southern France of 1722, where he was born into a noble family, to the cusp of what would be the deciding campaign that would fundamentally change the order of the world, had been a long one. As a youth, de Grasse spent a year at the naval academy in Toulon before leaving to enlist with the prestigious Knights of Malta. When the War of the Austrian Succession broke out in 1740, the 18-year-old returned to his passion for the sea and joined the navy, where he finally found his true calling. Service over several decades took him around the globe, from stations in the Mediterranean to as far away as India. By 1775, when the American Revolution was erupting in North America, de Grasse was in the Caribbean in command

National Park Service, Colonial National Historical Park, Yorktown Collection

Francois Joseph Paul, comte de Grasse-Tilly

of the 26-gun frigate *Amphitrite*. By 1779 he was leading a squadron under Charles-Hector, comte d'Estaing, and when that officer departed for France, the entire French fleet in the Caribbean was handed to him. By 1780, de Grasse was no longer young, and his once-robust health was in decline. The 58-year-old returned to his homeland late that year. By this time French authorities had decided to intervene directly into North America by inserting enough soldiers to swing the balance in favor of the Americans and away from their arch rivals. On March 22, 1781, Louis XVI elevated de Grasse to Rear Admiral and dispatched him back to the West Indies. And now, finally, he was off the Virginia Capes.[61]

The British fleet under Hood, pursuing from the West Indies by the direct route, had arrived a few days earlier. After vainly looking for signs of French vessels in the Chesapeake, he departed for New York, sending two frigates to hurry ahead should de Grasse appear in his absence. When the French admiral entered the bay on August 30, he captured one frigate and chased the other up the York River to Cornwallis before dropping anchor. Hood, meanwhile, reported at New York to his superior, Admiral Thomas Graves, and learned of de Barras's departure from Newport with eight ships of the line, four frigates, and eighteen transports bearing artillery. Seeking to prevent de Barras's union with de Grasse, Graves determined to move to the Chesapeake with Hood's squadron of fourteen ships and five of his own, some 1,400 guns and 13,000 seamen.

Graves joined the British Navy as a young teen and served on his father's ship in 1741. Fifteen years later he was court-martialed for failing to attack a large French ship, though he survived the ordeal with only a reprimand for an "error of judgment." In 1779, Graves was promoted to flag rank and dispatched to participate in war on the North American continent. In 1781, he was serving as the second-in-command of a blockading squadron under Admiral Marriot Arbuthnot. The news of the French activity prompted Graves to sail from New York on August 31. Five days later and much to his surprise, he arrived at the Chesapeake to find not de Barras—who remained at sea—but de Grasse, with his superior fleet of twenty-four ships mounting some 1,700 guns serviced by 19,000 seamen. His flagship, the *Ville de Paris*, mounted 110 guns and was the most powerful warship of its day. Most of the French ships were powerful 74s. Four other French vessels blocked the mouth of the York River and protected the continuing disembarkment at Jamestown of the West Indian troops under Claude Anne, Marquis de St. Simon, a

National Park Service, Colonial National Historical Park, Yorktown Collection

Admiral Thomas Graves

move begun on September 2. What followed was the most decisive naval engagement of the war.[62]

Despite his numerical inferiority, Graves offered battle. It is ironic that the decisive Battle of the Capes lasted only two hours and ended in a tactical draw. French guns roughly handled many British ships and seriously damaged a handful more, one of which Graves ordered scuttled, inflicting about 300 killed and wounded. British gunfire was not very effective, damaging four French ships and killing and wounding 200 men. Although the two opposing fleets remained within sight of one another for the next couple of days, no further battle took place. Graves, however, did not fulfill his objective of preventing de Grasse from cementing shut the mouth of the Chesapeake. Frustrated, Graves turned his fleet around and headed for New York.[63]

The victorious de Grasse opened communications with Lafayette, whose force was now near Williamsburg, and directed nearly eighty transport vessels to the head of Chesapeake Bay (near present-day Elkton, Maryland) to meet the greater part of Washington's and Rochambeau's approaching armies. The other troops marched to Annapolis. Some of them moved south on boats while the remainder took up the march along the west side of the Chesapeake. The horses of the Allies were also taken south by land. The entire force converged on Williamsburg. Cornwallis and his army were trapped.

Leaving the command to subordinate officers, Washington and Rochambeau rode on to Mount Vernon, the American general's first visit home in six years. On September 14, the two officers reached Williamsburg, where Washington assumed supreme command of both armies. Eight days later the troop transports began to arrive and unload their cargo at nearby Jamestown.[64]

Throughout the early stages of these developments, Cornwallis remained largely passive at Yorktown, essentially oblivious to the events closing in about him. The arrival of de Grasse's fleet, together with intelligence informing him of the Allied armies approaching from the north, shook him awake and prompted him to fortify his position.[65] Cornwallis's decision to remain at Yorktown elicited considerable criticism from his superior at New York. As Clinton later put it: "No orders under which He acted[,] no Instructions he had received[,] nor any intelligence [I] . . . had sent could justify his neglecting to beat [escape] an Army or detail which was coming to besiege him[.] He could not have lost twelve hours in making the attempt."[66]

But by now, escaping from the peninsula was nearly impossible. French naval dominance of the Chesapeake placed the British in a potentially desperate military situation. Superior French sea power permitted the convergence of Washington's land forces and made a clash with Cornwallis's army somewhere between the York and James rivers nearly inevitable. French and American siege guns were now secure on the James River, only six miles from the British garrison at Yorktown.[67]

Chapter 2

The Lion Comes to Yorktown

*T*hrough his success in the Battle of the Capes, Admiral de Grasse effectively secured the entrance of the York River against future British attempts to relieve Cornwallis's army by water. The Allied troops closing in on the isolated British garrison anticipated reducing the position by heavy artillery employed in the classic warfare style of the eighteenth century: the siege.

As defined by contemporary theorists, a siege occurs "when an army approaches a fortified place, and surrounds it on all sides, endeavoring to oblige the garrison to surrender, either by destroying the works of the fortification, or those which defend them."[1] Siege warfare differed from conventional modes of battle, subjecting both the besieged and besieging forces to fixed standards of endurance, determination, and procedure. Successfully prosecuting or surviving a siege required commanders on both sides to exercise considerable resourcefulness.

Leaders of the besieging army had to possess administrative acumen, unrelenting patience, and familiarity with all of the methodological tenets siege warfare embraced. On the opposing side, the assailed leader resisted the besiegers' efforts to dislodge his command and strove to instill and maintain confidence among his men under often trying conditions. Ideally, he possessed a thorough knowledge of defensive warfare, displayed constant vigilance, and worked in the face of tactical adversity to promote the security of his soldiers. The besieged men had to prepare themselves for hunger, disease, boredom, and prolonged exposure to the concentrated artillery attack of the besieging army. In addition, as the principal targets of the siege, the trapped soldiers faced the consequences of probable defeat, capitulation, capture, and punishment at the hands of the victors. The attacking army possessed the initial advantage in a siege. Besieging forces sometimes abandoned the siege for logistical reasons, because of changes in strategy, or because the objective turns out not to be worth the time and effort required for victory. Often, however, only the chance of outside intervention prolonged the hopes of the besieged, enabling them to last against desperate odds.[2]

Cornwallis at Yorktown

Yorktown, hugging the southern shore of its namesake river, came suddenly to life with the British occupation of August 1781. Although it had passed its peak as a tobacco port, it was still a bustling and promiment town. And now, with the end of summer approaching, the Virginia port city began to awaken to its destiny in world history. As described by contemporary observers, Yorktown consisted of about 200 buildings, including several churches and an attractive red brick courthouse. It was founded in the late 1600s as a port for shipping tobacco and other supplies to Europe. Four principal avenues surrounded the environs of Yorktown and offered access to the community. Stretching west was the Williamsburg Road, which basically paralleled the York River and led to the town of Williamsburg about twelve miles distant. Goosley Road diverged from this route just west of Yorktown and ran east to intersect a third highway, Hampton Road, which stretched from Yorktown south and east to Hampton. A secondary road entered Yorktown from the east. It, too, bordered the river for much of its distance.[3]

Yorktown afforded the British both advantages and disadvantages. On the river side, the high banks promised good protection from enemy ships should they manage to penetrate beyond British warships and ascend the York River to within striking distance of the town. However, the defenses on Gloucester Point on the northern shore (and in the narrowest part of the channel) were such as to make this possibility extremely unlikely. Gloucester Point served best by protecting Cornwallis's ships (and others that might arrive to help him), and offered a safe haven should a retreat from Yorktown become necessary.[4]

On the landward side, however, Cornwallis's defensive possibilities were more problematic. On the right (or generally west) of the town, Yorktown Creek ran down to the river, cutting through several broad ravines and leaving an area of boggy swampland for a distance up from its mouth. Below (or generally south of) Yorktown was Wormley Creek. In addition to a large dammed pond, the curvy waterway cut several deep ravines around the outer limits of the community as it followed its marshy course to the York about two miles below Yorktown. Together, York and Wormley creeks presented a network of ravines, ditches, and bogs that in appearance approximated the tongs of a giant caliper flanking the town. Between the streams lay broad and fairly level but high terrain that stretched for nearly half a mile, covered by trees and grass and traversed by Goosley Road. Approaching the town—especially from the northwest—would be difficult but not impossible for a besieger. In some places, the ravines of York and Wormley creeks were deep enough to hide a sizeable enemy almost up to the village itself. If an adequate defense of Yorktown was to be maintained, the construction of an outer British perimeter was of prime importance.[5]

*   *   *

By August, the gathering circumstances for Lieutenant General Charles Cornwallis were neither readily apparent nor altogether alarming. The forty-two-year-old soldier had weathered much of the conflict with the Americans since 1776. Educated at Eton and Cambridge, he had served as an ensign in Germany during the Seven Years' War. He was later elected to the House of Commons, and gained a seat in the House of Lords upon succession to his late father's earldom. There, Cornwallis had argued vigorously *against* the tax repression being foisted upon the colonies. He did not support American independence, however, and when war broke out the soldier took up arms in 1776. By the time of the Yorktown Campaign, he could boast of having participated in nearly every major British operation in North America.

Impatient and assertive, Cornwallis disagreed over policy matters with both equals and superiors alike—including Lieutenant General

Lieutenant General Charles Cornwallis

Henry Clinton, with whom he suffered an enduringly strained relationship. As major general, Cornwallis fought on fronts stretching from the Carolinas to New York, had been bested by Washington at Princeton, New Jersey (for which he drew Clinton's criticism), and had served under General Howe at Brandywine and during the capture of Philadelphia. Following a respite in England during the first half of 1778, Cornwallis returned to America after Howe's resignation. He stepped ashore as a lieutenant general and second in command to Clinton. At Clinton's urging, Cornwallis sailed back to London in December to seek reinforcements. When he returned to America without the requested support, a frustrated Clinton attempted to resign, but his resignation was denied. The rift between the two men widened and deepened. Communications between them were, at best, strained.

In May 1780, Cornwallis took part in the capture of Charleston before his singular surge through the Carolinas in preparation for his invasion of Virginia. A brave and spirited senior commander and a skilled administrator, Cornwallis proved an accomplished tactician and an aggressive fighter—perhaps too aggressive, as Nathanael Greene demonstrated at Guilford Court House. He was not a particularly astute strategist, however, a factor that doubtless contributed to his looming predicament at Yorktown.[6]

Cornwallis's decision to fortify Yorktown was not a novel one. Its strategic location had been recognized since the town's founding in 1691. Defensive arrangements of one sort or another had existed there long before the British took up residence in 1781. Fear of attack from the York River shortly after the town was established prompted the erection of a battery on the waterfront, which complemented an earlier one built on the Gloucester side to ward off water-borne enemies. In 1710-11, a threatened attack by the French caused the governor of Virginia to order construction of a strong fort with artillery at Yorktown to aid in the protection of the colony.[7] By 1755, the batteries at Yorktown and Gloucester Point, and a fort at the mouth of the James River, constituted the sole coastal defenses of Virginia. They saw no action either against enemies or pirates, but their location assumed greater significance after the beginning of the Revolutionary War.

Yorktown's strategic importance was recognized at the outset of the war. In June 1776, the Virginia Council of State ordered the village garrisoned with state militia. The troops did not remain long, however, and the barracks erected at the post were empty much of the time.[8] "Here is a battery of 12 pieces of heavy cannon to command the River and a Company of artillery stationed here," wrote an observer in 1777, "but they make a sorry appearance for so respectable a corps, as the Artillery ought to be."[9]

That same year a hospital was erected for soldiers stricken with smallpox in the epidemic of 1777.[10] By the spring of 1778, however, the state council manifested some concern over the poor condition of the works. They acted to remedy the problem after receiving a recommendation to extend the fortifications for use by the Allies both at Yorktown and Gloucester Point.[11] The works had been improved by the winter of 1779-80, when the French erected fortifications at Yorktown to protect several of their vessels that had found refuge in the York River after encountering a severe storm en route to the West Indies.[12] Although the garrison remained in a depleted state through much of the war, the Yorktown fortifications served as an active post manned by Virginia militia until the time of Cornwallis's arrival.[13]

British designs on Yorktown were discerned by the townspeople as early as April 1781, when Colonel John Simcoe and his Queen's Rangers, an outfit whose ranks were largely filled with Loyalist sympathizers, raided the place. Apprehension mounted anew when Cornwallis personally surveyed the potential defenses of the town in late June.[14]

Now, as Cornwallis undertook to establish a joint army-naval station in accordance with Clinton's wishes, many of the townspeople departed, some no doubt with portentous thoughts as to the fate of their community. As of late August, Cornwallis believed it would take him at least six weeks to properly establish the base. The hot and humid climate was hard on his men, as was the lack of entrenching tools. Oblivious to the Franco-American forces closing in by land and sea, the British general casually sent dispatches to Clinton requesting hundreds of spades and shovels and a wide assortment of carpenter supplies to aid in erecting defensive works.[15]

On August 30, any illusions of security Cornwallis entertained were abruptly shattered with the discovery of French warships in the mouth of the York River. The vessels, described by one observer as "a French 74, a 64-gun ship, and a frigate," had driven the British frigate *Guadaloupe*, the sloop *Bonetta*, and some small boats back into the neck of the river.

One Hessian captain viewed the alarming proceedings from his post on the Severn River. Fearful the ships would move up the York at high tide and bombard the port, he sent runners with the news to Cornwallis.[16] The next day a naval lieutenant, escorted by a handful of dragoons, rode to Old Point Comfort and counted between 30 and 40 enemy vessels anchored within the capes.[17]

The appearance of the French caused considerable consternation in the British ranks. Cornwallis's army was not ready to defend Yorktown, and he did not yet have a viable strategy in place to do so. The work on fortifications, which had progressed slowly because of disagreeable heat and a seemingly indifferent attitude, now went ahead at a furious pace. "Now, head banged head in Yorktown and Gloucester," recalled one officer. . .

> *Now*, they hastily began to unload all the magazines and guns which had been brought from Portsmouth, but which—through negligence and laziness—were still on board the ships lying at anchor in the York River between the two towns. Now, if the French had been in better readiness, or perhaps, had better intelligence, the ships could be shot to pieces.[18]

Cornwallis now more fully recognized his strategic predicament—especially with the news that French soldiers had arrived at Williamsburg to reinforce General Lafayette. News from the north was that General Washington was approaching Virginia with his army. If true, it would compound Cornwallis's troubles manifold.[19] The British navy obviously no longer plied the coastal Atlantic waters unmolested, and relief from that direction appeared remote. Worst of all, the nearby enemy land forces severely limited Cornwallis's alternatives.

The first week of September passed with feverish activity as the British commander sought to reinforce his position. The fortifications at Gloucester Point were nothing more than weakly constructed piles of sand, and efforts were directed toward improving these and procuring lumber from surrounding plantations for gun emplacement platforms.[20] During the night of September 9, an American detachment from Lafayette's army harassed the British outposts at Gloucester, but no serious fighting occurred.[21]

Lieutenant Colonel Banastre Tarleton

Cornwallis's position grew increasingly untenable as the first two weeks of September came and went. Admiral Graves's failure to defeat de Grasse and secure British access by sea hoisted a sword above Cornwallis's neck. The daily news he received was rarely uplifting, usually ominous, and included regular dispatches concerning the disposition of troops under Lafayette and the continued approach of enemy troops under Washington and Rochambeau. Determined to press west and scout the enemy, the British general dispatched Lieutenant Colonel Tarleton and his mounted command to reconnoiter Lafayette's position.

As far as the Allies were concerned, Banastre Tarleton was the most hated enemy soldier operating in the colonies. The 27-year-old native of Liverpool hailed from the upper middle class and studied law at the universities of Liverpool and Oxford. When the spendthrift blew through the fortune bequeathed to him by his father in less than one year, he convinced his mother to buy a cavalry officer's commission for him in 1775 in the King's Dragoon Guards, the First Regiment of the Green Dragoons. By the summer of 1778, the young officer was a lieutenant colonel in the North American conflict in command of a mixed cavalry-light infantry legion almost entirely composed of American Loyalists. At the head of the British cavalry during Sir Clinton's Southern campaign, Tarleton's aggressive service helped capture Charleston and score a victory at Monck's Corner. The fields in the South were well-suited to his hard-hitting mounted tactics, but his fight in South Carolina at Waxhaws on May 29, 1780, forever branded him as a butcher of prisoners and wounded, and tarred the horseman with several nicknames, "Bloody Tarleston" being but one. Although he denied the report there is little doubt atrocities occurred. Dashing in manner and boasting a swarthy complexion, Tarleton was also possessed of a terrible temper and impetuousness that resulted in his sharp defeat at the Battle of Cowpens in January 1781. Still, Tarleton's Legion was one of the best trained and equipped outfits in the British Army, and Cornwallis rightly relied upon his expertise and field savvy.

After riding west to reconnoiter the approaching Allies for Cornwallis, Tarleton returned and advocated, as he usually did, an immediate attack to escape the closing network of enemy troops. His advice was sound. Instead, Cornwallis waited, hoping the British navy under Admiral Lord George Rodney could somehow slip troops from

Clinton through the French blockade. The attitude of the usually aggressive Cornwallis changed during those September days from one of active and energetic leadership to a strange mixture of reliance on others and passivity.[22]

If Cornwallis continued sitting passively in Yorktown, his options for viable action would diminish by the day. He was enough of a general to realize this, and after consulting with his officers finally decided to heed Tarleton's advice. An attack on Lafayette might compel the young Frenchman to fall back and allow the British sufficient room to fight their way toward Richmond. The James River effectively blocked any retreat south to the Carolinas, so a surprise movement against Lafayette seemed to be Cornwallis's only, and perhaps best, recourse.

Two main plans were advanced to accomplish this design. One was to march the army along the Williamsburg Road under cover of darkness and strike the Marquis at dawn, before he could bring his field artillery to bear. The other plan was to send 2,500 men in small boats up the York River to Queen's Creek—which flowed from the area of Williamsburg—and strike Lafayette from the rear in a surprise flanking movement. Cornwallis also had the option of executing both plans simultaneously.[23] Both plans were based on the belief that any such movement would go undetected by Lafayette—an extremely illusory supposition.

On September 16, just as Cornwallis and his subordinates settled on a strategy to attack and escape the tightening Allied noose, a dispatch dated ten days earlier arrived from Clinton. Admiral Robert Digby and his warships, advised Clinton, would be off the coast "any day," and he (Clinton) would be sending 4,000 men from New York to effect Cornwallis's relief. Cornwallis postponed his offensive.[24]

This welcome information tended to support Cornwallis's own philosophical view of the situation: he had taken up his position at Yorktown on Clinton's orders to establish a defensive station—orders he had carried out against his better judgment. In effect, he transferred responsibility for its success or failure to Clinton, who was nearly three hundred miles away. "The place is in no State of defense," Cornwallis wrote his superior on the 16th of September. "If you cannot relieve me very soon, you must be prepared to hear the worst."[25] This sharp bit of news did not sit well with Clinton, who had no reasonable way to fully assess the situation from his post in New York. Cornwallis's refusal to mount an attempt to escape the growing encirclement was a convenient means of placing the fate of his army in Clinton's distant hands. As his position became increasingly desperate, the general depended entirely upon Clinton for either reenforcements or extraction.

Events picked up momentum as September passed. During the night of the 17th, American reconnaissance parties harassed and alarmed British outposts.[26] In the early morning darkness of September 22, Cornwallis sent fire ships against the French vessels blocking the mouth of the York River. "The sight was worth the trouble to see!" remembered Captain Johann Ewald, a one-eyed Prussian who had lost his left eye in a duel in 1770. "The [fire] ships were set on fire and illuminated the area so brightly that we could easily detect the French ships at anchor in the very dark night. But since the fire ships had been ablaze too soon, the enemy ships cut their cables and sailed away."[27]

As the days passed, Cornwallis pushed ahead with his fortifications at Gloucester Point and Yorktown. He confidently expected relief at any time. Two days before his experiment with the fire ships, his nominal strength stood at 8,885 men, excluding sailors attached to the armed British ships and the twenty-four transports and smaller vessels anchored off Yorktown. The addition of the seamen, who numbered 840, brought Cornwallis's strength in mid-September to 9,725 men. In addition, some 1,500 to 2,000 slaves were used to help build defenses.[28] The effective strength of his land force, however, was much lower (and was reflected as such in Cornwallis's official strength reports). Without the 840 sailors, the strength of the British army in Virginia fluctuated little over the months and averaged only about 5,500 men.

Between June and October, Cornwallis reported his effective strength as follows:

>   June 1, 1781: 5,312
>   July 1,1781: 5,250
>   August 1, 1781: 5,580
>   Sept. 1, 1781: 5,316
>   Oct. 1, 1781: 4,987[29]

The British force arrayed at Yorktown included a number of well-established units of untarnished reputation. The organization of the British Army under Cornwallis was as follows:

Headquarters

Lieutenant General Charles, Earl Cornwallis, Commanding

Lieutenant Colonel Lord Chewton, Aide-de-Camp

Major Alexander Ross, Aide-de-Camp

Major Charles Cochrane, Acting Aide

Major John Despard, Deputy Adjutant General

Major Richard England, Deputy Quartermaster General

Assistants: Captains Colin Campbell and Valiancy, Lieutenant Thomas
Oldfield, and Ensign St. John

Lieutenant Alexander Sutherland, Chief Engineer

Assistants: Lieutenants Henry Haldane and Stratton

Mr. Perkins, Commissary

Majors Edward Brabazon, John Manley, J. Baillie, and Francis Richardson

Engineers

Detachments Royal Engineers: Lieutenant Alexander Sutherland

Artillery

Detachments Royal Artillery: Captain George Rochefort

Captain-Lieutenant: Edward Fage

Cavalry

British Legion: Lieutenant Colonel Banastre Tarleton

Queen's American Rangers: Lieutenant Colonel John Graves Simcoe

Light Infantry

Lieutenant Colonel Sir Robert Abercrombie, Commanding

Major Thomas Armstrong

Brigade of Guards

Brigadier General Charles O'Hara, Commanding

Yorke's Brigade

Lieutenant Colonel John Yorke, Commanding

70th Foot: Lieutenant Colonel Henry Johnson

23rd Regiment, Royal Welsh Fusiliers: Captain Charles Apthorpe

33rd Foot: Lieutenant Colonel John Yorke

71st Foot: Lieutenant Colonel Duncan McPherson

Majors Patrick Campbell and James Campbell

Dundas's Brigade

Lieutenant Colonel Thomas Dundas, Commanding

43rd Foot: Major George Hewitt

66th Foot: Major Francis Needham

80th Foot: Lieutenant Colonel Thomas Dundas, Major James Gordon

Ansbach-Bayreuth Regiment

First Battalion: Colonel F. A. V. Voit Von Salzberg

Second Battalion: Colonel F. J. H. C. von Seybothen

Hessian Troops

Régiment Prince Héréditaire (Erbprinz):
Lieutenant Colonel Matthew von Fuchs
Régiment von Bose: Major O'Reilly.
Jägers: Captain John Ewald

Detachments

Pioneers

North Carolina Volunteers: Lieutenant Colonel John Hamilton[30]

As the preceding order of battle makes clear, Cornwallis was noticeably deficient in field grade officers. Besides himself, there was only one other general officer present, two colonels, twelve lieutenant colonels, and a similar number of majors in the entire Yorktown garrison.[31]

All of these officers and men concentrated defensively around Yorktown and Gloucester Point offered a tantalizing reward for the converging French and American columns, whose manpower totaled nearly three times that of the British force. The approaching contest was acquiring the characteristics of a one-sided enterprise—which was exactly what the Allies wanted.

Chapter 3

The British Positions

S oon after his arrival at Yorktown, Cornwallis directed his chief engineer, Lieutenant Alexander Sutherland, to draw up plans for fortifying Gloucester Point.[1] Work on this project began almost immediately, both because the point was more exposed than Yorktown and because holding it was essential to the control of both the town and the river. Thus Yorktown's defenses, at least initially, became a secondary defensive consideration; the community's height above the water made it less susceptible to attack by enemy gun ships. In addition, the works at Yorktown were not improved or added to immediately because of the relative dearth of entrenching tools needed for their erection.[2] Available spades and shovels were used instead to raise tenable works in the sandy soil of Gloucester Point.

The Gloucester Point Fortifications

To erect these works on Gloucester Point, Cornwallis dispatched Lieutenant Colonel John Simcoe. It was a good choice. Simcoe was educated at Exeter, Eton, and Oxford before joining the 35th Foot in 1771. His father was killed at Quebec in 1759, and he almost suffered a similar fate at Brandywine in 1777, where he was seriously wounded. He had extensive field experience and was a proven leader. His command consisted of a detachment of the 80th Infantry, some light companies of the 23rd and 82nd regiments, one regiment of Hessians, the Jägers, the Volunteers from North Carolina, and Simcoe's own Queen's Rangers. Together with Tarleton's Legion, which would later join them, this force numbered about 775 men. Once across the river, Simcoe led his rangers on foraging expeditions to the north, raids that proved successful in the face of the half-hearted efforts of the Virginia militia to disrupt them.[3]

Gloucester Point was an integral part of Cornwallis's defensive strategy. Without it, Yorktown could not be held. It was also fortified first, and viewed as a possible "escape" route. Far fewer troops served on Gloucester Point, however, so fewer firsthand accounts recorded about events that took place there have survived. Much of what we know today about the fortifications erected across the narrow peninsula come from Allied and British maps drawn in 1781. From these representations and the handful of firsthand accounts that exist, we know Simcoe's troops raised four redoubts based on Sutherland's specifications.

The first three of these—Redoubts 1, 2, and 3 as numbered left to right—ran on an west-east line across the peninsula. The first redoubt held one 24-pounder cannon, Redoubt 2 at least three 6-pounder pieces, and Redoubt 3 but a single 6-pounder. The ground in front of these works was described by one eyewitness as "clear and level for a mile." Redoubt 4, however, which was not armed with artillery, was directly southeast of Redoubt 3 and was anchored upon the York River. A creek wrapped its way inland east of the redoubt, which made the works even more defensible. Three batteries interrupted the redoubt chain. Comprised of four 6-pounders, Battery 1 protected the recessed right flank between Redoubts 3 and 4. Battery 2, with the same armament, protected the far left flank of the line. It was erected near the water on the eastern side of the peninsula on the left side of Redoubt 1. The last gunnery position, Battery 3, was armed with six 18- pounders and two 12-pounders and positioned deep inside British lines between Redoubts 2 and 3 and faced in a southeast direction to command approaches from downriver. Deep in the southwest corner of the peninsula west of Battery 3 was a small redoubt overlooking a swampy morass; east of Battery 3 between it and Redoubt 4 a small redan was erected. The outer redoubts were connected by a shallow entrenchment extending the length of the works. In front were small picket redans and a line of strong abatis, which consisted of

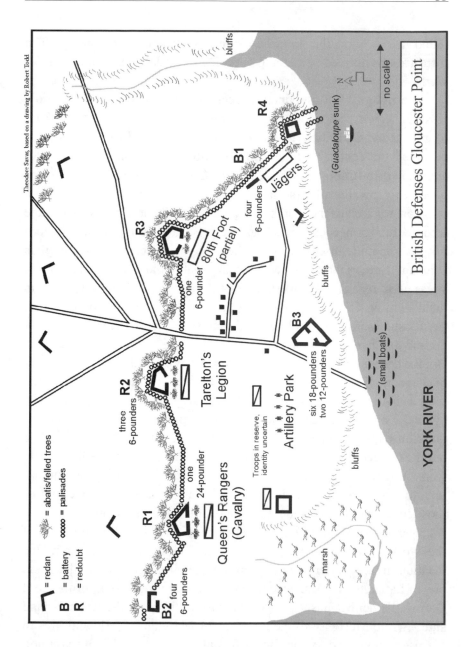

Theodore Savas, based on a drawing by Robert Todt

bluffs

R4

B1

Jägers

four
6-pounders

R3

one
6-pounder

80th Foot
(partial)

R2

three
6-pounders

Tarelton's
Legion

one
24-pounder

R1

Queen's Rangers
(Cavalry)

B2 four
6-pounders

= redan = abatis/felled trees

B = battery ooooo = palisades

R = redoubt

B3

six 18-pounders
two 12-pounders

Artillery Park

Troops in reserve,
identity uncertain

(Guadaloupe sunk)

(small boats)

marsh

bluffs

bluffs

bluffs

YORK RIVER

N

no scale

British Defenses Gloucester Point

felled trees with the branches pointing toward the enemy. The fortifications formed something approaching a large L-shaped line of works.

The right side of this line was secured by Captain Johann Ewald's Hessian Jägers. Simcoe's Rangers took the left side, and the 80th Regiment and the Prince Hereditaire Regiment (later, Tarleton's Legion) occupied the center. The right of the Gloucester Point line was later augmented by troops under Lieutenant Colonel Thomas Dundas, sent over by Cornwallis after the siege began.[4]

Construction of the works at Gloucester Point apparently lacked the resourcefulness needed for such an enterprise, and Sutherland drew scorn for his seeming insensibility to their proper erection. "The English Vauban [Sutherland]," wrote Captain Ewald mockingly, "laid more stress upon repairing the work afterward than on doing it thoroughly in the beginning. . . . Any sensible engineer thinks in advance of palisades, assault stakes, fascines, palings, and saucissons before he starts to break ground; but here, one thinks about it first when the work is constructed." But the dalliance was not without purpose. "What is the reason?" Ewald questioned. "The engineer gets a daily allowance of one pound sterling as long as his work lasts; hence, it is to his advantage if it drags on." The cynical Ewald—who had studied military engineering and authored a book on tactics—believed the French navy could have easily knocked out the Gloucester Point defenses had they known how weak they really were. Whether erection of earthworks at Yorktown promised similar lucrative rewards remains unknown, although the flimsy condition of those fortifications throughout the siege at least hints as much.[5]

Captain Ewald would have likely agreed with the Allied opinions of the works Cornwallis was erecting on Gloucester Point. From his location in Gloucester County, James McHenry, a native of Ulster and one of Lafayette's aides, watched as the works slowly took form. "Lord Cornwallis neither pushes his works with rapidity on the water or land side," wrote McHenry to the governor of Maryland. "[H]e appeares to despise armour and to confide in his natural strength. Would you not, after all this, be surprised to hear good news from this quarter?" General Wayne did not think Cornwallis was seriously intending to hold the peninsula, and believed he would give it up entirely once the siege began in earnest. "[T]hey have one or two little works to preserve a communication with the Country," wrote the vainglorious general with the fierce temper to a friend, "but they will certainly evacuate that side as soon as the investiture is complete." Indeed, for a time Lafayette believed Cornwallis was merely preparing a logistical point from which he could move his army north.[6]

The British Works at Yorktown

In late August, when the Gloucester Point defenses were finally completed, digging began across the river according to designs submitted by Sutherland and approved personally by Cornwallis.[6] Sutherland's plan called for the construction of an inner, or main, line of works around the town, bolstered by an irregular ring of detached outer fortifications to guard the approaches and impede any Allied advance. This design took maximum advantage of the surrounding terrain, especially of the two deep and swampy ravines cutting the ground around Yorktown. These natural obstructions allowed Cornwallis to build weaker entrenchments than he otherwise would have in areas bordering the ravines.[7]

In preparing the advance works, the engineers ordered the trees along the York and Wormley Creek ravines felled.[8] The outer works went up at varying distances from the town, depending on the topography and their potential vulnerability. The works west of Yorktown were erected about 700 yards distant, while those to the south and southeast stood within 300 yards of the inner defenses. Cornwallis fully realized the importance of these outer detached redoubts and concentrated much of his engineering effort on them, as he might be forced to hold them while completing the inner lines.[9] "Cornwallis employs his army night and day in fortifying York and Gloucester," General Edward Hand wrote to a friend on September 17. Hand was a native of Ireland who had served as a surgeon's mate and then ensign in the 18th Royal Irish Regiment before resigning to practice medicine in Philadelphia. Since February last, Hand had been acting as Washington's adjutant general. Cornwallis also knew the raised tract between the York and Wormley ravines—the so-called "gorge"—was of crucial importance because that was where the roads from Hampton (and the sea) and Williamsburg converged. With diligent effort, Cornwallis was confident he could hold the gorge until Clinton's promised relief arrived.[10]

After September 20, when work began in earnest on the main line of fortifications directly around Yorktown, the houses outside the projected perimeter were torn down to aid in the erection of entrenchments, to remove all potential conveniences for the enemy, and to clear away any obstacles that might hinder British artillery fire. These houses, wrote one German soldier, "were torn down in the little city of Yorktown because they were a hindrance outside of our lines."[11] Although the soldiers, assisted by a large number of captured slaves who had been promised their freedom, worked incessantly on the main fortifications, time eventually ran out. Cornwallis's inner line was not complete when the siege opened, primarily because of the insufferable heat, the relatively few entrenching tools available, the lack of sufficient time to accomplish the task—and, perhaps, Sutherland's own personal motives.[12] The work was also occasionally disrupted by the appearance of Virginia troops who fired on the British without warning. Cornwallis sent Tarleton to maneuver beyond the lines, check the enemy militia, and keep them from interfering with his army's progress.[13]

In order to fully understand the Yorktown siege, it is important to grasp and appreciate the defenses erected by Cornwallis and his men around Yorktown in their effort to keep the Allies at bay. What follows is a detailed discussion of these defenses, the archaeology surrounding those that have been studied closely, and a discussion of the field fortifications that have been reconstructed. It is important for the reader to realize that no two historical maps agree in all details as to the exact number, location, and armament of the British fortifications.

The Interior Line

Yorktown's hastily built inner defenses (those closest to the town itself) encompassed an area approximately 1,200 yards long and 400 yards deep, comprising a total perimeter length of some 2,000 yards. Eight redoubts, numbered from right to left, guarded the perimeter of the main works and extended through and around the town in semicircular fashion from river shore to river shore.[14]

Cornwallis's engineer decided upon several different types of construction for the main line of fortifications. On the more vulnerable eastern and southern side of Yorktown (the left side of the British line),

Sutherland devised a system of large strong earthworks and parapets running together in a single line. On the British right flank or western side, where an enemy attack was less likely because the broken terrain would make it nearly impossible to form large masses of men, a palisaded line of earthworks was erected. This inner line was protected by detached redoubts and batteries erected in front. Beyond these at scattered strategic points were additional detached entrenchments that made up what is traditionally known as "the outer line."

"The whole position," wrote French engineer Louis Floxel de Cantel, Chevalier d'Ancteville in his journal,

> was formed of earthworks, with parapets twenty feet in thickness, all fraised [sharpened stakes], with ditches eight feet deep, enveloped or covered by well constructed abatis, which Lord Cornwallis had caused to be built immediately after the arrival of the fleet of Monsieur de Grasse. It appears that he had first made detached works, which he joined together later, seeing that he had the time. He worked later on the interior works of a second line at the left. His right being covered by a ravine impracticable for an attack, he had constructed there only detached works and batteries, joined together by a line of timbers, placed upright and firmly sunk in the ground, with continuous terraces behind.[15]

The Western Inner Defensive Line

Along the far right or northwest of town, where an assault was unlikely, two redoubts supported by a battery were constructed outside the main wall of works. Redoubt 1 was on the right closest to the water

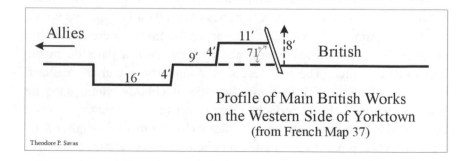

Profile of Main British Works
on the Western Side of Yorktown
(from French Map 37)

Theodore P. Savas

protecting the main Williamsburg Road, Redoubt 2 was directly southwest astride a secondary road also leading to Williamsburg, and Battery 10 was between the two forts. Both redoubts were, according to Tarleton, "furnished with fraizing and abbatis," and fascines were probably also employed. Since Redoubt 1 was in front of the line of works held by the German Erbprinz Regiment, elements from that outfit likely manned the fort as well. The 17th Regiment lined the parapets behind Redoubt 2. Each probably held about 100-man detachments. Battery 10 held four pieces of undetermined size that could reach and thus support the Fusiliers' Redoubt, a strong outer work about 800 yards to the northwest along the York River. Behind Battery 10 was the 23rd Regiment.[16]

In the rear of these three structures was a line of fortifications with a log stockade about eight feet above the ground and above that a parapet four feet high with a base fourteen feet thick at the bottom and eleven feet at the top. This part of the line, remembered Tarleton, "consisted . . . of redoubts and batteries, with a line of stockade in the rear, which supported a high parapet of earth." Much of this portion of the line did not have a ditch on its outside face. On the extreme right was a row of palisades (a strong fence made by driving stakes into the ground), probably with a gate near the Williamsburg Road, that ran along the marshy bottom of the Yorktown Creek ravine to the stream's confluence with the river. This portion of Cornwallis's inner line had five openings cut into it along its length. Whether they were defended with wooden gates, or relied on the redoubts out front is unknown. A log palisade finished the line as it stretched away to the river, blocking access along the beach to enemy troops operating there.

The southwestern-facing portion of the inner line of the Yorktown defenses formed a long and wide semi-circle consisting of two more redoubts (3 and 4) and two more batteries (8 and 9), all connected with a continuous parapet. Apparently, this part of the line was erected with a ditch cut in front, fraised berms, and perhaps even a palisade in the bottom of the ditch. The line here was manned by a pair of Ansbach battalions. General O'Hara's own Brigade of Guards would soon be squeezed between them. Redoubt 3 was larger than Redoubt 4. It is not believed that either redoubt held artillery. The number of weight of the guns in the two supporting batteries, numbered 8 and 9, vary according to the source consulted. Together they probably accounted for nine or ten

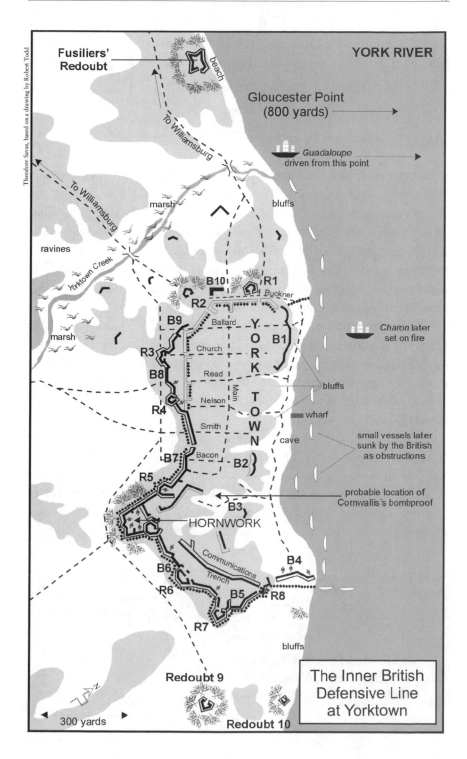

Theodore Savas, based on a drawing by Robert Todd

Fusiliers' Redoubt

beach

YORK RIVER

To Williamsburg

Gloucester Point
(800 yards)

Guadaloupe
driven from this point

To Williamsburg

marsh

bluffs

ravines

Yorktown Creek

marsh

B10

R1

Buckner

R2

Charon later
set on fire

B9

Ballard

Y-O-R-K-T-O-W-N

B1

R3

Church

B8

Read

bluffs

R4

Nelson

Main

wharf

Smith

cave

small vessels later
sunk by the British
as obstructions

B7

Bacon

B2

R5

probable location of
Cornwallis's bombproof

B3

HORNWORK

Communications Trench

B4

B6

R6

B5

R8

R7

bluffs

Redoubt 9

300 yards

Redoubt 10

**The Inner British
Defensive Line
at Yorktown**

pieces. All four of these strong points faced Yorktown Creek and its network of ravines, roads, and trails that passed through this area into the town.[17]

The Eastern and Southern Inner Defensive Line

Cornwallis knew the weakest portion of his line was south and east of Yorktown, where the ground was open and would allow for a strong infantry attack as well as the construction of regular siege parallels. This part of the inner line contained more redoubts and batteries connected by a fraised parapet, but with neither the stockade nor abatis found on the right side of his line. Instead, two large forward redoubts (9 and 10, which are discussed in detail below) were erected to guard the weaker approaches from the south and southeast.

This portion of the line consisted of Redoubts 5, 6, 7, and 8 (with the latter fortification holding the far left of the British line not far from the York River). Redoubt 5 probably boasted some artillery, as did Redoubt 6, which was easily the largest of the four strong points. Redoubt 7 was erected directly behind Redoubt 9, and Redoubt 8 (a small square structure) anchored the line.

A similar number of batteries were erected to sweep the open ground along this portion of the line. These were numbered sequentially 4, 5, 6, and 7, with Battery 4 supporting Redoubt 8 near the York River, Battery 5 farther south between Redoubt 7 and 8, and so on. Many pieces of artillery were also deployed along the entire parapet line as deemed necessary.

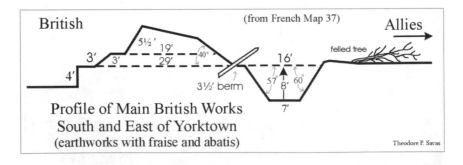

Profile of Main British Works
South and East of Yorktown
(earthworks with fraise and abatis)

Battery 4 was primarily constructed as a land battery to support advanced Redoubt 10 (which is discussed in detail below), but could also be employed as a water battery in case the French sailed within range. Its exact armament has not been determined, though it probably held seven guns. Battery 5 supported both outlying redoubts (9 and 10) and probably held six pieces of artillery. Battery 6 was tucked into the line immediately to the right of Redoubt 6, its fire able to concentrate against the axis of advance along the Hampton Road. Its armament probably consisted of four guns. The last of the four, Battery 7, was well to the northwest on the far side of the Hornwork (see below), and was likely armed with ten pieces of artillery.[18]

The Hornwork

Just left of center along the main inner line of the works, the British built a large "hornwork," which jutted out to the south on a slight ridge to command Hampton Road (which bisected the Hornwork) and other approaches along the gorge. The right side (the Hornwork's eastern face) was about 500 feet long and its left (which faced generally southeast) was about 350 feet long. The Hornwork was ditched and fraised (sharpened stakes) and was the only part of the left side of Cornwallis's inner line ringed with abatis. Carved along its parapet were embrasures for cannon. Like all the Yorktown works, it was built according to the tenets of the era. Bracketed by Redoubt 5 on its right and Battery 6 / Redoubt 6 on its left, and studded with artillery, the Hornwork was a powerful stronghold considered by some who mapped the defenses as a giant battery itself.[19]

The Water Batteries

The bluffs facing the broad face of the York River was where British sailors constructed and then manned three water batteries, numbered, as one might expect, Battery 1, Battery 2, and Battery 3.[20]

By far the largest of the trio was Battery 1, which incorporated old Fort Hill in its construction. Facing northeast with only water in its front, this broad battery stretched from the far right side of the British line (from near Redoubt 1) across three city blocks to Read Street. Exactly what pieces gave it its fire power is in some doubt. It probably contained some 26 pieces, many or perhaps all drawn from British warships. Battery 2, the next largest of the three water batteries, was erected on a bluff north of Bacon Street. Its armament is also uncertain, with some sources showing a dozen iron 12-pounders and another nine 18- and 9-pounders. The smallest, Battery 3, was thrown up on the next bluff southeast and held either three or four pieces of artillery (either 12- or 18-pounders, depending on the source).[21]

What we do know with certainty is that Cornwallis did not bring much artillery with him from the Carolinas. In order to arm these batteries, he was forced to strip the frigates *Charon* and *Guadaloupe* (44 and 28 guns, respectively), of many of their cannon.[22]

In all, the British mounted some sixty-five cannon in these works. Apparently only one of the pieces was larger than an eighteen-pounder. The British also established within their main works a concentric line of ditches and parapets with logs arranged vertically to protect the confined encampment area. The interior space behind the main inner works was so narrow—only about 600,000 square yards—it caused congestion among Cornwallis's soldiers, besides being easily subjected to enemy enfilade fire. To minimize the latter problem, earthen traverses were thrown up and extended from the parapets inward toward the town to separate concentrations of troops or guns. Their purpose was to absorb a shell blast or ricocheting ball and so confine its damage.[23]

Close by, but beyond the main works and guarding the right front overlooking Yorktown Creek ravine, were several detached picket redans, some armed with light ordnance. Within the circle of entrenchments, Lord Cornwallis chose as his headquarters the fine brick home of "Secretary" Thomas Nelson, a retired colonial official whose nephew, Thomas Nelson Jr., was the newly-elected governor of Virginia and commander-in-chief of the state militia. The Nelson house stood along Hampton Road near the edge of town just within the British line.[24]

In the final analysis, the main British works at Yorktown were not substantial enough to withstand a lengthy siege. Cornwallis's initial delay in beginning entrenchments at Yorktown ultimately worked against him. British security rested largely with the outer line of fortifications, or the advance works. The development of these structures began earlier than those of the main line and seemed to entail a thoroughness of construction not apparent elsewhere. Designed to face the brunt of an Allied approach, the British outer defenses assumed a more substantive character than the more transitory entrenchments set tightly around Yorktown.

The Outer Detached Defenses

Yorktown's outer works consisted of seven major earthen fortifications, several lesser ones, numerous field artillery emplacement and troop positions, and a clear field of fire before them.

The most powerful British outer work was a star-shaped redoubt. It was known as the Star or, more commonly, Fusiliers', Redoubt after a contingent of 150 British troops from the 23rd Regiment, Royal Welsh Fusiliers who built and manned it for a time with the assistance of a contingent of marines. Although other units were rotated into the stronghold, the name stuck.

The Star or Fusiliers' Redoubt

The four-pointed fieldwork stood atop the high cliff overlooking the York River about 800 yards west of the main line. It was defended at long range by a British artillery battery 600 yards away on Windmill Point and by whatever ships could support it from the river. The structure effectively covered the British right flank against incursions along the river road from Williamsburg, which nearly brushed up against the redoubt's southern extremity as it drew a line between a ribbon of Yorktown Creek and the river. As one historian notes, the fort "marked the outermost limits of the British right flank." The stronghold also provided protection against possible enemy thrusts in the areas of Yorktown Creek and Ballard Creek, between which two streams the fortification stood, and the approach of enemy sorties along the beach front above Yorktown.[25]

The star-shaped redoubt was a commonly used earthwork during the Revolutionary War—especially by the Americans, who adapted it from the French. The British, however, rarely used this type of earthwork, for they recognized its inherent weaknesses.[26] "It is rather wonderful that such works should obtain commendation," explained one theorist about

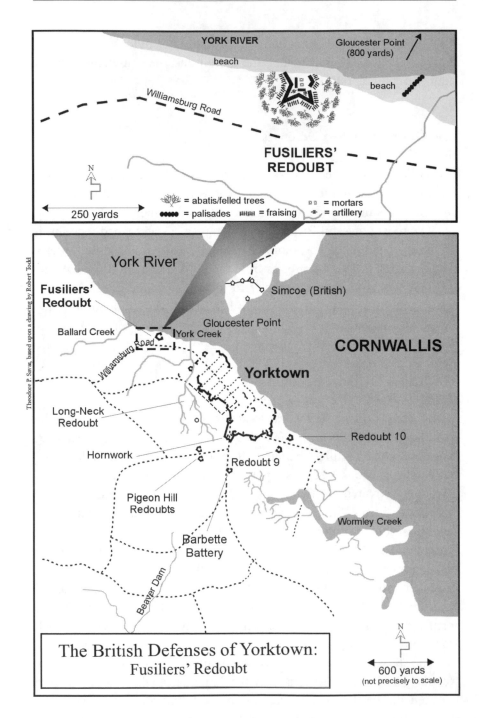

= abatis/felled trees
= palisades
= mortars
= fraising
= artillery

250 yards

FUSILIERS'
REDOUBT

YORK RIVER

beach

Gloucester Point
(800 yards)

beach

Williamsburg Road

The British Defenses of Yorktown:
Fusiliers' Redoubt

600 yards
(not precisely to scale)

star forts, "and a preference to the [square] redoubt, if it is considered that they are not of much greater defence, are more difficult in the construction, and give less inward space in proportion to their perimeter."[27]

Although such forts differed in overall size and exact design, depending on the number of troops intended to defend them and where they were constructed, an average star redoubt during the eighteenth century would have had a parapet six feet or more high and from nine to eighteen feet thick at the top, depending on whether the structure was intended to resist cannon or musket fire. The ditch surrounding the redoubt was at least six feet deep, and probably deeper. Dirt from the ditch went both to raise the epaulement and to form a glacis and covered way along the outside of the ditch. In cases where the parapet was especially high, around seven or eight feet, the glacis might accordingly be raised as high as five feet.[28] Abatis surrounding such an outpost was essential, but did not need to be exceptionally strong. Its purpose was to make the defending troops less liable to surprise attacks by an enemy and more likely to defend the work with dispatch.[29]

In laying out a star redoubt, the engineers first decided on the desired number of points. They varied in design from four to eight points. Fewer points were preferred and usually made for a stronger fortification. Once the number of points was determined, the size was calculated and the basic geometrical shape plotted on the ground. Next, the points were located, a process accomplished by simple mathematics and linear division.[30]

As noted earlier, the Fusiliers' Redoubt was built by members of the Royal Welsh Fusiliers (23rd Foot) commanded by Captain Charles Apthorpe. To them Cornwallis assigned the responsibility of defending the work and thus his right flank. Throughout the siege, members of the 23rd enthusiastically supported their creation.[31] During the latter stage of the siege, command of the redoubt was turned over to Lieutenant Colonel Henry Johnson, who occupied the structure with successive detachments of 190 men, suggesting a perimeter of at least that many yards. According to one account, the redoubt was armed with three coehorns and two twelve-pounders, the latter probably fired en barbette, or over the top without embrasures cut for each gun.[32]

The redoubt possessed four points—two of which ended in a truncated manner along the edge of the cliff. According to most

The Fusiliers' Redoubt as it appeared immediately after its reconstruction in the 1930s. The reconstruction was based upon careful historical research and archaeological excavations. For more views of this redoubt, see Appendix 1, views 1 and 2. *National Park Service, Colonial National Historical Park, Yorktown Collection*

contemporary maps of the siege, the Fusiliers' Redoubt was situated very close to the edge of the bluff. In some instances, the structure is depicted as having little or no parapet on the side fronting the York River, and in at least one case, the side by the bluff is protected by only a row of palisades.[33] Quite possibly, this side consisted of palisades sunk in the earth, stockade fashion, and supported on the inside by earth raised against them in the same manner as the right side of the line of the British main defenses around Yorktown. The entrance, or gorge, stood in the reentrant angle at the rear of the redoubt opposite Yorktown Creek.[34] A large traverse guarded the entrance inside the redoubt.[35]

Although most maps agree the redoubt was surrounded by two rows of abatis, many suggest the rows did not completely encircle the star but instead rested their ends on the edge of the cliff.[36] One contemporary map shows the abatis placed across the Williamsburg Road near the redoubt.[37] Several reveal that the abatis rows were connected at intervals by more felled trees, and one journal states they were intervally joined by "picketed buttresses," which comprised logs fixed with sharpened stakes. According to Captain Ewald, the abatis surrounding the Fusiliers' Redoubt was "of pointed apple or peach trees."[38] The structure was also fraised all along its perimeter.[39]

Below the Fusiliers' Redoubt and midway between it and Yorktown Creek on the beach, the British built a row of palisades extending from the bluff to beyond the water's edge.[40] The redoubt received additional support from a reserve of troops of the 23rd stationed close by in the Yorktown Creek ravine near Williamsburg Road.[41] Additionally, one map depicts what might be a small tented encampment area on the beach below the redoubt—perhaps a supply depot for the troops defending the Fusiliers' Redoubt.[42]

The Fusiliers' Redoubt played such an important role in the British defense of Yorktown that, in early 1935, the government began reconstructing the fortification so that visitors could imagine how the earthwork looked in 1781. Workers determined the actual site of the structure by digging cross-sectional trenches, a process that revealed areas in the soil that had been disturbed by the original excavation in 1781. From this information, the general trace of part of the redoubt became apparent. Constant erosion of the river bluff since 1781 had destroyed an estimated forty percent of the redoubt site, but it was decided to proceed with the reconstruction of what remained.

Specifications for the dimensions of the redoubt were based on the established partial perimeter and data gleaned from eighteenth-century technical manuals on earthen fortifications.[43]

The reconstructed work possessed a parapet seven and one-half feet high and eight feet thick at the top (superior talus). The interior and exterior slopes of the epaulement had to be modified to ensure a stable, permanent fixture, and a height-slope ratio of 1:1 resulted. The location of the entrance, or gorge, was believed to have been on the side least exposed to the enemy.[44] The entrance may or may not be a faithful reproduction of the original. Data yielded by historical maps indicated that the gorge was masked inside the redoubt by an earthen traverse rather than by palisades. In addition to the one at the entrance, other traverses were erected inside the work to reduce the effects of enfilading fire and to deflect the destruction wrought by bursting shells. Moreover, excavation of the moat ditch during reconstruction disclosed tentative evidence of the proper location of the gorge in the area now eroded away.

The floor of the redoubt was investigated archaeologically to a depth of two to three feet. Project Superintendent A. F. Booth, of the Civilian Conservation Corps, recorded what he found there:

> Various articles were found which were suitable for the museum. The dump where all refuse was buried was located and in addition, a grave containing three bodies was found, presumably those of three of the defenders which had to be buried at once as a large number of shell fragments were found among the bones. The bones were placed in separate concrete caskets, numbered and reburied in the same spot where they were found.[45]

The Fusiliers' Redoubt was a well-made and powerful fort that resisted every effort to capture it. Indeed, it remained in the hands of the British Army throughout the entire siege, and was surrendered only at the capitulation on October 19.

The Long Neck Redoubt

On the finger of land between the forks of Yorktown Creek above the morass (the area designated "long neck"), the British built a redoubt to cover the approaches leading through the ravines toward the right flank of the British position. This redoubt was small and based on information from contemporary maps, circular or octagonal in shape.[46] A circular structure would seem appropriate at this position, overlooking as it did the terrain along all its sides. As Lochee, the author of the influential 1783 *Elements of Field Fortifications* noted,

> the access will be more equally difficult in proportion as the redout [sic] has more faces: and it is on account of this that the circular form for the redout has the greatest number of advocates. Besides, all the points of the circumference of a circle being equally disposed, the soldiers post themselves throughout, which makes the space defended vary every moment, and so the enemy is no where in safety.[47]

Easily traced by moving string in concentric circles from a central axis, circular redoubts afforded greater floor space and were easily defended against assault. The maps are not unanimous on the presence of abatis around the Long Neck Redoubt, although the weight of the evidence suggests it existed.[48] Contemporary accounts contain no information bearing on the physical construction of this work or on its role during the days preceding the Allied investment, suggesting its use as a lookout by the British before the siege got underway. Tiny Long Neck Redoubt still exists today (now more commonly known as the "Untouched Redoubt."[49]

The Pigeon Hill Redoubts

Southeast of the Long Neck Redoubt is an area known variously as Pigeon Hill, Penny Hill, or Pigeon Quarter. Two strategic and conspicuous British advance redoubts (numbered for our purposes Pigeon Hill 1 and Pigeon Hill 2) were erected in this area about 500 yards from the Long Neck Redoubt. Pigeon Hill 1 stood a short distance north of Goosley Road, and Pigeon Hill 2 just south of it. The structures were separated by 250 yards, and each watched over the main route that stretched west toward Williamsburg. They also defended the western extreme of the throat of land running between the York and Wormley Creek ravines.

Information on the Pigeon Hill Redoubts is at best sketchy.[50] Neither seems to have been solidly constructed in the sandy loam or erected with a very thick parapet. Both needed considerable reinforcement after the Allies captured them—probably with fascines, which consisted of cylindrical bundles of small sticks used to strengthen the ramparts. Later, when the British abandoned these outposts, a French officer inspected them to get a feel for what they might expect when they confronted the main line closer to Yorktown. He was not impressed. "They are not solid; the parapets are not thick, and are made of sandy soil which obliges them to be propped up lest they fall down; but the abatis," he continued, "are excellent, having no other fault but being made of pine [which is] easy to set on fire."[51] The outposts also served to support each other, but neither seems to have been strongly manned by the British. Later, of course, the redoubts served to protect the French and American encampment area to the south. Neither structure saw any major action during the siege.[52] Perhaps most important, the Pigeon Hill Redoubts symbolized the confusion of the British leadership in the face of the Allied advance on the town, as evidenced by their precipitate evacuation by the British.[53]

According to nearly all of the historical maps, the Pigeon Hill redoubt north of Goosley Road was pentagonally shaped with the principal point toward the road and the entrance on the side facing Yorktown. Nearly every map depicts a single row of abatis around the structure.[54] This redoubt has not been reconstructed. If it were, the design would doubtless conform to the precepts expounded by the eighteenth-century theorists, with a parapet at least six feet tall and between three and twelve feet wide at the top, with the latter thickness probably evident along the southern and westernmost faces. Such an outer redoubt could have had even smaller dimensions—a four- to five-foot tall parapet, for example—if it was erected to withstand only fire from light artillery pieces rather than from siege ordnance.[55]

Much data concerning Pigeon Hill 1 can be derived from comparative information relative to Pigeon Hill 2, which has been reconstructed on the Yorktown field. This outpost was square in design according to the historical maps, although archaeological investigation has disclosed that certain sides were made longer than others, giving the work a rather unequal appearance; its salient angles were less than forty-five degrees.[56] Almost all the maps confirm the placement of a single row of abatis around the redoubt.[57] Pigeon Hill 2 was built to hold about seventy-eight men, based on the formulation that each man occupied a yard of perimeter, or twice that figure if double file was used. Based on the former number, this redoubt had an internal circumference of roughly 234 feet. Historical evidence, however, suggests neither of the Pigeon Hill outposts was ever occupied to capacity. The British assigned only 24 men to each of these advance works. After the Allies captured them, Rochambeau sent 100 grenadiers to one and 50 to the other, but no distinction was ever made as to which structure received which lot of French soldiers.[58]

The interior of the redoubt measured 3,310 square feet. Around the inside was a drainage ditch twelve inches wide by thirty to thirty-six inches deep to carry off rainwater. The parapet height and thickness differed markedly from one side to another. The side facing northeast stood the customary six feet high and was five feet thick at the top. Conversely, that facing southeast measured five feet high and three feet, 8 inches in thickness at the top.[59] Presumably, the archaeological disclosures reflected the condition of the redoubt after the French took it over, for the improvements necessarily included reinforcing the work on the sides facing Yorktown and constructing a new entrance. Furthermore, archaeological findings preparatory to reconstruction revealed that the British intended the southeast face to be the rear of the work. At that point, both the ditch and epaulement were smaller, probably because at one time an entrance stood there.[60]

Pigeon Hill 2 appears to have been well guarded by the British. Its northeast face was covered by the sister structure across Goosley Road, the easternmost angle drew protection from batteries in Yorktown and in the Hornwork, and the southeast side was covered by a light battery on a hill near Hampton Road.[61]

It is possible that one or both Pigeon Hill redoubts possessed light-caliber guns. Journals of the siege mention grapeshot being fired at the investing army, but there is no positive proof it came from guns stationed in these redoubts. Thor Borresen, the research technician responsible for designing the reconstructed work at Pigeon Hill in 1940, believed the outposts were indeed so armed and planned the reconstruction accordingly.[62] At least one contemporary source, however, suggests that neither Pigeon Hill redoubt ever contained artillery.[63] It seems more likely the fusillade of grape and canister shot that met the French and Americans came from light pieces mounted between and near the Pigeon Hill works. The powder magazine that Borresen postulated for the redoubt could have been used to service these adjacent light pieces.

Reconstruction of Pigeon Hill 2 included a powder magazine typical of the period of the siege, complete with a fascine-type floor and a roof covered with fascines, dirt, and rawhide.[64] In addition, Borresen proposed such embellishments as a bell tent, a shelter or hut, and a fireplace in the reconstructed work. Such conclusions were conjectural, however, and essentially lacked either the archaeological or historical data necessary to support them.[65]

The Hampton Road Battery

About 760 yards southeast of the Pigeon Hill Redoubts, to the left of Hampton Road and just below its present intersection with Virginia State Highway 704, the British erected a battery for field artillery to command the road in front.[66] Most of the maps indicate that this was a small work or redan open at the gorge; some make a distinction between its shape when the British Army occupied it, and after the Allies took over and the Americans converted it into a redoubt.[67] According to one map, two nine-pounders were placed in the work; another suggests that these were fired barbette fashion (i.e., without embrasures).[68] The British placed abatis only around the front, or southern face, of the structure, and some maps show it lying across Hampton Road. Baron Ludwig von Closen, a Bavarian captain in the Royal Deux-Ponts and aide to Rochambeau, later called the structure "a bonnet battery," which was a two-faced outwork with a salient angle. The battery was ditched and probably fraised like the other outer works, although there is no direct evidence of this.[69] South of the battery, and between it and the Pigeon Hill advance works, the trees had all been cut down, their ends pointing outward to further impede an advancing enemy.[70]

During the Allied occupation, the Americans constructed a V-shaped extension on the rear of the British work, cut an entrance in the former front face, and ended up with a pentagonal-shaped redoubt.[71] Apparently, the new occupants did not alter or add to the abatis around the structure, believing they were reasonably safe from assault because of their distance from the British main works.

This British battery and the Pigeon Hill Redoubts were the sole earthworks raised to cover the 1,500-foot "gorge" of land between the heads of York and Wormley creeks. However, the British planned to strengthen this area with the addition of at least three more works. One of these would have been erected between Pigeon Hill 2 and the field battery along Hampton Road. Two others would have been built, one to the south and another to the southeast, in order to consolidate the area. According to a map of these contemplated structures prepared by Cornwallis's chief engineer (probably) after the siege, the additional "redoubts would have rendered his [Cornwallis's] exterior position respectable[,] holding at the same time . . . [the Pigeon Hill works] and within 300 yds of [the] marshes."[72]

Redoubts 9 and 10

Two structures (known today as Redoubts 9 and 10) defended Yorktown's southeastern flank, which was the weakest stretch of the British main works. Whether the British considered them part of the inner defensive line is unknown, but they played a key role in defending that line. One American officer—the only eyewitness to say as much—claims a narrow ditch connected the redoubts to the main line. Between them ran a secondary road to the home of a man named Moore, slightly more than a mile to the east. Located roughly 350 yards east of the main works and 330 yards south of its neighbor, Redoubt 9 was a pentagonal structure possessing a ditch, palisades, fraising, and a surrounding single row of abatis. Larger than its sister work situated at the edge of the bluff overlooking the York River, Redoubt 9 covered the left front approach extending along the northern arm of the Wormley Creek ravines.[73]

Both works were critical to British security. As long as they held, Cornwallis could direct his attention to the Williamsburg roads in front. If they fell, however, they would expose the weakest part of the British stronghold to enemy attack.[74] Neither work, despite their fraising and abatis, was as soundly constructed as the Fusiliers' Redoubt on the right of the British position. Because they were detached from the main line of fortifications, each structure depended to a large degree on the other, as

Redoubt 9 as it appeared in the 1930s after its reconstruction while awaiting sodding. For more views of Redoubt 9, see page 250 and Appendix 1, views 18 and 20. *National Park Service, Colonial National Historical Park, Yorktown Collection*

well as on the main works behind them, for protection.[75] There is evidence that two howitzers were mounted in Redoubt 9, and some accounts claim approaching Allied troops in that quarter were greeted by grapeshot fired by guns in the work.[76] Redoubt 9 was manned during the siege by about 125 British soldiers sent from the main works, a figure borne out by the 103-yard inside perimeter of the redoubt disclosed during archaeological excavation prior to its reconstruction.[77]

Archaeology has also confirmed the location of the British gorge—or entrance—in the rear of the work facing Yorktown. After the redoubt was captured by the French on the night of October 14, this entrance was filled in and a new one cut in the northeast face.[78] Besides abatis and fraises, the redoubt had a palisade ditch.

"These forts or redoubts were well secured by a ditch and picket, sufficiently high parapet, and within were divisions made by rows of casks ranged upon end and filled with earth and sand," remembered American officer Ebenezer Denny.[79] There is a further possibility that sandbags were used to bolster the redoubts, although no direct mention of them or of gabions (usually a cylindrical wicker basket filled with dirt and stone) being used as part of the British fortifications has been located. At least 1,000 sandbags were among the property surrendered by the

British at Yorktown, and it is feasible such items would have been routinely used in the erection of redoubts.[80]

Archaeological work and reconstruction of Redoubt 9 was conducted between October 1936 and September 1937. This work positively determined the location of the structure by locating the previously disturbed soil, and eight human skeletons were found buried within the site.[81] Reconstruction began on the basis of available historical and archaeological evidence and on the theoretical evidence suggested by the technical manuals.[82] The redoubt dimensions incorporated into the reconstructed earthwork were bascially identical to those utilized in those reconstructions discussed earlier.

Redoubt 10 was called the "Rock Redoubt" by the Americans. It was about 700 feet away from, and somewhat smaller than, its companion to the southwest. Redoubt 10 was square-shaped with abatis, fraising, and palisades, and erected on the bluff overlooking the river. Approximately 70 British soldiers manned this station until their capture by the Americans on the night of October 14.[83] The "Rock Redoubt" was armed with two or three cannon placed to fire on enemy ships ascending the

Redoubt 10 as it appeared during the bicentennial celebrations. For another photo of Redoubt 10, see Appendix 1, view 17. *National Park Service, Colonial National Historical Park, Yorktown Collection*

river; consequently, the structure was fitted with three embrasures along the side nearest the bluff.[84]

Historical maps confirm the shape of Redoubt 10 and also the presence of fraising and abatis, as do most journals recounting the events surrounding the structure and leading to its surrender.[85] The British Engineers' map shows abatis on the sides facing away from the river, but none between the redoubt and the edge of the cliff.[86] Abatis placed in this manner emulated that around the Fusiliers' Redoubt and apparently allowed for access of supplies and relief troops up the sloping bluff from the beach. Along this route the men had protective cover, and could thus avoid the open ground between the main works and the "twin redoubts." Furthermore, at least one map suggests the strip of beach running into the water immediately below Redoubt 10 was corduroyed, possibly to facilitate the conveyance of men and provisions by small boats from the waterfront at Yorktown.[87]

After Redoubt 10 fell on the night of October 14, the Americans added their own armaments and directed the fire against Cornwallis's main line.[88] Complete reconstruction of Redoubt 10 has been impossible because of erosion to the riverbank on which the earthwork originally stood. Only part of the ditch encircling the structure remained when the partial reconstruction began.[89]

Lesser Works Covering Southeastern Front

Redoubts 9 and 10 completed the network of major British fortifications guarding the main position at Yorktown. Several smaller works, however, supported these and covered the approaches on the north side of the Wormley Creek ravine. Contemporary maps differ as to whether two or three redans were built on the tongue of land below the Smith residence overlooking the upper reaches of the Wormley ravine. Most maps indicate three fleches there (simple fieldworks consisting of two faces forming a salient angle pointing outward and open at the rear).[90] A British headquarters plan, however, indicates the presence of only two such works, each armed with a pair of three-pounders.[91]

Farther down Wormley Creek, beyond its millpond on the north side of the big bend of the stream, the British soldiers raised three more redans specifically designed to cover the road crossing the dam at that point. One of these was situated directly opposite the crossing, the others flanking it on bluffs located across arms of the ravine to the right and left. These stations were occupied by sailors taken from British vessels anchored in Yorktown harbor.[92] All three works were documented in 1934, and at least two still exist.[93] Another work, slightly southwest of these and nearly opposite an upper dam, may still be seen today.[94]

Besides these redans, some maps suggest still other earthworks in the area. At least three maps confirm a redoubt, complete with abatis, near the edge of the southernmost extension of Wormley Creek ravine at a location that evidently became the American field hospital.[95] What appears to be a long earthen epaulement is situated southeast of the Moore house, as if to cover one of the arms of the Wormley ravine cutting into that area.[96] These works probably played a subordinate—if indeed any—role during the siege of Yorktown. Possibly the latter position was erected, then abandoned, during early British operations in the vicinity. The chances are also that the British abandoned this work once the direction of the Allied attack became apparent.

In order to consolidate the British outer position around Yorktown, troops and light artillery were placed strategically to intercept the enemy from all directions. Between the advance fortifications in the gorge, trees were felled with their branches outward to form abatis. Historical maps explicitly show the terrain leveled of all timber on both sides of Wormley Creek ravine and along its tributaries.[97] The area all around the Yorktown Creek ravines was similarly treated, as was the area west of the Fusiliers' Redoubt and along the south side of Williamsburg Road.[98] The British put more abatis for a length of almost a mile across the secondary route running from Goosley Road into Yorktown, besides destroying the small bridge fording Yorktown Creek by that approach.[99]

Defending the River

With his forces separated into contingents at Yorktown and Gloucester Point, Cornwallis saw the immediate importance of ensuring British domination of the intervening stretch of river. Under no circumstances could the French Navy be allowed to reach the waters above the British position. It was also feared that Washington's force might attempt a landing from the York River. In addition to the erection of the Water Batteries (previously discussed), commencing September 16, Cornwallis's troops began sinking British transport vessels to prevent any French naval incursions directly offshore.[100] At least twenty-nine ships—transports and victualers—were scuttled in the shallow water around Yorktown, the line of wrecks forming an arc between the rows of stockade extended from the fortifications into the water at either end of the town. General Hand observed the events and informed a friend on September 17, "[Cornwallis] has drawn up his ships to the shore, moored them hand and stern, landed their guns, and cut up their sails for tents, and has given orders to bury or sink them on the first attack."[101]

To secure the area of lower Yorktown Creek and to support the Fusiliers' (Star) Redoubt, Cornwallis ordered two warships with a total gun complement of 72 pieces to take station directly offshore from these locations. The *Charon*, which carried 44 12- and 18-pounders, hovered off the mouth of Yorktown Creek under the commander of the naval forces immediately at Cornwallis's disposal, Captain Thomas Symonds. Slightly upstream was moored the *Guadaloupe*, originally carrying 28 12- and 9-pounders.[102] Both vessels occupied dangerous positions, being subject to direct attack by well-placed enemy artillery. Neither vessel, moreover, was armed to capacity, for many of their guns had been stripped for use in the water batteries around Yorktown.

Most of the smaller craft were clustered across the strait off the southeast shore of Gloucester Point, while some hugged the beach before Yorktown.[103] One American who viewed Cornwallis's preparations on the river described the scene this way:

> Ten or twelve large merchant ships have been sunk before York, and piles have been driven in front of these vessels, to prevent our ships from approaching the Town sufficiently to debark Troops, which they are infinitely afraid of. The *Charon* and *Guadeloupe* [sic] are moored before York, in such a manner as to defend the Town rather than the passage of the River.[104]

The British located their cemeteries inside the stockade at either end of the enclosed beach. Before September 30, the burial ground was west of Yorktown, but on that date an observer noted, "the Burial Ground for the Right Wing is within the Stockade close to the Water side, the same on the left Wing."[105]

By late September, Cornwallis had amply secured his outer position on land and water and turned his attention almost completely to improving his faltering main inner works. The outward redoubts—Fusiliers' on the right, the Long Neck and Pigeon Hill outposts, Hampton Road barbette battery in the center, and Redoubts 9 and 10 on the left—amply ringed Yorktown. Detached redans guarded York and Wormley creeks and their adjacent ravines, and felled trees further blocked approach into the area.

Soldiers, Batteries, and Abatis Bolster the Outer Defenses

Besides the outer works and auxiliary defenses, parts of the British Army covered the terrain around Yorktown with troops and cannon. On the right supporting the Fusiliers' Redoubt and protecting the approaches of Yorktown Creek were detachments of the 23rd Foot (Royal Welsh Fusiliers) Regiment. Safeguarding the gorge behind the Pigeon Hill Redoubts and the barbette battery near the junction of Goosley and Hampton roads were the 76th and 80th regiments. A battalion of each unit aided by light artillery closed Goosley Road to the Allies.

Between the Pigeon Hill structures and to the right of Goosley Road stood two 12-pounders. Four 3-pounders and a like number of 6-pounders stood on either side of the highway about one-quarter mile to the east. At the junction of the roads, Cornwallis's Light Infantry manned four more light pieces—two 3-pounders and two 6-pounders. To their left, behind and covering the northward arm of Wormley Creek ravine, was the German Ansbach Regiment, and to its left was placed the 71st Foot. Across and south of Wormley Creek, Tarleton's cavalry guarded the approaches. Midway between the regiments, sealing the gorge and the British main works, General Charles O'Hara's Guards took early station. Farther left, near Redoubt 9, the Regiment von Bose fulfilled a similar supportive function.[106]

Inside the main works, digging continued as the British prepared to receive the Allies. Magazines were placed at or near every battery and gun emplacement within the works, though historic maps fail to locate them with any specificity. A larger strategically located magazine (or magazines) for holding much of the powder would have been located inside these works—but where? Some postulate it was inside a cave cut

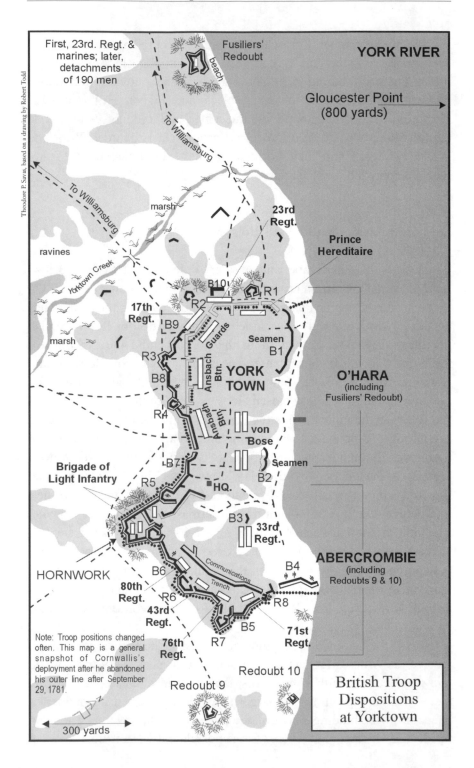

First, 23rd. Regt. &
marines; later,
detachments
of 190 men

Fusiliers'
Redoubt

beach

YORK RIVER

To Williamsburg

Gloucester Point
(800 yards)

To Williamsburg

ravines

marsh

23rd
Regt.

**Prince
Hereditaire**

Yorktown Creek

B10

R1

R2

17th
Regt.

B9

Guards

Seamen

B1

marsh

R3

Ansbach Btn.

**YORK
TOWN**

O'HARA
(including
Fusiliers' Redoubt)

B8

R4

Ansbach Btn.

von
Bose

**Brigade of
Light Infantry**

B7

Seamen

B2

R5

HQ.

B3

33rd
Regt.

ABERCROMBIE
(including
Redoubts 9 & 10)

B4

HORNWORK

B6

Communications

Trench

80th
Regt.

R6

43rd
Regt.

R8

B5

71st
Regt.

Note: Troop positions changed
often. This map is a general
snapshot of Cornwallis's
deployment after he abandoned
his outer line after September
29, 1781.

76th
Regt.

R7

Redoubt 10

Redoubt 9

300 yards

**British Troop
Dispositions
at Yorktown**

Theodore P. Savas, based on a drawing by Robert Todd

into the marl bluffs near the water (also known as "Cornwallis's Cave"). The natural cavity was excavated before the war to form a natural storage place. There is no evidence, however, that it was ever used for this purpose. Large magazines may have been located on the slope of the bluff or in one of the many ravines that led to the Lower Town (that area closer to the water). Indeed, Rochambeau noted after the war that his guns opened on enemy magazines located "on the slope of the hill, by the river." Sutherland, Cornwallis's engineer, noted on his rather vague map the presence of two magazines, one behind Redoubt 2 on the right side of the main line or in a ravine farther on.[107]

Just as the locations of the large magazines are uncertain, so too are the locations where the British established their hospitals to care for the ill and wounded. Some were transported across the water to Gloucester Point or to ships anchored off shore. The county courthouse, which the French utilized after the siege as a hospital, may have also been used for the same purposes by the British, but no definitive evidence on this has yet been found.[107]

Regardless of where he placed his hospitals and magazines, once the inner fortifications were complete, and after Cornwallis withdrew from his outer position, command of the main works was divided between two senior officers: General O'Hara assumed command of the right of the line, and Lieutenant Colonel Robert Abercrombie the left. On the right side facing upstream, Cornwallis posted the Regiment Prince Hereditaire (Erbprinz) and part of Lieutenant Colonel John Yorke's Brigade (General O'Hara's Brigade of Guards was essentially in reserve at this time). Facing downstream inside the works on the eastern flank were the 71st Foot and Colonel Thomas Dundas's Brigade. The 33rd Foot, along with the German Regiment von Bose, faced the York River, while Abercrombie's Light Infantry occupied the post of honor in the Hornwork.

Some of these positions changed during the course of the fighting, as Cornwallis altered the disposition of his forces. Some units were brought over from Gloucester Point to support the line, while others, like Tarleton's, were sent to the north shore in response to arising exigencies.[108]

His defenses planned, if not exactly readied, Cornwallis awaited the advance of the forces under General George Washington.

Chapter 4

Washington Takes Command

s Cornwallis and his men labored on their defenses, Major
General Lafayette sent parties of Continentals and militia to
keep an eye on their efforts. The Americans watched as the
enemy dug sand and dirt, cut down trees, sharpened stakes,
and erected their fortifications at Gloucester Point and Yorktown.
Lafayette reported the British general's every move, and contemplated
what he would do next.

"There is no doubt," wrote Lafayette early in August, "but that the
principal post will be at York."[1] The American presence did not greatly
bother or deter Cornwallis, who continued his work safe in the
knowledge that his own force was vastly superior to the Frenchman's and
that after the hot season passed, his troops would be secure.[2]

Cornwallis's confidence received a staggering blow when Admiral de
Grasse entered the mouth of Chesapeake Bay on August 30 with a large
contingent of French soldiers to augment Lafayette. These soldiers,
commanded by St. Simon, continued up the James River in longboats and
came ashore at Jamestown in the early morning darkness of September 2.[3]
The new division from the West Indies comprised the Regiments
Touraine, Agenois, and Gatenois, commanded, respectively, by the
Viscount de Pondeux, the Marquis d'Andechamps, and the Marquis de
Rostaing. The Regiment Touraine was nearly 150 years old. Lafayette's

father had fallen in 1759 leading it at the Battle of Minden, Germany. The Regiment Agenois outranked the others in terms of longevity. The Gatenois had seen previous service in the American war, having covered the withdrawal of French soldiers before Savannah, Georgia. As a young man, General Rochambeau had served in the Gatenois in Germany.[4] All of these troops, about 3,000 strong, joined Lafayette at his Williamsburg base on September 8.[5]

The arrival of these new soldiers was not without complications, however. General Wayne, hurrying to a nighttime appointment with Lafayette, was mistakenly shot by one of the new arrivals. As Wayne recounted the incident:

> About 10 o'clock at night I arrived in the vicinity of his Encampment, when I was challenged by a Sentry & made the usual answer—but the poor fellow being panic struck & mistaking us for the British, immediately fired his piece & shot me in the middle of the thigh—the ball fortunately Only graized [sic] the bone, & lodged pretty near the Opposite side to which it entered—the whole camp was alarmed & I had some difficulty (wounded as I was) to prevent the whole of the advanced guard from firing upon me.[6]

Yet even such adverse circumstances failed to dampen Wayne's optimism at the prospect of reducing Cornwallis's army. "We have the most glorious certainty, of very soon Obliging Lord Cornwallis, with all his Army to Surrender prisoners of War," wrote Mad Anthony. "[E]verything is in readiness to commence the siege, our army is numerous & in high spirits, the French are the finest body of troops I ever viewed, & harmony & friendship pervades the whole."[7]

Generals Washington and Rochambeau reached Williamsburg and joined Lafayette on September 14, having ridden overland from Mount Vernon. Despite their unification of purpose, the two army leaders hailed from very different backgrounds.

By 49, the tall and imposing Washington had become the quintessential American military leader, tried and proven over the course of the long and bitter struggle since 1775. The humble Virginian reflected his agrarian roots and managed to present a calm demeanor that inspired confidence among his cadre and filtered down through the ranks. As a military man, he lacked significant formal education and came to the position through the schools of hard experience. As a major and colonel in 1753-1754, Washington reconnoitered French positions in western Pennsylvania until surrendering Fort Necessity. He later accompanied British General Edward Braddock against the French, and following that officer's death in July 1755, safely withdrew the surviving forces. Thereafter, Washington served in Virginia's House of Burgesses, and in 1758 resigned his colonel's commission to marry and become a farmer at Mount Vernon. After 1763, however, Washington opposed British taxation policies, renewed his involvement in militia activities, and in 1774 and 1775, served as a delegate from Virginia to the First and Second Continental Congresses.

Washington's accrued knowledge of military affairs, together with his perceived administrative faculties and political connections in the vital Virginia colony, made him the logical man to elevate to commander-in-chief of the Continental armies in 1775. A more challenging task as a commander would be difficult to conceive. In the opening actions, he checked the British in Boston and New York, but met with a serious defeat on Long Island that nearly ended the war. The battlefield embarrassment forced him to withdraw his fledgling army into Pennsylvania. A risk taker by nature, Washington assumed the offensive against British positions at Trenton in December 1776, and again in January at Princeton, New Jersey. These daring winter attacks captured supplies and prisoners—and frustrated Cornwallis's efforts to catch him. In the next year, Washington fell back before General William Howe's move on Philadelphia and in a hard fight at Brandywine was defeated in September 1777. Still, the determined general mustered his men and struck back forcefully against Howe's base encampment at Germantown the following month. His tenure at the head of the army during these harrowing days of the British invasion was not completely secure. Indeed, he survived attempts to replace him in command, especially following the American victory of General Horatio Gates over Lieutenant General John Burgoyne at Saratoga.

Washington's confidence grew following the alliance with France in 1778, and the quality of training of the American forces increased dramatically. New thrusts against the British succeeded in New Jersey, and at Monmouth his command inflicted heavy casualties, although General Clinton succeeded in reaching and occupying New York City. Thereafter, dogged by insufficient troops and supplies, Washington

Independence National Historical Park

General George Washington

could only harass the British and monitor their movements while supporting Nathanael Greene's and Lafayette's operations in the South. The arrival of French troops under Rochambeau in July 1780, however, changed the strategic equation and permitted a resurrection of a more aggressive strategy against the British in New York—that is, until circumstances in the South presented an opportunity that changed everything. By 1781, armed with the promise of French assistance,

National Park Service, Colonial National Historical Park, Yorktown Collection

General Jean Baptiste Donatien de Vimeur, comte de Rochambeau

Washington's confidence soared. His dogged persistence through the previous five years, during which he had shown the mettle of leadership amid great adversity, had strengthened his character, resolve, and patience. Although he knew anger, his sense of duty and morality, together with the nobility of his personal appearance and simple gestures, inspired others in his presence. By the fall of 1781, Washington was at the height of his military prowess.[8]

Many of Washington's characteristics were mirrored in the enthusiastic Rochambeau, who was a capable administrator, tactful, diplomatic, and conversant. Like the commander-in-chief, the Frenchman was a brave military leader. He too had amassed exceptional experience in the art of war in European conflicts stretching back almost 40 years to the War of the Austrian Succession (1740-48). As a colonel, Rochambeau garnered invaluable siege warfare credentials in that conflict, and had been badly wounded at Lauffeldt in 1747. In the Seven Years War (1756-1763) he took part in the siege of Minorca and other major battles, and distinguished himself at Minden in 1759. Thereafter, Rochambeau served as inspector of cavalry, implementing training and discipline in the army command, and later took charge of a military district in France. He was promoted to lieutenant general in 1780 to command the expeditionary force sent to North America. As part of the international tandem about to confront the British at Yorktown, Rochambeau brought needed experience, support, and vibrancy in leadership and bearing to the Allied command.[9]

Once at Williamsburg, Washington immediately began preparations for a movement against Yorktown. The next day, the American general notified Admiral de Grasse of the immediate need to transport the Allied soldiers from the upper reaches of the Chesapeake, the vessels sent earlier having been used mainly for carrying ordnance and supplies. Meanwhile, the armies had marched from Head of Elk to Baltimore and Annapolis to await transport. Anticipating just such a situation, de Grasse had already sent ships under Admiral de Barras to convey the soldiers. As a result, Rochambeau's men began landing on September 18 at Archer's Hope on the James River south of Williamsburg. The first Americans debarked two days later.[10]

Realizing the vital need for de Grasse to retain his position at the mouth of Chesapeake Bay, Washington and Rochambeau visited the admiral and solicited his promise to remain and assist the land forces until the end of October. The two generals returned to Williamsburg on September 22, pleased with de Grasse's agreement. The same day, the admiral sent heartening word that artillery and provisions were beginning to arrive, and for several days the heavy siege pieces were unloaded at Trebell's Landing on the James, two miles below the mouth of College Creek. The noose was slowly but surely closing around Cornwallis.[11]

Gloucester Point remained a central cause for concern among the Allied commanders. They believed Cornwallis planned to use it not only as a place of deposit for supplies foraged throughout the Gloucester countryside, but also as a possible route of escape for his soldiers from Yorktown.[12] To forestall both schemes, Washington had earlier ordered more troops to Gloucester Point, possibly with the belief, as one officer expressed it, that "when he [Cornwallis] comes to be Closely Invested he will certainly Evacuate that side."[13]

Washington dispatched several hundred cavalry, infantry, and an artillery company to Gloucester Point under Louis Armand de Gontaut-Biron, duc de Lauzun. Lauzun's Legion was a foreign corps consisting of men from at least 15 European countries (including Ireland, Poland, Russia Denmark, Hungary, and Germany). Only one-third were French. Lauzun's cavalry contingent had ridden overland from the Head of Elk and down the peninsula between the York and Rappahannock rivers directly for Gloucester Point. His infantry and artillery reached that point by way of West Point. The legion backed by 1,500 militia under Brigadier General George Weedon, a former tavern owner and veteran of the French and Indian War, whose militia were already present at Gloucester to monitor British activities there.

Washington would later dispatch Brigadier General Claude Gabriel de Choisy to take charge. Choisy proved a good choice. His age is open to speculation (his date of birth has gone unrecorded), but his military credentials were solid. As a brigadier general he had campaigned against the resistance during the First Partition of Poland, and distinguished himself at the siege of Cracow in 1772. A confidant of Rochambeau, he had accompanied the general to America. On October 4, about 800 French marines arrived to aid Choisy at Gloucester Point, loaned by de Grasse expressly for that purpose.[14]

*   *   *

The armies congregating around Williamsburg and south of the former capital presented striking contrasts in composition, training, and appearance. In their white breeches and jackets, stockings, and low-cut shoes, the French infantrymen drew notice seconded only by that accorded the deep blue waistcoats worn by their countrymen's artillery and special corps. But even the infantry and artillery troops paled next to Lauzun's legionaries, who were decked out in the boldest shades of red and green imaginable. Nearly all the French soldiers wore the black, three-cornered cocked hats popular in eighteenth-century Europe, and most of their regimental standards were divided by white crosses, with each quarter sporting a different color.[15]

American uniforms, by contrast, offered greater variety than those of the French and reflected the diversity of units composing that army. Most Continental infantry units wore dark blue coats with various colors of facing, such as red, white, light blue, and buff, corresponding to individual regiments. The light infantrymen were similarly garbed, but wore shorter coats and leather caps. Continental artillerymen dressed in dark blue or black coats faced with yellow satin, while cavalrymen wore short coats, buckskin breeches, spatterdashes or boots, and either the familiar cocked hat or a leather helmet decorated with a feather or a hair broach. American drummers wore uniforms in which the regimental colors were reversed (i.e., the drummer's coat was the color of the facing of the unit coat).[16] Staff officers often wore different colored feathers in their hats for identification purposes.

Because of the difficulty in acquiring new uniforms or material with which to make them, the clothing of many army units, and especially the militia, was in a bedraggled condition by this late date. "They wear loose breeches and some have shoes," noted French engineer Chevalier d'Ancteville, "but a great many are without them."[17] Washington's personal unit, called the Commander-in-Chief's Guard, was responsible for the safety of the general's person and baggage. It exhibited a distinctive white flag bearing a pictorial motif and a green scroll with the inscription "CONQUER OR DIE."[18]

By September 26, all of Washington's and Rochambeau's soldiers had arrived. Williamsburg teemed with a motley assortment of uniform colors and styles, languages, and dialects. The French auxiliary force contributed seven infantry regiments (Bourbonnois, Royal Deux-Ponts, Saintonge, Soissonois, Touraine, Agenois, and Gatenois), one artillery battalion (Auxonne), ten artillery companies of the Metz Regiment, plus some additional artillery troops with St. Simon, and a legion of horse and foot troops. All told, Rochambeau's army numbered more than 7,800 men. The 800 troops loaned by de Grasse and placed under Choisy brought the final French land complement involved in the Yorktown operation up to 8,600 men.[19]

The size of the American force is subject to debate. Early authorities placed the figure between 5,000 and 9,000 men. A more recent and sound analysis puts the total number of Continental and militia present at Yorktown at roughly 14,000.[20] This figure encompasses one regiment and two detachments of artillery, two cavalry units, Lafayette's light infantry division, Continental infantry divisions under Major Generals Benjamin Lincoln and von Steuben, a sizable contingent of Virginia State Militia commanded by General Thomas Nelson Jr., several detachments of sappers and miners, and a number of recruits from Delaware.[21]

Included with the militia were several hundred mountaineers, or "Sons of the Mountains," a motley assembly of hardened outdoorsmen armed with rifles and a worthy reputation. "[They] form an excellent corps of sharpshooters, very competent to skirmish in the brush but not at all to fight in line formation," observed Chevalier d'Ancteville. "Very few of these troops have tents and almost all of them camp under temporary shelters made of branches covered with dried foliage or bark. They are all sober and patient and subsist entirely upon corn meal." The French engineer was impressed with how easily these men absorbed "privations and delays without murmuring," and how capable they were of "sustaining great fatigue and long marches, and these, of course, are admirable and most desirable qualities for an organization of real light infantry. They are," he concluded, "all soldierly looking, and, for the most part, big men."[22]

American and French Disposition and Order of Battle

All told, the Allied force gathered at Williamsburg was probably broken down and numbered as follows:[23]

Continentals (Washington)

Command and Staff: 25

Artillery: 325

Cavalry: 110

Sappers and Miners: 50

Delaware Company: 60

Brigadier General John Peter Gabriel Muhlenberg's Brigade: 1,280

Brevet Brigadier General Moses Hazen's Brigade: 1,200

Colonel Elias Dayton's Brigade: 1,400

Brigadier General James Clinton's Brigade: 1,180

Brigadier General Anthony Wayne's Brigade: 1,550

Brigadier General Mordecai Gist's Brigade: 1,100

Total Continentals: 8,280

Militia

Brigadier General George Weedon's Brigade: 1,500

Brigadier General Edward Stevens's Brigade: 1,600

Brigadier General Robert Lawson's Brigade: 1,640

Lt. Colonel Charles Dabney's State Regiment: 200

Total Militia: 5,535

French (Rochambeau)

Lieutenant General Jean-Baptiste-Donatien

Comte de Rochambeau's troops: 4,000

Major General Marquis de St. Simon's troops: 3,800

Brigadier General Claude-Gabriel, Duke de Choisy's

Troops from de Grasse's fleet: 800

Total French: 8,600

Grand Total / Nominal Strength: 21,820

We can safely estimate that some 1,500 Americans and 600 French were absent due to sickness or other reasons at any given time, and that the militia probably numbered no more than 3,500 effectives. Therefore, the reasonable effective strength under Washington at Williamsburg was approximately 18,000 men, compared to Cornwallis's 5,500.[24] Under Washington's supreme command, the Allied armies became a single force capable of acting efficiently against a wily and skilled opponent.

The Allied Order of Battle and Command Responsibilities

When they reached the environs of Yorktown, the American Continental and militia units were assigned the right wing of the Allied army south and southeast of the town. This wing was commanded by General Benjamin Lincoln (despite Lafayette's entreaties to Washington to let him command it). The Continentals formed three divisions of two brigades each, commanded, respectively, by Lincoln, Lafayette, and von Steuben. The militia made up a fourth division under Brigadier General Thomas Nelson, Jr. The various artillery units fell into a single brigade under Brigadier General Henry Knox, who was designated the army's chief of artillery. The mounted force, the detachments of sappers and miners, and the Delaware recruits all served with the newly formed right wing.[25]

The army's left wing, which was deployed south, southwest, and west of Yorktown, consisted of the entire French Army of seven infantry regiments, plus artillery and cavalry. The infantry regiments were assigned two each to three brigades, with the remaining regiment operating separately. Lieutenant Colonel François Marie d'Aboville, the French chief of artillery, commanded the artillery contingent of 600 men. Lauzun and his 600 legionaries completed the French complement.[26]

By September 27, the disposition and order of battle of the Allied armies was as follows:[27]

I. Headquarters and Staff

General George Washington, Virginia, Commander-in-Chief

Major General Frederick William Augustus Henry Ferdinand,
Baron von Steuben, Prussia, Inspector General

Brigadier General Henry Knox, Massachusetts, Chief of Artillery

Brigadier General Edward Hand, Pennsylvania, Adjutant General

Brigadier General Louis Le Begue de Presle Du Portail,
France, Chief Engineer

Colonel Jonathan Trumbull Jr., Connecticut, Secretary

Colonel Samuel Elbert, Georgia,
Superintendent of Materials in the Trenches

Colonel Ephraim Blaine, Pennsylvania, Commissary General

Colonel Timothy Pickering, Massachusetts, Quartermaster General

Lieutenant Colonel Henry Dearborn, New Hampshire,
Assistant Quartermaster General

Lieutenant Colonel Tench Tilghman, Maryland, Aide-de-Camp

Lieutenant Colonel David Humphreys, Connecticut, Aide-de-Camp

Lieutenant Colonel David Cobb, Massachusetts, Aide-de-Camp

Lieutenant Colonel William S. Smith, New York, Aide-de-Camp

Lieutenant Colonel John Laurens, South Carolina, Aide-de-Camp

Doctor James Craik, Virginia, Chief Physician and Surgeon

II. Right (American) Wing

Major General Benjamin Lincoln, Massachusetts, Commanding

First or Right Division

Major General Marie-Jean-Paul-Joseph-Roch-Yves-Gilbert du Motier,
Marquis de Lafayette, France, Commanding

Major William Barber, New Jersey, Division Inspector

Advance Guard

1. Pennsylvania Volunteer Battalion Riflemen,
Major William Parr, Pennsylvania, Commanding

2. 4th Regiment Continental Light Dragoons,
Colonel Stephen Moylan, Pennsylvania, Commanding

3. Armand's Partisan Corps, Colonel Charles Armand Tuffin,
Marquis de la Rouerie, France, Commanding

First or Right Brigade (1st Division)

Brigadier General John Peter Gabriel Muhlenberg, Virginia, Commanding

Captain John Hobby, 10th Massachusetts, Brigade Major

First Battalion (eight Massachusetts companies)

Colonel Joseph Vose, Massachusetts
Major Cabel Gibbs, Rhode Island

Second Battalion (one Rhode Island, two Massachusetts, and
five Connecticut companies)

Lieutenant Colonel Jean Joseph Sourbadère de Gimat, France, Aide-de-Camp
Major John Palsgrave Wyllys, Connecticut

Third Battalion (one New Jersey and five New Hampshire companies)

Lieutenant Colonel Francis Barber, New Jersey
Major Joseph R. Reid, Second Canadian Regiment

Second or Left Brigade (1st Division)

Colonel and Brevet Brigadier General Moses Hazen, Canada, Commanding
Captain Leonard Bleeker, First New York, Brigade Major

First Battalion (one Connecticut and four Massachusetts Companies)

Lieutenant Colonel Ebenezer Huntington, Third Connecticut
Major Nathan Rice, Massachusetts

Second Battalion (two New York and two Connecticut Companies)

Lieutenant Colonel Alexander Hamilton, New York
Major Nicholas Fish, New York

Third Battalion (one Massachusetts, one Connecticut,
and four New Hampshire Companies)

Lieutenant Colonel John Laurens, South Carolina, Aide-de-Camp
Major John H. Cumming, New York

Second Canadian Regiment (Hazen's)

Lieutenant Colonel Edward Antill, New York
Major Tarleton Woodson, Second Canadian

Second or Center Division

Major General Baron von Steuben, Prussia, Inspector General, Commanding
Major Galvan, Massachusetts, Division Inspector

First or Right Brigade (2nd Division)

Brigadier General Mordecai Gist, Maryland, Commanding
Captain Lilburn Williams, Third Maryland, Brigade Major

Third Maryland Regiment. Lieutenant Colonel Peter Adams, Maryland

Delaware Recruits, Captain William McKennan
(temporarily annexed to the Third Maryland)

Fourth Maryland Regiment. Major Alexander Roxburg, Maryland

Second or Left Brigade (2nd Division)

Brigadier General Anthony Wayne, Pennsylvania, Commanding[28]
Lieutenant Richard Fullerton, Pennsylvania, Brigade Major

First Pennsylvania Battalion. Colonel Walter Stewart, Second Pennsylvania

Major James Hamilton, Pennsylvania
Major William Alexander, Pennsylvania

Second Pennsylvania Battalion. Colonel Richard Butler, Fifth Pennsylvania

Lieutenant Colonel Josiah Harmar, Pennsylvania
Major Evan Edwards, Pennsylvania

Virginia Battalion. Lieutenant Colonel Thomas Gaskins, Third Virginia

Third or Left Division

Major General Benjamin Lincoln, Massachusetts, Commanding

First or Right Brigade (3rd Division)

Brigadier General James Clinton, New York, Commanding
Captain Aaron Aorson, First New York, Brigade Major

First New York Regiment. Colonel Goose Van Shaick, New York

Lieutenant Colonel Cornelius Van Dyke, New York
Major John Graham, New York

Second New York Regiment. Colonel Philip Van Cortlandt, New York

Lieutenant Colonel Robert Cochran, New York
Major Nicholas Fish, New York (detached)

Second or Left Brigade (3rd Division)

Colonel Elias Dayton, New Jersey, Commanding.

Captain Richard Cox, First New Jersey, Brigade Major

First and Second New Jersey Regiments (combined)
Colonel Mathias Ogden, New Jersey

Lieutenant Colonel William De Hart, New Jersey
Major John Hollinshead, New Jersey

First Rhode Island Regiment. Lieutenant Colonel Jeremiah Olney,
Rhode Island, Commanding

Major Coggeshall Olney, Rhode Island
Major John S. Dexter, Rhode Island[29]

III. Left (French) Wing [30]

(The precise order of battle of the French Army is not clear. The following principal
officers and units comprised the French forces at Yorktown.)

Lieutenant General Jean-Baptiste-Donatien de Vimeur, comte de
Rochambeau, Commander of the King's Forces in America

Major General Francois-Jean Beauvoir,
chevalier de Chastellux, Marechal de Camp

Brigadier General Claude-Gabriel, Duke de Choisy

Brigadier General de Beville, Quartermaster General

Colonel Commandant François Marie d'Aboville, Chief of Artillery

Colonel Commandant Desandrouins, Chief Engineer

Colonel-en-Second Donatien-Joseph de Vimeur,
Viscount de Rochambeau, Adjutant General

Lieutenant Colonel Francois-Louis-Arthur-Thibaut, comte de Menonville,
Aide-de-Camp, First Deputy Adjutant General

Lieutenant Colonel de Tarlé, Intendant

Hans Axel von Fersen, Aide-de-Camp

Marquis de Vaubon, Aide-de-Camp

Marquis de Damas, Aide-de-Camp

Charles Malo François, comte de Lameth, Aide-de-Camp

Guillaume-Mathieu, comte Dumas, Aide-de-Camp

M. de Lauberdière, Aide-de-Camp

Baron Ludwig von Closen, Aide-de-Camp

M. Claude Blanchard, Commissary General

M. de Baulny, Finance Officer

M. de Ronchamp, Provost Marshal

M. de Mars, Superintendent of Hospitals

M. de Coste, Chief Physician

L'Abbe de Glesnon, Chaplain

M. Robillard, Chief Surgeon

Engineers
Detachments

Colonel Commandant Desandrouins, Chief Engineer

Lieutenant Colonel Querenet de La Combe

Major de Palys

Artillery
Detachments

Colonel Commandant d'Aboville, Chief of Artillery

Adjutant Manduit

Cavalry
Lauzun's Legion

Brigadier General Louis Armand de Gontaut-Biron, duc de Lauzun

Count Arthur Dillon

Brigade Bourbonnois

Major General Antoine Charles de Houx,
baron de Viomenil (Charles Gabriel), Marechal de Camp

Régiment Bourbonnois.
Colonel Anne-Alexander-Marie-Sulpice-Joseph de Montmorency,
Marquis de Laval

Colonel-en-Second Donatien-Marie-Joseph de Vimeur, Viscount
de Rochambeau, Adjutant General

Lieutenant Colonel de Bressolles

Major de Gambs

Régiment Royal Deux-Ponts
Colonel Christian de Forbach (German: von Forbach),
Comte de Deux-Ponts (German: Zweibrücken)

Colonel-en-Second, comte Guillaume de Deux-Ponts
Lieutenant Colonel Baron d'Ezbeck (German: von Ezbech)
Major Desprez

Brigade Soissonois

Maj. Gen. Joseph Hyacinthe du Houx, comte de Viomenil, Marechal de Camp

Régiment Soissonois.
Colonel Jean-Baptiste-Louis-Philippe
de Felix d'Olieres, comte de Saint-Maisme

Colonel-en-Second Louis-Marie, Viscount de Noailles
Lieutenant Colonel d'Anselme
Major d'Espeyron

Régiment Saintonge.
Colonel Adam-Philippe, comte de Custine

Colonel-en-Second Armand-Charles-Augustin, La Croix,
comte de Castries de Charlus

Lieutenant Colonel de La Vatelle andMajor M. Fleury

Brigade D'Agénois

Major General Claude-Anne, Marquis
de Saint-Simon Montbléru, Marechal de Camp

Régiment d'Agénois
Colonel Antoine-Joseph-Eulalie,
comte de Beaumont d'Autichamp

Lieutenant Colonel Pierre-Marie, Chevalier Du Lau d'Allemans

Major Pandin de Beauregard

Regiment Gatenois
Colonel Juste-Antoine-Henry-Marie-Germaine,
Marquis de Rostaing

Colonel-en-Second Jacques-Eleonor, Viscount de Béthisy
Lieutenant Colonel de l'Estrade
Major de Tourville

Separate Regiment

Régiment Touraine
Colonel Mestre-de-Camp Henry-Francois Liamont, Viscount de Pondeux

Lieutenant Colonel de Montlezun
Major de Ménonville[31]

IV. Intermediate Line

Right

Artillery Brigade. Brigadier General Henry Knox,
Massachusetts, Chief of Artillery, Commanding

Detachment, First Continental Artillery. Lieutenant Colonel
Edward Carrington, Virginia

Second Continental Artillery. Colonel John Lamb, New York

Lieutenant Colonel Ebenezer Stevens, Massachusetts
Major Sebastian Bauman, New York

Detachment, Fourth Continental Artillery
Captain Patrick Duffy, Pennsylvania

Center

Engineers. Brigadier General Du Portail,
Chief of Engineers, Commanding

Detachment, Sappers and Miners. Captain James Gilliland, New York

Left

First Virginia State Regiment Infantry in Continental Service.
Colonel Charles Dabney, Virginia, Commanding

V. Reserve or Second Line

Militia Division. Brigadier General Thomas Nelson Jr.,
Virginia, Commanding

Right Brigade. Brigadier General Robert Lawson, Virginia

Left Brigade. Brigadier General Edward Stevens, Virginia

Weedon's Brigade. Brigadier General George Weedon, Virginia

Lewis's Rifle Corps. Colonel William I. Lewis, Virginia

Rear Guard

Major James (Joseph?) R. Ried, Second Canadian Regiment,
Commanding Rear Guard and Camp Guard[32]

Disposition of Troops around Williamsburg

Prior to the march on Yorktown, the Allied force was stationed around Williamsburg. Lafayette's troops quartered themselves just west of town near St. Simon's light artillery between the roads to Jamestown and Richmond. St. Simon's troops encamped across the Richmond Road, while farther along the route were units of Royal Deux-Ponts (Zweibrucken in German, meaning two bridges). A guard of St. Simon's volunteers took station near the mill above Capitol Landing on Queen's Creek. North of Williamsburg, closer to the landing, were posted some soldiers of the Regiment Bourbonnois. Rochambeau's main force guarded the eastern flank of the city and his artillery covered the western edge. The principal units of the American Army were stretched for about one mile east of Williamsburg along the road to Yorktown. Advance units of French and Americans were positioned farther east closer to Yorktown. These troops secured the former capital against hostile

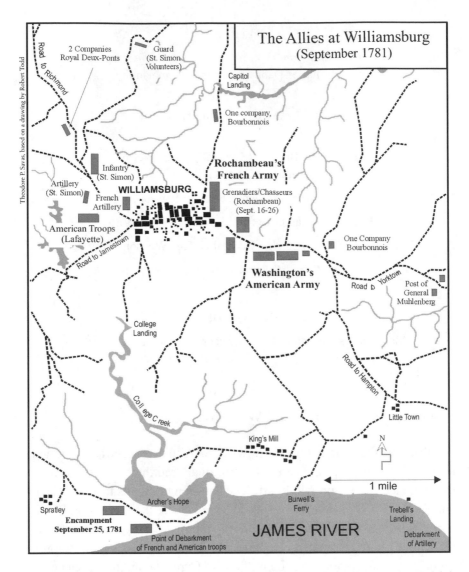

Theodore P. Savas, based on a drawing by Robert Todd

The Allies at Williamsburg
(September 1781)

Road to Richmond

2 Companies
Royal Deux-Ponts

Guard
(St. Simon
Volunteers)

Capitol
Landing

One company,
Bourbonnois

Infantry
(St. Simon)

Artillery
(St. Simon)

French
Artillery

WILLIAMSBURG

American Troops
(Lafayette)

Road to Jamestown

**Rochambeau's
French Army**

Grenadiers/Chasseurs
(Rochambeau)
(Sept. 16-26)

**Washington's
American Army**

One Company
Bourbonnois

Road to Yorktown

Post of
General
Muhlenberg

College
Landing

College Creek

Road to Hampton

Little Town

King's Mill

N

1 mile

Spratley

**Encampment
September 25, 1781**

Archer's Hope

Point of Debarkment
of French and American troops

Burwell's
Ferry

JAMES RIVER

Trebell's
Landing

Debarkment
of Artillery

incursions while concentrating their resources to lay siege to the British garrison just 12 miles away.[33]

On September 27, the entire army marched east of Williamsburg and encamped for the night in order of battle. Washington issued precise orders governing the next day's march to Yorktown. He dictated it would begin at 5:00 a.m., at which time the troops would move out in a procession of one column still arrayed in battle order. The advance guard received specific directions for leading the march through the heavily wooded region; Washington was keenly aware of the danger of a surprise assault against his marching army.[34]

*   *   *

Although aware of the closing Allied armies, Cornwallis was confident he would be reinforced or withdrawn. As his enemies approached Yorktown, Cornwallis worked to bolster his principal fortifications around the city. Governor (General) Thomas Nelson made a request to the British commander that Yorktown citizens be permitted to leave. "I have not the least objection to any of the Inhabitants at present in this place going out with their Families & effects," replied Cornwallis courteously. "Nor to those who formerly resided here sending for their Wives & Families, who will likewise be permitted to take their effects with them, and any Waggons that you think proper to send to adjust them will be received at our Out-post on the Hampton Road."[35]

Exactly how many Yorktown citizens took advantage of this opportunity is unknown, but those who decided to remain with Cornwallis would soon come to regret their decision.

Chapter 5

Investment

*F*riday, September 28, broke clear with the promise of another intolerably hot and humid day before the Allied armies of France and the United States reached Yorktown. The soldiers struck camp before dawn and set out on the march at daybreak, leaving a detachment of 200 men behind in Williamsburg to mind the hospital and stores.[1]

Leading the combined force was the Virginia corps of riflemen under Colonel James Lewis and the light dragoons of Colonel Stephen Moylan, followed by Brigadier General John Peter Gabriel Muhlenberg's infantry with attached field artillery. The French advanced guard units were composed of St. Simon's grenadiers and chasseurs led by Colonel Anne-Alexander-Marie-Sulpice-Joseph de Montmorency, Marquis de Laval.[2] Behind them marched the American Continentals, followed by the French auxiliaries, all as prescribed in Washington's marching orders. The militia served as the army's reserve. Two miles out of Williamsburg the militiamen turned right onto the Harwood Mills Road (Warwick Road), tramping southeast as an escort for the wagons Washington had managed to find to transport provisions and entrenching tools. His own vehicles and horses had not yet reached the front, and the troops were hard pressed to make do with the limited transportation available.[3]

The main Franco-American column continued along the direct Williamsburg-Yorktown Road, passing by the old Halfway House Ordinary located about midway between the communities. The march was slow and tiring, the heat oppressive. Men staggered in the sandy roadbed and collapsed. Most of the officers lacked horses and were forced to share the privations of the foot troops. The French soldiers halted frequently. The Americans stopped at least twice during the trek, once for a period of two to three hours.[4] "I can testify to having suffered every affliction imaginable," recalled a French officer. "We left nearly 800 soldiers in the rear. Two fell at my feet and died on the spot." Baron von Closen noted in his journal, "The day was so hot and the sand was so burning that the troops suffered a great deal."[5]

Soldiers were under strict orders from Washington to turn back any surprise attacks by the British with bayonets alone, "that they may prove the Vanity of the Boast which the British make of their particular prowess in deciding Battles with that Weapon."[6] To the surprise of many, the troops marched through the dense pine and cedar forests, tramping past occasional areas cleared for homes and crops, without any sign of the enemy. The artillery train did not accompany the column, the pieces of light ordnance instead scattered throughout the units to be ready to use in case of ambush. A mile beyond Halfway House the road forked in three directions. The Americans took the center route along a road that led toward Munford's Bridge to the south. The French remained on the main Williamsburg Road and continued toward Yorktown, which was only another four miles distant. The Jolly Pond Road, which broke off due south, connected a mile away with the Warwick Road upon which the militia was marching with the wagons. Near Munford's Bridge (which was broken and had to be repaired), the American Army rejoined General Thomas Nelson's militia and together the units moved forward along Grove Road toward Yorktown. Although British cavalry detachments were occasionally spotted by the advance guard, no determined resistance was met during the movement.[7]

First Blood

The French army arrived within two miles of Yorktown about 3:30 p.m., having advanced by the most direct route. The soldiers approached the outskirts through a wooded area along the Williamsburg Road with some cultivated ground breaking away to their right.[8] As they neared the route's juncture with Goosley Road, the troops fanned out left and right to cover their sector of the front. British Light Infantry pickets under Colonel Abercrombie were there protecting a work party. When the French pickets were spotted, word was dispatched to Yorktown that the enemy was in sight.[9] The French advance was not without bloodshed. British troops occupied a number of advance posts in the area between Goosley Road and the Fusiliers' Redoubt, all of which served to protect the right flank of Cornwallis's line at Yorktown. As the French guards mounted a reconnaissance of the ravines around the British position, a shower of grapeshot from a distant battery sprayed through their ranks. Exactly where it came from is unknown, but the French wisely fell back beyond range to the forest edge.[10]

Finally meeting determined resistance, General Rochambeau ordered Baron de Viomenil forward with six 4-pounders to support the grenadiers and chasseurs under de Laval, test the enemy resolve, and scout the terrain. Fifty mounted hussars led the advance as his guns unlimbered and opened fire. The guns dispersed perhaps 50 enemy soldiers and killed several of Tarleton's horses arrayed on the distant plain. The French counter-thrust caused the British to withdraw to the protection of the Pigeon Hill Redoubts guarding Goosley Road, which allowed the French reconnaissance of the terrain west and southwest of Yorktown to proceed without further molestation.

The French light artillery continued firing sporadically throughout the afternoon. Three German officers positioned in the British outer works were killed by two 4-pounder iron balls. Farther left, Rochambeau's soldiers stretched out their flank to the York River and probed the Fusiliers' Redoubt without a serious effort to capture it. Meanwhile, French grenadiers under comte de Lameth kept a close watch on the strong outer works at Pigeon Hill. Rochambeau's cautious troops had yet to lose a man in the advance.[11]

The British were anxious to begin the action. "There was but one wish," remembered one of Cornwallis's officers, "that they would advance."[12] An aged Scottish highland lieutenant drew his sword and uttered, "Come on, Maister Washington, I'm unco glad to see you; I've been offered money for my commission, but I could na think of ganging' hame without a sight of you. Come on."[13]

The Scotsman would soon have his wish, for Washington and the entire American wing of the Allied army were rapidly approaching. Having taken a more indirect route than the French, the head of the Continental and militia column emerged from the forested roads about 3:45 or 4:00 p.m. This was just a short time after Rochambeau's army, and at approximately the same time the French were forcing the withdrawal of Cornwallis's pickets. This area was familiar to Washington, for Yorktown stood on land once owned by his American ancestors; in his youth the general had gambled on cockfights there.[14]

Moving along Grove Road, the Americans approached Yorktown from the southwest before leaving the highway and proceeding toward a section known as Nelson's Quarter (both Governor and "Secretary" Nelson owned land there). The troops stopped at Beaverdam Creek, or Great Run, because the British had destroyed the bridge over the swampy morass at that point. Across the marshy rivulet on the open plain between Beaverdam and Wormley creeks, Banastre Tarleton's green-clad legion, assigned to reconnoiter the Americans, paraded on the ground Washington's engineers intended to occupy. According to Tarleton, his advance sentinels had informed him the Americans were moving against the left flank of his cavalry (apparently near the junction of the Hampton and Warwick roads). The cavalry leader quickly mounted his men and formed them into three squadrons in front of the British center. "In this situation," he wrote, "they watched for an opportunity of striking at any detachment who might pass the Hampton road; but the enemy were cautious and cannonaded the legion dragoons across the morass, who retired to Moore's house, within the outward position." Watching Tarleton's cavalry deploy was Colonel St. George Tucker, who remembered that a meadow some 300 yards wide separated the opponents. "4 field pieces were brot. Down to the Brow of the Hill to drive him off, & cover some pioneers who were sent to repair Munford's Bridge where the Army were to cross," wrote the colonel, "[and] the second shot produced the desired effect." The combination of grapeshot and musket balls sent Tarleton scampering toward Yorktown. Washington's sharpshooters also engaged in a lively contest with Hessian soldiers, a deadly game of sport that would last throughout the evening.[15]

Once it was safe to do so, the Americans repaired the bridge over Beaverdam Creek, as well as others that were either missing or destroyed.

Bridge-building lasted all night, and some of the soldiers were probably detailed to make fascines (cylindrical bundles of small sticks) for that purpose. Fascines would have served to support log stringers laid across the stream, being both flexible enough to withstand cannon weight and porous enough to allow running water to pass through.[16] One bridge was fixed almost immediately and some of the soldiers, including Muhlenberg's light infantry, crossed to the east side.[17] The Americans concluded their investment the next day after the bridges were repaired. That night, Muhlenberg's advance pickets took station well in front of the morass. Their commander, General Muhlenberg, "was tall, strikingly handsome, and courtly." Behind them, the Continentals and militia doubled on part of the French line, deployed along Great Run, and rested on their arms without cover of any kind, ready for any possible emergency. Some of the troops ran down hogs in the woods and enjoyed roasted pork that evening, while others sought drinking water to slake their thirst.[18]

By nightfall, the right side of the British position (west and southwest of Yorktown) was fully dominated by the soldiers of Rochambeau. Near the fork of Goosley Road, on either side of Williamsburg Road, were the Regiments Gatenois and Agenois, one north of the highway, the other south. The units were ordered to erect three redoubts "big enough to hold 200 men, in each of which two four-pounder campaign guns could be placed as well as two cannon 'a la Rotain,'" as protection against British sorties.[19] The Gatenois Redoubt overlooked Ballard Creek, and presumably thwarted any flanking movements of the British by that route. Guarding the rise between York and Ballard creeks was the Regiment Touraine, situated well back from the danger posed by the Fusiliers' Redoubt. The unit erected a long protective epaulement (earth wall) along its front, overlooking a branch ravine of Ballard Creek and to the left of the Williamsburg Road.[20] South of these regiments—two of which, Agenois and Gatenois, composed the Brigade Agenois—near an area called Lowell's Quarter, were the regiments of Saintonge and Soissonois (Brigade Soissonois). To the east, a thin wood separated these regiments from those of the Royal Deux-Ponts (whose ranks were populated by German troops) and Bourbonnois (Brigade Bourbonnois), camped west of Grove Road.

Thus placed, the French units closed all the principal highways and plantation roads leading in and out of Yorktown from the west and southwest. Because intervening forest thwarted communication between Brigades Agenois and Soissonois, Major General comte de Viomenil (substituting for St. Simon, who was sick at Williamsburg, and not to be confused with Major General Baron de Viomenil) ordered a swath cut through the thickets to facilitate contact—"a communication big enough for an advance through it by platoons."[21] Viomenil led the grenadiers and chasseurs out in front. By nightfall, the French circumvallation ran from near the York River on the far left around to the morass opposite the British center.[22] The enemy, as Rochambeau later described it, was confined "to within pistol-shot of their works."[23]

During their inspection of the British position the afternoon of September 28, Washington and Rochambeau drew the attention of enemy cannoneers. "The shots seeming rather to have been in their honor than to interfere with their operation," noted one observer.[24] Neither man was hurt by the barrage, and both managed to get a good look at Cornwallis's fortifications. They appeared both extensive and apparently strong—the result of industrious digging by his soldiers in recent weeks.[25] On the basis of intelligence gained from reconnaissance, British deserters, and his officers stationed along the James River who told him the water at Trebell's Landing was deep enough to land the siege guns, Washington estimated siege operations would commence by October 1—a mere four days away.[26] "I fear we shall have little Hope to starve him into a Surrender," Washington wrote Nathanael Greene of his prospects against Cornwallis. "My greater Hope is, that he is not well provided with Artillery and Military Stores for such Defence, not having had in Contemplation, the Situation to which he is now reduced."[27]

The next morning, his bridges repaired, Washington marched the rest of his troops in column across the swampy morass and extended the American sector farther to the right toward the Wormley Creek ravines and the York River. The line was behind another morass to the left of Beaverdam Creek (Great Run), whose marshlands served to divide the Americans from the French, and to the right of the southern arm of Wormley Creek, within one-half mile of Cornwallis's fortifications guarding the left bank of that stream. British cannon fire impeded the investment slightly, although the Americans exchanged a lively musket fire for much of the day with Ansbach soldiers deployed across their front. Most of the British artillery fire directed at Washington's troops came from one of the Wormley Creek redans and from the barbette battery emplaced on Hampton Road. "A nine pound and a three pound shot paid us a visit in camp," wrote Lieutenant William Feltman in his journal. Washington's officers ordered light ordnance forward to return the fire. The damage inflicted was light, however, because the encampment, for the most part, was beyond the range of the enemy guns. Unfortunately for one American infantryman, however, the range was perfect and cost him his leg. He was apparently the only casualty sustained by the Americans during this period.[28]

The Americans Deploy

The American troops lay on their arms before the enemy until about 3:00 p.m., when they were ordered to move a short distance back to establish their encampment about one mile from Cornwallis's outer works. Pickets were sent forward to watch the British.[29]

General Benjamin Lincoln, second in command to Washington and in charge of the entire right wing, set up his headquarters on the right on the American line close to Wormley Creek (about 500 yards below the mill dam). The 48-year-old former member of the provisional congress and prosperous tiller of the soil was a member of the Massachusetts militia for more than two decades when war broke out in 1775. By the summer of 1776 he was training state troops around Boston and New York as a major general of militia. Washington took an interest in the man, whom he described to congress as "an excellent officer, and worthy of your notice in the Continental Line." Though he did not have a formal commission, by February of 1777 Lincoln was a major general in the Regular Army. Washington's faith was not misplaced. Lincoln played a major role in the Saratoga victory in the fall of 1777, where he suffered a leg wound that kept him out of the field for nearly a year. As the commander of the Southern Department, Lincoln was forced to surrender Charleston, South Carolina, in May of 1780, though the fault of its loss lay with others. When the time came to march the American men to Yorktown, Lincoln was tapped to lead them. Solid and dependable, Lincoln was utterly without the flash and pomp of so many others in the army.

Immediately to Lincoln's left at Yorktown, Lafayette's light infantry division (composed of Muhlenberg's and Hazen's brigades) made camp

Independence National Historical Park

Major General Benjamin Lincoln

on land owned by a "Mr. Inges." Lafayette's men were the closest American troops to the British. The French officer established his headquarters behind his division just east of the Hampton Road. Nelson placed the Virginia Militia (composed of Stevens's and Lawson's brigades) as a second line directly behind Lafayette's men on the property of a "Mr. Smith."

Lincoln's division (composed of Dayton's and Clinton's brigades) held the center of the American line, which ran between Hampton and

Warwick roads on the Allen and Dedman property. The corps of sappers and miners took station in an intermediate position between Lincoln's soldiers, on the right of the men from New York and on the left of the Rhode Island and New Jersey troops.

The last American division was under Baron von Steuben, who was born in the magnificent German fortress at Magdeburg while his father was stationed there as an engineer. By 17, von Steuben was an officer in the Prussian army, where he served during the Seven Years' War as a line

Independence National Historical Park

Major General Frederick William Augustus, Baron von Steuben

and staff officer before being assigned to the General Staff and attached to the headquarters of Frederick the Great. His staff experience would later prove of immense value to the Americans. For reasons that remain a mystery, he was dismissed from the service as a captain in 1763. Service as a chamberlain at the court of Hohenzollern-Hechingen earned him the title of Baron. In 1771, Steuben followed his insolvent prince to France, where he hoped to improve his fortunes. Unable to do so and now utterly broke, both men returned to Germany in 1775. Unable to garner a foreign commission, von Steuben ended up in Paris, where Benjamin Franklin (who recognized the value a Prussian-trained general staff officer could provide to the nascent American army), recommended his services to Washington. Although he spoke only broken French and not a word of English, von Steuben dedicated himself to the American cause and the results unfolded on the battlefield at Monmouth and elsewhere. At Yorktown, at the head of a veteran division, the staff officer was a step closer to his dream of a field command.

Von Steuben's division was composed of Anthony Wayne's and Mordecai Gist's brigades. It took up a position left of the Warwick Road in advance of General Knox's artillery and the quartermaster facilities. Knox established his headquarters well behind the American artillery west of the Warwick Road.

About three-quarters of a mile west of Knox, not far from where the American left flank and French right flank came together, was where Washington established his headquarters. The position was fully two and one-half miles from the British outer works. It was from this point that he would exercise supreme command over the Allied forces. Washington's Life Guard occupied the surrounding ground.[30]

To protect his army against surprise assaults by the British, Washington ordered Brigadier General Louis Le Begue de Presle Du Portail to see to the erection of small earthworks before each brigade in the manner of the French. This line of countervallation (essentially light trenches guarded by low parapets) served to secure the camp guards who might warn of enemy attack.[31]

As Washington tightened his position around the British, he sent troops to reconnoiter Cornwallis's defenses. On the right flank, Muhlenberg's brigade was ordered to cross the boggy ground in its front. "The First brigade . . . crossed a small morass and paraded in order of battle, marched a small distance in front," remembered Captain James

Duncan of Hazen's command. "The enemy, not firing," continued Duncan, "they wheeled to the right and took their post in the line; a picket was now turned out . . . which advanced in front nearly halfway to the enemy, until they were obliged to retreat by the fire of a field piece from the enemy's [main] works."[32]

The feint was designed to feel enemy strength on the ground where the British had camped the day before. Having withdrawn from the area between the redoubts, Cornwallis's stomach for mounting a strong resistance appeared to be waning.[33] Having verified this, Washington and Rochambeau spent the rest of the day conducting surveys of the British entrenchments and deployment. Careful attention was paid to the outer works at Pigeon Hill and those along the Hampton Road. The capture of the former structures was considered vital to the Allied plans to confine the British within their main line of fortifications. "A Bridge is making to cross the Morass opposite Pigeon hill, which place I conjecture will be taken by storm, within a few days—it is a very commanding post, and must be possest [sic] by us," wrote American Captain John Pryor to a friend.[34]

During the day, the Americans exchanged sporadic musket fire with the British troops occupying the forward redoubts. According to one account, American riflemen killed "ab't Eight of the Enemy in their works."[35] The broad reconnaissance cost the Americans three killed and three wounded.[36]

"A large, deep ravine, cut by a stream [Wormley Creek], borders half the position on the right, for a distance of [approximately 1600 yards]. The enemy had made abatis around it; in front the ground was strewn with felled trees, clear to the swampy [York] Creek which empties into the river York," wrote Chevalier d'Ancteville, a French soldier who penned one of the outstanding firsthand accounts we have of the Yorktown Campaign. The early reconnaissance of the enemy lines, he wrote, revealed substantial information:

> [T]wo redoubts [at Pigeon Hill], with fraising and enclosed with abatis, extended toward the center above the ravine, leaving between them the [Goosley] road to York. These redoubts occupied the high ground some distance from the town. About [700 yards] in front of them the ground fell away in a slope toward the country. Their left was covered by three batteries placed likewise at

[600-800 yards] from the town, with abatis in front, on the highest ground. Finally, they were supported by a wood filled with light infantry, with a masked battery in the wood on the bank of the river at the extremity of their left [right?], covered by a Creek [York] which served them as a ditch. The declivity in front of these pieces prevented our gathering information on the works which the enemy had constructed behind them and with which they had covered the town of York.[37]

The intelligence gleaned during the reconnaissance helped Washington appreciate the strengths and weaknesses of Cornwallis's position. It was obvious to the American leader that the British outer position commanded a nearly unobstructed view of the main defenses around Yorktown. Moreover, according to his subordinates, the earthworks surrounding the village itself appeared weaker than expected and probably comprised an enclosure too large for Cornwallis to adequately maintain with his limited force. The British left (opposite the American wing of Washington's army) possessed a field of fire superior to either the right or center of the line, and was reinforced by two detached redoubts (9 and 10). These structures, with their fraising and abatis, stood perhaps 350 or 400 yards from the main Yorktown works. Washington also realized the soil around Yorktown was sandy enough to make the construction and maintenance of strong earthworks very difficult without great quantities of fascines and gabions.[38]

Washington's reconnaissance of the terrain between the Allied armies and the British position was necessary before siege operations could begin. The all-day reconnaissance was triggered by the reluctance of Admiral de Grasse to allow ships to venture upstream beyond the British in order to safeguard the York River above Yorktown. The admiral's decision apparently altered Washington's original operational plan. "Spent this day in reconnoitering the enemys [sic] position, and determining upon a plan of attack and approach which must be done without the assistance of the Shipping above the Town," he penned in his diary on the evening of September 29, "as the admiral (not withstanding my earnest sollicitation [sic]) declined hazarding any Vessels on that Station."[39] The entry suggests Washington had earlier planned to attack the British from above their position, with approach trenches being prepared near banks of the York River above the Fusiliers' Redoubt. De

Grasse's refusal to send ships to cover this operation from the river (principally because his vessels might be needed should another British fleet arrive, and because he feared the British gun batteries and fire ships), spoiled Washington's original design.[40]

On that Saturday, the French consolidated the positions they had assumed the day before. The Santo Domingo regiments guarded the left of the Allied line and completed their redoubts and the communication line through the woods between the Regiments Agenois and Saintonge. In addition, a small earthwork—indicated as a redan on historical maps—was raised between the bridges crossing Great Run and just before the encampment areas of the Regiments Soissonois and Deux-Ponts. On the extreme left near the river, French patrols of the Regiment Touraine surveyed the Fusiliers' Redoubt and guarded against a surprise attack by the enemy in the area of Ballard Creek.[41] Late that afternoon, units of French grenadiers and chasseurs belonging to the Agenois and Gatenois regiments, respectively, staged an attack on part of Tarleton's Legion deployed in their front. They succeeded in forcing the legion to withdraw under the cover of an advanced British artillery battery. Seven rounds of shot from several 18-pounders dispersed the French and ended the assault.[42]

By evening, the French units camped on the ground they would occupy for the duration of the siege. Further tightening the investment, the Brigade Bourbonnois, consisting of the Regiments Deux-Ponts and Bourbonnois, moved forward from behind the marsh of Baptist Run and joined the other brigades in line.[43] To the right and a bit south across Grove Road, the French artillery took up camp close to the extreme left of von Steuben's American division. Rochambeau established his headquarters southeast of the artillery on the north side of Jones Run, about one-third of a mile east of Washington's tent.[44]

The American Continentals and militia, together with the French regulars and volunteers, had enclosed Cornwallis, sealed every major avenue of escape on Yorktown's landward side, and now looked to the commencement of the siege they hoped would produce the British general's capitulation. At Gloucester Point, one mile across the York River, Lauzun joined with General Weedon to keep close watch on the enemy and to guard against British attempts to break out of the tightening vice. The Allies would not complete their investment there until after the fight at the Hook on October 3.

As the Allied forces made camp and while officers from both armies completed a reconnaissance of the ground between them and the British, twelve qualified military engineers were broken into three groups, two of which were French and commanded by Lieutenant Colonel Querenet de La Combe because vice Colonel Desandrouins was ill in Williamsburg. The other group, which also contained Frenchmen, was headed by Du Portail of the American Army. As assigned, the three engineer divisions, detailed respectively to the commands of Washington, Rochambeau, and St. Simon, consisted of the following:

First Division of Engineers
M. de Gouvion, Lieutenant Colonel, U.S.A
Chevalier Doire (Doyre; d'Oyre), Captain, Royal Engineer Corps
Baron de Turpin, Captain, Royal Engineer Corps
M. de Plancher (Planchet), Lieutenant, Royal Engineer Corps

Second Division of Engineers

M. Palys de Montrepos, Major, Royal Engineer Corps
M. Crublier d'Opterre (d'Opter; d'Aubeterre),
Captain, Royal Engineer Corps
M. de Rochefontaine, Captain, U.S.A.
M. de Fourrageola, Lieutenant (?), Engineer
of Santo Domingo, with St. Simon

Third Division of Engineers
Chevalier Cantel d'Ancteville (d'Aneteville),
Royal Engineer Corps, with St. Simon
M. de Garavaque (Caravagne; Garavagne),
Captain, Royal Engineer Corps, with St. Simon
M. de Bouhan (Bouan), Lieutenant,
Royal Engineer Corps, with St.Simon
M. de Geaut, Lieutenant,
engineer of Santo Domingo, with St. Simon[45]

The main task of the engineers during the initial stages of a siege was to render the terrain suitable for the artillery operation against the enemy fortifications. If all went well, the imminent siege of Yorktown in September 1781 promised to become the supreme example of the coordination of American and French heavy weaponry to force a British capitulation.

Allied Artillery

The siege would also provide the ultimate test for the American artillery, a fledgling service just five years old by 1781. In 1776, the American artillery corps consisted of less than 600 men roughly organized into independent companies. The branch was later reorganized into four artillery regiments. By 1780, the regiments contained 10 companies. The total authorized strength for the artillery in 1780 was 2,646 men, but its effective strength was about 1,000 fewer than that number.[46]

The man chiefly responsible for the development of the American artillery corps was Henry Knox. The 31-year-old Massachusetts native had joined the militia at 18 and lost two fingers on his left hand three years later when his musket exploded. A Boston bookseller prior to 1775, Knox was an ardent supporter of independence and belonged to a Massachusetts artillery company when fighting broke out at Lexington. He fought with Artemus Ward at Bunker Hill in June of 1775, and his innovative spirit and intelligence quickly attracted the notice of several superiors. In November of that year, Knox was promoted to colonel and tapped to head the Continental Regiment of Artillery. The determination and ability of this eight-fingered bookseller was on display when Washington sent him north to Fort Ticonderoga to bring back artillery captured there. Knox helped haul back by sled the artillery and shot (some 120,000 pounds) across 300 miles of rough terrain, ending what he called the "noble train of artillery." It was a difficult feat, well performed. The guns helped Washington end the siege of Boston in 1776.

Thereafter, Knox took part in virtually every major battle in the Northern theater. His artillery played a major role in the winter battles of 1776-1777 at Trenton (after which he was appointed brigadier general) and Princeton. A talented administrator, Knox established the Springfield Massachusetts Arsenal and the Academy Artillery School in Morristown, New Jersey (the forerunner for West Point). He continued directing and improving the burgeoning artillery arm of the United States throughout the war. The colonial long-arm finally came into its own at Monmouth in June 1778. At Yorktown, Knox had before him a true test to match his genius for organization.[47] The Bostonian was guided in his development of the American artillery system by the French, who were

Brigadier General Henry Knox

by the late eighteenth century widely recognized as the finest artillerists in Europe.[48]

The development of artillery as a military science had accelerated in many European capitals since the middle decades of the eighteenth century.[49] By the 1780s, the French were considered the preeminent masters—largely because of the early planning by Sébastien le Prestre de Vauban and others—and because the French Army possessed a great number and variety of field and garrison pieces, some of which arrived in America with Rochambeau in 1780. While French artillery practice exercised considerable influence over its evolving American counterpart, so did the British long-arm—especially in regard to the actual manufacture of cannon in the American states.

Probably the prime British contributor to American artillery thought and development was John Muller, the English theorist whose *A Treatise of Artillery* (1757) appeared in Philadelphia as early as 1779 as the American artillery corps labored in the throes of its initial reorganization. Appropriately dedicated to "George Washington, General Henry Knox and Officers of the Continental Artillery," the printed edition of Muller's work became the sole English language technical manual accessible to the American army. Eleven copies of Muller's book were included in an inventory of American artillery supplies taken at the start of the 1781 campaign. As the standard British authority on the subject, the book exerted a measurable impact, and Britain's artillery procedures were soon emulated in the former colonies.[50]

Muller's recommendations—including those pertaining to the calibers of guns—were strictly adhered to by the Americans during the Revolutionary War. Consequently, the earliest gun foundries cast a wide variety of calibers, despite the fact that the English themselves had modified many of Muller's suggestions.[51] At the war's outset, Knox's artillery consisted primarily of old and outmoded British weapons either left over from the colonial government or taken from British ships. Calibers reflected the weight of the ball fired, and the young American artillery boasted as many as thirteen calibers at the beginning of the revolution. Of these calibers, the 4-, 8-, 12-, 18-, and 24-pounders predominated.[52]

French pieces were also used, which added to the diversity of the artillery arm because their calibers differed from the British. French guns used by the Americans had to be either re-bored to British specifications or altogether segregated from other pieces.[53]

American foundries for the home production of cannon, mortars, and howitzers grew quickly following the curtailment of imports at the opening of the conflict with Britain. Notable contributors to the American artillery were foundries located in eastern Pennsylvania: the Durham Iron Works, producers of cannon tubes and ordnance, and the Warwick and Cornwall furnaces, which manufactured sixty 12- and 18-pounders in 1776.[54] Foundries in Philadelphia produced both iron and bronze guns early in the war, but the center for Continental Army cannon manufacture became Springfield, Massachusetts.[55]

After the Franco-American Alliance of 1778, more French bronze pieces arrived across the Atlantic along with vast quantities of French shot, shells, and black powder. Washington's artillery soon comprised a contingent of bronze and iron mobile field guns ranging from 3- to 12-pounders and a large number of howitzers whose calibers were five-and-one-half and nine inches, as gauged by the diameters of their muzzles. Iron siege pieces consisted of 18-, 24-, and 32-pounders (none of the latter pieces were used at Yorktown) that fired round iron shot, grapeshot, and canister.[56] (For a detailed examination of French-related artillery issues, see Appendix 5.)

Allied Camp Life at Yorktown

The encampment location of both the French and American armies before Yorktown was nearly perfect. It possessed many of the qualities outlined for a good camping position in the theoretical manuals of the day. Washington had decided where to place his force on the basis of maps and suggestions of his engineers even before he reached Yorktown.[57] In order to make such recommendations, Washington's officers relied heavily on the systematic measures devised by von Steuben and published in 1779 as *Regulations for the Order and Discipline of the Troops of the United States*.[58] Although there is no direct reference to this work in regard to the encampment at Yorktown, the fact that it existed, coupled with von Steuben's presence with the American soldiers, indicates strongly that its tenets were adopted by at least the right wing of the besieging army. The French heeded similar regulations governing the art of setting up an encampment (called castrametation). In either case, the armies were subjected to the rudiments of European discipline in the manner of laying camp.

Washington's two headquarters tents, the shelters in which he had directed American operations for the previous five years, arrived September 29 and were pitched well beyond enemy artillery range.[59] Other baggage also reached the American troops that day. Before the sun set, the designated unit areas were dotted with tents of varying sizes able to accommodate between eight and sixteen soldiers.[60] The troops always laid out their camp in order of battle, and the quartermaster general always assigned blocks of ground to the various brigade units. Brigade quartermasters allotted sufficient space to the regiments and regimental quartermasters, and assigned tracts to their respective company units.[61] Within the detailed space, noncommissioned officers and privates of a company pitched their tents in two ranks separated six feet from each other, with two-foot intervals between each tent.

At Yorktown, there are indications that not all the soldiers had tents—a shortage that necessitated the erection of some brush shelters. Junior grade officers located their tents twenty feet behind their men, while field commanders placed their shelters another thirty feet behind their subalterns.[62] Unit support offices, such as regimental surgeon, paymaster, and quartermaster, were placed well to the rear of the field officers. Sutlers set up their tents between the kitchens. When they arrived, the horses and wagons were stationed in a line twenty feet beyond the kitchens. Latrines for the two ranks thus arranged were dug 300 feet before and behind the respective ranks. Camp guards took post about 900 feet in front of, and in back of, their regiment's lines, while a quarter guard was positioned forty feet from the wagons.[63]

Most of the functions of the established army camp were controlled by drumbeats, with a specific beat for specific duties. The beats for camp, as for combat, began on the right of the line and were taken up by the successive drummers who, in turn, relayed the signal to the left until the entire army, regiment, or battalion was apprised of the order.[64] General drumbeats affecting various aspects of camp life at Yorktown included the following, as stipulated by von Steuben:

> — The General is to be beat only when the whole are to march, and is the signal to strike the tents, and prepare for the march;

— The Assembly is the signal to repair to the colours. The March for the whole to move;

— The Reveille is beat at day-break, and is the signal for the soldiers to rise, and the centries to leave off challenging;

— The Troop assembles the soldiers together, for the purpose of calling the roll and inspecting the men for duty;

— The Retreat is beat at sun-set, for calling the roll, warning the men for duty, and reading the orders of the day;

— The Tattoo is for the soldiers to repair to their tents, where they must remain till reveille beating next morning;

— To Arms is the signal for getting under arms in case of alarm. The Parley is to desire a conference with the enemy.[65]

Each morning, the soldiers assembled at the beat of the drum for inspection of their persons and their dress. Each day the men responded to drumbeats for roll call and parade, and even for drinking water, which was distributed to those desiring to fill their canteens only after the appropriate drum signal had been sounded.[66] The drumbeat fairly dominated life in eighteenth-century army encampments.

Cleanliness and sanitation were paramount considerations for the maintenance of a healthy (and especially stationary) army. It was the regimental quartermaster's duty to make sure the area surrounding an encampment was kept free of unhealthy litter. He also insured that old sinks were filled up and that new ones were dug at three-to-four-day intervals. Dead animals were required to be buried at least one-half mile from camp, and the commissary received directions to butcher cattle at least fifty yards behind the wagons and to cover the entrails immediately. For personal cleanliness among their troops, unit officers daily inspected the tents to make certain "that no bones or other filth be in or near them." As an added precaution against disease, the soldiers struck their tents in good weather and aired their bedding daily.

Two problems facing Washington upon his arrival at Yorktown threatened to compromise the health of his soldiers: a shortage of drinking water and disease. Good water was scarce because the British had spoiled much of what was available. "To stop the advance on York, Lord Cornwallis, instead of attacking our column as a soldier would have done," recalled an offended French officer, "had recourse to ruses such as only savage Indians are capable of employing. He had thrown into the wells heads of steers, dead horses, and even the bodies of dead negroes."

The result was that the Allies were short of fresh water. "It could have been molested in a more worthy manner," concluded the Frenchman.[67]

Another manifestation of this crude form of British germ warfare appeared in Cornwallis's effort to spread the dreaded smallpox among the Allies. Washington urged preventive measures in his morning orders of September 29. "Our ungenerous enemy having as usual propagated the small pox in this part of the Country, the Commander in Chief forbids the officers or soldiers of the Army having any Communication with the Houses or Inhabitants in the neighbour-hood or borrowing any Utensils from them."[68] Malarial fever, which was transmitted by mosquitoes, also infected the field armies. By the end of the siege, several hundred soldiers had been stricken and were gathered at Williamsburg, where an army hospital was established in the Governor's Palace.[69]

To handle casualties suffered in the field, both the Americans and French established hospitals in the American encampment area. The American wing was set up in the vicinity of Lafayette's headquarters just north of Hampton Road under the supervision of Virginian Dr. James Craik, the army's chief physician and surgeon. Other surgeons on Craik's field staff included Drs. James Thacher and Aeneas Munson. Southwest of the American hospital and east of Warwick Road, the French set up a medical unit under their Physician-in-Chief M. de Coste, and Surgeon-in-Chief M. Robillard. The French superintendent of hospitals was M. de Mars. This hospital stood just across the highway from the right flank of von Steuben's division. The site was selected because it was located almost directly behind what would become the French sector of operations on the siege line, and because of its proximity to a main thoroughfare conducive to the transportation of wounded soldiers. Both armies conveyed their wounded and sick by ambulance to the evacuation hospital at Williamsburg.[70]

The Allied Artillery Parks

The French traced the ground for their park of artillery midway between Grove Road and Beaverdam Creek (Great Run) and one-half mile west of von Steuben's division (though the French heavy ordnance had not yet arrived). Rectangular in shape, the park measured roughly 700 feet along its front and 300 feet on its sides. The artillery encampment was placed to the right rear of the park, which would contain not only the heavy siege pieces of the French, but the carriages and limbers to transport them and powder carts and ammunition wagons for their service. An artificers' laboratory (where skilled craftsmen labored) stood nearby, and a guard unit protected against enemy sabotage. The entire French artillery park and encampment was on property owned by Nelson. The chief of artillery, Lieutenant Colonel François d'Aboville, made his headquarters in the Nelson plantation house. M. Manduit served as adjutant of the French artillery, and M. Nadal as director of the French park. Several hundred yards behind the park, the French traced the ground they would use during the siege as their cemetery.[71]

The American artillery park was located a short distance to the left of Warwick Road, somewhat behind von Steuben's division and to the right of Beaverdam Creek. According to contemporary maps, it was similar in arrangement to the French park. And like the French, the American artillery park also had to await the arrival of siege ordnance from Trebell's Landing on the James River. Henry Knox's artillery command camped immediately in front of the park. Behind it was established the artificers' workshop and the central ammunition magazine. Generally, the artillery and engineers' depots were established closest to the front in order to best serve the forces in a siege. The facilities of commissary and quartermaster, while vital to the well-being of the troops, necessarily occupied secondary stations to those of the artillery and engineers. Consequently, they were placed farther to the rear.[72]

*   *   *

Other preparations were underway for the imminent receipt of the heavy artillery from the James River six miles away. Special attention was paid to the construction of bridges across the streams and marshes so the guns and their horses would not encounter any problems en route to the newly established parks. Even the older wooden bridges had to be reinforced in order to withstand the great weight of the cannon that would rumble across them on the way to the front. While detailed building knowledge of these bridges is lacking, it seems probable they were fashioned from wooden beams and heavy planks, perhaps made from timber already growing in the area and easily accessible for that use.

Theoretically, construction probably conformed somewhat to that outlined by the German engineer Johann Gottlieb Tielke:

> When a bridge is to be made for baggage-wagons and artillery, the principal beams or trunks must be very strong; and at least four of them will be necessary, even if it should not be above six or eight feet in breadth. As soon as they are properly placed at equal distances, rafters or planks must be laid cross them, and fixed to the ground. . . . The centre of the upper planks must cover the joints of those below; and if there is reason to apprehend that the pressure of the wheels may be too great, they must have their usual covering of earth, and a sufficient quantity of straw under it. The same precaution may be taken before they trust to old or weak wooden bridges; because the elasticity of the straw will add . . . much to their security.[73]

At Trebell's Landing, part of Knox's artillery brigade under Colonel John Lamb, who was second-in-command of the American artillery, prepared to help unload the American supplies and equipment from 64 sloops and schooners that had borne it from the head of Chesapeake Bay. Some of the French siege guns had also arrived from that point and were anchored off College Creek below Williamsburg. When a problem arose because insufficient skows and flatboats were available for the army to transfer the guns and stores to shore, the troops simply confiscated whatever vessels were available.[74] Soldiers were warned, however, against robbing or otherwise maltreating citizens. "Any Soldier who shall be detected in such MalPractices may depend on being punished, without being tried by a Court-Martial," was how an order of September 29 read.[75]

Once enough flatboats were gathered, the troops proceeded to unload the artillery and its provisions. Supplies for the artillery included the following items:[76]

Garrison carriages	Grape shot
Traveling carriages	Cannister shot
Mortar beds	Port fires
Various shells	Rammers & Sponges
Powder in barrels	Kegs of "Oyl"
Cannonballs	Tar barrels

Smith's equipment	Spare carriage wheels
Paper cartridges for cannon	Coins
Fuses	Wagons
Slow match	

Other military articles off-loaded included muskets, bayonets, musket cartridges, barrels of flour, flints, quartermaster and clothier stores, and numerous carpentry and entrenching tools.[77] Washington still had to await the arrival of the horses, which were still en route overland from Baltimore, before the artillery or any of these provisions could be sent on to Yorktown.[78]

While waiting for the artillery to advance from the James, Washington refused to waste time preparing to open trenches before the enemy. In his evening orders of September 29, he called for 1,200 men to parade on the morrow for work with the engineers. He also directed the quartermaster general to furnish the troops with 500 spades, 100 pickaxes, and 400 axes, hatchets, or bill hooks.[79] Siege preparations, announced the Virginian, would begin immediately.

Throughout Allied ranks morale remained high. A general feeling of impending victory pervaded both armies. "Unbounded confidence is reposed in our illustrious commanders," confided Dr. James Thacher, "the spirit of emulation and military ardor universally prevail, and we are sanguine in our expectations that a surrender of the royal army must be his Lordship's fate." Though he did not have the benefits of a formal education, the short, thin and good-natured doctor was a skilled writer and reliable observer of military affairs.[80]

Cornwallis Reacts

Ironically, Washington's opponent was just as sanguine. Lord Cornwallis fully believed relief from Sir Henry Clinton would arrive soon. His first full day exposed to the investing armies, however, had cost him numerous casualties, especially among the men stationed at the advanced posts. "This morning about 10 o'clock Private Zeilmann of Quesnoy's Company was mortally wounded on his picket post by a small musket ball and he died soon afterwards. I helped bury him," wrote one of Cornwallis's German soldiers in his diary. "About 12 o'clock, noon,

Private Haemmerlein, also of Quesnoy's Company, was wounded on this same post. The ball was cut out from between his two shoulder blades. I saw it and helped hold him. At other times also on this post were 1 private, Gruenbeck of Eyb's Company and 3 others from the Ansbach Regiment, severely wounded," he continued. "Today over 30 men were shot and wounded on the English and Hessian detached outposts."[81]

Reports like these from the front caused Cornwallis some discomfort. But his hope in ultimate success was bolstered at dusk on September 29, when a ship from Clinton arrived after slipping undetected through the French naval blockade at the mouth of the York River. A messenger sought out Cornwallis with a dispatch that made the general's spirits soar. The message promised that 23 ships of the line bulging with 5,000 soldiers would leave New York to solidify Cornwallis's position. "There is every reason to hope we start from hence the 5th October," Clinton informed his subordinate.[82]

The euphoria of the moment that gripped Cornwallis was brought to earth by the reality of his situation at Yorktown. Cognizant of the increased prospects for more casualties in his outer works as the Allies tightened their investment, Cornwallis was aware that losses along that line would jeopardize his inner position. Much would depend on the aggressiveness of his opponent. Could he hold out until Clinton's promised help arrived? His options were not inviting. If he spread his troops evenly along his main line, he would invite an Allied concentration that, with a determined assault, could effect a catastrophic breakthrough. Conversely, if he concentrated his men at selected points, he risked exposing large segments of his line to Washington's hardened veterans. The American and French combined strength also limited Cornwallis's options, for the Allies could mass great numbers of troops before any given point of his line while simultaneously maintaining their encirclement at all other points. These questions made Cornwallis's disposition along his outer works that much more important to his survival, for the casualties he suffered there meant fewer soldiers were available to hold Yorktown. By withdrawing from the advanced posts, however, Cornwallis could conceivably conserve enough strength to ward off the Allies until Clinton arrived with reinforcements. The decision was a weighty one, for a withdrawal would make it easier for Washington to formally open siege operations.[83]

There was also another reason to withdraw. The advance of the American wing from south of Yorktown toward the dam on Wormley Creek threatened to turn his position. The move, wrote Cornwallis, "could not fail of turning my left flank in a short time." Although he inked these words three weeks later and thus with hindsight, the general was an experienced soldier and was well aware on September 29 of the deficiencies of his position.[84]

Later that evening, Cornwallis penned a reply to Clinton. "[Y]our letter . . . has given me the greatest satisfaction. I shall retire this night within the works, and have no doubt, if relief arrives in any reasonable time, York and Gloucester will be both in possession of his Majesty's troops."[84]

It was a bold move, and perhaps a bit of a hasty one as well, for Cornwallis was rolling the dice and gambling that relief would arrive before the pounding guns of the Allied artillery batteries could be brought up to breach his main defenses around Yorktown.

Chapter 6

The Noose Tightens

*T*he night of September 29 passed in relative quiet, interrupted occasionally by the deep-throated boom of British cannon. The artillery fire went unanswered by the Allies. Ahead of the French and American encampments, pickets approached as close to the enemy redoubts at Pigeon Hill as prudence allowed. Sometimes the patrols of the British encountered those of the Allies, and when they did a brief but lively skirmish would illuminate the darkness for a few minutes before fitfully dying out.[1]

Sunday broke clear and warm. At sunrise Lieutenant Colonel Alexander Scammell, field officer of the day, advanced on horseback to reconnoiter changes in the British outer position made during the night. As he approached the vicinity of the Fusiliers' Redoubt and lower Yorktown Creek, the New Hampshire officer became separated from the picket guard accompanying him. In the ensuing confusion, Scammell mistook a party of Tarleton's dragoons under the command of a Lieutenant Cameron for his own guard and fell in with them. It took but a few moments for the surprised enemy to realize their good fortune, and when they did, they promptly captured the startled officer. Whether or not Scammell tried to resist is unknown. What is known is that a treacherous episode followed his capture.

One of the legionnaires advanced behind Scammell as he was being led toward Yorktown. According to an eyewitness account, the British soldier "put his pistol near his [Scammell's] back & shot him. The ball enter'd between his hip bone & his ribs & lodg'd in him."[2] Another firsthand source described the incident in more detail:

> Two of them [the British legionnaires] addressed him in rather harsh terms, the one seized his bridle and the other presented a pistol to his breast. Thus situated he [Scammell] acknowledged himself a prisoner, when a third rode up, presented his pistol close enough to burn his coat, and shot him in the back; a fourth made a stroke at him with his sword, but the shot having weakened him, he fell from his horse, and the intention of the villains was frustrated.[3]

The British soldiers rushed the seriously wounded Scammell into Yorktown, where Cornwallis's surgeons treated and dressed his wound. That afternoon, a soldier in a red coat with a white flag crossed into the Allied lines with a letter from Scammell explaining that he was being paroled and requesting his servant and clothing be forwarded to the hospital in Williamsburg. Scammell rested there and hope for his recovery grew. On October 6, however, his condition took a turn for the worse and at 5:00 p.m. that afternoon he died. According to most sources, Scammell was a courageous and well-liked officer, and thus his death cast a pall on American morale that lasted several days. "This was the severest blow experienced by the allied army throughout the siege: not an officer in our army surpassed in personal worth and professional ability this experienced soldier," wrote Lieutenant Colonel Henry ("Light-Horse Harry") Lee. "No officer of Colo. Scammell's rank that has been killed or died in the Army has been more, if so much, lamented by all ranks as he is," grieved Lieutenant Colonel Henry Dearborn, who succeeded Scammell in command of the 1st New Hampshire. Asa Redington, a soldier in the same New Hampshire unit, could not have disagreed more with these assessments. "When he was sent [wounded] to Williamsburg . . . none of his men became enthusiastic about volunteering to accompany him, but Uriah Ballard finally consented to go," wrote Redington after the war. "In a few days Scammel [sic] was dead, and none of his men regretted his loss, for they said it was a just punishment for the undeserved punishments he had inflicted on them while exercising his extreme tyranny. Patriotic men who thought they were American soldiers were shown that they were mere dogs in that colonel's estimation."[4]

Whether a tyrant or beloved officer, the tragedy of Scammell's capture and shooting was shortly followed by the arrival of good news for the Allies. Noting a lack of movement in the British redoubts at Pigeon Hill, some French grenadiers and chasseurs (light infantry) marched forward at about 8:00 a.m. to investigate. To their surprise, they found both structures empty, abandoned during the night by Cornwallis's soldiers.[5] Further inspection revealed that the two-gun battery at Hampton Road, as well as all the redan units bordering the north side of Wormley Creek, had also been abandoned. Of the outer line entrenchments, only the Fusiliers' Redoubt on Cornwallis's far right flank along the York River remained in British hands.[6] It was a stunning and unexpected development.

When news of the enemy withdrawal reached Rochambeau, the disbelieving officer rode forward immediately to survey the ground. He directed 100 chasseurs and grenadiers of the Regiment Bourbonnois to occupy one of the Pigeon Hill Redoubts, and 50 chasseurs of the Regiment Deux-Ponts into the other.[7] Both structures were hidden in the woods, so the soldiers approached cautiously in case the British were lurking nearby in the hope of launching an ambush.[8] As the French soon discovered, however, the British had indeed abandoned the entrenchments. Rochambeau posted the remaining grenadiers and chasseurs of the Brigade Bourbonnois behind the redoubts on sloping ground to better shelter themselves from Cornwallis's steady artillery fire.

Almost as important as the earthworks abandoned by the enemy ("within point blank shot of their main works," wrote Colonel St. George Tucker) was the ravine of Yorktown Creek, now unobstructed for nearly its entire length. Not only did it comprise a superior defense, but its stream promised water for the Allied work forces.[9] As Rochambeau's soldiers solidified the Pigeon Hill position, American light infantry moved forward in two lines of battle on the right center of the line to occupy the abandoned battery adjacent to Hampton Road. The troops expected a feint from the British, but nothing like it occurred.[10]

Cornwallis's artillery fired throughout the Allied advance, though with little effect. Although the Americans and French did not know it, the

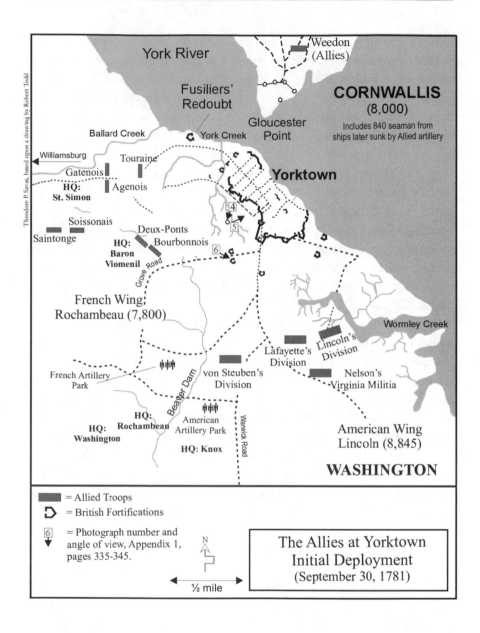

York River

Weedon
(Allies)

Fusiliers'
Redoubt

CORNWALLIS
(8,000)

Includes 840 seaman from
ships later sunk by Allied artillery

Ballard Creek

York Creek

Gloucester
Point

Yorktown

Williamsburg

Touraine

Gatenois

HQ:
St. Simon

Agenois

Soissonais

Saintonge

Deux-Ponts

HQ:
Baron
Viomenil

Bourbonnois

Grove Road

French Wing:
Rochambeau (7,800)

Wormley Creek

Lafayette's
Division

Lincoln's
Division

French Artillery
Park

Beaver Dam

von Steuben's
Division

Nelson's
Virginia Militia

HQ:
Rochambeau

HQ:
Washington

American
Artillery Park

Warwick Road

American Wing
Lincoln (8,845)

HQ: Knox

WASHINGTON

= Allied Troops

𝔻 = British Fortifications

6 = Photograph number and
angle of view, Appendix 1,
pages 335-345.

N

½ mile

The Allies at Yorktown
Initial Deployment
(September 30, 1781)

Theodore P. Savas, based upon a drawing by Robert Todd

British were greatly concerned that Washington would occupy the abandoned outer works and then launch a direct attack against the main line—something Cornwallis's men were ill-prepared to withstand. "An assault was more to be apprehended before ten o'clock that morning than at any precedent or subsequent period till the completion of the second parallel," remembered cavalry commander Tarleton. "The unfinished state of the works, the want of abatis, the badness of the position, and the difficulty of arranging both the troops and the artillery, would have rendered the attempt not very hazardous, if General Washington had either been acquainted with these circumstances, or had reason to doubt the superiority of the French navy in the American seas."[11]

Such fears proved unfounded. Incredulous at their good fortune in the inexplicable development, Washington and Rochambeau surveyed their new acquisitions and readied them for occupancy by their own troops. The works at Pigeon Hill were weaker than expected, built in a sandy area with especially thin parapets. Rochambeau decided they needed reinforcement and ordered his soldiers to convert and bolster the redoubts for their own use. The surrounding abatis proved stout, although its construction from flammable pine trees meant it could be easily destroyed.[12]

Cornwallis's precipitate withdrawal from the detached outer works to his front produced considerable speculation on the part of the Allies. Washington wrote to Congress that the abandoned fortifications commanded "in a very near advance almost the whole remaining line of [the British] defence." "We must believe that he feared being assailed in the rather extended position that he had fortified," wrote Baron von Closen."[13] General Wayne ridiculed the retreat as "not only unmilitary but an Indication of Confused precipitation." Chevalier d'Ancteville was probably closer to the mark when he wrote: "Whether the enemy feared to occupy such a great front . . . or that they had need to perfect and join together their inner works, which seems likely, they abandoned the redoubts of the center and the batteries of the left."[14]

Count Deux-Ponts was surprised by the withdrawal and harshly condemned it, claiming "that the enemy ought to have kept these redoubts until they were forced to abandon them. . . . It would have compelled us to feel our way, and would have held us in doubt." It was valuable land, believed Deux-Ponts: "The places evacuated allowed us to see . . . all the land which surrounds the town . . . It is clear that the approaches are as easy as possible." The consensus of opinion on the tactical value of the move was summarized by Washington's adjutant general. Edward Hand maintained the British withdrawal "will save us much time and trouble, as it at once gives us ground which is as advantageous as that the Enemy possesses, and greatly shortens our approaches." Quartermaster General Colonel Timothy Pickering agreed when he wrote his wife the news: "The enemy have abandoned some of their outworks, which will probably, in some degree, shorten the siege." Count Hans Axel de Fersen, a Swedish statesman serving as Rochambeau's aide-de-camp, blamed Clinton for the retreat more than he did Cornwallis, "for he had express orders from General Clinton to shut himself up in the body of the place." Still, concluded the Swede, the withdrawal was a "fault."[15]

Other benefits the Allies derived from the British evacuation included the ability to shorten their own line by moving its center forward even with Goosley Road and the Wormley Creek ravines, the opportunity to further restrict Cornwallis within the confines of his main works, and most important, the chance to move the Allied artillery closer to the British position once it could be brought to bear.[16]

While general agreement prevailed as to the relative advantages for the Allies after the British pullback, a variety of explanations for the withdrawal existed, all of them to a certain extent applicable. One was that the British lacked sufficient numbers to maintain their outer fortifications.[17] Another was that Cornwallis feared the Allies might turn his left and somehow interject themselves between his outer defenses and his main line.[18] A third reason—completely plausible as later events proved—was that the abandonment constituted but a preparatory move in an elaborate escape plan by which the British would cross by boat to Gloucester Point and fight their way through the Franco-American force stationed there. Frenchman Brisout de Barneville spoke for many when he wrote in his journal, "we fear that the enemy may cross the river one clear night and throw himself on M. de Choisy, making up his mind to travel by land in order to give us the trouble (very great) of looking for him." If escape was on his mind, Cornwallis might also attempt to concentrate enough men to break out somewhere along their right flank and flee up the peninsula toward Richmond. Some Allies worried that Admiral de Grasse's refusal to post ships above Yorktown would bode ill if Cornwallis selected the latter escape route.[19] "I am far from laughing at the idea of the enemy's making a retreat," Lafayette informed Washington. "It is not very probable; but it is not impossible." Washington did not think it likely Cornwallis could successfully slip away, but felt compelled to caution General Weedon at Gloucester to keep an eye on the enemy "on every point."[20]

Cornwallis's decision to abandon his outer position provoked as much comment among his own officers as it did among the Allies. Tarleton was not overly enthusiastic about the withdrawal, believing it premature. As far as he was concerned, the posts were strong and well defended by an appropriate number of British troops. Precious time could have been purchased had Cornwallis chosen to fight for every yard of land pending Clinton's arrival, believed Tarleton, for the only reasonable alternatives open to the Allies were to either storm the posts—an effort that might or might not have been successful—or conduct regular siege approaches toward them. Either solution could have delayed the British surrender by several days or longer, which might have been long enough for Clinton's soldiers and navy to relieve him.[21]

Cornwallis decided instead to spare the redoubts and thus save lives to defend his main position—banking heavily in the process that Clinton would appear in time to relieve him. The British general later explained his motives to Clinton this way in a letter dated October 20, 1781:

> After remaining two days in a strong position in front of this Place in hopes of being attacked, upon observing that the enemy were taking measures which could not fail of turning my left flank in a short time, & receiving on the second evening your letter of the 24th of Sept': informing me that the relief would sail about the 5th of October, I withdrew within the Works . . . hoping, by the Labour & firmness of the Soldiers, to protect the defence until you could arrive.[22]

This course proved as injurious to Cornwallis as that which he sought to avoid by his withdrawal. As Tarleton later put it, "to coop the troops up in the contracted and unfinished works of Yorktown, unexpectedly hastened the surrender of the British army." It is difficult to argue with him.[23]

British fears of a general American-French attack on the main works around Yorktown heightened around 10:00 a.m., after the Allies discovered Cornwallis's withdrawal. One event in particular caused many to believe a major attack was in the offing. Buoyed by the unexpected withdrawal of the Pigeon Hill redoubts, about 100 French light infantry volunteers belonging to St. Simon's command, under Baron de Viomenil's leadership, charged forward in an effort to seize the Fusiliers' Redoubt. Two companies of grenadiers and chasseurs of Agenois supported the movement. No artillery fire to soften the enemy position preceded the effort. St. Simon's men pushed forward recklessly, skirmishing with the British pickets positioned outside the redoubt who had been sniping at the French in an effort to retard their movement. The attackers drove them out of hiding, but in so doing drew musket fire and grapeshot from inside the redoubt. The lead and iron chilled their ardor, though only briefly.

The French troops tried again, this time pushing ahead "sword in hand" through the abatis all the way to the ditch of the fort. The troops of the 23rd Foot held their fire until the French soldiers gained the ditch, and then promptly sent them back toward their lines under a fusillade of lead balls backed by a few rounds from the two 12-pounder guns and three coehorns positioned inside the fort. The eruption of artillery, coupled with heavy musketry, alerted everyone on both sides that a heated fight was underway, and Allied and British eyes as far away as Gloucester Point watched the unfolding event with rapt interest.

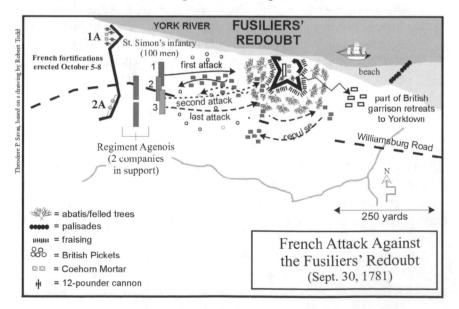

French Attack Against
the Fusiliers' Redoubt
(Sept. 30, 1781)

Unready to call it quits, the French attacked a third time. The thrust drew the same heavy level of defensive fire, but this time they succeeded in forcing some of the British hiding on the sides and beyond the redoubt into retreat. Colonel St. George Tucker, an attorney, trader, inventor, and French-speaking militia commander serving as Governor Thomas Nelson, Jr.'s liaison with the French army, watched as the fleeing redcoats fell back in confusion, "running very hastily across the sandy Beach into the town."[24]

Would the Fusiliers' Redoubt be cut out and captured so easily? The ace in the hole for the defenders proved to be naval firepower. Anchored in the York River, the frigate *Guadaloupe* joined with the land batteries and opened on the French pursuers. The noise and smoke was tremendous and helped drive them back in disorder, this time for good. Militia leader Weedon witnessed the event from his position across the river on the Gloucester peninsula. As he explained the affair in his homespun style to Washington two days later, "the Shiping [fired] When they Se our men runing after theirs."[25]

Some of the British believed they had beaten back a full-scale attack and inflicted heavy casualties. Hessian Stephen Popp wrote in his journal that more than 400 French soldiers had been killed in just fifteen minutes. Almost as confused as the young German was the calculation by a British intelligence officer claiming the Allies left 189 corpses on the field.[26]

Though some of the fighting was conducted at relatively close quarters, St. Simon's casualties were extraordinarily light, with but one or two men killed and less than a dozen wounded. Among the latter was M. de Bouillet, an officer with the Agenois unit whose leg was struck and broken by a cannonball. The attack was not a complete loss, however, for the French had succeeded in driving the enemy pickets from the field, securing in the process more advantageous ground in front of the redoubt. According to one account, under a flag of truce, the British allowed unarmed French to advance and remove their casualties.

Watching the advance, Rochambeau ordered forward the Brigade Bourbonnois to a new camp in the woods one-half mile in front of its earlier station. The Regiment Touraine took the advance post, well ahead of Agenois and Gatenois. The move completely sealed the river road to Williamsburg. If Cornwallis had been seriously entertaining an exit along that axis, it would now be much harder for him to effect a retreat along the York River.[27]

Almost simultaneous with the French move on the Fusiliers' Redoubt was an American feint on Cornwallis's left against Redoubts 9 and 10. One British naval officer concluded the Allies intended to storm the flanking redoubts on either side of Yorktown.[28] However, the American effort headed by Major Joseph R. Reid of Muhlenberg's Brigade was disrupted by some well-aimed artillery fire, which forced the troops to retire without accomplishing anything.[29]

The Allies Reconnoiter and Prepare

Throughout Sunday morning Washington, Du Portail, and several engineers inspected the ground the enemy had so willingly handed them. The engineers traced an intermediate redoubt midway between the structures at Pigeon Hill and Hampton Road before moving forward to inspect the terrain intended for the first parallel and its batteries. During the steady bombardment of Cornwallis's artillery—"about 40 cannon to the hour," remembered Captain James Duncan—Washington and his escort made a close reconnaissance of his new acquisitions and of the intervening tracts. Occasionally British shot struck nearby, causing the covering parties to scatter. The scene reminded one Continental officer "of a play among the boys called Prison-base."[30]

Throughout, Washington appeared unruffled by the cannon fire. With Du Portail and the engineers, he surveyed one of the captured redoubts surrounded by a dense wood of poplar trees. While they were there, an enemy cannonball whizzed over the heads of the party. Another sped by and lodged in the earth just 50 feet away. The shots were a little too close for comfort, and most of the officers prudently set their spurs and rode toward the rear. Washington alone remained, calmly watching the British through a spyglass. The enemy artillery ceased fire.[31]

The Allies could not answer the British, for their own heavy guns were still awaiting the arrival of horses to transport them to the front from Trebell's Landing.[32] In preparation for the pieces, on September 30 General Knox sent Captain Thomas Shilds on a mission to obtain the wood required to construct the artillery platforms to hold them. It may have seemed a mundane task, but upon the captain's shoulders Knox balanced a heavy responsibility. "You are, with the vessels appointed for

Independence National Historical Park

Brigadier General Louis Le Begue de Presle Du Portail

that service, to proceed with all possible dispatch to Somerset on the Eastern shore of Maryland," instructed Knox,

> and there load them with all the oak plank from 2 to 3 inches [thick] & from end 12 or 18 feet in length which you can find and also with as much pine plank from 1 to 3 inches as well [will?] complete the loading of said vessels. The plank being absolutely essential in the operations against the enemy, every method must be made use of to obtain it, and in case a sufficient quantity of it can not otherways be

had you are hereby authorized to impress as much as shall be wanting. . . . The great necessity for these articles will I hope be a sufficient inducement for you to make All possible dispatch to return to this place, at which you will inform me . . . the instant of your arrival.[33]

The Allies passed the afternoon making other preparations to open the siege against Cornwallis. The French began altering the outposts on Pigeon Hill while the Americans took steps to convert the Hampton Road battery into a redoubt and break ground on the planned intermediate structure.[34] The entire Allied position on the gorge was approximately 950 yards from the nearest British soldiers posted in the Hornwork on the southwest side of the Yorktown line.

Learning that day of British Admiral Digby's arrival at New York, and apprehensive lest Clinton should soon arrive to aid Cornwallis, Washington accelerated his schedule as much as possible. Twelve hundred Americans were ordered into the forest to collect materials for making fascines and gabions. The general ordered a like number to parade the next morning, 400 to work on reinforcing the Pigeon Hill structures, 800 to continue fashioning fascines and gabions.[35]

As the Allies consolidated their gains, spread out their camps, and otherwise readied themselves for the great military undertaking before them, Washington again entreated Admiral de Grasse to provide him with the means to tactically secure Cornwallis. Once more he requested the French admiral post ships in the river above Yorktown. Although de Grasse again rejected that course, he did agree to loan 800 marines from his vessels for duty on Gloucester Point. He politely asked in return that Washington make no additional requests that would reduce the strength of his fleet.[36]

Washington also turned down Lafayette's repeated requests that he be named second in command. General Lincoln, who held that position, should be transferred to Gloucester and command there, maintained the Frenchman. Lincoln's departure would leave Lafayette in charge of the entire American wing. Washington demurred courteously but firmly, and Lincoln remained in charge of all United States forces.[37]

During the afternoon, Washington issued various orders affecting the administration of the Allied forces. Henceforth, soldiers not assigned to reconnoitering parties were to refrain from independently inspecting the enemy works. "The curiosity of such persons often interrupts the observation of officers particularly charged with this Business," wrote the general.[38] Deserters from the British ranks were to be checked scrupulously to prevent those infected with smallpox from spreading the disease. He also ordered the army's surgeons "to be particularly attentive to removing without an Instants delay any soldier in whom the symptoms of the small pox may appear."[39] Washington also directed that "All officers and others are strictly forbid for obvious Reasons to wear Red Coats." Why anyone near the front on the Allied side would consider donning red was never addressed.[40] The commanding general also appealed to the personal honor of his soldiers when he told them, "The Liberties of America and the Honor of the Allied arms are in our hands. Such objects must excite a patriotic emulation in the greatest actions, and exertions. Their consequences will amply compensate every danger and Fatigue."[41]

Baron von Steuben served as Officer of the Day. Earlier, Washington ordered a picket of 24 officers and 300 men to take post in the gorge between the abandoned outer works and the ground previously camped on by Tarleton's command.[42] These pickets composed the day cordon and were positioned to prevent a surprise thrust by the British garrison. As dusk approached, Muhlenberg's brigade, supported by some of Hazen's and Wayne's soldiers, assumed picket duty. With their French counterparts under de Viomenil, the American sentinels advanced and spread to the left and the right so that the British were completely hemmed in throughout the night.[43] As the pickets peered through the darkness, the Allies continued adapting Pigeon Hill to their purposes and at the same time broke ground to build new structures to aid in further covering their approaches between the hill and the Wormley Creek ravine. In converting the Pigeon Hill redoubts, the French essentially reversed the fronts; that is, they filled in the former British openings and cut new ones in the opposite walls.

The outer earthworks—those gained fortuitously and those constructed by the French and Americans—completed the counter-vallation Washington had prescribed for protecting the army's encampment. In the darkness, workmen cut forest boughs with which to fashion fascines necessary for bolstering the existing Pigeon Hill structures and building new ones. Meanwhile, 400 Americans paraded forward with spades, shovels, and pickaxes to the spots selected earlier by Washington's engineers. On a specified signal they began throwing up earthen defenses, their labor accompanied by an occasional musket shot and the deep-throated rumble of a distant cannon.[44]

Farther to the right on the gorge between York and Wormley creeks, 200 American laborers went to work converting the British barbette battery into a redoubt, a process accomplished by closing its entrance and raising its parapet to a protective height for American soldiers.[45] A majority of the contemporary maps suggest this structure, as altered by the Americans, was pentagonal in shape.[46] If the fleche-shaped battery contained only three sides (as at least two maps indicate), then the Americans erected only two sides in closing its entrance. The British had placed abatis only on the southern sides to face an Allied rush from that direction, but the Americans evidently either moved it north of the redoubt or continued it completely around the structure.[47]

To the left of the former British battery and about equidistant between it and Pigeon Hill, 200 American soldiers started work on another redoubt. This earthwork was near the edge of one of Yorktown Creek's sprawling arms and more exposed to British artillery than the fortification on its right.[48] Cornwallis's guns remained silent throughout the night as the noisy work continued. "I am at a loss to account for it," marveled Captain James Duncan, "for the moon shone bright, and by the help of their night glasses they must certainly have discovered us."[49]

The expected bombardment came after daylight on the first day of October, when the British unleashed three artillery pieces in an effort to impede progress on the two American redoubts.[50] "We were very much annoyed by the shot from the British Artillery, which after having wounded several of our men, we adopted the precaution to establish men in different places on the work, to watch the flash of the Enemy's guns," wrote a New York soldier who participated in raising the intermediate earthwork. "[W]hen we immediately cry out 'a Shot'—on which each man took care of himself, by jumping off the works into the trenches, or as best he could."[51]

Baron de Turpin, a captain of engineers, directed the construction on this work, which ended during the night of October 3.[52] Historical maps indicate a palisaded pentagonal-shaped redoubt without abatis, which perhaps suggested the confidence the Allies felt relative to their security from British sorties.[53] Otherwise, the maps disclose very limited information about this structure.[54] In addition to building new earthworks and strengthening old ones, the Allies also completed work on bridges over the marshes and on communication routes among the various troop encampments.[55] During the daylight working hours, the British continued to mount efforts to disrupt the Allies with artillery fire. "The Enemy endeavored to retard these operations by playing on our men who were at work," reported General Nelson. It was ineffective, however, and Allied casualties were light. "We have not returned one shot."[56]

Cornwallis, meanwhile, continued buttressing his defenses around Yorktown. The withdrawal from the outer position severely limited his access to timber, so the general directed his men to begin dismantling houses for the lumber they needed to strengthen the line. Lieutenant John Bell Tilden of Pennsylvania was on picket duty the night of September 30. He remembered hearing the British work, "a confused noise of tearing down buildings to make fortifications."[57]

As Cornwallis struggled to prepare his main earthworks to resist the Allied artillery, Washington remained confident of ultimate success and incited his troops to rise to the occasion at hand:

> The advanced season and various considerations render it indispensably necessary to conduct the attacks against York with the utmost rapidity, the General therefore exhorts and requires the Officers and soldiers of this Army to pursue the duties of their respective departments and stations with the most unabating ardor; the present moment offers in prospect the epoch which will decide American Independence and the Glory and superiority of the Allies.[58]

Chapter 7

The Lion at Bay

*F*or almost a week after the British withdrew from the redoubts on the gorge and from those around the ravines of York and Wormley creeks, the Allies labored toward their objective of opening trenches and commencing the siege. The first days of October passed warm and humid, but were not hot enough to delay Washington's operations. All day Monday, October 1, the British sent scores of balls and shells flying in an effort to disrupt Allied progress on their line of countervallation. At one point, recorded an Allied officer, "the enemy fired two eight-inch shells. One burst over our heads, the pieces of which flew among us but did no harm. The other struck the ground and burst fifty yards in our rear "[1]

The cannonade lasted into the evening, diminishing after dark to about ten rounds per hour. Casualties were light and totaled but two men, both apparently bystanders killed near the American works. At 9:00 p.m., Lincoln's division relieved Lafayette's and the construction continued. The workers were protected against a surprise attack by General Wayne's brigade of Pennsylvanians and Virginians.[2]

The workers at the redoubts absorbed most of the attention of the British artillerymen. The distraction kept the redcoats from firing on Washington's reconnaissance party as it scouted the terrain to determine where to establish the first siege parallel. That afternoon, Washington,

General Du Portail, and several other engineers crossed the mill dam at Wormley Pond. Captain James Smith's company of Pennsylvanians acted as a guard to prevent a sudden British sortie that might capture or injure Washington. The group approached unmolested to within 300 yards of the enemy position at Redoubt 9. After surveying the terrain, the party returned safely to the Allied line. The intensive study of the ground below Yorktown clarified for Washington how the siege should progress.[3]

To formulate effective siege plans, Washington drew heavily upon the experience of Rochambeau, and less so upon von Steuben. Both officers had been wartime adversaries during the Seven Years' conflict in Europe more than two decades earlier. Washington's reliance upon Rochambeau's advice made sense, for that officer had taken part in fourteen sieges before his arrival at Yorktown. Von Steuben's only significant siege experience had been at Prague when he was but fourteen years old; Yorktown would be his last.[4] Washington also relied upon the expertise of Generals Knox and Du Portail, his chief engineer, for the successful conduct of the siege would require close cooperation between the artillery and engineering departments.

The Siege Gets Underway

On October 1, Washington approved the directing plan of the siege. Du Portail's engineers busied themselves that day plotting the first parallel 800-1,000 yards from the British fortifications, the normal distance for that line in siege operations against a fortress. Although Yorktown was defended by outer works rather than permanent fortifications, the engineers believed it was correct to place the line at that distance because of "the strength and reputation of the [British] garrison." To adequately protect the parallel, the engineers proposed four equidistant infantry redoubts along its length.

Utilizing available topographical features, they planned to stretch the line from the steep bank of the York River on the far right of the Allied line to the Yorktown Creek ravine south of Yorktown. When complete, the parallel would face the left and left-center of the British position, the area deemed most vulnerable to an Allied assault. Because security and secrecy were vital to success, only Washington, Rochambeau, and a few of their high-ranking officers knew specific details about how the siege would progress.[5]

During the day, Knox, Colonel d'Aboville, and their officers rode along the planned parallel and marked the prolongations for their projected batteries. The ride probably took place late in the day when afternoon shadows better revealed the faces of the British batteries.

British artillery fire was steady through much of the day. "A warm fire continued all this day," recalled a Pennsylvania captain, "about 40 Guns to the hour, on an average & 10 by night to the hour. 2 men only kill'd one of them in ye works." Although the fire was heavy, it was not effectively delivered, and even the British realized it. Bartholomew James, a lieutenant from the *Charon* and commander of a land battery designated No. 5 by the British, seemed equally impressed with the effects of the barrage and the resilience of the enemy. "The enemy constantly throwing up works, and all our batteries cannonading their working parties, which in great measure impeded their operations, though they were," he concluded in his diary, "from their great numbers, carried on with astonishing briskness."[6]

The artillery officers also helped select sites for the distribution of ammunition. Colonel Samuel Elbert, superintendent of materials, located positions intended for the trench depots where fascines, saucissons, gabions, hurdles, sandbags, and the various tools for the siege would be deposited. The French depot was planned for the left side of the parallel, on a small rise between two ravines at the head of Wormley Creek, on ground beyond the observation of the British. The American depot, almost one-half mile to the right, lay in another ravine extending from Wormley Creek. Far to the rear, the French and American field hospitals equipped and plotted ambulance routes from the projected parallel.[7]

Twelve hundred American soldiers continued on fatigue duty, making siege items and working on the American redoubts. The French joined in the work, the artillerymen making gabions and saucissons, while the rest of Rochambeau's army constructed fascines. At 5:00 p.m., the 3rd Maryland Regiment reported for nighttime picket duty in the American sector.[8]

At Trebell's Landing, several miles southwest of Yorktown on the James River, the siege guns continued to be unloaded from numerous transport vessels. On October 1, horses and teams finally began arriving from the north. To expedite the movement of the heavy ordnance,

Washington dispatched his personal vehicles to the landing to aid in their transport. At his request, other officers did the same. Having left Trebell's several days before, some mortars and cannon reached the American lines October 1-2. The general lack of draft animals, which had to take a circuitous route to the landing, coupled with the stumpy ground to be traversed, slowed the arrival of the artillery for several days.[9]

In his General Orders for October 1, Washington dictated measures governing the welfare of his forces. He knew the army's strength depended upon the health of the soldiers, writing that "Every possible attention ought to be paid to the preservation of it."[10] Smallpox continued to worry him. It was also on the minds of the men in the ranks as well, including Joseph Plumb Martin, a Connecticut enlistee who had been with the army since the age of 15 in 1776. It was during these early days of the siege that hundreds of blacks were turned out of the British garrison, many of them stricken with the disease. Some had been seized during Cornwallis's earlier maneuvers through Virginia and had been employed to build fortifications at Yorktown and Gloucester Point; others had joined the British Army in the hope of securing freedom. Low on food supplies, Corneallis sent them out of Yorktown—including those inflicted with the deadly illness. Allied troops found them dead and dying, individually and in groups, throughout the woods around the community.[11] Washington also directed his quartermaster general to secure enough straw for his men to sleep on, and instructed all of his officers to make certain their men were amply provided with the basic provisions. Each man was to be issued a gill of rum daily, and the unit commissaries received orders to maintain "a constant supply of Rum" specifically for that purpose.[12]

Despite the imminent siege, most aspects of army camp life continued as usual. "A genl Court Martial of which Colo Dayton is appointed President," read an entry from the Orderly Book, "will assemble to morrow morning [at] 10 o'clock at the Judge advocates marquee 100 yards south east of the Bridge over bever dam Creek for the trial of Captain Duffy of the 4th Regt of Artillery and such other persons as may come before them."[13]

As his men labored on the siege entrenchments, struggled to haul supplies and ordnance to the front, stood picket duty, and attended court martial hearings, Washington tried to put himself in Cornwallis's position. As he saw it, Cornwallis had essentially run out of options. He would eventually be forced to either fight his way out up the peninsula or attempt to flee across the York River. Once again, Washington pleaded with de Grasse to post ships above Yorktown. Only by that action, the general argued, would the investment be complete. Otherwise, he explained, "the British remain masters of the navigation for 25 miles distance above them, and have by their armed Vessels intercepted supplies of the greatest value on their way to our Camp." All this, said Washington, was happening "at a most critical time."[14] Moreover, the stationing of French vessels upstream would expedite the commander's communication with the Allied force on Gloucester Point. As it was, messages passed between the commands only after being borne over a roundabout route nearly ninety miles long.[15]

The possibility of Cornwallis's escape haunted the Virginia commander. Cornwallis, he wrote de Grasse, "[B]y embracing a leading wind and tide and stealing a march [might] proceed unmolested to West point [Virginia], where upon debarking his troops he will have the Pamunkey on one flank and the [Mattapony] on the other, and that finally he may by mounting the greatest part of his men and [making] successive forced marches, push his way, with a compact disciplined Army thro a Country whose population is too scattered to be collected for sudden opposition and [which would] make it impossible for us to overtake him." There were many who believe this, Washington continued, as it appears "the only means of safety, and it is certain that unless the investment is completed as abovementioned, he will have it in his power either now or in a last extremity [to escape]."[16]

Anticipating a negative response from de Grasse—which he subsequently in fact received—Washington urged the admiral to at least move his ships farther upstream, "and take a more menacing position with respect to the Enemy on our right."[17] The French fleet, anchored in Lynnhaven Bay, adroitly guarded the entrance to Chesapeake Bay and the mouths of the York and James rivers. The chance that an enemy fleet might enter and ascend either stream appeared exceedingly remote. On Gloucester Point, troop reinforcements from the French navy joined those of Lauzun and General Weedon in confining the British and severely restricting their foraging operations. Sporadic musketry erupted around Gloucester as patrols of Allied marksmen clashed with the British advanced pickets. There, too, Cornwallis appeared penned in by the Allies.[18]

Despite Washington's concern, the British at Yorktown and Gloucester Point were beginning to feel the hopelessness of their situation. As early as October 1, signs of Cornwallis's growing distress reached the Allies. From deserters, the Americans learned that sickness was rampant inside the British garrison. One estimate held that 1,500 of Cornwallis's soldiers were ineffective due to illness. The troops also lacked ammunition, and rations had been cut by one-third.[19] Even forage for Cornwallis's horses had begun to run dangerously low and the general had settled on the expedient of slitting their throats and casting the carcasses into the river. "About four hundred Horses . . . may be seen floating about in the river or lying dead on the Shore," observed Colonel Tucker.[20]

On Tuesday, the British resumed their heavy cannonade designed to retard Allied work on the redoubts to their front. Two new batteries directed the fire of 18-pounders toward the Americans still building the intermediate earthwork near Pigeon Hill. Between sunrise and sunset, some 300 to 500 British cannonballs passed among the Allies. To some, it seemed as if the sky was raining lethal metal. As Captain John Pryor reported, "We are making out approaches, tho' under and infernal Hot Cannonaid—upwards of 2000 Balls have been fir'd at us to day." The inability to respond irked the soldier. "In a day or two our first parallel will be form'd, by which time, I hope our heavy Cannon will be ready to play on them—as yet we have not return'd a single shot." Regardless of the exact number the British expended, it was the most severe cannonade experienced by the Allies since the investment began. As one would expect, casualties increased. A random shot on the night of October 2 killed four out of five men in an American patrol composed of Pennsylvanians; many believed a deserter informed the enemy of the patrol's position. Another took off the hand of an unlucky Maryland soldier.[21] Guarding against an enemy sortie, workers on the American redoubts devised a system of signs and countersigns that were employed with success during the night.[22]

In a move designed to conserve ammunition, the British occasionally simulated fire by igniting black powder in the embrasures of their batteries, causing the Allies working at the redoubts to run for cover. Cornwallis's artillery, though, continued taking its toll. A member of the militia was struck by a ball as he stood atop a parapet hurling verbal defiance at the British.[23] Neither were musicians immune to the enemy fire. "A drummer, rather too curious in his observations, was this day killed with a cannon ball," reported an American captain.[24] During the afternoon, at least one man deserted to the British and four enemy cavalry horses fled the garrison at Yorktown and were picked up by American soldiers.[25]

More American cannon and artillery stores arrived on October 2. Because of the necessity for fixing roads and bridges to accommodate the heavy pieces, their transport continued at a painfully slow pace.[26] Nevertheless, Knox appeared optimistic. "We hope to open our batteries in three days," he notified the Board of War.[27]

Meanwhile, Washington pressed the troops onward in their labors. Under the command of Brigadier General James Clinton, Lincoln's division went on fatigue duty on October 2. The First Brigade spent the day making fascines and gabions. A Maryland regiment went on picket duty in the evening.[28] Armed with hatchets, mallets, axes, and bill hooks, the Allies trimmed boughs and branches and fashioned them into defensive accouterments.[29] "We made fascines and gabions," an American sergeant recalled, "the former, bundles of brush, and the latter are made in this manner, viz.—after setting sticks in the ground in a circle, about two feet or more in diameter, they are interwoven with small brush in form of a basket; they are then laid by for use, which is in entrenching."[30] At suitable points behind the front, the soldiers deposited their products and at supply dumps collected the tools needed for conducting siege warfare. In addition to the standard tools of the trade, they picked up planks, stakes, and frames to construct and reinforce embrasures.[31]

While British heavy weapons directed shot and bombs against the Allies, Cornwallis's soldiers worked hard to improve their surrounding stockade and to establish communication routes from the different redoubts to the main Hornwork.[32] "The Enemy have pull'd down almost every Wooden House in Town," observed an American officer, "& I suppose we shall knock down every Brick one, so that the Town between us will be demolished entirely."[33] Toward dusk, a German soldier watched as an American galley exploded near the mouth of the York River, cause unknown. Shortly thereafter, a British guard boat, having slipped through the French blockade, arrived with more dispatches from Clinton saying the fleet would soon embark to Cornwallis's relief.[34] At about 10:00 p.m., British ships in the York commenced a steady fire toward the Allies. As each gun discharged, a long tongue of fire licked out into the darkness before disappearing in a cloud of sparks and smoke. The fiery water-based barrage was short-lived, designed only to cover the passage over the river of Tarleton's legion, which was ordered to Gloucester Point to assist the troops foraging beyond the Allied units stationed on the point.[35]

*   *   *

Wednesday, October 3, dawned cool and cloudy and an easterly wind refreshed the Allied soldiers still finishing the approaches. More ordnance and stores arrived from the James River and spirits rose in anticipation of at last answering Cornwallis's pesky artillery.[36] British firing was not as intense as it had been, and caused little destruction among French and American troops. One shot could have spun the campaign and the war in a different direction, and almost did. A New Hampshire chaplain, Israel Evans, was standing near General Washington just as an enemy cannonball plowed into the earth nearby, showering Evans's hat with the sandy loam. "Mr. Evans," Washington softly addressed the agitated chaplain, "you had better carry that home and show it to your wife and children."[37]

Desertions continued. On the Allied side, two French soldiers and one American leaked their way over to the enemy.[38] As a deterrent to such activity, Washington decreed that "Every deserter from the American troops . . . who shall be found within the Enemies Lines at York, if the place falls, will be Instantly hanged."[39] Two more British soldiers also deserted the garrison at Yorktown, bringing further word of Cornwallis's growing plight.[40] Work continued apace on the unfinished defenses about the town, they said, and some 200 more artillery horses had been killed because of want of forage and because Cornwallis determined not to release the animals for capture by the Allies.[41] Dumped into the York, the carcasses bobbed out with the tide only to return with it a few days later to clutter the beach with decaying matter. By their return, remarked one officer, "it seemed as if they wanted to cry out against their murder after their death."[42]

Fight on Gloucester Point: The Battle of the Hook

Prior to the opening of the French and American batteries, the principal engagement between the Allies and the British at Yorktown occurred that Wednesday morning on the plain of Gloucester. The engagement that ensued occurred at what was called "the Hook" of Gloucester Point when a column of men under Tarleton was returning from a successful foraging expedition and encountered the Allies. It was one of the few direct actions during the Yorktown Campaign, and the most important combat on the far side of the river.

For almost two months the British had essentially had a free hand in looting the Gloucester countryside. Simcoe's cavalry and his German infantry supports were professionals at the top of their game. General Weedon headed 1,500 Virginia militia (infantry and cavalry). Of these, only Lieutenant Colonel John Mercer's men in his Select Battalion of Virginia Militia, Continental Army veterans all, could boast of extensive military service. The balance of Weedon's command was poorly-trained. The last thing Weedon envisioned was a pitched fight against a seasoned enemy. On September 24, he received badly-needed reinforcements when Lauzun's Legion arrived. The legion was organized into two squadrons of hussars (about 320 mounted troops, including officers), and another three companies, one each of grenadiers, chasseurs, and artillery. The entire legion numbered about 620 men. On September 29, Choisy arrived with 800 marines on loan from de Grasse. Because he ranked Weedon, Choisy assumed command of the entire Allied force at Gloucester. Opposing them as the siege began was the British garrison under Lieutenant Colonel Thomas Dundas.[42]

Lauzun was not an admirer of the 58-year-old Choisy, who had been sent by Rochambeau as a result of Lauzun's complaints about Weedon's reluctance to engage the enemy. Choisy was "a good and gallant man," wrote Lauzun, but "ridiculously violent, constantly in a rage, always making scenes with everyone, and entirely devoid of common sense." Soon after his arrival, he continued, Choisy "began by finding fault with General Weedon and all the militia and told him that they were cowards. [Within] five minutes," continued Lauzun, "they were almost as much afraid of him as of the English, which is certainly a great deal to say." Weedon, a former innkeeper and militia leader, had been reluctant to lead an offensive against the British and had been content to maintain a

National Park Service, Colonial National Historical Park, Yorktown Collection

Louis Armand de Gontaut-Biron, duc de Lauzun

sufficient distance between the armies. Weedon, Lauzun later wrote, had "blockaded Gloucester in a drole [sic] way; he was more than 15 miles from the enemy's posts, frightened to death, and did not dare to send a patrol half a mile from his army. He was the best man alive and all that he desired was to take no responsibility." Lauzun also labeled Weedon "an officer of sufficient merit, but who detested fighting. . . and went in deadly fear of coming under fire."[43]

The new French commander was not about to sit back and let the enemy rampage around the countryside, though his command was not well equipped and most of the men had never fired a shot in anger. Many were without shoes, and according to Choisy, few had tents, kettles, or even mess tins. Only Lauzun's men and Mercer's Battalion had seen action, and the former's experience had been of the skirmish variety only.

On October 1, Choisy made preparation to ease his entire command closer to the British main line. Once organized, he moved out from Gloucester Court House in search of the enemy. The next day, Weedon informed Washington of these developments and expressed concern over the lack of artillery. "We have not a single Field piece to our whole Troops except two small Canon belonging to the Duke [Lauzun], not more than two pounders." Later that day Weedon wrote to Washington again, telling him they would drive more deeply toward the enemy with a force that "will be adequate, I hope to anything short of Lord Cornwallis' main body."[44]

Though Weedon was leery about directly engaging the British (telling Lauzun he would not move so close to the enemy lines again, "as I had no desire to be killed"), Lauzun relished the thought of combat. With Choisy in charge, he boldly grasped the opportunity to meet his English adversary—the recently arrived green-clad (and much despised) Banastre Tarleton. Lauzun would have his wish the next day, when British Colonel Dundas sent his cavalry leader to accompany what he hoped would be the last and largest foraging expedition before the Allies completely restricted their movements.

Early on the morning of October 3, the Allies prepared to break camp and "take a position in the Neighbourhood of Abingdon Church, which is the nearest position we can take for want of water," wrote Weedon. Because of a lack of wagons, Choisy divided his command. Weedon formed two battalions of light infantry and one of grenadiers, all under the command of Lieutenant Colonel John Mercer, plus cavalry under Colonel Webb. According to Weedon, this force was "annexed" to Lauzun's Legion. Choisy would take the balance of the command with him. Mercer's command, together with one company of Lauzun's French Hussars under comte Arthur Dillon, marched along the York River Road. (The entire Second Squadron of Lauzun's hussars was armed with lances.) Choisy and the rest of the Allies traveled in the same direction down the Severn Road, with the balance of Lauzun's Legion well in the lead. The British were also moving that morning, and on the same side of their defensive works as the Allies. Dundas had "led out detachments from all the corps in his garrison to forage the country in front," remembered Tarleton, whose men had been shuttled to Gloucester Point just 24 hours earlier to provide cover for the important foraging expedition. It did not take long for one combatant to find the other.[45]

A captain of the Gloucester militia named Phil Taliaferro sent a rider with an important dispatch to Choisy, alerting him that "A party of the Enemy are now At Mrs. Whitings & have sent out to collect the Cattle & Sheep adjacent, there being no one to oppose them. I thought proper to send this information to you." By this time Choisy's column was within a few miles of Dundas's soldiers, who had loaded their wagons with Indian corn and were rolling back to Gloucester about 10:00 a.m. Some 240 men from Tarleton's Legion covered the rear of the rolling column, which was also guarded by men from the 17th Regiment of Light Dragoons, a mounted infantry company from the 23rd Regiment, Royal Welsh Fusiliers, and Simcoe's Queen's Rangers.[46]

Dundas seems to have learned of the presence of the Allies at about the same time. Lieutenant Cameron (the same officer who had been in charge of the patrol responsible for killing Alexander Scammell) had been sent by Tarleton to patrol the rear. The lieutenant spotted "a column of dust, and afterwards some French hussars," remembered Tarleton. The enemy spotted by Cameron was Lauzun's advance, near where the Severn Road (upon which Lauzun and Choisy traveled) converged with the York River Road (upon which Mercer's militia marched). The confluence of these avenues formed a mile-long lane about four miles from the tiny village of Gloucester. It was in this area, "the Hook" (where the Guinea Road now meets Route 17), that Tarleton deployed the balance of his legion, the Queen's Rangers, and the 17th Regiment of Light Dragoons in a stand of woods. He then rode to join Cameron at the front.

Lauzun, meanwhile, had also been hunting his adversary. "I went forward to learn what I could," he later wrote. "I saw a very pretty woman at the door of a little farm house on the high road; I went up to her and questioned her; she told me that Colonel Tarleton had left her house a moment before; that he was very eager to shake hands with the French Duke. I assured her, that I had come on purpose to gratify him."[47]

As Lauzun wrote, "I was not a hundred steps from the house when I heard pistol shots from my advance guard." The fight was on! "I hurried forward at full speed to find a piece of the ground where I could form a line of battle." On Lauzun's left were some woods, and on his right an open field. Enclosed fields bordered the single road. He caught sight of Tarleton's horsemen—"the English cavalry in force three times my own"—and the fight began in earnest when Lauzun launched an attack.

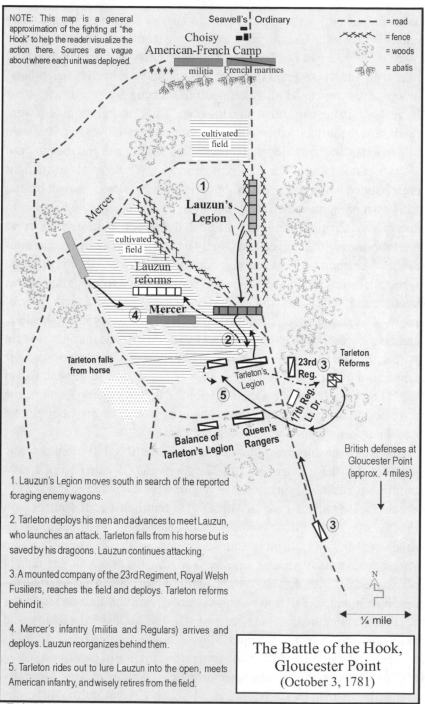

NOTE: This map is a general approximation of the fighting at "the Hook" to help the reader visualize the action there. Sources are vague about where each unit was deployed.

Seawell's Ordinary

Choisy
American-French Camp

militia   French marines

- - - = road
xxxx = fence
= woods
= abatis

cultivated field

① Lauzun's Legion

Mercer

cultivated field

Lauzun reforms

④ Mercer

Tarleton falls from horse

② Tarleton's Legion

23rd ③ Reg.

Tarleton Reforms

17th Reg. Lt. Dr.

⑤

Balance of Tarleton's Legion

Queen's Rangers

British defenses at Gloucester Point (approx. 4 miles)

③

1. Lauzun's Legion moves south in search of the reported foraging enemy wagons.

2. Tarleton deploys his men and advances to meet Lauzun, who launches an attack. Tarleton falls from his horse but is saved by his dragoons. Lauzun continues attacking.

3. A mounted company of the 23rd Regiment, Royal Welsh Fusiliers, reaches the field and deploys. Tarleton reforms behind it.

4. Mercer's infantry (militia and Regulars) arrives and deploys. Lauzun reorganizes behind them.

5. Tarleton rides out to lure Lauzun into the open, meets American infantry, and wisely retires from the field.

N

¼ mile

The Battle of the Hook, Gloucester Point
(October 3, 1781)

Theodore P. Savas

Tarleton spurred his mount and led his men in a countercharge. Once contact was made, Lauzun remembered, "a continual crackling noise arose." The charge of the dragoons had left Choisy and the infantry well to the rear, and the result at the front was an old-fashioned hand-to-hand contest with swords and pistols at point blank range.

Just before the two sides came together, Tarleton and his mount were knocked to the ground when one of the horses ridden by one of his men was wounded and stumbled into them. "Tarleton saw me and rode toward me with pistol raised," Lauzun remembered. "We were about to fight single handed between the two troops when his horse was thrown by one of his own dragoons pursued by one of my lancers. I rode up to him to capture him." British dragoons waiting in the woods witnessed the event and responded with a ragged and largely unorganized charge to save their leader. "[A] troop of English dragoons rode in between us and covered his retreat; he left his horse with me." Once extricated from his dangerous situation and remounted, the bruised Tarleton launched a hasty pair of probing charges against Lauzun's men, though without breaking his line. Realizing it was time to withdraw, the British leader rode for the woods in his rear. Fortunately for Tarleton, Captain Forbes Champagne and his company of 40 mounted infantry belonging to the 23rd Regiment, Royal Welsh Fusiliers, had just reached the field. Tarleton ordered Champagne to dismount his men "and placed them in a thicket on [the] right." Tarleton reformed his dragoons behind them.

Lauzun's cavalrymen pursued closely until confronted by the dismounted 17th Regiment of Light Dragoons and Captain Champagne's men from the 23rd Regiment, all of whom were deployed in the skirt of timber. Against them Lauzun launched a few half-hearted attacks on horseback, without effect. With that, Lauzun also pulled back. As he withdrew, Mercer's Virginia militia arrived on the field and Lauzun formed behind the American infantry. Tarleton, his dragoons adequately reorganized, prepared to take on Lauzun again. When he spotted the American infantry, Tarleton swung his cavalrymen around on the left of the 17th Regiment of Light Dragoons in the hope of detaching and drawing Lauzun out into the open.[48]

Mercer's men had by this time formed a solid line of battle and sent at least one volley in the enemy's direction. American lead mortally wounded a British lieutenant named Moir. The line of militia, leavened with a battalion of Continental soldiers, stood its ground and impressed everyone in sight—including the enemy. Wise enough to know he had more of a fight on his hands than he wanted, Tarleton retired toward Gloucester Point. Through Lauzun's wishful eyes, his own charge "overthrew a part of his [Tarleton's] cavalry and drove him within the entrenchments of Gloucester." The balance of Choisy's column reached the field about 30 minutes after the firing sputtered to a fitful close.[49]

As is so often the case, the number of killed and wounded varies by source. Lauzun's Legion alone lost three men killed (two outright, one mortally) and 16 wounded including Lauzun's executive officer Dillon. Mercer's mixed infantry command lost two killed and 11 wounded. Tarleton reported one infantry officer killed and a dozen wounded and captured. Lauzun, however, put British losses from all causes at 50, which is probably closer to the truth.[50]

As one might expect, both Choisy and Lauzun were ecstatic. That same afternoon from a tavern called Seawell's Ordinary, Choisy penned a brief report in his unique writing style and dispatched it to Washington:

> Sir,
>
> I have the hounor to inform you that by our arrival at Saoul's Tavern we have met with the ennemi who was in number about 500 men Cavalry and Infantry, that the Cavalry of the Duc of Lauzun has attaqued them, pierced throug and that we have had a great advantage on them We can esteem they have 30 men killed or wounded The 200 men grenadier Americans who were the only Infantry advanced enough to have part in the affair and who have behaved excedingly well have killed one officer who was at the head of the Infantry of the ennemi. T'is a general report that Tarleton has been wounded. The ennemi have retired to Gloucester and we are quickly in our Camp where I expect you will join to morrow as we have al. Agreed.
>
> I have the hounor to be your Most humble servant,
>
> Choisy

Washington was just as elated by the encounter and issued general orders the next day that included the following:

. . . The General Congratulates the Army upon the brilliant success of the Allied Troops near Gloucester. He requests the Duke de Lauzern to accept his particular thanks for the Judicious disposition and the decisive Vigour with which he charged the Enemy, and to communicate his Warmest Acknowledgements to the Gallant Officers and men by whom he was so admirably seconded. He feels peculiar satisfaction at the inconsiderable loss on our part, that no ill effects are to be apprehended from the Honorable Wounds which have been received in this affair, and that at so small an Expence, the Enemy amounting to six hundred Horse and foot were compleatly repulsed and Reconducted to their very lines.

Although the British foraging wagons had managed to escape, Washington's claim of a "brilliant success" at the Hook was not without foundation. Strategically speaking, the combat was most significant. Dundas's command was now tightly corked on Gloucester Point, making foraging beyond their defensive lines no longer feasible. The victory also severed Cornwallis's line of communications between the narrow peninsula and the open country to the north, and effectively sealed off any possible escape by that quarter. If anything would have made Allied morale soar and Cornwallis's sag, it would have been Tarleton's capture or tactical defeat; both had been within reach. Just learning the hated officer had been knocked from his saddle put smiles on Allied faces and increased morale. Something no one knew at the time was that Tarleton's active military career ended at the Hook, and he would never again lead men in combat. The day following the battle, Choisy pushed his men forward to within a mile or two of the British works.[51]

Preliminary Work to Open the First Parallel Continues

On the Yorktown side of the river, meanwhile, Allied preparations went on throughout Thursday, October 4. By then, the army's work horses had arrived after their 400-mile overland trek, and more heavy artillery and ordnance supplies reached the American and French parks before Yorktown. Movement of the heavy guns was slow and hard work. Horses, hitched two abreast per piece, sometimes could not muster the strength needed to haul the particularly heavy cannon, and the soldiers themselves often pushed and pulled the guns over rough terrain. At the artillery parks, the pieces were dragged into position with the aid of oxen confiscated from local inhabitants.[52] A doctor with the army hospital at Williamsburg sent a tongue-in-cheek note to Colonel John Lamb regarding the emplacement of the heavy guns. He learned with pleasure, he wrote Lamb, "that you are very busy in getting your great folks to speak to the Earl [Cornwallis]—I long to hear them open their mouths."[53]

While optimism in ultimate victory increased with arrival of the siege guns, the realization sank in quickly that the weapons could not be brought to bear for several more days. By some estimates, the ordnance would not be ready to fire before the tenth of the month. Planning for the first parallel, however, continued.[54]

Generals Knox and Du Portail, and Colonels Desandrouins and d'Aboville, traced the batteries and lines in preparation for constructing the parallel and placing the artillery. General Muhlenberg's brigade of the First Division reported at 6:00 a.m. to make fascines in the woods, continuing in that duty until 5:00 p.m. that afternoon.[55] The Allied redoubts on the gorge were completed by the morning of October 4. At the extreme left of their position near the York River, the French began building a battery from which to unleash artillery fire against the British Fusiliers' Redoubt, and particularly against British shipping that continued to harass French working parties with long-range naval fire.[56]

British artillery fire against the American and French fortifications that day was steady and concentrated largely against the American intermediate redoubt and the former British work at Hampton Road. "Cannonade as usual pretty heavy from the British, faint from us," wrote an American soldier in his diary. The French troops occupying the reinforced structures at Pigeon Hill drew little of this fire.[57] When night arrived, soldiers from both Allied armies advanced closer to the British works. Several skirmishes erupted between these patrols and those sent out by Cornwallis. The rattle of muskets continued through much of the night, and the British cannon roared incessantly.[58] The movement was nothing more than a ruse launched with the intent of having the British reveal the location of their batteries, which in turn aided the French and Americans in placing their own guns.[59] The nocturnal effort cost one Continental his life.[60]

When the sun rose the following morning, the Allies hoisted their respective national standards over the earthworks on the gorge.[61] The sight of the enemy flags did not sit well with the British, whose guns continued to slowly but steadily fire on the ring tightening around them. Although most of the cannon balls smacked the dirt entrenchments or sailed overhead and dropped harmlessly into the rear areas, a few managed to find their mark. An American soldier was lying on the ground using his knapsack as a pillow when a ball knocked it from under his head. The shot killed the man, but left his body unmarked.[62] Near the American intermediate redoubt, a Pennsylvania corporal named Organ was on picket duty when a 9-pounder shot "carried off part of his Hips." He lingered in agony for a time before expiring.[63] Cornwallis continued firing without abatement, for there was little else he could effectively do to disrupt the besiegers.[64] "In a day or two," Colonel Tucker wrote his wife, "it is expected we shall return the Compliment with Interest."[65]

As Tucker penned his lines, the big Allied artillery pieces were beginning to arrive and be organized in ranks in the French and American artillery parks. The guns were available, but Washington patiently awaited their proper emplacement on the siege line before answering the British. Teams continued to stagger in from Trebell's Landing, their wagons laden with mortar bombs, cannonballs, powder, and ordnance equipage. Behind the parks, in the artificers' camps and magazines, soldiers readied the materials of war and prepared cartridge ammunition for the cannon.[66]

Fatigue details from Hazen's Brigade roamed the woods and fashioned more fascines, saucissons, and gabions. The articles were gathered and brought toward the front for use in making approaches. Lafayette served as Officer of the Day.[67] Demonstrating his ongoing concern for the health of his men, Washington ordered the unit commissaries to either bury "Offall [sic] and other Offensive matter" or suffer arrest. He also directed that a detail be raised to see to the removal and burial of a number of dead horses "and other putrid bodies" from within the encampment areas.[68]

News of naval matters also filtered into Allied lines on October 5. Captain Thomas Symonds, Cornwallis's naval commander, had posted guard boats below Yorktown to alert the garrison if de Grasse's blockading French ships attempted to move upriver. Three fire ships (vessels packed with flammable materials that would be set afire and directed into enemy craft) were ready to intercept them. More detailed news was extracted from a captured British boat captain who told Washington's officers that up to a dozen merchant ships had been deliberately sunk off Yorktown, and that wooden piles had been driven into the riverbed to prevent enemy ships from unloading troops. Two powerful British frigates, *Charon* and *Guadeloupe*, were anchored off the town to defend it instead of the passage of the river. While all of this was interesting to Washington, the most important intelligence concerned Cornwallis's apparent inability to extricate his command promptly. If he wanted to evacuate his garrison from Yorktown to Gloucester Point, continued the boat captain, there were not enough boats for him to accomplish the task in a single night.[69]

Also on October 5, heartening news for the entire Allied army arrived: nearly a month earlier on September 8, Major General Nathanael Greene and some 2,000 men had defeated a slightly larger British army under Colonel Alexander Stewart at Eutaw Springs, South Carolina.[70] The news caused St. George Tucker to write his wife Frances, "If our success here should correspond with his at the South, I have no doubt that a speedy peace must be the result of the present Campaign. We have everything to hope, and less than we ever had heretofore to fear. In short I think nothing but the Intervention of a superior providence can save the British Army at York."[71]

* * *

As each hour passed, preparations for the formal opening of the siege neared completion. Engineers finished their plan on a topographical chart showing the projected parallels with their collateral works, the enemy defenses intended as the targets of French and American siege guns, and the intervening terrain that had determined the engineers' and artillerists' proposed course of action. The problem now was to turn the design into reality with some degree of exactness, a task usually accomplished with more difficulty than precision.[72]

To strangle Cornwallis's army, the first parallel was erected with its right flank resting near the York River below the town. The line was concave in design and ran for some 2,000 yards south, southwest, west, and finally northwest to the swampy ravines of Yorktown Creek, where the line's left flank was anchored near Goosley Road almost directly opposite the British Hornwork. The average distance of this line from the enemy's inner defenses was about 800-1,000 yards, except opposite

Redoubts 9 and 10, whose presence forced the Allies to "bow" their line out at that point, which increased the distance to more than 1,000 yards.

Why was the first parallel erected southeast of Yorktown? Simply put, it was the only viable place for effective siege operations. The nature of the terrain around the Yorktown Creek ravine on the Allied left west of town, while valuable as natural cover, precluded a concentrated offensive effort from that direction. British batteries in the town, naval gunfire, and the Fusiliers' Redoubt on the enemy right flank effectively commanded that sector, which discouraged the Allies from making any serious direct approaches in that quarter. Cornwallis's left flank, therefore, appeared more vulnerable and offered more favorable open terrain for an Allied attack than any other part of the British line.

After careful reconnaissance, the engineers decided to place the right side of the first parallel farthest from the enemy's main fortifications because of the presence of the detached Redoubts 9 and 10. Artillery fire from those obstacles could disrupt Allied entrenchment operations in that quarter. Situated at a distance of 600 yards, the first parallel would be too far away to be subjected to effective small arms fire or grape and canister shot. The distance also served to discourage enemy sorties. Heavy artillery placed in this first parallel could systematically destroy Cornwallis's earthworks. Moreover, the line cut across the heads of the lateral arms of the Wormley Creek ravines, and so allowed for easy access via these natural approaches from the encampments. The actual excavation of this parallel was designed to proceed under the protective surveillance of troops posted in the Pigeon Hill Redoubts overlooking Yorktown Creek, and in the recently completed American works.[73]

The news continued to worsen for Cornwallis. Tightening the investment on the river, Admiral de Grasse at last responded favorably to Washington's request for ships farther upstream to menace the British garrison and discourage a British escape. On October 5, two French ships of the line sailed into sight downriver from the Allied armies and the enemy.[74]

The Allies originally planned to open the first parallel Friday night, October 5. Frequent intimations that this was the case appear in the contemporary sources. The reason excavation did not begin on the trench that evening remains a mystery. "Six regiments were ordered to hold themselves in readiness to march this evening," wrote Dr. Daniel Shute. "Did not march, reason unknown." Wayne wrote much the same thing:

"Six Regts . . . one from the right of each Brigade were warned for particular duty to parade at 4 0 Clock P.M. but countermanded until further orders."[75] Lieutenant Colonel Jeremiah Olney led his 1st Rhode Island Regiment forward for picket duty that night in the American sector.[76] The night was dark, cloudy, and rainy— perfect for such an enterprise. The British may have divined Allied intentions and foiled the initial effort. "I was at the outpost on the night of the 5th-6th," remembered Rochambeau aide Baron von Closen. "And as the enemy knew all the siege preparations that we were making, he suspected that we would open the trench that night, which brought upon me bombs, balls, and royals [mortars], all these and more."[77]

More likely than not, the reason for the increased cannonade—as well as for Washington's change of mind about opening the trenches that night—rested with his engineers and their desire to gain additional knowledge of the locations of the British batteries. "The night of the 5th-6th was passed like the preceding [nights]," observed Deux-Ponts, "with the same patrols and the same cannonading."[78] In addition, the engineers probably needed more time to mark the ground for the batteries in accordance with their findings. If the inclement weather held as Washington expected it would, the Allies could begin digging the following night under similar favorable conditions.

Although the digging was postponed, the parallel was located that night. Soldiers from three American regiments acted as a covering party and advanced deep into "no man's land"—far ahead of the proposed parallel. Once they were safely deployed, American sappers and miners followed the engineers in the blowing rain and traced the projected line with strips of pine wood laid end to end.[79] Similar operations were underway in the French sector.

An American soldier who participated in this project recorded a memorable experience that windy and rainy night that he would never forget:

> We had not proceeded far . . . before the engineers ordered us to desist and remain where we were and be sure not to straggle a foot from the spot while they were absent from us. In a few minutes after their departure, there came a man alone to us . . . and inquired for the engineers. The stranger inquired what troops we were, talked familiarly with us a few minutes, when, being informed which way

the officers had gone, he went off in the same direction, after strictly charging us, in case we should be taken prisoners, not to discover to the enemy what troops we were. We were obliged to him for his kind advice, but we considered ourselves as standing in no great need of it. For we knew as well as he did that sappers and miners were allowed no quarters, at least are entitled to none, by the laws of warfare. . . . In a short time the engineers returned and the afore-mentioned stranger with them. They discoursed together some time, when by the officers often calling him, 'Your Excellency,' we discovered that it was General Washington.[80]

By Saturday morning, October 6, the Allies had finished essential preparations for opening their trenches and establishing their artillery to batter Cornwallis's defenses. They were now waiting only for the next nightfall and an overcast sky to insure success in drawing their line ever closer and within striking distance of the main British fortifications. The huge siege guns resting in the rear, hoped Washington, would soon become the determining factor in his drive to force a surrender. "In thirty Days from the opening of our Batteries," wrote Tucker to his wife, "I am sanguine enough to hope that we shall see the British Standard at the Feet of the Commander in Chief of the Allied Armies."[81]

Chapter 8

On the Verge

*F*rench Admiral de Grasse smiled to himself as he listened with pleasure to what he believed was a bombardment of the British lines on the evening of October 5. He took up his pen and wrote a short letter to Rochambeau. "All the evening and night I have heard a considerable noise. Evidently, you are tuning your instruments to accord with those of Lord Cornwallis. Make him dance lively for me."[1]

De Grasse's belief that the Allies had begun "tuning" their siege guns was premature, but only slightly so. Before long, Washington's big guns would be in position to pound the British into submission. That prospect awaited only the completion of the first parallel and the erection of earthworks to support it. All indications pointed to success in the endeavor. The weather continued cloudy with intermittent rain and wind from the east and southeast. Hopes were that the clouds would not break after dark because moonlight would reveal the Allied entrenching operations to the enemy. These fears proved unwarranted, however, for rain fell throughout the day and long into the night.[2]

The day seemed to offer little in the way of accomplishment as far as Pennsylvania Captain James Duncan was concerned, for he scribbled in his journal, "nothing extraordinary happened this day."[3] In fact, preparations behind the scene continued apace as everyone looked forward to the next step of the siege—the actual opening of the first parallel. Saturday passed slowly, with the troops of the French and American armies whiling away the hours in quiet anticipation of things to come. Early in the morning two Pennsylvania and two Maryland regiments, together with some of the militia, set out to make more gabions. The principal task these men (and others) faced was moving the great quantities of fascines, gabions, and other component materials already fashioned as close as possible to the line of the first parallel without disclosing the effort to probing British eyes.[4]

To aid General Henry Knox for the duration of the siege, Washington assigned Lieutenant Colonel Dabney's Virginia Regiment, the Delaware recruits, and 160 of Nelson's militia to duty with the American artillery. "They will encamp in the park, and take their orders from Genl Knox," directed Washington.[5]

That morning, the commander also issued a lengthy document entitled "Regulations for the Service of the Siege." The detailed directive, prepared with the close help of von Steuben, comprised 54 paragraphs of instruction governing the conduct of the armies during the ensuing operations. The articles had been translated from a French model used at previous sieges in Europe, with appropriate modifications reflecting the situation at hand.[6] The American soldiers, the vast majority of whom had never taken part in a siege and never would again, probably found the regulations more difficult to comprehend than their French counterparts.[7]

The articles are instructive and help us appreciate how Washington conducted the siege, and how the men and officers were directed to comport themselves. Here is a sampling of these writings:

> An Officer of Rank will be appointed by the Commander in Chief to act as Superintendent of the deposit of the trenches, for the following important Services during the whole Siege, viz. to take Charge of all the sand Bags, Faschines [sic], gabions, Huddles [sic] and other materials Deposited at the place which the Engineers will appoint & keep an accurate state of them.

> The trenches shall be Relieved every 24 hours unless a particular order to the Contrary by the Genl in which Case the Relief shall be in the rear of the other.

All the troops either Relieving or Relieved will march with Drums Beating, Colours Flying, & carry arms to the place from whence they are to file off, when they will Support arms.

The Officers will cause each Soldier to work in his place to enlarge the trench, & Strengthen the epaulement.

No honours to be rendered in the trenches when the Commander in Chief & Genl Officers of the trenches visit them. The Soldiers will stand to their arms, facing the Epaulement & Ready to mount the Banquette.

The Gabions are to be 3 Feet high including the end of the Pickets, which are to enter the Ground, they are to have 2 Feet & a half Diameter, and be formed of nine pickets each of two & a half Inches Circumference interlaced with Branchery stripped of leaves to be equally closed at Top & Bottom, in order that they may be not longer at one end than the other.

The Huddles shall be six feet long & 3 Feet wide, and shall be made of nine Pickets each of two Inches & a half to 3 Inches Circumference, equal distant from each other, and interwoven with stronger Branchery, than that employed for the Gabions.

The Faschines to be 6 Feet long and 6 Inches [through] this to be made of Branchery, the twigs of which are to be crossed, to be bound with withs [sic] at each end & the middle to each Faschine, 3 Pickets of three feet long, & 2 or 3 Inches diameter.

Each Soldier going to the trenches, either to mount Guard or to work shall take with him a Faschine to be left on the deposit of the trenches.

The Fatigue men are to march near each other & Observe the greatest silence when the engineers place them.

In the saps, Batteries & other Places ajacent [sic] to the deposit of Powder no Soldier is to be permitted to smoke.

In case of a Sally the Fatigue men are to retire Briskly into some part of the trenches, where they may not embarrass the troops, they are to retire in Preference to the places, where there [sic] arms were lodged.[8]

The Opening of the First Parallel

By late that afternoon, final dispositions had been made for the important events planned for after nightfall. The engineers had completed their tracings, and with the help of French and American artillery officers, the projected placement of batteries along the parallel had been accomplished. "Everything being prepared for opening Trenches[,] 1,500 Fatigue men and 2,800 to cover them, were ordered for this service," Washington jotted in his diary.[10] The order of the previous afternoon was revived: one regiment from the right of each American brigade would assemble at 5:00 p.m. A like number of soldiers from the French contingent would also assemble at that time.[11]

Both armies established rotating command schedules by which senior officers succeeded one another in command on a daily basis. General Lincoln took charge of the American sector on October 6, Lafayette would succeed Lincoln the following day, and von Steuben would assume command of the line on October 8. Similarly, Baron de Viomenil commanded the French troops on the line at the outset, which alternated on succeeding days with St. Simon and then de Viomenil once again. This sequence of command for both armies was slated to last throughout the siege.[12]

The assembly of the soldiers for duty that evening was marred by the arrival of news from Williamsburg that Colonel Alexander Scammell, the officer who had surrendered and was then shot at point-blank range by a British officer, had succumbed to his wound. By this time, the British cannon fire had tapered off until it was nearly silent.[13]

The French and American forces detailed for the honor of opening the trench numbered roughly 4,300. Six American regiments paraded about 6:00 p.m. on the plain near where Lieutenant Colonel Tarleton's old camp had been situated. The French grouped a short while later. Their designated force consisted of two battalions each from the Regiments Bourbonnois and Soissonois, besides 250 men each from the Regiments Royal Deux-Ponts, Saintonge, Agenois, and Gatenois. Some 1,500 soldiers were assigned the actual excavation of the trench line, while another 2,800 French and Americans advanced far ahead in armed detachments to serve as covering parties to guard the workers against attacks from the British garrison. Brigadier Generals Wayne and James Clinton assisted Lincoln in preparing his command; the able Phillipe

Jarreck, the comte de Custine, helped ready de Viomenil and his French troops.[14] By dusk all was in order. "You may depend upon its being a Night of Business," wrote Colonel John Lamb of the proceedings about to begin.[15]

At 8:00 p.m., the soldiers detailed to guard the workmen stepped off into the rainy night to a point 100 yards beyond the pine strips marking the proposed parallel. Once there, they lay down on the wet earth and peered out into the inky darkness. From this line, small patrols crept closer still to the main British line, ready to sound the alarm should Cornwallis choose to mount a sortie. Although we do not know their specific orders, the French and American patrols were probably instructed to aggressively drive back into the main garrison any British soldiers sent out to disrupt the digging of the first parallel. While the covering parties made their dispositions, the workers remained far in the rear. They formed their units into lines commanded by their own officers, but under the general supervision of the engineers of Du Portail and Lieutenant Colonel Querenet de La Combe. On orders from the engineers, the workmen marched to the materiel deposits emplaced during the preceding days. Once there, they picked up fascines, gabions, and entrenching tools such as spades, shovels, and pickaxes. Once equipped, they marched forward on the open plain and aligned themselves at three- to four-foot intervals along the outlined parallel.

The men had not yet begun to dig when Washington appeared, riding through the rainy evening not far from where he had ridden the previous night. The general dismounted and took up a pickaxe, which he thrust deeply into the earth. It was a ceremonial motion, one soldier recalled, so "that it might be said, 'Gen Washington with his own hands first broke ground at the siege of Yorktown.'"

Thus inspired, the men began to dig. The most detailed reminiscence of the digging of the first parallel was left by soldier Asa Redington of the 1st New Hampshire:

> I was one of the intrenching party that marched onto the ground about 9 o'clock in the evening. Besides our knapsacks, guns and bayonets, we had intrenching shovels, and began digging where we found a line of split white pine strips stretching along the ground, marking out the line to intrench. Our men formed in line, taking three feet distance, laid down their arms and knapsacks a few feet in

the rear, and began to break ground. Not a word or a whisper was uttered—nothing but silent work. [16]

Work proceeded as silently as possible. There was no talking, and the steady patter of rain effectively muffled the noise of spades and pickaxes digging deeply into the soaked sandy loam. Wagons loaded with sandbags moved along the line, their cargo utilized to strengthen the balky soil. Draft horses pulled cannon and other heavy ordnance toward the developing parallel. The trench and four supporting redoubts (two in the French sector, two in the American) progressed swiftly, largely because the British failed to detect what was happening and continued to direct light artillery fire toward their own abandoned outer works at Pigeon Hill and those recently completed by the Americans in that locale. Cornwallis was utterly unaware that 1,500 men were digging a siege parallel a mere 600 yards from his main line of defense.

When the trench was waist-deep, the soldiers stationed ahead serving as guards were ordered to fall back. Some took station in the unfinished trench, but the majority moved to the rear and sat on the ground, cradling their weapons in soaked exhaustion. The fatigue parties worked on in relief arrangement. [17]

Occasionally men became separated in the darkness, as did the medical personnel assigned to accompany the working parties. To Dr. James Thacher's inconvenience and embarrassment, he quickly learned the line of Allied guards provided an effective ring around the trench line:

> Having advanced about half a mile, [all] of a sudden a party of armed men in white uniforms rose from the ground, and ordered us to stop; they proved to be the rear guard of the French. The officer demanded the countersign, which I was unable to give, and as we could not understand each other's language, I was detained under considerable embarrassment till an officer who could speak English was called, when producing my instruments and bandages, and assuring the French officer that I was surgeon to the infantry, he politely conducted me to my station. [18]

As Washington oversaw the labors on the first parallel, work on other entrenchments went forward on the extreme left of the Allied line. About 500 yards from the Fusiliers' Redoubt, the unbrigaded Regiment Touraine continued erecting a battery near the cliff overlooking the York

River. To guard against British sorties there, French laborers, supervised by two engineers, began digging a trench in the form of a flying sap that extended from the unfinished battery south across the Williamsburg Road to the mouth of a ravine. By some accounts, this small line of entrenchment was considered to be the end of the main parallel, interrupted by the undulating ravines of York Creek. The purpose of the battery, explained a French engineer, was twofold: "to disturb the advanced redoubt of the right wing of the besieged and to keep away the War Ships which might have taken them [the French] from the rear."[19]

On the night of October 6, however, this distant sector of the front played an important part in the Allied effort to open their first parallel, though it did not unfold exactly as Washington and Rochambeau had planned. Washington ordered the French stationed along this section of the front to launch a feint in order to divert Cornwallis's attention away from his left flank, where the Allied workmen labored on the first parallel. The diversion never materialized. Between 8:00 and 9:00 p.m. that evening, watch dogs in the Fusiliers' Redoubt began barking, and their racket was quickly taken up by dogs up and down the British line. A deserter from the French Hussars slipped into the British lines. The traitor alerted the enemy of the progress his countrymen were making opposite Cornwallis's right flank near the river. When word arrived inside the Fusiliers' Redoubt, the men there launched a signal rocket. The result was a furious British cannonade against the laboring Touraine soldiers. The French were forced to temporarily abandon their entrenchments. "The enemy discovered this approach very early and paid it a good deal of attention," recalled Lieutenant Verger, a German fighting in the largely German Deux-Ponts Regiment, "though they did not know about our grand approach and did not fire on it, contenting themselves, as in previous nights, with firing on their abandoned redoubts . . . behind our works."

In addition to driving back the workers, the British bombardment critically injured an artillery lieutenant when his thigh was ripped off by a cannonball. Six grenadiers and a soldier from Regiment Agenois also sustained wounds. The mortally wounded French officer was 25-year-old Chevalier de La Loge, who died three days later. According to a friend, the lieutenant "[was] charming and witty, he was very erudite, not only in his profession, but in poetry as well. We often saw his poems in the Almanach des Muses.'" Cornwallis commended the men of the 23rd

Regiment defending the Fusiliers' Redoubt, noting their "uncommon gallantry." The French, however, had not launched an attack and had done nothing beyond responding with a brief cannonade from their unfinished battery.[20]

It seems almost impossible to believe the French deserter who so willingly informed the British of the pending French attack and their entrenching activities was oblivious to the real intent of the Allies—to open their first parallel below the town. Perhaps the secret was indeed that well kept, in which case neither the French nor American soldiers realized what was unfolding that night. This seems most unlikely, however, for the troops surely knew the excavation was planned to commence that evening—especially in light of the order cancelling the work parties the previous day. It is also possible this entire episode was part of the planned "false attack" mentioned in so many firsthand reports of the activities that night. The deserter could have been an actor in an elaborate ruse, purposefully designed to distract the attention of the British from operations against their far left. If so, the stratagem followed theoretical recommendations flawlessly.[21]

Whether intentional or otherwise, the diversion allowed the French and American workmen on the first parallel to press on without interruption. Rain continued falling, and the fatigue details easily removed the freshly softened earth throughout the night. Probably three-quarters of the soldiers worked with spades and shovels, while the remaining workmen wielded pickaxes.[22]

The excavation followed closely the prescriptions of the technical publications of the day. As a leading French theorist put it:

> It oftens happens, that the opening of the trenches is unknown to the besieged for some hours; nay, sometimes for the whole of the first night of work. . . . Every exertion should, therefore, be made to establish the whole of the first parallel during this night, together with the communications between it and the depots of the trenches. In general, the parapets of the trench are so forward when day breaks, as to shelter the battalions of the guard, who retire behind them. The workmen are relieved at day break by others, who go on with the work.[23]

Through the night the Allies kept working, digging their entrenchments and improving them. It was back-breaking work, but the men seem to have complained little, appreciating the implications of a successful night's work. They also set gabions in a row along the side of the ditch nearest the British garrison and cast dirt from the trench into the baskets to form the beginning of a parapet.[24]

Documentary evidence of the construction of the first Allied siege linc at Yorktown is rare, probably because personnel considered the work of digging the parallel an almost routine matter. Most existing references to the excavation mention dimensions that are compatible with those cited in the technical manuals of the period. According to one soldier, "this parallel is ten feet wide and four deep, which made a sufficient cover for our men."[25] Another reference is contained in the journal of Daniel Trabue, who served earlier in the war as a Virginia soldier and returned to the army as a sutler for the Yorktown Campaign: "It was a sight to see a plain old field, with men in it working with . . . spades making a ditch. Then throwing the dirt in front. The Ditch would be about 10 feet wide."[26] "The soil was light and sandy, and we worked like beavers all through the night," marveled Asa Redington. "Before daylight came we had a half-mile of trench four feet deep and eight wide, which completely covered us from the cannon shot of the British."[27]

By the time the first parallel was perfected several days later, recalled an observer, it consisted "of a large ditch, broad enough for carriages to travel in, about four feet in depth, and covered by a rampart of gabions, or cylindrical baskets, fixed upon the ground, by means of projecting stakes, filled and covered over with loose dirt, and forming a height of about seven feet on the side toward the enemy."[28] Archaeological investigations of the French sector of the first Allied siege line confirm the average dimensions given in the historical accounts: the trench measured about 10 feet wide and registered a maximum approximate depth of four feet.[29]

As the trench progressed, so did the four redoubts planned in the line. The French and American soldiers tasked with erecting them followed the dimensions earlier plotted on the terrain with stakes and tape by the engineers. The British, meanwhile, continued their fire against the redoubts already constructed on the gorge, doing little harm to the parties busily entrenching farther ahead. Occasionally, rockets burst overhead and the Allies feared discovery as the flares lighted the earth below. In an attempt at deception, a group of American guards, posted close to a morass, built large bonfires and walked back and forth before them so the British might see them and direct their artillery away from the workers.

The men on fatigue duty were relieved in shifts by men coming from the rear. When that happened, explained Asa Redington, "We were permitted to take some sleep in the rear of our works. I went back a few rods, laid down on the grass, and spread my blanket over me." It would be a fitful nap for the New Hampshire native. "In a few minutes, a cannon ball came directly over me, and like a gust of wind threw my blanket right off. Then I made a new bed nearer our breastworks . . . and got some sound sleep."[30] Although there were several close calls like the one suffered by Redington, not a single American, worker or guard, was killed or wounded during that critical night of work. "Let gratitude abound in our hearts for this remarkable instance of the divine goodness," rejoiced a chaplain with the troops.[31] By morning, the men were soaked from the constant drizzle and a northwest wind chilled them uncomfortably, but they had the warming satisfaction of success burning within them.[32]

Excavation of the French part of the parallel differed negligibly from that of the Americans. On the left or French side, the trench was traced on the ground with fascines rather than white pine stripping. The troops employed gabions according to normal digging procedure, filling the receptacles with dirt to form the parapet of the line. Armed troops stationed in ravines to the front and rear guarded the workers from a surprise thrust by the British.[33] The ravines greatly aided the French and precluded the need for tunnels to communicate with the line from the rear.[34] Digging was somewhat retarded by the presence of many tree stumps, presumably left from timber previously cut by the British to form abatis on the gorge and around the Yorktown Creek ravines.[35]

Casualties among the French on this part of the line were light: an officer of the Regiment Royal Deux-Ponts sustained a small contusion, while a soldier from that unit incurred a more dangerous wound.[36] Such scant losses were deemed "a circumstance the more fortunate, as the wounded would have been unprovided with straw to lie on, and linen rags for the dressing of their wounds."[37] Work on the line continued at a vigorous pace. "The activity of the workmen and the natural looseness of the soil," commented a participant, "to our great astonishment, put the parallel into a state to receive the troops on the next day."[38]

By the time the sun was ready to peek above the horizon on October 7, the Allies had completed enough of the parallel to secure them from British artillery fire. "The work was executed with so much secrecy and dispatch," penned a happy and relieved Washington in his diary, "that the enemy were, I believe, totally ignorant of our labor till the light of the Morning discovered it to them."[39]

Dawn, October 7

The sight that met Cornwallis's eyes the morning of the seventh must have been disheartening. The Allied line lay squarely before him—an uninterrupted earthwork running across the entire plain below Yorktown. Cornwallis was enough of a general to know exactly what it portended. He also knew it was already of sufficient depth and strength to allow work to continue behind it virtually without interruption.

Most Allied soldiers anticipated that hell in the form of artillery fire would rain down upon them as soon as the British realized what was transpiring. It did not. Cornwallis' instead rolled out two field guns and lazily lobbed cannonballs into the newly completed entrenchments—a wholly useless waste of powder and shot, for the fire did no damage. Why Cornwallis reacted in this manner is unknown, for he failed to disclose any rationale for it. One historian theorizes that he may have been hoarding his ammunition in the hope of being able to hold out until Clinton arrived with reinforcements. Another was more blunt in his assessment, claiming simply, "Cornwallis, little dreaming that he should be compelled to stand a siege, was unprepared for it."

Colonel Tucker thought the British might indeed be hoarding powder and shot, for the enemy had resorted to a clever method of interrupting Allied work without expending a cannonball. "The Enemy have for some days had recourse to an Expedient for interrupting our men at work without wasting their Ammunition, by flashing a small Quantity of powder near the mussles of their Cannons," he wrote in his journal. This trick, he continued, is frequently mistaken for the fusing at the Touch-hole," which was all that was needed to convince Allied workers to stop and take cover.

During the light artillery response the Americans found diversion in watching an English bulldog run out of the enemy garrison in playful pursuit of the bounding iron shot. Some of the officers wanted to capture the canine and send him with a note back to his masters. "But," as one soldier lamented, "he looked too formidable for any of us to encounter." Other diversions were of the more deadly variety. On the other side of the lines, German Private Johann Conrad Döhla found himself in the trenches playing a game of cat and mouse with American patrols operating in no-man's land. "The rifle men, or American Jäger," he scribbled into his journal, "crawl around so close that the balls from the long rifles they carry fly over our lines, but do no harm."[40]

One of these patrols was led by Captain Thaddeus Weed of the 2nd Connecticut Line (sometimes known as 5th Company). Weed was working his men carefully toward the British line when he came face-to-face with what he later remembered as a 200-man enemy picket force, complete with a pair of light field pieces. Weed and his men high-tailed it for the rear, where Weed nearly jumped into a French trench instead of an American one. The enemy did not follow the fleeing colonials, though if they had, remembered a British soldier, "our orders were to . . . give them our fire, then charge [with] Bayonets and meet them." The precipitate flight disgusted Captain James Duncan. "They were fired upon by the enemy, never returned a single shot and retreated into our works in the utmost disorder," he wrote in his diary. "Captain Weed, who commanded the picket, was again ordered out, but the enemy had retired. How he will be answerable for his conduct time will discover." Whether he was answerable at all is not evident from existing records.[41]

While the pickets of both sides pushed and prodded at the other to gain a temporary advantage, work on the first parallel continued without respite. The British cannonade gradually grew in strength as if slowly awakening to a realization of what had transpired during the night. American and French laborers pressed on to improve their defenses, revetting the sides of the trench while digging it deeper. The redoubts also took shape. Early that morning, a number of guard batteries composed of light field ordnance were rushed into the parallel as an added repellant to any attack Cornwallis might launch. Elsewhere, preparations proceeded with feverish dispatch. Artillery platforms were under construction in the American camp. In the artificers' camps, soldiers stacked cannonballs, loaded shells, and readied cartridge ammunition to send against the British once the batteries were finished and the heavy guns emplaced. Before long, the "horrid fire" of the enemy subsided to a "scattered fire of musketry, and a feeble fire of artillery." Little damage was done to the Americans, but the French lost several men wounded. Later in the day, an American officer had his leg torn off by a British cannonball. Marveling at the slight losses suffered thus far, Colonel Richard Butler of the 2nd Pennsylvania Battalion remarked, "the siege appears to be no more than an experimental movement."[42]

Opinions on the length of time the Allies might expect to work on Cornwallis during their "experimental movement" were not as optimistic as Butler suggested. "Sixteen days of open trenches are talked of," James McHenry wrote to General Greene. "I am not sanguine. I see difficulties: and yet, I think we shall take his Lordship."[43]

A traditional ceremony marked the formal opening of the trenches and the start of the siege on October 7. A ritual passed down through the centuries in Europe, the event entailed an elaborate entrance into the trench by the soldiers to the beating of drums, with muskets at carry and banners unfurled. When they arrived at their specified stations, the men implanted the flags upon the parapet in accordance with ancient war customs.

The ceremony at Yorktown began precisely at 11:00 a.m. Scheduled to relieve Lincoln's troops, Lafayette's division—the brigades of Hazen and Muhlenberg—assembled on the right of the division encampment so the soldiers could advance to the line through the Wormley Creek ravines without exposing themselves to the British. The division commander for the day (in this case Lafayette) served as Officer of the Day. His subordinate, the division inspector, was referred to as "Major of the Trenches."

On the left at Yorktown, the Regiments Agenois and Saintonge simultaneously prepared to relieve their predecessors in the trench of the French sector.[44] The French troops followed a procedure similar to that of the Americans; Lafayette and General Hand inspected the division. Thereafter, the Major of the Trenches arranged the men in order with respect to their particular assignments and stations. With drums to the front and rear of the column, and with flags flying, Lafayette's division marched at noon from the Grand Parade before his encampment across the mill dam of Wormley Creek and into the parallel. Once inside, the soldiers changed their weapons from "carry" position to "support." They marched to a steady beat on to their respective posts and hoisted their colors on the breastwork. While Lafayette's soldiers advanced into the parallel, Lincoln's departed at another point as their own drums kept time.

Unable to restrain themselves at such an impertinent sight, the British gunners greeted Lincoln's replacements with the best deluge of cannon fire they could muster.[45] The loud bark of the guns died out almost as suddenly as it had begun when Cornwallis's soldiers witnessed a jaw-dropping sight. Lieutenant Colonel Alexander Hamilton, commanding the Second Battalion of Hazen's Brigade, ordered his infantry to mount the epaulement and, fully exposed to whatever guns the enemy might open on them, execute the manual of arms from Baron von Steuben's *Regulations*. Incredulous at what their eyes beheld, many of the British held their fire. "Although I esteem him one of the first officers in the American army," wrote Captain James Duncan in his diary, "[I] must beg leave in this instance to think he wantonly exposed the lives of his men."[46] However impetuous, the incident sparked repeated emulation throughout the balance of the siege.

Not long after Hamilton's bold exhibition, Colonel Philip Van Cortlandt, a civil engineer by trade and a member of the Provincial Congress in 1775, paraded his 2nd New York Regiment, complete with unfurled banners and beating drums, dangerously close to the main British line. Thankfully, von Steuben diverted the enemy's attention from bombarding Van Cortlandt's men with shot and shell by directing a feint attack against another section of the front. The stern Von Steuben ultimately fell victim to the lure of bravado, directing his own troops through a similar escapade in the face of Cornwallis's artillery.[47]

With his troops in place this same day, Lafayette issued a directive on how to deal with an enemy sortie. If attacked, he explained, his men were to fire one volley with their muskets and then charge over the parapet and meet the enemy bayonet to bayonet.[48]

In the French sector, work went on throughout the day as laborers struggled to finish the parallel and two redoubts. The line there was not quite as advanced as it was under the Americans, largely because of differences in the slope of the terrain and because of the stumpy ground in the vicinity of Yorktown Creek. Four hundred men (two battalions) of Regiments Agenois and Saintonge relieved the trench at noon, while two other battalions took up supporting posts in ravines to the rear of the line. Field guns stood along the parallel at appropriate intervals. Major

General Francois-Jean Beauvoir, chevalier de Chastellux, an outstanding scholar-soldier who had accompanied Rochambeau to America, was appointed Major General of the Day in the French side of the parallel. He was third in command of the French army.[49]

Locations for the batteries having been determined, that evening 400 French night workmen joined the artillerymen in beginning the construction of four earthworks. Five hundred more laborers worked to perfect the redoubts and to build communication trenches to the batteries, the commanding nature of the ground dictating their erection behind, rather than ahead of, the parallel. A detached battery was also begun at this time across the Yorktown Creek ravine, while that being constructed at the far left, near the river, was finished during the night of October 7 and was ready to fire by morning.[50]

The four parallel batteries begun in the night by the French were described by an officer, Gaspard de Gallatin, as follows:

> A big battery [to be] composed of 4 16-pounders, 2 mortars of 12 inches, 4 mortars of 8 inches, 2 howitzers of 8 inches, a little behind the parallel and a little to the left of the Hampton highroad.

> A battery of 4 24-pounders, also behind the parallel and to the right of the ravine on which it rests.

> One of 3 24-pounders, in the direction of and behind the extremity of the parallel.

> One of 3 24-pounders, to the left of the ravine on which the parallel rests.[51]

While the French progressed in building their batteries, so did the Americans. At 9:00 p.m., American work parties advanced about 40 yards beyond the parallel and commenced preparations for the erection of two batteries, one large unit on the extreme right close to the York River (actually begun the night of October 8), and one on the left of the American sector nearby the adjacent position of the French.[52]

Some of Nelson's militia moved close to the British line to distract the enemy with random sniping from their muskets. In the darkness, two American patrols stumbled into each other and shooting erupted. One man was killed and a workman on the line had his foot shot off by a cannonball.[53] Several alarms occurred in the night. In one instance, 200 British pickets with two field pieces encountered an American patrol and drove it at an angle back into the French part of the line. The British party, however, stayed beyond musket range of the new trench line and retired safely.[54]

Besides their new work on the batteries, the Allies also endeavored to improve the parallel through revetment, and to complete the four infantry redoubts. Ever cognizant of "a numerous garrison, under the orders of an enterprising man," the French and Americans built redoubts designed to ward off enemy assaults against the parallel. The structures were ditched and palisaded, and palisades were also placed across the entrances in the rear of the works.[55] At the same time, the parallel proper was deepened and widened and its sides strengthened with the addition of fascines and gabions. Men worked to repair the breastwork when it became damaged by British artillery fire. Drainage (a necessary consideration in construction of the line), was accomplished primarily through the existence of numerous small ravines, the heads of which occasionally intersected the excavation. Ideally, the inside base of the trench parapet contained a banquette (shelf) for the soldiers to stand on so that they might fire at an onrushing enemy with their muskets raised over the top, but without having to expose much of their bodies. Occasionally, along its length workmen cut apertures into the rear wall to hold sundry necessities like water, musket ammunition, and first aid equipment. Blinds (wooden barrels filled with sand) stood at irregular intervals in the trench as protective devices against balls from exploding bombs. These were also commonly used in the redoubts.[56]

Men stationed in the parallel for long periods also needed access to latrines. Vauban, the French military engineer who revolutionized the art of siege warfare and the construction of fortifications, urged that holes be dug in the earth some distance behind the line and screened by epaulements erected for that purpose. "In this manner," wrote Vauban, "you can prevent your people from having to go too far away, from getting themselves killed needlessly, and from infecting the trenches."[57]

Theoretical Considerations

Of all the work performed that memorable night, the construction of the batteries for Washington's siege pieces commanded the most attention and stretched well into the next day and night. While specifics of the character and dimensions of these batteries are not available, the engineers almost certainly adhered to the guidelines imposed by experience and related by the technical treatises of the day. The work was well defined and batteries were raised in two to three days, and sometimes sooner.

Vauban recommended communication trenches running to the location of the proposed battery be dug the first night, and that the front line of the battery be marked. "There you should set up a double row of gabions six feet high and five feet in diameter; fill them and the spaces between them carefully with dirt dug from the trench so no gaps remain." On the following day, work could ensue under this cover to build and assemble the artillery platforms, while during the night, laborers could work to thicken and raise the parapet and strengthen it with fascines. The next day would then be allotted to readying the platform, and after dark, the embrasures cut and the guns mounted.[58]

Guided by such ideas, and under supervision of the engineers, the laborers staked out the position of the battery parapet (based on prolongations of the enemy's batteries to be enfiladed), and work began on excavating the ditch, the dirt being thrown into the area designated for the parapet. In sandy soil, such as at Yorktown, the parapet should have been at least 25 feet thick. Normally the linear dimensions of a battery were based on the number of ordnance pieces intended to occupy the structure, with between 15 and 20 feet assigned for each weapon. Typically, a gun battery would possess a parapet uniformly seven-and-one-half feet high, though actually the height might visibly undulate because of varying ground level. If the battery was built on level ground, this would be reflected in a parapet of equal height throughout.[59]

The parapets of the batteries and redoubts at Yorktown, at least those of the French, seem to have possessed berms (probably five or six feet wide) on the exterior sides. Archaeological investigations disclosed that the distance between the scarp walls and interior excavations of particular structures was much greater than the maximum parapet width recommended in eighteenth-century fortifications manuals. Moreover, dirt excavated archaeologically from the frontal ditch could have been raised to the probable parapet height only if the ditch's width conformed to the theorists' recommended standards.[60]

The American batteries, placed in advance of the newly-dug first parallel, also needed connecting trenches back to the line. These ran about 10 or 12 feet wide and four to five feet deep. Batteries also required powder magazines. Usually one magazine sufficed in a battery harboring cannon alone. In a structure designed for mortars and howitzers, in addition to cannon, two or three magazines were built adjacent to one another. To conserve powder, some officers urged the barrels be spaced intervally behind the batteries in such a way so that if a barrel might occasionally be lost, the total quantity would not be threatened with destruction by being contained in one large magazine.[61]

During the two to three days allotted to raising artillery batteries, workmen performed other duties beyond merely building earthen walls to surround the guns. They also cut embrasures, the spaces or openings through which the artillerists directed the muzzles of the guns against the enemy. In addition, they rammed the earthen floor, excavated it slightly if necessary, and otherwise firmed the ground to receive the heurtoirs, the heavy wooden artillery platforms. Finally, when all was ready, the siege weapons themselves were brought up. A platform consisted of a heurtoir and a number of timbers, or sleepers, pressed into slots prepared in the earth perpendicular to the parapet and topped with planks for the carriage wheels to roll on. Although most manuals specified five sleepers per cannon platform, those excavated archaeologically at Yorktown consisted of only three. Moreover, archeologists disclosed that most of the American battery sleepers were crooked and partly rounded, apparently hewn by ax and saw from timber grown locally. Sleeper impressions excavated at Yorktown measured from 12 to 15 feet long. The former probably comprised the length of howitzer platforms, the latter, cannon platforms. The direction of the platform conformed to that of the heurtoir, the large guide timber placed at the base of the parapet and against which the carriage wheels ultimately rested. A platform of 12 feet slanted four feet toward the epaulement to avoid too great a recoil; a platform of 14 feet dipped six feet toward the parapet.

Placed in a somewhat trapezoidal fashion, cannon batteries measured roughly 15 feet wide at the rear and nine feet wide at the front. Mortar platforms for pieces of 10- and 12-inch caliber contained sleepers measuring six feet in length and six or seven inches square. These platforms were placed horizontally on the ground with no slope.[62] The merlons (those parts of the epaulement lying between the embrasures) had to be lined with saucissons, as did the base of the wall up to the genouillere, the height of the parapet at which embrasure openings first appeared. Gabions, placed in rows, were also used to strengthen the parapet.[63] Normally, two men accomplished the work of revetement (the lining of a ditch or erection of a retaining wall), one to place the fascines or saucissons, and another to stake them firmly in position. Ideally, a battery was revetted inside and out. However, safety, economy, and expediency frequently necessitated such treatment for the inside only.

As experts in siege craft made plain, the construction of these fortifications was a precisely detailed and elaborate affair. According to Lochee, author of *Elements of Field Fortifications*, the number of 10-foot-long and one-foot-thick saucissons needed to line the interior of a typical parapet was 160. Here is how he reached that number: "[160 would suffice] for as each side of the work measures 25 yards with a height of 4 feet and ½, each side will require 5 rows of 8 saucissons each, or 40 saucissons; and consequently 4 times that quantity, or 160, for the whole interior slope; each saucisson requiring 5 stakes, the number of stakes will be 800."[64]

These duties were not undertaken haphazardly, as Frenchman Louis de Tousard wrote in his influential book *American Artillerist's Companion, or Elements of Artillery*. The labor required at Yorktown to prepare for an effective siege required meticulous attention to detail, and probably proceeded as systematically as Tousard set forth:

> The battery is seldom raised above two feet and a half high the first night: the merlons are traced. . . . At break of day this [first] working party is relieved by another consisting of half their number; they enlarge the ditch all the day, throwing up the earth to form the battery or merlons, if traced. When the embrasures have not been marked out, the senior officer plants the pickets at sunset for determining their direction, and completes the tracing of the merlons at the arrival of the fresh working party, which should be as numerous as in the preceding night. . . . During this [second] night also the platforms are laid, and some guns brought to the battery, if they be covered from the enemy's fire during the next day. The following day and night are employed in constructing the powder

magazines, completing the batteries, and preparing every thing for opening them on the third morning at sunrise.[65]

The object of the batteries of the first parallel in a siege was to demolish the enemy's defenses. Intervening distances between the Allies and the British varied from 750 to 1,260 yards. This distance required that Washington bring his heaviest pieces to bear on the farthest targets along the enemy line. At Yorktown, the Allies hoped to destroy the British parapets and knock out the embrasures for enemy cannon. This required direct firing. Random and ricochet firing also helped grind down and ruin enemy works, and could also strike Cornwallis's men behind their lines well to the rear. This type of cannonade would "carry confusion into places where there could be no suspicion of [artillery fire] . . . ever reaching," explained one expert.[66] The psychological impact from such firing was always devastating.

With precisely these objectives in mind, Washington's engineers and artillery officers supervised construction of the first parallel earthworks.

The Structures of the First Parallel

Compared to the batteries, redoubts, and other structures that would eventually be raised in the second parallel, those of the first line permitted more refinements. The reason why was simple: at a greater distance, work on batteries and redoubts could take longer and involve greater detail in construction. Therefore, the fortifications of the first parallel generally followed recommended procedures and accepted specifications. In other words, artillery was spaced more exactly (between 18 and 20 feet between each) than in a second parallel where, because of the proximity to the enemy, every effort was concentrated in getting the guns into position and firing before enemy shot and shell knocked them out of commission.

The first Allied siege line at Yorktown was established between October 6 and 9. In order to explain each in detail, but in a manner easily understood, a numbering sequence from left to right in the line has been assigned to identify each structure so it can be easily cross-referenced with fortifications on the accompanying maps, and the maps in this text. For example, the letter "A" assigned to a number means the structure was part of the first parallel, and the lower the number, the farther to the left it was located. Thus 1A was the fortification on the far left of the first parallel. The letter "B" will be used later in the text to identify structures in the second parallel.

From contemporary descriptions provided in documentary materials (chiefly maps), the structures were erected as follows:

Structure 1A. This battery (see map on page 124) held the far left of the first line next to the York River. Begun on the night of October 5, it was finished by about noon on October 8. It possessed two sections, one of cannon and the other of mortars and howitzers. A consensus of the historical maps indicates the cannon consisted of four 12-pounders, while the other ordnance comprised three mortars and four howitzers. There is no detailed information regarding the calibers of these latter weapons.[67] One map claims this battery fired hot shot (heated shot designed to ignite ships) against the British shipping from two 24-pounders brought in expressly for this purpose.[68]

This battery consisted of two parapets that met in a salient angle near the riverbank. Because the entrenchment was so near the precipice, there was a fear the battery might collapse. Therefore, the French workers probably observed a safety margin of at least 50 feet from the edge of the bank when placing the heavy weapons.[69] The left part of the structure harbored the cannon and was commanded by a captain named Boisloger. The right side held the mortars and howitzers and was commanded by a Captain Bonnay.[70] Most maps concur that Battery 1A was connected to Battery 2A, a short distance to the south, by a strip of trench bisecting the Williamsburg Road. This battery formed what the French termed the left extremity of their part of the first parallel.[71]

Structure 2A. Situated immediately to the right of the Williamsburg Road (see map on page 124), at the south end of the trench running from 1A, this battery apparently contained two mortars of undetermined caliber.[72] This small unit was commanded by the same Captain Bonnay who had command of the mortar/howitzer section in Battery 1A.[73]

Structure 3A. This French battery was detached from those located on the main French parallel. It was situated on the high ground west of the Yorktown Creek ravine that approaches the left end of the French sector. Its location offered an unobstructed view of the British defenses. Four bronze 24-pounders stood in this earthwork when it was completed.[74]

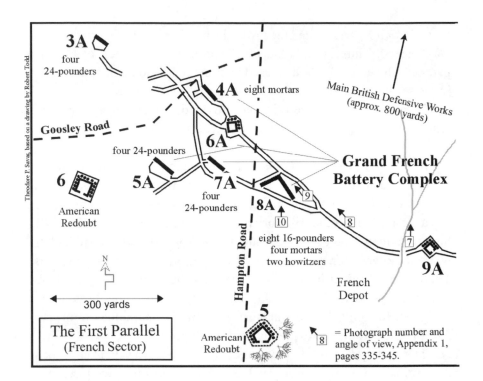

3A four 24-pounders

4A eight mortars

Main British Defensive Works (approx. 800 yards)

Goosley Road

6A

four 24-pounders

6 American Redoubt

5A   **7A**
four 24-pounders

Grand French Battery Complex

8A
eight 16-pounders
four mortars
two howitzers

9

10   8

7

9A

French Depot

N

300 yards

The First Parallel
(French Sector)

5
American Redoubt

8 = Photograph number and angle of view, Appendix 1, pages 335-345.

Hampton Road

Theodore P. Savas, based on a drawing by Robert Todd

Two historical maps disclose a small trench to the right and rear of Battery 3A. This was almost certainly a communications passage into the work from the ravine on the right. One map indicates the French placed a corps of grenadiers and chasseurs in the Yorktown Creek ravine for the purpose of supporting the left side of the first parallel. Battery 3A was under the command of Captain Francois Olivier d'Hemery.

While it was not part of the Grand French Battery complex (see below), this unit can be considered a peripheral structure of that larger battery. Battery 3A opened on the British on October 11. Its firepower contributed to that of the Grand French Battery and shared some targets with the guns and mortars of its neighboring complex of earthworks to the east. Battery 3A stood approximately midway between the end of the siege line and Redoubts 3 and 4 at Pigeon Hill. The unit joined the adjacent branch ravine via a strip of communication trench extending southeastward from its rear.[75]

Structure 4A. The principal sector of the first parallel began just to the right of the Yorktown Creek ravine. Here, the French constructed a powerful tight complex of gun batteries generally referred to as the Grand French Battery—the strongest artillery unit erected during the

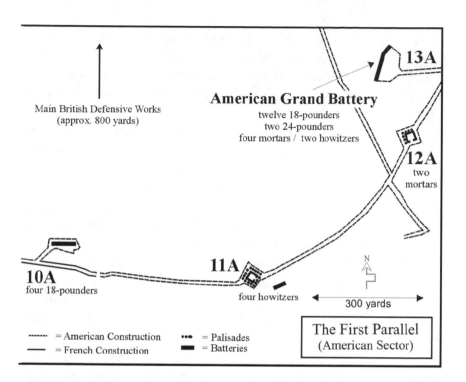

entire siege. Essentially, the Grand French Battery encompassed Structures 4A through 8A, or four batteries and one redoubt, and dominated the gorge area between York and Wormley creeks.

Battery 4A, on the extreme left of this complex, almost touched Goosley Road. It was established near that avenue's intersection with Hampton Road and according to contemporary maps, had a capacity for eight mortars. Some of this ordnance may have been moved, for some maps suggest only six or seven mortars were emplaced there.[76] Gaspard de Gallatin reported seven mortars in Battery 4A, which was begun the night of October 8 or the following morning, later than the other structures. Unlike the other French fortifications, it was built ahead of the parallel, closer to the British line. Of the eight pieces usually cited for Battery 4A, three were 12-inch mortars and five were 8-inch.[77] They were in the charge of a French officer named Chanteclair.[78]

Structure 5A. Four bronze 24-pounders occupied Battery 5A, which was located approximately 600 feet almost directly behind (or southwest) of Battery 4A.[79] The unit was commanded by Captain of Bombardiers Pierre Garret de Maisonneuve.[80]

Structure 6A. This was one of two redoubts built into the parallel in the French sector to hold infantry troops ready to repel British sorties against the line. Palisaded in its ditch and at its entrance, the redoubt was roughly square-shaped, with one salient angle facing toward the British, one in the rear of the line, and the other two joining the parallel at the east and west sides of the structure.[81] An entrance was evidently located along the left rear side.[82] Redoubt 6A was closest in proximity to the mortar battery (4A), which was just north and slightly east.

Structure 7A. This French battery held four bronze 24-pounders and stood a short distance west of Hampton Road behind (south and slightly west) of Redoubt 6A and northeast of Battery 5A. The unit was commanded by a French captain named Francois-Justin Josserand.[83]

Structure 8A. This fourth and last battery (fifth structure) was the largest of the Grand French Battery complex and was the farthest east of the French batteries. Like Battery 1A, it was divided into sections for cannon, mortars, and howitzers. Battery 8A was shaped like a wide inverted V, with the angle pointing north and facing the British defenses. The short left arm of the structure contained four cannon, while the longer right arm contained mortars, howitzers, and four more artillery pieces.

While most of the maps agree the cannon in this unit numbered eight 16-pounders,[84] archaeological excavation of the site (discussed in detail in Appendix 4) raises some intriguing questions concerning the placement of the armament in 8A.

There is considerable disagreement as to the number of mortars and howitzers. Some maps indicate six mortars present, while others indicate four mortars and two howitzers.[85] One map clearly indicates there were eight mortars and six howitzers in this part of the battery. Another accounts for six mortars and two howitzers, besides the four cannon at the extreme right of the mortar section (these cannon in addition to twelve pieces located in the left arm, according to this particular map).[86] While discrepancies such as these may appear misleading, it should be remembered that these first parallel batteries were in constant use through most of the siege. As a result, it is more probable than not that the composition of the armament inside these batteries changed during the siege. Constant adjustments and refinements of the artillery must have occurred that caused certain pieces of ordnance to be transferred again and again to meet arising exigencies. Thus, the maps are not necessarily wrong; at different times the batteries probably contained the ordnance specified for a particular unit when a certain map was being prepared.

The maps do not reveal the particular calibers of the mortars and howitzers in Battery 8A. Because of its size and diverse weaponry, Battery 8A was administered jointly by three officers. The four (and possibly five) guns on the left were under the command of Captain Jean-Baptiste de Maurecourt of the Auxonne Artillery Regiment. The howitzers and mortars in the left part of the right arm were commanded by Captain Nicolas Barthelemy, while the remaining four 16-pounders in the right section of the right arm were under Captain Bernard de Neurisse.[87]

Just to the right of Battery 8A, in the ravine between it and Redoubt 9A, there appears to have been a slight break in the parallel. The ravine enters the line from the French depot behind the parallel. The break, which was small—perhaps several yards across—seems to have been an access route for troops entering the line from the rear. What appears to be a short length of epaulement several feet in front of the break probably served as a traverse to hide the opening from British eyes.[88] Several maps show a secondary road leading in from Hampton Road and entering the line at this point, suggesting it was a major artery into the parallel for supplies, soldiers, and even the siege artillery.[89] The legend of one map suggests it was at this point the French and American night workers advanced preparatory to opening the trench on the evening of October 6. The legend reads: "Opening of the trenches in a hollow, the Americans pushed toward the right, the french the left."[90] Traditionally, this break in the line has marked the division of labor between the Allied armies. One map, however, places the right flank of the French construction much farther to the right, to include that part of the parallel before which the Americans erected Battery 10A.[91] American troops evidently occupied that section of the parallel excavated by their Allies, the French.

Structure 9A. This redoubt, strategically situated in the parallel to the immediate right of, and above, the ravine leading from the French deposit, served to guard the supplies and at the same time watch over the break in the trench that might admit an enemy sortie. Square-shaped, with its salient angle forward as in Redoubt 6A, this structure possessed a palisaded ditch and a similarly protected entrance.[92]

About 300 yards to the rear of the west side of the Grand French Battery, there seems to have been a short detached section of trench running for 100 yards in a southeastern direction.[93] While its exact purpose remains unknown, the trench seems to have passed through a slight rise or hillock in the area, leading to speculation that it served to protect troops advancing into the French sector via the west end of the Grand French Battery. Also, the ditch lies rather midway between the Pigeon Hill Redoubts and the American intermediate redoubt. It could also have served to contain troops supporting these structures.

Structure 10A. This American battery, the first American structure adjacent to the French sector and about 170 yards east of 9A, stood well in advance of that part of the parallel apparently constructed by the French.[94] The unit mounted, at most, five or six 18-pounders, although the majority of maps indicate this battery held only four such guns.[95]

Structure 11A. The first of two American redoubts was palisaded the full length of its perimeter. Like its French counterparts, the structure was erected in the parallel to guard the line against enemy assault. Located about 325 yards east of 10A, it was either triangular or square-shaped, with a salient angle forward and an entrance at the rear. This structure guarded the American trench depot established nearby.[96] Added security to this vital station was present in the form of a small battery of four howitzers behind an epaulement to the right rear of Redoubt 11A.[97]

Structure 12A. According to historical maps, the second American redoubt appeared much like Redoubt 11A. It was erected in the parallel, about 400 yards northeast of 11A. It had palisades guarding its ditch and rear entrance.[98] This square structure seems to have been armed with from two to four mortars in a small bomb battery.[99]

Structure 13A. The structure held the far right of the first siege line about 125 yards north of 12A. This American battery had a capacity for twelve 18-pounders, two 24-pounders, two howitzers, and four mortars. Begun the night of October 8, this so-called American Grand Battery stood near the riverbank far in advance of the parallel, to which it was connected by a lengthy communications trench. Figures disagree regarding the weaponry complement of this battery, again reflecting the shifting of ordnance during the siege as conditions warranted.[100] General Knox's specially improvised carriages for mortars were used in Battery 13A.[101]

As should be readily apparent from the preceding description, Washington's first parallel was a powerful line. How or whether Cornwallis could deal with it remained to be seen.

*   *   *

While construction of these batteries and refinement of the trenches and redoubts went on, the British kept up a light but annoying artillery fire. On October 8, a Continental officer jotted a mere six words in his journal to describe British efforts to disrupt the work on the first parallel: "The accustomed Blazing away at us."[102]

In the morning twilight of that day, an American patrol brought muskets to bear against several British outposts guarding the left of Cornwallis's defenses.[103] The clash resulted from information gleaned from a British deserter, who outlined for the Americans the location and habits of Cornwallis's patrols in that area of the line. Bartholomew James, a naval lieutenant and commander of a land battery, recalled how a squad of Americans moved against one of these outposts, drove the men into the woods, and then filtered all the way to the ditch of the Hornwork, where they "persuaded the officers they were deserters." Once the officers climbed up on the works, continued James, the Americans—in an unusually cruel gesture—"fired at and [killed] two of the officers of the 43rd."[104]

The British cannonade on October 8 was primarily aimed at interrupting progress on the gun batteries. The disruption it wrought was more irritating than substantive, and Allied casualties remained light: one American soldier had his arm blown away by a cannonball as he mounted the parapet of a battery, two Pennsylvanians were killed by British shot fired en ricochet, and two Marylanders were wounded. The French lost several men killed and wounded.[105] As a precaution, American soldiers posted sentinels on the epaulements. According to Daniel Trabue's journal, "they kept a man on the watch, and when they saw a match going to their [British] Cannon our men would fall down in the Ditch, and you could hear the Ball go by. Sometimes it would skip along on the ground, and bury the men in the Ditch, but in general they would not be hurt."[106]

Command Reorganizations and the Placing of the Artillery

During the day, Washington issued numerous orders to his command to better deal with the latest developments. Colonel Elias Dayton's New Jersey troops were formed into a battalion under Colonel Mathias Ogden.

Similarly, the New England regiment of the late Alexander Scammell was split into two battalions and placed one each under Lieutenant Colonels Ebenezer Huntington and John Laurens. Ogden's new command was directed to make 33 saucissons, a like number of gabions, 110 fascines, and 330 pickets. Lieutenant Colonel Francis Barber's Battalion of New Jersey and New Hampshire troops performed the same service.[107] After the eighth day of the month, however, component materials were furnished by the various corps as apportioned by Adjutant General Hand. Thomas Nelson's militia also experienced a change in its organization when it was divided into thirds, with each segment expected to do duty in 24-hour shifts.[108]

By the afternoon, several of the Allied batteries were completed and it was time for the workers to emplace the artillery. The pieces arrived over bad roads from the James River, dragged by horses or pulled in wagons. That evening, they were laboriously pushed and pulled through the trenches and hoisted into the batteries by soldiers, for it was feared horses that close to the front might rear or otherwise lose control under British firing and damage the guns. Von Steuben's division assumed trench duty at noon and marched into the parallel with the usual flourish of drums rolling and flags flying in the breeze. The baron himself directed his trench guards to keep their men assembled with muskets at the ready—especially after dark. He fully expected Cornwallis to launch a sally that night, and the careful and experienced officer instructed his men that if attacked, they should fall back eight paces behind the parallel and strike suddenly with bayonets after the British soldiers entered the trench.[109] If the sortie occurred in the French wing, plans were readied for von Steuben's Maryland Brigade to "immediately march out of the trenches and attack the flank of the Enemy."[110]

In the French sector, the batteries went up rapidly. St. Simon and Custine relieved the trenches with the Regiments Gatenois and Royal Deux-Ponts. Grenadiers of Soissonois and Saintonge provided auxiliary troops. After nightfall, as the guns were being dragged into position, several hundred French workmen continued perfecting the trench and batteries and prepared two more openings into the parallel at the left approach resting on Yorktown Creek ravine.[111] The entire line, remarked an observer, began "to wear a threatening appearance."[112]

The growing optimism coursing through Washington's army generated vigorous discussions as to the fate of Cornwallis. Would he surrender quickly without a fierce fight or make a bloody stand? Pennsylvanian Lieutenant William Feltman was not as sanguine as some of his comrades and wagered silk stockings with another officer "that Cornwallis and his army, would not be prisoners of war by this day [in] two weeks."[113]

The manner in which Cornwallis handled his guns only increased speculation within Washington's army. British artillery fire slackened considerably on October 8, leaving the Allies to wonder about the intentions and the conditions inside the British camp. "The enemy seem embarrassed, confused, and indeterminate," observed the 5th Pennsylvania's Colonel Richard Butler. "Their fire seems feeble to what might be expected. Although we have not as yet fired one shot from a piece of artillery, they are as cautious as if the heaviest fire was kept up."[114] That night, the British guns sent shot almost randomly into the American batteries that were being built, again with but scant effect. Again in the darkness, American patrols scouting ahead of the parallel clashed with British troops. Across the river at Gloucester Point, a brief skirmish erupted between pickets of the opposing armies.[115]

With the Allied artillery batteries nearing completion and almost ready to respond to Cornwallis's guns, it was time for General Knox, the army's chief of artillery, to step up and assume a more prominent role in the unfolding drama. The Massachusetts officer had supervised the recent transportation of Washington's ordnance and supplies from the north. As the siege lines were drawn ever more tightly around Yorktown and Cornwallis, Washington found himself relying more and more on the abilities of the 31-year-old officer from Boston. Knox, as Washington knew, spoke passable French. The ability to communicate effectively in both languages at Yorktown proved invaluable to the Allies, for it helped coordinate artillery operations with Rochambeau more seamlessly than would otherwise have been possible. Aware of Washington's expectations of him, Knox stepped up and gladly accepted his responsibilities.[116]

The opening of the guns was scheduled to begin on October 9. The meticulous Knox was determined that his field officers knew exactly what was expected of them. "A Field officer of artillery," he directed on October 8, should be appointed every day to Command in the Trenches, to be relieved every twenty-four hours. He will pointedly attend that the firing is well directed according to the object, and that the utmost coolness and Regularity is observed. Upon every occasion where it shall be practicable, the Recochet firing of shots and shells must be practiced. This mode has a vast superiority over all others, and is much more economical. The officers of Artillery in the Batteries are to level every piece themselves.[117]

Knox also mandated that an artillery field officer would be appointed each day to direct the American artillery park, and that the officer "shall order all the necessary Repairs to be executed, of the Carriages which may be damaged—to have the Shells, Shott, and every species of ammunition replaced which have been expended during the day in the Batteries."[118]

Lieutenant Colonel Ebenezer Stevens, a Massachusetts artillery officer, was ordered to supervise the artillery park on October 9—the day the guns were scheduled to open fire. The trenches on that day would be under the command of Colonel Lamb, a veteran officer who had lost an eye at Quebec in 1775.[119]

While cognizant of his vital role in the siege, Knox was realistic in his appraisal of the capacity of the first parallel guns to damage the British works and artillery. If General Lincoln, the commander of the American wing, was laboring under any illusion that the American artillery fire would be completely effective, Knox threw cold water all over the idea. "Our first parallel is nearly finished, the batteries are establishing in it and to my surprise and sorrow I perceive an idea prevailing, which I think it ought never to have existed, that the enemy are materially to be annoyed by our fire," he wrote Lincoln. "At the distance our batteries might be . . . you may not expect one shot in four will take place or that one in that number will even hit the [British] works and shells will be much less certain." Knox urged Lincoln to make his views plainly known to Washington, and firmly believed the purpose of the first parallel was little more than a cover for the construction of a second and closer parallel that would play the decisive role in the siege to capture Cornwallis:

I think sir that we have nothing rationally to expect from our present batteries but a cover while we are erecting others in our next parallel—So that these I think ought rather to have that for their object and so be constructed as best answer this purpose. After the first batteries are completed I hope no time will be lost between that and our opening our second parallel—but time is precious [and] it must not be wasted in vain expectations,—besides if the second parallel is soon commenced every body will see the purpose of the first and none will be disappointed in want of success from our present line of batteries.[120]

Although the batteries of the first parallel ended up inflicting more damage than Knox anticipated, he was right: a second line would have to be opened. Washington knew this as well, for the Yorktown operation was a classic siege in the European tradition, dictated by a progression of constricting siege lines. Of course, Cornwallis's response to the first parallel would play a significant role in determining when (and perhaps even if) a second line could be constructed.

As Lieutenant Colonel François Marie d'Aboville readied the French line of guns, Henry Knox adjusted his batteries and confidently rode along his mighty line of guns in anticipation of fine tuning his instruments of war. His hour was finally at hand.

Chapter 9

The Guns of October

*T*he opposing armies shivered under a crisp chill during the night of October 8. The dawn of the following morning brought warmer temperatures, and by midday the sun appeared from behind overcast skies. At 9:00 a.m., Lafayette's light infantry struck their tents and moved them to the right and ahead of the American encampment, closer to the Wormley Creek ravines and the American wing of the first parallel.[1]

On the far right side of the line, the American Grand Battery neared completion. By this day it contained (subject to change as exigency dictated) three 24-pounders, three 18-pounders, two 8-inch howitzers, and, reported Lieutenant William Feltman, "two ten and a half inch mortars fixed upon carriages (and not upon beds) in order to throw the shot horizontal into the enemy's works, and there to burst and destroy their works. We have six of those mortars; they were invented by Gen. Knox and proved to be of effect."[2]

Final Preparations

Spirits were high throughout the Allied army—perhaps higher than at any time during the long and bloody war. Despite soaring morale and the pending opening of the Allied bombardment, defections to Cornwallis's army continued. Several French deserters told the British that General Washington planned to build further approaches and provided sketchy information on the strength and composition of the Allied forces.[3]

Allied defections were not unique. A British deserter crept into Allied lines to inform his hosts that Cornwallis—in an obvious move to allay growing suspicions among his troops—had told his men the Americans lacked siege artillery, had only field ordnance to work against the British, and that the French vessels lingering in the distance sought only tobacco and would soon leave the area. According to the deserter, however, Cornwallis's soldiers already had begun to doubt the general's word.[4]

The first part of the day passed uneventfully. British cannon, mortar, and howitzer fire lazily arced its way toward the Allied line, but the toll in damage to earthworks or lives lost was light. James McHenry, Lafayette's aide, wrote the governor of Maryland that the guns were almost ready to open fire, and would likely do so "this afternoon." American and French troops, meanwhile, continued toiling on to perfect their defenses, with the latter using a large number of sandbags to strengthen their fortifications.[5] At 1:00 p.m., the trenches were relieved in the American sector by General Benjamin Lincoln's division and in the French by the Regiments Bourbonnois and Soissonois under Count de Viomenil. French auxiliary troops were the chasseurs of Agenois and Gatenois.[6] "The Regt is for the Trenches, and Drums are Beating to arms. I must leave you," Lieutenant Jacobus Swartwout, Jr. ended his letter to Captain Barnardus Swartwout, "and take up my Sword."[7] A barrage of enemy shot and shell met the relieving troops as they marched into the trenches, and in an attempt to spare lives, Washington ordered an end to excessive martial exhibitions with drums and flags. Henceforth, the parallel would be relieved in absolute silence and at a different hour so as to deceive the British.[8]

In the early afternoon, American fatigue parties went into the woods to prepare more fascines, gabions, and saucissons.[9] Still later, the troops were instructed to make palisades, "12 feet long & pointed at one end," for the purpose of fortifying the ditches around the redoubts of the parallel.[10] General Wayne's brigade was ordered to deliver 200 palisades along with 60 saucissons (nine to 18 feet long), 80 fascines, and 800 pickets or stakes.[11] The proportional quantities of siege components, as before, were to be furnished by the particular units assigned to make them. At the behest of his engineers, Washington directed that the articles be placed in areas behind the trenches by 5:00 that evening.[12] Hoping to dissuade spectators from the ranks from unintentionally interfering with progress on the works, the commander directed that "Persons whose duty does not Call them to the trenches, and who Assemble there merely to indulge Curiosity are to walk on the reverse of the trenches, that they may not interrupt the works."[13]

This directive proved all the more necessary as the soldiers labored to haul the big siege pieces through the trenches and into position in the batteries. To prevent the British gunners from narrowing their fire against a selected Allied unit, none of the batteries of the main parallel was allowed to open or unmask their embrasures and commence shooting. In this respect the Allies at Yorktown followed theoretical tenets almost to the letter, ideas drawn together in two volumes in 1820 by Charles Francois Antoine Lallemand in his important *Treatise on Artillery*:

> A Battery must not be opened the instant its cannon are mounted, because this would draw upon it the whole undivided fire of the place, that would-infallibly destroy it; it must remain silent, on the contrary, until the whole of the batteries are finished, they should then be unmasked at the same instant, and the enemy[,] attacked from every point, in front, in flank, and in rear, can no longer act with the same precision, and is obliged to scatter his fire, which is in that way much less fatal to the besiegers.[14]

Washington originally planned to abide strictly by this rule—and he did, in fact, observe it to a point. Evidently, he proposed to wait until 80 pieces could open on Cornwallis simultaneously. He modified his designs somewhat on October 9 when he realized the Grand French Battery would not be perfected before the next day. Washington still hoped to deliver a modicum of Allied power, perhaps to dispel the false rumors of the Allied inferiority Cornwallis was spreading among his troops, and to increase doubts as to their immediate future.[15]

The Opening of the Guns

By 2:00 p.m., American batteries 10A (near the left end of the American side of the line) and 13A (the American Grand Battery on the far right near the York River) were finished and ready to open on the enemy.[16] Despite one American soldier's contention that the French "had completed their batteries a few hours before us," such was not the case.[17] According to a French officer, "we were delayed by the lack of vehicles and horses to pull our guns and ammunition caissons. The Americans had all they needed and, when they were finished with them, lent us their horses and wagons. They had made every effort to be ready before we were; however, since their resources were greater, this was not difficult."[18] Despite the lack of horses and vehicles, St. Simon managed to finish his battery (1A) near the river on the far left of the first parallel a full day ahead of the others. As such, he was ready and anxious to fire on the British ships hovering off the mouth of Yorktown Creek while protecting the Fusiliers' Redoubt on the British right.

With the principal line batteries approaching completion, General Washington relented and, because of their excellent preparation, gave the French permission to open their embrasures and turn the guns of this unit full force on the enemy. Shooting commenced at 3:00 p.m., about one hour after the time General Knox reported the two American batteries (10A and 13A) finished, and two hours before the American ordnance in the American Grand Battery opened on Cornwallis. The shot and bombs from the four 12-pounders, three mortars, and three howitzers in French Battery 1A immediately drew British attention to their right. The small mortar battery (2A) south of Williamsburg Road and connected by a trench to 1A also probably discharged rounds at this time, although direct mention of this unit's firing does not appear in the sources.[19]

The fire from these French pieces was so accurate and deadly—especially from the 100-pounder mortar bombs—that the frigate *Guadaloupe* and sloop *Formidable*, both moored to cover the Fusiliers' Redoubt, cut their cables and withdrew for security's sake to the Gloucester side of the river. The *Charon* moved down in front of Yorktown. Once these warships pulled away, the French turned their pieces to batter the right side of the enemy fortifications around Yorktown, though with scant effect. They also sent bombs to set afire the double abatis surrounding the Fusiliers' Redoubt, probably in preparation for an assault by chasseurs. But the 120 British soldiers of the 23rd Regiment, aided by about 40 marines, stoutly defended their fortress against the bombs and cascading balls, and the redoubt seems to have sustained but little damage. British cannon fell silent for long intervals during the French bombardment, almost as if Cornwallis, perplexed by the attack against his right, was trying to anticipate the next point of assault.[20]

It was not long in coming. At approximately 5:00 p.m., scarcely two hours after the French barrage began, the American Grand Battery (13A) on the right of the line closest to York River opened a direct assault against the British left and front. As an American standard was being unfurled on the parapet, Washington himself ignited the fuse of an 18-pounder cannon and stood clear as the piece boomed forth the first American artillery salute to Cornwallis's gunners.[21] The lone ball sped through the air and dropped with fatal effect. "I could hear the ball strike from house to house," reported Colonel Philip Van Cortlandt of the 2nd New York Regiment.[22] Washington's shot finally crashed into the wooden structure where a coterie of officers had gathered for dinner. The round killed British Commissary-General Perkins and tore the leg from Lieutenant Charles Robertson, quartermaster and adjutant of the 76th Regiment. Perkins's wife, seated between these men, luckily escaped injury. At least one other officer was wounded.[23]

Following Washington's devastating first shot, the other artillery in Battery 13A (two other 18-pounders, three 24-pounders, four mortars, and two howitzers) opened fire.[24] The battery, commanded by Captain William Ferguson of the 4th Continental Artillery, lobbed its deadly missiles into Yorktown with steady precision as the gunners sought to adjust and correct their pieces so they would cause the most damage to Cornwallis's works. From this battery, bombs were dispatched from the 10-inch mortars mounted on reinforced howitzer carriages personally designed by Henry Knox, although it is unclear how many of these pieces saw action.

While Washington's pieces opened on the British, the French continued blazing away at the enemy's right flank. French flags whipped and snapped in the early evening breeze all along the parapet. The 24-pounders in the French battery on the left of the parallel (3A) joined in the action about this time, but the Grand French Battery complex (structures 4A-8A) remained silent pending final completion. The Grand

French Battery was almost ready and would join the grand bombardment the following day.[25]

The first Allied artillery bombardment offered Washington's soldiers an opportunity to release their frustrations and pent-up emotions after the long and arduous days of preparation. "This day, this happy day, we return'd their fire," wrote a relieved Pennsylvania soldier.[26] Lieutenant Swartwout of New York noticed that the batteries "are now opened with an unusual briskness from both Cannon and Mortars."[27] Colonel St. George Tucker watched the opening of the guns stationed along the first parallel with deep interest and entered his observations in his journal:

> At five this Evening the continental Standard was hoisted at our Battery on the Right—a discharge of Cannon instantly ensued— One or two shells were discharged from eight Inch Howitzs without effect falling many yards short of the Enemy's works. Our Cannon were so well directed that the first shot after the general Discharge struck within a foot of the Embrasure of the Enemys [sic] works on the right. Several succeeding shot were lodged in their works further to the left. [28]

The first Allied fire confirmed Knox's expectations, for numerous rounds fell far short of their mark and plowed the earth before the enemy glacis. This was especially true of the French artillery on the left, while the American guns in Battery 13A enjoyed relatively more success. The American guns, however, were directed against the British occupants of Redoubts 9 and 10, which were closer to Battery 13A than the right side of Cornwallis's earthworks were to the French pieces concentrated against them. In other words, French missiles had a greater distance to cover to reach their mark. "Our cannon were well aimed," claimed Rochambeau's aide-de-camp Hans Axel, comte von Ferson, "but the balls, without doing great damage, were buried in the sand of the [British] fortifications."[29]

By a process of adjustment, both American and French artillerists soon improved the results of their firing. One theorist reported that the American gunners marked with chalk on the platforms along the wheels before firing a piece, a process enabling them, "if the piece had been well directed, to put the carriage exactly in the same place again."[30] Under instructions to make each shot count, Washington's officers personally aimed the artillery. Deserters from the British ranks reported the gratifying news of steadily increasing casualties among Cornwallis's soldiers. "We were informed that our shells did considerable execution in Town, and we could perceive that our shot, which were directed against the enemy's embarzures, injured them much," Washington wrote the President of the Congress. Even worse for the British, the Allied fire was beginning to dismount their artillery.[31] "I now beheld the cannon, those infernal machines, playing with the utmost fury," wrote an American observer in his journal. "I saw the rapid bullet striking or rebounding from the redoubts of the enemy, and driving thro' the air the planks and timber, which formed the embrasures for the great guns." The view was similar from across the lines. Lieutenant James watched the destruction wrought by the big guns and later wrote, "The slaughter was great."[32]

Operation of the Allied ordnance naturally differed somewhat from theoretical precepts. Basically, however, the French and Americans adhered to the tenets of such European masters as Vauban. The purpose of the first batteries was to dismount enemy artillery by the best means possible, namely, by enfilading ricochet fire and by direct, or point-blank, fire. Secondary to ruining the enemy guns was destroying his embrasures and earthworks, driving soldiers back from the ramparts, and disrupting communication between the line and the rear. Ricochet firing was especially effective in enfilading the face of the British works and causing havoc behind the line. Bombs and shells from mortars and howitzers aided this destructive enterprise, while other cannon supplied both direct and oblique firepower to further reduce the earthen entrenchments and knock enemy guns out of commission.[33] The heavy 18- and 24-pounders proved especially useful in ricochet firing and in breaching enemy works.[34]

Distance played a significant factor in the ultimate success of the Allied guns ensconced in and near the first parallel. The 24-pounders, with a range of 1,120 to 1,340 yards, were of immense value along that distant line. Mortars could be adjusted to fire bombs at ranges of between 670 and 1,670 yards, and long-range howitzers had the capability of sending shells up to 1,120 yards distant.[35]

On October 8, General Knox penned an unusually philosophical epistle to General Lincoln in which he addressed the limitations and wide variety of issues they would likely encounter that would hinder the operation of his mortars. "In the schools they may not be [effected] when every circumstance remains nearly the same," Knox began.

> In the first you may not expect the same exactness, where the different quality of the powder changed by the different state of the air, the different state of the platforms—the different degrees of heat in the mortar—the different sizes of the shells, not all cast in the same mould-the different weight of those cast in the same mould from different metals—The difference of those cast in the same mould from the different grade of their surfaces and the different state of the powder more or less compressed in the chamber are among the evils, which in the field it will be difficult to guard against, and which will form in some measure to show how little we may expect from the effect of shells thrown at this distance.[36]

Based upon Knox's observations and practice in the field, the most satisfying results might be more reasonably expected and obtained from larger cannon than from other ordnance types—especially when the targets sought were the British batteries encircling Yorktown proper. All the American ordnance could easily reach the British positions in the detached redoubts scarcely 500 yards distant. On the basis of the lines of fire depicted on various historical maps of the siege, the majority of shooting from American Battery 13A was directed against these outer works rather than against the Yorktown entrenchments.[37]

Guns cast during the 1700s were not always reliable or even durable. Indeed, many guns were constructed of inferior metal. As a result, they were fired at ten-minute intervals whenever possible. If guns were fired more rapidly, the barrels would "droop." Each gun ceased fire after a three-hour stint, during which period the inside of the barrel was treated with a mixture of water and vinegar to clean out the tube. Gunners considered it hazardous to their health to fire more than 50 shots from a gun during a 24-hour period because of possible adverse effects on the metal.[38] These considerations almost certainly were observed by the Allied artillerists at Yorktown. Actual firing of the pieces, whether cannon, mortars, or howitzers, comprised a series of distinct procedures that the gunners practiced with exactness to the strict verbal commands of responsible officers.[39]

American and French artillery continued the deadly cannonade, even when darkness began to blanket the landscape on October 9. The fury and duration of the fusillade registered serious concern among Cornwallis's troops. The Allies, recorded German Private Döhla, "deprived us of the suspicion which we formerly had that they had only their regimental cannon and could, in view of the dense woods and swamp, bring up no heavy guns."[40] Cornwallis answered the French and American guns by opening three batteries along his front, and throughout the night firing from both sides echoed across the plain and lit up the night sky.[41]

By all accounts, the Allies succeeded in inflicting far more damage to the British works than the British managed in return. Colonel Richard Butler of the 5th Pennsylvania wrote that both French and American "shot and shells flew incessantly through the night, dismounted the guns of the enemy, and destroyed many of their embrasures."[42] One Continental officer remembered the nocturnal display this way: "a number of shells from the works of both parties passing high in the air, and descending in a curve, each with a long train of fire, exhibited a brilliant spectacle."[43] Still, the British kept up as lively a response of mortar and cannon fire possible, which served to keep the occupants of the siege line on the alert.[44] Gradually, as the shadows deepened into darkness, the guns of both armies tapered off until late in the night, when direct firing ceased altogether. Fitful ricochet firing continued apace, however, for Washington was determined to exert constant pressure to prevent the enemy from repairing their disfigured entrenchments.[45]

Under cover of night, General Rochambeau's engineers went to work. Four hundred French laborers began the risky task of planting the newly-fashioned palisades in the ditches in front of the redoubts, a job requiring exposure of Allied flesh to British gunfire. French soldiers also worked to improve their earthworks and establish firm communication with the rear. American troops spent the night engaged in similar enterprises.[46]

The Day After: October 10

If Cornwallis was apprehensive at the obvious superiority in firepower the Allies had attained, he must have wrung his hands in despair when the sun rose over the Virginia peninsula on October 10. The remaining American and French batteries were finally finished, and at 9:00 a.m. the Allies launched a thunderous artillery assault that dwarfed that of the previous afternoon and evening. The bombardment sent British soldiers careening back from their epaulements in perplexed trepidation. On the siege line, Knox's soldiers brought to bear the several 18-pounders in Battery 10A on the left side of the American sector. Colonel Gerard d'Aboville's Frenchmen leveled three British 24-, 18-, and 16-pounder artillery pieces, in addition to mortars and howitzers, from the Grand French Battery and its satellite units.[47]

The barrage of shot and shell stormed into the British works from the well-aimed pieces. "Several parapets can already be seen with their tops damaged," wrote Deux-Ponts, "and we know, from the reports of several deserters, that the enemy has been much astonished at the firing of our batteries, and that our shells, especially, disturb him much."[48] So incessant was the Allied firepower that after but one hour, the British guns ceased to respond at all: the weapons were either too damaged to fire, or their gunners' positions along the works had become too hazardous to maintain.[49] In return, the Allies suffered only a handful of casualties. And their guns kept firing.[50]

The Grand French Battery (the tight complex of works comprising structures 4A-8A) played a large role in silencing the enemy guns. The French "battery" extended from an area slightly east of Hampton Road to a point on the west side of that route at the edge of the Yorktown Creek ravine, a line stretching approximately 1,000 feet from east to west.[51] Give or take three or four guns, approximately 30 pieces of artillery occupied the complex. These five separate structures and their large weapons poured forth a heavy and concentrated fire that ripped apart Cornwallis's earthworks and drove their occupants to ground or killed and maimed them. The success of this effort helped convince Washington to immediately begin the approaches necessary to establish a second, closer, parallel.[52]

The total artillery complement of any particular structure at any given time must be speculative, for the weapons were shifted continuously to respond to shifts of British ordnance. Throughout the siege, changes took place among the batteries of the Allies and the British. Each side sought to anticipate the other in placing its artillery where it would be the most effective. In this manner, a six-gun battery one day might become a four-gun unit the next. The result is that few contemporary accounts agree as to the number and types of weapons serving in a particular battery.[53]

Even archaeological investigation has failed to determine the exact type or quantity of armament that occupied a structure at a given time. At most, this work has revealed the maximum number of platforms that could be erected in a single battery, but could not determine the number of pieces actually contained therein. Although weapons were shifted from one battery to another, there is no evidence the platforms followed the pieces, except when siege ordnance and equipment was transferred from the first to second parallel. Neither archaeology nor history, however, can at this point definitively state how many artillery pieces actually occupied a structure at a precise moment during the siege.[54]

*   *   *

For most of the daylight hours of Wednesday, October 10, the Allies delivered a continuous barrage from their artillery mounted along the parallel. Their targets were the British batteries positioned in the Hornwork and along Cornwallis's left flank. The guns and mortars in Batteries 1A and 2A attacked the British right and the Fusiliers' Redoubt. The advanced enemy positions in detached Redoubts 9 and 10 also drew significant attention, especially the former structure with its threatening armament of howitzers that sent explosive shells crashing among the Allies. Three historical maps, two American (largely duplicative of one another) and one French, clearly indicate the objectives of the artillery fire of the principal batteries of the first parallel.[55]

In the French sector, the 24-pounders of Battery 5A directed shot toward the fortifications to the left of the British Hornwork, while those in Battery 7A sent shot against the British line east of the Hornwork. As suggested by the diversity of its ordnance, Battery 8A sent shot and shell hurling in different directions. The cannon in the left section of the battery directly targeted the Hornwork and adjacent works; howitzer and mortar shells fell in the area of British Redoubt 9. American Battery 10A, using only 18-pounders, fired its missiles chiefly into the stretch of fortifications built to protect Cornwallis's left flank, but reserved some fire for both of the detached enemy redoubts. The bombardment of the cannon, mortars, and howitzers located in Battery 13A on the far right end of the line was primarily directed to beat down the defenses of the detached works, although occasionally shot found its mark at the extreme left end of the British line close to the water's edge. By all accounts, the

24-pounders in French Battery 7A, part of the Grand French Battery complex. This view looks northwest behind the battery. Yortown and the British defenses are about 800 yards to the right. The Hampton Road is behind the camera position. *National Park Service, Colonial National Historical Park, Yorktown Collection*

Allied cannonade severely raked that portion of the enemy works from the Hornwork east to the York River. Those structures were the most accessible to French and American fire.[56]

Trying to determine exactly how many pieces of artillery were brought to bear against Cornwallis's garrison is a frustrating exercise. An undated sheet located among General Knox's papers dealing with the siege of Yorktown claims the American artillery totaled 45 weapons: 27 18-pounders; three 24-pounders; 10 10-inch mortars (six to be fitted with howitzer carriages), two 8-inch mortars, and three 8-inch howitzers. According to this notice, prepared in Knox's hand, "the french [sic] can furnish" 28 pieces, comprising 12 24-pounders; eight 16-pounders; four 12-inch mortars; and four 8-inch mortars. No mention is made of French howitzers. Based on this reference, American and French artillery at Yorktown numbered 73 pieces.[57]

Whatever their exact number, the Allied guns, mortars, and howitzers caused much destruction to the British fortifications and confusion and turmoil among the soldiers manning them. The bombardment probably inflicted the greatest damage on October 10, when nearly all the batteries unleashed a steady fire. "Bombarding and Cannonading exceedingly heavy from the American and French Batteries all this day and night," observed Captain Swartwout.[58]

British return fire was substantially less than what it had been the previous day, but close calls abounded. As one soldier wrote another that day, "I am as yet well, but like to have lost my hat by a 12 pds. Yesterday."[59] The subdued fire of the enemy was a direct result of the effectiveness of the Allied guns in general, and those of the French in particular, in closing the British embrasures. Washington complimented the skill of Rochambeau's gunners, who used newer weapons and better ammunition than the Americans. As Claude Blanchard, Rochambeau's

This close-up view of the east side of the British Hornwork was taken from outside the line looking northwest. The 24-pounder guns from Battery 7A (part of the Grand French Battery complex pictured on the preceding page) bombarded this portion of the line on October 9 and 10. *National Park Service, Colonial National Historical Park, Yorktown Collection*

commissary general, observed, the Americans "did not approach the perfection of our [French] gunners, who were the admiration of General Washington; it is true they had perfect instruments, so to speak; the cannons were new and the balls perfectly suited to their calibre." Another witness echoed this observation: "The [French] artillery men made every discharge take effect by the exactness of their aim, and their alertness in working the guns." Washington's praise of the French embarrassed Knox. American shot was poorly made and their bombs frequently fell short of the mark or failed to burst on schedule, though the fault did not lay with the American artillerist. Knox's artillery improved its fire as the siege progressed, and by the end of the campaign his gunners could take pride in having contributed mightily to the final result.[60]

By midday October 10, the British reply was virtually nonexistent. Cornwallis's guns averaged but six rounds per hour through the balance of the day. With his embrasures either constantly damaged or closed to avoid detection by the Allied artillerists, Cornwallis was forced to respond with his mortars—especially during daylight hours. "They threw many bombs and royal grenades," remembered a French officer, "and at night they established flying batteries. During the day they ordinarily withdrew their cannon, and placed them behind the parapet."[61]

"The difference of the two [Allied and British] firings could easily be distinguished; that of the enemy was slow and regular, while ours was brisk and well supported," reported St. George Tucker. Unless Cornwallis could devise a system to compete with and quell such an onslaught, wrote the 3rd Connecticut's Lieutenant Colonel Ebenezer Huntington to a friend, the Allied artillery "must inevitably . . . oblige him to surrender."[62]

Many of the men cooped up inside Yorktown must have felt the same way. Early that morning, wrote the always observant Private Döhla, because of the intensity of the fire, "we had to change our camp and pitch our tents in the earthworks . . . . One could not avoid the horribly many cannon balls either inside or outside the city. Most of the inhabitants . . . fled . . . eastward to the bank of the York River." Hessian Stephen Popp also noted in his journal the movement of the camp and heavy pounding. "They threw bombs of from 100 to 200 pounds. Their howitzers and cannon balls were all 18, 24, and 48 pounds," he wrote with some understandable exaggeration. The outfit stationed behind Popp in the second line, the Hessian von Bose Regiment, "had a bad position because of the bombs and shells. Therefore they had many dead and wounded," continued Popp. "The light infantry which stood in the horn works had the most dangerous spot and lost the most men. All the marines and sailors from the ships were divided up in the trenches and batteries where they had to help with the work."[63]

Particular targets for the French bombardiers on the afternoon and evening of October 10 were the British powder magazines believed located along a hill near the river.[64] The fire was heavy and accurate. "The bomb shells from the besiegers and the besieged are incessantly crossing each others' path in the air," recalled Dr. James Thacher, who left a graphic account of the mortar fusillade. "They are clearly visible in the form of a black ball in the day, but in the night, they appear like fiery meteors with blazing tails, most beautifully brilliant, ascending majestically from the mortar to a certain altitude, and gradually descending to the spot where they are destined to execute their work of destruction." The methodical science behind gunnery fascinated the doctor. "It is astonishing with what accuracy an experienced gunner will make his calculations, that a shell shall fall within a few feet of a given point, and burst at the precise time, though at a great distance. When a shell falls," Thacher continued, "it whirls round, burrows, and excavates the earth to a considerable extent, and bursting, makes dreadful havoc around. I have more than once witnessed fragments of the mangled bodies and limbs of the British soldiers thrown into the air by the bursting of our shells.[65]

Daniel Trabue, the former Virginia soldier-turned-sutler, remembered the same bombardment and left a similar record of its spectacular nature:

> Some of the mortars [sic] were throwing their bomb shells, and they would go in a blaze, then turn a sommersault [sic] and fall down in the Fort. The report was as loud when it struck the ground as when it came out; the same also, when it bursted, the bombs flying in a circle.... The shells were made of pot metal like a jug ½ inch thick, without a handle, & with a big mouth. They were filled with powder, and other combustibles in such a manner that the blaze came out of the mouth, and keeps on burning until it gets to the body where the powder is, then it bursts and the pieces fly every way, and would kill whoever it hits. There were so many flying and falling in

the Fort that we had no Doubt but that we were paying them well for their mischief to us.[66]

Frenchman Claude Robin described the physical and psychological impact the "slow and destructive bomb" inflicted on men unlucky enough to be caught on the receiving end of the discharge. The explosives, he wrote,

> sometimes burying itself in the roofs of houses, sometimes when it burst, raising clouds of dust and rubbish from the ruins of the buildings, at other times blowing the unfortunate wretches, that happened to be within its reach, more than twenty feet high in the air, and letting them fall at a considerable distance most pitiably torn. Such terrible sights as these fix and captivate the attention, and fill the mind at the same instant with trouble, wonder and consternation.

According to Robin, deserters claimed the British garrison was "in the utmost confusion; not knowing where to fly, death seizes them even in the arms of sleep; and the General [Cornwallis], uneasy at the discontent of the Hessians, no longer confides his advanced guard to any but the English soldiers."[67]

Captain William Stevens of the 2nd Continental Artillery reported similar scenes resulting from howitzers fired en ricochet: "Several of the enemy were blown to pieces, and some of their limbs were seen from our batteries, flying in the air." According to Stevens, "Those shells which lodged in their parapet, when bursting . . . made a greater havock than the cannon shot did, by shaking the works similar to the springing of a mine."[68]

The increasing casualties suffered by the British was a secondary benefit to the Allies, whose primary purpose at this stage of the siege was to dismount and silence enemy guns—an effort that was succeeding admirably (and almost certainly beyond Knox's expectations). In fact, the Allies could not have anticipated a more propitious beginning for their operation, given the largely circumstantial nature of events that had brought about the growing good fortune of their arms.[69]

It seemed as if the Allies could do little wrong. Improperly aimed artillery fire that overshot the Yorktown fortifications took a toll among the British shipping that was moored off Gloucester Point.[70] "These ships were miserably ruined and shot to pieces," remembered Johann Conrad Döhla.[71] To better secure his position on the river side, Cornwallis promptly sank more than a dozen additional vessels close to shore.[72]

Distressed at the turn of events, many Yorktown residents saw their homes destroyed by bounding shot and exploding shell that set fires raging along the line. Many inhabitants who had chosen to remain in the village now fled with their choice holdings to the riverbank, where they proceeded to dig shelters under the sand cliffs. "But there also they did not stay undamaged," recalled Döhla, "for many were badly injured and mortally wounded by the fragments of bombs which exploded partly in the air and partly on the ground, their arms and legs severed or themselves struck dead." Many blacks also died along the waters of the York. Credible evidence exists that the town's women and children were crossed over to Gloucester Point in an attempt to avoid the terrible Allied bombardment.[73]

Along the left part of the line, British soldiers suffered heavily from the constant rain of shot and shell. Many bombs fell directly in their camp, doing great mischief. British troops later recounted their experience in the barrage to Daniel Trabue: "When a shell fell on the ground it would sink under the ground so deep that when it burst, it would throw up a wagon load, or even more of Dirt." Those that fell on a house," continued Trabue's account, "Tore it to pieces. The British had a number of holes and Pits Dug all over the Fort, some large and some small with timber in the top edge; when the soldiers would see a shell coming near them they could jump in one of the pits and squat Down until it had burst." According to British accounts, "When a shell would fall on any hard place, so that it would not go under the ground, a soldier would go to it and knock off the fiz, or neck, and then it would not burst. The soldier then received a shilling for the act."[74]

British officer Samuel Graham observed the terrible destruction firsthand and wrote about it in his postwar memoir: "On the 10th scarcely a gun could be fired from our works, fascines, stockade platforms, and earth, with guns and gun-carriages, being all pounded together in a mass." Lieutenant James well understood how guns and carriages and platforms could be "pounded together in a mass," and wrote in the third person about the destruction of his own battery in the main line of works behind detached Redoubt 9: "This evening, the enemy, having mounted some more of their artillery, totally silenced No. 5 battery, commanded by the first lieutenant of the *Charon*, who with his men was obliged to quit it, the shot and shell having dismounted his guns and tore up his platforms." James also recorded that a "general" infantry attack was launched "under cover of their cannon, and the enemy again repulsed." There was no such Allied infantry attack, although aggressive patrols were constantly in place probing and pushing against the British lines. The Germans, however, were indeed becoming demoralized by the iron rain battering everything around them. "The Hessians gave way twice in front of my works on this night," wrote James, "and the cannonade continued with a degree of warmth seldom equaled and not to be described." James continued:

> The remainder of the night passed in a dreadful slaughter, and we [were] occasionally employed in throwing up the works the enemy knocked down. Several parts of the garrison was in flames on this night, and the whole discovered a view awful and tremendous.[75]

As one might expect from this sequence of horrific accounts, the mounting casualties and damage in and around Yorktown wreaked havoc with British morale and their ability to retaliate in any meaningful manner.[76] Cornwallis's earlier calculations about how long he might be able to withstand the Allied encirclement until help arrived from General Clinton were now moot; the opening of Washington's first parallel changed the equation entirely. The question was now one of how long he and his command could survive under the incessant Allied artillery barrage—an entirely different question. In the course of a handful of hours, Cornwallis's situation had utterly changed, and it looked exceedingly grim.

*   *   *

At noon on October 10, Lafayette's light infantry division relieved the trenches in the American sector of the first parallel. The Agenois and Saintonge regiments took their place along the French part of the line.[77] It was at this time the British responded to a flag earlier sent into their lines, supposedly at Washington's direction. The intercourse concerned "Secretary" Thomas Nelson, who had retired from public life in 1775. The elder Nelson was the uncle of the governor and Virginia militia commander of the same name, and it was the senior Nelson's home, located behind the Hornwork, that Cornwallis had taken as his personal headquarters. At the behest of the secretary's two sons, who were serving with the American army, Washington sent word to Cornwallis asking that the old man, who as a patiot had openly supported the rebellion, be spared the tumult and danger of the siege and passed through the lines to the American side. Realizing the Allied battering guns now threatened to topple the secretary's home, Cornwallis respected the request, even though the British commander must have known the old man could provide his enemy with valuable information.

At noon sharp, a white flag rose above the beleaguered enemy works announcing a respite of arms while the elder Nelson was transported by two British soldiers across the plain. The gout-afflicted 65-year-old former Commonwealth official was taken to Washington's headquarters tent, where he was immediately questioned by officers. A black servant who had accompanied the old man through the lines managed to smuggle out the family silver concealed in a blanket.[78]

Washington received valuable intelligence from Nelson about Cornwallis's state of affairs. The Allied artillery, explained the secretary, was having a devastating effect. Deaths and injuries were mounting. One of his own servants had been struck and killed by flying shot while standing in the Nelson living room. He reported that many soldiers, including officers, had joined the citizens in refuge beneath the cliffs bordering the York River. Cornwallis had personally sought shelter in a recess near the foot of the secretary's garden. At Gloucester Point, continued Nelson, Tarleton and Simcoe had ordered more than 1,000 horses destroyed because of a lack of forage. Both men, moreover, had fallen sick and had been unable to actively lead their men in recent days. In addition, observed Nelson, Lauzun kept the British at Gloucester Point completely hemmed in and restricted in movement.[79]

All of this was welcome news to Washington and his officers, but the most important news concerned the arrival that very day of a message from Clinton to Cornwallis. Just how Nelson became privy to such information is unknown, but his word was never in doubt. Two British majors in a 12-oar whaleboat had eluded the French fleet and arrived with dispatches. Admiral Digby, with 30 ships of the line, would soon set out to attack de Grasse. With Digby were reinforcements under Clinton to relieve the Yorktown garrison. From Cornwallis's perspective, Clinton's message to him was both ambivalent and profoundly disheartening. "I am doing every thing in my power to relieve you by a direct move, and I have reason to hope, from the assurances given me this day by Admiral Graves, that we may pass the bar [at New York] by the 12th of October, if the winds permit, and no unforeseen accident happens," waffled Clinton. "This, however is subject to disappointment, wherefore, if I hear from you, your wishes will of course direct me and I shall persist in the idea of a direct move, even to the middle of November, should it be your Lordship's opinion that you can hold out so long." However, continued Cornwallis's superior, "[if] when I hear from you, you tell me that you cannot [hold out], and I am without hopes of arriving in time . . . I will immediately make an attempt by Philadelphia."[80]

This news elated the Allies, for it offered the first hint that Clinton might not arrive in time to save Cornwallis. The scent of capitulation, though yet faint, wafted in the October air.[81]

The news also gave incentive for pushing ahead with the siege and further pressuring Cornwallis into surrender before help should appear from the sea. In the American camp there began a renewed effort to build a reserve of siege materials for furthering the approaches. Von Steuben's entire division spent the afternoon on fatigue in the woods preparing fascines, gabions, saucissons, and palisades for the coming advance.[82] Washington renewed his instructions governing the sizes of these materials and their proportional preparation by organizational units. His directions called for 2,000 fascines, 600 gabions, 600 saucissons, and 6,000 stakes to be made by the American command for immediate use. The troops were also required "to keep that quantity always in readiness by replacing the daily consumption."[83]

In the French sector, meanwhile, Rochambeau's soldiers worked to improve their redoubts and communications trenches and to maintain their batteries. Baron de Viomenil led these operations, accompanied by two battalions each of the Regiments Agenois and Saintonge. French casualties remained light throughout the day.[84] On the far left hugging the York River, French troops in Battery 1A made prepared hot shot (solid balls heated to ignite ships) for use against the British warships still endeavoring to support the Fusiliers' Redoubt. Anticipating a possible probing attack in that quarter preparatory to an all-out escape attempt by Cornwallis up the Williamsburg Road, Rochambeau directed two battalions of St. Simon's volunteers to take up a position behind the bluff battery in the ravine formed by Ballard Creek.[85]

The British Attempt to Flank the Allies at Gloucester Point

Washington and his generals knew Cornwallis's situation was rapidly deteriorating. The possibility that he might attempt to escape from Yorktown caused them no little concern. What would the wily British general attempt? The answer was a move against the Allies arrayed against him at Gloucester Point. That morning, even before the French artillery began roaring into action, eight flatboats loaded with British soldiers had moved upstream in an effort to land on the Gloucester shore and flank the Allies who had pinned the British on Gloucester Point. Choisy's well-posted command detected the movement, and his field artillery spoiled the effort to get around the Allied flank. Battery 1A on the bluff above Yorktown joined in the effort to disrupt the enemy flatboats. The soldiers on one boat began to panic as iron balls rained down around them. They hurriedly rowed their craft to the nearest Gloucester beach and splashed ashore in utter confusion to join the troops there under Tarleton and Simcoe. This was probably the barge that was captured and, according to one source, held a 4-pounder field piece. The other boats. meanwhile, dodged the cannon shot and bursting mortar shells in their wild effort to return to shore. Miraculously, every man returned safely A second similar attempt may have been launched that same night; if so, it also came to naught.[86]

Digging Toward a Second Parallel

The possibility of Cornwallis's escape or relief from the outside world made it imperative that Washington press his advantage quickly. Preliminary work had already begun to locate approach trenches and to start their construction so that a second siege line could be drawn closer to Yorktown—one that would force Cornwallis into submission. Allied engineers spent most of the night of October 10 gathering data for starting the approaches for the new line. The date for establishing the second line was moved forward, at least in part in response to the recent intelligence about Clinton's plans to reinforce Cornwallis.[87]

Although the Allied artillery firing from the first parallel had been effective, it had not driven the enemy troops from the two detached British redoubts (9 and 10) guarding the left flank of Cornwallis's position. That failure was not lost on the American and French soldiers, who realized a direct assault to gain the works was now all but inevitable.[88]

The construction of the zigzag approach trench in preparation for the construction of a second parallel lay in the province of the French, for until Redoubts 9 and 10 fell, it would be difficult to advance from the American section of the line below Yorktown. The French approach probably began sometime during the overcast night of October 10. The line was started near where the Goosley and Hampton roads intersected above the Grand French Battery. The trench was driven straight east across the Hampton road in the general direction of British Redoubt 9. Less than 300 yards from its beginning point the trench angled sharply northwest and continued for a slightly longer distance in that direction. Angled obliquely to protect the sappers from enemy enfilade, the approach trench was brilliantly designed so that either section, if extended, would pass at least 40 yards in advance of any British fortification.[89]

Primary responsibility for advancing the approach rested with the chief sapper. Armed with pickax, shovel, fascines, and gabions, he pressed ahead behind a specially constructed gabion five feet in diameter by six or seven feet high and stuffed with fascines and earth to protect him from musket fire. As he advanced the trench, the chief sapper staked fascines and gabions along either or both edges, depending on the direction of enemy fire, and filled them with the excavated earth. He left a trench about one-and-one-half feet wide at the top by two feet deep for succeeding sappers to enlarge.[90]

The second sapper followed on the heels of the first, with others following him. Each followed procedures prescribed by fortification theorists. The second sapper widened and deepened the trench by about six inches. The third and fourth sappers did the same, carefully digging out and down the same distance. By the time they finished, the trench was about three feet deep and three feet wide at the top, but only two feet wide at the bottom, "on account of the talus that is left on both sides of this ditch, from the excavation of which sufficient earth has been gathered, to form, toward the place [besieged], an epaulement which can only be penetrated by cannon ball."[91]

When the first four sappers finished, a fifth took up the task. He was responsible for staking a revetment of fascines to further strengthen the sides of the trench, while a sixth sapper steadily moved supplies forward to insure that the advance workers had complete access to materials. It was a laborious, dirty, and dangerous job, but one essential to victory.[92]

The Night of the Hot Shot

Work on the approaches to a second parallel was grounded in a sense of urgency. Cornwallis had already indicated his growing desperation by launching his recent flatboat debacle. The best way to prevent him from retreating by water was to destroy Cornwallis's surviving ships, and this the Allies set out to accomplish. The British general had already scuttled many of his smaller craft in order to establish a water barrier through which Allied vessels could not navigate. French gunners were prepared to cripple his remaining vessels with hot shot fired from two powerful 24-pounder cannon moved from the Grand French Battery for use near the York River in Battery 1A.[93]

The principal reason hot shot—cannonballs heated red hot—was used against enemy vessels was because the missiles set wooden craft ablaze. If well or luckily aimed, they could enter the powder room and obliterate all aboard.[94] Heated shot was also an effective way to sow confusion in enemy ranks, destroy wooden houses, powder magazines, and ammunition dumps behind enemy lines. Firing hot shot, however, was extremely dangerous and required the utmost precaution.

First, gunners placed the powder charge in the cannon barrel and rammed it home. Next, they covered the charge with a wad followed by a piece of turf or a cushion of water-soaked hay. After the muzzle of the piece was slightly elevated and sponged out, the cannon shot—heated on a special furnace and grate—was removed with tongs when it was red hot and placed directly into the gun muzzle. As soon as it was inside, another gunner ignited the charge. The discharge sent the scorching ball flying toward its objective.[95]

At 8:00 p.m. on October 10, Rochambeau's cannon in Battery 1A began tossing hot shot at Cornwallis's remaining ships. A principal target was the 26-gun frigate *Guadaloupe*, which had begun a series of menacing maneuvers designed to forestall a French ground attack against the Fusiliers' Redoubt. Driven off by the glowing balls, any one of which could have fatally ignited the warship, the *Guadaloupe* sought refuge under the Yorktown cliffs. The more powerful *Charon* was not as fortunate. The 44-gun frigate was set ablaze by the burning round shot. Most of her ordnance had been removed for use in the land batteries, but she was still a valuable prize nonetheless. While attempting to flee, the burning *Charon* collided with a transport and the conflagration quickly spread to other vessels. The frigate drifted slowly across to Gloucester Point, where she burned to the water's edge and sank.[96]

"The whole night was nothing but one continual roar of cannon, mixed with the bursting of shells and rumbling of houses torn to pieces," wrote Captain James Duncan in his diary.[97] Another observer was even more graphic, noting how burning ships lit the sky over the York River and billowing black smoke funneled up to meet low-lying clouds. Spectators assembled on housetops under risky conditions to watch the scene revealed by the licking flames in the harbor.[98]

The view of Cornwallis's ships burning and the fireworks etching their way across the sky produced more emotion-filled descriptions than any other single event of the siege. "Never could a more horrible or more beautiful spectacle be seen," reported a senior French officer. "On a dark night, the ships with all their open portholes discharging sheafs of fire, the cannon shots that were going off, the appearance of the whole roadsted, the ships under topsails flying from the burning vessels, all that formed a terrible and sublime spectacle."[99]

As was so often the case, Dr. Thacher found himself in an excellent position to watch the unfolding historic action, which on this night he labeled "this splendid conflagration." The ships, he wrote,

> were enwrapped in a torrent of fire, which spreading with vivid brightness among the combustible rigging, and running with amazing rapidity to the tops of the several masts, while all around was thunder and lightning from our numerous cannon and mortars, and in the darkness of night, presented one of the most sublime and magnificent spectacles which can be imagined. Some of our shells,

National Park Service, Colonial National Historical Park, Yorktown Collection

Twice during the twentieth century, underwater archaeology was conducted on the British ships sunk in the York River. Here, one of the cannons, perhaps from the 44-gun frigate *Charon*, is hauled from the muddy water.

overreaching the town, are seen to fall into the river, and bursting, throw up columns of water like the spouting of the monsters of the deep.

Yet another witness, this one unnamed, recorded that the scene "afforded an awful and melancholy sight. The *Charon* was on fire from the water's edge to her truck at the same time. I never saw any thing so magnificent."[100]

By daylight, before Cornwallis's remaining ships had weighed anchor and repaired out of range to the Gloucester shore, the French hot shot battery had succeeded in firing two more transports as well as a corsair of 20 guns.[101] The Allied siege pieces now dominated the waters off Yorktown. Unwilling to risk serious injury or destruction, British ships remained well to the north beyond danger.

The morning sun greeted a stunned Cornwallis. British ships lay smoldering and steaming in the harbor if they floated at all. His naval support was all but gone. His ramparts, the only thing that protected him from the aggressive and well-led Allied army, were damaged in many places, and his exhausted and demoralized soldiers were laboring to repair them before the Allies renewed their onslaught. Flames flickered in the ruins of houses destroyed during the night by Washington's relentless artillery.[102] Cornwallis's only consolation—and it was a minor one—was that British fire ships had temporarily scattered the French vessels hovering near the mouth of the York River.[103] If Clinton's promised relief had been at hand, Cornwallis might have had reason for hope. But alas, it was not.

The victor of Camden and Guilford Court House was enough of a general to know his situation had deteriorated significantly during the night. The worst was yet to come.

Chapter 10

The Earth Trembles

*D*espite growing optimism among the Allied rank and file that
Lieutenant General Charles, Lord Cornwallis, was tiptoeing
along the brink of disaster, Washington was wisely
unwilling to leave anything to chance. Although his
opponent's capitulation appeared more likely with each passing day,
Washington knew that as long as the possibility of relief remained, the
normally aggressive Cornwallis was not about to simply lay down his
arms and surrender. If relief did not arrive, It was much more likely that
Cornwallis would make a determined attempt to break free.

Thus far, the artillery along the first parallel had been successful in
battering the British defenses. The guns had also wrecked much of the
enemy's shipping and driven off those ships that remained. Washington
hoped to draw the ring tighter still, to place the chance of Cornwallis's
escape beyond all rational consideration. He still hoped to convince de
Grasse that all was well on the river above Yorktown, and that the
stationing of French warships there was all that was needed to seal Lord
Cornwallis's fate.

Possibly in ignorance of the maneuvers performed by British fire
ships the night before, Washington tried to convince the French admiral
these dangers had passed and that Cornwallis no longer possessed
facilities for constructing such vessels.[1] He also wrote him on the evening

of October 11 of his design to open a second parallel because, as he put it, "the Enemy's conduct has continued passive beyond our expectation."[2]

The French admiral remained unconvinced of the wisdom of the Virginian's request. In deference to him, however, de Grasse sent two of his officers to inspect the state of Cornwallis's water defenses and the river near Yorktown.[3] Other than the frigate *Guadeloupe*, which still hugged the cliffs near the town, Washington assured de Grasse, "there remains no other armed Vessel of consequence. I submit to your Excellency whether two frigates will not answer all the purposes of the station above York."[4] The admiral still vacillated, refusing to commit his force in so active a manner. The Frenchman was wary of the arrival of Admiral Robert Digby's fleet from New York; if it arrived, he wanted every warship at his disposal available to meet the threat.

While de Grasse pondered his decision, the Allies increased their artillery barrage against the British in Yorktown. After the awesome nighttime bombardment, Lieutenant James scribbled in his journal, "I now want words to express the dreadful situation of the garrison . . . . Upwards of a thousand shells were thrown into the works [during the] night, and every spot became alike dangerous." The situation was not about to improve with the coming of daylight. By midday Thursday, more than 50 guns and mortars were playing on Cornwallis's besieged garrison.[5]

The French gunners were still outperforming their American counterparts, however, a situation General Knox blamed on faulty ordnance. "Knox damns the Pennsylvania shells, as not being well cast, varying greatly in weight, and especially for not being proved," remarked one officer. "As proof of the latter, he observed that the cores have not been well cleaned out; so that, if they in fact passed a proof, it is not a full evidence that they are sound, as any holes might be stopped up by the remains of the cores."[6]

One special target was the Yorktown residence of militia General Thomas Nelson. He was invited into an American battery by Lafayette, who asked Nelson which building he would like the cannons directed against. "There, to that house," Nelson indicated, pointing toward an imposing brick structure beyond the British earthworks. "It is mine, and, now that the Secretary's is nearly knocked to pieces, is the best one in town. There you will be almost certain to find Lord Cornwallis and the British Headquarters."[7] The answer surely surprised Lafayette, but he took the officer at his word and issued the order. Within a few minutes, American balls were tearing into the structure. Some lodged in the sturdy brick walls, where they remain to this day. The Nelson house was damaged extensively, but survived the siege.

Deserters continued to trickle into the Allied posts to tell of the dreadful effect of the cannonballs and bombs on Cornwallis's garrison. The ceaseless fire was taking an immense human toll, and casualties continued to climb.[8] On October 11, the newly completed French mortar battery 4A, located west and slightly ahead of the other structures comprising the Grand French Battery, finally went into action, adding its deadly 12-inch bombs to the cacophony of noise and destruction. Their main focus was to set fire to the abatis around British Redoubt 9. Structure 3A, with its four 24-pounders on the knoll west of the Yorktown Creek branch ravine also opened fire.[9]

"I saw with astonishment today on my watch how the enemy cannon balls of 24 and more pounds flew over our whole line and the city into the river," wrote Hessian Johann Döhla, who recorded one of the best accounts of the Allied barrage of October 10 and 11—the heaviest two days of bombardment during the entire siege. "[T]hey often struck through 1 and 2 ships, and indeed even struck 10-12 times in the water; yes, some even went clear across the river to Gloucester, where they even injured some soldiers on the beach." The level of artillery and mortar fire was heavier than he had ever witnessed, and he would never again see such a sight in his life:

> I saw bombs fall into the water and lie there for five, six-eight and more minutes and then still explode, which was so repulsive and horrible in the water that one can scarcely believe it. It showered upon the river bank the sand and mud from, below; if one sat there, it felt like the shocks of an earthquake. The fragments and pieces of these bombs flew back again and fell on the houses and buildings of the city and in our camp, where they still did much damage and robbed many a brave soldier of his life or struck off his arm and leg. I had myself a piece of an exploded bomb in my hands which weighed more than 30 pounds and was over three inches thick.[10]

Döhla also wrote about the casualties suffered in his German unit: "On the left wing with the detachment stationed in the outermost redoubt was killed on the 11th of October Grenadier Schoenlein by a howitzer ball, while Grenadier Buehlmann and Private Menzel of Eyb's Company were wounded in this redoubt, from the Onsbach regiment also a man was completely blown to pieces by a bomb which fell on him."[11]

The seeming imbalance of the surviving accounts regarding the effect of the bombardment reflects the gross disparity in the actual exchange of iron. Cornwallis's gunners could barely get near their pieces to respond to the blanket of Allied firepower. British earthworks crumbled faster than their owners could repair them. More cannon were dismounted and broken with each passing hour.[12] An astonishing admission recorded by a French soldier summed up the effectiveness of Cornwallis's artillery when he wrote, the British return fire slackened "to such a degree that it really was not dangerous."[13]

Despite the overwhelming (some would say surprising) success achieved by the guns of the first parallel, Washington's soldiers expressed their eagerness to move ahead with a second parallel. Knox's negative view of the potential of American ordnance firing from the substantial distance of the first parallel drew adherents, despite obvious evidence to the contrary. Still, the effectiveness of the American gunnery paled when compared to that of the French. "Though I am ready to acknowledge their abilities, yet I do not imagine they can work miracles," explained one officer who echoed what had apparently become familiar sentiment in Allied circles regarding the first batteries:

> We know what has, in times past, been the effect of British cannon against our earthen defences, and I cannot think ours to be essentially different. At the present distance of our batteries (say 500 yards), they might fire till Christmas without materially lessening the enemy's force. The shells, falling in a variety of places, are doubtless troublesome, and do some mischief. I am impatient to get nearer to the enemy, that our work may be more speedily accomplished, and our ammunition not thrown away.[14]

Behind the lines, meanwhile, routine camp life continued. Requests for food supplies, forage, and liquor to support the army went out with regularity.[15] American officers tried by courts-martial colleagues who had violated one or more of the "Rules and Articles of War." Captain Patrick Duffy of the 4th Continental Artillery was found guilty and sentenced to be dismissed from the service for "drawing a Sword on Capn

Ballard and attempting to Stab him, and firing a Pistol at him when unarmed, also for a most disgraceful breech of Friendship, in seizing from Lt Blewer a loaded pistol & snapping the said at him."[16] Lieutenant William Munday of the 2nd New York Regiment was likewise dismissed for "wilful disobedience of orders and neglect of duty."[17]

Problems with discipline and morale plague every army to one degree or another, but the actions of a few malcontents at Yorktown did nothing to slow down the Allied juggernaut.

The Second Parallel

Digging their way closer to the enemy was the immediate objective of the French and Americans on October 11, and most of the activity that day was directed with that end in mind. Baron von Steuben's division assumed trench duty in the American sector promptly at 11:00 a.m. The troops relieved by von Steuben's soldiers repaired to the rear and began making more fascines and gabions.[18] Along the French line, Major General de Chastellux took command and made similar preparations to advance another parallel.[19]

Anticipating the opening of the second parallel that evening, and fearing a sortie by the British, von Steuben issued orders that no soldier would be permitted to lay down that night; instead, each would remain alert with musket in hand. Von Steuben was with his men at the front in the company of General Wayne at 4:00 p.m. when Count Deux-Ponts rode up and presented the compliments of Baron de Viomenil, the French officer commanding on von Steuben's left.

"General von Steuben," began Deux-Ponts. "General de Viomenil observed, while visiting the trenches, that your division is extremely weak, and as it is probable the enemy might make a sortie tonight, he would be pleased to reenforce your left wing with from 500 to 800 men, if you think it necessary."

Within earshot of General Wayne, von Steuben offered his reply. "Count Deux-Ponts, you may tell General de Viomenil I do not want any reenforcements, and if the enemy should attack me, I shall answer for being able to hold the battery until he can arrive to support me." Before Deux-Ponts left, the Prussian added, "Tell General Viomenil that if he is

Independence National Historical Park

Brigadier General Anthony Wayne

attacked, he can rely on me to support him with 800 men in two columns."

Once Deux-Ponts had ridden away, Wayne remarked, "General, you have only 1,000 men in your entire division!"

"No doubt of it," replied von Steuben, "that is my calculation too. But if it should so happen, I should, on my own responsibility, leave 200 men to defend the battery, and with the remaining 800 attack forthwith in two columns."

Though it is difficult to picture the Prussian officer with a smile on his face or a twinkle in his eye, on this occasion it is certain he had both. "If I am guilty of a certain amount of gasconade with regard to the number of my men, it is for the honor of his country."

With that, Wayne took the baron by the hand and, turning to address the officers present, exclaimed, "Now, Gentlemen, it is our duty to make good the exaggeration of Baron Steuben and to support him just as if he had double the number of troops he has."[20]

* * *

By dusk, all was in readiness for beginning the new parallel. Nelson's militia advanced to man the first line while von Steuben's men prepared to start the second.[21] The zigzag approach had been pushed ahead 200 yards by French laborers until the end lay within 360 yards of the closest British line fortification and on a level with the detached enemy Redoubts 9 and 10. The forward part of the approach trench was now beyond the effective supporting distance of the Allied artillery, and the French engineers proceeded to trace the parallel from its head.[22] The menacing posture of Redoubts 9 and 10 prevented them from projecting the line all the way to York River. Work on the second parallel would necessarily be limited to the left sector until these two enemy structures could be stormed and captured.

After sunset and in complete silence, von Steuben's men moved forward armed with shovels, spades, grubbing hoes, gabions, and fascines.[23] They passed across the low ground extending in front of the ravine forming the French supply depot of the first parallel (just to the west of Battery 9A). There, at about 8:00 p.m., they began breaking the sandy turf along a short zigzag approach trench and a truncated section of what would become the second parallel.[24]

Farther left, about 750 Frenchmen from the Regiments Gatenois and Deux-Ponts also moved ahead, some through the approaches and some by way of the natural cover of the Yorktown Creek morass. The French were charged with completing the greater part of the parallel, their section extending from the edge of Yorktown Creek ravine east to a juncture with the Americans near the latter's zigzag approach.[25]

According to fortification experts, the second parallel should always be constructed with a thicker parapet, more solidly revetted than the first because of its closer proximity to enemy cannon.[26] Instead of wooden strips to lay out the line, gabions served to trace it. "These gabions, even when empty," explained one theorist, "will stop the course of a musket bullet."[27] Placed side by side, the gabions were filled and covered with excavated dirt and formed the foundation for the parapet.

Covered somewhat precariously by the distant guns of their first line of batteries, the French and Americans dug hurriedly through the night. "In one hour's time we had ourselves completely covered, so we disregarded their [British] cannonading," wrote Lieutenant William Feltman of Pennsylvania in his journal. The British did their best to disrupt the digging. "[T]hey discharged a number of pieces at our party, but they had but little effect, they only wounded one of our men," remembered the Pennsylvanian. As it turned out, the danger came not from the front but from the rear. "We were in the center of two fires, from the enemy and our own, but the latter was very dangerous; we had two men killed and one badly wounded from the French batteries, also a number of shells bursted in the air above our heads, which was very dangerous to us. We dug the ditch three and a half feet deep and seven feet in width."[28]

The Americans ended their sector of the second parallel slightly more than 300 yards from the western side of British Redoubt 9. This accomplishment, devised by Washington's engineers, was substantial. Not only had the men advanced the second parallel on schedule, they also cut in half the distance required for a direct attack against the enemy earthwork, should such a bold move become necessary. In order to resist an enemy enfilade from the direction of Redoubt 9, von Steuben's soldiers raised a strong epaulement at the end of the line facing the British earthwork.[29] Colonel Richard Butler of the 5th Pennsylvania took direct command of approximately 600 American workmen while General Wayne guarded their efforts at carving out and building up the second parallel with two battalions of Pennsylvania troops.[30] Cornwallis's guns, as best they could, blazed away at the first parallel, evidently unaware of the new thrust by the Allies.[31] "The opposition from his Lordship [is] by no means equal to our expectations, considering his high character, for bravery, military skill and activity," remarked Washington's secretary.[32]

General Rochambeau's French finished most of the second parallel that night. In addition to the four battalions of Gatenois and Royal Deux-Ponts, auxiliaries composed of grenadiers and Chasseurs of the

Regiment Saintonge, along with 800 night fatigue men, assisted in building the parallel.[33] The trench in their sector stretched farther west than the first line and rested on the edge of the morass leading toward Yorktown Creek. Like the first parallel, the second bisected Hampton Road and extended east to meet the American sector. The French portion measured more than 650 yards in length, or three times as long as the part completed by the Americans under von Steuben. French engineers also traced the positions of redoubts on the line that would be necessary to protect workers preparing the artillery batteries. Amid the explosions of British guns, the French soldiers forged on.[34]

At one point during the night there occurred another unsuccessful attempt by St. Simon's volunteers to take the Fusiliers' Redoubt opposite the far left of the Allied line. German Captain Johann Ewald of the Régiment von Bose firmly believed the French stormed the redoubt and were driven back. "The besiegers have . . . attempted to take the advanced redoubt by a coup de main during the night," he wrote in his diary, "but were driven back with bloody heads." Viscount Rochambeau, the son of the French commander, also wrote about that attack: "It should be pointed out that since our first parallel was very close to the left side of the enemy's fortifications, the enemy imagined that the attack in setting up the second parallel would come at this point, and we surprised them with our activities which broke on their center." The push against Cornwallis's "center" and the Fusiliers' Redoubt, if there was such a thrust, was almost certainly a feint designed to divert British attention away from the real action taking place on the growing second parallel.[35] French losses that night consisted of four men killed or wounded, most or all of whom were probably felled by Allied ordnance.[36]

In addition to digging the parallel, the workmen hurriedly raised the parapets of the redoubts and even began palisading the ditches in expectation of British countermeasures to the advance. Already some cannon were being hauled forward to provide a modicum of artillery support to the newly established line.[37]

The second parallel thus progressed rapidly, and the French soldiers worked strenuously to perfect it and give it utility. De Chastellux witnessed the apparent surge of French adrenalin that night as he watched Rochambeau's troops labor through the night. These men, he said, "seemed to become rivals to each other . . . Even the obscure common soldier, whose life and death is equally consigned to oblivion, strove to outdo his renowned officers in . . . daring enterprizes, and went up in defiance of the enemy to the very edges of their intrenchments." The general also praised the unarmed worker. "The miner," he explained, "with the axe in his hand, advanced with a determined step through a shower of grape-shot to cut down the tree at his leisure, which perhaps shielded him from destruction."[38]

The French soldiers and workers manifested bravery in the face of fire from British howitzers and royal mortars that proved surprisingly ineffective. More dangerous to the French were their own gunners, who fired over their heads from behind them. The short-fused bombs were discharged at low elevations that severely threatened, and in some instances harmed, the Allied workers.[39] "Our shot and shells going over our heads in a continual blaze the whole night," wrote an American soldier. "The fight was beautifully tremendous."[40] At one point in the night the French gunners suspended their fire for fear of hitting friends, at which time the British managed to get off a flurry of fire. Cornwallis's gunfire slackened quickly once the French adjusted their ordnance and resumed shooting.[41]

As the workers labored and the heavy weapons did their work, both sides sent out foot patrols to probe and feel the enemy. The result was a fitful exchange of musketry between the lines, the shots lighting up the darkness with sudden bursts of deadly ground-level fireworks.[42] Inside Yorktown, Cornwallis's troops huddled and waited under the steady rain of exploding shells and bounding solid shot. So swift and hard came the Allied barrage that the British gunners were at a loss as to how to effectively get off rounds of their own. "The noise and thundering of the cannon, the distressing cries of the wounded, and the lamentable sufferings of the inhabitants, whose dwellings were chiefly in flames," wrote Lieutenant James in his journal, "added to the restless fatigues of duty, must inevitably fill every mind with pity and compassion who are possessed of any feelings for their fellow creatures."[43]

Dawn, October 12

If Cornwallis harbored any illusions that the Allies would remain content behind their first parallel of earthworks, they were quickly dispelled when British eyes peered across the Yorktown plain at daybreak on Friday, October 12. Before him was a second parallel running east to west for some 750 yards. Soldiers guarding the line were drawn completely undercover, fully hidden from British arms.[44] "This business [constructing the second parallel] was conducted with the same secrecy as the former," explained Washington. The British "did not by their conduct and mode of firing, appear to have had any suspicion of our Working parties till day light discovered them to their Picquets."[45]

Once the second line was spotted, the British released a thunderous volley of mortars, shells, and musket balls against the new earthworks in the hope of impeding further work on the line. Cornwallis's gunners also fired a tremendous amount of grapeshot, along with grenades discharged from royals (mortars). This time the ordnance had the desired effect—at least temporarily. The barrage was effective enough to force Allied workers to hunker down and all but cease their labors.

Even as his guns were firing, Cornwallis was casting his eyes about for infantry assistance. With a second parallel so close to his works, he knew his line was highly vulnerable to an infantry assault. He needed more soldiers to defend his position. There was only one place from which he could draw reinforcements: Gloucester Point. Lieutenant Colonel Thomas Dundas was ordered to move immediately to Yorktown with part of his brigade. The move left Banastre Tarleton in charge at Gloucester Point, for Lieutenant Colonel John Graves Simcoe, his superior, had been ill and was still too sick to command in the field.[46]

The British cannonade, so effective in the short-term, withered away and virtually ceased once the French and American artillery zeroed in on the enemy gun positions. As the sun rose higher that morning, Allied heavy weapons located and sank yet another British vessel, this one a fire ship. More deserters slipped and crawled their way through the line to report on the widespread damage behind the Yorktown fortifications.[47]

The principal focus of this new round of fire was directed against the beleaguered Hornwork, the large segment of entrenchments protruding south overlooking Hampton Road. The barrage, reported Lieutenant James, was notably destructive:

> In 52 minutes after my arrival in the hornwork the enemy silenced the three left guns by closing the embrasures, shortly after which they dismounted a 12-pounder, knocked off the muzzles of two eighteens, and for the last hour and half left me with one 18-pounder

with a part of its muzzle also shot away, with which I kept up a fire
till it was also rendered useless.[48]

Most of the damaging fire originated with the French mortar battery
4A and two of the gun units composing the Grand French Battery, 7A and
8A. About 9:00 a.m., however, fears grew that the latest round of firing
might inflict serious harm upon the 300 workmen laboring in broad
daylight in the second parallel. After some discussion, the firing from
these batteries was suspended. Once again the British were quick to take
advantage of the respite and opened vigorously with their own ordnance.
The French responded with their guns in Batteries 3A and 5A, units
whose fire were less likely to strike laborers in the trenches.[49]

American batteries also contributed to the barrage. An examination
of the ordnance fired from a few of the American batteries paints a picture
of the intensity of these actions. From October 11 to 12, Battery
13A—the stronghold along the river on the far right dubbed the
American Grand Battery—fired 336 24-pounder shot, 263 18-pounder
shot, 199 10-inch mortar shells, 159 8-inch and 94 five-and-one-
half-inch howitzer shells. The mortar battery behind Redoubt 12A
expended 166 10-inch shells, while gunners inside Battery 10A, on the
extreme left of the American sector of the first siege line, discharged 450
18-pounder balls. The quantity and variety of this ordnance is compelling
evidence of the unrelenting character of the Allied firepower at
Yorktown, and speaks to the enormous supply of ammunition at their
disposal.[50]

Early this same morning, October 12, Washington's officers began
seriously contemplating the reduction of British Redoubts 9 and 10.
Their capture would permit the Allies to prolong and complete the second
parallel all the way east to the York River. The capture of these exposed
structures would also allow Washington to tighten his grip around
Yorktown and complete the siege in customary fashion.

During the brief cessation of fire that morning, Rochambeau and his
son boldly set forth to inspect the enemy defenses about Redoubt 9. Both
returned safely. Rochambeau reported that the redoubt's abatis and
palisades were still strong and evidently unaffected by the Allied
artillery. "We must redouble our fire to break them and destroy the top of
the parapet," he told his aides. "We shall see to-morrow whether the pear
is ripe."[51] It was beginning to be clear that artillery alone was not going

to drive the British out of the two strong redoubts. If they were going to be taken, it would have to be done with the bayonet.[52]

As Rochembeau inspected the enemy fort, American troops on his right worked to improve their position, armed with a growing sense of success and anxious to get on with the final dislodgement of Cornwallis. Baron von Steuben and his subordinate Anthony Wayne were standing close together watching the men work when a British shell struck the line. The men fairly stumbled over each other getting to cover, with von Steuben hitting the ground first and Wayne falling on top of him. "I always knew you were brave, General," explained von Steuben to the Pennsylvanian as he stood up and brushed himself off, "but I did not know you were perfect in every point of duty; you cover your General's retreat in the best manner possible."[53]

The general feeling among the Allies on October 12 was that their guns would be in position along the second parallel to attack in two days. At that time, the final drive for the capture of Yorktown would take place. "I am fully convinced," concluded General Lincoln, "that the Siege will not last more than 12 days more and that Cornwallis & his troops must in that time be ours."[54]

A buzz of activity consumed the day. At noon, Lincoln's division took its turn in the new line, drums beating and colors flying in proclamation of this latest insult to British arms. Cornwallis's working guns sent out a short but noisy greeting without the desired effect.[55] Von Steuben's troops, relieved of trench assignment, renewed their labors behind the lines making palisades—items of vital utility for the redoubts of the second parallel—while more fatigue men worked until 5:00 p.m. fashioning still more fascines, gabions, and saucissons for the supply depot. The Virginia Militia joined the Regular troops in improving the new fortifications.[56] St. Simon, with Count de Custine, took over the French command. Labor in that sector was performed by two battalions each from the Regiments Bourbonnois and Soissonois, supported by auxiliaries of the Gatenois and Agenois units.[57] "Never did greater harmony subsist between two Armies than between the French and American," wrote Adjutant General Edward Hand. "Their only [contention] is who shall do most."[58]

That night, the Allies resumed the work on the new redoubts that had been disrupted by enemy musket fire during the day. Work also began on establishing the new batteries from which final reduction of Cornwallis's

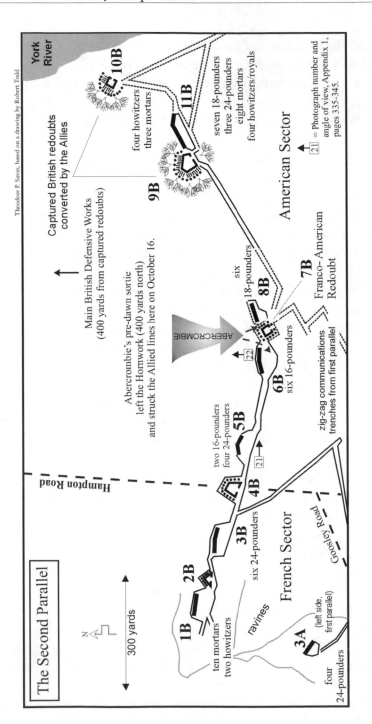

The Second Parallel

Theodore P. Savas, based on a drawing by Robert Todd

York River

10B

four howitzers
three mortars

9B

11B

seven 18-pounders
three 24-pounders
eight mortars
four howitzers/royals

Captured British redoubts
converted by the Allies

Main British Defensive Works
(400 yards from captured redoubts)

Abercrombie's pre-dawn sortie
left the Hornwork (400 yards north)
and struck the Allied lines here on October 16.

American Sector

21 = Photograph number and
angle of view, Appendix 1,
pages 335-345.

ABERCROMBIE

8B

six
18-pounders

7B

Franco-American
Redoubt

22

6B

six 16-pounders

zig-zag communications
trenches from first parallel

5B

two 16-pounders
four 24-pounders

21

Hampton Road

4B

3B

six 24-pounders

Goosley Road

French Sector

N

300 yards

1B

2B

ten mortars
two howitzers

ravines

3A

(left side,
first parallel)

four
24-pounders

garrison would hopefully be realized. The night passed with precarious uncertainty for the American laborers, for the British were now directing their bombs and grenades with greater precision. Several Allied soldiers died as a result, and many Frenchmen fell wounded. Though deadly and stressful, work on the second parallel continued. Surrounded by darkness and occasionally the target of shell, mortar, grenade, or musket fire, the soldiers finished the parallel and its three palisade redoubts, widened the zigzag approaches to allow for the movement of more supplies and troops, and began construction on five batteries, four in front of the French section and one before the shortened American sector.[59]

Because of their exposed positions, the batteries had to be erected as quickly as possible and guns slipped into them to play immediately upon the town. The most important of these were the ricochet and mortar batteries, situated so that the besieged could be enfiladed with telling effect. "These batteries," explained artillery expert Louis de Tousard in his important work *American Artillerist's Companion, or Elements of Artillery*,

> should be completed in 24 hours, as they have no embrasures and their tracing does not require the same precaution; wherefore, 14 or 16 are allotted to every 20 feet; the epaulement can be made with many fascines, and the trench enlarged as much as may be necessary, even sunk three or four feet: passages of communication are made round the rear, to prevent any embarrassment; and the powder magazine is constructed in the space between this communication and the battery.[60]

The Initial Structures of the Second Parallel

Just as was done with the structures comprising the first parallel, a numbering sequence (from left to right in the line) has been assigned to identify each structure so this text can be cross-referenced with the fortifications on the accompanying maps, and visa versa. For example, the letter "B" assigned to a number means the structure was part of the second parallel, and the lower the number, the farther to the left it was located. Thus 1B was the French fortification on the far left of the second parallel. The letter "A" was used earlier in the text to identify structures in the first parallel. What follows is a brief description of the initial structures of this line. A more detailed explanation, including armaments, is found later in the book once the line was completed by the capture of Redoubts 9 and 10 and erection of American Battery 11B.

Structures 1B, 2B, and 3B: The French batteries on the second parallel began at the far left of this new line. All three (1B, 2B, and 3B) were west of Hampton Road and east of the Yorktown Creek ravine, upon which the parallel rested. Battery 1B, a mortar-howitzer emplacement, was about 300 yards west of Hampton Road and the same distance north of the Grand French Battery complex. Structure 2B was next in line to the east, the first French redoubt in the second parallel. Battery 3B, a six-gun structure, was only a short distance west of 2B.

Redoubt 4B straddled Hampton Road.

Battery 5B, a second cannon battery designed to hold six pieces, was erected a short distance east of the Hampton Road.

Battery 6B was plotted out by Rochambeau's soldiers about 125 yards east of Battery 5B. This powerful 6-gun emplacement was erected at the eastern end of the French sector.[61]

Franco-American Redoubt 7B was built next to Battery 6B, where the zig-zag communications trench entered the second parallel.

Battery 8B, the sole American battery along the second parallel (until the fall of Redoubts 9 and 10 and erection of Battery 11B between them), joined Redoubt 7B on its right (or eastern) side. The Allies concentrated two batteries and one redoubt in this area because it was where the American and French lines joined, and a nearby ravine was used to funnel troops and supplies to the front—prime targets for an enemy attack.

The new second line was vulnerable to attack throughout this phase of the construction. Once these batteries and forts were completed and equipped, however, the Allies would be in a position to exert tremendous pressure against the trapped British. "As soon as our Batteries on the Second Parallel are completed," wrote Edward Hand in reference to Cornwallis's troops, "I think they will begin to Squeak."[62]

In point of fact, Cornwallis had long since begun "to squeak." The American and French artillery in and along the first parallel played incessantly on the British earthworks ringing Yorktown. On the 13th, more Allied fire was directed against Redoubts 9 and 10 and against the Fusiliers' Redoubt on the other end of the line, all with hope of burning and smashing the abatis surrounding these structures and damaging their

An aerial view of some of the reconstructed works from the second parallel looking southwest. In the left foreground is Battery 8B, the only American battery on the second line until the capture of Redoubts 9 and 10 and the erection of Battery 11B between them. In the center is Franco-American Redoubt 7B. Note the zig-zag communications trench running from it to the left of the picture. On the far right is French Battery 6B. A deadly British pre-dawn attack struck this sector of the Allied line on October 16. *National Park Service, Colonial National Historical Park, Yorktown Collection*

palisades, fraises, and epaulements. Defections from the British ranks grew, with 14 deserters entering the Allied lines on October 13 to report upon the confused state of affairs in Cornwallis's camp.[63] One Hessian soldier described the effects of an exploding bomb that hurt four men, two of them mortally. The British light infantry, stationed in the Hornwork, suffered an inordinate number of deaths and injuries.[64] From October 12 to 13, Allied guns rained a hail of shot and shell upon the enemy never before witnessed on the American continent.[65]

*   *   *

While these batteries and those of the French in the first parallel continued to rake the British lines, Washington concentrated on advancing his ordnance closer to finish off Cornwallis's obviously weakening resistance. Most of the American guns, for the moment, would have to remain in the first line until the American sector of the second was prolonged and completed. That, in turn, depended upon the speedy capture of the detached British works that blocked the way and thwarted progress: Redoubts 9 and 10.

Time, however, was not Washington's friend. The Virginian needed to capture the redoubts, finish his second line, and crush Cornwallis before General Clinton arrived with reinforcements or withdrew the Yorktown and Gloucester troops, and before Admiral de Grasse's time expired and he returned to the West Indies. The pair of redoubts, therefore, was the key for concluding the siege and forcing a surrender. By October 13, everyone in the Allied command structure agreed that only a direct assault against these strongholds would accomplish the desired objective. The terrain helped dictate this conclusion, for the ground between the second line and the British redoubts was not well suited to the further erection of batteries.[66] Only by taking the enemy structures, concluded one officer, could American guns "level the way, cut off palisades, and beat down other obstructions."[67]

Saturday passed routinely, with the French and American armies engaged in gathering component siege materials to complete the batteries and, at the appropriate time, extend the second parallel to the York River. That afternoon, Pennsylvania Colonel Stephen Moylan marched his 4th Regiment Continental Light Dragoons south along the Hampton Road,[68] probably to watch for any British presence in the James River and spread the alarm should any trouble arise in Washington's rear. Also behind the lines, a general court once again convened, found three men guilty of infractions of the war articles, and sentenced two of them to death. The third was "sentenced to receive 25 lashes on his naked Back four mornings successively, amounting in the whole to 100 lashes."[69]

Discipline problems, however, were remarkably low considering the size of the armies surrounding Yorktown. Problems of supply were more severe, and unit quartermasters and commissaries worked endlessly to insure proper commodities reached the troops. By early October, many items were in short supply, including shoes, clothing, ammunition for the militia, and flints for their weapons.[70] Even firewood became scarce. Washington was forced to issue orders restricting the soldiers' "pernicious practice" of burning fence rails stripped from the fields around Yorktown.[71] A shortage of tents in some commands prompted the general to direct redistribution of the shelters so "the troops sharing the same danger and fatigue, may enjoy equal benefit."[72] While liquor comprised part of a soldier's authorized ration, its distribution had to be carefully regulated in the camps around Yorktown. "The Commanding Officer is astonished, that altho' he has repeatedly Issued Orders, to prevent the Soldiers' Wives selling Rum, the practice is still continued," complained Colonel John Lamb of the 2nd Artillery Regiment, who was remonstrating against unbridled profiteering from the article, which might jeopardize the performance of his troops. "He earnestly calls on each Officer, to exert himself, to prevent it in future; as it is not only injurious to the Service; but, disreputative to the Regiment."[73]

More of a problem than the control of liquor sales was that of furnishing adequate clothing for the American troops, and especially for those of the militia. Military commander Nelson constantly called upon the officials of Virginia to meet not only the needs of his state, but those of the Allied Army as a whole. Nelson even acted on requests from the French Army for forage for its horses,[74] although his prime commitment remained to his own command. From his headquarters in front of Yorktown, Nelson addressed pleas to the Virginia delegates in Congress to provide clothing for his men, complaining, "The few Troops we have now in the Field are not fit to be seen."[75] Colonel Charles Dabney of the 1st Virginia State Militia Regiment wrote to another officer, "Pray let me hear when there is a probability of drawing clothing for the soldiers—they are very naked and are get'g sickly."[76]

Colonel Dabney was not exaggerating the sickly condition of his men. Washington himself claimed in a note dated October 14, 1781, that clothes for his dragoons were desperately needed, citing the authority of the regimental surgeon who "assures me 100 of the Men are literally naked at this advanced season." Illness was spreading through the French and American armies, and the wide variety of diseases threatened to reduce the effectiveness of Washington's command. With or without proper clothing, medical stores were woefully inadequate to combat the problem. The clinging humidity of the peninsula combined with hot days and cold nights to produce a host of illnesses ranging from the common cold to malarial fever. At one time, as many as 400 French soldiers were carried sick on the rolls. The Allies had thus far eluded the dreaded smallpox.[77]

Matters on the far side of the lines were even worse. Cornwallis's troops suffered from a variety of illnesses, including smallpox which, when added to the effects of the Allied artillery, further depleted British effective strength and morale. Allied soldiers encountered more corpses on their patrols as black men and women were mercilessly sent out of Yorktown to wander and die from disease or starvation. "Almost every Thicket affords you the Disagreeable prospects of a Wretched Negroes Carcase brought to the earth by disease & famine," wrote General Hand to a friend. "The Poor deluded Creatures were either so much afraid of the displeasure of their owner that they voluntarily starved to death or were by disease unable to seek sustenance."[78] Sickness and the lack of proper facilities and medical provisions to combat it plagued both sides throughout the siege.

At noon on October 13, Lafayette's light infantry division moved forward into the lines and relieved the troops of Lincoln.[79] Baron de Viomenil took charge in the French sector of the second parallel with the Regiments Agenois and Saintonge assisted by the grenadiers of Soissonois and Royal Deux-Ponts. After dark, work resumed building the new line. Some 300 French soldiers perfected the redoubts and trench system while another 300 began work on the new batteries everyone hoped would bombard the British into submission.[80]

In the American sector, Lafayette sent one regiment from the first parallel to relieve the guards on the right flank of the second parallel. British gunfire increased to a heavy level in response to these moves, and injuries increased among the Allies. An American captain and a private were killed at the outset of the barrage. Two more soldiers were wounded when they stopped to collect working tools.[81] The firing remained steadier than usual through the afternoon and into the night, during which time the French lost a half-dozen men killed and more than 25 wounded. "[T]he fire of the enemy this Night became brisk, both from their Cannon and Royals and more injurious to us than it had been," noted Washington in his diary. "[S]everal men [were] killed and many wounded in the Trenches, but the Works were not in the smallest degree retarded by it." A French officer commented on the same bombardment when he wrote, "the enemy seemed to have been saving up their ammunition for the second parallel. It was of very small caliber and very effective, being fired at short range."[82] All of these losses took place on the line. Surprisingly, no casualties were suffered during the daring attempts by

French grenadiers to set fire to the abatis and palisades bordering the British fortifications. Three efforts to accomplish that objective failed, but the grenadiers returned unscathed.[83]

Work on the French batteries progressed satisfactorily despite the human casualties incurred on the line. One of the units, probably Battery 3B, was built as a combination reverse and ricochet battery.[84] The Chevalier d'Ancteville compared the role expected of the second parallel batteries to that of the first ones:

> By these dispositions we . . . placed ourselves in position to bombard them [the British] by direct, reverse, and cross fire. Up to this time we had only counter-batteries. One could not procure ricochets, except by prolongation, on a flattened front too close to obtain the desired effect. It was necessary to restrict ourselves to fire from above, to ruin the abatis and the fraises; to cut down the parapets with our guns and howitzers and mortars; to fill the enemy's works with shells and bombs, and to throw these into their camp, in order to occasion heavy losses; to instill terror by an unremitting fire. [Now it became our objective] to let daylight into their works and put ourselves in position to force them, if their resistance should become too stubborn.[85]

Sometime between 9:00 and 10:00 p.m., American workers on the right side of the second line began building Battery 8B. British heavy weapons fire, up to this time trained mainly on the French activity, vigorously attended the new endeavor.[86] "It happened to be our lot to lie in the trenches just in the rear of the battery exposed to all their fire; and now were I to recount all the narrow escapes I made that night it would almost be incredible," observed Captain James Duncan in his diary. He continued:

> I cannot, however, but take notice of a remarkable and miraculous one indeed. About midnight the sentry called "A shell!" I jumped up immediately to watch the direction, but had no suspicion of its coming so near until it fell in the center of the trench, within less than two feet of me. I immediately flung myself on the banques among some arms, and although the explosion was very sudden and the trench as full of men as it could possibly contain, yet not a single man was killed and only two of my own company slightly wounded.[87]

American casualties increased sharply as a result of the British effort, even as Battery 8B neared completion the following day. Rather than withdraw to avoid exposure to enemy artillery, as the Allies had done on previous occasions, the soldiers building Battery 8B bravely pressed on. For some, it was a costly decision. At dawn, the British greeted them with a barrage of grapeshot and shell. Ten men from a single Continental regiment were killed or wounded in a matter of minutes while working or guarding the second parallel.[88] While each loss was painful to someone, overall losses remained low and were far below what Washington and his officers had anticipated suffering. Unfortunately for many French and American soldiers, that was about to change.

Chapter 11

Night of Heroes

*E*arly on the Sunday morning of October 14, a redcoat entered the American lines. According to the deserter, Lord Cornwallis had suffered a crisis in command that threatened to compound his troubles. The British infantrymen, claimed the turncoat, refused to work on the entrenchments any longer. As an inducement to get his men back to their labors, Cornwallis spoke optimistically of the arrival of relief from New York, and had promised a cask of wine for each regiment.[1] News of these conditions in the enemy's camp gave the Allies even more hope that the end of the siege was within reach.

Preparing for the Attack

In addition to the good news of the crumbling conditions inside the Yorktown garrison, a feeling of anticipation filled the air. Something big was afoot. As General Washington's officers made private plans, the Allied camps buzzed with rumor. "This evening it is reported there is something grand to be done by our Infantry," Lieutenant William Feldman wrote in his journal.[2] Despite the secrecy surrounding the pending attack, most of the men were by now aware that any large-scale infantry action would probably involve the detached British redoubts that blocked progress on the second parallel. Their capture would all but guarantee an American victory at Yorktown.

Allied soldiers and workers anxiously pushed ahead, erecting batteries and improving their fortifications, dangerously exposing themselves to exploding British shells and a hail of deadly shot. Injuries and deaths increased along the lines. Since arriving at Yorktown, the Americans had lost only 15 killed and 29 wounded. French casualties through the afternoon of October 14 were substantially higher at 52 killed and 134 wounded.[3] The work performed that morning by the American fatigue party drew fire from several Hessian sharpshooters posted in their front, but colonial marksmen quickly silenced the enemy musketry.[4] About noon, von Steuben's division replaced Lafayette's in the trenches.[5] The French line was commanded by de Viomenil and de Custine; the Regiments Gatenois and Royal Deux-Ponts relieved the sector, later supplemented by four companies of Bourbonnois.[6]

Until October 14, most of the serious fighting at Yorktown had been conducted by artillery and mortar fire. While the big guns still had a large role to play, it was now time for the infantry to step forward and take a direct hand in the reduction of Cornwallis's defensive network. Before the foot soldiers could be used, however, the defenses around Redoubts 9 and 10 had to be softened up enough to make a successful attack more likely. Washington directed artillery from the first parallel batteries to pound and burn the abatis, palisades, and salient angles of those structures. On the far left, St. Simon opened a swift cannonade against the Fusiliers' Redoubt, a fire designed to create uncertainty in Cornwallis's mind as to the direction from which the next Allied maneuver might originate. Throughout, the British remained passive.[7]

Through more than half the day, French and American ordnance kept up a steady bombardment. From October 13 to 14, the American batteries (10A, 12A, and 13A) expended nearly 700 rounds of solid shot, shell, and mortar fire.[8] By 2:00 p.m. that Sunday, Washington's engineers informed him that his guns had had the desired effect, and that an assault on Redoubts 9 and 10 was now entirely practicable.[9]

Redoubt 10 (the so-called "Rock Redoubt"), the most distant of the pair, was located on the cliff above the York River. The British fort was square-shaped and smaller than Redoubt 9, a pentagonal stronghold 225 yards to the southwest. They were manned by details from the 33rd, 43rd, 71st, 80th, von Bose, and Prince Hereditaire regiments. Major James

Campbell commanded the men in Redoubt 10, while Lieutenant Colonel Duncan McPherson was in command inside Redoubt 9. According to the British orderly book for the 43rd Foot, 208 men held the redoubts. Probably 60-70 men manned Redoubt 10, with the balance holding the larger structure. Both were surrounded by ditches, abatis, palisades, and fraises. Their interiors were partitioned by stacked rows of casks filled with dirt and sand. Sandbags lined the tops of the parapets.[10] Despite the Allied day-long fusillade against their defenses, Redoubts 9 and 10 stood relatively unscathed as nightfall approached on October 14.

That afternoon, Washington's officers assembled to plan the assault. The meeting was filled with some dissension, principally among the French, who alone wanted to manage the strikes on both redoubts. When it became obvious that this idea was going nowhere, the conference degenerated into an acrimonious argument between Lafayette (arguing on behalf of the Americans), and de Viomenil (for the French) regarding whose troops were better soldiers.[11] Eventually, however, a decision was reached and the Allied officers fleshed out the details of the plan. It was agreed that two major attacks would be launched, one against each redoubt. Two feint attacks, one against the Gloucester Point works and the other on the far left of the Allied line, would distract the British.

The most difficult assignment fell to Baron de Viomenil, whose objective was Redoubt 9—by far the stronger of the two outposts. Count Guillaume de Deux-Ponts would lead the ground assault with 400 grenadiers and chasseurs of Regiments Gatenois and Deux-Ponts.

Lafayette's objective was Redoubt 10. The strike force selected for that honor was composed of light infantry pulled from three regiments: Lieutenant Colonel de Gimat's mixed battalion of men from Connecticut, Massachusetts, and Rhode Island (the latter were taken from Olney's 1st Rhode Island and included a large number—perhaps a majority—of black troops); Lieutenant Colonel Alexander Hamilton's New York and Connecticut battalion; and soldiers from Lieutenant Colonel John Laurens's New Hampshire, Connecticut, and Massachusetts battalion. The American column numbered about the same as the French: 400 men, plus a party of sappers and miners who would advance and clear a path for the attacking column. Reserves were selected from French and American units to follow up the assault or defend against a counterattack should the effort fail.[12]

A dispute as to who should lead the column threatened the success of the effort even before it began. Lafayette chose Gimat, who was described by an American captain as a "bold Frenchman" and Lafayette's favorite staff officer. It was not an unreasonable selection, but it deeply offended Alexander Hamilton, who believed that as Officer of the Day, he deserved the honor of leading the assault. Unable to convince Lafayette otherwise, Hamilton appealed directly to Washington and requested that he intercede on his behalf.

The French officer chosen by Lafayette was a native of Gascony and the son of a French military officer. Unlike Hamilton, Gimat had made a career in the military. At the young age of 14, he joined the service in 1761 as an ensign in the Guyenne Regiment. Befriended years later by Lafayette, he joined that officer's staff and sailed with the marquis for America, where he was given the rank of major. Early in 1781, Washington gave Gimat command of a light infantry battalion in Lafayette's Division, and now his mentor had tapped him to lead the entire assault column against Redoubt 10.

Hamilton's early years were vastly different. The future and first Secretary of the Treasury of the United States was born in the British West Indies, orphaned at 11, and apprenticed to a New York merchant who quickly recognized the young boy's genius and arranged for a formal education. A staunch and early supporter of independence, Captain Hamilton raised a company of artillery and as part of Knox's artillery regiment, led it with tremendous bravery and skill in the fighting for New York City and again at Trenton. Because Hamilton wielded a pen as skillfully as he did a cannon, Washington made him his personal secretary and aide-de-camp. Although he was an outstanding staff officer, Hamilton chafed for an active field command. In 1781, Washington finally acquiesced and assigned him to lead a light infantry battalion in Lafayette's Division. And so the matter stood.

For reasons that remain unclear, Washington countermanded Lafayette's selection of Gimat and gave the nod to Hamilton; Gimat would lead his own men—and only his own men—in the upcoming attack. Hamilton's own battalion was placed under the command of Major Nicholas Fish of New York. As the overall commander of the effort, to Hamilton would go any glory derived from a successful assault.[13]

The French and American batteries slowed their rate of fire as dusk approached. Across the river at Gloucester Point, Choisy prepared his men for what was supposed to be a feint against the British lines to distract Cornwallis. Instead, the French general readied his men for a more serious attack. Axes were distributed among the American militiamen to cut through the enemy palisades in front of the Gloucester Point works. The bold effort, however, was a spectacular failure. The soldiers moved out well, but quickly encountered a barrage of British fire that sent them stumbling rearward for cover. Choisy fell back to a position held by Lauzun and his cavalrymen, leaving behind 12 men killed and wounded in the fruitless effort.

Almost simultaneous with Choisy's failed Gloucester Point action was the planned movement against the Fusiliers' Redoubt. Whether it was a feint designed to draw Cornwallis's eyes and attention to the far right side of his line, or an all-out attack to capture the fort, is not clear. The night before, a party of French soldiers had crept into no-man's-land and set fire to the abatis protecting the redoubt. The anticipated conflagration failed to materialize, however, because the obstructions were comprised mainly of fruit trees instead of pine. Whether an attack or feint, it began and ended quickly. When it was over, sixteen men had been killed and wounded.

Later, several French officers explained the effort was indeed planned as a ruse, and at least one blamed de Custine, the commander of the Regiment Saintonge, for failing to vigorously open the feint as he had been ordered to do. According to this source, de Custine's effort did not even get underway until *after* Redoubts 9 and 10 had been carried. Baron von Closen, one of Rochambeau's aides, was sharply critical of de Custine:

> Instead of carrying it out at 7:30, he did so at 8:30, when all was quiet. Why? No one knows. A friend of mine from the Soissonnais regiment assured me that M. de Custine had drunk too much, and as I myself had sometimes seen him in that condition, I had no trouble in believing it. He got off with 24 hours' arrest and many jests. But this bad joke cost 9 men from the Soissonnais company of chasseurs and provoked once more a discharge of musketry from the cordon of the [British] fort.

Contemporary French maps of the siege, however, may tell a different story. They indicate the French intended to extend a line of works east from the Fusiliers' Redoubt, which of course could not have been done unless they were planning to capture the stronghold. Fortunately for the Allies, the outcome of the feint/attack was not critical to the success of the overall plan to reduce and capture Redoubts 9 and 10.[14]

The American Attack against Redoubt 10

The French and American guns fell silent in the growing darkness. A dense fog settled over the landscape. Half an hour passed. On the right side of the American sector, Hamilton organized his troops. Washington addressed them briefly in tones of encouragement, inciting them to bravery. You must "act the part of firm and brave soldiers," instructed Washington. "I thought then that his Excellency's knees rather shook," remembered Captain Stephen Olney, who led a company of men in the 1st Rhode Island, "but I have since doubted whether it was not mine."[15]

Around 7:00 p.m., six shots were fired from one of the French redoubts—the signal to start the attack.[16] Both columns, one French and one American, moved out simultaneously. Hamilton's American assault force, composed of the battalions under Gimat and Hamilton (Fish), and part of Laurens's, moved forward in two columns quickly and quietly from a position at or near the American Grand Battery (13A) of the first parallel. Because the watchword was silence and speed, muskets were unloaded; the redoubts were to be taken at the point of the bayonet.[17]

"[We] marched in good order. Many, no doubt, thinking, that less than one quarter of a mile would finish the journey of life with them," remembered Captain Olney. The moment of reckoning was at hand, and some of the men were a bit shaken at the prospect. "I had a chance to whisper to several of my men (whom I doubted,) and told them that I had full confidence that they would act the part of brave soldiers," recalled Captain Olney. "Let what would come," he continued. "[I]f their guns should be shot away, not to retreat, but take the first man's gun that might be killed."[18]

Gimat's battalion occupied the traditional post of honor at the front of the attacking column. It was composed of five companies from

Lieutenant Colonel
John Laurens

*Independence National
Historical Park*

Connecticut, two from
Massachusetts, and one
from Rhode Island. If
Gimat fell in the effort,
Major John Palsgrave
Wyllys, a native of
Connecticut, would then
assume command. This
same battalion had held
Anthony Wayne's right flank at the Green Spring engagement on July 6,
1781, and was recognized as the oldest and most experienced of the three
assaulting battalion organizations. Formed behind Gimat was Hamilton's
battalion, led this night by Major Fish. It consisted of two New York and
two Connecticut companies. Lieutenant Colonel Laurens led part of the
late Alexander Scammell's old unit—one company from Connecticut
and one from Massachusetts.

Laurens's task was to sweep his 80 soldiers left to take Redoubt 10
from the rear in order to prevent a retreat toward Yorktown by its
occupants. With Hamilton's force was a party of sappers and miners
under Captains James Gilliland and David Kirkpatrick, which moved
ahead of the soldiers to remove abatis and obstacles from the column's
path. Lafayette remained in reserve, where the rest of his troops under
Brigadier Generals Peter Muhlenberg and Moses Hazen awaited the
outcome of the assault. Two battalions under General Wayne stood ready
to support the attack of either the Americans or the French. Knox sent

forward four 3-pounders under Captain William Stevens to aid in the onslaught, if needed.

The advance moved out in the murky darkness, muskets empty and bayonets locked firmly in place. "When we had got about half way to the redoubt we were ordered to halt, and detach one man from each company for the forlorn hope," recalled Captain Olney. "My men all seemed ready to go. The column then moved on; six or eight pioneers in front, as many of the forlorn hope next, then Colonel Gimat with five or six volunteers by his side, then my platoon, being the front of the column." British gunners spotted the movement when the men approached the abatis and assailed Hamilton's troops with a thunderous discharge of grapeshot, shells, and iron cannonballs, apparently without noticeable effect. Approaching the smaller redoubt from the southeast, Hamilton's enthusiastic soldiers charged even before the sappers and miners could clear a path for them. Over the tangled abatis they plunged, tearing weakly-planted and damaged palisades from the earth. The previous artillery barrages had damaged the outer defenses, one witness recalled, leaving holes "large enough to bury an ox in." Somehow they managed the ditch and its obstructions, clawed their way through the fraises, and mounted the parapet—all with such suddenness that the British and German soldiers inside found themselves abruptly overwhelmed. One of the first to enter the structure was Lieutenant John Mansfield, who led 20 men from the 4th Connecticut in the forlorn hope at the tip of the attacking column. A British defender lunged at Mansfield and wounded him with a bayonet thrust. Hamilton later urged a commendation be awarded the young officer for his bravery.

Captain Olney led the assault of Gimat's Battalion. As they approached the front of the line of abatis, the British leveled their weapons and delivered what Olney later remembered as a "full body of musketry." The flash and crash of enemy fire triggered a resounding "huzzah!" from the Americans. Figuring the order for silence had now been broken by everyone, Olney joined in, shouting, "See how frightened they are, they fire right into the air!" As the captain and his men waited, the squad of pioneers began swinging their axes and cutting off the abatis, which had been crafted from the trunks of trees, the trunk fixed to the ground and the limbs sharpened to impale unlucky attackers. "This seemed tedious work, in the dark, within three rods of the enemy," remembered Olney, who ran some distance to the right to look for a way

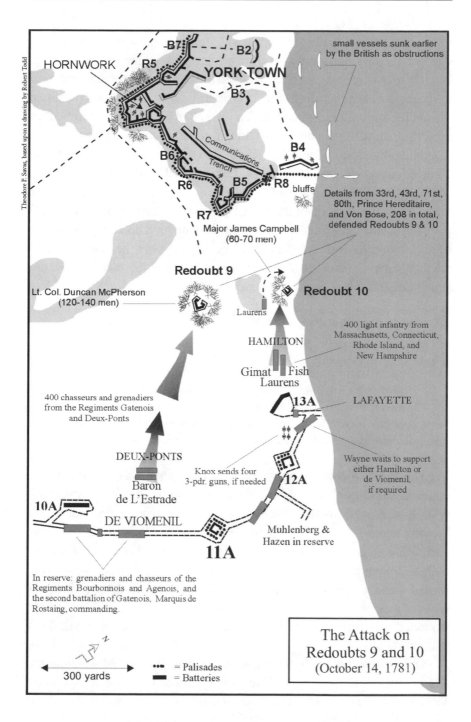

Theodore P. Savas, based upon a drawing by Robert Todd

B7   B2 }

HORNWORK   R5   YORK TOWN

B3

small vessels sunk earlier
by the British as obstructions

B6   Communications   B4

R6   B5   R8   bluffs

R7

Major James Campbell
(60-70 men)

Details from 33rd, 43rd, 71st,
80th, Prince Hereditaire,
and Von Bose, 208 in total,
defended Redoubts 9 & 10

Redoubt 9

Lt. Col. Duncan McPherson
(120-140 men)

Redoubt 10

Laurens

HAMILTON

400 light infantry from
Massachusetts, Connecticut,
Rhode Island, and
New Hampshire

Gimat   Fish
Laurens

400 chasseurs and grenadiers
from the Regiments Gatenois
and Deux-Ponts

13A   LAFAYETTE

DEUX-PONTS

Baron
de L'Estrade

Knox sends four
3-pdr. guns, if needed

12A

Wayne waits to support
either Hamilton or
de Viomenil,
if required

10A

DE VIOMENIL

11A

Muhlenberg &
Hazen in reserve

In reserve: grenadiers and chasseurs of the
Regiments Bourbonnois and Agenois, and
the second battalion of Gatenois, Marquis de
Rostaing, commanding.

N

300 yards

••• = Palisades
▬ = Batteries

The Attack on
Redoubts 9 and 10
(October 14, 1781)

to slip through. Unable to find a way through the obstructions, and worried his own men would get through first without him, Olney hurried back. With a way now clear, he managed to push through in the very front of the mass of attackers and enter the ditch, a dozen or so of his own men stumbling and yelling with him. The brave officer calmly climbed up onto the parapet and yelled out "in a tone as if there was no danger, 'Captain Olney's company, form here!' On this I had not less than six or eight bayonets pushed at me," he remembered. Using his espontoon (thrusting spear or half-pike) Olney parried several attempts to skewer him. Unfortunately, one of the British bayonet thrusts snapped the blade from his own weapon, and several enemy bayonets "slid along the handle of my espontoon and scaled my fingers; one bayonet pierced my thigh, another stabbed me in the abdomen just above the hipbone."[19]

Olney left this account of his experience:

> One fellow fired at me, and I thought the ball took effect in my arm; by the light of his gun I made a thrust with the remains of my espontoon, in order to injure the sight of his eyes; but as it happened, I only made a hard stroke to his forehead. At this instant two of my men, John Strange and Benjamin Bennett, who had loaded their guns while they were in the ditch, came up and fired upon the enemy, who part ran away and some surrendered; so that we entered the redoubt without further opposition.

The hand-to-hand-fighting along the parapet was a wild affair, remembered Olney. One of his sergeants, Edward Butterick, was stuck with British steel in the stomach, though the wound did not prove life-threatening. Another, Sergeant Brown, had fired his musket and was attempting to reload it when a British infantryman jabbed him in the hand with his bayonet. Private Peter Barrows suffered a terrible disfiguring wound when a lead ball passed through his mouth, shattering his lower jaw. "My company, which consisted of about forty . . . had five or six wounded . . . [But] I believe we had none killed," reported an amazed but thankful Olney.

Other casualties included Captain Thomas Hunt of Massachusetts, also of Gimat's Battalion, and Gimat himself, who was shot in the foot by a musket ball before he could get past the abatis. He was wounded "about the first fire of the enemy," wrote Olney, "and I suppose it took all the volunteers to carry him off, as I never saw any of them afterwards." David Kirkpatrick of the sappers and miners was likewise felled by the British as he tried to negotiate the ditch. A member of Hamilton's forlorn hope, Sergeant William Brown of the 5th Connecticut, was shot through the hand. For his gallantry, Brown was later awarded a special "Honorary Badge of Military Merit," which in later years became known as the Purple Heart—the first American military award given for valor regardless of rank.[20]

Major Fish advanced his men slightly to the left of Gimat's force and also took part in the storming of the redoubt. Lieutenant Colonel Laurens, meanwhile, led his 80-man column around and into the rear area of the fort. The timing of the entire proceeding was as close to textbook perfect as possible. To their credit, the British and German defenders had tried to repel the lightning attack, but with so few men and so little advance warning, there was little they could do to stop the flood of Americans pouring into the ditches, over the parapet, and into the fort. Those who were not cut down inside fled out the rear, where many were intercepted by Laurens's men, who almost completely blocked the back of Redoubt 10. Captain Stephen Betts of the 3rd Connecticut, who was with Laurens in the flanking movement, was wounded during that maneuver. The captured included three officers (including Major Campbell of the 71st Foot), and 17 soldiers; the balance made good their escape. Alexander Hamilton exhibited conspicuous courage during the attack, as did Colonel Charles Armand Tuffin and other volunteer officers of the legion, each of whom offered an example of coolness and discipline the command proudly emulated.

Guarding against the unexpected, Lafayette directed yet another battalion forward, this one under Lieutenant Colonel Francis Barber, consisting of New Hampshire and New Jersey troops. Barber was ordered to support Hamilton, consolidate his stunning success, and repel any counterattack Cornwallis might launch. The entire effort, from beginning to end, had consumed barely ten minutes. Redoubt 10 was securely in the hands of the Americans.

As one might expect, Hamilton was jubilant at his victory and, all things considered, the cost in human lives was not excessive: nine men had been killed and 25 wounded. The enemy lost eight soldiers killed and wounded and some 20 captured. Contemporary accounts claim Hamilton's men were instructed not to take prisoners, this in retaliation for British atrocities against American captives earlier in the war. Whether this is true has not been conclusively determined. Many witnesses claimed the enemy begged for their lives. According to one account, a New Hampshire captain tried to kill British Major Campbell, but was personally restrained by Hamilton from completing the deed. If the British did indeed plead for their lives, did liquor account for their actions? The wounded Captain Olney thought so. "I believe they were all half drunk; in this condition, the British soldiers generally fight," he wrote with exaggeration. "We had not been in the redoubt more than five minutes, when Charles M'Afferty, an Irishman, and pretended Freemason, got out a bottle of wine, and invited me to drink. Who but an Irish or Englishman would have thought of such a thing?" asked Olney, who was deemed mortally wounded by the surgeons. "When my wounds came to be examined, next day, that on my left arm, which gave me most pain when inflicted, was turned black all round, three or four inches in length; neither skin nor coat broken," Olney wrote in his diary. "The stab in my thigh, was slight, that in front, near my hip, was judged to be mortal, by the surgeons, as a little part of the caul protruded. I was carried to the hospital at Williamsburgh, twelve miles, and in about three weeks my wounds healed, and I joined the regiment." In addition to the handful of prisoners, three small caliber cannon were also taken in the attack.[21]

"There was not an officer nor soldier whose behavior, if it could be particularized, would not have a claim to the warmest approbation," exuded Hamilton. "The enemy are entitled to the acknowledgment of an honorable defence," he added. Not every American deserved Hamilton's praise. New Hampshire Private Asa Redington recounted an embarrassing example of cowardice during the attack against the redoubt:

> A Sergeant in our company, a fine, big, strapping man, who rather boasted of his physical powers, dropped down at the first fire, singing out 'Oh, God, I am a dead man!' Our men charged right over him, and after the works were taken, details were sent back to pick up the dead and wounded, but this Sergeant could not be found. At sunrise next morning he joined the company, safe and sound. This kind of dodging duty was too much for our Captain Chase to stand, so he disarmed the Sergeant, tied onto him, a wooden sword, and had him paraded up and down the American lines as a skulker.

It was so humiliating to the Sergeant that he was taken sick, and in a week was dead.[22]

The attack on Redoubt 10 generated a substantial amount of patriotic fervor and considerable renown—to say nothing of controversy—for its participants. Hamilton received the combat glory he so coveted by leading the dramatic and successful assault. The far-sighted officer was well aware that successful combat provided a wonderful foundation for political ambition—which Hamilton possessed in spades. His enhanced reputation created some jealousy among his associates, chief among them Peter Muhlenberg, the Pennsylvania general who led the First Brigade of Lafayette's Division in a supporting role during the attack. In his hastily written report, Hamilton committed the unpardonable sin of omitting reference to Muhlenberg's role in the action, an error for which Muhlenberg in later years manifested much displeasure. The general's supporters (largely his grand-nephew and biographer, who were one and the same) cited his being wounded at the head of the storming party as the principal reason Hamilton's report went uncontested. They failed to discredit Hamilton's credibility, however, for regardless of how they spun the account, it was Hamilton and not Muhlenberg who had commanded the entire body of men responsible for taking Redoubt 10. As was borne out by the evidence, efforts to discredit the young New Yorker simply lacked substance.[23]

As soon as Hamilton had secured the earthwork and stationed his reserve troops, Lafayette hurried forward. He dispatched a message to de Viomenil of the French attacking force: "I am in my redoubt. Where are you?" De Viomenil's troops were pinned down by enemy musket fire a short distance from Redoubt 9, waiting while French pioneers cut through the abatis barricade surrounding it. "Tell the Marquis I am not in mine," replied the baron, "but will be in five minutes!"[24]

The French Attack against Redoubt 9

The 400 chasseurs and grenadiers of Regiments Gatenois and Deux-Ponts (which had benefitted from an infusion of enlisted men to bring them up to strength) departed their trenches for Redoubt 9, apparently somewhere on the right of Battery 10A in the American sector of the first parallel. The movement began at precisely the same time Hamilton's party left to begin its assault. "No one knew what all of this meant," wrote Georg Daniel Flohr, a German serving in Regiment Deux-Ponts, "but we found out rather quickly." Flohr was the son of a butcher and a small farmer from Sarnstall in the Duchy of Zweibrucken. He had joined the regiment in June 1776, two months before his 20th birthday, never imagining he would be fighting the British half-way around the world in North America.[25]

The men were led by the very able Count Deux-Ponts, in whom de Viomenil expressed unbridled confidence, and his subordinate, Lieutenant Colonel Baron de L'Estrade. The men in the attacking force received well wishes from the troops remaining behind, a gesture that touched Deux-Ponts deeply. "That moment seemed to me very sweet," he wrote, "and was very elevating to the soul and animating to the courage."[26]

Each soldier carried with him 60 rounds of ammunition, and the attacking force moved forward in column by platoons across ground personally reconnoitered that afternoon by Deux-Ponts. The men had orders to remain silent, threatened as Georg Daniel Flohr remembered, "with the loss of their lives." Nor were they to stop and assist the fallen. Officers following in the rear did so armed with a directive to kill any cowards who broke for safety. Two sergeants, eight carpenters, and 50 chasseurs of Regiment Gatenois led the way, most of the latter armed with fascines to aid in crossing the ditch. Eight more chasseurs carried ladders for scaling the parapet. Following the Gatenois chasseurs were the grenadiers of that regiment. A column of grenadiers and chasseurs of the Regiments Bourbonnois and Agenois, and the second battalion of Gatenois commanded by Marquis de Rostaing, all in reserve. In addition, two 4-pounder pieces manned by the French were posted in the area between Redoubts 9 and 10 to reinforce the grenadiers and chasseurs, if needed. Baron de Viomenil remained in the rear with the support troops where he might better oversee developments.

A British sentry on the left issued a challenge, but no one answered. The men continued moving forward. As Deux-Ponts approached the target in the darkness, a startled "Wer da?" ["Who goes there?"] jumped from the throat of one of the German sentinels stationed on the left. Again, no one answered. The French instead did as they were directed and forged ahead under strict orders not to fire their weapons before gaining the top of the parapet, nor to enter the structure except on explicit directions to do so. According to Flohr, the German repeated the question three times before leveling his musket and shooting into the threatening darkness. A volley of musketry issued from the British redoubt as Deux-Ponts's troops halted before the sturdy abatis protecting the earthwork. The surprise attack was no longer a surprise.

"It was as bright as daylight, but we ignored the firing and kept marching," wrote Flohr after the war. Wounded men screamed for assistance as their comrades ran at the double-quick. Despite the heavy Allied artillery bombardment of the previous days, the wooden barrier had not been visibly weakened. According to Deux-Ponts, it remained "strong and well preserved." A French general proclaimed the abatis was in "much better condition than it was hoped to find it." Indeed, wrote a French engineer, the line was "still unbroken." Stunned by this discovery, the French holding the vanguard of the assault force wielded their axes with every ounce of energy they could muster, knowing their lives hung in the balance. The British and Germans, meanwhile, continued shooting into the darkness at the stymied soldiers; French casualties grew at an alarming rate. "[W]e fell just like snowflakes," Flohr remembered. "One could think that it rained bullets." Deux-Ponts agreed, adding that the delay "cost us many men and stopped us for some minutes."

After several awkward and dangerous minutes, the carpenters pulled the outer abatis away. Deux-Ponts and his men surged forward the remaining 25 paces to the ditch, into which they poured by the score. Stuffed into the depression, remembered Flohr, we remained "without protection from the fire out of the redoubt." Although unshielded from the heavy fire, the British and German soldiers aimed too high, and most of the shots missed their mark. Above the French heads were the heavy palisades, which the carpenters chopped at with their axes in an effort to open passages into the fort. Using their ladders to surmount the ditch as well as hands and feet, the men wiggled and pulled their way up the inside face of the ditch. Only then did Deux-Ponts give the order to fire.

French officer de Lameth was the first to reach the crest, where he met a burst of Hessian gunfire that wounded him in both knees. He fell back into the ditch. L'Estrade also rolled into the ditch when a soldier lost his foothold and fell backward against him. Some 200 onrushing French soldiers trampled over L'Estrade, a veteran of numerous sieges in

National Park Service, Colonial National Historical Park, Yorktown Collection

Redoubt 9 (top) held perhaps as many as 140 British and Hessian soldiers when it was attacked by Count Deux-Ponts and 400 French chasseurs and grenadiers on the night of October 14. This aerial view looking southwest shows the reconstructed earthworks, including the adjoining American Battery 11B (dubbed the new Grand American Battery), which was erected following the capture of Redoubts 9 and 10. For more images of this portion of the Yorktown works, see Appendix 1, views 15, 16, 18, 19, and 20.

Europe. Somehow he emerged from the fray unscathed except for a few bruises and a bit of embarrassment. Straining to reach the epaulement, Deux-Ponts grasped the extended arm of one of his young lieutenants, Jean François de Sillegue, who hoisted him to the top. The count reached the crest in time to see his helper buckle and fall with a mortal injury. Many of the British were armed with axes, "and with them split the heads of many of us right through the middle as we climbed up."

According to Flohr, Baron de Viomenil cut quite a picture in the midst of the murderous melee. The officer was "girdled with a leather belt over his uniform, in which he had stuck two pistols on each side and he had a saber in his hands." The baron informed his men that the soldier "who should reach the top of the redoubt before him and reach his hand down to him, would be remembered by him and be given a good reward."

The French drove relentlessly forward but stopped to deliver a musket volley into a Hessian-led bayonet charge. With that, they leaped into the redoubt. Accounts differ as to what happened next inside the redoubt. Many of the Germans had taken refuge behind barreled partitions in the fort and began surrendering. They quickly realized "that everything was lost," recalled Flohr. Deux-Ponts's men gave a loud cheer, "Vive le roi!," which was immediately taken up by the troops behind them. The screams of the wounded and unwounded, intermingled with the continuing discharge of weaponry, may have prevented the French officers from gaining immediate control of their men. Redoubt 9 was designed to hold about 200 men. Now, its 120 defenders were joined by several hundred French, all jammed together into a fort with a circumference of only 103 yards, their emotions locked into survival overdrive. According to Flohr, what followed is what often resulted in hand-to-hand affairs in small spaces—a period of savagery. This episode differed from similar events in that French may have killed French.

"The soldiers everywhere were so enraged and excited that our people killed each other," Flohr explained. Members of the Regiment Gatenois, who had white uniforms and had suffered the heaviest losses at the head of the attack, "struck down everyone who wore blue coats. Since the Deux-Ponts regiment also wore blue, very many were stabbed to death that way. Some of the Hessian and Ansbach troops wore uniforms almost identical to ours," continued Flohr, "and the English wore red, which in the dark of night seemed blue as well, and things went very unmercifully that night." So heavy were the dead and dying that carpeted the inside of the redoubt by the time the officers resumed command, Flohr concluded, that "one had to walk on top [of the bodies]." How many were killed by friendly fire and steel is unclear, but the German observer put the number at 20.

Because of the delay in penetrating the abatis and the carnage once inside the stronghold, French casualties were much higher than those suffered by the Americans at Redoubt 10. That is about all everyone agreed upon. According to Deux-Ponts, one officer was killed and three wounded, and another 21 from his regiment and 56 from Gatenois were killed and wounded (81 men total). Flohr put the number at 41 killed and 41 wounded. The best approximation puts French losses at 15 killed and 77 wounded. Among the dead were Lieutenant de Sillegue and Captain de Barthelot of the Gatenois regiment. Captain de Sireuil of the same unit was injured with a broken leg. Staffer de Lameth suffered wounds to his kneecap and thigh. The seriously wounded were treated on the spot, while others were conveyed by ambulance wagon to the field hospital and some on to the hospital at Williamsburg. The British lost 18 soldiers killed and between 37 and 50 captured (depending upon the sources). Most of them, with their commander, Lieutenant Colonel Duncan McPherson, eluded the French and escaped. The French also captured two small howitzers and some hand grenades.

Deux-Ponts's troops carried Redoubt 9 in perhaps one-half hour—or twenty minutes longer than it took Hamilton to take Redoubt 10. The reasons why are obvious: the French target was larger, its defenses stronger, and it held at least twice as many defenders. Most accounts from immediately after the war to the present draw a striking contrast between the attacking columns, with the Americans led by Hamilton gallantly mobbing over the obstructions to get at the British, while the French professionals stood and waited for their sappers to cut through the defenses, suffering needless losses in the process. However, Flohr's recently discovered manuscript suggests that many of the losses suffered by the French *may* have been self-inflicted during the melee inside the fort—something Deux-Ponts and other French writers would never have publically acknowledged. Also, neither French effort against the other parts of Cornwallis's line (the Fusiliers' Redoubt and across the river at Gloucester Point) had been carried off well. "The success of the French attack was marred by unnecessary blunders," concludes historian Robert A. Selig, the researcher who found and first used Flohr's recollections to advantage. These blunders, he continued "if widely known, would have greatly damaged the image of the professional soldier that the French were anxious to maintain." Whether Flohr's account of what happened inside the redoubt are accurate will never be known with certainty.

Once the structure was secure, de Viomenil rushed forward to prepare a defense against an expected British effort to retake it. Already, Cornwallis's artillery was beginning a tremendous fire in retaliation for the loss of the key positions. A counterattack seemed imminent. Looking over the parapet, Deux-Ponts was nearly struck by a ricocheting cannonball that hurled sand and gravel into his eyes. Unable to see, he removed himself to the rear to seek medical attention, ending his participation in what he later termed "the happiest day of my life."[27]

Washington, with Knox and Lincoln and their aides, monitored the progress of the attacks from an exposed position in the Grand French Battery. Fearing for the safety of his chief on the open ground, Colonel David Cobb urged Washington to step back. "Colonel Cobb," answered Washington as he calmly scanned the foggy darkness, "if you are afraid, you have liberty to step back."[28] A short time later, a musket ball struck a cannon and rolled down it to fall at Washington's feet, eliciting more concern for the commander's safety. Knox grasped his leader's arm, exclaiming, "My dear General, we can't spare you yet," whereupon Washington responded, "It is a spent ball, and no harm is done."[29]

When the assaults were over, Washington evinced pure delight at their outcome. "The work is done, and well done," he told Knox, turning to his servant William to ask for his horse.[30] Later, he noted in his diary his great joy at the Allied victory over the redoubts: "The bravery exhibited by the attacking Troops was emulous and praise worthy. Few cases have exhibited stronger proofs of Intripidity [sic], coolness and firmness than were shown upon this occasion."[31]

*   *   *

Behind the Yorktown defenses, Cornwallis's troops mobilized to beat back a general offensive. The suddenness and vigor of the Allied attacks left them bewildered and apprehensive. "There must have been 3,000 men, French and Americans . . . who undertook this assault," believed Conrad Döhla. "At this occurrence the alarm was sounded through our entire camp; all the troops were ordered out onto the ramparts. The whole left wing gave out some musketry fire. We expected that they would close in on our left wing in order to storm our entire line."[32]

According to Colonel Butler of the 5th Pennsylvania, following the capture of the redoubts the Allies purposefully spread an alarm "around the British line in order to ascertain what weight of fire they could produce [in reply]." Contrary to other reports, Butler claimed the enemy response "proved very faint." Most accounts, however, agree British artillery poured forth a tremendous response to the attack, and the Allies lost many men on the night of the 14th to shot and bombs directed against the captured redoubts. Together with the continuous heavy musket noise, the guns created an infernal racket. "Such firing never was heard in America," recorded one witness. "You would have thought Heaven and Earth were coming together."[33]

Some of Cornwallis's troops fleeing the captured redoubts were cut down in the hail of shot from their own Yorktown works. One German soldier was found in three pieces. The enemy fire effectually delayed and impeded the Allied plan to complete their second parallel.[34] Through the night, more soldiers defected from the British ranks.[35] Cornwallis's ammunition supply dipped lower still. His defenses had deteriorated under the incessant Allied cannonade and were now alarmingly weak. By this time, reported a British naval lieutenant, they were "scarcely tenable."[36]

Completing the Second Parallel

The capture of Redoubts 9 and 10 gave the Allies significant advantages in terms of closing the distance to the main enemy line and gaining a solid position on terrain level with that occupied by Cornwallis in Yorktown.[37] The latter advantage would be of profound benefit once guns were established on the conquered ground. As soon as the redoubts were deemed secure and it was determined the anticipated counterattack would not materialize, the Allies quickly set to work to consolidate their gains.

Almost immediately, fatigue groups set forth to complete the second parallel in the dark night of October 14-15. Five hundred of Rochambeau's Frenchmen followed a flying sap dug along the ground

350 yards between the epaulement to the east of American Battery 8B and the structure just taken by Deux-Ponts and their countrymen. American troops of Lafayette's Division joined those of von Steuben's (Wayne's Brigade) under Colonel Walter Stewart in excavating a trench linking Redoubts 9B and 10B together (the captured British redoubts formerly designated 9 and 10). Simultaneously, troops in the American sector of the first parallel began digging an extensive communications trench 760 yards long toward Redoubt 10B near the York River. This trench branched forward from the first line near the American supply depot just west of Redoubt 12A.[38]

"Each man of the fatigue party carried a fascine, [and] a shovel or a spade," wrote Lieutenant Feltman, "and the remainder of our Division went as a Covering party to our troops who stormed the works."[39] Another man present remembered that "every officer and soldier took his shovel and spade and after placing a tier of gabions, went to digging to fill them up as fast as possible." Within 45 minutes, the troops were under cover. "Easy digging; light sandy ground," wrote Pennsylvania major Ebenezer Denny in his diary.[40]

By 10:00 p.m., the Regiment Bourbonnois entered the line as a guard unit to ward off British sorties. Elsewhere on the parallel, 200 more French laborers worked to ready the batteries and perfect the communications to the rear previously established. By dawn, the second parallel with its concomitant network of communication lines was completed all the way east to the York. Throughout this construction period, British guns blazed away. Most of the shot and shell flew harmlessly above the heads of the Americans, but the French workers, farther west along the new parallel, sustained exceptionally heavy losses.[41]

Completion of the second parallel during the night of October 14-15 marked a waning in importance of the first line. The batteries of the first parallel had admirably fulfilled the mission for which they had been established, namely, to cripple the enemy guns so as to permit the creation of a second, closer and more dangerous, approach. Henceforth, the first parallel assumed a supportive function. October 14 was its final day of decisive service.[42]

The Allies shared ardent hopes on Monday, October 15. The capture of the enemy redoubts launched the week on an optimistic note. French and American soldiers watched diligently for growing signs of

Cornwallis's trauma, anticipating what could now only be his inevitable capitulation. Early that morning, Washington issued a formal congratulatory message to his men:

> The Commander in Chief congratulates the Allied Army on the Success of the Enterprize last evening against the two important works on the left of the enemys line: He requests the Baron Viomenil who commanded the French Grenadiers and Chasseurs and the Marquis de la Fayette who commanded the American Light Infantry to accept his warmest acknowledgments for the excellency of their dispositions and for their own Gallant Conduct upon the occasion and he begs them to present his thanks to every individual officer and to the Men of their respective Commands for the Spirit and Rapidity with which they advanced to the Attacks and for the admirable Firmness with which they supported themselves under the fire of the Enemy without returning a shot.[43]

And well might Washington be elated by the victory pulled off by his troops. Not only did the taking of Redoubts 9 and 10 close off Cornwallis's left flank to the river and permit extension of the second Allied parallel, but it also gave Washington an excellent position from which his guns would command British communication lines across the river to Gloucester Point. Moreover, strategically placed cannon and mortars would soon be able to bombard the waterfront of Yorktown and enfilade much of the enemy position.[44] Once the new batteries were completed and ready for use, ricochet firing would become the order of the day. "It is the surest way to keep the besieged from having any cover and to disconcert their batteries," noted one observer.[45]

In the morning, Colonel Philip Van Cortlandt of Lincoln's division advanced his New Yorkers to occupy the redoubt captured by the French. His troops moved forward with drums rolling and banners flying, an affront that brought forth a deadly volley from Cornwallis's gunners. The hail flew past Van Cortlandt's soldiers, doing them no harm, though it killed two bystanders, one French and one American. Baron von Steuben put a stop to the display just as Van Cortlandt entered the redoubt; the British ceased their cannonade.[46]

One of the first things the Allies did after taking Redoubts 9 and 10 was arm them so that they might direct a distracting fire against the British while the second parallel was being readied to receive its artillery.

Two 8-inch howitzers were placed in Redoubt 10B by the cliff overlooking the York River. Two more howitzers went into Redoubt 9B, along with a mortar. The placement of the ordnance required that new entrances be cut in the walls of the fortifications facing away from the British. At the same time, the British gorges on the sides facing Yorktown had to be closed.[47]

The work on either side of the structures proved exceptionally dangerous in daylight, and one of the fatigue party undertaking the task on Redoubt 9B was killed almost instantly when an enemy 9-pounder ball bounded across the plain and tore his leg off at the thigh. Another soldier, peering along the embankment of the structure, was ordered to get down. "As he slid down," recollected Van Cortlandt, "the ball that was intended to kill him, and which would have passed through his body if he had remained, passed over his head; and either the wind or the sand, as it passed without breaking his skull or skin, produced his death in an instant, as he fell dead in the trench— no mark but blood-shot head and face."[48]

Besides the howitzers, Redoubt 10B also received two 18-pounders the following day, while Redoubt 9B was subsequently fitted with two 10-inch mortars and two royals.[49] The two howitzers placed in each structure during the day did not fire until 5:00 p.m.[50]

As work continued to convert the redoubts for use by the Allies, Washington strengthened his new position by erecting yet another powerful artillery battery with which to pummel Cornwallis's position. About 9:00 a.m. the day after the successful assault, members of the Pennsylvania line began building a large battery (designated 11B) adjacent to Redoubt 9B on the northeast side almost directly opposite a British gun unit now precariously guarding Cornwallis's left flank in the main Yorktown line.[51] The existence of a large natural depression in the terrain between the two captured redoubts (9 and 10) precluded the erection of the battery on that ground, compelling instead the selection of the site adjoining Redoubt 9B. The addition of a strong complement of ordnance to Redoubt 10B helped compensate for the apparent weakness in that part of the line.[52]

Because of the depression, the parallel between the redoubts was not straight, and instead curved to a left oblique around the edge of the hollow. The ditch at the rear (the former front) of Redoubt 9B was incorporated by the Allies as part of the second parallel and was continued into what became Battery 11B to the right of the structure. The line connecting Redoubt 9B with Redoubt 10B converged with the communications trench from the first parallel at the same southernmost corner of the latter earthwork.[53] As laid out the morning of October 15, Battery 11B was designed to mount 22 guns, although the structure was not filled to capacity before Cornwallis's capitulation.[54]

Most of the day on October 15 was spent preparing new works and perfecting others to receive their designated armaments. The French worked swiftly, and in the course of the day removed all their artillery platforms from the first parallel for transport to the second.[55] The dismantling of the American Grand Battery (13A) and the American gun unit (10A) on the left of the sector also began October 15.[56] Four guns, probably from the former battery, were moved forward that night into the still unfinished Battery 11B, while two more howitzers were put in Redoubt 9B, perhaps temporarily.[57] That the Allies considered arming the section of the parallel that harbored their recent gains appears obvious. Redoubts 9B and 10B became the focal points of Allied construction on the line. Consequently, they likewise represented special targets for Cornwallis's artillerists. The Allies labored with great vigor to complete this section and arm it adequately enough to withstand the British cannonade.[58]

The passage of a flag from Cornwallis early on the morning of the 15th evoked excitement within Allied lines. Whatever its significance may have been was seemingly lost to protocol. Cornwallis's gunners continued firing even as the anonymous red-coated bearer scurried across the short distance dividing the armies—an indignity the Allies would not tolerate. Lafayette hurried a note back across the plain citing the impropriety of His Lordship's action, eliciting in reply a quick apology. However, the exchanges ended, and whatever substance they might have produced disappeared.[59]

At noon, Lincoln's Division, with drums beating and banners waving, relieved Lafayette's weary soldiers.[60] Two battalions each of the Regiments Bourbonnois and Soissonois took over in the French sector, although as evening approached, soldiers of the Agenois unit replaced those of the Bourbonnois because of their all-night vigil following the assault on the redoubts. De Chastellux took command of the French troops in the trenches.[61] Lively rounds of musketry and grapeshot met the relieving soldiers, a greeting Washington himself experienced when he inspected the newly-won redoubts during the day.[62]

Behind the lines, the Allies attended to routine matters. The late Scammell's effects were auctioned off while men toiled to prepare the new batteries that would help avenge his loss.[63] "Our works which [we] are now creating within 200 yards of theirs will probably be opened this Evening," Colonel Tucker informed his wife. "And then my Lord beware of your Head."[64]

Late in the afternoon, the Allies started their cannonade from the second parallel, even though the batteries lacked final perfection and all the ordnance had not yet been moved ahead from the first line. Indeed, it appears that throughout the day, even while the second batteries were readying, those of the first kept up a menacing fire to protect the workers in the new line. Captain Stevens, commanding Battery 13A, reported expending 130 24-pounder shot, 91 18-pounder shot, 50 8-inch shells, 19 five-and-one-half-inch shells, and 31 10-inch shells—just on October 15. Captain Gercom, in charge of the two mortars in Redoubt 12A, reported 25 10-inch shells expended, and Captain Thompson, commanding Battery 10A of the first parallel utilized 150 18-pounder shot.[65]

Just what second parallel units opened fire on the evening of the 15th (other than the howitzers mounted in the captured redoubts) is uncertain. Several accounts state the batteries were not ready to open, while others appear nebulous as to whether they mean new batteries distinct from the captured redoubts mounting armaments. Lieutenant Swartwout, for example, wrote that "some of our Bomb Batteries being in compleat order, a fierce Bombarding is commenced from them in our works."[66] Lieutenant Tilden, on the other hand, referred to "our second line having no batteries erected on it as yet, tho' a number will be in two days time."[67] Daniel Shute reported simply, "Batteries in . . . [second parallel] opened," while General Wayne recorded only a bit more specifically that "two small batteries were opened this evening."[68] In all likelihood, the redoubt howitzer units were considered batteries by some and not by others. With such variance of definition, the statement of Lafayette's aide that "by tomorrow we expect to open some batteries within 200 yards of his Lordship" is correct.[69] The redoubt units were evidently seen as holding devices until the more substantial line batteries could be finished.

The damage inflicted on Cornwallis's position by Allied artillery on the 15th, while not as extensive as preceding barrages, was nevertheless ample. A French mortar shell burned another British frigate that exploded with a shock that "made the earth shake," remembered Ebenezer Denny.[70] Another bomb fell on a regimental bake oven and wounded several German soldiers tending it.[71] The British gunners answered with a brisk fire of royal mortars and small-caliber cannon that dealt scant harm to the Allies.[72] The sky was filled with crisscrossing shot and shell. Asa Redington remembered counting 10 missiles in the air at one time. "Some of our big bombs," he observed, "exploded in the British works and sent some of their pieces back into our works."[73]

That night the Allies slackened their fire, though the enemy did not reciprocate.[74] "Throughout the night we were amused by cannon fire, and especially by endless royal bombs," remembered von Closen of the French Army. One of Closen's workers near Redoubt 2B, second parallel, was struck by a shell that "took off the thick skin from the heel of his foot, just as if it had been cut off with a razor."[75]

The steady discharge of his light guns and mortars was all Cornwallis had left to offer the Allies. He knew full well the capture of Redoubts 9 and 10 made his situation in Yorktown virtually untenable.

"Last Evening the Enemy carried my two advanced Redoubts on the left by Storm, and during the Night have included them in their Second Parallel, which they are at present busy in perfecting," wrote Cornwallis to Clinton on October 15. It was the clearest warning to date he had dispatched to that officer. Cornwallis continued:

> My Situation now becomes very critical. We dare not shew a Gun to their old Batteries, and I expect their new ones will be open to-Morrow Morning. Experience has shewn that our fresh earthen Works do not resist their powerful Artillery, so that we shall soon be exposed to an Assault in ruined Works, in a bad Position and with weakened Numbers.

In what must have been a painful admission for such a proud soldier, Cornwallis announced that he was beyond help: "The Safety of the Place is therefore so precarious that I cannot recommend that the Fleet and Army should run great Risque, in endeavoring to save us."[76]

Cornwallis was admitting the inevitability of his capitulation. Only an act of sheer desperation, aided by unparalleled good fortune, would save his army now.

Chapter 12

Hopes Bright and Dim

*C*ornwallis's artillery fell silent about 4:00 a.m. on Tuesday, October 16. Some 350 of his soldiers filed out of the Hornwork portion of the British lines and walked silently across the plain in front of the works. They moved stealthily in the growing twilight of dawn so as not to draw the attention of Allied troops guarding the second parallel. The attacking party was composed of a detachment of the Royal Foot Guards, the 80th Company of Grenadiers under Lieutenant Colonel Lake, and a light infantry unit headed by Major Thomas Armstrong. Lieutenant Colonel Robert Abercrombie, the officer in charge of the left side (southern and eastern defenses) of the main works at Yorktown, oversaw the sortie effort.

The attack was intended to cripple the unfinished French and American batteries (6B and 8B) set squarely opposite the left center of Cornwallis's line—batteries whose fire threatened to breach the British works preparatory to a general storm of Yorktown by the Allies.[1] The bold effort was in response to news that French naval reinforcements had been sighted in Chesapeake Bay, and signaled a new echelon of desperation stirring within Lord Cornwallis. If well executed, substantial damage could be inflicted upon the enemy, and the siege perhaps lengthened. But the sortie had little hope of lasting success, and represented no more than a nod to tradition.[2]

The choice of Abercrombie to lead the assaulting column was a good one. The lieutenant colonel was a hardened veteran of the French and Indian War and had fought in many of the American Revolution's earlier battles. During the siege, he commanded his light infantry battalion as well as the left wing of Cornwallis's embattled army. Abercrombie divided his strike force into two columns. The first consisted of Grenadiers from the Royal Foot Guards and Colonel Lake's 80th Company (with Lake in command of this half of the attack), while the other was comprised of Major Armstrong's "elite" light infantry. The British approached the new parallel. In advance were pickets from the Regiment Agenois. Behind them was the Regiment Soissonois, which was entrusted with holding this portion of the line.

The advancing British met with more immediate success than Cornwallis likely anticipated. "They fell upon a picket of the Agenois Regiment whom they massacred, took the captain prisoner, and entered the trench where the Soissonnais put up only a halfhearted resistance, abandoning the place of army and the redoubt to the advancing enemy," recalled Jean-Baptiste-Antoine de Verger of the Regiment Deux-Ponts.

Abercrombie's sortie had perfectly aimed and pierced the joint in the Allied line between the target batteries at the juncture of the French and American sectors. Once inside, one column turned right and passed through an unobstructed communications trench and, without warning, broke upon unfinished Battery 6B, which was supposed to be guarded by a captain and 50 soldiers of the Regiment Agenois. Few, if any, were there because most of the French defenders were asleep in adjacent Redoubt 7B, or absent. Pretending to be an American relief unit, the British leaped over the parapet and began stabbing the sleeping Frenchmen with their bayonets. Shocked and bloodied, many of the Agenois men fled, leaving the attackers behind with a free hand to spike the four guns in the battery. This they did using their bayonets, which they hurriedly drove into the vent holes of unmounted 16-pounders. Once deeply inserted, the soldiers snapped them off.

Meanwhile, the other British column moved left and encountered American Captain Joseph Savage's men in Battery 8B, which was occupied by 100 soldiers belonging to the 2nd New York, the 1st Continental Artillery, and Lieutenant Colonel Dabney's Virginia Militia. The British approached the battery in the lingering darkness and one of the officers shouted out, "What troops?"

Lieutenant Colonel Robert Abercrombie's men charged across this field and struck the Allied line (in the distant trees) during their pre-dawn attack on October 16. This view looks south from the British line. The distance across the field was about 400 yards. For more examples of the terrain over which Abercrombie attacked, see Appendix A, views 21 and 22. *National Park Service, Colonial National Historical Park, Yorktown Collection*

"French!"

"Push on, boys, and skin the bastards!"

With that command the British charged forward and engaged some of Savage's men in hand-to-hand combat, scattering the Americans and spiking three 18-pounders with their bayonets. The commotion drew the attention of Viscount de Noailles, who was behind the batteries with the trench guard of Soissonois. De Noailles immediately comprehended what was happening and led a charge of shouting Frenchmen into the fray to rout the British and send them scurrying back toward their own works. De Noailles's soldiers succeeded in bayoneting eight of the assailants and capturing six others. According to Hector St. John de Crèvecoeur, a French aristocrat who wrote on life in America, many of the British dead were the spikers themselves.

The British, however, had inflicted significant casualties on the French, who had been caught utterly off guard by the sally. Accounts differ as to the numbers lost. De Crèvecoeur claims the French lost eleven killed and 37 wounded, while others put the loss at five officers and a dozen soldiers killed or wounded, with a captain taken prisoner. Cornwallis inflated the casualty toll when, on October 20, he wrote Clinton that the French lost about 100 men in the pre-dawn attack. On the American side, one man was taken prisoner, two were killed, and three were wounded (one mortally). Following the return of Abercrombie's assault force to its own lines, Cornwallis's artillery opened all along his fortifications.[3]

The entire episode seems to have been mismanaged on both sides. Apparently, Major General de Chastellux had been informed by a deserter that a sortie was going to occur, and the soldier even designated the point along the line where the assault might be expected.[4] The British found the French battery deserted because its gunners had been sent to retrieve two artillery pieces that had overturned in the trench en route from the first parallel. The Agenois soldiers, left to guard Redoubt 7B, were permitted to sleep, and took every advantage of the order to do so. "The negligence of the Agenois regiment was the sole reason for the surprise of the redoubt and of the adjoining [French] battery," concluded Baron von Closen.[5] Although the point of the attack seems to have been well chosen, Abercrombie can also be faulted for having launched the sortie without the careful planning it deserved. The reason the British spiked the Allied guns with their bayonet points was because they had taken along wheel nails, which were too large for the cannon vents, instead of the correct steel spikes made expressly for that purpose.[6] The British left the decided impression among some of the French that "they were nearly all drunk," and for that reason they failed in their attempt. The French admitted they were notably unprepared for the assault, despite the obvious caution that should have been exercised. As one officer put it, "We must confess that we hardly dreamed of being attacked that night."[7]

Any advantage Cornwallis gained in the sally proved illusory. The strong counterattack by the French destroyed the British drive and sent it scurrying back to Yorktown with loss. The guns spiked by the enemy with bayonets were easily restored to working order by simply prying loose the bent metal. Soon after the British soldiers reached their lines the three American 18-pounders were able to operate again. They delivered a sharp fire in defiance of the failed enemy effort.[8] "Within an hour," reported a German officer, "they battered our works so badly in the flank and rear that all our batteries were silenced within a few hours."[9] It took the French a few hours longer to extricate the bayonet points and finish mounting their cannon, but by 9:00 a.m., all was ready and their guns opened a ricochet fire along Cornwallis's front line. British artillery did not respond.[10]

The early morning attack was a wasteful exercise and accomplished nothing other than to make the Allies acutely aware of the desperate straits of their enemy. "This action, though extremely honorable to the officers and soldiers who executed it, proved of little public advantage," Cornwallis concluded, "for the cannon having been spiked in a hurry, were soon rendered fit for service again, and before dark the whole parallel and batteries appeared to be nearly complete."[11]

The Second Parallel's Composition, Armament, and Archaeology

The construction of the second parallel batteries was a hazardous occupation. From all indications, it proceeded in a hurried fashion; the considerable detail of construction undertaken by units of the first line was lacking in the second. Cannon were brought forward while the batteries were being erected. Some were mounted and opened rapidly upon the enemy even before adequate space to contain them had been prepared. Consequently, the artillery pieces in the second parallel batteries were often crowded. Theoretical considerations succumbed to practicality along the new line. The proximity to the enemy artillery, enabling greater accuracy on their part, proved an overriding deterrent to the incorporation of detail normally built into earlier earth works.[12]

From all accounts, the second parallel was not completely finished before the siege ended. Some batteries and parts of others opened fire on October 16 and 17, but others simply remained forever unfinished. As it neared final form on the 16th, the second Allied parallel before Yorktown measured approximately 1,250 yards east to west. Two lengthy trenches from the second line communicated with the first parallel and the deep Allied rear areas. The French held the one on the west, comprised of two ditches meeting midway between the parallels to form a 90-degree angle.

The other, joining the easternmost points of the American sectors of the two lines, ran about 830 yards and partially bordered the York River. At the junction of the French and American sectors was a zigzag trench that ran a short distance back toward the first line to open into a broad ravine that afforded cover and permitted the movement of men and supplies from the rear to the front. This trench was dug by the American troops on the night of October 11.[13]

Archaeological examination of this zigzag revealed that it covered 400 feet of ground and joined the main trench near the southeastern side of Redoubt 7B. The ditch measured about 10 feet wide and its overall excavated length was 660 feet.[14] At least one historical map also shows the spot where the American excavation ended because of the presence of the two British-held detached redoubts (9 and 10). This spot appears as a slight southern extension in the main trench, and was situated across a ravine between Battery 8B and Redoubt 9B.[15]

The completion of the second parallel following the capture of Redoubts 9 and 10 permitted the Allies to concentrate on the construction of their new batteries and the perfection of their entrenchments. By October 16, six batteries for heavy siege pieces were either built or underway along the line. In addition, three redoubts stood at fairly equal intervals within the left, or French, sector. Redoubts 9B and 10B, taken from the British in the assault the night of October 14, were ordered converted into small batteries with siege ordnance that could effectively harass Cornwallis's left flank.

Battery 1B: At the extreme western end of the second parallel, this large mortar-howitzer battery faced the British Hornwork. Erected on October 14, the earthwork was designed to hold at least 10, and possibly 12, mortars and two howitzers.[16] How many pieces opened from Battery 1B is unknown. However, an American soldier claimed the structure contained eight 13-inch mortars, two royals, and one 8-inch howitzer, all made of bronze.[17] According to at least one contemporary map, a powder magazine was built in the area between the armament and the main line to support these weapons.[18] Battery 1B was commanded by two French officers: the left was under Vouges de Chanteclair, the same officer who had commanded the mortar battery 4A in the first parallel; Captain Nicolas Barthelemy took charge of the right, after having commanded the mortars and howitzer of Battery 8A in the earlier line.[19]

Redoubt 2B: Just a handful of yards east of Battery 1B stood Redoubt 2B, one of the first fortifications established along the second parallel. Most of the maps showing any detail indicate that Redoubt 2B was triangular, with its apex facing the British line.[20] The actual dimensions of this redoubt are unknown, but map representations suggest the unit was considerably smaller than Redoubt 4B on the same line. Redoubt 2B was palisaded in its frontal ditch.[21]

Battery 3B: The French constructed this cannon battery a short distance to the right of Redoubt 2B. It contained six bronze 24-pounders, all of which began playing against the British lines on October 16.[22] This unit was commanded by an officer named Joster. Its fire helped seal off Hampton Road and, according to contemporary map descriptions, stood in front of the parallel, which circled around behind the battery.

Redoubt 4B: This fortification directly blocked the way out of Yorktown and bisected the Hampton Road. It was much larger than Redoubt 2B, and was likewise guarded by a stout line of palisades placed in its ditch. From its depiction on contemporary maps, Redoubt 4B represented in shape a triangular structure with a drastically truncated apex—a trapezoidal, misshapen-square arrangement. Its gorge lay along its southern side and provided access into the main parallel.[23] Redoubts 2B and 4B served as guard posts to protect the batteries of the line against enemy incursions.[24]

Battery 5B: This gun emplacement stood a short distance east of Redoubt 4B and was the first Allied structure erected completely east of Hampton Road on the second parallel. Every historical map agrees this unit harbored six cannon.[25] Four of these appear to have been 24-pounders; the remaining pieces were 16-pounders.[26] However, Lieutenant William Feltman reported the armament slightly differently, claiming Battery 5B contained four 18-pounders (he meant 16-pounders) and two 24-pounders.[27] During excavation of the battery site preparatory to reconstructing the earthwork, however, only four cannon emplacement positions were found (it was determined that two of these were for howitzers). Thor Borresen, the man assigned to reconstruct some of the Yorktown works, concluded in 1940 that it would have been entirely possible to crowd two additional guns into this battery. He suggested that the two pieces might have been mounted on platforms placed directly on the ground without sleepers.[28] Given the circumstances governing the hurried construction of the second parallel, this conclusion seems wholly plausible. Battery 5B was commanded by a French officer named Morcour.[29]

Battery 6B: Next along the line stood Battery 6B, the French unit that constituted one of the primary objects of Lieutenant Colonel Abercrombie's bloody pre-dawn sortie on the morning of October 16. Battery 6B held six bronze 16-pounders, four of which had been spiked by the British in an operation so clumsily executed that the weapons were back in use a few hours later.[30] The principal purpose of this unit and of the nearby American battery 8B (as Cornwallis knew when he ordered the sortie against them) was to try and breach the British works in preparation for a general Allied assault upon them.[31] Battery 6B was in the charge of Captain Bernard de Neurisse, who moved forward from command of the right section of Battery 8A in the first parallel.[32]

Archaeological work completed on the middle part of the second parallel has disclosed that this earthwork possessed a frontal ditch about 80 yards long, and that the gun emplacement area measured roughly 20 yards wide from the parapet. Almost midway along the rear of the battery, in the area between the unit proper and the parallel behind, the French built a powder magazine that was connected by a 20-foot trench to the gun emplacement position.[33] Once its cannon were un-spiked and fully mounted, Battery 6B delivered powerful volleys that pummeled Cornwallis's works and contributed greatly to the British commander's decision to surrender.

Redoubt 7B: Battery 6B was separated from American Battery 8B by the fully palisaded Redoubt 7B, which was occupied by French troops of the Agenois Regiment at the time of Abercrombie's sortie. Evidently built by the Americans (and hence often referred to as the Franco-American Redoubt),[34] 7B was square (or rather diamond- shaped), with its foremost salient angle facing the British. Its right facet closely joined the left of American Battery 8B, and its obvious purpose was to serve as a guard for the breach batteries on either side.[35] Redoubt 7B was established directly in the second parallel, and the Allied zigzag communications trench entered this line immediately to the right rear of the structure. Its outer palisaded perimeter measured approximately 90 yards, while its longest side, the northernmost one, ran about 27 yards.[36]

American Battery 8B: Adjoining Redoubt 7B on the east was Battery 8B, which completed the fortification complex in the middle of the second line. Begun on the evening of October 13, 8B held six artillery pieces, iron 18-pounders all.[37] Three of these were spiked by the British in their sortie on the morning of the 16th. These three pieces were immediately repaired and opened against the enemy. The others did not fire until the morning of October 17.[38] Battery 8B's guns joined those of 7B in attempting to breach the British works.[39]

Archaeological examination completed in the 1930s revealed that this unit (8B) was a sunken battery. The bottoms of the embrasures of Battery 8B were at about ground level. The gun emplacement area was large enough (54 yards long) for six cannon, but the height of the unit must have been almost entirely excavated in order for the pieces to function properly with adequate cover.[40] At the east end of the battery, the parapet made a right angle and continued for approximately another 27 yards—apparently a protective measure against the British armaments in Redoubt 9B before its capture the night of the 14th. It is possible that this battery mounted naval carriages, as Thor Borresen suspected, because the space behind the platform area was not sufficient to allow for recoil and reloading the weapons. Rather than the 21.5 feet of back space necessary for an 18-pounder, the area in Battery 8B measured fully three feet less than that required for proper functioning of the pieces.[41]

Redoubt 9B: The long strip of parallel running between Battery 8B and Redoubt 9B—roughly 400 yards—was the longest exposed section on the entire line. Lacking either redoubt or battery protection throughout its length, this segment undoubtedly received substantial infantry reinforcement, perhaps even more following the enemy assault on the morning of the 16th. Redoubt 9B, fitted with armaments after its capture, covered the intervening terrain between the British and Allied lines and dissuaded attacks in that quarter. Following its capture, Redoubt 9B was modified by the Allies. The British entrance was closed and a new one was cut in the side facing away from Yorktown. The structure retained its original pentagonal shape along with such conventional British-constructed defensive components as palisades, fraising, and abatis.[42] Some of the historical maps show abatis only on the sides of the redoubt facing Yorktown;[43] certainly much, if not all, of the abatis was removed from the back of the structure if it interfered with the excavation of the Allied connecting trenches. The inner perimeter of Redoubt 9B was 103 yards, which permitted occupation by 198 men (including six men for each of the howitzers mounted in the work).[44]

During the 1930s, the redoubt was archaeologically examined and reconstructed to approximate its original condition before its capitulation to the Allies on the night of October 14.[45]

Redoubt 10B: Perched atop the cliff overlooking the York River, Redoubt 10B significantly commanded enemy movements on the water between Yorktown and Gloucester Point. Smaller than its neighboring earthwork to the west, Redoubt 10B was square rather than pentagonal in shape. It, too, was taken in the Allied assault of the 14th, and its captors armed it and used it as a battery to blast away at Cornwallis's works. At least three contemporary maps have Redoubt 10B containing (at most) four howitzers and three mortars during the tenancy of the Allies.[46] The structure seems also to have been partly ringed with abatis on the sides facing away from the river,[47] and had the proper fraising and palisading to impede an enemy's advance.[48] Probably all of these were modified with the Allied occupation beginning on the night of the 14th. Redoubt 10B has been only partially reconstructed because of the erosion of the site through the years since 1781.[49]

Battery 11B: Washington's soldiers built Battery 11B directly adjacent to the right side of Redoubt 9B. Battery 11B was a large work slated to contain much of the artillery to be moved forward from the American Grand Battery (13A) in front of the first parallel. Most maps agree that once established, Battery 11B was able to hold at least a dozen heavy cannon of the 18- and 24-pounder variety, plus a number of mortars and howitzers.[50] One detailed American map, however, clearly notes that Battery 11B was "designed for" seven 18-pounders, three 24-pounders, four howitzers, eight 10-inch mortars, and 10 five-and-one-half-inch royal mortars. Part of this complement opened on October 16, although the battery was not finished before the British surrendered.[51] According to Lieutenant Feltman, only sixteen pieces were placed in operation by October 18: 10 18-pounders, three 10-inch mortars, one eight-inch howitzer, and two royals.[52]

Construction of this half-sunk earthwork (11B) began early on October 15 and originally incorporated part of the parallel connecting the two captured redoubts. Work involved widening the line and raising the parapet with fascines and gabions to a sufficient height and width to guard against the British artillery fire. An archaeological investigation in 1940 of Battery 11B revealed evidence of 11 platforms, 10 of which measured 15 feet in length and were located close to the base of the epaulement. The 11th platform measured 12 feet long and was situated 12 feet back from the parapet, suggesting a howitzer was placed there. Eight feet to the right the gun emplacement ditch grew deeper, indicating the mortars were probably fired from that point. In all likelihood, they were mounted to shoot horizontally from the carriages designed by General Knox. The two royals were installed beyond this area. Near this point, the emplacement ditch joined the new second parallel that had been dug along the rear of Battery 11B and continued on to join Redoubt 10B.[53]

While the spacing between the archaeologically disclosed platform sleeper impressions of Battery 11B did not follow technical precepts of the time—which called for at least 15 feet between armaments—there appears to have been ample reason for the departure. In the judgment of Thor Borresen, the Allies worked to get four guns forward from the first line as soon as possible. These four pieces were probably moved up during the night of the 15th and crowded closest to Redoubt 9B. Then, as they engaged the enemy on the night of October 16, two more guns were advanced and placed at a greater distance from the first four pieces in order to not interfere with the gun crews firing them. Likewise, the spacing between the sixth and seventh platforms indicates that night firing determined their placement by workmen. Construction of the embrasures reflected and compensated for the disparity in spacing the guns.[54]

No platforms were found in the area consigned to the royal mortars, but these weapons required none. They were mounted stationary on wooden blocks and could be moved by two men to any new position in their part of the battery.[55] Apparently, the soldiers did not erect a powder magazine behind the cannon section, although it seems one was started in the rear of the howitzer-mortar part of Battery 11B. The magazine was unfinished at the time of Cornwallis's surrender.[56]

Thus established, the second parallel and its component artillery units offered a powerful new position from which to pummel the British. The only question was whether it would be sufficient to induce Lord Cornwallis to surrender his forces. The French and American armies were closing rapidly, and Cornwallis was now deeply mired in the worst military predicament of his career. Without immediate aid, the British position promised to collapse.

On the far right of Cornwallis's line, the French planned an action against the last outer stronghold, the thus-far resilient Fusiliers' Redoubt. The French had already begun tracing a network of trenches extending forward from their line between Batteries 1A and 2A. The principal sap was designed to approach almost to the abatis around the Fusiliers' Redoubt. Once the British defenders of that structure were routed, another battery was planned for its southwest corner straddling Williamsburg Road.[57] These guns would have greater access to the British works guarding Cornwallis's right flank around Yorktown. This design never progressed beyond the planning stage, however, and the fort that so effectively preserved Cornwallis's right throughout the siege remained in British hands until the capitulation.

*   *   *

On October 16, Lafayette's infantry took a position in the American sector of the second parallel.[58] Most of the day was spent completing the batteries before shifting the remaining ordnance from the old line to the new line. All the while, the weapons already in place at various key points along the parallel barked forth ominous warnings to Cornwallis and his men.[59] The Allies were making "every preparation for a serious and terrible fire tomorrow from [an] increased number of batteries and [from] artillery in much nearer approach than hitherto," explained Jonathan Trumbull, the Connecticut native who had replaced Alexander Hamilton on Washington's staff in February 1781.[60]

During the day Washington issued two important orders governing the conduct of the siege. One directed that future relief troops not announce their movements with the customary drumbeats, but instead march forward silently with colors furled and arms at trail until they reached their stations.[61] The second was designed to keep the parallel clear of human obstruction at all times:

> The Commander in Chief having observed that the trenches are constantly crouded [sic] by Spectators, who by passing and repassing prevent the men from Working and thereby greatly impede the Operations of the Siege, He therefore Orders that no Officer who is not on duty shall hereafter enter the Trenches except General Officers and their Aids. And that no Inhabitant or person

not belonging to the Army be suffered to enter the Trenches at any time without permission from the Major Genl of the Trenches.[62]

Along the French sector, Rochambeau's soldiers worked diligently to strengthen their fortifications. St. Simon and his subordinate, de Custine, commanded two battalions each of the Regiments Gatenois and Saintonge, with auxiliary workers composed of the grenadiers of Agenois and Gatenois. Eight hundred more workmen would enter the trenches after dark to perfect the French earthworks.[63] Sometime in the afternoon, St. Simon was hit in the ankle by a round of grapeshot that crippled him. The French officer faltered briefly before ordering his troops to carry him into the second parallel, where he continued to command the sector for the duration of his tour.[64]

A humorous event occurred during the afternoon of the 16th while Knox was debating Alexander Hamilton on the merits of a Washington directive that called for the men to yell "A shell!" whenever one of the enemy missiles landed in the works. Hamilton thought the system was unsoldierly, but Knox rigorously defended it as in the best interests of the men's lives. As the two were discussing the situation, a pair of bombs struck inside the redoubt in which the men were standing. "Instantly the cry broke out on all sides, "A shell! A shell!" and [there was] a scrambling and jumping to reach the blinds and get behind them for defense," wrote Aeneas Monson of Connecticut who witnessed the event. "Knox and Hamilton were united in action, however differing in word." Both men scrambled behind the blinds, but Hamilton made a point to position himself behind Knox—"Knox being a very large man and Hamilton a small man," explained Monson. Knox did not take kindly to acting as a human obstruction and a struggle ensued. The two men rolled over and Knox, being much stronger, threw Hamilton toward the hissing shells. Aghast, Hamilton scrambled back once more behind the blinds. "All this was done rapidly, for in two minutes the shells burst and threw their deadly missiles in all directions. It was now safe and soldierlike to stand out," recalled Monson. "Now," began Knox, "what do you think, Mr. Hamilton, about crying 'shell'? But let me tell you not [to] make a breastwork of me again!"[65]

By now, the combination of French and American artillery had nearly destroyed all British shipping in the York River. Cornwallis himself had scuttled or dismantled many of his own vessels, sinking them to protect his command from a French assault from the water. French hot shot and American guns had damaged or destroyed other enemy vessels until few remained to threaten an Allied naval advance up the York River. By October 16, Washington had conceived of a new plan that would block the stream above Yorktown. He had even managed to convince the reluctant Admiral de Grasse that he could safely station a ship above the village. The danger of enemy fire ships, the Virginian told to the admiral, could be obviated by using rowboats to guard the French ship in its station. In fact, continued Washington, he had already ordered boats from up the York. Additional flat-bottomed craft had been hauled overland from the James River, and the army at Gloucester had also been busy collecting boats for de Grasse's use. Only the quickening surge of events prevented this plan from ever fully materializing.[66]

The Allies spent the evening of the 16th watching for another enemy assault against their lines. Strong detachments stood guard in each of the new batteries. When completed, these units delivered a heavy barrage of fire against the weakened British front while hundreds of French and American soldiers hurried the rest of the armaments forward. The October Virginia air turned cold when a storm front moved in, and a heavy rain pelted the opposing armies.[67]

In the growing darkness, Knox directed all of his cannon to fire vigorously at once to violently shatter the enemy defenses and breach Cornwallis's works.[68] "The parapets were tumbling down, from the effects of the bombs," French engineer Chevalier d'Ancteville wrote in his journal. "The fraises were flying in pieces. We were preparing an assured route for a forward movement to take the place by storm. Twenty-four hours of our fire fixed the moment for it."[69]

The view from the receiving end of the Allied artillery fire was eerily similar. "By the force of the enemy's cannonade, the British works were tumbling into ruin," a British soldier recorded. As far as he could determine, Cornwallis's steadily worsening situation was irretrievable. "Not a gun could be fired from them, and only one eight inch, and little more than 100 coehorn shells remained. They were in many places assailable already; and if the fire continued a few hours longer, it was the opinion of the engineer, and principal officers of the army, that it would be madness to attempt to maintain them." There exists little doubt that the Allied bombardment on the night of October 16 was very severe. "Some of the oldest officers and soldiers in both armies concurred in declaring," wrote one historian of the siege, "that they had never witnessed a more heavy and continual discharge of artillery than that which now took place."[70]

Much of this destructive fire hailed from Cornwallis's former Redoubts 9 and 10, the powerful detached works that once guarded his left flank, but were now in the hands of the Allies. Between October 15 and 16, the Americans firmly established themselves in Redoubts 9B and 10B and expended a considerable amount of ammunition. In Redoubt 9B, for example, Captain Peter Nestle of the 2nd Continental Artillery commanded two 10-inch mortars and two coehorns. His weapons consumed 59 10-inch shells, 30 coehorn shells, and 10 bags of grapeshot. Between these redoubts General Knox placed two more 10-inch mortars—perhaps his specially designed pieces—under a Lieutenant Troop. These weapons fired 56 rounds during this 24-hour interval. Redoubt 10B, commanded by a lieutenant named Gardner, contained two 8-inch and two 5.5-inch howitzers that dispensed 43 and 75 shells, respectively.[71]

Cornwallis Attempts an Escape

The fire from these structures and the others facing the British front was simply devastating. For Cornwallis, the moment of sheer desperation had finally arrived. If he remained where he was, his lines would be breached and open to enemy attacks. He was running low on food, short of ammunition, indeed, all the supplies required to feed and equip a large field army under protracted siege conditions. He knew now with certainty that reinforcements were not going to arrive in time, and if he wanted to save his army, he would have to take matters into his own hands. After considerable thought, Cornwallis decided to cross the bulk of his command over the York River to the Gloucester shore, leaving behind his baggage and a detachment under Lieutenant Colonel Henry Johnson to capitulate for the citizens and for the many wounded and sick soldiers who would necessarily be left behind.

Cornwallis secretly directed that 16 large boats and their crews be readied at 10:00 p.m. to carry the first of three contingents across. He determined three trips would suffice to remove the healthy remaining soldiers of his command. Even if he made it across the river, Cornwallis was not out of the woods. Once the fording was complete and a junction made with Tarleton (who had been apprised of the plan, one he had long argued Cornwallis should pursue), British artillery on Gloucester Point would blast an exit through the Allied forces of General Choisy. If all went well, Cornwallis's soldiers would charge through the cordon before dawn and escape to the north, leaving Washington stranded on the peninsula beyond the York River. It was at this point when Admiral de Grasse's shunning of Washington's entreaties to station a ship above Yorktown threatened to work to Cornwallis's favor. The possibility the Allied commander so dreaded—Cornwallis's last-minute escape across the York—was on the verge of being attempted. Fleeing the clutches of the Allies, the British could either strike north to join Clinton around New York, or move toward the Carolinas via Richmond.[72]

But Cornwallis had not reckoned with nature, which both helped shield the movement and eventually ensured its failure. At the appointed hour the embarkment of the first troops began. Sixteen boats pushed off from Yorktown and moved silently through the water. Within them were British light infantry, part of the Guards, and a segment of the 23rd Regiment. Three hundred German soldiers, meanwhile, slipped into the battered Hornwork to occupy that portion of the line evacuated by the light infantry. During the passage the weather turned sour and a violent storm arose. Rain and high winds tossed the boats about on mounting waves. The Allies seem to have been unaware of the escape attempt, at least during its early stages. "To our great luck," wrote German Captain Ewald, "the weather was so frightful that the enemy could not discover anything of all this."

Within an hour most of the troops, some likely quite seasick, reached Gloucester Point. Two boatloads of British soldiers never reached the far shore. To their dismay, the wind blew them downstream, where they were captured by waiting American soldiers. The heavy weather also prevented the scheduled return to Yorktown of the boats for the evacuation of the next round of men. The threads holding together Cornwallis's last-ditch plan were unraveling quickly.[73]

By midnight, the squall had ruined Cornwallis's attempt at escape. The storm abated after 2:00 a.m., but the boats—by now scattered or capsized—were no longer available. Only after daybreak could enough be reassembled to return the soldiers from Gloucester Point to Yorktown. The passage back across the York River in broad daylight under Allied artillery fire was a perilous one, though the British managed to arrive safely. Back in Yorktown by noon on the 17th, the men resumed their dreary fatigue in what was left of the crumbling British fortifications. "Thus expired the last hope of the British army," Tarleton succinctly concluded.[74]

Cornwallis's attempt to flee had failed dismally. As his boats bobbed and tossed across the rising waves the night of October 16, his spirits ebbed—the end was indeed at hand. Behind the American sector, Knox wrote his wife: "The fate of the enemy draws nigh—I hope in 10 or 12 days, we shall with the blessing of heaven terminate it."[75]

Chapter 13

Britain against the Sky

*B*y coincidence, Wednesday, October 17, 1781, was the fourth anniversary of the British surrender at Saratoga, New York. Loyal Americans honored the historic occasion with music and appreciative toasts, with most only vaguely aware of the momentous events taking shape in tidewater Virginia. Some more fully appreciated their significance. An American chaplain with the army at Yorktown remembered that on "this day four years [ago], Burgoyne and his whole army surrendered to the United States; that signal instance of the smiles of heaven, and what we now have in prospect, should make us very thankful to Almighty God." Events now at hand promised to eclipse the 1777 victory over Johnny Burgoyne's army.[1]

Throughout September General Clinton had grappled with the problem of how best to accomplish the relief of Cornwallis's army. His efforts were stifled by ongoing debate among his military and naval advisors, and because of his own refusal to fully comprehend the gravity of Cornwallis's predicament and act accordingly. Clinton convened councils of war almost daily to discuss the situation, but no hard and fast action could be agreed upon. Admiral Thomas Graves could not repair his fleet as quickly as was required, having but recently returned from his encounter with Admiral de Grasse off the Virginia Capes. Graves believed, moreover, that his preparations would not be finished before

October 8, and perhaps not even before the 12th. Clinton notified Cornwallis that even this date might be premature for the actual departure of reinforcements from New York. Despite Cornwallis's admonitions, Clinton adhered to the fatuous opinion that the situation of the British Army in Virginia was no cause for significant alarm. As late as October 19 Clinton wrote Lord George Germain in England, "I still flatter myself that, notwithstanding the Rapidity of the Enemy's Progress and our having been delayed by the necessary Repairs of the Fleet so far beyond the expected Time, it may yet be in the Power of our joint Exertions to relieve his Lordship."[2]

By the middle of October, however, essential agreement had been reached between Clinton and Cornwallis regarding the signals to be employed when the relief expedition arrived in Chesapeake Bay. The British admirals were optimistic of their chances for slipping past the French vessels at the mouth of the Chesapeake. According to Clinton, "The Admirals . . . seemed all convinced that as the French Fleet guarding the passage (in Crescent) between the Horse shoe and middle ground sands could not in such tides way avail themselves of the springs on their Cables: The British Fleet had every advantage of passing them and taking up a Position near the entrance of York River."[3] Once there, Clinton would announce his approach by firing the squadron's guns,[4] to which Cornwallis would respond by stating his condition through a series of alternating smoke columns and gun reports.

The signals agreed upon by these men were quite elaborate and took into account a variety of circumstances. If Cornwallis was still at Yorktown when Clinton arrived, he would send up "one great smoke" and discharge one gun at single-minute intervals. If Cornwallis believed Clinton should land on the northern shore of the York, he would make two smoke columns and fire two guns at two-minute intervals. "Three Smokes & Three Guns close fired at Six minutes Interval" meant Clinton should land at Newport News, while "Four Smokes and Four Guns close fired at Eight minutes Interval" dictated that Clinton should land at Jamestown. Furthermore, "if a smoke or fire appears on Cape Henry, a Boat is sent for the Person who makes [it], If he produces Two Half pence it denotes that Lord Cornwallis has left York Town."[5]

Alas, all of this planning and hoping was moot. Clinton's procrastination made any chance of relief virtually impossible. By the morning of October 17, Cornwallis had exhausted all hope of being rescued. His men were weary and their numbers greatly reduced to the point that they could not relieve each other at the defenses. Holding out longer meant only that more Allied artillery would tear into his works and kill and wound more of his men. Before long, the French and Americans would batter openings into the line and storm the garrison without quarter. Any compensating advantages would be lost in an unconditional surrender. At this stage, the welfare of his soldiers determined Cornwallis's course. And it was the right one: he would negotiate a surrender that would be as advantageous as possible to his command.[6]

If there lingered any doubt within Cornwallis's mind about when the Allies intended to storm his fortifications, French and American artillery eliminated it when a heavy new barrage welcomed the dawn of October 17. The fresh and fierce blast up and down the line smashed into the defenses and shook them violently. The Allies were going to pay a personal visit as soon as possible.

"The whole of our works are now mounted with cannon and mortars, not less than one hundred pieces of heavy ordnance have been in continual operation during the last twenty-four hours," wrote an American surgeon. "The whole peninsula trembles . . . We have leveled some of their works in ruins and silenced their guns; they have almost ceased firing." A German soldier agreed with the doctor's assessment, scribbling in his diary, "The cannonade from the enemy this morning is completely astounding." To this "astounding" fire the British could only respond with intermittent shots from their small mortars. During the night one of these bombs struck a French magazine in the second parallel, exploding 1,500 pounds of black powder into a giant mushroom of flame, dirt, and debris. Remarkably, no one was harmed by the tremendous explosion, although the French lost several killed and wounded after dawn from other causes.[7]

Batteries 1B and 5B began serious work this day. Washington entered in his diary, "The French opened another Battery of four 24s. and two 16s. and a Morter Battery of 10 Morters and two Howitzers." Structure 11B—dubbed the new American Grand Battery— continued Washington, fired with "12 24 and 18 prs. 4 Morters and two Howitzers."[8] From October 16 to 17, Battery 11B expended no less than 135 rounds of 24-pounder shot, 32 rounds of 18-pounder shot, 257 10-inch mortar shells, and 104 8-inch bombs. On the left of the American sector, Battery 8B used 68 rounds of 18-pounder shot during the same period.[9]

Most of the fire along the Allied line was directed toward reducing the area around the British Hornwork and Cornwallis's left flank. Mortar and howitzer bombs discharged from Redoubts 9B, 10B, and Battery 11B fell along Yorktown's beach. Those from the French unit 1B dropped into the Hornwork. Few cannon shot reached to the right of the British line, the only section of Cornwallis's defenses that remained relatively secure from Allied fire.

"General Lord Cornwallis himself came into our camp and went at once into the horn and observed the enemy coming so close," wrote German Private Popp. The British commander was inspecting the closing enemy noose and the state of affairs inside the critical Hornwork. The tremendous shelling that made the peninsula tremble also shook Cornwallis, who wrote a detailed letter about his state of affairs to Clinton three days later. "Our works . . . were going to ruin, and not having ben able to strengthen them by Abbatis, nor in any other manner than by a slight Fraizing, which the enemy's Artillery were demolishing wherever they fired." Conversations with his engineer and other officers confirmed what he already knew: "that they were in many parts very assailable in the forenoon, & that by the continuance of the same fire for a few hours longer, they would be in such a state as to render it desperate with our numbers to attempt to maintain them. We at that time could not fire a single Gun, only one eight Inch & little more than one hundred Cohorn Shells remained."

Reluctantly, Cornwallis concluded that a successful defense "in our situation was perhaps impossible." By this time, he explained to Clinton, "the place could only be reckoned an entrenched Camp, subject in most places to enfilade, & the ground in general so disadvantageous, that nothing but the necessity of fortifying it as a post to protect the Navy could have induced any person to erect Works upon it."[10]

The First Flag

Baron von Steuben's division was scheduled to relieve Lafayette's men in the trenches on the 17th.[11] On the left that day, de Viomenil was slated to command battalions of the Regiments Bourbonnois and Royal

Deux-Ponts.[12] Shortly past 10:00 a.m., before the relief forces took station and in the face of the vigorous new assault from the Allied guns, Cornwallis sent out a flag. As is almost always the case when dealing with the precise time a particular event transpired, the hour at which Cornwallis's first flag appeared is subject to some dispute within contemporary accounts. Most American journals at the time (or recorded shortly thereafter) place the event at precisely 10:00 a.m., or very close to that time. This includes Washington's own diary. Others place the time at "between 10 and 11." At least one French journal (that of Gaspard de Gallatin) claimed the British flag emerged from Yorktown at about 10:00 a.m. Other accounts place the event later in the afternoon.[13]

Regardless of the time, the event itself was an important moment in American history. The American and French soldiers must have guessed the intention behind the act when an enemy drummer, beating a chamade,[14] appeared on the British parapet before Yorktown. "Had we not seen the drummer in his red coat when he first mounted, he might have beat away till doomsday," wrote Lieutenant Ebenezer Denny in his diary. "The constant firing was too much for the sound of a single drum; but when the firing ceased, I thought I never heard a drum equal to it—the most delightful music to us all." A red-coated officer joined the drummer. He lifted his hand and began waving something: it was a white handkerchief.

When no one shot in their direction, the plain intention of the handkerchief-waving obvious to all, the officer and drummer boy climbed down the parapet and walked slowly toward the Allied line, all the while the drummer beating his chamade. One by one Allied guns fell silent, whether on order or word of mouth is unknown. An American officer ran out of the works toward the advancing duo and sent the drummer back to his own lines. The white handkerchief was tied over the eyes of the British officer, who was ushered forward to meet Lafayette in the American entrenchments.[15] The officer was then quickly escorted to Washington's headquarters in a nearby house, where he delivered Cornwallis's message: "I propose a Cessation of Hostilities for 24 hours, & that two Officers may be appointed by each side, to meet at Mr. Moore's house to settle terms for the Surrender of the Posts of York & Gloucester." One can only imagine the emotions coursing through Washington's body as he read these words.[16]

The British officer was returned to his lines, and a signal gun in one of the American batteries announced the resumption of the Allied bombardment. Washington was not about to give his enemy a full day of respite unless his terms of surrender were tendered in writing. The British had not expected the Allied batteries to open again, or at least so soon and without warning. Several "[who] were on the parapets and had not expected this," wrote one observer, were killed and wounded. The firing stopped when another British flag moved across the plain: the same officer who had delivered Cornwallis's initial proposal was returning for Washington's response, which he and his staff had discussed and crafted during his absence. Washington wrote, "I wish previously to the Meeting of Commissioners that your Lordship's proposals in writing, may be sent to the American Lines for which Purpose, a Suspension of Hostilities during two Hours from the Delivery of this Letter will be granted."

The artillery fire from both sides recommenced and lasted, except for two or three short periods when messages were exchanged, through most of the afternoon. Cornwallis, perhaps a bit indignant because he could not draft his proposals within the short two-hour timeframe offered by Washington, sent a more concrete framework of what he had in mind about 4:30 p.m. "The basis of my proposals will be, that the Garrisons of York and Gloucester shall be Prisoners of War with the customary Honuors," explained Cornwallis. The British soldiers, he continued, "shall be sent to Britain & and Germans to Germany, under engagement not to serve against France, America, or their Allies until released, or regularly exchanged, that all Arms & public Stores shall be delivered to you . . ." [17]

Though Washington was not inclined to parole his prisoners under the terms offered by Cornwallis, he concluded the specificity of his opponent's offer, coupled with his enemy's weak bargaining position, meant "there would be no great difficulty in fixing the terms." Therefore, wrote Washington, "hostilities were suspended for the Night and I proposed my own terms to which if he agreed Commissioners were to meet to digest them into form."[18]

Washington's terms were harsher than Cornwallis expected. The Allied commander was not about to return home the King's army and bluntly said as much. For Washington it was a matter of avenging the ill-treatment General Clinton had inflicted upon the American garrison at Charleston, South Carolina in 1780, when he refused to allow it to surrender with the full honors normally extended to a defeated enemy. "The same Honors will be granted to the Surrendering Army [Cornwallis's] as were granted to the Garrison of Charles Town," insisted Washington. Individual soldiers would be allowed to keep personal items, and officers their sidearms. Everything else would be turned over to the Allies. Cornwallis had 120 minutes to decide before hostilities once again commenced. As Washington assumed he would, Cornwallis responded favorably and agreed to impose a further cessation on his artillery beginning at 5:00 a.m. the next morning.[19]

Some of the Allies remained suspicious of Cornwallis's motives. "[W]e shall soon know whether the whole is a farce—or if his Lordship is in earnest," wrote Washington's secretary Jonathan Trumbull.[20] Work in the trenches reciprocally ceased late in the day and soldiers from both armies mounted their works and stood quietly surveying the desolate scene around them.[21] The British were indeed in earnest.

In the York River harbor, some of Cornwallis's command labored to unload the few ships still afloat before sinking them. During the day, the frigate *Guadaloupe* was scuttled and sunk, and the man-of-war *Fowey* was towed into shallow water where carpenters bored holes in her hull. About 7:00 p.m., a tragic accident occurred that momentarily broke the evening calm. Some drunk British artillerymen were loading bombs to be used in the event fighting erupted again the next day. One of them foolishly entered a powder magazine carrying a flame, whereupon the magazine and a dozen British soldiers were immediately blown to pieces.[22] This lone event marred the first night of relative calm the armies had experienced in nearly two weeks.

Thursday, October 18: Negotiations Continue

The truce was extended as planned on Thursday. At dawn, the strains of Scottish bagpipes wafted over the undulating plain of Yorktown. The regimental band of Royal Deux-Ponts returned the serenade. The rising sun found many hundreds of Allied soldiers crowded along the length of their earthworks facing British troops likewise arrayed along the battered ramparts of Yorktown. Colonel St. George Tucker, Nelson's aide, described the scene in his journal, remembering how the men of both sides stood and stared at their former opponents. "On the beach of York

The Moore house, located near the York River about one mile from the British works ringing Yorktown. Here, on October 18, 1781, the Allied commissioners negotiated with Cornwallis's aides the "Articles of Capitulation" that ended the siege and virtually conceded American independence. The house is preserved today by the National Park Service.

National Park Service, Colonial National Historical Park, Yorktown Collection

hundreds of busy people might be seen moving to and fro." Tucker could see the ships Cornwallis had ordered sunk littering the river, "the masts, yards and even the top gallant masts of some might be seen without any vestige of hulls." Near Gloucester Point was the remainder of the British shipping. "Even here the Guadaloupe [emphasis in original], sunk to the water's edge, showed how vain the hope," concluded Tucker.[23]

Washington appointed two commissioners to represent Allied interests. One was his aide-de-camp Lieutenant Colonel John Laurens of South Carolina, whose own father was even then imprisoned in the Tower of London. Laurens would represent the Americans. General Rochambeau selected Viscount de Noailles to represent the French. These two plenipotentiaries were authorized to negotiate with two officers of equal rank chosen by Cornwallis. Both sides agreed the meeting would take place at the Moore home located behind the first parallel near the river approximately one mile from the British defenses around Yorktown.[24]

Flags now passed between the armies with such regularity that the customary drumbeats were eventually discontinued. Laurens and de Noailles reached the Moore house ahead of their counterparts and waited for the British to arrive. The British envoys arrived a short time later. Cornwallis had selected his aide, Major Alexander Ross, and Lieutenant Colonel Thomas Dundas of the 80th Regiment. And so the deliberations began.[25]

Evidently, Washington anticipated a smooth settlement and was prepared to receive a British surrender that day. He readied one detachment each of French and American soldiers with instructions to occupy the enemy fortifications at the appropriate time. As the hours slowly slipped by, the realization grew that the negotiations were not unfolding as smoothly as he had expected. The Allied troop detachments fell back into their respective sectors.[26]

In the trenches, von Steuben continued to command that afternoon, having refused as a point of military etiquette to be relieved by General Lincoln's division. Citing European precedent, von Steuben claimed that since his troops were serving in the trenches when negotiations for the surrender began, they had the right to continue on duty until the capitulation ended. To Lincoln's dismay, Washington sustained the baron in the matter. Likewise, the Regiments Bourbonnois and Deux-Ponts continued their duty in the French sector until the enemy flag over Yorktown was taken down for the last time.[27]

In case the negotiations collapsed, Allied artillery stood poised and ready to resume fire at a moment's notice. Although not all of the second parallel batteries were finished, enough ordnance was now available to level a final, crippling fire against Cornwallis's crumbling ramparts should Washington decide an assault was necessary. Lieutenant Feltman of the 1st Pennsylvania counted 60 pieces of armament in the batteries attached to the second parallel before Yorktown.[28]

Prospects for renewing the siege became increasingly remote as the day passed. At the Moore house, negotiations dragged on as Cornwallis tried to obtain the least offensive arrangements for the surrender of his army. Dundas and Ross delayed the proceedings with arguments over many of the proposed articles of capitulation.[29] One particular area of dispute concerned the formal surrender ceremony. Cornwallis's agents demanded the same terms accorded General Burgoyne at Saratoga, where the Americans allowed the British Army to march out with colors flying. Laurens and de Noailles adamantly stood their ground and denied these repeated requests. The humiliating and recent capitulation of Lincoln's army at Charleston was fresh in their minds, too.[30]

Laurens and de Noailles did concede, albeit reluctantly, some honors of war for the British stationed at Gloucester Point. These troops, maintained Ross, had remained largely unmolested through the siege and unlike the garrison at Yorktown, were not immediately threatened by Choisy. In other words, they did not really need to surrender. In rebuttal, Laurens argued the Gloucester troops composed part of the single Yorktown garrison. A compromise was reached that allowed Lieutenant Colonel Banastre Tarleton's cavalry to ride forth with swords drawn, but the infantry would surrender with cased colors—the same as those at Yorktown.[31] Just as Washington desired, the Allied commissioners steadfastly refused to allow Cornwallis's soldiers to be paroled and shipped to England.[32]

Another controversial article dealt with the question of the Loyalists, those Americans who had chosen to support the Crown and as a result had earned Washington's undying contempt. The Allied commander rejected Cornwallis's request for immunity for the Loyalists serving with his army—most of whom served with Lieutenant Colonel John Graves Simcoe's "Queen's Rangers." According to Washington, that matter, as well as the persons involved, lay completely within the jurisdiction of the United States government. Washington yielded somewhat, however, in placing the sloop *Bonetta* at Cornwallis's disposal to carry dispatches and private property to General Clinton. The vessel could proceed, *without inspection*, subject only to being delivered to de Grasse upon its return. Washington was providing Cornwallis a means to convey the Loyalists under him to New York, which allowed Washington to retreat gracefully from his own previously announced determination to hang all deserters found in Yorktown.[33]

Slow progress was made, but the negotiations continued through the day and into the night. About midnight, the commissioners—who knew they were close to an agreement but had not yet fully reached one—informed their superiors of the state of affairs and the truce was extended to 9:00 a.m., October 19. Both sides tentatively agreed on a draft set of Articles of Capitulation to be submitted for Cornwallis's approval.[34] Despite the long delay, the day's negotiations evoked general optimism among the Allies. Hamilton of the 1st Pennsylvania wrote his wife of the recent events and concluded joyfully, "Tomorrow Cornwallis and his army are ours."[35]

The armistice continued through the night. By morning, hundreds of civilians, apprised of the epochal events taking form, had assembled in wagons and carriages from miles around to witness the surrender of the British Army.[36] Shortly after daybreak, Laurens dispatched a message to the British envoys outlining the procedures for capitulation:

> [I] am instructed to inform you that the Generals of the Allied Army will be at the Redoubt on the right of our second parallel at 9 o clock—this morning—when they expect to receive Ld Cornwallis's definitive Answer and sign the Capitulation. The Works on the York side as mentioned last night, to be delivered immediately after signing—those at Gloucester as soon as a message can be sent to them. The Garrison of York to march out at 12 o clock and that of Gloucester at 2 in the afternoon.[37]

The times specified were soon thereafter revised by Washington, probably because the armies required more time to organize for the surrender ceremony. He notified Cornwallis that he expected the Articles signed by 11:00 a.m., and the British garrison to march out three hours later.[38]

Near the appointed hour, the British general and his naval commander, Captain Thomas Symonds, held the final document before them. In what must have been the most painful signature of his life, Cornwallis dipped his quill into an inkwell and affixed his name to the surrender document; Symonds did the same, and it was sent to the Allied leaders waiting in Redoubt 10B. There, Washington studied the signatures and wrote nine simple words and the date: "Done in the trenches before York Town in Virginia, Oct. 19 1781." He signed the paper "G. Washington." Rochambeau signed for the Army of France, and Admiral Louis de Barras for the French Navy in place of de Grasse, who could not be present.[39]

With these signatures, the siege of Yorktown formally ended.

The Surrender Ceremony

Occupation of the British fortifications began within the hour. About noon, the enemy troops lowered the Union Jack and evacuated their works, marching for their camps behind the lines. Two battalions, one each of French and American soldiers, marched forward from the second parallel to enter two British redoubts located on the east side of Yorktown near the river (Nos. 7 and 8). Major James Hamilton of the 1st Pennsylvania commanded the American party of 100 infantrymen; the Marquis de Laval headed a like number of French grenadiers of Bourbonnois. Hamilton advanced to the redoubt on the right and took possession of it, whereupon young Lieutenant Ebenezer Denny prepared to plant his flag on the parapet. His efforts were interrupted by von Steuben, who had accompanied the party into the British lines. The baron rudely grabbed the standard from Denny's grasp and planted it himself— an action that provoked the ire of Colonel Richard Butler, who watched the episode from the rear. The baron's hubris in pilfering Denny's flag nearly triggered a duel between Butler and von Steuben; only the intercession of Washington and Rochambeau prevented it.[40]

Before long, the French standard waved over the left redoubt and Allied picket troops advanced to complete the occupation in the British earthworks all along the line. More Allied troops blocked the Hampton Road into Yorktown to halt traffic and communications until Allied officers of the various departments completed an inventory of the property and stores remaining with Cornwallis's army. Pennsylvania troops, meanwhile, began leveling the French earthworks straddling Hampton Road.[41] These comprised Redoubt 4B of the second parallel, plus sections of the French communication trenches and the French sector of the first parallel.

While the occupation of the British works was underway, Cornwallis issued several paragraphs of thanks to his troops in the third person. "Lord Cornwallis cannot express enough the gratitude due the Officers and Soldiers of this Army for their good [performance] on every occasion while he had the honor to command them," he began, "but especially for their extraordinary courage [and] resolution in their defense of these posts. He sincerely laments [that] your exertions were not sufficient to withstand the numerous artillery which you have had to stand against. The blood of the noblest man will not have been in vain." He went on to explain that they would not be sent home as they had hoped—"This alone could not be ratified"—though he assured he had "taken pains" to see they would be well provided for in captivity. Finally, Cornwallis outlined how the surrender ceremony would take place, and how he expected his men would be "parading in the finest and grandest order."[42]

The Allied armies of France and the United States, meanwhile, paraded in a field before forming three ranks deep about 20 yards apart along Hampton Road. The French aligned themselves on the west side of the road, and the Americans on the east. The Allied formation began at about the point where the second parallel intersected the highway and stretched south for nearly a mile on either side of Hampton Road. Edward Burke, who witnessed the surrender, wrote that "the American & french Army formed two lines of Order of Battle from the head of our Works along the road which led out of the Town."[43]

Rochambeau's soldiers stood resplendent in their newly-donned white uniforms of long coats and waistcoats with various colored lapels designating the regimental organizations. "The French troops appeared very well," remarked a German soldier. "They were good looking, tall, well-washed men." Soissonois soldiers had red lapels that complemented light blue collars and yellow buttons; the troops of Bourbonnois wore crimson lapels, set against pink or green collars, and white buttons; those of Saintonge were similar to the soldiers of Soissonois, with sky blue collars and yellow buttons; Touraine soldiers sported violet lapels and collars and yellow buttons; Agenois troops had violet lapels also, but displayed deep yellow collars and white buttons. Some might have worn uniforms with grey lapels. The men of Royal Deux-Ponts wore blue coats with blue collars and light yellow lapels. Black gaiters pulled over white broadcloth encased the Frenchmen's legs. The colors of France, a golden fleur-de-lis embroidered on a white silken background, undulated in the breeze at the head of each regiment.[44]

In striking contrast to the French stood the American Continentals, proudly at attention but wearing shabby blue uniforms that were, for the most part, ragged and soiled. The militia wore a motley assortment of uniforms and a potpourri of leather hunting shirts and breeches, clothes associated with backwoodsmen along the frontier. American regimental standards waved over the line while the music of a French military band, the only one in America, helped the soldiers pass the time until the British appeared.[45]

A modern photo of a segment of the fenced trace of Surrender Road. The British and German soldiers exited their defenses following Cornwallis's capitulation, marched down this road, and yielded their arms and standards in a meadow known today as Surrender Field. *National Park Service, Colonial National Historical Park, Yorktown Collection*

On the right of the American line, nearest the Yorktown garrison, Washington waited on horseback with his general officers. Rochambeau, de Barras, and the principal French military and naval officers sat their horses on the far side of the road, facing the Americans.

When Cornwallis's army emerged from the Yorktown fortifications, it did so late and probably from a gate east of the Hornwork. Exactly where and when is not clear. With the Allies in control of a string of enemy redoubts along the eastern portion of the line, the British and German troops may have walked out between Redoubts 6 and 7. There is also a possibility they came out just to the west of Battery 7. As historian Erwin N. Thompson put it, "Not only was this gate more centrally located, but just outside lay a spur (west of the hornwork) to the Hampton Road, down which they would march." A contemporary map suggests as much. Unfortunately, determining the exact point is not possible at this late date.[46]

When the exit of the army took place varies widely depending upon the source consulted. According to Lieutenant Swartwout, the British

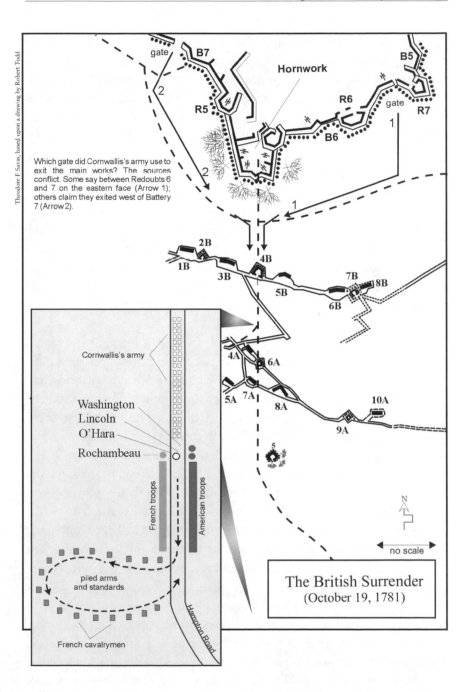

Theodore F Savas, based upon a drawing by Robert Todd

gate
B7
B5
Hornwork
2
R6
gate
R5
R7
B6
1

Which gate did Cornwallis's army use to exit the main works? The sources conflict. Some say between Redoubts 6 and 7 on the eastern face (Arrow 1); others claim they exited west of Battery 7 (Arrow 2).

2
1

2B
1B
4B
3B
7B
8B
5B
6B

Cornwallis's army

Washington
Lincoln
O'Hara
Rochambeau

French troops
American troops

piled arms
and standards

French cavalrymen

Hampton Road

4A **6A**
5A **7A**
8A
10A
9A
5

N

no scale

The British Surrender
(October 19, 1781)

Army tramped out of Yorktown "at one o'clock P M." General Henry Knox vaguely referred to the event as occurring at "about two o'clock," a time Baron von Closen also remembered as being accurate. Based upon other credible sources, these recollections can confidently be discarded as too early. The general consensus is that the Yorktown garrison marched out about 3:00 p.m.—one hour after the time specified by Washington. A German soldier quoted Cornwallis's orders as specifying that precise time (3:00 p.m.), and he was indeed correct, for 3:00 p.m. was the time Cornwallis recorded in his message to this men. Frenchman Brisout de Barneville agreed that was the hour, as did Virginia Militia officer Colonel William Fontaine, who recorded his recollections of the surrender just one week after the event. Several other observers were less precise and believed it was even later. Hessian Lieutenant Jakob Ernst Kling put the time at "between 3 and 4:00." German Johann Radler wrote his mother two months later that the British marched out "at about 4 o'clock."[47]

Regardless of the gate from which it emerged or the hour at which it did so, there are three matters no one disputes: the British army was but a shadow of its former self, looked grand in clean and bright uniforms, and Lord Cornwallis was not within its ranks. The capitulating army had been terribly whittled down by disease and casualties and no longer resembled the powerful force that had originally entered Yorktown. Large numbers of men, roughly one-half, remained sick or wounded in the town.[48] The many hundreds who paraded, however, boasted clean uniforms, having taken the time to don their finest. The officers with their yellow collars, cuffs, lapels, and silver buttons contrasted with red waistcoats, white sashes, and white breeches looked picture perfect. Cockades and silver lace on the hats complemented the silver loops on their coats. The artillerymen wore blue coats and black-laced hats, while the infantrymen dressed in the bright red waistcoats that had come to symbolize the enemy of the Allies. The Hessian regiments mostly wore blue uniforms of a shade approaching that used by many of the Americans.

Cornwallis—a general in the most respected army in the world forced to surrender to a Virginia planter untrained in the art of war—may have been too embarrassed by the episode to take part; he also may have simply been ill. Dr. Thacher scoffed at his absence. "We are not to be surprised that the pride of the British officer is humbled on this occasion," he wrote in his journal, "as they have always entertained an exalted opinion of their own military prowess and affected to view the Americans as a contemptible, undisciplined rabble." Thacher was not finished:

> But there is no display of magnanimity when a great commander shrinks from the inevitable misfortunes of war; and when it is considered that Lord Cornwallis has frequently appeared in splendid triumph at the head of his army, by which he is almost always <u>adored</u>, we conceive it incumbent on him cheerfully to participate in their misfortunes and degradations, however humiliating; but it is said he gives himself up entirely to vexation and despair.

Brigadier General Charles O'Hara had the duty of leading the British in Cornwallis's stead.[49]

O'Hara's own Guards held the vanguard. Behind them tramped the infantry regulars in regimental numerical order. Cavalry followed, with the German units bringing up the rear, Hessians first and the Ansbachs thereafter. Once formed into ranks, the drums rolled and the British platoons began their melancholy procession along Hampton Road toward the twin waiting columns of victors. "The road through which they marched was lined with spectators, French and American," remembered Harry Lee. "On one side the commander-in-chief, surrounded by his suite and the American staff, took his station; on the other side, opposite to him, was the Count de Rochambeau, in like manner attended."[50]

Washington had refused to allow the British to follow custom and play an American or French march during the surrender; Lincoln, after all, had not been allowed to play British music when he surrendered his army at Charleston. That they played something is not in doubt. What they played, however, is of no little debate.

Article III of the terms of surrender specifically state that Cornwallis's garrison would march out with "Colors cased & Drums beating a British or German march." Did this mean drums only? Fife and drums? Lieutenant Swartwout remembered the British "Drums beating, to them an unpleasant march." Lieutenant Denny agreed, adding that the "drums beat as if they did not care how." Colonel Richard Henry "Light Horse" Lee wrote simply that the drums beat a British march. Many others agreed with Lee, including General Washington, Lieutenant de Verger of the Deux-Ponts regiment, and Adjutant General Hand. Other accounts muddle the issue. About three weeks after the surrender, German Lieutenant Jakob Ernst Kling wrote that the army "marched to military music to where the enemy armies paraded in line. We marched with drums beating and colors cased." Remembered another German soldier, "We marched to military music in platoons through the enemy lines, while our drummers beat the march." According to yet a third German soldier, Johann Döhla, "[D]rums and fifes [were] playing." Cornwallis's own message to his troops, issued immediately before they marched, plainly stated "the entire army with marital music will march out in front of the trenches . . ." American Edward Burke, who watched as the British passed by, wrote a friend that "they marched . . . to the Sound of Musick, not Military Marches, but of Certain Airs, wch. had in them so peculiar a strain of melancholy." Something seems to have been played besides beating drums—but what?

Most accounts today claim British musicians played a native piece some recognized as "The World Turned Upside Down." Indeed, nearly every American child has been taught as much in school. Popular accounts notwithstanding, there is little credible evidence to support this claim. Asa Redington, who was present with the 1st New Hampshire, reported the name more than fifty years after the war when he wrote, "the British bands played that old tune about the world being turned upside down." There are other problems with this specific recollection in addition to the passage of so much time. At least one historian has demonstrated that the first specific reference to this particular tune did not appear in print until the 1820s in a secondary account of the war, and the source for the information was a man who was in Europe at the time of the surrender. "The World Turned Upside Down" was a popular tune of the period and had numerous ballads and verses written to it, including "When the King Enjoys His Own Again." The melody, moreover, was indeed a melancholy one and therefore seems to fit with contemporary accounts and the solemnity of the occasion. "Americans seized on the 'Upside Down' version because it so exactly fitted their view of the event," concluded historian Thomas Fleming. What was played that day so long ago will probably never be known with certainty.

Whatever was played, the slow-moving column advanced to the dirge-like strains, the soldiers "heavily burdened with their effects" and with their muskets at arms. At the head marched the British color-bearers, their flags furled and cased as agreed. General O'Hara, on horseback, led the procession. "Universal silence was observed amid the vast concourse," remembered Harry Lee, "and the utmost decency prevailed: exhibiting in demeanor an awful sense of the vicissitudes of human life, mingled with commiseration for the unhappy." Lee's sketch of the solemn ceremony would be echoed by others 84 years later describing another surrender ceremony at Appomattox Court House, one in which his son would play a prominent role.[51]

As O'Hara approached the awaiting Allies, Guillaume Mathieu, Count Dumas, Rochambeau's aide-de-camp, rode forward to meet him. O'Hara asked for Rochambeau, and Dumas directed him to the head of the French column arrayed west of Hampton Road facing east toward the line of Americans. "Guessing his intention," recalled Dumas, "I galloped on to place myself between him and M. de Rochambeau, who at that moment made me a sign, pointing to General Washington who was opposite to him." O'Hara knew Washington was the commander of the Allied army, and his intent to either slight the Virginian or avoid him altogether was unsuccessful, for Rochambeau would have none of it. Dumas conducted O'Hara across the road to where Washington was waiting. O'Hara apologized for the error and for Cornwallis's absence from the ceremony.[52] According to at least one account, the British general extended Cornwallis's sword for Washington's acceptance. The Allied commander demurred. "Never from such a good hand," he said, and referred O'Hara to Benjamin Lincoln. If Cornwallis was going to send a subordinate to surrender, O'Hara could surrender to a subordinate. Lincoln took the sword, symbolically held it a moment, and then returned it to O'Hara. With that, Lincoln guided his mount into the road and led the British to the site selected for the disarmament.[53]

Some of the Allied soldiers who watched Cornwallis's troops file by left vivid impressions of the event. One Virginia officer observed that "their knees seemed to tremble, and you could not see a platoon that marched in any order." There is little doubt that some of the British were intimidated by the number of Allies who lined the road. "We saw all these soldiers with surprise and were astonished over this multitude of people who [had] besieged us," remembered Lieutenant Kling.[54] Two Americans believed the disordered march by so many of the British soldiers was the result of intoxication.[55] Dr. Thacher, who witnessed the

John Trumbull's *The Surrender of Lord Cornwallis, 19 October 1781*, was painted ca 1787-1828. Trumbull, who served as an American officer during the war, combined extensive research with artistic liberties to depict the surrender scene.

procession from horseback, remembered "a disorderly and unsoldierly conduct, their step was irregular, and their ranks frequently broken." Light Horse Harry Lee, however, recalled the event quite differently: "[The] captive army . . . moved slowly in column with grace and precision."[56]

"I detest the British Army, and despise from my Soul the mass of unfeeling men w[ch] compose its Officers," wrote civilian observer Edward Burke as he vented his emotions in a contemporaneous letter to a friend. "But their pride, insolence and insults," he continued, "their present situation in w[ch] all ranks of them discover a condescention and humility bordering on that of a Spaniel; this, I say, is a good Lesson, & is one instance of the inconstancy of fortune, & of the strange Vicissitudes in the Affairs of this World."[57]

A writer to the New Jersey *Gazette* described the surrendering troops this way:

The British officers in general behaved like boys who had been
whipped at school; some bit their lips, some pouted, others cried;
their round, broad-brimmed hats were well adapted to the occasion,
hiding those faces they were ashamed to show. The foreign
[German] regiments made a much more military appearance, and
the conduct of their officers was far more becoming men of
fortitude.[58]

Sullen, drunk, or both, the troops continued on between the French
and Americans drawn up either side of Hampton Road for a mile or more.
Kling was impressed by the manner in which the Allies had arrayed
themselves. The French "paraded splendidly. . . . Their general was
mounted in front on a charger which was splendid with silver harness and
looked handsome." On the left, he noted, stood the colonials. "[F]irst the
American regular troops, after them the Virginia militia, who were not a
match for the former as day from night." The dejected column marched
on the road through the second siege line, through the zig-zag approach
trench, past the first parallel and beyond the old British barbette battery
converted to a redoubt by the Americans. No major incident marred the
procession.[59]

At the end of the Allied ranks, the defeated column swung to the right
off the road and entered a broad cultivated plain designated as the
surrender field. The ground lay in a roughly triangular space bounded on
the east by Hampton Road and on the south and west by secondary routes
leading into that highway from the area of the Allied encampments.[60] In
the field were mounted French Hussars formed in a great circle, and into
this ring marched the British color-bearers.[61] Twenty-eight regimental
officers of Cornwallis's army advanced in line formation and halted six
paces opposite a like number of American sergeants posted to receive
their flags. When ordered to deliver the colors the British demurred; an
impasse arose. The British, wrote Asa Redington, "were disposed to
resent the idea of surrendering their flags furled, and to noncommissioned officers." The stalemate was broken by Alexander
Hamilton. The lieutenant colonel directed an American ensign to receive
the colors. The junior officer took them one by one and handed each to an
American sergeant. The impasse was broken.[62]

Behind came the soldiers, filing into the circle of French cavalrymen
to ground their muskets and drop their cartridge boxes, swords, drums,

Surrender Field today, looking northwest. The British and German troops advanced into this field from the right, laid down their arms and handed over their standards (the center of this photograph), and circled around toward the fence in the foreground before walking back to Yorktown. *National Park Service, Colonial National Historical Park, Yorktown Collection*

and other musical instruments. As a courtesy to the vanquished, British and Hessian officers were allowed to retain their sabers and soldiers were permitted to keep their knapsacks. Washington, Rochambeau, and the other Allied leaders sat their mounts silently and watched. Another spectator was Washington's stepson, Captain John Parke Custis, who served as an aide-decamp to the commander at Yorktown. Stricken with the fever that was shortly to kill him, Custis witnessed the surrender from a carriage, much against the advice of army physicians.[63]

Admiral Louis de Barras, who was present to represent the French Navy, was not an accomplished equestrian. Nevertheless, he weathered his steed well until his mount suddenly stretched forward to relieve himself. De Barras appeared shaken. "Good heavens!'" he exclaimed. "I believe my horse is sinking!"[64]

The disarmament lasted more than one hour. Doctor Thacher, a keen observer and chronicler of the goings-on at Yorktown, as usual was not overly impressed by the comportment of the enemy. "The spirit and pride of the British soldier was put to the severest test: here their mortification could not be concealed," he penned in his journal. "Some of the platoon officers appeared to be exceedingly chagrined when giving the word 'ground arm,' and I am a witness that they performed this duty in a very unofficer-like manner, and that many of the soldiers manifested a sullen temper [emphasis in original], throwing their arms on the pile with violence, as if determined to render them useless. This irregularity, however, was checked by the authority of General Lincoln." Other witnesses noted that many of the men openly wept as they passed by the growing pile of weapons and accouterments.[65] "The English," wrote French Commissary General Claude Blanchard, "displayed much arrogance and ill humor during this melancholy ceremony, they particularly affected great contempt for the Americans.[66]

"After having grounded their arms and divested themselves of their accouterments," explained Thacher, "the captive troops were conducted back to Yorktown and guarded by our troops till they could be removed to the place of their destination."[67] Their route into the fortifications was the same in reverse, and so the men were threaded back through the Allied ranks along the Hampton Road into Yorktown, where they took quarters in their tents, guarded by American infantrymen and French grenadiers. "I am glad that the [surrender] convention was made because the enemy armies were so great that our situation was hopeless," Johann Radler wrote his mother. The Germans were more favorably disposed towards the Allies than were the British. "The French soldiers and the American regulars were fine looking troops, but the militia were dirty, unruly, and easily bribed—bad soldiers and greedy men," remarked Lieutenant Kling, who was also quite happy the Allies had "made such an accord with us. The French were to us very friendly, the officers as well as the soldiers. It was also likewise with the Americans."[68]

Following the surrender of the Yorktown garrison, French guards took possession of the earthen defenses west of Hampton Road, while their American counterparts occupied the fortifications east of the road.[69]

Surrender at Gloucester Point

Across the York River at Gloucester Point, the British capitulated in accordance with stipulations in the surrender documents that called for a ceremony nearly identical to that completed at Yorktown. Unfortunately, no contemporaneous firsthand accounts of the surrender ceremony at Gloucester Point have been located.[70] We do know the ceremony offered a few noticeable differences than the one conducted at Yorktown. Because it was surrendering on its own accord and not because of the Allies arrayed against it, the garrison received special privileges. Tarleton and his cavalry were allowed to ride out with their swords unsheathed, and the trumpets from the garrison's band were permitted to play a British or German marching tune. All colors, however, remained furled. Washington directed Choisy to send forward at 1:00 p.m. one detachment of French and one of Americans, each to possess an enemy redoubt on the British perimeter. Concerned lest the Virginia militia become unruly during the ceremony, Washington counseled Choisy to appoint capable officers and watch matters closely. When all was ready, the Gloucester Point garrison, instructed the Allied commander,

> is to march out at three o'clock with shouldered Arms, Drums beating a British or German March, the Cavalry with their Swords drawn, and the Colours of the whole cased; to a place which you will be so good to appoint, in front of the posts, where they will ground their Arms and afterwards return to their encampment.[71]

Tarleton commanded the British forces at Gloucester Point. Because of the time lapse in transmitting messages across the river, Choisy had not yet received a copy of the Articles of Capitulation. In an unusual gesture, Tarleton visited the Frenchman's headquarters early in the afternoon to demand a copy of the Articles before he surrendered. The French officer conveyed the request to Washington, adding, "I hope likewise your excellency will acquaint me with them."[72]

Tarleton and his troopers had inflicted wanton injury and damage upon residents from Virginia through the Carolinas, and Tarleton feared for his personal safety at the hands of vengeful American militiamen—a concern he freely communicated to Choisy. He was right to be worried, for there were any number of men who would have hung him from the nearest tree or shot him where he stood. The French general indulged his adversary's concerns and assigned Lieutenant Colonel John Mercer's battalion of Virginia Militia, along with Lauzun's Legion, to formally represent the Allies at the surrender ceremony. Thus preoccupied, the militia could pose little threat to Tarleton's well-being.[73]

At 3:00 p.m., about the time the capitulation of the British at Yorktown was getting underway, the garrison at Gloucester Point emerged from its earthen defenses. Tarleton's legionnaires paraded on horseback with their swords drawn. Simcoe's Rangers led the long column of red-coated infantrymen and blue-uniformed Germans. Following their grounding of arms, the prisoners passed back behind the fortifications. A contingent of Mercer's Battalion moved forward and occupied the redoubts of the British line.

With the disarmament at Gloucester Point, the British capitulation was complete.[74]

Aftermath

The immediate aftermath of the surrender appears to have been rife with disorganization. Even as General O'Hara prepared to take supper with General Washington, chaos layered inside deep emotions gripped the tip of the Yorktown peninsula. "Much confusion and riot among the British through the day," noted Lieutenant Denny in his diary.[75] According to Denny, many of the vanquished resorted to drinking and vented their anger and frustration throughout the afternoon and well into the night. One British soldier bayoneted and killed an American sentinel, while others tried forcibly to break open provisions but were repulsed by the American patrols.[76] Everywhere in Yorktown lay stricken blacks, dead or dying of smallpox compounded by other sicknesses.[77] "Never was [I] in so filthy a place," wrote Denny. "Vast heaps of shot and shells lying about in every quarter, which came from our works."[78]

After nightfall, a group of 17 Hessian soldiers entered the fallen garrison, supposedly survivors of a 1,000-man contingent that had marched north from South Carolina and had stumbled into the Allied troops posted around Williamsburg. Most of them had been captured, but the dutiful remnant had pressed on to Yorktown to join Cornwallis. A cordon of French soldiers guarded the Germans from Americans bent on divesting them of their equipment.[79]

The rampant disorganization that marked the hours after the capitulation afforded both sides an emotional release from the trauma experienced over the past few weeks. The confused dispositions undoubtedly reflected manifestations of the joy and grief felt by the men over the recent developments. A realization of the broader implications of Cornwallis's surrender was surely comprehended by many of the men on both sides. But for the present, factors of personal safety and survival overrode inclinations to reflect too deeply upon the event. There would be time for that soon enough.

Scarcely two weeks later, a young French soldier expressed precisely these sentiments in a letter home:

> You may imagine, my dear Mother, the mingled feelings of joy, contentment and gratitude to the Almighty which fill our hearts. We feel that we have not fought in vain. Any regret I may have had through all these years because I did not enjoy the privileges of an officer, but remained a simple volunteer, have vanished and trouble me no more. I know now that I have been an actor in events which the world and history will never forget.[80]

Chapter 14

Broken Sword

*T*he days immediately following Cornwallis's surrender were disordered ones. The Allied forces confronted manifold problems regarding the organization and disposition of the prisoners, property, and supplies they had captured. On October 20, General Washington issued a congratulatory message extolling his army and navy for the splendid and historic victory. Admiral de Grasse, he said, was "an Admiral whose fortune and talents ensure great events." The French West Indian troops were "an army of the most admirable composition both in Officers and men . . . and their Cooperation has Insured us the present signal success."[1]

"This important affair has been effected by the most harmonious concurrence of circumstances that could possibly have happened," Henry Knox wrote in a letter to John Jay echoing Washington's sentiments. "A fleet and troops from the West Indies under the orders of one of the best men in the world—An Army of American and French troops marching from the North River 500 miles—and the fleet of Count de Barras—all joining so exactly in point of time, as to render what has happened almost certain."[2]

Similar feelings appeared in nearly all the correspondence sent from the Allied camps during this time. "The play, sir, is over," wrote Lafayette, intoning his usual histrionics. "The fifth act has just been closed."[3] "After this commencing stroke, what English general will ever think of conquering America?"[4] In a message to the Virginia delegates in Congress, General Nelson expressed weighed optimism: "This Blow, I think must be a decisive one, it being out of the Power of G. B. to replace such a number of good Troops."[5]

October 21 was a day of general thanksgiving, and Washington called on his troops to observe the occasion with the "seriousness of deportment and gratitude of heart" it demanded.[6] He dined that evening with his senior French and American officers aboard de Grasse's *Ville de Paris*, where many toasts were drunk in honor of the victory.[7] To complete the rejoicing, Washington, in an unprecedented gesture, pardoned all soldiers then under arrest or in confinement.[8] For the next several days, American troops heard speeches and discourses all praising the glorious event bestowed by a doting providence that seemed to indicate the end of British rule in America.[9]

In stark contrast to the levity of the Allied troops was the despair displayed by the senior British officers. Cornwallis penned a lengthy report describing to Clinton the developments that had culminated so disastrously in his surrender.[10] Captain Thomas Symonds broke the news to Admiral Thomas Graves: "I am very Sorry to inform you," he wrote, "that the Garrison of York, and the Vessels that remained in the River, surrendered to the Enemy by Capitulation yesterday afternoon, after a siege of 17 days."[11] The messages would depart on the sloop *Bonetta*, as specified in the Articles, once that vessel was readied to begin the voyage north.

Suspecting Cornwallis's intention to use the craft to convey Loyalists from Yorktown, General Nelson politely addressed the British commander, asking him to search the *Bonetta* for blacks and "Refugees from this State" before the vessel sailed.[12] According to one account, an American officer demanded to inspect the *Bonetta* before it left Yorktown, but was restrained from doing so by French officers who insisted on strict compliance with the surrender terms regarding the craft.[13] As stipulated in the Articles, all enemy shipping (eventually the *Bonetta* as well, despite its temporary retention by the British command) passed into the hands of the French Navy. The seamen found only 16 other craft intact (four cutters and 12 transports), and they set to work repairing and otherwise salvaging what little else remained, including the frigate *Guadaloupe*.[14]

Casualties

As a post-siege quiet settled over the ruins of Yorktown, both sides assessed their losses in killed and wounded during the combat. According to the evidence that remains (and it is not complete), the Allies appear to have sustained 389 casualties; this number includes both officers and men. French casualties account for the majority of this number because of the resistance they encountered at Redoubt 9 on the night of October 14, and because they lost more men than did the Americans during the pre-dawn enemy assault two days later. Accordingly, one French officer and 59 men were killed during the course of the siege, and 17 officers and 177 men wounded, for a total of 254. The Americans reported 135 casualties: one officer and 27 men killed, and 10 officers and 97 men wounded.[15] The relatively light nature of Allied casualties at Yorktown can be explained by the systematic procedure under which siege warfare was conducted in the 18th century. Had the struggle continued and included a grand assault into the breached enemy works, the casualties would have been much higher.[16]

Sickness had also contributed to reduce the effective strength of the Allied armies by the time of the surrender. Out of a total force at Yorktown numbering something less than 20,000 men, some 1,700 Americans contracted illness or injury of one sort or another, and 1,000 of these were absent from duty and probably receiving treatment in Williamsburg. Possibly as many as 1,700 French soldiers were likewise stricken. Effective Allied strength by the end of the siege was probably around 18,000 men present for duty.[17]

Compared to those of the Allied army, the British suffered severe losses during the siege. By their own computation, casualties numbered 156 officers and men killed and 326 wounded in the defense of Yorktown (including Gloucester Point). Seventy men were listed as missing, many of whom had deserted to the Allies. The British figure did not include Cornwallis's aide, Major Charles Cochrane, who technically belonged to another command, nor does it include Commissary Officer Perkins, who was also killed. As in the case of the lists of Allied casualties, the British tabulation of their dead did not include those wounded who later died from their injuries. Other contemporaneous documents paint an even gloomier picture. One German report, for example, claims British losses were substantially higher at 309 killed and 595 wounded. At least one report seems to substantiate this last claim.[18] In addition, more than 1,500 soldiers were sick or otherwise indisposed on the day of the surrender.[19]

The number of British officers and men who fell into Allied hands as prisoners of war was 7,087. In addition to this figure were 84 soldiers captured by the Allies during the attacks on Redoubts 9 and 10 and during the British assault of the 16th, plus 80 camp followers and 840 naval prisoners taken from the enemy vessels in the York River. All told, the grand total of British captives amounted to 8,091.[20]

Besides the British prisoners, the Allied victors claimed virtually Cornwallis's entire military equipage. During the entire day following the surrender, parties of American and French troops busily collected and inventoried the various stores and munitions taken in their conquest. Soldiers were sent across the river to Gloucester Point to help gather all sorts of accouterments.[21] Despite an observation by one Allied soldier that "there were only 10 balls and a bomb" left in Yorktown, much remained for the Allies to appropriate.[22] The spoils included twenty-four regimental standards (six British—two each from the 43rd, 76th, and 80th regiments—and 18 German). The Queen's Rangers smuggled their colors out to safety. Four British Union Jacks were also turned over, as were 32 German camp colors and 41 British camp colors. The British military chest was found to contain £2,116 6d., and the number of vessels either intact or damaged in the York River was considerable.[23] The Allies also garnered several hundred horses, a number of wagons with teams, and British commissary stores of pork, bread, and flour.[24]

Allied confiscation of armaments and various types of military equipage overshadowed other spoils and symbolized the completeness of Washington's victory. A list of articles in the Henry Knox Papers probably accounts for most of the small arms and accouterments given up by British and German soldiers during the surrender ceremony October 19. These consisted of the following:

2,800	Muskets with Bayonets
57	Muskets without Bayonets
51	Good Drums
4	Damag'd drums
2,689	Cartridge Boxes
1,013	Swords
12	Bugal [sic] horns

28	Serjt Halberts[25]
729	Bayonet belts
804	Tin Canisters
7	Fife Cases
16	Drum Slings
80,000	Musket Cartridges
5	Axes[26]

Most important was the seizure of all the British heavy ordnance at Yorktown and Gloucester Point. Accounts vary as to the exact number of cannon, mortars, and howitzers taken, but Knox's enumeration of the captured pieces is probably the most precise. In a return compiled after the surrender, Knox accounted for 244 such weapons, including 168 bronze and iron cannon of assorted calibers, most of them mounted on garrison or ship carriages, plus 23 mortars, and 15 howitzers. Also included were one amusette, six swivel guns, and 31 carronades, light pieces mostly mounted on traveling carriages.[27]

Some of the armaments, notably three 13-inch mortars, one 16-inch mortar, and several howitzers, belonged to the state of Virginia and had been captured previously during Cornwallis's drive south.[28] The French reclaimed one mortar, five howitzers, and four bronze 9-pounders lost to the British during the fight at Point of Forks, Virginia, in June 1781.[29] Most of the captured ordnance went north with the Allies when they left Yorktown. Some of the pieces needed repair. These, and others, were left in Philadelphia where carriages were built for them. Something that came as a surprise to the Allies was the abundance of British food supplies found inside Yorktown, which included 35 tons of flour, 30 tons of bread, 10 tons of beef, 37 tons of pork, plus coffee, sugar, and more than 1,200 gallons of alcohol.[30]

As the Allies collected the surrendered military stores and weapons of the British, they tabulated their own artillery ammunition expenditures from October 9-17. The final figures were staggering. The Americans fired a total of 3,312 rounds from their 18- and 24-pounder artillery pieces, and 2,178 rounds from their mortars and howitzers. French gunners had been even more profligate with their powder and shot. During the course of the siege they sent 6,378 rounds of 12-, 16-, and 24-pounder shot into Yorktown, along with 3,569 bombs from mortars and howitzers. The grand total of ammunition discharged against

Cornwallis's works by Allied artillery was 15,437 rounds. This works out to an average of more than 1,700 rounds per day, or 71 rounds per hour—nearly one shot every minute from the beginning of the siege until the end.[31]

From all appearances, the French and American fire that raked Yorktown for nine days had been devastating. Everywhere houses lay in rubble, bodies were strewn in disarray, and buildings still standing bore vivid imprints of their days under Allied artillery fire. "I will never forget how frightful and disturbing was the appearance of the city of York, from the [British] fortifications on the crest to the strand below," wrote a French officer in a graphic account of the destruction wrought by the heavy weapons. "One could not take three steps without running into some great holes made by bombs, some splinters, some balls, some half covered trenches, with scattered white or negro arms or legs, [and] some bits of uniforms. Most of the houses [were] riddled by cannon fire, and [there were] almost no window-panes in the houses." Sutler Daniel Trabue agreed. "It was a truly Dreadfully shocking sight to see the damage our bomb-shells had Done." According to Lieutenant Verger of the Deux-Ponts Regiment, "The din and disorder caused by our bombs in the town defy description," though that did not prevent him from providing one: "Hardly a house remains that is not destroyed, either wholly or in part, by shells or bombs. One could not go ten steps without meeting the wounded and dying, destitute negroes abandoned to their fate, and corpse after corpse on every hand."

Hector St. John de Crèvecoeur psychologically stepped back from the devastation by noting simply that the Allies had "destroyed the small and unattractive town. There was only one pretty house, and that was not spared." Chaplain Claude Robin, another Frenchman, was a bit more taken aback by the destruction. The "unfortunate little town," he wrote with no little understatement, was in a shambles. "[I] saw many elegant homes shot through and through in a thousand places, and ready to crumble to pieces; rich household furniture crushed under their ruins [and] the carcases of men and horses."[32] Baron von Closen noted the apprehension of the local residents who feared even more of their property was about to be lost at the hands of the victorious American soldiers.[33]

At the same time, the citizens began tallying their own losses from the British occupation of Yorktown and its environs. Damage claims filed later by the townspeople reflected the destruction, impairment, or confiscation by Cornwallis's troops of various homes, warehouses, boats, fencing, forage, animals, slaves, and other personal property.[34] Tempers flared in the days following the surrender as citizens sought to take, sometimes forcibly, articles previously appropriated by the enemy. Lieutenant Colonel Banastre Tarleton found himself publicly humiliated when a man brandishing a wooden stick accosted him in the street of Yorktown, demanding the return of the horse he was riding. Utterly without authority over the locals, Tarleton meekly gave up the animal, much to the amusement of the watching crowd.[35]

While officers of the defeated and victorious armies surveyed their conditions, collected supplies, and figured their losses in the wake of the capitulation, the soldiers of France and America labored to restore some order to the countryside around Yorktown. On October 27, Washington ordered patrols out to search the area and "see that all dead carcases . . . in and about Camp are immediately buried." Washington continued:

> A Sergeant and 12 men from the Baron Steubens [sic] Division will this day Patrol from their left to the Forks of the road above Head Quarters for the above purpose. . . . Like parties will be immediately sent from General Lincoln's and the Marquis de la Fayettes [sic] divisions, the former to scour the ground between York town, Tarleton's old camp and the right of the French Camp, the latter in front of their own camp extending to the river and as high up as the east end of York.[36]

The Fortifications

The principal task of the Allies during the last days of October entailed leveling their entrenchments around Yorktown. The job was scarcely designed to appease local property owners. Washington's primary objective in ordering the works demolished was to prevent their falling into British hands should Clinton arrive with troops, somehow reverse the situation, and lay siege against the Allies.[37] As early as October 20, men of the Virginia Militia were employed in tearing down the American fortifications.[38] On that same day, Washington directed that a search be made for all available axes to facilitate the project.[39]

The general demolition seems to have begun October 22 for the Americans, and not until November 1 for the French.[40] The difference may be accounted for by the fact that General Rochambeau's troops were slated to remain at Yorktown through the winter months. The leveling was perhaps delayed until some determination could be made as to what works the French wanted retained.[41] On October 24, Washington ordered 200 men from General Muhlenberg's Brigade to "parade tomorrow morning at seven o'clock on the right of the first Parrallel to Level the works. . . . Application must be made to the Quarter Master General this evening for tools."[42]

The work proceeded by rotation of brigades.[43] On the 26th, General Wayne's unit was assigned to fill in the trenches, but rainy weather forced a halt to the work. Wayne's Brigade resumed this unwelcome duty the next day; on the 28th, Clinton's Brigade took over, joined by Colonel Mathias Ogden's Regiment of Dayton's Brigade.[44] The work to level the American earthworks went on through October 31.[45]

The next day, the French began demolition of their works, including their sectors of the first and second parallels and the two redoubts at Pigeon Hill. On November 6, the French began a new line of entrenchments inside Yorktown and on Gloucester Point, contracting the former British positions to suit their needs for the forthcoming winter. Two batteries, each containing 18 pieces of artillery, were established below Yorktown, while a unit of 12 pieces, guarded by a redoubt, was erected at Gloucester Point.[46]

Despite the work of the Allies in late October and early November, many of the earthworks in and around Yorktown remained more or less intact after the troops withdrew from the area. In the spring of 1782, the French departed for Rhode Island and the works still standing were looked upon as a nuisance by the people of the community. That summer, a movement was undertaken to get the Continental Army to complete their removal, but the proposal succumbed to Governor Benjamin Harrison's desire to maintain the entrenchments for emergency purposes. Shortly thereafter, the governor changed his mind, fearing their reoccupation by British forces should warfare erupt anew. Accordingly, the Council of State ordered 500 men from Elizabeth City, Warwick, James City, New Kent, York, and Gloucester counties to proceed to Yorktown for the purpose of dismantling the surviving earthworks. The plan was stymied by the county magistrates and by the lack of suitable accommodations at Yorktown for all the men.[47]

The matter was not allowed to die, however. In July 1783, a leading Yorktown citizen, David Jameson, proposed to a Virginia delegate to Congress that blacks be sent to complete the demolition. The people of Yorktown, he said, ought not have "to bear at their very doors Mounds of Earth which prevent a free circulation of the Air, and Ditches of stagnant putred [sic] water."[48] Black workers, believed Jameson, might best accomplish the task because they "will obey Command," unlike many undisciplined Continental soldiers. Nor would they require extensive and expensive billeting.[49] But the money-poor central government refused, citing instances where other states had torn down fortifications within their borders without Congressional aid.[50]

And so the earthworks at Yorktown remained long after their occupants left. Most gradually disappeared over the years, succumbing to wind and water erosion. During the Civil War, when Confederate forces occupied the village, some of the old British works were incorporated in a new line ringing Yorktown. Many of the Confederate additions are still visible. By the time of the centennial observance of the siege of Yorktown in 1881, most of the major Allied entrenchments were no more. "A few of the redoubts, which were erected by each army, are still remaining, but the principal fortifications are almost quite obliterated," observed Henry P. Johnston in 1881. "[T]he plough has passed over some of them, and groves of pine trees sprung up about others, though, during the siege, every tree near the town was destroyed. The first and second parallels can just be traced when pointed out by a person acquainted with them in a more perfect state."[51]

Few of the original Allied works exist today.[52]

Disposition of Prisoners

Another major task of the victorious forces after the surrender involved the disposition of the several thousand British soldiers who were now prisoners of war. Washington originally hoped to move the men out of Yorktown as quickly as possible the day after the surrender, but the plan was delayed until an accounting of the captives was completed and high-ranking British officers had received paroles.[53] In addition, an outbreak of dysentery had weakened many, the men were tired, and the sick and injured required treatment. Some of the latter remained in Yorktown after the other prisoners departed. They received aid from British medical personnel allowed to stay with them.[54]

Relations between victors and vanquished gradually became amicable, especially those between the British and French. The Welsh Fusiliers won particularly warm praise from French officers for their stout and complete defense of the Fusiliers' Redoubt, which never fell during the siege.[55] When the British left Yorktown, Cornwallis solicited and received financial help from Rochambeau, who graciously turned over part of what remained in the French military chest.[56]

Relations between the British and Germans and the Americans, however, remained strained, their mutual antagonism over the issue of independence the root cause of the unpleasantness. "In general, the French conducted themselves very well toward us," recalled Hessian Private Döhla, "but the Americans. . . . None were permitted in the city or in our lines, for the French grenadiers had strongly surrounded all our works and also Yorktown and allowed no one inside, because they feared the American militia . . . might also steal from us and plunder us." Americans might well have had plunder on their minds, for they had suffered heavy losses of life and property at the hands of the very soldiers now subordinate to them. The matter of the Loyalists plagued American consciousness, and only served to aggravate their disdain for Cornwallis's troops.[57]

Many of the high-ranking officers of the British Army managed to avoid the perils and discomforts American prison camps held for the defeated. By virtue of the recognized military custom of "parole," they signed statements promising good behavior until officially "exchanged." A typical parole affidavit, sworn to by numerous British officers after Yorktown, was that signed by Major Alexander Ross, one of Cornwallis's aides de-camp:

> I, Alexander Ross, Captain in His Britannick Majesty's 45th Regt.
> of Foot, & Major in His Army.
>   Do Acknowledge myself a Prisoner of War to the United States
> of America, & having permission from His Excellency General
> Washington, agreeable to Capitulation to proceed to New York &
> Charleston, or either, & to Europe.

Do pledge my Faith and Word of Honor, that I will not do or say any thing injurious to the said United States or Armies thereof, or their Allies, until duly exchanged, I do further promise that Whenever required by the Commander in Chief of the Army, or the Commissary of Prisoners for the same, I will repair to such Place or Places as they or either of them may require:

Given under my Hand at York Town 29th Octr 1781

A Ross[58]

Under similar measures, Cornwallis was granted parole and eventually returned to London. There seems to have been some discussion regarding Cornwallis's singular status as commander of the defeated army. One report held that there existed sentiment among the Americans favoring Cornwallis's retention until Minister John Laurens, imprisoned in London, won release. One faction in Congress even wanted the general to hang in retaliation for atrocities committed by his troops in the Southern colonies.[59] Cooler heads prevailed, however, and Cornwallis was allowed to proceed to New York and, ultimately, home to England. Before he left, however, he enjoyed celebrity status as the most popular officer in Yorktown. Many of the high-ranking Allied officers nearly embarrassed themselves by doing all they could to dine and rub elbows with the defeated general. The illness (if that was what had kept him from participating in the surrender ceremony) seems to have been short-lived. Indeed, so plentiful were the invitations that Lord Cornwallis could not attend them all; condolences penned by his secretary attest to his popularity.

While Cornwallis was dining and chatting in comfort, the rank and file of the surrendered army, together with some of their officers, began a long and generally miserable trek north on October 21. The column tramped through Williamsburg the following day. Guarded by Virginia militia, the prisoners continued on through Fredericksburg, where they drew rations before departing for Red House, Ashby's Gap, and into the Shenandoah Valley to their destinations at Winchester, Virginia, and Frederick, Maryland. The journey took many days, and on arrival at the American prison camps the men found the accommodations wanting. The prisoners numbered almost as many as the respective populations of the two communities, and barrack facilities of any substance were sorely lacking. With but scant shelter, the Yorktown captives and their guards set about erecting cabins. Maintaining the prison posed many troubles, for the British could not be allowed to work the fields for fear they might escape. At the same time, their prolonged confinement encouraged disease.[61]

Once most of the British had left, American regulars stepped into Yorktown and cordoned off the city to the French. De Crèvecoeur was not amused. "The magazines at York were filled with every kind of stores," he later wrote. "Most of the French officers were in great need of basic necessities." After several days the French were allowed back inside Yorktown, "but by then they [the Americans] had plundered everything and there was nothing left." De Crèvecoeur, observed one historian, was unaware that all of the captured British stores, including ammunition and weapons, were considered to be American property. Those Allies not lucky enough to be allowed to scrounge for plunder were given the odious task of burying hundreds of rotting horse carcasses, most of which had washed out of the York River and were decomposing on the sandy beaches.[62]

*   *   *

One final dash of irony remained. On the morning of October 24, three days after the majority of British prisoners left Yorktown, Admiral Thomas Graves and General Clinton appeared off the Virginia Capes with ships and troops to relieve Cornwallis. Washington learned of the fleet's arrival the same day and warned Admiral de Grasse of the threat. Delayed by his own indecisiveness, physical ailments, and Graves's problems in refitting his ships, Clinton had not left New York until October 19—the same day Cornwallis surrendered. Unaware of the capitulation, Clinton directed Graves to prepare to break through de Grasse's fleet and send small boats to cruise the shoreline for information.

Eventually, news from the pilot of the 44-gun frigate *Charon,* which had been burned and sunk by heated shot on October 10, reached the fleet's flagship. The pilot had left Yorktown on October 18, the day after Cornwallis proposed a cease-fire, and "had not heard any firing since the day before." The news distressed Clinton, who spent the next few days seeking confirmation of the intelligence. By October 29, he and Graves were convinced they were too late. "We do not of course seek an action, having lost the only object that could justify it," " Clinton wrote that same day in a message to the Allies at Gloucester Point.[63]

The British fleet turned back toward New York.

Chapter 15

Endings, Beginnings

With the subjugation of the British at Yorktown, Washington hoped to retain his powerful army and navy combination to liberate the Southern port cities of Charleston and Savannah; both still remained firmly under British control. So pressing was this objective that he appealed to de Grasse the day after the surrender, asking him for cooperation and the use of his fleet. The admiral's direct answer on October 25 was not what the Virginian wanted or necessarily expected to hear. Prior instructions from the French government, explained the admiral, necessitated his departure for the West Indies. Therefore, he was unable to commit his ships for further extended maneuvers along the coast.[1]

Without French naval support, Washington believed that complete victory in the South was unattainable, and without victory there, the long war would likely drag on indefinitely. Without other recourse, Washington began disassembling and repositioning his land force. On November 4, the same day de Grasse embarked for Santo Domingo with St. Simon's West Indian troops, the Pennsylvania, Maryland, and Virginia soldiers of Wayne and General Mordecai Gist marched southward under Major General Arthur St. Clair to meet up with Major General Nathanael Greene's command. De Grasse left four vessels to guard the entrance to the York and James rivers. Washington himself left Yorktown and rode to Williamsburg that same day.[2]

The American troops who had remained behind after the militia escorted the British and German prisoners inland departed Yorktown about November 1 to winter on the Hudson. Captured stores and ordnance were transferred to West Point at Head of Elk. Most of the militia units were soon disbanded. Only the French army of Rochambeau and some siege artillery remained behind to guard Yorktown, where some spent the winter. These included the Regiment Soissonois, plus the chasseurs and grenadiers of Saintonge. Lauzun's Legion took post at Hampton, while three companies of Royal Deux-Ponts wintered at Jamestown. The rest of the French army and its headquarters occupied Williamsburg until the summer of 1782 when, in mid-August, Rochambeau's entire force returned to Rhode Island.[3]

News of the Allied success at Yorktown spread rapidly. On the day of the surrender, Washington dispatched an aide, Lieutenant Colonel Tench Tilghman of Maryland, to notify Congress of the victory. Tilghman crossed Chesapeake Bay and rode to Philadelphia, reaching the capital during the early hours of October 24. He was nearly arrested as he sought to awaken Thomas McKean, the President of Congress. Before long the bells of Independence Hall sounded forth the news and Philadelphia came alive with excitement. Congregations of thankful citizens poured into churches and prayed. In the streets, flags and banners waved and guns barked in recognition of Cornwallis's jaw-dropping defeat. A fireworks display to honor the occasion was postponed for two days by rain, but the city otherwise bustled with celebration. On November 3, a more dignified ceremony marked the arrival in Philadelphia of the captured enemy standards, which were respectfully placed before Congress and the Ambassador of France. If anyone doubted the victory, seeing the standards in the flesh made them believers.[4]

Similar demonstrations took place in other communities as the news spread like a wild fire. At Poughkeepsie, New York, cannons were fired, bonfires were lighted, and cheers and prayers of thanksgiving commemorated the victory.[5] The good feelings inspired by the news from Yorktown were evident everywhere. Journals carried laudatory remarks for the Allies, and contemptuous comments for the British. It is fair to say that many in the country did not think highly or kindly of Cornwallis. "It is sincerely to be wished, for the sake of humanity," editorialized the *New York Journal*, "that his lordship had made a more obstinate defence, that the Allied army, obliged to storm his works, might have offered up him and his troops as a sacrifice to the violated rights of humanity!"[6] The *Maryland Gazette* ran an open letter to Cornwallis, purportedly written by an American soldier, which railed against the British general's previous actions:

> The philanthropy of America would be highly gratified in paying your lordship the tribute due an enlightened and humane soldier, did your conduct deserve such treatment; but as her justice obliges her to view you in the odious light of a cruel leader and an unprincipled plunderer, it would be impious in her to treat you with generosity or delicacy. As an American soldier I consider it a virtue to imbitter your captivity, by recalling to your remembrance the follies which have led to your present catastrophe, and to hold you up as an object of universal detestation, by surrounding you with an assemblage of your crimes. . . .[7]

Oratory likewise abounded. Nathan Fiske told an assembly at Brookfield, Massachusetts, "I cannot forbear being gratified . . . at the mortification and astonishment of the haughty nation of Britain, of the Ministry, and of their tyrannical Prince, when the fatal news comes like a sudden thunder-clap to their ears."[8]

For the American people, Yorktown represented at once the aspirations and successful resolve of the United States to gain independence. The site of the triumph became hallowed ground in American eyes. Scores of people flocked to the scene of the momentous conflict that many properly sensed had decided their future. Even Indian chiefs were ushered over the field by proud Americans who, reveling in the glory of Yorktown, sought to "make them [the Indians] sensible of the late great capture of the British Army."[9] Within weeks of the event, Yorktown symbolized both the ratification by force of the Declaration of Independence, and its tacit recognition by British arms.

British Bickering: Clinton vs. Cornwallis

If Cornwallis's surrender at Yorktown marked the perceptible wane of British power in North America, the military decisions leading to the event spurred continuing debate centering on the protagonists of the losing side—Clinton and Cornwallis. The former's failures during the weeks leading up to the surrender were readily apparent (especially in hindsight) and, almost immediately there developed around him an onus of blame and responsibility for the catastrophe. "The British Army that moved from New York to relieve Lord Cornwallis is returned," an American officer informed General Nathanael Greene in December, "and report says that Sir Henry Clinton has disappeared, conjectured by some that he has drowned himself."[10] Clinton was not about to take the blame of history's pen easily. Instead, he set his sights squarely on Cornwallis in an effort to shift the encumbrance. Cornwallis returned it in spades, and the dispute between the two men festered until their deaths.

Of course, responsibility for the disaster rested with both men, but it also went well beyond them. In the British government, Colonial Secretary Lord George Germain had philosophically favored Cornwallis and failed to support Clinton, his chief commander in North America. "I am persuaded that had I been left to my own plans," wrote Clinton in his autobiography four years later, "and a proper confidence had been earlier reposed in me, the campaign of 1781 would not probably have ended unfortunately."[11] Perhaps. But Clinton himself had been overcautious, too much of a defensive strategist, and a largely inactive leader when action was required to bring about an British victory. Further, he was too late in discerning Washington's movement south to Virginia. Physical ailments added to his lethargy, and his army and navy hierarchy often engaged in petty factionalism at the most crucial of times. Decisions were put off, and even when reached, their requisite actions were delayed time and again.[12]

Clinton's incompetence, however, was compounded by failings on the part of Cornwallis. Headstrong and independent, Clinton's Southern commander took too literally the favoritism implied by the home government. His arrogance in this respect produced a breach between him and his superior in New York. While Cornwallis proved a bold and meticulous tactician, his boldness emerged at inopportune moments and the failure of Clinton to exert strict supervision over his subordinate only encouraged his independence of movement and judgment. Cornwallis's selection of Yorktown as a post to insure the protection of British ships was a precarious choice. He found himself hemmed in by terrain advantageous to his assailants, and by water that retarded extrication of his command. He began his defensive works late and dawdled, all the while sending requests and assurances to Clinton, until his escape from the gathering Allied threat was beyond possibility. Probably his greatest shortcoming in the 1781 campaign was in his inability to comprehend (or easy dismissal of the risk) that by selecting Yorktown, the fate of his army hinged utterly on the success of the British Navy. Cornwallis courted the disaster that came to him at Yorktown.[13]

To be sure, other factors contributed to the decline of British affairs in the Yorktown Campaign. The rift between Clinton and Cornwallis was complemented by Admiral George Brydges Rodney's return to England when his presence was critically needed. Graves's failure to win control of the entrance to the Chesapeake, and his later delays in leaving New York, plus British Rear Admiral Samuel Hood's own failure to locate de Grasse and to perceive his intentions, all pointed up the lack of teamwork that in the end helped give the Allies their historic victory.[14]

*   *   *

Contrasted with the British facility for ineptitude and mismanagement, the Allies exhibited a cohesion of purpose paralleled by an admirable ability to coordinate their maneuvers toward the desired objective. Washington's campaign worked because of an interplay of careful design and good fortune. The close cooperation between de Barras's and de Grasse's fleets, St. Simon's volunteers, Rochambeau's French troops, and Washington's American command made victory possible. Cooperation between the French and Americans in the prosecution of a successful siege—itself largely dependent on French weapons, expertise, and enterprise—assured the triumph of the campaign. After many years of misfortune punctuated by large losses and small gains, Washington had at last acquired and utilized the military components of success.

Yorktown to the End of the Revolution

The Revolutionary War did not end with the surrender at Yorktown. The British continued to hold New York, Charleston, Savannah, and a host of smaller garrisons around Lake Champlain and the Great Lakes. London was still supporting some 26,000 British troops on the North

American continent, including 9,000 in Canada. Washington was determined to prosecute the war to a successful conclusion, and was looking forward to pressing forward around the New York headquarters of the enemy forces. He urged continued Congressional support for his army as a means of encouraging the French to stay the course.[15] In the meantime, he concentrated his available forces around New York and Charleston. The minor skirmishes that flared up sporadically for the duration of the war cost at least 397 more Americans their lives and wounded another 230. The resolution that had previously characterized British warfare in America, however, had forever waned.

The news of Cornwallis's sound defeat shocked London into immediate reconsideration of its North American policy. The war had proved extremely costly and the replacement of so many troops to offset the losses at Yorktown became a questionable proposition. Other factors appeared to jeopardize the very existence of the British Empire. Military setbacks reached London's ear from India, where French forces menaced. In Florida, Spanish troops expelled British soldiers, and early in 1782, Spain again threatened Gibraltar, putting it under siege. In the West Indies, Admiral de Grasse's victories left only Jamaica, Antigua, and Barbados in British control. Violence erupted in Ireland over the establishment of an independent Parliament. Even the Dutch were fighting Britain, which had declared war on Holland in 1780 because its vigorous merchant trade with North America had proven invaluable to the colonials. By 1782, the British were finding it difficult to maintain a credible presence in the North Sea and the real threat existed that ships belonging to the Dutch East India Company would assist the French in India. Old World rivals were chipping away at the empire while the contest in America was draining away its blood and treasure.[16]

Beset by pressures at home and abroad, and confronting prospects of military and economic setbacks should the American struggle drag on, Parliament early in 1782 authorized George III to end the war. On March 4, a resolution carried "that the House would consider as enemies to his Majesty and the Country all those who should advise, or by any means attempt, the further prosecution of offensive war on the Continent of North America for the purpose of reducing the revolted Colonies to obedience by force." In a final embarrassment, Clinton was recalled from America and replaced by General Guy Carleton, who arrived in New

York in May 1782. His mandate was to suspend offensive operations until a complete political solution could be finalized.[17]

Peace commissioners met in Paris for the first time in April 1782. The United States was represented well by Benjamin Franklin, John Jay, and John Adams. France, which was in even worse economic straits than its arch rival England, was also willing to strike a deal. Spain held out while Gibraltar hung in the balance. After months of negotiations, the preliminary articles were signed by commissioners of Great Britain and the United States in January 1783. The following month, Britain announced a cessation of hostilities in North America. The Continental Congress approved the provisional document on April 15, 1783, and the treaty was formally signed on September 3, 1783. The agreement required Congress to return the ratified document to England within six months. On January 14, 1784, Congress ratified the articles comprising the Treaty of Paris, thereby officially establishing the United States as an independent and sovereign nation.

The American commissioners negotiated a very beneficial treaty. In addition to independence, it granted the new young country all the land east of the Mississippi River, and included clauses that bound Congress to urge state legislatures to compensate Loyalists for property damage incurred during the war. It also allowed British creditors to freely collect debts accrued before the war began. England—diplomatically isolated, militarily weak, and economically stricken—desperately needed the breathing room offered by the treaty. War with its neighbors would come again, and soon enough.[18]

With the Treaty of Paris, the achievements of the American Revolution, largely made possible by the stunning victory at Yorktown, were legitimized forever.

Thereafter

Robert Abercrombie was indeed a soldier's soldier. The officer who led the bloody pre-dawn sortie was promoted to colonel in 1782 and made an aide-de-camp to the King. More fighting awaited him in India, where he distinguished himself during nine years of campaigning. As a major general, Abercrombie succeeded Cornwallis in India as commander-in-chief. He died in 1827 at the age of 87—the oldest general in the British army.

James Barham was not mentioned by name in the text, but in so many ways he personifies the thousands on both sides who soldiered in anonymity and will remain unknown to history forever. He was born on May 18, 1764, in Southhampton County, Virginia. According to his pension affidavit, he served as "a private in the companies commanded by Captains Whitehead, Myrick and Taylor in the Regiment of Virginia militia commanded by Col. Blount or Parker, and was drafted at Southampton County Virginia on or about 1779." Barham was in Whitehead's Virginia Militia when it moved into Yorktown one day before Cornwallis' official surrender. After the war, Barham lived in Kentucky and Tennessee before moving to Missouri to be near his children. He died in Stoddard County on January 8, 1865—two months before a letter from President Lincoln arrived congratulating him on being the "last survivor of the Revolutionary War."

Writer, soldier, poet, philosopher, and scholar *Major General Francois-Jean Beauvoir, chevalier de Chastellux* spent three years in America, where he soaked in as much of the culture and new way of life as possible. He joined philosophical and scientific societies and was awarded honorary degrees from The College of William and Mary and the University of Pennsylvania. His book *Travels in America* is a priceless study of social life in the 1780s. He died in France in 1788 from a sudden illness while traveling in Normandy. He was 54.

Little is known of the postwar life of *Claude Gabriel de Choisy*. During the French Terror, he sided with the Royalists and was imprisoned. He died a short time later.

Henry Clinton returned to England in disgrace, the loss at Yorktown and indeed the thirteen colonies hung largely around his neck. His efforts to obtain a formal inquiry to clear his name came to naught. After initial political setbacks, he won a seat in Parliament in 1790, and three years later was promoted to full general. In 1794 he was made governor of Gibraltar, where he died two days before Christmas, 1795.

To Clinton's everlasting chagrin, *Charles, Lord Cornwallis* returned home as a hero. Though defeated at Yorktown, most believed the unfortunate combination of the arrival of the French and Clinton's timidity had more to do with sealing his doom than his own limited strategic abilities. Cornwallis was formally exchanged and assumed the military duties associated with constable of the Tower. In 1786, he was appointed commander-in-chief of India, defeated Tippoo Sultan, and carved out a solid resume as a capable administrator. He was made the 1st Marquess Cornwallis in 1793 and returned to England the following year. Three years later he was made governor-general of Ireland, and in 1805 returned to India in ill health. He died there that October.

Thomas Dundas, who helped negotiate the surrender at Yorktown, was breveted colonel and his regiment disbanded. He was later commissioned a major general and led an infantry brigade against the French in the Caribbean in the early 1790s. He died of fever there in 1794.

Washington's invaluable chief engineer at Yorktown, *Louis Du Portail*, was praised by his superior in a letter to the President of Congress and promoted to major general the month after Yorktown fell.

Du Portail returned to service with the French army and served in a wide variety of posts including Minister and Secretary of State for War. With the French Revolution well underway, charges were brought against him and after two years in hiding he fled to America, where he took up residence on a farm outside Philadelphia. Du Portail was trying to return to France in 1802 when he fell ill and died. He was buried at sea.

Prussian officer *Johann Ewald* almost perished from dysentery on Long Island following the surrender at Yorktown. He returned to Germany and was eventually elevated to lieutenant colonel and given command of a jäger corps in Denmark. After becoming a member of the Danish nobility and a major general, he battled Joachim Murat during the early years of the Napoleonic Wars. Ewald died a lieutenant general in 1813 after a brief illness. His book about his experiences during the American Revolution remains one of the best of its kind.

Swede Hans Axel, comte von Ferson, Rochambeau's aide-de-camp, returned to France from Sweden after the American Revolution in an attempt to save the French royal family from the guillotine. He was unsuccessful. Von Ferson had been a favorite of the French court at Versailles, and was so close to Marie Antoinette that rumors abounded the pair had been lovers. He returned to Sweden and died there in 1810.

Jean Joseph de Gimat, who Lafayette had chosen to lead the attack against Redoubt 10 but whose selection was overridden by Washington, left the army early in 1782 on a leave of absence. The French promoted him to colonel later that same year and he was given a regiment on the island of Martinique. He later became governor of the island of St. Lucia in 1789. Gimat was mortally injured leading his corps against the British on the night of June 19-20, 1793.

Though *Francois Joseph Paul Compte de Grasse* enjoyed extraordinary luck during 1781, it did not hold. On April 12, 1782, he lost the 13-hour Battle of the Saints in the Caribbean against Admiral Rodney (the same officer he had earlier outsmarted off North America). De Grasse's flagship, *Ville de Paris*, was crippled and boarded, and he was captured. Seven of his 29 ships of the line were sunk and 3,000 men were killed or wounded. Paroled, he sought long and desperately to clear his name—an effort that infuriated Louis XVI, who bluntly told de Grasse to retire. He was back in favor two years later, but fell ill on the eve of the French Revolution and died in Paris in 1788. His country estate was burned by the rabble and four cannon sent to him from Yorktown by Congress in 1784 were hauled away and melted into Revolutionary coin.

Alexander Hamilton was brevetted a colonel in September 1783 and left military service three years later. Politically ambitious, he spent one year in Congress and practiced law in New York before drafting the report that led to the Constitutional Convention, where he urged the formation of a strong centralized government. Most of the invaluable *Federalist* papers came from his pen. Hamilton is best known as the first Secretary of the Treasury (1789-1795), a key member of Washington's cabinet and staunch political foe of Thomas Jefferson. Hamilton resigned in 1795, resumed the practice of law, and worked the political system from outside the official reigns of government. On July 11, 1804, he was mortally wounded in a duel with political rival Aaron Burr and died the next day. He was 47.

Washington's adjutant general, *Edward Hand*, was breveted a major general on the last day of September, 1783. He resigned again to take up his practice of medicine in Philadelphia. A staunch Federalist, he served in Congress for a short time and as inspector of revenue for a decade (1791-1801). Unfortunately, when problems with his accounts arose, a petition to sell off his lands to make up the difference was filed in court. The stress brought about a stroke that killed him in 1802.

A few months after his brilliant handling of the artillery at Yorktown, *Henry Knox* was appointed major general in March 1782 and succeeded Washington as commander-in-chief from December 1783–June 1784. Knox served as secretary of war under the Articles of Confederation and remained in the post in the Washington administration until 1794. Often described as profane, forceful, meddlesome, and pompous, the "Philadelphia nabob"—Knox threw extravagant parties—played a major role in winning American independence. The 56-year-old father of 12 had survived battles in several states and hardships untold, only to die when a chicken bone stuck in his intestines. The papers he left behind are invaluable for any serious study of the war.

After Yorktown, *Marquis de Lafayette* sailed for Europe in December 1781. He was assembling French and Spanish troops in Spain when the American Revolution drew to a fitful close. He never asked to be repaid the $200,000 he had spent to support the colonial cause. Lafayette returned to America in 1784 and helped advise Thomas Jefferson during his tenure as U.S. minister to France. Back in France,

Lafayette was widely recognized as one of the most popular men in his country. Elevated to lieutenant general, he was removed from command of an army during the war against Austria in 1792 for political reasons and sought refuge in Belgium. Arrested for his dangerous views on democracy, Lafayette spent the next five years in various dungeons in Germany and Austria. Napoleon freed the financially ruined officer in 1797. Spurning offers of high office, he spent the next two decades farming outside Paris. In 1824, President Monroe invited Lafayette back to the United States, where he was greeted by enthusiastic crowds. He died ten years later in Paris.

John Laurens, the promising young South Carolinian who had helped negotiate Cornwallis's surrender terms at the Moore house, rode south after Yorktown to meet his end. He was killed in his home state at Combahee Ferry, one of the final and utterly insignificant skirmishes of the war. The date was August 25, 1782.

Louis Armand de Gontaut-Biron, duc de Lauzun was promoted after the war to lieutenant general and served with the French Revolutionary government until 1793, when he fell out of favor and was arrested after failing to show enough energy in putting down a counterrevolution. He was sentenced to death. Lauzun offered wine to his jailer at the prison, telling him, "You must need courage in your profession." The aristocrat was beheaded on New Year's Eve, 1793.

Benjamin Lincoln must have taken some satisfaction away from Yorktown after having been forced himself to surrender at Charleston, South Carolina in 1780. He was appointed secretary of war just days after the Yorktown siege ended, and remained in that post until war's end. Other offices, both state and federal, came his way until 1809, when he retired from public service. He returned to Massachusetts and died one year later.

Lafayette aide *James McHenry* served for 13 years in the Maryland state legislature and represented his state at the Constitutional Convention, where he took copious notes that are today invaluable for the study of that body. He served as secretary of war for both Washington and Adams. His later arguments led to the establishment of a standing army. McHenry's son also served as a wartime volunteer and took part in the 1814 defense of a Baltimore stronghold named after his father. The bombardment of Fort McHenry inspired Francis Scott Key to pen the "Star-Spangled Banner."

After serving as a brigade leader under Lafayette, Pennsylvania native *John Muhlenberg* was breveted major general and retired from the army in November 1783. He held several state offices, served in Congress and as a customs collector, and died in 1807. Outside his home state, he is not well known, but Muhlenberg was one of the many steady unsung heros of the war. His statue can be found in Philadelphia.

Militia officer *Thomas Nelson, Jr.*, who directed artillery fire against his own home in Yorktown, lost his fortune with the American victory for he had donated virtually all of his money to feeding and equipping soldiers to defeat the British. Married with 11 children, he died of asthma at 51. At his direction, he was buried in an unmarked grave so his creditors could not find his corpse and hold it for ransom. His descendant, the novelist Thomas Nelson Page, erected a headstone reading, "He gave all for Liberty."

Charles O'Hara, Cornwallis's second-in-command at Yorktown, returned to England with a burnished military record and an assortment of wounds that nagged him until his death. Ten years after his return he was made lieutenant governor of Gibraltar, and was later promoted to lieutenant general. O'Hara was captured again, this time in November of 1793 in France at Fort Mulgrove, Toulon, by a young and relatively unknown French officer named Napoleon. O'Hara was exchanged for none other than Rochambeau two years later. Promoted to full general, he was given the post of Gibraltar, which he administered well. He was a popular guest at parties and well known for his wit and impeccable manners. He died in 1802 a wealthy man, and left the money to two local women for their support and to help feed and educate his illegitimate children.

Comte de Rochambeau left the Chesapeake Bay for the Biscay coast of France in January 1783. Louis XVI showered the officer with commendations and royal privileges. A variety of important military posts tossed him up into the rank of Marshal of France in 1791, but he was arrested and would have been beheaded had not Robespierre himself felt the sting of the guillotine against the nape of his neck. Rochambeau spent his final years writing his memoirs, which appeared in two volumes in Paris in 1809. He died four years later. Without Rochambeau's willingness to work with Washington and accord him the respect he deserved as a superior officer, the cooperation between the French and

American armies would never have culminated with victory at Yorktown.

After performing well at Gloucester Point, *John Graves Simcoe* of the Queen's Rangers sailed back to England and retired to his estate. He was elected to Parliament ten years later and appointed lieutenant governor of Upper Canada. In 1794, he was commissioned a major general. Simcoe was in command of the garrison at Santo Domingo when the Napoleonic Wars opened. Appointed commander-in-chief in India in 1806, he fell sick at sea, returned, and died that same year.

Commanding a division at Yorktown was the closest Prussian *Baron von Steuben* would ever get to his deep desire to have a field command of his own. Granted American citizenship in 1783, he was discharged the following year and took up residence in New York City. Because he was expecting some $60,000 from Congress for his military service, he spent freely and went deeply into debt. Only the kind acts of Alexander Hamilton and others saved him from financial ruin. Von Steuben died in 1794. He never married. His property was willed to his aides.

Paroled and returned to England, *Banastre Tarleton* was promoted to lieutenant colonel of Light Dragoons and spent the next two decades bouncing in and out of parliament as a Liverpool representative. He proved a better cavalry leader than politician. The first edition of his recollections of the 1780 and 1781 campaigns was issued in 1787. It is a valuable, if self-congratulatory, account. Tarleton is remembered most for his merciless treatment of civilians and prisoners. He died without an heir in January 1833.

James Thacher left military life to take up the scalpel as a civilian in Plymouth, Massachusetts. He penned several medical-related titles, but his brilliance transcended medicine, as evidenced by books he wrote on agriculture, bee-keeping, and the paranormal. His invaluable military journal was first published in1823, and has been reprinted many times. He died in 1844 at the age of 90.

Unlike so many who fought in the upper echelons of command, the military event for which *Anthony Wayne* would be most remembered had yet to take place. After a brief stint in Georgia he returned to Pennsylvania and sat in the State Assembly and was selected as a delegate to the Constitutional Convention. On Washington's request, "Mad" Anthony Wayne led 2,600 men into the Ohio wilderness in 1792 to subdue the Indians and throw out the British. He built Fort Defiance, and near modern-day Toledo won a decisive victory over Delaware, Shawnee, and Canadian Indians at the Battle of Fallen Timbers in 1794. He died at Presque Isle, Pennsylvania, on December 15, 1796. In 1808, his son decided to move the remains to the family burial plot in Radnor, Pennsylvania. When the general was disinterred, however, his corpse was found in a remarkable state of preservation. Because it would not withstand a wagon journey, a doctor cut the general's body into pieces and boiled off the flesh in a large kettle, sending home the bones for burial.

Colonel St. George Tucker returned to Petersburg after the war to practice law. His beloved Fanny, to whom he wrote so many letters, died in 1788 after delivering their sixth child. Tucker married again and had three more children, though all died very young. A brilliant legal mind, he taught law at The College of William and Mary and became a judge in Richmond. He installed the first bathroom in Williamsburg, was an avid astronomer, and an expert gardener. Tucker died in 1827. His in-depth letters and journals are indispensable to the study of the period.

George Weedon, the Virginia militia general so despised by Choisy, returned to Fredericksburg after the war and died there in 1793. His papers about his service shed substantial light on the role of the militia.

Rochambeau's second-in-command and the victor of the attack against Redoubt 9, *Baron de Viomenil*, was (like so many of his comrades in America) a Royalist. He was severely wounded in the left knee on October 10, 1792, defending Louis XVI against a Parisian mob. He never fully recovered and died four months later.

After refusing an offer to make him king, *George Washington* attempted in vain to retire from public life. He served as president of the Constitutional Convention, and when a new government was organized, Washington was the unanimous selection for our first chief executive. He took office in April of 1789 and was reelected in 1792. He refused a third term. During his presidency he supported Hamilton's financial ideas, put down Indian uprisings in the Northwest territory, and tread lightly in international matters in an effort to maintain neutrality in a world spinning into another major global war. After his famous "Farewell Address" in 1796, Washington retired to Mount Vernon. When war with France seemed inevitable, he was made commander-in-chief once again, but died (perhaps from a throat infection and poor medical treatment) after only a single day of illness. He did not leave any direct heirs.

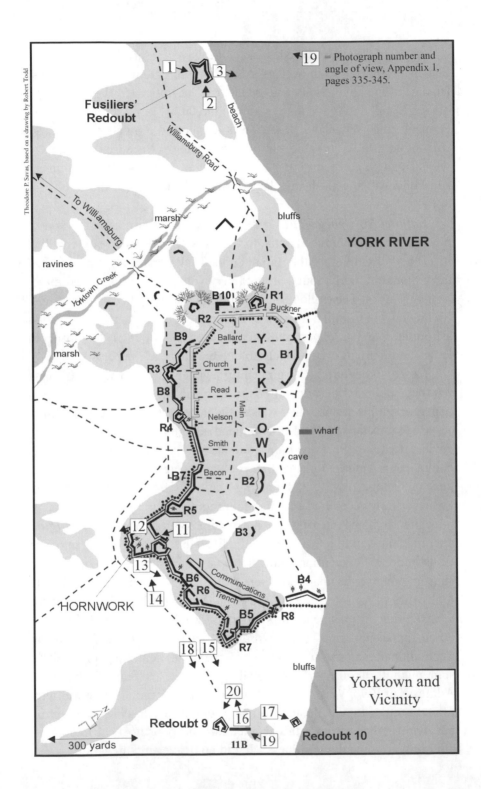

19 = Photograph number and angle of view, Appendix 1, pages 335-345.

1 3
2

Fusiliers' Redoubt

beach

To Williamsburg

Williamsburg Road

marsh

bluffs

YORK RIVER

ravines

Yorktown Creek

marsh

B10 R1
Buckner
R2
Ballard
B9

Church
R3

Read
B8

Nelson
R4
Main

Smith
R5

Bacon
B7

12 11
13
B6
HORNWORK 14
R6 Communications
Trench
B5
R7

Y
O
R
K
T
O
W
N

B1

wharf

cave

B2

B3

B4

R8

18 15

bluffs

20
Redoubt 9 16 17
19 Redoubt 10
11B

300 yards

Yorktown and
Vicinity

Modern Photographic Gallery

1. The Allied view of the Fusiliers' Redoubt (from the southwest). Behind it only a short distance is the bluff leading down to the York River.

2. Another view of the Fusiliers' Redoubt, this one from the east, or British, perspective. The York River is to the right, just out of the camera angle.

3. The York River and Gloucester Point from Fusiliers' Redoubt.

4. The untouched redoubt. This is the only surviving British redoubt on the battlefield today. It overlooks Yorktown Creek (see next image).

5. Yorktown Creek behind the unfinished British redoubt (looking southeast). An outstanding example of one of the natural barriers before Yorktown. The British Hornwork was about 400 yards beyond the left-center of this image.

6. The southernmost Pigeon Hill Redoubt (reconstructed in the 1970s). The overgrown sides are clearly visible in the center of the image in front of the main line of trees.

7. The view looking north toward the inner British defensive line (the distant tree line) from the French positions along the first parallel. The line of works in the middle distance is the second Allied siege parallel.

8. Looking west along the line toward Battery 8A (part of the Grand French Battery complex) in the first parallel just east of Hampton Road.

9. Another view along the Grand French Battery (8A) looking west toward the Hampton Road. The British line was about 800 yards north (to the right).

10. This view looks north from inside Battery 8A of the Grand French Battery. Note the field piece in the left-center and the mortar on the left.

11. Inside the Hornwork. This view looks southwest across the remains of the British earthworks toward the distant second Allied siege line (the tree line in the far left distance).

12. The view from atop the Hornwork looking generally south toward the second Allied siege line, which was positioned in the distant trees.

13. The British inner line looking generally east along the front of the works. The protruding eastern face of the Hornwork is immediately behind the photographer. (See 14 below for a view back toward this camera angle.)

14. The British inner line. This reverse view shows the eastern face of the Hornwork (center distance), and the ditch and face of the inner main works.

15. Battery 11B (Grand American Battery) in the second line, as it appears through a telephoto lens looking east from the inner British line about 300 yards distant. Captured Redoubt 9 is just beyond the right side of this image.

16. The opposite view from 15 (above) without a telephoto lens, looking northwest from Battery 11B (Grand American Battery) toward the British inner line 300 yards away.

17. A northern view of Redoubt 10, captured by the Americans on October 14. The York River is just beyond the trees. Redoubt 9, captured by the French that same night, is 150 yards behind the photographer.

18. Redoubt 9 from the inner British line, about 300 yards distant.

19. Looking south by southwest inside Battery 11B (the Grand American Battery) in the second siege line. American guns began firing from this position on October 16, 1781, pulverizing Cornwallis's main line of works.

20. Captured Redoubt 9, looking south by southeast from the British inner line. Battery 11B (the Grand American Battery) is just out of view on the left.

21. This view looks east along the rear of the second siege line (reconstructed) from near Battery 5B toward Battery 6B and Franco-American Redoubt 7B. Abercrombie's pre-dawn October 16 sortie covered the ground in the distance (from left to right) and struck the Allied line at the stand of trees on the right.

22. A close-up view of the British Hornwork looking north from Battery 6B, where Abercrombie struck the Allied line. The British left these works pictured here and crossed this ground, heading directly toward the camera.

The Washington and Cornwallis Correspondence

This appendix includes copies of the correspondence between General Washington and Lord Cornwallis, October 17-18, 1781. It is drawn from copies in the Henry Clinton Papers, William L. Clements Library, University of Michigan.

* * *

York in Virginia
17th Octr: 1781.

Sir

I propose a Cessation of Hostilities for twenty four hours, & that two Officers may be appointed by each side, to meet at Mr. Moore's house to settle terms for the Surrender of the Posts of York & Gloucester.

I have the honour to be, Sir

Your most obedient & most humble Servant

/Signed/   Cornwallis

His Excellency
General Washington
Commanding the combined America Forces of France and America

*   *   *

Camp before York
17th Octr: 1781.

My Lord

I have had the honour of receiving your Lordship's Letter of this date.

An ardent desire to spare the further effusion of Blood, will readily incline me to listen to such terms for the surrender of your posts, as are admissible.

I wish, previous to the meeting of Commissioners, that your Lordship's proposals in writing, may be sent to the American Lines: For which purpose a suspension of hostilities during two hours from the deliver of this Letter will be granted—I have the honour to be. My Lord

Your Lordship's

Most obedient & Most humble Servant

/Signed/ G. Washington

Lieut: General
Earl Cornwallis

*   *   *

York in Virginia
17th October 1781/2 past 4 P.M.

Sir

I have this moment been honoured with Your Excellency's Letter, dated this day.

The time limited for sending my Answer will not admit of entering into the detail of Articles, but the Basis of my proposals will be, that the Garrisons of York and Gloucester shall be Prisoners of War with the customary honours, And, for the convenience of the individuals which I have the honour to command, that the British shall be sent to Britain, & the Germans to Germany, under engagement-not to serve against France, America, or their Allies untill released, or regularly exchanged, That all Arms & publick Stores shall be delivered up to you, but that the usual indulgence of Side Arms to Officers, & of retaining private property shall be granted to Officers and Soldiers, & that the interests of several Individuals, in civil capacities & connected with us, shall be attended to.

If your Excellency thinks that a continuance of the Suspension of hostilities will be necessary to transmit your Answer, I shall have no objection to the hour that you may propose.

I have the honour to be, Sir

Your most obedient & Most humble Servant

/Signed/   Cornwallis

His Excellency General Washington
Commanding the combined Forces of France and America

*   *   *

Camp before York
18 Octr: 1781.

My Lord

To avoid unnecessary discussions and delays, I shall at once in answer to your Lordship's Letter of yesterday, declare the general Basis upon which a definitive treaty of Capitulation may take place.

The Garrisons of York and Gloucester, including the Seamen, as you propose, shall be received Prisoners of War. The condition annexed of sending the British and German Troops to the parts of Europe to which they respectively belong is inadmissible Instead of this; they will be marched to such parts of the Country as can most conveniently provide for their Subsistence, and the benevolent treatment of Prisoners which is invariably observed by the

Americans will be extended to them. The same honors will be granted to the surrendering Army as were granted to the Garrison of Charlestown.

The Shipping & Boats in the two Harbours with all their Guns—Stores, Tackling—Furniture and Apparel shall be delivered in their present State to an Officer of the Navy appointed to take possession of them.

The Artillery—Arms—Accouterments, Military Chest, and publick Stores of every denomination shall be delivered, unimpaired, to the Heads of Departments to which they respectively belong.

The Officers shall be indulged in retaining their side Arms, and the Officers & Soldiers may preserve their Baggage & Effects, with this reserve, that Property taken in the Country will be reclaimed.

With regard to the Individuals in civil Capacities, whose Interests your Lordship wishes may be attended to, untill they are more particularly described, nothing definitive can be settled.

I have to add, that I expect the Sick and wounded will be supplied with their own Hospital Stores, and be attended by British Surgeons particularly charged with the care of them.

Your Lordship will be pleased to signify your determination either to accept or reject the proposals now offered, in the course of two hours from the delivery of this Letter, that Commissioners may be appointed to digest the Articles of Capitulation, or a renewal of hostilities may take place.

I have the honour to be My Lord

Your Lordship's Most obedient and humble Servant

G. Washington
His Excellency
Lieut: General Earl Cornwallis

*   *   *

York in Virginia
18 Octr. 1781.

Sir

I agree to open a treaty of Capitulation upon the Basis of the Garrisons of York & Gloucester including Seamen, being Prisoners of War, without annexing the condition of their being sent to Europe; But I expect to receive a Compensation in arranging the Articles of the Capitulation for the surrender of Gloucester in it's present state of defence. I shall in particular desire that the Bonetta Sloop of War may be left entirely at my disposal from the hour that the Capitulation is signed to receive an Aide-de-Camp to carry my dispatches to Sir Henry Clinton, such Soldiers as I may think proper to send passengers in her, to be manned with fifty men of her own Crew, & to be permitted to sail without examination when my dispatches are ready, Engaging on my part, that the Ship shall be brought back, and delivered to you if she escapes the dangers of the Sea, that the Crew & Soldiers shall be accounted for in future Exchanges, that she shall carry off no Officer without your consent, nor publick property of any kind; And I shall likewise desire that the Traders & Inhabitants may preserve their property, and that no person may be punished or molested for having joined the British Troops.

If you chuse to proceed to Negociation on these grounds I shall appoint two Field Officers of my Army to meet two Officers from you at any time and place that you think proper, to digest the Articles of Capitulation.

I have the honour to be

Sir

Your most obedient &
Most humble Servant

/Signed/   Cornwallis

The Articles of
Capitulation, October 19, 1781

His Excellency
General Washington
Commanding the combined Forces of France and America

Articles of Capitulation settled between His Excellency General Washington Commander in Chief of the combined Forces of America & France, His Excellency the Count de Rochambeau Lieutenant General of the Armies of the King of France Great Cross of the Royal & Military Order of St. Louis, commanding the auxiliary Troops of His most Christian Majesty in America, His Excellency the Count deGrasse Lieutenant General of the Naval Armies of His most Christian Majesty Commander of the Order of St. Louis, Commanding in Chief the Naval Army of France in the Chesapeak, on the one part. And The Right Honorable Earl Cornwallis Lieutenant General of His Britannick Majesty's Forces, Commanding the Garrisons of York & Gloucester and Thomas Symonds Esq—Commanding His Britannick Majesty's Naval Forces in York River in Virginia on the other part.

Article 1

The Garrisons of York & Gloucester including the Officers & Seamen of His Britannick Majesty's Ships as well as other Mariners to surrender themselves Prisoners of War to the Combined Forces of America & France; The Land Troops to remain Prisoners to the United States; The Navy to the Naval Army of His most Christian Majesty.

Article 2nd

The Artillery, Arms, Accouterments military Chest & publick Stores of every denomination shall be delivered unimpaired to the Heads of Departments appointed to receive them.

Article 3^d

At Twelve O'Clock this Day the two Redoubts on the left Flank of York to be delivered the one to a Detachment of American Infantry, the other to a Detachment of French Grenadiers. The Garrison of York will march out to a place to be appointed in front of the Posts at 2 OClock precisely with Shouldered Arms, Colors cased & Drums beating a British or German March. They are then to ground their Arms and return to their Encampment where they will remain until they are dispatched to the places of their Destination. Two Works on the Gloucester Side will be delivered at one O'Clock to detachments of French & American Troops appointed to possess them. The Garrison will march out at 3 O'Clock in the Afternoon, the Cavalry with their Swords drawn Trumpets sounding & the Infantry in the manner prescribed for the Garrison of York. They are likewise to return to their Encampment until they can be finally marched off.

Article 4th

Officers are to retain their Side Arms. Both Officers & Soldiers to keep their private Property of every kind, & no part of their Baggage or Papers to be at any Time subject to search or Inspection. The Baggage & Papers of Officers & Soldiers taken during the Siege to be likewise preserved for them. It is understood that any Property obviously belonging to the Inhabitants of these States, in the possession of the Garrison, shall be subject to be reclaimed.

Article 5th

The Soldiers to be kept in Virginia Maryland or Pensylvania, & as much by Regiments as possible & supplied with the same Rations of Provisions as are allowed to Soldiers in the Service of America, a Field Officer from each Nation, to wit, British Anspach & Hessian, and other Officers on parole in the proportion of one to fifty Men, to be allowed to reside near their respective Regiments, to visit them frequently & to be Witnesses of their Treatment, & that these Officers may receive & deliver Clothing & other Necessaries, for which Passports are to be granted when applied for.

Article 6th

The General, Staff & other Officers, not employed as mentioned in the above Article, & who chose it, to be permitted to go on Parole to Europe, to New York, or to any other American Maritime Posts, at present in the Possession of the British Forces, at their own Option, & proper Vessels to be granted by the Count de Grasse to carry them under Flags of Truce to New York within 10 days from this date if possible, and they to reside in a district to be agreed upon hereafter until they embark. The Officers of the Civil departments of the Army & Navy to be included in this Article, Passports to go by Land to be granted to those to whom Vessels cannot be furnished.

Article 7th

Officers to be allowed to keep Soldiers as Servants according to the common practice of the Service. Servants not Soldiers are not to be considered as Prisoners 4 are to be allowed to attend their Masters.

Article 8th

The Bonetta Sloop of War to be equipped & navigated by it's present Captain & Crew, & left entirely at, the disposal of Lord Cornwallis from the hour that the Capitulation is signed to receive an Aid de Camp to carry dispatches to Sir Henry Clinton, & such Soldiers as he may think proper to send to New York to be permitted to sail without Examination when his dispatches are ready. His Lordship engaging on his part, that the Ship shall be delivered to the Order of the Count deGrasse if she escapes the dangers of the Seas. That she shall not carry off any public Stores, any part of the Crew that may be deficient on her Return & the Soldiers Passengers to be accounted for on her Delivery.

Article 9th

The Traders are to preserve their property & to be allowed three Months to dispose of or remove them & those Traders are not to be considered as Prisoners of War.

The Traders will be allowed to dispose of their Effects, the Allied Army having the Right of Preemption. The Traders to be considered as Prisoners of War on parole.

Article 10th

Natives or Inhabitants of different Parts of this Country at present in York or Gloucester are not to be punished on Account of having joined the British Army.

This Article cannot be assented to being altogether of Civil Resort.

Article 11th

Proper Hospitals to be furnished for the Sick & wounded, they are to be attended by their own Surgeons on Parole and they are to be furnished with Medicines & Stores from the American Hospitals.

The Hospital Stores now in York & Gloucester shall be delivered for the use of the British Sick and Wounded. Passports will be granted for procuring them further Supplies from New York as occasion may require. And proper Hospitals will be furnished for the Reception of the Sick and wounded of the two Garrisons.

Article 12th

Waggons to be furnished to carry the Baggage of the Officers attending the Soldiers and to Surgeons when travelling on Account of the Sick, attending the Hospitals at publick Expence.

They will be furnished if possible.

Article 13th

The Shipping and Boats in the two Harbours with all their Stores, Guns, Tackling & Apparel shall be delivered up in their present State to an Officer of the Navy appointed to take Possession of them, previously unloading the private Property, part of which had been on board for Security during the Siege.

Article 14th

No Article of the Capitulation to be infringed on pretext of Reprisals, and if there be any doubtful Expressions in it, they are to be interpreted according to the common meaning and acceptations of the Words.

Done in the Trenches before
York   October 19th 1781.

/Signed/

G. Washington
Le Cte.de Rochambeau
Cornwallis   Le Cte.de Barras en mon
Th^{s}. Symonds   Nom et celui du Cte.de Grasse.

The Archaeology of the Grand French Battery Complex

Archaeology has played a significant role in accurately establishing the location of the first and second parallels and of the different redoubts and batteries built along their lengths, including the Grand French Battery complex. Prior to the 1930s, when archaeological work was inaugurated at Colonial National Historical Park, maps and participant accounts provided the sole evidence of the positions of the Allied fortifications. Archaeological digs confirmed many of those positions and afforded certain knowledge of the way those structures appeared during their brief existence in 1781.

Similar work completed in the 1970s provided even more insight into the method of construction of the Allied earthworks in general, and in those constituting the Grand French Battery in particular. Moreover, this work has uncovered a great many artifacts—cannonballs, pieces of exploded shells (in some cases live shells), and various implements and entrenching tools. The intensive archaeological investigations preceded reconstruction of the earthworks from designs based largely on that data and on historical evidence contained in contemporary sources and pertinent technical publications. Colonial research technician Thor Borresen ably summed up the significance of this project in a statement as compelling now as when it was first delivered: "The evidence will always testify that we knew where the fortifications were and what they looked like and that supposition was replaced by fact. It can never be stated that the time taken for such reconstruction was wasted."[1]

The soil type in the area of the Grand French Battery aided the archaeological examination there immensely. The topsoil on that part of the field is composed of a sandy loam about 12 to 14 inches deep atop a stratum of yellow clay. In the process of erecting earthen fortifications on this ground in 1781, the soil was disturbed in the initial excavation for the entrenchments. Following the siege, the parallels were leveled and the mixed sand, clay, and loam dirt was used as backfill in the trenches. When archeologists began their work more than 150 years after the siege, historical maps guided them to the approximate locations of the first parallel and the Grand French Battery. By scraping away the topsoil at selected points in a series of exploratory cross-section trenches, workers revealed a distinct outline of the fortifications as formed by the mixed backfill of clay, loam, and sand. Once the original line and its batteries were located, archaeological excavation proceeded.[2]

The contrast between the disturbed and the undisturbed soil allowed archeologists, by removing the disturbed soil, to gauge the depth of the siege trenches and thus the approximate height of the epaulements. The contrast in soils has also disclosed sleeper impressions in the artillery batteries, palisade holes in the frontal ditches of redoubts, and even what might be tent pole and stake holes in certain structures.

In the 1930s, archaeological work concentrated on that part of the Grand French Battery and its communicating trenches east of Hampton Road. From 1973 to 1975, an archaeological team headed by Dr. Norman Barka of The College of William and Mary, Williamsburg, Virginia, accomplished the delineation of the remainder of the Grand French Battery, or those structures located west of Hampton Road. Much of the work of both periods dealt with investigation of the service trenches adjoining the first parallel, as well as of the parallel itself. Under Barka's guidance, approximately 1,100 feet of communication trench was examined, along with about 450 feet of the siege line in the area between Hampton and Goosley roads. The main parallel served to guard infantry and to screen the movement of supplies and troops passing into the line from the nearby French depot, or from a communication line in the rear.

East of Hampton Road, archeologists discovered that the main trench varied in width from roughly nine to 12 feet, with the widest part of 15 feet presumably used as a passing point for troops, wagons, and artillery. The communication lines excavated west of the highway revealed a width of from six to eight feet, and a depth of approximately three feet.[3]

Battery 8A, the reconstructed portion located just east of Hampton Road (today's Virginia Highway 704), comprised the largest component of the Grand French Battery complex. At least 14 artillery pieces were mounted in this unit. From all indications, its construction in 1781 adhered to orthodox procedures advanced in the technical publications, the only deviations being caused by sloping ground. Battery 8A thus consisted of a partial frontal (or moat) ditch, a parapet cut in places by embrasures, a banquette along the inside perimeter, and the essential artillery emplacement platforms. Neither palisades nor fraises seem to have been used in the battery, perhaps indicating French confidence in their firepower capability against possible enemy sorties.[4] Throughout its length the epaulement of Battery 8A was revetted with saucissons. Gabions strengthened embrasures before the cannon positions.[5] Artillery placed in Battery 8A directed its fire against the Yorktown defenses, especially in the area of the Hornwork and against the detached enemy positions at Redoubts 9 and 10.[6] The structure's location was perfectly placed on the high terrain: it permitted the establishment of weapons just within range of the British works, yet remote enough to make surprise assaults unlikely.[7] Moreover, troops stationed in the siege line directly ahead of Battery 8A experienced no real danger because of the structure's commanding height above the surrounding ground (though their position might be jeopardized by the malfunction of an artillery piece or the discharge of a "short round").

From archeologists and historical sources, the interior configuration of Battery 8A has been accurately determined. The unit consisted of three sections (one each for cannon, mortars, and howitzers) separated by traverses. Directly behind the battery ran a support trench that extended into the area from across Hampton Road. At Battery 8A the trench diverged, its left extremity forming a moat ditch bordering the left epaulement of the structure for its entire length and finally joining with the main siege line. Similarly, the right arm of the support trench continued east behind Battery 8A to join the siege line a short distance away.[8] Another frontal ditch partially paralleled the right epaulement, causing speculation that its prime purpose was to provide dirt for raising the parapet of the structure in the mortar and howitzer sections. The battery parapet at its base possessed a maximum thickness of about 16 feet, a figure commensurate with the distance of the battery from British artillery (about 700 yards).[9] Apparently, the rear support trench was dug after the battery itself was completed, and was used as a recess into which the artillerymen might retire in case of a British surprise attack. The support trench measured about three feet deep and four or five feet wide. Dirt excavated from the ditch was used to erect a parapet with a slope that was sodded.[10]

Immediately adjacent to Hampton Road in Battery 8A was the section containing the heavy siege cannon. Archaeological knowledge gained from excavating the site, and historical knowledge gained from period artillery fortification treatises, provide a fairly accurate description of the armament in this part of the battery. Excavation of Battery 8A disclosed sleeper impressions and numerous stake holes showing the exact locations of the gun platforms. Stakes were used to help keep the big cannon in place and to prevent excessive recoil of the pieces. The first weapon situated at the extreme left in Battery 8A was either a large 24-pounder rigged to fire en barbette (i.e., over the parapet, without an embrasure) or a 16-inch stone mortar, a type normally used for defensive purposes and not known to have been used by the French at Yorktown. Whichever weapon was used, it was apparently mounted to fire at angles above 180°, was fitted to work on an iron track, and was located about 10 feet behind the epaulement.[11] About 18 feet east of this cannon (the spacing between ordnance in the Grand French Battery followed the technical prescriptions almost precisely) lay another, its platform evidently touching the base of the epaulement in the customary manner. This piece is believed to have been a 24-pounder, and it is speculated that a platform without the customary sleepers stood at that point.

The next two guns in the battery were probably 16-pounders. Archeologists revealed sleepers for these pieces measuring 15 feet long and four inches thick; each platform emplacement measured eight feet wide, while the sleepers for each were spaced 18 inches apart in the usual manner for 16-pounders.[12] For the latter three cannon, the archaeological evidence and the embrasures later cut through the reconstructed parapet indicate angles of fire directed toward the area of Cornwallis's line just to the right of the Hornwork.[13] Throughout the whole length of the gun section of Battery 8A the parapet seems to have generally conformed to specifications recommended by the theorists. The floor of this part of the structure was dug more than three feet below ground level; archeologists therefore disclosed numerous stake marks placed in the course of revetting the base of the epaulement with fascines. Gabions were probably likewise staked along the upper parts. Just beyond the last cannon emplacement and at the angle of the parapet, evidence in the form of numerous stake holes indicated the presence of a revetted traverse.[14]

Beyond the traverse lay the mortar section. However, the first weapon in the section was not a mortar but a 24-pounder field gun rigged to fire en barbette.

This gun, by the direction of the hole left by its trail piece, fired over the angle formed by the traverse meeting the parapet. The carriage wheels of the piece probably rested on logs, for no evidence of a platform was discovered.[15]

Seven feet away from this gun stood a small mortar of unknown dimensions. Archeologists disclosed the presence of three short sleepers, each measuring about two feet long by one foot wide. This mortar was evidently a portable unit that could be removed to various positions in Battery 8A. The discovery of a longer sleeper impression immediately behind this portable mortar and parallel to the parapet caused considerable speculation among investigators as to what had transpired there. "Apparently what had happened in this section of the battery, was that the guns [mortars] were all set in position at night and in accordance with regular practice were set at right angles to the parapet," wrote one investigator. "In the morning it was discovered that a mistake had been made and the platforms had to be changed around to correct the angles of fire, with the exception of this one which was small enough and did not necessitate moving the whole thing."[16]

This conjecture was based on the discovery that the next two small mortar platforms had originally been placed perpendicular to the parapet but had been changed in order to achieve the right angle of fire needed for shells to reach the Hornwork.[17]

Next to these mortars was a large one, possibly with a 13-inch bore, because the excavation completed at this site revealed two very deep sets of sleeper impressions, again suggesting the entire platform was moved in changing the angle of fire of the piece.[18] Probably another 13-inch mortar, possibly a naval weapon mounted on a swivel platform, was placed in the right of the section, as suggested by the depth of the sleeper excavations there.[19] The parapet of the mortar section required no embrasures to facilitate shooting the piece. As excavated, the front wall of the section stood nearly perpendicular and lacked the slope characteristic of the cannon section.[20] Archeologists did not discover a traverse at the end of the mortar section to separate it from the howitzers.[21]

Adjoining the mortar section, the howitzers lay farthest east in Battery 8A and opened into the *boyau* (support trench) constructed along the entire rear length of the structure. Archaeological work uncovered evidence of two howitzer platforms, apparently without sleepers, on sloping ground a considerable distance back from the parapet, positioned to fire over the epaulement rather than through it. Given the angle of the parapet opposite the howitzers, it was concluded that these weapons trained their fire against the British-held Redoubts 9 and 10 rather than against the Hornwork.[22]

Situated between the battery proper and the support trench running along its rear were four magazines designed to hold the powder, shot, and shells needed to serve the various armaments. The magazine serving the cannon section was the largest and was built at the end of a trench leading back from those pieces at the approximate middle of the section. The trench entered into a pit measuring 6 x 9 feet at the bottom and 9 x 12 feet at the top. Presumably the pit was covered with logs and/or fascines, together with a thick two- to three-foot layer of earth to render it secure against bomb explosions. The interior floor was probably lined with saplings and fascines to keep the powder barrels and shot dry. Also, a special pit in the floor served to collect moisture resulting from rainfall. Possibly the entrance to the magazine was protected with a thick wooden door, although heavy tarpaulins might have been used for this purpose.[23]

Similarly, directly behind the mortar battery, a trench led back to a nest of three smaller magazines constructed to support the ordnance in that section. During the archaeological work conducted in these magazines, it was found that the soil in two of the structures contained stains caused by the presence of black powder. It was surmised that one magazine served to store the powder, another served to load bombs and drive fuses, while the third held the loaded shells until they were needed in the battery.

The first magazine, the largest of the group, was rectangular and measured 10 feet long by five feet wide; the second and third were square-shaped and measured 5 x 5 feet. All three magazines had a depth of about four feet.[24] These structures were also probably lined and covered with logs, fascines, and dirt. Strangely, no powder magazines were found to serve the howitzer section of Battery 8A, encouraging speculation that the magazine to serve these weapons was somehow contained in the parapet near the easternmost end of the fortification.[25]

As 1934 drew to a close, reconstruction work began on Battery 8A. Company 1351 of the Civilian Conservation Corps undertook the project following the completion of the archaeological excavations. A number of artillery emplacement platforms, fashioned of concrete to simulate wood, were laid during the reconstruction and still exist in the present structure.[26]

The remaining units of the Grand French Battery complex (Structures 4A, 5A, 6A, and 7A) have been excavated more recently than Battery 8A. A team from the College of William and Mary, under the supervision of Barka, located and delineated Battery 7A a short distance west of the highway. This structure also stood on high ground behind the main siege line, but was connected to the other parts of the complex through a network of communication trenches. A narrow support trench curved around the rear of Battery 7A and, widening, continued east to border the rear of Battery 8A about 90 yards away. Another trench departed from the left rear of the work to connect behind with Battery 5A; yet another swung west and forward 67 yards to meet the siege line a short distance behind Battery 4A and to the left (west) of Redoubt 6A. Archeologists revealed a 79-foot long frontal ditch for Battery 7A that varied between nine and 12 feet in width at the top and between five and six feet at the bottom. Sides of the ditch possessed an inward slope angle of 50 to 60 degrees. The floor of Battery 7A was evidently sunk about two and one-half feet below ground level at the base of the parapet and sloped gradually upwards toward the south, away from the gun positions. Archeological estimates place the width of the gun emplacement area at about 40 feet, its length at 85 feet. The parapet, cut through with embrasures, probably measured about five-and-one-half feet in height above normal ground level. Battery 7A contained four 24-pounder cannon. The archeologists found evidence of three platforms and room for a fourth in the emplacement area. Very shallow sleeper impressions were discovered, with groups of three sleepers used for each platform. Individual sleepers measured between 10 and 12 feet in length, and between six and 12 inches in width. Each sleeper grouping spanned six feet at its maximum width, and measured 22 feet from the center of one to that of another.[27]

Some 93 yards southwest of Battery 7A stood another four-gun unit. Battery 5A was connected with 7A by a communications trench that joined its eastern side by means of a narrow connecting trench. The communications trench also served as an egress out of the Grand French Battery, as well as an entrance into the complex from behind the lines. Battery 5A possessed a commanding elevation over the conterminous terrain. Archaeological examination of the area revealed minimal data, largely because much of the ground has been malevolently disturbed. Archeologists discovered evidence of the frontal ditch, however, a roughly V-shaped section measuring 45 yards long, three to 10 feet wide, and two to three feet deep. All evidences of the parapet, gun platforms, artillery emplacement ditch, and connecting trench, if indeed they ever existed, were obliterated by the operations of a bulldozer in the area and have thus been lost.[28]

North and slightly west of Battery 7A along the main siege line stood 6A, a large redoubt of triangular shape. This structure, as examined by archeologists, consisted of an interior area sunk roughly two feet below the general ground surface, and a frontal ditch of varying dimension. Along the northeast and northwest sides of the work, the ditch measured from five feet to 10 feet wide and five feet deep. Investigation of the bottom of the ditch in this area facing the British line revealed the existence of a narrow palisade trench containing a series of closely spaced postholes. The frontal ditch continued around to the southwest side of Redoubt 6A, but the south side incorporated the main siege line, which at this point measured 10 feet in width. The ditches along these latter sides were considerably shallower than the former, each possessing a depth of about four feet. Furthermore, neither the south nor southwest ditches contained palisades, the placing of which would have constituted a needless exercise at that distance from the British. Archeologists proved the interior of Redoubt 6A was separated from the surrounding ditch by distances varying from 11 to 18 feet, suggesting the presence of a parapet of unequal thickness along its base. The parapet seemingly would have been thickest along the northwest side. A corridor cut through the epaulement at the rear (south) side formed the gorge that led into the siege line proper. At the center of the interior floor, investigators found evidence of a fire-burned area, indicating the French occupants of the structure maintained a fire for cooking and warming themselves during chilly weather. The interior of Redoubt 6A had maximum measurements of 54 feet by 40 feet. Including the parapet, the structure measured 105 feet by 91 feet.[29]

The last unit in the Grand French Battery complex, and one of the last to open fire on the enemy (October 11), was located west of Redoubt 6A and close to the edge of Goosley Road. Battery 4A was a mortar unit sunk below ground level about five feet. Archeologists have revealed the component parts of this work in much detail: the unit consisted of a narrow frontal ditch running about 90 feet in length, about four-and-one-half to 10 feet in width, and five feet at its greatest depth. About 25 feet behind the frontal ditch was the sunken mortar emplacement ditch. The presence of seven artillery pieces in Battery 4A is indicated by the discovery of seven groupings of sleeper impressions (some historical maps show eight mortars.) These impressions suggest that the platforms each measured between seven and nine feet square. Despite the sunken nature of the emplacement ditch, it seems likely at least seven feet of earth was piled upon the parapet, making it slightly taller than 12 feet on its interior slope. Such height is plausible since the exposed status of Battery 4A ahead of the siege line possibly made it more readily accessible to British sorties than were other units of the complex. Without the added height, British soldiers in such an assault would have encountered a parapet but two feet high. The epaulement probably measured four feet high on the exterior slope and about 12 feet high on the interior.

Because of the nature of its armament, Battery 4A had no embrasures. At its easternmost edge the artillery emplacement ditch abruptly narrows to form a support trench that angles sharply back to join the main siege line. Between the emplacement ditch and the support trench were two powder magazines. They were joined together by a short trench crossed by a narrow corridor that cut from the mortar position back to the support trench in its rear. The west magazine was the larger of the two, measuring about 10 feet on each side and four feet deep. The other was circular, approximately six feet in diameter and three feet deep. The position of Batteries 5A and 7A, far behind the parallel on elevated terrain, posed little danger to the occupants of Battery 4A because shot thrown from the cannon passed high overhead.[30]

On the high ground west of the Yorktown Creek branch ravine that approaches on the left end of the French sector, Rochambeau's engineers constructed battery 3A to hold four cannon, evidently 24-pounders. While it was not part of the Grand French Battery complex,[31] this unit is best considered a peripheral structure. Opened October 11, its firepower contributed to that of the Grand French Battery and it shared some targets with the guns and mortars of its neighboring earthworks to the east. Battery 3A stood approximately midway between the end of the siege line and Redoubts 3 and 4 at Pigeon Hill. The unit joined the adjacent branch ravine via a strip of communication trench extending southeastward from its rear.

Besides the array of French armament that opened on Cornwallis the morning of October 10, more American cannon, mortars, and howitzers joined in the bombardment. These were located in Battery 10A and Redoubts 11A and 12A. Battery 10A was built a short distance east of the French guard redoubt (9A) overlooking the ravine supply depot. Commanded by Captain Thomas Machin of the Second Artillery, Battery 10A held at least four, and possibly five, 18-pounders.[32] Lafayette and his guest, General Thomas Nelson, witnessed the first fire of this battery.[33] According to a return of ammunition expended in the structure the day of October 10-11, the armament consumed 240 cartridges firing a like number of cannonballs.[34]

In Redoubt 12A, nearest the American Grand Battery (13A), Knox's artillerists installed two 10-inch mortars. At 5:00 p.m. on October 10, their bombs joined those from Battery 13A in wreaking havoc on the British works.[35] Forty shells were sent toward the enemy from Redoubt 12A between October 10 and 11.[36] Many of these undoubtedly dropped on British Redoubt 9, which lay well within range of the mortars.[37]

Structurally and functionally, Redoubt 12A probably approximated Redoubt 11A, some 400 yards west along the siege line. The earthwork comprised an infantry guard post built to defend the American supply depot in the ravine directly east. Presumably, the shape of Redoubt 11A was roughly triangular, or perhaps square, somewhat similar to Redoubt 6A in the French sector. The location of Redoubt 11A was determined from documentary sources and confirmed archaeologically at the time of the early work on the Grand French Battery. Major examination of the site did not occur, however, because its location was centered along the fairway of a golf course constructed there during the 1920s. Situated farthest from the British works of any Allied structure of the first siege line (1,136 yards from Cornwallis's main fortifications, 666 yards from British Redoubt 9), Redoubt 11A did not play a special role during the siege and acted only as a link in the chain of works that deterred Cornwallis from attempting a direct frontal assault. Associate Historical Technician Thomas M. Pitkin postulated that the structure possessed a frontal ditch of 10 to 16 feet in width and six feet in depth, utilized palisades there and at the gorge, and had an interior perimeter along the parapet of "somewhere between 50 and 150 yards."[38]

To the right rear of Redoubt 11A, and practically a part of that structure, stood a small battery for howitzers or cannon. This battery was perhaps erected later than the redoubt. Records of expended ammunition indicate neither shot nor shells for this structure for either October 10 or 11. However, at least six maps verify the existence of the unit and all specify four artillery pieces operating in it.[39] Archaeological excavation in the area of Redoubt 11A is needed to determine with certainty the existence and nature of this battery and its artillery complement.

Much could also be learned through archaeological examination about Battery 13A—the American Grand Battery. This so-called "first shot battery," where Washington signaled the beginning of the bombardment from the first parallel, was the largest of all American earthworks built during the siege. From the time it opened on the afternoon of October 9 through the next day, Battery 13A exhausted the following stores:

81 Twenty four pound cartridges
101 Eighteen pound . . . Do.
90 Flannel Cartridges, for 10 Inch Mortars
54 Flannel Cartridges, for 8 Inch Howitzers
81 Twenty four pound shot

101 Eighteen . . . Do
90 Ten Inch Shells
54 Eight Inch Do
364 Wadds
18 Port-Fires
1 # Meal Powder
2 Hanks slow Match[40]

The report covering ammunition expended in Battery 13A over the period of October 10-11 accounted for 180 24-pounder shot, 140 18-pounder shot, 30 10-inch shells, and 40 8-inch shells fired against Cornwallis.[41] The marked increase in firepower over that recorded in the previous report reflected the unit's first full day of operation.

The Artillery at Yorktown

Field, Siege, and Ship or Garrison Pieces

Cannon fell into three categories. An army on the move utilized field guns, lighter in weight than the standard siege pieces and consequently shorter with thinner bore walls than the heavier guns. Because of the necessity for firing these weapons hurriedly in emergency situations, field pieces were mounted on light two-wheeled carriages. Field guns ranged in caliber from 3- to 24-pounders.[1]

By contrast, siege cannon were usually heavier, designed to batter and breach the enemy defenses, and displayed calibers ranging from 3- to 42-pounders, although 18- and 24-pounders were most widely desired by artillerists in siege conditions. Mounted on two-wheeled traveling carriages built larger than those for field guns, siege pieces could be employed in combinations against a fortified place, yet they were mobile enough to be moved into succeeding parallels and usually proved the key determinant in the outcome of the contest.[2]

Ship and garrison cannon, on the other hand, were quite immovable and were usually employed to defend either a fortress or a vessel. Their small-wheeled, low-slung carriage made mobility difficult. Heavy and cumbersome, garrison guns were dismounted by hoists and placed on wagons or on a special carriage for removal elsewhere.[3]

Iron and Bronze Guns

Guns were also classified according to their construction—either iron or bronze. Although contemporary works speak of brass rather than bronze, the alloy employed often contained copper and tin and sometimes even zinc. The result was a bronze piece.[4] Bronze guns were much more expensive than iron ones: a bronze 24-pounder cost more than twice as much as an iron piece. But the durability of bronze over iron compensated for this disparity. Moreover, a worn-out bronze gun might be recast time and again, while an iron piece could only be sold for scrap purposes. In a siege, bronze guns could withstand great heat during lengthy cannonades, while iron pieces could not.[5]

French Ordnance

Most of the French siege pieces used at Yorktown were made of bronze. French units of weight and measure differed slightly from the British (and American): the French inch was a bit longer than the American; the French *livre* weighed a little more than the American pound. As a result, French ordnance was slightly larger than the American and British pieces of the same caliber.

For example, the French 8-pounder actually equaled in nearly all respects the British 9-pounder.[6] In terms of artillery caliber, the French Valliere System brought a degree of standardization to French weaponry. Since 1732, French pieces had been organized into calibers of 4-, 8-, 12-, 16-, and 24-pounders. Mortars were categorized into 8- and 12-inch varieties, and all the ordnance assigned specified weights, lengths, and proportions. The Valliere System even prescribed specifications for the elaborate ornamentation on the gun barrels that came to characterize French artillery. The various designs accomplished a utilitarian purpose, allowing for easy identification of the pieces. Under the Valliere System, the breeches of the various caliber weapons were designed accordingly:

    4-pounder: face in a sunburst
    8-pounder: monkey's head
    12-pounder: rooster's head
    16-pounder: Medusa's head
    24-pounder: Bacchus

In addition to these decorative aspects, all Valliere pieces were easily recognized by the handles of the guns, which were always sculptured to represent dolphins. All functional and design distinctions among French field, siege, and garrison pieces were abandoned for the sake of standardization and uniformity.[7]

Per caliber, the Valliere guns all looked alike and remained identical in weight:

Caliber / Weight in Pounds

4-pounder / 1,265
8-pounder / 2,310
12-pounder / 3,520
16-pounder / 4,620
24-pounder / 5,940[8]

Most of the French guns used at Yorktown in 1781 seem to have been of the Valliere design.

A reorganization of French artillery began in France during the Revolutionary War. This produced a new design that forsook the decorative attributes of the Valliere System in favor of a smoother, more streamlined appearance. Known as the Gribeauval System, the new French ordnance type seems not to have found extensive use in America, and its presence at Yorktown in 1781 is debated.[9]

Gun Carriages

The carriages on which the field and siege guns used at Yorktown rested were themselves often elaborate devices. American gun carriages were fashioned from young, pliable oak whenever obtainable; otherwise, from walnut and chestnut. For the large wheels, elm, beech, and hickory were used.[10] Traveling carriages transported nearly every caliber, including the frequently used 18- and 24-pounders. Whenever weight threatened to strain or break a carriage, the guns were shifted into large block carriages or wagons for movement. Sometimes four-wheeled carriages called trucks were utilized to move pieces. These truck, or garrison, carriages were standard equipment for ordnance aboard ships. Field and siege carriages, fixed at their trail to a two-wheeled limber, were pulled with their gun cargo by horses or oxen whose number for the task was commensurate with the weight of the piece being towed.[11]

John Muller, the English theorist and author of *A Treatise of Artillery* (1757) computed the number of animals required to transport guns of different calibers:

> A 3 pounder requires but 1 horse, a 6 pounder 2, a 12 pounder 3, and a 24 pounder 6, of the light [field] sort; and the heavy [siege] 3 pounder 4 horses, the six 7, the twelve 10, and twenty-four 17, or 18.[12]

Besides carrying the cannon, gun carriages conveyed much of the gunners' equipment attached to hooks on the heavy wooden cheeks. The carriages were fixed with rings and bolts to facilitate moving of the piece by men in the field. To insure stability and to resist wear, the wood at stress points was reinforced with iron stripping.[13] The guns and carriages were nearly always painted, the cannon tubes and mountings normally black and the carriages gray or red-brown. By 1780, it appears that some carriages were being painted blue. By 1783, that color had become standard on American carriages as it had on the French.[14]

Firing Cannon

The proper firing of field and siege cannon during the late 18th century required intelligence and vigilance on the part of officers and gunners. Some understanding of scientific trajectory was necessary to accurately discharge the pieces and to gauge their success against the enemy. Because of their metallic composition, the cannon could not be fired infinitely without pause, for the heat would otherwise cause the tube to bend or even burst. The softening of the metal also widened the touchhole of the piece, creating too large a vent for the powder and thus diminishing the thrust of the projectile.[15]

As French artillery theorist Guillaume Le Blond noted,

> A 24 pounder may be fired 90, 100, or even 120 times in 24 hours, as is usually done in sieges, which is 5 times an hour; but great care must be taken to cool, or refresh the piece, after firing 10 or 12 times. This is done by dipping the maulkin [sponge] into water, and passin it several times up and down the bore of the piece.[16]

Powder and Cartridges

The propellant for all artillery was black powder, composed of saltpeter (potassium nitrate), charcoal, and sulphur at a 75:15:10 ratio.[17] The amount of powder in a charge fluctuated according to the distance from the enemy and the type of fire intended. For battering opposing defenses, the usual charge comprised one-third the weight of the shot. For ricochet firing, the powder charge varied with the distance.[18]

By the time of the Revolutionary War, advances in artillery component materials rendered the task of firing a piece much easier. Flannel and paper cartridges that utilized measured powder charges appeared and quickened the loading process. Cylindrical time measures permitted exactness in determining the charge to be placed in the cartridge and expedited the entire firing process. The paper or flannel cartridge burned at discharge and its residue was cleaned out after several firings.[19]

Further embellishment of the firing procedure appeared in the form of fixed ammunition that combined ball and propellant into one unit. Fixed ammunition developed from the invention of the sabot, a wooden disc slightly hollowed on one side to accommodate the base of the shot, which was attached with tinned iron cross straps. The sabot replaced the traditional cannon wad and provided a base for attaching a flannel powder bag or cartridge. The advent of fixed ammunition was made possible by the standardization of artillery calibers. Similarly, grapeshot and canister (or case) shot became fixed ammunition, too, and like cannonballs, were used almost exclusively in situations demanding rapid firing. For normal shooting, siege and field guns employed a semi-fixed load incorporating a separated projectile and powder bag.[20]

Elevation

Aiming the guns took time and demanded precise mathematical calculation. Simple direction was considered first during the erection of the cannon platforms, and usually was set before the guns arrived in the battery. The distance involved necessitated elevating the pieces to heights appropriate for striking particular targets. A gunner's quadrant aided the aiming process. Shaped like a carpenter's square with a quarter-circle joining the lengths, the quadrant allowed an artillerist to determine the correct angle of elevation for his cannon. The gunners accomplished the elevation with the aid of a quoin, a small wooden wedge driven between the cannon breech and the carriage bed. The device raised the rear of the breech and lowered the muzzle to the properly calculated position.[21] Siege gun elevation normally stayed under 12 degrees.[22]

Elevation was closely correlated with the powder charge to enable a cannon to hit enemy targets. Furthermore, guns that fired point-blank necessarily lacked the distance achieved with elevation of the pieces, as the following table demonstrates:

Caliber	Distance (Point Blank) in feet	Distance (Elevated 45°) in feet (greatest extent of range)
2-pounder	370	3,709
4-pounder	741	7,419
6-pounder	1,978	19,783
8-pounder	803—989	8,902—11,128
12-pounder	927—1,112	10,880—12,364
24-pounder	1,051—1,978	12,550 —14,837
32-pounder	1,236—1,442	14,837[23]

Artillerists also had to keep in mind that greater elevation of the piece resulted in more inaccurate fire.

Types of Fire

Eighteenth-century theorists delimited two general types of fire based on the course of discharged shot and on the overall topography of the target site. Grazing fire was that in which the discharged cannonball directly paralleled the horizon, destroying all in its path. Plunging fire was that which arced significantly in its course or which traveled from a higher to a lower area. Destruction from plunging fire was limited to what was hit near the point of contact.[24] Within this framework, artillerists classified the functional responsibilities of their pieces.

The purpose of direct firing was to dismount opposing guns and destroy the enemy fortifications. Direct firing most often occurred from the first parallel to cover the advancing of the approaches and the construction of later parallels. With his guns out of commission, the enemy exposed himself to further artillery and musket attack from the second and third lines.[25] Direct firing constituted an enfilade whenever the attack was part of a concerted sweeping operation, either direct or flanking in character, wherein the besiegers' shot raked along the inside of the enemy parapet.[26]

The term "enfilade" could also apply to ricochet firing, in which the powder charge of the guns was diminished to the point where the shot merely cleared the muzzle to bounce ungracefully over the intervening terrain and along the face of the opposing works. Guns fixed to fire en ricochet in a siege were elevated between eight and 12 degrees to obtain maximum effect. In the field, where the principal targets would likely be infantry or cavalry, guns firing ricochet were seldom elevated beyond three degrees.[27] In either case, the discharged shot "goes rolling and bounding, killing and maiming all it meets in its course, and creates much more disorder by going thus slowly along, than it could if thrown from the piece with great violence and speed."[28] As Tielke put it, a ball sent forth in ricochet fashion would "do incredible mischief wherever it goes."[29]

Most destructive of all forms of cannon fire, however, was that resulting from guns situated to cross fire. Two or more gun batteries arranged for cross fire unleashed merciless barrages of shot against enemy fortifications that crippled the opposing artillery and usually led to the breaching of the enemy defenses. The target battery of a besieger's cross fire rarely survived intact.[30]

Hot Shot

For action against enemy shipping, offensive artillery often resorted to the use of hot shot—red-hot cannonballs fired to set enemy vessels ablaze. Shot was heated in a pit excavated in the ground four feet deep and six feet in diameter. The gunners built a fire in the pit in which they placed the shot. Meantime, the cannon was attentively readied with a quantity of powder, wadding, and either a wooden disc or a thick chunk of sod, to prevent premature ignition of the powder charge by the heated ball. The artillerymen fired the piece as soon as the hot shot was heated and before it cooled to the point of ineffectiveness.[31] When practiced with skill and patience, firing hot shot had a telling effect on enemy shipping and gunboats and took a toll in lives and equipment that often foretold final defeat.

Auxiliary Equipment

Special equipment aided in maneuvering and actually firing the cannon. There appeared little difference between the apparatus for siege cannon and that for the field type. One manual enumerated the items necessary to the performance of field artillery:

> 1st. A lint-stock, 2d. A portfire-stock, 3d. A powderhorn and hammer, pincers, priming wyers and gimblets; these are fixed in the gunners [sic] belt: 4th a tubebox and thumb-case; this is made of leather, which the bombardier [gunner] puts on his left thumb, to prevent the heat of the piece, in quick firing, from burning him: 5th. A haversack, 6th. A spunge and rammer, 7th. A ladle, 8th. A worm: sometimes the ladle and worm are fixed on one staff: 9th. A sett of drag ropes, 10th. A trail spike, to guide the piece with, or tiller, which is a more suitable term-for it, as the gunner steers the piece with it. . . . Also, limbers, gears, horses, &c.[32]

Maneuvering the heavy cannon around in a battery was accomplished with the aid of drag ropes and handspikes. The latter were large wooden crowbars sheathed in iron that helped in moving the gun carriage and in lifting the breech for insertion of the quoins during elevation. Handspikes for siege cannon measured about six feet in length; some were fitted with rollers at the end so that the heavy trail of the carriage might be raised and moved with relative ease.[33]

Loading the Piece

When cartridges were either unavailable or not being used, a long-handled lanterne, or ladle, accomplished the process of loading powder into the breech of the piece. Fashioned of thin copper, the ladle served both as a powder measure and as the best means of getting the propellant into the weapon.[34] The thumb-piece mentioned above in the quoted material was very important to prevent burns to the gunner who stopped up the vent during the loading procedure. As described by Tousard, the thumb-piece was "a kind of small bag, about three inches square, made of strong skin or leather, and stuffed with hair: one of the sides is recovered with a piece of leather, so that the cannoneer may lodge his fingers in it while stopping the vent."[35]

The loaders next pushed the powder, wad, and shot home with a cylindrical, long-handled wooden instrument called a rammer. Usually made of elm, the rammer exhibited variously-spaced marks on its handle to permit the loaders to see whether the components of the charge were exactly seated.[36] In the American Army (though not in the French) the rammer was sometimes mounted on the same handle as the sponge, a somewhat smaller cylinder covered with lambskin and used to swab water into the barrel to cool and clean it after each firing. Sponging insured that no sparks lingered in the breech and muzzle to set off ensuing rounds. Sometimes, instead of the lambskin-covered cylinder, the sponge consisted of a bristle brush. The diameters of both the rammer and sponge equaled exactly that of the shot for a particular caliber piece.[37]

Igniting the Charge

The artillerist ignited the charge at the touchhole with the aid of slow match, or cord match, a three-strand cotton rope impregnated with saltpeter and treated with lead acetate and lye to burn at a rate of four or five inches an hour. Occasionally slow match was produced from flax tow or smooth hemp. The cannoneer firing the gun held the slow match in a lintstock, a wooden forked stick three feet long, in order to stay clear of the recoil of the piece.[38] The slow match was applied to the loose priming powder at the vent of the gun.

By the middle of the 18th century, portfires began to be favored over slow match in discharging cannon. Portfires were thin cylindrical paper cases containing a highly flammable mixture of gunpowder, saltpeter, and sulphur fixed in a consistency of linseed oil. Some portfires were created in molds, while others were simply rolled and filled by artificers in the field. Portfires burned with a flare and produced extremely hot flames. In place of the lintstock, portfire stocks served to light the priming powder. Portfire stocks made from sheet iron measured about 11 inches in length.[39]

Sometimes priming tubes replaced the loose, black priming powder. These devices were narrow tin tubes containing portfire substances. When paper or flannel cartridges were used instead of loose powder in the charge, sharpened priming tubes were inserted in the vent of the piece to prick the cartridge and provide access for ignition. Priming tubes usually measured between 4 and 6-1/2 inches in length. During the Revolutionary War, the American artillery employed both the slow match and portfire means of discharging cannon.[40]

Cleaning the Piece

Another indispensable piece of cannon apparatus was the worm, or wormer. Long-handled like the sponge and rammer, the wormer in effect was a type of double corkscrew used to clean wads and residue of cartridges from the bore after firing. Occasionally wormers were fastened to the same pole as the sponge, enabling a piece to be washed and wormed simultaneously.[41]

Gun Crews

These men brought experience and skill to their work. By the time of the Revolution, British and French gunners were among the finest in the world. British and Hessian crews were so expert they could fire up to 14 shots per minute (though this meant they had elimated most of the drill—usually because of an extreme danger of being overrun by the enemy). The French performed equally well.[42] By Yorktown, American artillerymen had approached expertise with their weapons, and won plaudits from the French during the siege.

Duties

Generally, field gun crews were larger than those for servicing siege pieces. A field gun crew consisted of 14 or 15 men, each assigned a specific task. Numbers 1 through 6 were mostly unskilled and controlled the drag ropes to maneuver the piece. When the cannon was ready for firing they stood three on either side of the carriage wheels. Number 7 cleaned and sponged the barrel between shots and rammed home the wad and shot. Number 8 stood opposite him, left of the muzzle, and placed the powder or cartridge and ball into the piece. The man designated number 9 thumbed the vent to keep out residue while number 7 worked the bore with sponge and rammer. Number 9 also primed the vent, either with loose powder or with a priming tube, and number 10 actually discharged the round with slow match or by means of a portfire. Numbers 9 and 10 stayed outside the wheels, clear of recoil, although 7 and 8 remained near the muzzle and had to keep their mouths wide open to protect their ear drums from the splitting blast of the cannon. No. 11 operated a handspike on the trail transom to aim the piece in accordance with an officer's directions. Another man, number 12, stood to the right rear of the piece with a water bucket and the lighted lintstock. Number 13 brought ammunition from a supply managed by number 14 and turned it over to number 8 for placement down the muzzle. Number 15 likewise managed an ammunition supply and at the same time looked after the limber horse.[43]

Most siege pieces were much too heavy to be maneuvered easily by drag ropes. Consequently, their crews became smaller. For example, a gun crew for a 24-pounder siege cannon numbered eight (occasionally nine) men.[44]

Commands

The gun crew completed its duties in an orderly manner by following the direct commands of an artillery officer. For a field gun these would have been the following:

— *Attention!*
— *Unlimber pieces! Secure side-boxes! Man out - the pieces!*
— *From right to left - dress! Advance spunge! Tend - vent!*
— *Spunge piece! Handle cartridge! Charge - Piece!*
— *Ram down - Cartridge! Prime!*
— *Take Aim! Fire!*
— *Change - Drag-ropes!* [sometimes indicated by a drum.]
— *Unhook - Drag-ropes!*
— *Mount - Side-boxes!*
— *Limber pieces!*
— *Shoulder rammer!*
— *Carry - Lint-stock!*[45]

For heavy siege cannon, the commands were:

— *Gunners and Matrosses! To your posts - march.*
— *Front - face.*
— *Prepare - battery!*
— *To -handspikes!*
— *Enter - handspikes!*
— *From - battery!*
— *To the knob - To the wedge!* [depending on whether a quoin or an
     elevating screw was used with the piece]

— *Lay down - handspikes!*

— *To - spunge! Stop - vent! To - cartridge!*

— *Spunge - gun!*

— *Return spunge! To - rammer!*

— *Cartridge - gun!*

— *Ram - cartridge!*

— *Shot - gun!*

— *Ram - shot!*

— *Return - rammer!*

This exercise with sponge and rammer was common in the French service; among American and British artillery it differed only slightly:

— *To - handspikes!*

— *Enter - handspikes!*

— *To - battery!*

— *Point - gun!*

— *Lay down - handspikes!*

— *Clear - vent! Prime!*

— *To - lintstock! To - wedge!*

— *March!*

— *Front - face!*

— *Lintstock - march!*

— *Make - ready!*

— *Fire!*[46]

The Mortars

Next to field and siege pieces in importance were mortars, whose large truncated bores threw exploding bombs on the enemy with deadly precision. The mortar's purpose, recorded Tousard, "is to throw hollow shells filled with powder, which, falling on any building, or into the works of a fortress, burst, and its fragments destroy every thing within its reach."[47]

The measurement across the mouth of the bore gave the caliber of particular mortars. By the late 18th century, calibers became standardized and ranged from an extreme 20-inch piece to one of only 4-1/2 inches. Most mortars used at Yorktown were 12-inch, 10-inch, and 8-inch. Weight varied with size, with the largest (13-inch) piece weighing 4,500 pounds. Mortars of the 12-inch variety weighed about 3,150 pounds, while 10-inch weapons ran anywhere from 1,620 to 2,050 pounds, depending on whether the piece was intended for medium or long-range fire. Mortars with an 8-inch bore weighed on the average 550 pounds.[48]

The smallest mortar, a 4-1/2-inch piece called a coehorn for its Dutch inventor, Baron Van Menno Coehoorn, became a favorite among troops because of its portability: two men could lift and transport it easily. A 5-1/2-inch piece (technically 5.8-inch), known as a royal, answered much the same purpose as the coehorn. In siege operations, however, both coehorns and royals remained subordinate to the heavy 8-, 10-, and 13-inch mortars commonly employed.[49]

Mortar Beds

Instead of using carriages, mortars were mounted on heavy wooden beds sufficiently strengthened with iron molding to withstand the direct vertical recoil of the pieces. Timber mortar beds were made in four sections, except those for the smaller coehorns and royals, which consisted of single blocks of wood. Basically, a mortar bed consisted of two stout wooden cheeks joined by two transoms. Some cheeks were manufactured of iron. Lacking wheels, mortar beds were transported on specially built mortar wagons or in slug carts. On arrival in a battery, the beds were set on level, square wooden platforms preparatory to receiving the mortar. American-made mortars usually had their beds permanently attached, unlike the French mortars, which could be removed from the beds for transporting.[50]

Knox's Mortar System

During the Siege of Yorktown, General Knox devised a system for firing mortars from carriages similar to those used for howitzers. The idea was not novel, having originated with one Count Buckeburg who invented traveling carriages for mortars in order to discharge bombs at low elevations in the manner of howitzers.[51]

William Stevens provided some data regarding the Knox enterprise at Yorktown:

> General Knox ordered . . . some 8 inch mortars mounted on carriages constructed similar to travelling carriages with truck wheels, which answered a very good purpose. But they require the carriages to be made very strong, as the trunnions being on the breech of the mortar, will naturally cause a greater pressure or shock, when fired, than it would do if the trunnions were more proportioned in the middle, as a howitzer.[52]

Essentially, the Knox mortar carriage differed from the standard howitzer type in that the recesses where the trunnions rested were greatly strengthened to better absorb the more direct shock of recoil.

Bombs

Mortars fired large hollow bombs made of iron and filled with varying amounts of black powder. On bursting, the mortar shell fragmented into a myriad of pieces, causing death or destruction to men, animals, and buildings. Bombs were of different weights; that for a 12-inch mortar weighed upwards of 150 pounds, while an 8-inch missile might weigh as much as 44 pounds or as little as 42.[53]

Bomb globes were pierced with a hole, or eye, into which artificers poured black powder. At the minimum, a 12-inch bomb took five pounds of powder to explode it, a 10-inch bomb three pounds, and an 8-inch bomb one pound. At the maximum, a 12-inch bomb could accommodate 17 pounds of powder, a 10-inch bomb 10 pounds, and an 8-inch bomb four pounds, one ounce.[54] The amount of powder placed in a bomb varied between these extremes according to need and the effect desired. To destroy earthen fortifications, for example, the sphere should be filled as full as possible; as an antipersonnel weapon, a moderate charge would suffice. "In a regular siege," wrote Tousard, "the charge for twelve inch bombs is from four to six pounds, and that for eight inch bombs from one to two pounds."[55]

The insertion of the fuse followed the charging of the bomb. For this, a special fuse driver and mallet were used to implant the frustum-like wooden fuse containing a composition of gunpowder, sulphur, and saltpeter.[56] The composition was inentionally slow-burning to allow the projectile to reach its target before bursting.[57] The larger mortar bombs had ring-type handles to facilitate moving them and loading them into the piece. Some mortar ammunition was marked for identification, and archaeology done at Yorktown has disclosed at least one French shell fragment displaying, in relief, a fleur-de-lis.[58]

Handling and Firing Mortars

Equipment

The articles used to tend mortars resembled some of those used for cannon. An iron ladle called a curette aided in cleaning the chambers of both mortars and howitzers. One end of the curette was spoon-shaped, while the other contained a concave scraper for removing rust and residue from the bore of the piece. A wooden spatula enabled the bombardiers to pack earth or wedges around the bomb in order to center the ammunition prior to firing it. Sponging the mortar was unnecessary because the nature of the bore enabled the men to reach into it with their hands to dislodge accumulated matter. A piece of heavy, coarse canvas was used to clean the inside of the bore. For loading the ring-handled bombs into the ten- and twelve-inch mortars, double S-shaped iron hooks were used.[59]

Loading

Mortars were fired according to strict procedures by a select corps of noncommissioned artillery officers called bombardiers.[60] These soldiers supervised the entire process of loading, directing, and discharging the weapons. Mortar chambers were loaded with black gunpowder; a 12-inch piece took five pounds at its fullest capacity, a 10-inch three pounds, and an 8-inch mortar one pound.[61] Once the charging was completed and a wad placed over the powder, the loaded bomb was carefully centered in the bore to rest directly on the wad or upon loose earth packed atop the wad. In either case the bomb, fuse outward, was steadied at the exact center with more dirt packed around it or with four to six wooden wedges appropriately placed. When dirt was used, both to cover the wadding and to center the bomb, the discharge was called "double firing" because the fuse of the missile had to be ignited prior to firing the mortar proper. When wedges alone were used to center the bomb, the fire of the discharging mortar triggered ignition of the bomb fuse.[62] In all likelihood, this safer process of firing mortars was practiced at Yorktown in 1781.

In flight, the discharged bomb left a trail of black smoke during the day and a rainbow of flames at night. The length of the fuse had to be coordinated with the intended length of the missile's flight in order to prevent either a premature or a belated explosion. Sentinels in the besieged garrison might give ample warning of approaching bombs, permitting the troops to dive for cover. If upon impact the missiles failed to explode, the men might try to douse the fuse with water or lessen its explosive impact by covering the bomb with sandbags thrown from a safe distance.[63]

Test Shooting

The besieging artillery could usually avoid much of this by conducting test shots in which proof bombs were fired and the seconds counted until they reached their targets. Then the elevation of the mortars and the fuse length of the bombs could be adjusted accordingly.[64] Elevation proved essential for good mortar performance, and bombs prepared for use against buildings, magazines, and enemy batteries were launched, not only with the greatest charges, but with the greatest height. In this manner the bombs acquired more force in their fall, which resulted in maximum shock and execution.[65] Bombs were never fired point-blank at a target, as Le Blond noted:

> As one of the effects of the bomb results from its weight, it is never discharged in the same manner as a ball from the cannon, that is, by directing or pointing the mortar at a certain object; but the mortar is a little inclined to the horizon, so that the bomb being thrown up obliquely, much in the same direction as a tennis ball struck by the racket, may fall upon the-place intended. . . .[66]

Commands

Four mattrosses assisted the bombardier in the discharge of a mortar. They responded to the verbal commands of the appropriate battery officer:

— *Bombardier and Matrosses, to your posts - march!*
— *To the Front - face!*
— *Prepare Battery!*

— To - handspikes!

— Enter - handspikes!

— To - battery!

— Lay down - handspikes!

— Clean - mortar!

— Raise - mortar!

— To - powder! To - bomb!

— Load - powder!

— Load - bomb!

— To - handspikes!

— Give - degrees! Point!

— Lay down - handspikes!

— Clear - vent! Prime!

— To - portfire!

— March!

— Front - face!

— Portfire - march!

— Make - ready!

— Fire!

— Bombardiers and Matrosses - to your posts - march! [if exercise is to be repeated] [67]

Howitzers and Grenades

Use of Howitzers

Somewhat more versatile than either cannon or mortars were howitzers, a 17th-century invention of the Dutch. These popular weapons could throw bombs at trajectories lower than mortars and higher than cannon, and were ideal for discharging bombs at an enemy en ricochet in the same manner as cannonballs.[68] Indeed, their use in firing bombs in this fashion endeared them to siege artillerists of the 18th century. The bomb, or howitzer, "hopps along the ground, and drops just over the enemy's parapet, destroying them where they thought themselves most secure."[69] Moreover, the howitzer was a light weapon and used a short-trailed, two-wheel carriage. Thus, it was highly mobile, and could be used to fire grapeshot and cannister shot besides bombs. Like mortars, howitzer size was gauged by the width across the muzzle. There were two main sizes, 6-inch and 8-inch. The latter howitzer weighed 2,625 pounds.[70]

Firing Howitzers

When the howitzer was fired with great elevations at stationary targets, its wheels were sometimes removed from its carriage and the mounting placed astride timbers on the ground to avoid shattering the carriage on recoil.[71] Howitzers were fired essentially like mortars, with the bomb placed in the bore after the weapon itself had been charged. Then the vent was cleared and the piece primed and fired, all on command of the responsible officer.[72]

Grenades

Another type of antipersonnel ordnance sometimes fired from mortars were hand grenades. These small hollow iron shells (sometimes made of tin or even papier mache) were filled with extra-fine powder and fixed with a wooden fuse. They measured about three inches in diameter and were generally hand thrown by soldiers, designated grenadiers, when nearly in contact with the enemy.[73]

The Artillery Park

During a siege, the artillery was organized in a special artillery park located behind the first parallel. From the artillery park, the guns and ammunition were advanced by wagons, horses, and by artillerymen who maneuvered the pieces in the trenches and batteries after the animals were detached. The park was guarded from enemy attack by 50 men drafted from the artillery corps.[74] Drum beats governed the movement of the pieces under the system adopted by General Knox and his staff in 1779. The firing of the artillery commenced on the right and moved through subsequent batteries to the left of the line.[75] Cannon, mortars, and howitzers, when expertly employed, constituted a formidable array of weaponry that sooner or later made capitulation of an enemy inevitable.

At Yorktown, the combination of fire from the elite French batteries and largely veteran American gun crews proved the principal factor in the defeat of the British Army under General Charles Cornwallis.

Endnotes

Chapter 1: The Campaign of the Allies

1. A handy chronological summary of the Revolutionary War is in *Harper's Encyclopedia of United States History, from 458 A.D. to 1902*, 10 vols. (New York: Harper and Brothers, Publishers, 1902), 7, pp. 410-415. Political background, personalities, and ideology of the war is in Bernard Bailyn, *The Ideological Origins of the American Revolution* (Cambridge, Mass.: Harvard University Press, 1967); Bernard Bailyn, *To Begin the World Anew: The Genius and Ambiguities of the American Founders* (New York: Alfred A. Knopf, 2003); John E. Ferling, *A Leap in the Dark: The Struggle to Create the American Republic* (New York: Oxford University Press, 2003); and A. J. Langguth, *Patriots: The Men Who Started the American Revolution* (New York: Simon and Schuster, 1988). A concise background is found in Gordon S. Wood, *The American Revolution: A History* (New York: Random House, 2002). For a concise reading of the individual engagements, see Theodore P. Savas and J. David Dameron, *A Guide to the Battles of the American Revolution* (New York, Savas Beatie, 2005).

2. Russell B. Weigley, *History of the United States Army* (New York: Macmillan Company, 1967), p. 42; Maurice Matloff, ed., *American Military History* (Washington: Office of the Chief of Military History, 1969), pp. 89-90; Marshall Smelser, *The Winning of Independence* (New York: New Viewpoints, 1973), pp. 322-323; Louis Clinton Hatch, *The Administration of the American Revolutionary Army* (New York: Longmans, Green, and Company, 1904), p. 113. For the army and its overall composition, see Charles Royster, *A Revolutionary People at War: The Continental Army and American Character, 1775-1783* (New York: Norton, 1981); Robert K. Wright, Jr., *The Continental Army* (Washington, D.C.: Officer of the Chief of Military History, 1983); and E. Wayne

Carp, *To Starve the Army at Pleasure: Continental Army Administration and American Political Culture* (Chapel Hill: University of North Carolina Press, 1984).

3. Matloff, *American Military History*, p. 94; Henry P. Johnston, *The Yorktown Campaign and the Surrender of Cornwallis* (New York: Harper and Brothers, 1881), p. 18; Trevor N. Dupuy, Curt Johnson, and David L. Bongard, eds., *The Harper Encyclopedia of Military Biography* (New York, 1995), p. 174. See also, generally, Henry Clinton, *The Narrative of Lieutenant General Sir Henry Clinton, K. B., Relative to His Conduct during Part of His Command of the King's Troops in North America: Particularly to That which respects the Unfortunate Issue of the Campaign in 1781* (London: John Debrett, [1785]).

4. Matloff, *American Military History*, p. 94.

5. Hoffman Nickerson, "Yorktown, 1781," *American Mercury*, 24 (September, 1931), p. 84.

6. Ibid., p. 83.

7. Piers Mackesy, *The War for America, 1775-1783* (Cambridge: Harvard University Press, 1965), p. 409.

8. Don Higginbotham, *The War of American Independence: Military Attitudes, Policies, and Practice, 1763-1789* (New York: The Macmillan Company, 1971), pp. 378-79. For a psychological assessment of Clinton and his role in the campaign of 1781, see William B. Willcox and Frederick Wyatt, "Sir Henry Clinton: A Psychological Exploration in History," *William and Mary College Quarterly Historical Magazine*, 16 (January, 1959), pp. 3-26; and also Willcox's evaluation in his *Portrait of a General: Sir Henry Clinton in the War of Independence* (New York: Alfred A. Knopf, 1962), pp. 492-524.

9. Johnston, *Yorktown Campaign*, p. 21; Higginbotham, *War of American Independence*, p. 376.

10. Johnston, *Yorktown Campaign*, p. 21.

11. Matloff, *American Military History*, p. 90; Jacob Harris Patton, "The Campaign of the Allies: The Surrender of Lord Cornwallis," *Magazine of American History*, 7 (October, 1881), p. 243.

12. Matloff, *American Military History*, pp. 90, 91.

13. Ibid., p. 91.

14. Ibid., p. 93; Johnston, *Yorktown Campaign*, p. 24. For a solid examination of this battle and its personalities, see John Hairr, *Guilford Courthouse: North Carolina* (Da Capo, 2003).

15. Matloff, *American Military History*, p. 93; Smelser, *Winning of Independence*, p. 321; Lucien Agniel, *The Late Affair Has Almost Broke My Heart* (Riverside, Conn.: The Chatham Press, Inc., 1972), p. 109. A standard treatment of Greene's campaign in the South, 1780-81, is in Henry Lee, Jr., *The Campaign of 1781 in the Carolinas* (Philadelphia, 1824; reprint ed., Chicago: Quadrangle Books, Inc., 1962). Greene has been unduly criticized for falling back into South Carolina instead of re-engaging Cornwallis. Actually, he occupied 7,000 British troops who eventually were sorely needed in Virginia. Agniel, *Late Affair*, p. 110. See also, John S. Pancake, *This Destructive War: The British Campaign in the Carolinas, 1780-1782* (Tuscaloosa:

University of Alabama Press, 1992); John Buchanan, *The Road to Guilford Courthouse: American Revolution in the Carolinas* (New York: John Wiley and Sons, 1997), and Lawrence E. Babits, *A Devil of a Whipping: The Battle of Cowpens* (Chapel Hill: University of North Carolina Press, 1998).

16. Matloff, *American Military History*, p. 94; Higginbotham, *War of American Independence*, p. 376.

17. Edward C. Haynes, "The Siege of Yorktown," *Chautauquan*, 15 (April, 1892), p. 3.

18. Ibid., pp. 3-4; Higginbotham, *War of American Independence*, p. 376; Matloff, *American Military History*, p. 94.

19. William B. Willcox, *The British Road to Yorktown: A Study in Divided Command*, reprint from *American Historical Review* (October, 1946), p. 2. An explanation by Cornwallis of his motives in moving into Virginia is contained in Johnston, *Yorktown Campaign*, pp. 26-28.

20. Agniel, *Late Affair*, p. 111; Johnston, *Yorktown Campaign*, p. 26.

21. Quoted in Charles E. Hatch, Jr., *Yorktown and the Siege of 1781* (Washington: United States Government Printing Office, 1957), p. 2.

22. Quoted in Alfred Thayer Mahan, *The Influence of Sea Power Upon History, 1660-1783* (Boston: Little, Brown, and Company, 1908), p. 385.

23. Higginbotham, *War of American Independence*, p. 376.

24. Reproduced in Henry Clinton, *The Narrative of Lieutenant General Sir Henry Clinton, K. B., Relative to His Conduct during Part of His Command of the King's Troops in North America: Particularly to That which respects the Unfortunate Issue of the Campaign in 1781* (London: John Debrett, [1785]), p. 50; See also Germain to Clinton, May 2, 1781, reproduced in *Johnston, Yorktown Campaign*, p. 19n.

25. Johnston, *Yorktown Campaign*, p. 29.

26. Nickerson, "Yorktown, 1781," pp. 81-82.

27. Hatch, *Yorktown and the Siege of 1781*, pp. 2-3; Franklin Wickwire and Mary Wickwire, *Cornwallis: The American Adventure* (Boston: Houghton Mifflin Company, 1970), p. 329. For Lafayette, see, Stanley J. Idzerda (ed.), *Lafayette in the Age of the American Revolution: Selected Letters and Papers, 1776-1790* (5 vols.; Ithaca, N.Y.: Cornell University Press, 1977-83), with Virginia covered in volume 4.

28. Hatch, *Yorktown and the Siege of 1781*, p. 3.

29. Higginbotham, *War of American Independence*, p. 378; Patton, "Campaign of the Allies," pp. 246-47; Haynes, "Siege of Yorktown," p. 2.

30. Hatch, *Yorktown and the Siege of 1781*, p. 6.

31. Ibid., pp. 3-4; Wickwire and Wickwire, *Cornwallis*, p. 326; Haynes, "Siege of Yorktown," p. 2; Patton, "Campaign of the Allies," p. 247; Agniel, *Late Affair*, p. 111.

32. Hatch, *Yorktown and the Siege of 1781*, pp. 4, 6.

33. Johann Ewald, "Diary of the American War," trans. and ed. Joseph P. Tustin, transcribed excerpts furnished by Joseph P. Tustin, Tuckerton, N. J., pp. 824-825. Wickwire and Wickwire place the reconnaissance on June 28. Wickwire and Wickwire, *Cornwallis*, p. 339.

34. Mackesy, *War for America*, p. 411; Hatch, *Yorktown and the Siege of 1781*, p. 6.

35. Hatch, *Yorktown and the Siege of 1781*, p. 7; Matloff, *American Military History*, p. 96.

36. Arnold Whitridge, *Rochambeau* (New York: Macmillan Co., 1965), p. 208.

37. Nickerson, "Yorktown 1781," p. 84; Hatch, *Yorktown and the Siege of 1781*, p. 7; Agniel, *Late Affair*, p. 113; Wickwire and Wickwire, *Cornwallis*, pp. 326-28; Mackesy, *War for America*, p. 411. Clinton later maintained that Cornwallis "was at liberty to add York Town as an additional security to old fort Comfort [sic] . . . but not to remove the station from James River to York River[.]" Clinton's marginalia notes in Charles Stedman, *The History of the Origin, Progress, and Termination of the American War*, 2 vols. (London: Printed for the Author, 1794), 2, p. 396. Copy in the Henry Clinton Papers, William L. Clements Library, University of Michigan, Ann Arbor.

38. Whitridge, *Rochambeau*, p. 208; Clinton, *Narrative*, pp. 22-23.

39. Quoted in Hatch, *Yorktown and the Siege of 1781*, p. 7. For a critical view of Cornwallis's decision against fortifying Old Point Comfort, see Willcox, *Portrait of a General*, p. 408. "Cornwallis [instead] chose . . . a position where an outnumbered British fleet would have maximum difficulty in reaching him and getting out again, and where the York River cut his army in two without providing an escape route." Ibid.

40. Robert Arthur, *The End of a Revolution* (New York: Vantage Press, 1965), p. 108.

41. Ewald, "Diary of the American War," pp. 825-26.

42. Arthur, *End of a Revolution*, p. 108.

43. Ibid., p. 109.

44. Ewald, "Diary of the American War," p. 856; Wickwire and Wickwire, *Cornwallis*, p. 353; Hatch, *Yorktown and the Siege of 1781*, p. 7.

45. Quoted in A. H. Burne, "Cornwallis at Yorktown," *Journal of the Society for Army Historical Research*, 17 (Summer, 1938), p. 72. The two battalions of the Ansbach-Bayreuth Regiment numbered, respectively, 432 and 412 men at Yorktown.

46. John Marshall, *The Life of George Washington, Commander in Chief of the American Forces . . . and First President of the United States*, 5 vols. (London: Richard Phillips, 1805), 4, p. 539; Charles E. Hatch, Jr., "Gloucester Point in the Siege of Yorktown, 1781," *William and Mary College Quarterly Historical Magazine*, 2d ser. 20 (April, 1940), p. 268.

47. Charles E. Hatch, Jr., *"York Under the Hill," Yorktown's Waterfront, Colonial National Historical Park, Virginia* (Denver: National Park Service, 1973), p. 58.

48. Quoted in Mackesy, *War for America*, p. 412; Henry Clinton, *Observations on Mr. Stedman's History of the American War* (London: John Debrett, 1794), p. 22. (This publication is affixed in the rear of Clinton's personal copy of volume 2 of Stedman's work in the William L. Clements Library, University of Michigan, Ann Arbor.). Despite his selection of the post as the best available, Cornwallis harbored serious reservations about its ultimate potential for defense. As he would later write with the benefit of hindsight, "A successful defense . . . in our situation was perhaps impossible, for the place could only be reckoned an intrenched Camp, subject in most places to enfilade, the ground in general so disadvantageous, that nothing but the necessity of fortifying it as a post to protect the Navy could have induced any person to erect Works upon it."

Cornwallis to Clinton, Oct. 20, 1781, Gold Star Box, Henry Clinton Papers, William L. Clements Library, University of Michigan., Ann Arbor.

49. Hatch, *Yorktown and the Siege of 1781*, p. 9.

50. Agniel, *Late Affair*, p. 112; Patton, "Campaign of the Allies," p. 247.

51. Nickerson, "Yorktown, 1781," pp. 81, 83; Clinton's marginalia notes in Stedman, *History . . . of the American War*, 2:397; Mahan, *Influence of Sea Power*, p. 388. Although it is customary to give de Grasse the rank of "Admiral," such a rank did not exist in pre-revolutionary France, though it generally corresponds to the American rank and so is provided to help facilitate understanding. De Grasse's official title was "lieutenant général des armées navales."

52. Smelser, *Winning of Independence*, p. 323; Nickerson, "Yorktown, 1781," p. 83; Higginbotham, *War of American Independence*, p. 381.

53. Nickerson, "Yorktown, 1781," pp. 83, 84; Mahan, *Influence of Sea Power*, p. 389.

54. Haynes, "Siege of Yorktown," p. 5; Higginbotham, *War of American Independence*, p. 380.

55. Higginbotham, *War of American Independence*, p. 380; Agniel, *Late Affair*, p. 112. Washington later maintained that he would not have laid siege to New York unless the garrison was sufficiently decreased in strength, because some great advantage was needed at that critical juncture "to revive the expiring hopes . . . of the Country." Furthermore, his imminent strike against the city was in reality a long-standing ruse designed for "inducing the Eastern, Middle States to make greater exertions in furnishing specific supplies . . . as well as for the interesting purpose of rendering the enemy less prepared elsewhere." Washington to Noah Webster, July 31, 1788, in *1781 Yorktown. Letter from Noah Webster to George Washington, and from George Washington to Noah Webster* (Brooklyn: Privately printed, 1881).

56. Nickerson, "Yorktown, 1781," p. 85.

57. Matloff, *American Military History*, p. 96; Higginbotham, *War of American Independence*, p. 380. A good discussion of the alternative strategies presented to Washington and the Allies contingent on British maneuvers in 1781 appears in Theodore Thayer, *Yorktown: Campaign of Strategic Options* (Philadelphia: J. B. Lippincott Company, 1975), pp. 3-50.

58. Patton, "Campaign of the Allies," p. 256; Washington to Webster, July 31, 1788, in *1781 Yorktown*.

59. Matloff, *American Military History*, p. 96; Higginbotham, *War of American Independence*, p. 380.

60. Agniel, *Late Affair*, p. 124; Smelser, *Winning of Independence*, pp. 323-24; Nickerson, "Yorktown, 1781," p. 85; Patton, "Campaign of the Allies," p. 257.

61. See Robert A. Selig, "François Joseph Paul Comte de Grasse, the Battle off the Virginia Capes, and the American Victory at Yorktown," *Colonial Williamsburg. The Journal of the Colonial Williamsburg Foundation*, vol. 21, No. 5 (October/November 1999), pp. 26-32, for outstanding information on this officer and run-up to this decisive naval action. See note 51, above, for a discussion of the rank of admiral in the French navy at this time.

62. Nickerson, "Yorktown, 1781," pp. 85-86; Haynes, "Siege of Yorktown," p. 6; Mahan, *Influence of Sea Power*, p. 389.

63. Mahan, *Influence of Sea Power*, p. 389; Matloff, American *Military History*, pp. 96-97; Higginbotham, *War of American Independence*, pp. 381-82; Smelser, *Winning of Independence*, p. 326; Nickerson, "Yorktown, 1781," pp. 86–87. For a concise account of this most significant encounter, see Christopher Ward, *The War of the Revolution*, 2 vols. (New York, 1952), vol. 2, p. 884-885. For a more popular version, see in Burke Davis, *The Campaign that Won America: The Story of Yorktown* (New York: The Dial Press, 1970), pp. 147-66.

64. Higginbotham, *War of American Independence*, p. 380; Haynes, "Siege of Yorktown," p. 6; Agniel, *Late Affair*, p. 124; Patton, "Campaign of the Allies," pp. 258-59; Smelser, *Winning of Independence*, p. 324.

65. Smelser, *Winning of Independence*, p. 259.

66. Clinton's marginalia notes in Stedman, *History . . . of the American War*, 2, p. 407. Clinton himself became convinced of the destination of the Allied force only on September 2, 12 days after its departure from the Hudson. Mahan, *Influence of Sea Power*, p. 389. A concise treatment of the Southern campaign of 1781 is in Howard H. Peckham, *The War for Independence: A Military History* (Chicago: University of Chicago Press, 1958), pp. 164-82. An outstanding popular and well-researched account of the Southern campaign can be found in Buchanan, *The Road to Guilford Courthouse*.

67. Mackesy, *War for America*, p. 428. For the importance of army-navy coordination during the Yorktown Campaign, see John F. Shafroth, "The Strategy of the Yorktown Campaign, 1781," *United States Naval Institute Proceedings*, 57 (June, 1931), pp. 721-736.

Chapter 2: The Lion Comes to Yorktown

1. John Muller, *A Treatise Containing the Elementary Part of Fortification, Regular and Irregular* (London: J. Nourse, 1746; reprint ed., Ottawa: Museum Restoration Service, 1968), p. 230.

2. Eversley Belfield, *Defy and Endure: Great Sieges of Modern History* (New York: Crowell-Collier Press, 1967), pp. 4, 5, 6.

3. See Charles E. Hatch, Jr., *Historic Resource Study, Yorktown's Main Street (From Secretary Nelson's to the Windmill), and Military Entrenchments Close In and Around the Town of York, Colonial National Historical Park, Virginia* (Denver: National Park Service, 1974), pp. 160-167.

4. Wickwire and Wickwire, *Cornwallis*, pp. 358, 365-366.

5. Hoyt, *Practical Instructions*, pp. 72-73; Arthur, *End of a Revolution*, p. 108.

6. Background on Cornwallis is drawn from Dupuy, *Harper Encyclopedia of Military Biography*, pp. 191-192. Standard biographies are in Franklin B. and Mary B. Wickwire, *Cornwallis: The American Adventure* (Boston: Houghton Mifflin Company, 1970); and (post-Revolutionary War) Franklin B. and Mary B. Wickwire, *Cornwallis: The Imperial Years* (Chapel Hill, NC: University of North Carolina Press, 1980). A

treatment of Cornwallis's operations in Virginia in the spring and summer of 1781 can be found in Gregory J.W. Urwin, "Cornwallis and the Slaves of Virginia: A New Look at the Yorktown Campaign," *International Commission of Military History Proceedings, Norfolk, Virginia, 2002*, John A. Lynn, ed. (Wheaton, Ill.: The Cantigny First Division Foundation, 2003), pp. 172-192.

7. Hatch, *"York Under the Hill"*, pp. 23, 24.

8. Ibid., pp. 27, 28; Hatch, *Yorktown and the Siege of 1781*, p. 37.

9. Quoted in Hatch, *"York Under the Hill"*, p. 28.

10. Hatch, *Yorktown and the Siege of 1781*, p. 37.

11. Virginia Council of State, *Journals of the Council of the State of Virginia*, ed. H. R. McIlwaine, 4 vols. (Richmond: Virginia State Library, 1932), 2:138.

12. Willcox, *British Road to Yorktown*, pp. 5-6.

13. Hatch, *Yorktown and the Siege of 1781*, p. 37.

14. Ibid.

15. Mackesy, *War for America*, p. 412. An order on August 23, 1781, by Cornwallis's chief engineer, Lieutenant Alexander Sutherland, asking for spades, shovels, nails, saws, chisels, chalk, squares, and smoothing planes, among other things, is in Henry Clinton Papers, vol. Aug. 23-Aug. 30, 1781, William L. Clements Library. Clinton claimed a disparity existed between the number of entrenching tools actually available for use by Cornwallis's army and the number he reported he had on hand. Wrote Clinton: "There appears to have been a misapprehension . . . as [to] the number of entrenching tools; which, though computed by his Lordship to be only about 400 . . . I find by his engineer's reports . . . to have been 992 on the 23d of August." *Observations on Mr. Stedman's History*, pp. 20-21. See also Ewald, "Diary of the American War," p. 866.

16. Ewald, "Diary of the American War," pp. 864-66.

17. Mackesy, *War for America*, p. 412.

18. Ewald, "Diary of the American War," p. 866.

19. Arthur, *End of a Revolution*, pp. 113-14.

20. Ewald, "Diary of the American War," p. 871.

21. Ibid., p. 874.

22. Higginbotham, *War of American Independence*, p. 381; Whitridge, *Rochambeau*, p. 209; Boatner, *The Encyclopedia of the American Revolution*, pp. 1,087-1,088.

23. Nickerson, "Yorktown, 1781," p. 86; Agniel, *Late Affair*, pp.. 127-28; Wickwire and Wickwire, *Cornwallis*, p. 361; Arthur, *End of a Revolution*, p. 114.

24. Wickwire and Wickwire, *Cornwallis*, p. 361; Agniel, *Late Affair*, p. 128. Clinton did not yet know about the recent Battle of the Capes—but Cornwallis was in full knowledge of the French navy in the Chesapeake and the outcome of that sea battle.

25. Quoted in Arthur, *End of a Revolution*, p. 114. Cornwallis believed that if he was relieved early enough, the combined forces might strike a decisive blow against the Allies that would end the war. Wickwire and Wickwire, *Cornwallis*, p. 364.

26. Ewald, "Diary of the American War," p. 877.

27. Ibid., p. 880.

28. These figures are taken from Douglas Southall Freeman's careful evaluation presented in *George Washington: A Biography*, 6 vols. (New York: Charles Scribner's Sons, 1952), 5:513-14. The Frenchman Cromot Du Bourg assigned the naval personnel an approximate figure of 1,500, which, in place of the 840 figure usually given, would boost the British force to a total exceeding 10,000. The figure given for land forces in the monthly strength report dated September 15, 1781, represented an inexplicable decline of 548 men from the previous month. Ibid.

29. Earl Cornwallis, *An Answer to That Part of the Narrative of Lieutenant-General Sir Henry Clinton, K. B., which Relates to the Conduct of Lieutenant-General Earl Cornwallis, during the Campaign in North America, in the Year 1781* (London: John Debrett, 1783), Appendix XX, following p. 236. Wickwire and Wickwire gives 5,129 officers and men as "present and fit for duty" at the opening of the siege in late September. In addition, there were 632 others from various small units and reduced detachments, like the guides and pioneers and some North Carolina loyalist volunteers. *Cornwallis*, pp. 366-67. See also "State of the Army in Virginia under the Command of Lieut. General Earl Cornwallis, 1st October 1781," Henry Clinton Papers, William L. Clements Library. Figures presented in this document are considerably at variance with those cited above.

30. Organization based on that given in Arthur, *End of a Revolution*, pp. 173-74, and Johnston, *Yorktown Campaign*, pp. 118-19.

31. Johnston, *Yorktown Campaign*, p. 111.

Chapter 3: The British Positions

1. Thor Borresen, "Orientation Report," p. 5.

2. Arthur, *End of a Revolution*, p. 109; Nickerson, "Yorktown, 1781," p. 88; Wickwire and Wickwire, *Cornwallis*, p. 358.

3. Borresen, "Orientation Report," p. 6; Wickwire and Wickwire, *Cornwallis*, p. 372; Thompson, *Historic Resource Study, The British Defenses of Yorktown, 1781, Colonial National Historical Park, Virginia* (Denver: National Park Service, 1976), pp. 67-68.

4. Arthur, *End of a Revolution*, p. 109; Johnston, *Yorktown Campaign*, p. 108; Hatch, "Gloucester Point," pp. 269-70; Stephen Bonsal, *The Cause of Liberty* (London: Michael Joseph Limited, 1947), p. 146. Detailed coverage of the British main works on Gloucester and Yorktown is presented in Thompson, *The British Defenses of Yorktown, 1781*, pp. 67-68.

5. Ewald, "Diary of the American War," pp. 7, 8; Joseph P. Tustin to Historian James Haskett, 1970, in the files of CNHP, Yorktown, Virginia.

6. James McHenry, *A Sidelight on History, Being the Letters of James McHenry, Aide-de-Camp of the Marquis de Lafayette to Thomas Sim Lee, Governor of Maryland. Written during the Yorktown Campaign, 1781* (Privately printed, 1931), p. 67-68; Letters to Robert Morris, 1775-1782," in *Collections of New-York Historical Society, for the*

Year 1778 (New York, 1879), p. 469; Thompson, *The British Defenses of Yorktown, 1781*, p. 67.

7. Stedman, *History . . . of the American War*, 2, p. 408; Arthur, *End of a Revolution*, p. 13; Thompson, *The British Defenses of Yorktown, 1781*, p. 70; Borresen, "Orientation Report," p. 3.

8. Ibid., p. 7.

9. Nickerson, "Yorktown, 1781," p. 88; Bonsal, *Cause of Liberty*, p. 147.

10. Bonsal, *Cause of Liberty*, p. 147; Wickwire and Wickwire, *Cornwallis*, p. 366; U.S., Congress, Senate, *The Story of the Campaign and Siege of Yorktown*, 71st Cong., 3d sess., February 17, 1931, S. Doc. 318, pp. 41-42 (hereafter cited as S. Doc. 318).; Edward Hand to Jasper Yeates, September 17, 1781, in "Letters to Robert Morris, 1775-1782," *Collections of New-York Historical Society, for the Year 1778* (New York, 1879), p. 469.

11. Borresen, "Orientation Report," p. 7; *"Wertgetreue Abschrift eines Tagebuchs eines markgräflischen Soldaten [über] den Aufenthalt in Amerika"* ["The true copy of a diary of a soldier of the Margrave (on) his sojourn in America."], trans. John Luzader, Historical Society for Middle Frankonia, Ansbach State Library, Ansbach. Germany; Johann Conrad Döhla, "The Journal of Johann Conrad Döhla, 1775-1785," typescript, dated September 1941, trans. Robert J. Tilden, in the library of CNHP, Yorktown, Virginia, p. 139.

12. Baron Ludwig von Closen, *The Revolutionary Journal of Baron Ludwig Von Closen, 1780-1783*, ed. and trans. Evelyn M. Acomb (Chapel Hill: University of North Carolina Press, 1958), p. 139n.

13. Agniel, *Late Affair*, p. 129.

14. Burne, "Cornwallis at Yorktown," p. 72.

15. "Journal of the Chesapeake Campaign," trans. Thomas M. Pitkin, transcribed copy in the library of CNHP, Yorktown, Virginia, p. 16; See also Warrington Dawson, "The Chevalier D'Ancteville and His Journal of 'The Chesapeake Campaign,'" *Legion D'Honneur* 3 (October, 1931), p. 94.

16. Thompson, *The British Defenses of Yorktown, 1781*, pp. 79-81. (This source is invaluable, and is the best study on the British defenses to date. It was relied upon extensively for this discussion). Burne, "Cornwallis at Yorktown," p. 72; Arthur, *End of a Revolution*, pp. 109-12; Johnston, *Yorktown Campaign*, p. 106; Robert Arthur, *The Sieges of Yorktown, 1781 and 1862* (Fort Monroe, Virginia: The Coast Artillery School, 1927), pp. 12, 13; Hatch, *Yorktown's Main Street*, pp. 106-7.

The Erbprinz Regiment, from Hesse-Kassel region, was also known as the Prince Hereditaire Regiment. This regiment arrived August 1776 in the American colonies and saw action in the New York area. The Erbprinz Regiment came to Virginia in March 1781 with troops under the command of British. Major General William Phillips. When Phillips died in Virginia, the unit was temporarily under the command of Brigadier General Benedict Arnold, who was commanding troops in the British army. A week later the unit came under the command of Cornwallis during the Virginia and Yorktown campaigns. During the Siege of Yorktown, the unit consisted of 404 men commanded by Lieutenant Colonel Mathew Fuchs. It lost an estimated 23 killed, 57 wounded and 16 missing during the siege. Some 147 men from the 17th Regiment of Foot (also known as the Leicestershire Regiment) participated at Yorktown. Formed in 1688, it was designated the 17th in 1751. It was under the command of Colonel Henry Johnson. Service in Nova Scotia followed the close of the war in America. Today, this unit is known as the 4th Battalion, The Royal Anglian Regiment. Colonial National Historical Park, Yorktown.

17. Banastre Tarleton, *A History of the Campaigns of 1780 and 1781, in the Southern Provinces of North America* (Dublin: Colles, Exshaw, White, H. Whitestone, Burton, Byrne, Moore, Jones, and Dornin, 1787), pp. 384-85; Arthur, *End of a Revolution*, p. 112. Borresen, "Orientation Report," p. 26; Hoyt, *Practical Instructions*, p. 73. Querenet de La Combe stated in his journal that the ditches and fortifications on the right were only partially protected by abatis. "Journal of the Siege of York in Virginia in October 1781," transcribed and translated copy of original in the United States Army Engineers Museum, Fort Belvoir, Virginia. Ouerenet de La Combe commanded the French Royal Corps of Engineers at the siege; See also Hatch, *Yorktown's Main Street*, p. 117.

18. Thompson, *The British Defenses of Yorktown, 1781*, pp. 81-82.

19. Ibid., p. 83.

20. Ibid.

21. Ibid; Hatch, *"York Under the Hill"*, p. 59; Hatch, *Yorktown's Main Street*, p. 111. See Symonds to Graves, September 8, 1781, in Thomas Graves, *The Graves Papers and Other Documents Relating to the Naval Operations of the Yorktown Campaign: July to October, 1981*, ed. French Ensor Chadwick (New York: Publications of the Naval History Society, 1916; reprint ed., New York: Arno Press, 1968), p. 104.

22. Bonsal, *Cause of Liberty*, p. 147; Johnston, *Yorktown Campaign*, p. 106; S. Doc. 318, p. 41; Agniel, *Late Affair*, p. 128; Arthur, *Sieges of Yorktown*, p. 13. Most of the British ordnance consisted of nine- and 18-pounders, with a smattering of six- and 12-pounders and an extremely limited number of howitzers and mortars.

23. Hatch, *Yorktown's Main Street*, p. 117. See also Borresen, "Orientation Report," p. 8.

24. Borresen, "Orientation Report," p. 20. The foundations of the "Secretary" Nelson House can still be seen at Yorktown.

25. Thompson, *The British Defenses of Yorktown, 1781*, p. 76. According to Johann Gottlieb Tielke, "The flanks are the weakest parts of every position, therefore great attention must be paid to their security, that they may neither be turned or commanded." *Field Engineer*, 1, p. 124. In view of this statement, the purpose of the British star redoubt along the lower Williamsburg Road is readily apparent. The origins of the 23rd Regiment of Foot begin in 1688. It was designated the Royal Welch Fusiliers in 1727, and 1751 received the designation of 23d Foot. The regiment was 140 strong at Yorktown and was under the command of Captain Charles Anthorpe. Today, the regiment is known as the Royal Welsh Fusiliers.

26. Lochee, *Elements of Field Fortification*, pp. 55, 60-61.

27. Ibid. See especially p. 60 for refutation of the angular advantages of star forts over square ones. Tielke echoed Lochee's sentiments: "Their salient angles are generally too narrow within, and the defence of the lines must be imperfect; because the shot can

never fly parallel to them, unless the soldiers fire obliquely." *Field Engineer*, 1, p. 242. See also ibid., 2, pp. 19-20.

28. Lochee, *Elements of Field Fortification*, pp. 55-56.

29. Tielke, *Field Engineer*, 2, p. 54.

30. Here is how German engineer Tielke described it: "Let fall a perpendicular from the centre of each side of your figure: that is to say, if it is a square, the perpendicular must be equal to one-seventh or one-eighth of the length of the side; if a pentagon, to one-sixth; and if an hexagon, to one-fifth. Draw a line from the ends of each face to that of its perpendicular. . . ." Construction of the parapet, banquette, ditch, and glacis followed along the lines plotted above. Ibid., 1, p. 282.

31. Johnston, *Yorktown Campaign*, pp. 107-8; Rowland Broughton Mainwaring, comp., *Historical Record of the Royal Welch Fusiliers Late the 23rd Regiment, or, Royal Welsh Fusiliers (The Prince of Wales's Own Royal Regiment of Welsh Fuzeliers)* (London: Hatchards, Piccadily, 1889), p. 103.

32. Johnson was commander of the 17th Foot, suggesting that some men occupying the Fusiliers' Redoubt actually belonged to that unit. Reference to the armament is provided by Captain Ewald in Tustin to Haskett, 1970, CNHP, Yorktown, Virginia.

33. Thompson, *The British Defenses of Yorktown, 1781*, p. 76.

34. Map 17F, Map Division, Library of Congress. The "F" following the map number indicates this map is of French origin. An "A" indicates American origin (Map 52A, for example), and a "B" stands for British (Map 30B, for example). For all subsequent references to contemporary maps, please refer to the numeric listing of these documents in the bibliography to determine the institution in which the original resides. Copies of most or all of these maps may also be found at Colonial National Historical Park (CNHP) in Yorktown, Virginia.

35. Ibid., Map 16F.

36. Ibid., Maps 1F, 15F, 16F, 18F, 24F, 30B, 31F, 32F, 33F, 34F, 37F, 41F, 45F, 48F, 49F, 53F, 59B; See also La Combe, "Journal of the Siege of York," p. 2.

37. Map 53F.

38. See Maps 17F, 19F, 28A, 31F, 32F, 37F, 54F, 62F; French engineers, "Journal of the Siege of York in Virginia," *Magazine of American History*, 4 (June, 1880), p. 450 (hereafter cited as Engineers' Journal); Ewald's quote is in Tustin to Haskett, 1970, in the file of CNHP, Yorktown, Virginia.

39. Engineers' Journal, p. 450; La Combe, "Journal of the Siege of York," p. 2; Tarleton, *History of the Campaigns*, p. 382; Map 45F; Thompson, *The British Defenses of Yorktown, 1781*, p. 77.

40. Maps 2F, 15F, 34F, 62F.

41. Ibid., Map 29B.

42. Ibid., Map 1F.

43. A. E. Booth, "Fusiliers Redoubt," MS, November 4, 1936, in the library of CNHP, Yorktown, Virginia, pp. 1-2. Compounding the problem of erosion, wrote Booth, "the sea wall which was placed at the foot of these cliffs necessitated the construction of such steep slopes that maintenance [of the reconstructed work] will be exceedingly difficult." Ibid.

44. Ibid., pp. 3, 6.

45. Ibid., p. 7; Interior traverses appear on Map 16F.

46. Many of the maps consulted show this structure as being in the shape of a pentagon. See, for example, maps 24F, 25B, 35F, 48F, 49F, 62F. The majority, however, suggest it was round. See, for example, maps 1F, 2F, 11F, 15F, 16F, 17F, 50B, 51B, 57B, 59B. At least one map, 7A, indicates it was square, while two, 6F and 61F, give it no more shape than a redan.

47. Lochee, *Elements of Field Fortification*, pp. 39-40.

48. See, for example, Maps 15F, 16F, 17F, 25B, 41F, 48F, 50B, 57B, 59B.

49. Borresen, "Orientation Report," p. 20; C. L. Coston to Floyd Flickinger, May 22, 1934.

50. Borresen, "Orientation Report," p. 8; The Pigeon Hill Redoubts, when viewed in relation to the course of York Creek, fulfilled Tielke's theoretical maxim that "if one end of a ravine reaches our encampment . . . while the other forms a debouche near the enemy; the heights on each side and the debouche itself should be defended by enclosed works." *Field Engineer*, 2, pp. 93-94.

51. Charles E. Hatch, Jr., "The Siege of Yorktown Opens," draft MS, undated, CNHP, Yorktown, Virginia, p. 7; Borresen, "Orientation Report," p. 8; Thor Borresen, "Report on the Proposed Reconstruction of a Pigeon Hill Redoubt," MS, dated October 27, 1939, in the library of CNHP, Yorktown, Virginia, pp. 2, 3-4. The observer was Count William de Deux-Ponts. See *My Campaigns in America: A Journal Kept by Count William de Deux-Ponts, 1780-1781*, trans. and ann. Samuel Abbott Green (Boston: J. K. Wiggin and William Parsons Lunt, 1868), pp. 135-36. Mention of the Pigeon Hill works and their role in consolidating the British outer line is in Tarleton, *History of the Campaigns*, p. 382. Specific mention of fraising and abatis for the structures is contained in Engineers' Journal, p. 449; La Combe, "Journal of the Siege of York," p. 1 (nearly identical to ibid.); and Closen, *Revolutionary Journal*, p. 139.

52. Borresen, "Pigeon Hill Redoubt," pp. 1, 2.

53. Thor Borresen, "Memorandum for the Regional Supervisor of Historic Sites," dated April 5, 1940, in the library of CNHP, Yorktown, Virginia, p. 4.

54. See Maps 1F, 2F, 11F, 15F, 16F, 17F, 19F, 24F, 25B, 26F, 28A, 29B, 30B, 31F, 32F, 33F, 34F, 36F, 37F, 41F, 45F, 48F, 49F, 50B, 51B, 53F, 61F, 62F, and especially 57B, the official British engineers' map.

55. Borresen, "Pigeon Hill Redoubt," pp. 6-7.

56. Ibid., p. 31; Maps 7A, 11F, 15F, 16F, 17F, 19F, 24F, 26F, 28A, 29B, 31F, 32F, 33F, 34F, 35F, 36F, 37F, 41F, 45F, 49F, 53F, 57B, 61F, 62F.

57. 1F, 2F, 15F, 16F, 17F, 19F, 24F, 25B, 29B, 30B, 31F, 32F, 33F, 34F, 41F, 48F, 49F, 50B, 53F, 57B, 62F.

58. Borresen, "Pigeon Hill Redoubt," pp. 2-3, 20.

59. Ibid., pp. 5, 10, 11-12.

60. Ibid., pp. 8-9.

61. Ibid., p. 8.

62. See ibid., pp. 9-10. Borresen theorized that the guns would have been situated to fire barbette fashion. "Memorandum for the Regional Supervisor of Historic Sites," pp. 2, 3.

63. Mathew Gregory, "Diary of Mathew Gregory at Yorktown, 1781, typescript, in the library of CNHP, Yorktown, Virginia, p. 1.

64. See Borresen, "Pigeon Hill Redoubt," pp. 13-15.

65. Ibid., pp. 16, 18, 22, 23, 25-26, 27, 28, 29. Much of the early work on the Yorktown Battlefield was accomplished by individuals untrained in the principles of archeological excavation. That Borresen managed to amass a considerable amount of information derived in a wholly unscientific manner is to his lasting credit. In most instances he coupled the data with historical facts and with those gained from sources on the theory of 18th-century siege warfare. In many cases his conclusions are acceptable. In some, however, they are tenuous and resulted purely from unsupported speculation on Borresen's part.

66. Tarleton, *History of the Campaigns*, p. 382.

67. Maps showing the field battery before conversion to a redoubt are 15F, 16F, 51B, 58B. Map 48F calls the structure a "redan of the English." See Closen, *Revolutionary Journal*, p. 139.

68. Maps 51B and 25B, respectively.

69. Closen, *Revolutionary Journal*, p. 139. See maps 16F, 17F, 19F, 24F, 32F, 33F. See also Engineers' Journal, p. 450.

70. Maps 11F, 49F.

71. Map 33F.

72. Map 57B.

73. Closen, *Revolutionary Journal*, p. 141; Maps 1F, 2F, 6F, 7A, 11F, 15F, 16F, 17F, 18F, 19F, 24F, 25B, 26F, 28A, 30B, 31F, 33F, 34F, 35F, 37F, 41F, 45F, 46F, 48F, 49F, 50B, 53F, 57B, 59B, 62F, CNHP, Yorktown, Virginia; Ebenezer Denny, *Military Journal of Major Ebenezer Denny, An Officer in the Revolutionary and Indian Wars* (Philadelphia: J. B. Lippincott and Company, 1859), p. 42.

74. Agniel, *Late Affair*, pp. 128-29.

75. U.S., Congress, Senate, *The Virginia Campaign and the Blockade and Siege of Yorktown, 1781, Including a Brief Narrative of the French Participation in the Revolution Prior to the Southern Campaign*, by H. L. Landers, 71st Cong., 3d sess., February 7, 1931, S. Doc. 273, p. 187 (hereafter cited as S. Doc. 273); Thor Borresen, "Final Report on Redoubt No. 9, Second Parallel," MS, dated December 23, 1938, in the library of CNHP, Yorktown, Virginia, p. 57. An interesting sidelight regarding the landscape in the area of Redoubt 9 concerns the existence of a "Remarkable Tree" located to the right of what was afterwards the Allied communication trench following the capture of Redoubts 9 and 10. This tree is depicted on an unusual sketch map entitled "This Place is what the Enemy had possession of. Within these lines is the Compact part of Little York in Virginia. Griffin Spencer, Lover of Learning and Ingenious Arts." Yale University Library, New Haven, Connecticut. Map 27F substantiates the existence of this "great tree" and also "two notable connected trees" standing nearby.

76. Borresen, "Final Report on Redoubt No. 9," p. 69.

77. Whitridge, *Rochambeau*, p. 219; Borresen, "Final Report on Redoubt No. 9," Plate 7. One account places 200 British in Redoubt 9, a likely figure if the soldiers occupied the work in double file. The figure would also have included 12 men to handle the two howitzers present. Ibid., pp. 77-78; Claude Blanchard, *The Journal of Claude Blanchard, Commissary of the French Auxiliary Army Sent to the United States During the American Revolution, 1780-1783*, trans. William Duane, ed. William Balch (Albany, 1879), p. 150.

78. Blanchard, *Journal*, Plate 4; Maps 25B, 30B, 50B, 57B, (all British maps). The British entrance has been placed elsewhere in the reconstruction.

79. Denny, *Military Journal*, p. 42. See Thomas Balch, *The French in America during the War of Independence of the United States, 1777-1783*, 2 vols. (Philadelphia: Porter and Coates, 1891), 1, p. 197, for a contemporary reference to palisades in Redoubt 9B.

80. Borresen, "Final Report on Redoubt No. 9," p. 63.

81. Ibid., pp. 48-49, plate 6. For a list of items disclosed by the archeological investigation, see ibid., pp. 49-50.

82. See ibid., pp. 51ff.

83. Whitridge, *Rochambeau*, p. 219; James R. Sullivan, "A Documentary Study of British Redoubt No. 10 in the Yorktown Battlefield in Colonial National Historical Park," MS, dated November 1952, in the library of CNHP, Yorktown Virginia, pp. 14-15.

84. "Abstract of Operations of the Campaign of the combined French and American Army 1781," Berthier Papers, Princeton University, copy translated by Laura Feller in the library of CNHP, Yorktown, Virginia.

85. For maps showing the square shape, the abatis, or the fraising, or a combination of two or more of these features, see lF, 2F, 6F, 7A, 11F, 15F, 16F, 17F, 19F, 24F, 25B, 26F, 27F, 28A, 30B, 31F, 32F, 33F, 34F, 35F, 37F, 41F, 45F, 48F, 50B, 53F, 57B, 62F, CNHP, Yorktown Virginia.

86. Map 57B. See also maps 33F, 34F, and 53F. 89. Map 2F, CNHP, Yorktown Virginia.

87. Maps 24F, 29B, and 49F, CNHP, Yorktown Virginia.

88. Map 2F, CNHP, Yorktown Virginia.

89. Borresen, "Orientation Report," p. 57.

90. Maps lF, 2F, 11F, 15F, 16F, 17F, 19F, 29B, 32F, 34F, 48F, 59B, CNHP, Yorktown Virginia.

91. Map 51B, CNHP, Yorktown Virginia; Borresen, "Orientation Report," p. 19.

92. Borresen, "Orientation Report," p. 19; Maps 1F, 19F, 32F, 48F, 51B. Several maps show four redoubts in this vicinity (2F, 15F, 17F, 58B), while some others show but two earthworks (11F, 29B), CNHP, Yorktown Virginia.

93. Memorandum, Coston to Flickinger, May 22, 1934.

94. Ibid.

95. See maps 6F, 11F, 49F, and 61F,CNHP, Yorktown Virginia.

96. Map 59B, CNHP, Yorktown Virginia.

97. Maps 1F, 25B, and 51B,CNHP, Yorktown Virginia; Borresen, "Orientation Report," p. 19.

98. Maps IF, 17F, 25B, 46F, 48F, 49F, 53F, CNHP, Yorktown Virginia. Tarleton, *History of the Campaigns*, p. 382; Hoyt, *Practical instructions*, p. 73.

99. Maps 1F and 26F, CNHP, Yorktown Virginia.

100. Ewald, "Diary of the American War," p. 877.

101. Borresen, "Orientation Report," p. 21; Maps 24F, 26F, 31F, 37F, 41F, 49B, 53F, 59B; Hatch, "York Under the Hill," p. 60. In the river at the time of the siege, including sunken vessels, the British had at least five warships (*Charon, Guadaloupe, Fowey, Bonetta,* and *Vulcan*), 29 transports, four sloops and brigs, one privateer, several schooners, and from 12 to 15 galleys. In addition, there were two ships captured from the Dutch, at least four private vessels, and a number of other boats and cutters, some of which were sunk. An American schooner, captured by the British in the James River, was also present. For a detailed enumeration of these vessels, see Homer L. Ferguson, *Salvaging Revolutionary Relics from the York River*, reprinted from *William and Mary College Quarterly Historical Magazine*, 2d ser. 14 (July, 1939), pp. 13-14; Edward Hand to Jasper Yeates, September 17, 1781, in "Letters to Robert Morris, 1775-1782," p. 469.

102. Ferguson, *Salvaging Revolutionary Relics from the York River*, p. 13; Map 29B. Archeological salvage work in the York River in 1934 and 1935 disclosed that the general type armament of the British warships was light guns of four- to six-pounder caliber. One 12-pounder was found, along with several swivel guns. Ferguson, *Salvaging Revolutionary Relics from the York River*, pp. 10, 12, 13.

103. Maps 1F, 11F, 18F, 24F, 25B, 26F, 29B, 32F, 34F, 61F, 62F.

104. George Washington Papers, vol. 185, Library of Congress.

105. Quoted in Hatch, *"York Under the Hill,"* p. 60. In July 1972, the remains of two British soldiers were found in the easternmost cemetery "approximately 150-feet upstream from the Point of Rocks and approximately 20-feet downstream from the remains of an old pier." Memo, Robert Madden, July 17, 1972, CNHP, Yorktown.

106. The British troop positions among the outer works appear most explicitly on Maps 25B and 51B. A good, though somewhat confusing, description based on these sources is in Borresen, "Orientation Report," pp. 19-21. Only the 2nd Battalion (188 men) of the 71st Regiment was present at Yorktown. Also known as the Highland Light Infantry, the 71st was formed in 1775 in Glasgow, Scotland, as a result of the American Revolution. It was disbanded after the war in 1783. Musketeer Regiment von Bose was the Musketeer Regiment Von Turmbach until 1778, when Major General C. von Bose became its new commander. Only 285 men were present from the unit at Yorktown.

107. Jean Baptiste Donatien, Comte de Rochambeau, *Relation, on Journal des Operations* (Colophon: A Philadelphie De l'Imprimerie de Guillaume Hampton, 1781; Facsimile: Americana Series; Photostat Reproductions by the Massachusetts Historical Society, No. 225. Boston, 1929) p. 5. Grace Church was used as a powder magazine (and damage claims were filed for the church). Thompson, *The British Defenses of Yorktown, 1781*, p. 84, note 59.

108. Edward M. Riley, "Preliminary Report on the Physical History of Yorktown, 1691-1800," typescript, 1940, CNHP, Yorktown, Virginia; Johnston, *Yorktown Campaign*, p. 130; Arthur, *End of a Revolution*, p. 113; Arthur, *Sieges of Yorktown*, pp. 13-14.

Chapter 4: Washington Takes Command

1. Lafayette to General Wayne, August 6, 1781, Wayne Manuscripts, vol. 14 (August 1781-January 17, 1782), Historical Society of Pennsylvania, Philadelphia. See also Lafayette to Wayne, August 16, 1781, in ibid.

2. Arthur, *End of a Revolution*, p. 113.

3. Whitridge, *Rochambeau*, p. 209.

4. Bonsal, *Cause of Liberty*, p. 145.

5. Hatch, *Yorktown and the Siege of 1781*, p. 15.

6. Wayne to "Dear Polly," September 12, 1781, Wayne Manuscripts, vol. 14 (August 1781-January 17, 1782), Historical Society of Pennsylvania.

7. Ibid. That the Allies were planning to lay siege to Yorktown is evident from this letter dated September 12, 1781. Other intimations of such a design appear in the correspondence of Colonel Thomas Butler, who wrote from Williamsburg on September 14 that preparations for a siege were underway and that "all we can do is to circumscribe the British till the army arrives." Quoted in Wright, "Notes on the Siege of Yorktown," p. 235. On September 23, a soldier noted, "we are preparing for a siege," while on the same date an officer wrote, "Every vigilance in preparation for a siege." Ibid. In all likelihood, the siege mentality had been prevalent ever since the Allies learned of de Grasse's presence off the Virginia Capes. Washington learned of the event September 5, the very day de Grasse and Graves battled for control of the Chesapeake. Washington to Greene, September 28, 1781, in George Washington, *The Writings of George Washington, from the Original Manuscript Sources, 1745-1799*, ed. John C. Fitzpatrick, 39 vols. (Washington: United States Government Printing Office, 1937), 23, p. 149.

8. This general overview of Washington's life and career is gathered from many sources. See, for example, J. C. Fitzpatrick, "George Washington," in Dumas Malone (ed.), *Dictionary of American Biography* (New York: Charles Scribner's Sons, 1936; 1964-), 10, pp. 509-527; R. Don Higginbotham, "George Washington," in Roger J. Spiller (ed.), *Dictionary of American Military Biography* (Westport, Conn.: Greenwood Press, 1984), 3, pp. 1,159-611,163; *Webster's American Military Biographies* (Springfield, Mass.: G. & C. Merriam Company, Publishers, 1978), pp. 464-467. For full-length treatments, beyond those mentioned elsewhere in this study, see, Richard M. Ketchum, *The World of George Washington* (New York: American Heritage Press, 1974); John E. Ferling, *Setting the World Ablaze: Washington, Adams, Jefferson and the American Revolution* (New York: Oxford University Press, 2000); Richard Brookhiser, *Founding Father: Rediscovering George Washington* (New York: Simon and Schuster, Inc., 1996); and Henry Wiencek, *An Imperfect God: George Washington, His Slaves, and the Creation of America* (New York: Farar, Straus, and Giroux, 2003). Perhaps the most in-depth and finely written biography of Washington remains Freeman's 6-volume opus *George Washington.*

9. Background on Rochambeau is in Dupuy, Johnson, and Bongard, *Harper Encyclopedia of Military Biography*, pp. 635-636. See also, Arnold Whitridge, *Rochambeau* (New York: The Macmillan Company, 1965).

10. Hatch, *Yorktown and the Siege of 1781*, pp. 15-16; Nickerson, "Yorktown, 1781," p. 87. Map 8F shows the area of College Creek around Williamsburg where the Allied Army debarked.

11. Nickerson, "Yorktown, 1781," p. 87; Hatch, *Yorktown and the Siege of 1781*, p. 16. Washington later reported to General Greene the situation of de Grasse by late September: "The Count de Grasse has, most happily and critically, effected a Junction with the Count de Barras from Newport, the conjoined Fleet are now in a good Position within the Capes of Chesapeake Bay, makg in Number 36 Capital Ships of the Line, four large french Frigates, with some smaller Ships, captured from the English. . . . Two British Frigates . . . have also been captured. . . ." Washington to Greene, September 28, 1781, in Washington, *Writings*, 23, p. 150.

12. Lafayette to Wayne, August 16, 1781, Wayne Manuscripts, vol. 14 (August 1781-January 17, 1782), Historical Society of Pennsylvania.

13. Wayne to President of Congress (?), September 13, 1781, in ibid.

14. Robert A. Selig, "The Duc de Lauzun and his Legion: Rochambeau's Most Troublesome, Colorful Soldiers," *Colonial Williamsburg: The Journal of the Colonial Williamsburg Foundation*, Vol. 21, No. 6 (December/January 2000). Lauzun himself arrived by ship, reached Williamsburg, and was sent to take charge of his cavalry at Gloucester. Cromot Du Bourg, "Diary of a French Officer, 1781," *Magazine of American History*, 4 (June, 1880), p. 445; *Engineers' Journal*, p. 449; Bonsal, *Cause of Liberty*, pp. 144-45; Arthur, *End of a Revolution*, p. 119.

15. Servan Malo, *The Men of Yorktown. Uniforms and Flags Drawn After Official Documents* (Paris: George Bertrand, 1918), pp. 5, 8-9.

16. Kemp, *American Soldiers of the Revolution*, pp. 12-13, 16, 25-26, 27, 28, 39, 47.

17. Chevalier d'Ancteville, quoted in Bonsal, *Cause of Liberty*, p. 145.

18. Ibid., pp. 15, 67. For descriptions of Revolutionary War uniforms, see Rene North, *Military Uniforms, 1686-1918* (New York: Grosset and Dunlap, 1970), pp. 22-27, and John Mollo and Malcolm McGregor, *Uniforms of the American Revolution* (New York: Macmillan Publishing Company, Inc., 1975), passim. By 1781, the authorized "Life Guard" for Washington consisted of 1 captain, 3 lieutenants, 1 surgeon, 4 sergeants, 3 corporals, 2 drummers, 1 fifer, and 136 privates. Baron von Steuben frequently used the unit as a demonstration group in teaching drill, and it came to be recognized as extremely proficient in that discipline. Fred Anderson Berg, comp., *Encyclopedia of Continental Army Units. Battalions, Regiments and Independent Corps* (Harrisburg: Stackpole Books, 1972), p. 135.

19. Johnston, *Yorktown Campaign*, p. 110; Freeman, *George Washington*, 5, p. 514;. Arthur, *End of a Revolution*, p. 159.

20. "Washington's American forces were more numerous than has been supposed," wrote Douglas Southall Freeman. "He had 7,290 Continental Infantry and staff of all grades, 514 artillerymen and 176 cavalry, a total of 7,980, plus 3,153 militia, an aggregate of 11,133. About 100 of these were absent sick, and approximately 700 were sick but

present. Washington's effectives thus were, roughly, 9,500." *George Washington*, 5, p. 514. Higher figures are presented in Arthur, *End of a Revolution*, p. 159. See also Johnston, *Yorktown Campaign*, p. 109.

21. Hatch, "Siege of Yorktown Opens," p. 6a (note); Johnston, *Yorktown Campaign*, pp. 108-9.

22. Chevalier d'Ancteville, quoted in Bonsal, *Cause of Liberty*, pp. 145-46.

23. Adapted from Arthur, *End of a Revolution*, p. 159.

24. These figures are arrived at arbitrarily, but with knowledge gained from the previous enumeration and from Freeman's estimates in *George Washington*, 5, p. 514. Freeman's breakdown was thus: 7,890 Continentals, 3,153 militia, and 8,600 French. Ibid. See also Whitridge, *Rochambeau*, pp. 211-212; S. Doc. 318, p. 43; and Nickerson, "Yorktown, 1781," p. 87, for lower estimates of the Allied strength. According to one rationale, the numerical advantage of the Allies was offset among the British "by large experience, by the prestige of Southern victories, by a well supplied magazine, and by the cheering expectation of an early reenforcement from New York." Edwin Martin Stone, *Our French Allies* (Providence: Providence Press Company, 1884), p. 430. One is hard-pressed to agree with Stone's assessment.

25. Arthur, *End of a Revolution*, pp. 117-18; Johnston, *Yorktown Campaign*, p. 108; Whitridge, *Rochambeau*, p. 212.

26. Arthur, *End of a Revolution*, p. 118; Whitridge, *Rochambeau*, p. 212. Johnston states that the organization of the American Continentals into brigades occurred on September 27. *Yorktown Campaign*, p. 108. Wright maintains the assignments took place as early as the 24th. "Notes on the Siege of Yorktown," p. 236.

27. Adapted from Asa Bird Gardner, arr., "Disposition and Order of Battle of the Allied Armies on the March from Williamsburgh, to the Siege of York," *Magazine of American History*, 7 (October, 1881), pp. 267-269; Arthur, *End of a Revolution*, pp. 166-171; and Johnston, *Yorktown Campaign*, pp. 112-115.

28. For Wayne's role in the Revolutionary War in general, and in the Siege of Yorktown in particular, see Charles J. Stille, *Major-General Anthony Wayne and the Pennsylvania Line in the Continental Army* (Philadelphia: J. B. Lippincott Company, 1893). The disposition of the various Pennsylvania units throughout the war is contained in John Blair Linn and William H. Egle, eds., *Pennsylvania in the War of the Revolution, Battalions and Line, 1775-1783*, 2 vols. (Harrisburg: Lane S. Hart, 1880).

29. For biographical information on American officers, see Francis B. Heitman, comp., *Historical Register of Officers of the Continental Army during the War of the Revolution, April, 1775, to December, 1783*, rev. ed. (Washington: The Rare Book Shop Publishing Company, Inc., 1914), and Mark Mayo Boatner, III, comp. *The Encyclopedia of the American Revolution* (New York: David McKay, 1966, rev. 1994). Data on particular American Army units that served at Yorktown appears in ibid., and in Berg, *Encyclopedia of Continental Army Units*.

30. The French position in the order of battle had been determined over a year previously in Paris during the negotiations that culminated in the arrival of Rochambeau's auxiliary force. Rochambeau had been directed to yield the right to the Americans. When the French and American forces united for the first time in July 1780,

the Americans assumed the right of the line. Wright, "Notes on the Siege of Yorktown," p. 236.

31. Data on some of the French officers who served at Yorktown is found in Heitman, *Historical Register*, pp. 644-668.

32. Considerable disparity exists between the chief sources used for this "Order of Battle." What is presented here is a composite of data provided in Gardner, "Disposition and Order of Battle of the Allied Armies," and Arthur, *End of a Revolution*. For example, Gardner's Second Division is Arthur's Third, and Gardner's Third Division is Arthur's Second. Moreover, Gardner designates the brigades commanded by Gist and Wayne (units of the Second Division, according to Gardner) as the First and Second Brigades, respectively. Arthur reversed their numerical designations. In instances where Gardner indicates line position (i.e., right, left and center), his disposition has been accepted. Arthur does not mention the formation of either the intermediate line, the reserve line, or the rear guard. The annexation of the Delaware recruits to the Third Maryland Regiment is mentioned in Washington's General Orders of September 27, in Washington, *Writings*, 23, p. 147. Washington's stated order of battle follows: "Muhlenberghs and Hazens Brigades to form The Division on the right under the Command of the Marquis de la Fayette, Waynes and the Maryland Brigade [Gist's], the Division of the centre for the present to be commanded by Baron de Steuben, Daytons and Clintons Brigades, that on the Left. The senior Continental Officer [Lincoln] will Command the Right Wing and his Excellency Count Rochambeau the Left Wing of which he will be pleased to make his own disposition." Ibid., pp. 146-47.

33. Maps 9F and 14F show the camps of the Allied armies near Williamsburg on September 26, 1781.

34. Wright, "Notes on the Siege of Yorktown," p. 236; Washington, *Writings*, 23, p. 147.

35. Cornwallis to Nelson, September 26, 1781, manuscripts collected by J. Pierpont Morgan, vol. 1, The Siege of Yorktown and Surrender of Cornwallis, Pierpont Morgan Library, New York City.

Chapter 5: Investment

1. Closen, *Revolutionary Journal*, p. 138. One account states that the troops marched at 4:00 a.m. "Journal of Jean-Francois-Louis, Comte de Clermont-Crèvecoeur," in Howard C. Rice, Jr., and Anne S. K. Brown, eds., *The American Campaigns of Rochambeau's Army, 1780, 1781, 1782, 1783*, 2 vols. (Princeton and Providence: Princeton and Brown University Presses, 1972), 1, p. 57. Another source maintains the march to Yorktown began as late as 8:00 a.m. "Journal of Jean-BaptisteAntoine de Verger,"in ibid., p. 138.

2. Washington's General Orders of September 27, in Washington, *Writings*, 23, p. 148; Arthur, *End of a Revolution*, p. 118; George F. Scheer and Hugh F. Rankin, *Rebels and Redcoats* (New York: The New American Library, 1957), p. 551.

3. George Washington, *The Diaries of George Washington, 1748-1799*, ed. John C. Fitzpatrick, 4 vols. (Boston and New York: Houghton Mifflin Company, 1925), 2, pp 261-262; Arthur, *End of a Revolution*, p. 118; Wright, "Notes on the Siege of Yorktown," pp. 236-237; DeB. Randolph Keim, *Rochambeau: A Commemoration by the Congress of the United States of America of the Services of the French Auxiliary Forces in the War of Independence* (Washington: United States Government Printing Office, 1907), p. 438.

4. Clermont-Crèvecoeur Journal, in Rice and Brown, *American Campaigns*, 1, p. 57; "Siege of York and Gloucester, Virginia," *American Museum* (June, 1787), p. 475. The column halted at noon before reaching Halfway House and spent two or more hours cooking dinner. Davis, *Campaign that Won America*, pp. 190-191.

5. Clermont-Crèvecoeur Journal, in Rice and Brown, *American Campaigns*, 1, p. 57. Johnston, however, describes this "a leisurely march of 11 miles under a fair sky." *Yorktown Campaign*, p. 105; Closen, *Revolutionary Journal*, p. 138.

6. Washington, *Writings*, 23, p. 147.

7. This account of the routes of the Allied Army from Williamsburg to Yorktown is compiled from Washington, *Diaries*, 2, p. 262; Clermont-Crèvecoeur Journal, in Rice and Brown, *American Campaigns*, 1, pp. 56-57; De Verger Journal, in ibid., p. 138; Dawson, "Extract from the Journal of Chevalier Dupleix de Cadignan," p. 3; Maps 9F, 14F, 21B, 23A, 40F, 47F, 60B; Johnston, *Yorktown Campaign*, p. 105; Keim, *Rochambeau: A Commemoration*, p. 438; Arthur, *Sieges of Yorktown*, p. 12; Wright, "Notes on the Siege of Yorktown," pp. 236-237; Borresen, "Orientation Report," pp. 16-17; Hatch, "Siege of Yorktown Opens," pp. 6a-6b; and Scheer and Rankin, *Rebels and Redcoats*, p. 552.

8. Charles E. Hatch, Jr., and Jerome A. Greene, *Historic Structure Report, Combined Study: Developed Sites and Colonial Rural Fences, Yorktown Battlefield, Colonial National Historical Park, Virginia* (Denver: National Park Service, 1975), p. 23, Illustration No. 4 (Historic Base Map).

9. Accounts differ as to when the French arrived before Yorktown, and how the early action unfolded. Some accounts put the time at 11:00 a.m., which is much too early, and some 6:00 p.m., which is much too late. A general consensus of the French recollections puts the time at between 3:00 and 4:00 p.m. See Closen, *Revolutionary Journal*, p. 138; Clermont-Crèvecoeur Journal, in Rice and Brown, *American Campaigns*, 1, p. 57; and Brisout de Barneville, "War Diary, May, 1780-October, 1781," *French-American Review*, 3 (October-December, 1950), typescript copy of pp. 269-78, dated May 11, 1953, trans. Herbert Olsen, in library of CNHP, Yorktown, Virginia, p. 271. According to Thompson, *The British Defenses of Yorktown, 1781*, p. 91, the advance British Light Infantry held fast and only fell back when the French unlimbered a few light artillery pieces and shelled them.

10. Bartholomew James, *Journal of Rear-Admiral Bartholomew James, 1752-1828*, ed. John Knox Laughton (London: Publications of the Naval Records Society, 1896), p. 118.

11. This account of the French role in the investment of Yorktown is based essentially on data contained in Washington, *Writings*, 23, p. 158; Barneville, "War Diary," p. 271; Dawson, "Extract from the Journal of Chevalier Dupleix de Cadignan," p.

3; "Abstract of Operations"; *"Wertgetreue Abschrift eines Tagebuchs eines markgräflischen Soldaten"*; Closen, *Revolutionary Journal,* pp. 138-139; Mathieu Dumas, *Memoirs of His Own Time* (London: Richard Bentley, 1839), pp. 62-63n; James J. Graham, ed., *Memoir of General Graham with Notices of the Campaigns in which He was Engaged from 1779 to 7801* (Edinburgh: R. and R. Clark, 1862), p. 58; and Johnston, *Yorktown Campaign,* pp. 105-106. Du Bourg stated that two four-pounders were used against the British. "Diary of a French Officer, 1781," p. 445. De Verger mentions "several field pieces." De Verger Journal, in Rice and Brown, *American Campaigns,* 1, p. 138. Clermont-Crèvecoeur, who commanded two of the guns, said the total number was six. Clermont-Crèvecoeur Journal, ibid., p. 57.

12. Graham, *Memoir of General Graham,* p. 59.

13. Quoted in ibid.

14. Captain John Pryor placed the time of arrival of each column at about 3:30 p.m., which seems correct. Pryor to Colonel William Davies, September 29, 1781, in William P. Palmer, ed., *Calendar of Virginia State Papers and Other Manuscripts, from January 1, 1782, to December 31, 1784,* 11 vols. (Richmond: Virginia State Library, 1883), 2, p. 508. Washington indicated the time as "about noon," which was much too early. Washington, *Diaries,* 2, p 262.

15. Washington to General William Heath, October 1, 1781, in Washington, *Writings,* 23, p. 157; Washington, *Diaries,* 2, p. 262; Closen, *Revolutionary Journal,* p. 139; Keim, *Rochambeau: A Commemoration,* p. 439; Edward M. Riley, "The History of the Founding and Development of Yorktown, Virginia, 1691-1781," MS, dated March 20, 1942, in the library of CNHP, Yorktown, Virginia, p. 281; Johnston, *Yorktown Campaign,* p. 106; Arthur, *End of a Revolution,* p. 119; Tarleton, *History of the Campaigns,* p. 383; Tucker, "Journal kept by Col. St. George Tucker," p. 6. The brief contact with Tarleton's Legion on the afternoon of September 28 was not the first the Americans experienced with the illustrious cavalry leader. That morning, an American reconnaissance party belonging to Wayne's Brigade had a sharp engagement with Tarleton near Wormley Pond. Colonel Walter Stewart reported the occurrence: "This morning some of Tarletons Horse came within our Centrys in pursuit of Capt Herd with 20 Men[.] The Centrys fir'd, and the Guard having Let Capt. Herds party pass Wheel'd again to the right & left & threw in a Heavy fire[.] They on this retreated a small distance, but Our having accounts that they were 1500 strong prevented us Attempting to Cross the Mill dam." Stewart to Wayne, September 28, 1781, Wayne Manuscripts, vol. 14 (August 1781January 17, 1782), Historical Society of Pennsylvania.

16. Thor Borresen, Memorandum to the Acting Park Historian, March 27, 1939, on Bridges, CNHP, Yorktown, Virginia.

17. Captain John Pryor to Colonel William Davies, September 29, 1781, in Palmer, *Calendar of Virginia State Papers,* 2, p. 508; Wright, "Notes on the Siege of Yorktown," p. 237; "Siege of York and Gloucester, Virginia," p. 475.

18. Barnardus Swartwout, Jr., "The Journal of Barnardus Swartwout Junr. during the American Revolution from Nov. 1777 to June 1782—as Copied and corrected by himself in 1834," Swartwout Folder, New-York Historical Society, New York City; La Combe, "Journal of the Siege of York," p. 1; Axel de Fersen, "Journal of Operations," *Magazine*

of American History, 3 (July, 1879), p. 439; Freeman, *George Washington*, 5, p. 345; Davis, *Campaign that Won America*, pp. 193-194. For a description of the historical terrain in this locale, see Hatch and Greene, *Developed Sites and Colonial Rural Fences*, pp. 16, 19, 20.

19. Dupleix de Cadignan, "Journal of Chevalier Dupleix de Cadignan," Warrington Dawson Papers, in the library of CNHP, Yorktown, Virginia. All of these structures remained as late as 1853. The Gatenois redoubt was still in existence in 1934. Borresen, "Orientation Report," pp. 12-13. The redoubt built north of the Gatenois position was "a pentagonal redoubt about 75 feet across. It is very shallow, being not much more than 30 inches between the top of the parapet and the bottom of the interior." Memorandum, C. L. Coston to Mr. Flickinger, May 22, 1934, in files of CNHP, Yorktown, Virginia. Map 12F shows a redan before the Agenois. Map 2F also shows such a redan, but places two small redoubts before the Gatenois.

20. Maps IF, 46F.

21. De Cadignan, "Journal of Chevalier Dupleix de Cadignan"; Dawson, "Extract from the Journal of Chevalier Dupleix de Cadignan," pp. 3-4; Borresen, "Orientation Report," p. 13.

22. Arthur, *End of a Revolution*, p. 119.

23. Rochambeau's account in Dumas, *Memoirs of His Own Time*, p. 62; Keim, *Rochambeau: A Commemoration*, p. 439.

24. Dawson, "Extract from the Journal of Chevalier Dupleix de Cadignan," p. 3. The cannon shots may well have come from British ships anchored in the York River, because Brisout de Barneville maintained he heard reports from the vessels at five o'clock. "War Diary," p. 271.

25. Arthur, *Sieges of Yorktown*, p. 12.

26. Washington, *Writings*, 23, p. 149; Freeman, *George Washington*, 5, p. 345; Davis, *Campaign that Won America*, p. 193. Some of the officers sent to sound-test the waters of the James recommended that the artillery be debarked at the marshy peninsula called Mulberry Island. Trebell's Landing, a short distance upstream, was chosen probably because of its proximity to Yorktown and because the water there was also deep enough to accommodate the French transport vessels. See letter written from the James River, near Mulberry Island, September 28, 1781, in "Extracts from the [John] Lamb Papers Relating to the Yorktown Campaign," transcribed copy (from the Lamb Papers in the New-York Historical Society) in the library of CNHP, Yorktown, Virginia, p. 13; See Map 4B for historical orientation to the Chesapeake Bay-James River-York River complex.

27. Washington, *Writings*, 23, p. 150.

28. Tarleton, *History of the Campaigns*, pp. 383-84; Washington to President of Congress, October 1, 1781, in Washington, *Writings*, 23, p. 158; Viscount de Rochambeau, "The War in America: An Unpublished Journal (17801783)," in Jean-Edmond Weelen, *Rochambeau, Father and Son: A Life of the Marechal de Rochambeau*, trans. Lawrence Lee (New York: Henry Holt and Company, 1936), p. 230; Roger Lamb, *An Original and Authentic Journal of Occurrences During the Late American War, from its Commencement to the Year 1783* (Dublin: Wilkinson and

Courtney, 1809), p. 376; Reuben Sanderson, "Diary of the March from the Hudson to Yorktown, and Return, by Lieutenant Reuben Sanderson, Fifth Connecticut Continental Line, on Duty with Scammell's Light Infantry Corps," in Johnston, *Yorktown Campaign*, p. 171; Jonathan Trumbull, "Yorktown, Virginia, Aug. 12-Nov. 5, 1781," *Proceedings of the Massachusetts Historical Society*, 1st ser. 14 (18751876), p. 335; Ebenezer Wild, "Journal of Ebenezer Wild," *Proceedings of the Massachusetts Historical Society*, 2d ser. 6 (1890-1891), pp. 151-152; Octavius Pickering and C. W. Upham, *The Life of Timothy Pickering*, 4 vols. (Boston: Little, Brown and Company, 1867-1873), 1, p. 302; William Heath, *Heath's Memoirs of the American War* (1798; reprint ed., New York: A. Wessels Company, 1904) p. 329; "Journal of the Siege of York in Virginia by a Chaplain of the American Army," *Collections of the Massachusetts Historical Society*, 9 (1804), p. 104; *Pennsylvania Packet*, October 16, 1781, quoted in *Magazine of American History*, 6 (January, 1881), p. 40; Stedman, *History . . . of the American War*, 2, pp. 408-409; Arthur, *End of a Revolution*, p. 119; Freeman, *George Washington*, 5, p. 347. Captain John Pryor to Colonel William Davies, September 29, 1781, in Palmer, *Calendar of Virginia State Papers*, 2, p. 508; William Feltman, "The Journal of Lieut. William Feltman, of the First Pennsylvania Regiment, from May 26, 1781 to April 25, 1782, embracing the Siege of Yorktown and the Southern Campaign," *Pennsylvania Historical Society Collections*, 1 (May, 1853), p. 315; Deux-Ponts, *My Campaigns in America*, p. 134; "Journal of Lieut. William Feltman," p. 316. The calibers indicated are precisely those of the British guns mounted in the barbette unit at Hampton Road and in the Wormley Creek redans.

29. Wild, "Journal of Ebenezer Wild," p. 151; "Siege of York and Gloucester, Virginia," p. 475; Swartwout, "Journal of Barnardus Swartwout," p. 34; Johnston, *Yorktown Campaign*, p. 120; S. Doe. 318, p. 44; Davis, *Campaign that Won America*, p. 195.

30. James Duncan, "Diary of Captain James Duncan, of Colonel Moses Hazen's Regiment, in the Yorktown Campaign, 1781," *Pennsylvania Archives*, 2d ser. 15 (1890), p. 747; Pennsylvania Packet, October 16, 1781, quoted in *Magazine of American History*, 6 (January, 1881), 41; Catherine R. Williams, *Biography of Revolutionary Heroes: Containing the Life of Brigadier Gen. William Barton, and Also, of Captain Stephen Olney* (Providence: Published by the Author, 1839), p. 274; S. Doc. 318, p. 46; Borresen, "Orientation Report," p. 14; Stone, *Our French Allies*, p. 423; Arthur, *Sieges of Yorktown*, p. 14; Arthur, *End of a Revolution*, p. 121; Keim, *Rochambeau: A Commemoration*, p. 444; Johnston, *Yorktown Campaign*, pp. 130-131. For biographical treatments of Lincoln and von Steuben, see Boatner, *The Encyclopedia of the American Revolution*, pp. 635-636, 1,055-1,057. Von Steuben's grandfather inserted the "von" in the family name.

31. Wright, "Notes on the Siege of Yorktown," p. 230; Washington, *Writings*, 23, p. 152; William S. Stryker, *New Jersey Continental Line in the Virginia Campaign of 1781* (Trenton: John L. Murphy, 1882), p. 16; "Orderly Book kept during the Siege of Yorktown, Va. Sep. 26-Nov. 2, 1781," photostatic copy of the original (Henry E. Huntington Library, San Marino, California) in the library of CNHP, Yorktown, Virginia, p. 11. Muller defined the line of countervallation as "the work made by an army

which besieges a place between their camp and the town, to cover it against any enterprise of the garrison." *Treatise Containing the Elementary Part of Fortification*, p. 224.

32. "Diary of Captain James Duncan," p. 746.

33. Wright, "Notes on the Siege of Yorktown," pp. 237-238.

34. Captain John Pryor to Colonel William Davies, September 29, 1781, in Palmer, *Calendar of Virginia State Papers*, 2, p. 508.

35. Ibid.

36. Du Bourg, "Diary of a French Officer, 1781," p. 445.

37. "Journal of the Chesapeake Campaign," pp. 14-15. A highly questionable "du Chesony Diary," also in the CNHP library, appears to be an almost complete word-for-word copy of the d'Ancteville journal.

38. Freeman, *George Washington*, 5, pp. 347-349. Regarding the terrain before Yorktown, one observer noted that "the country about York is exceedingly level, a rise of five yards is called a hill. Our lines are about the same height of the enemy's [British]." Connecticut Gazette, October 19, 1781, quoted in *Magazine of American History*, 6 (January, 1881), p. 42.

39. Washington, *Diaries*, 2, p. 262.

40. See Wright, "Notes on the Siege of Yorktown," p. 237.

41. Dawson, "Extract from the Journal of Chevalier Dupleix de Cadignan," p. 5; Barneville, "War Diary," p. 272; see Maps 1F, 2F, 6F, 59B, 61F.

42. James, *Journal*, p. 119; Davis, *Campaign that Won America*, p. 196; "Diary of French naval operations in America, January 5, 1779–September 2, 1782," MS Division, Library of Congress, translated typescript copy in the library of CNHP, Yorktown, Virginia, pp. 190-191.

43. Engineers' Journal, p. 449.

44. The disposition of the French line as of September 29 appears in Stone, *Our French Allies*, pp. 422-23; Keim, *Rochambeau: A Commemoration*, pp. 444-445; Arthur, *Sieges of Yorktown*, pp. 14-15; and Arthur, *End of a Revolution*, p. 121.

45. Adapted from d'Ancteville, "Journal of the Chesapeake Campaign," p. 14; Balch, *French in America*, 2, pp. 12, 13, 14; Heitman, *Historical Register*, pp. 644-668.

46. Weigley, *History of the United States Army*, p. 69.

47. Biographical treatments of Knox are in North Callahan, "Henry Knox, General Washington's General," *New-York Historical Society Quarterly* 44, (April, 1960), pp. 151-166; Noah Brooks, *Henry Knox, A Soldier of the Revolution* (New York: G. P. Putman's Sons, 1900), and Dupuy, *Harper Encyclopedia of Military Biography*, p. 410.

48. Higginbotham, *War of American Independence*, p. 382.

49. Ibid.

50. Harold L. Peterson, *Round Shot and Rammers* (Harrisburg: Stackpole Books, 1969), p. 57; Albert Manucy, *Artillery Through the Ages: A Short Illustrated History of Cannon, Emphasizing Types Used in America* (Washington: Government Printing Office, 1949), p. 10.

51. Peterson, *Round Shot and Rammers*, p. 57. In 1764, the Board of Ordnance in England acknowledged 11 calibers for cannon: ½-, 1-1/2-, 3-, 4-, 6-, 9-, 12-, 18-, 24-, 32-, and 42-pounders. Ibid., p. 41.

52. Alan Kemp, *American Soldiers of the Revolution* (London: Almark Publishing Company, Ltd., 1972), p. 45.

53. Peterson, *Round Shot and Rammers*, p. 57.

54. Kemp, *American Soldiers of the Revolution*, p. 45.

55. Ibid. American cannon were generally of simple design and sometimes even crude. Some, especially the bronze pieces, were more elaborate and exhibited ornamentation similar to the European manufactures. Certain guns were stamped "US" and "UC" (United Colonies) and some displayed the date and place of manufacture and the maker's name. Peterson, *Round Shot and Rammers*, p. 60.

56. Manucy, *Artillery Through the Ages*, p. 10.

57. Wright, "Notes on the Siege of Yorktown," p. 230. The encampment site before Yorktown approximated the ideal prescribed by Hoyt: "In the choice of a post the general rules to be attended are, that it be convenient for sending out parties, to reconnoitre, surprise, or intercept the enemy; that if possible it have some natural defence, as a wood, river, or morass, in front or flank." *Practical Instructions*, p. 33. See also Tielke, *Field Engineer*, 1, p. 123.

58. The full citation reads: *Baron Friedrich Wilhelm Ludolf Gerhard Augustin Von Steuben, Regulations for the Order and Discipline of the Troops of the United States* (Philadelphia: Styner and Cist, 1779).

59. David Riggs, Colonial National Historical Park; Raymond, Richard D. and Loreen Finkelstein, "George Washington's Field Tents: The Challenge of Preserving and Interpreting a National Treasure in the 21st Century," in *Cultural Resource Management*, Vol. 23 (No. 3, 2000), pp. 3-5.

60. Dawson, "Extract from the Journal of Chevalier Dupleix de Cadignan," p. 5; Charles F. Antoine Lallemand, *Treatise on Artillery*, 2, p. 329. The tent for eight soldiers measured 12 feet long by eight feet wide, with tent poles six-and one-half feet long. Those for more soldiers ran 20 feet long by 13 feet wide, with but six-and one-half foot poles. Ibid.

61. Steuben, *Regulations*, pp. 76-77; Lallemand, *Treatise on Artillery*, 2, p. 328.

62. For details of this troop placement, see Steuben, *Regulations*, pp. 78-79.

63. Ibid., pp. 79-80.

64. Ibid., pp. 90-91.

65. Ibid., pp. 91-92.

66. Ibid., pp. 85, 87, 88-89.

67. Ibid., pp. 83, 85, 86; *Mercure de France*, December 1781, quoted in Bonsal, *Cause of Liberty*, p. 144.

68. "Orderly Book kept during the Siege of Yorktown," p. 10. By 1781, many Continental soldiers had been immunized to smallpox by vaccination, a process that had become routine as early as 1777. C. Keith Wilbur, *Picture Book of the Continental Soldier* (Harrisburg: Stackpole Books, 1969), p. 77.

69. The Williamsburg hospital (the Old Palace) was of stone, measured 40 by 130 feet, and had two wings each 30 feet wide and 50 feet long. Louis C. Duncan, *Medical Men in the American Revolution, 1775-1783* (Carlisle Barracks, Pennsylvania: Medical

Field Service School, 1931; reprint ed., New York: Augustus-M. Kelley, Publishers, 1970), p. 351.

70. Stone, *Our French Allies*, p. 431; Arthur, *Sieges of Yorktown*, p. 15; Arthur, *End of a Revolution*, pp. 121-122. Dr. Craik was ordered to specifically watch Lafayette and stay near at hand in case the marquis was wounded. Duncan, *Medical Men*, p. 351.

71. Rock L. Comstock, Jr., "The French Artillery Park at Yorktown: A Report and Exhibit Plan," MS, dated January 13, 1957, in the library of CNHP, Yorktown, Virginia, pp. 1, 4, 5, 13; Borresen, "Orientation Report," p. 13; Johnston, *Yorktown Campaign*, p. 116. The French Artillery Park was laid out on September 30. Closen, *Revolutionary Journal*, p. 140; See also Hatch, "Siege of Yorktown Opens," p. 10.

72. Wright, "Notes on the Siege of Yorktown," p. 230. Maps showing the location of the artillery parks and the placement of troops around them are 1F, 2F, 6F, 7A, 11F, 15F, 17F, 18F, 19F, 24F, 26F, 29B, 32F, 33F, 41F, 46F, 49F, 52A, 59B, 61F.

73. *Field Engineer*, 1, pp. 39-40, 41, 45-46.

74. Letter from unidentified correspondent, dated September 28, 1781, James River, in "Extracts from the Lamb Papers," in the library of CNHP, Yorktown, Virginia, p. 13.

75. Orderly Book, Second Artillery (August 4-October 13, 1781), Lamb Papers, New-York Historical Society, copy in the library of CNHP, Yorktown, Virginia.

76. "An account of Ordnance & Ordnance stores ship'd on board of several Vessels at the head of Elk, bound to James River," dated 1781, Henry Knox Papers, Massachusetts Historical Society, Boston, photostatic copy in the library of CNHP, Yorktown, Virginia (hereafter cited as Henry Knox Papers [CNHP]).

77. Ibid.

78. Arthur, *Sieges of Yorktown*, p. 15. The French mustered only 30 wagons and 180 artillery horses while waiting for their equipment to arrive from the north. It came October 5. By September 30, almost all of Rochambeau's artillery had reached Trebell's Landing. Rochambeau, *Relation, or Journal des Operations*, p. 4; Freeman, *George Washington*, 5, p. 353; De Verger Journal, in Rice and Brown, *American Campaigns*, 1, pp. 138-139.

79. Washington, *Writings*, 23, p. 152.

80. James Thacher, *A Military Journal during the American Revolutionary War, from 1775 to 1783*, 2d ed. (Boston: Cottons and Barnard, 1827), p. 270.

81. Döhla, "The Journal of Johann Conrad Döhla," p. 139.

82. Quoted in Wickwire and Wickwire, *Cornwallis*, p. 369. Much controversy later centered on the words "to hope" in this letter. Cornwallis accepted the total message as final, believing that help would embark October 5. Clinton, however, always maintained that the indefiniteness was purposely intended. As he later put it, "My words were [that] there is every reason to hope the Fleet would sail the 5th Octr as the tides were then high. These are the words of the letter." Clinton's marginalia notes in Stedman, *History . . . of the American War*, 2, p. 409. See also Johnston's evaluation in *Yorktown Campaign*, p. 332.

83. Wickwire and Wickwire, *Cornwallis*, p. 370; Arthur, *End of a Revolution*, p. 120; Nickerson, "Yorktown, 1781," p. 88; Agniel, *Late Affair*, p. 129; Bonsal, *Cause of*

Liberty, p. 148. For a slightly different view of Cornwallis's reasoning, see Burne, "Cornwallis at Yorktown," pp. 73, 74.

84. Cornwallis to Clinton, October 20, 1781, Clinton Papers, William L. Clements Library.

85. Quoted in Burne, "Cornwallis at Yorktown," pp. 73, 74.

Chapter 6: The Noose Tightens

1. Denny, *Military Journal*, pp. 40-41; Gregory, "Diary of Mathew Gregory at Yorktown, 1781," p. 1.

2. Henry Dearborn, *Revolutionary War Journals of Henry Dearborn, 1775-1783*, ed. Lloyd A. Brown and Howard H. Peckham (Chicago: The Coxton Club, 1939), p. 219. Lieutenant Colonel Dearborn was an Assistant Quartermaster General and a medical doctor. Frederic Kidder, *History of the First New Hampshire Regiment in the War of the Revolution* (Albany: Joel Munsell, 1868), p. 100; Tarleton, *History of the Campaigns*, p. 386.

3. Colonel William S. Smith to Colonel Samuel B. Webb, October 10, 1781, in John Austin Stevens, "The Allies at Yorktown, 1781," *Magazine of American History*, 6 (January, 1881), p. 21.

4. Dearborn to Meshech Weare, October 11, 1781, in Johnston, *Yorktown Campaign*, p. 175. Other than those sources already mentioned, this account of the Scammell affair is essentially drawn from data presented in Philip Van Cortlandt, "Autobiography of Philip Van Cortlandt, Brigadier General in the Continental Army," *Magazine of American History*, 2 (May, 1878), pp. 293-294; Sanderson, "Diary of the March from the Hudson to Yorktown," in Johnston, *Yorktown Campaign*, p. 171; Benson J. Lossing, *Pictorial Field Book of the Revolution*, 2 vols. (New York: Harper and Brothers, Publishers, 1855), 2, p. 309; Johnston, *Yorktown Campaign*, p. 123; S. Doc. 318, p. 45; Arthur, *End of a Revolution*, p. 120; and Davis, *Campaign that Won America*, pp. 198-200. Scammell had served as Adjutant General of the Continental Army in 1780. Early in 1781 he took charge of the 1st New Hampshire Regiment. For a biographical sketch of Scammell, see Kidder, *History of the First New Hampshire Regiment*, pp. 102-104; *Memoirs of the War in the Southern Department of the United States*, rev. ed. (New York: University Publishing Company, 1870), p. 496; "Narrative of Asa Redington," typescript copy from an unidentified source, in the library of CNHP, Yorktown, Virginia, p. 12. Redington was from Wilton, New Hampshire. He enlisted February 27, 1781, and was discharged in December of that year. Kidder, *History of the First New Hampshire Regiment*, p. 154.

5. Barneville, "War Diary," p. 272. The commander of the French bivouac, M. le Baron d'Esebeck, noted the British evacuation and reported it to Rochambeau in the morning. Closen, *Revolutionary Journal*, p. 139. Evidently the withdrawal occurred just before dawn. The troops that took Scammell constituted the rear guard for the evacuation. "Siege of York and Gloucester, Virginia," p. 475.

6. De Fersen, "Journal of Operations," p. 439; General Nelson to David Jameson, October 1, 1781, in Thomas Nelson, Jr., *Letters of Thomas Nelson, Jr., Governor of Virginia* (Richmond: Virginia Historical Society, 1874), p. 47; Palmer, *Calendar of Virginia State Papers*, 2, p. 513; Deux-Ponts, *My Campaigns in America*, pp. 134-35; Balch, *French in America*, 1, p. 188. Captain Ewald, who was stationed with the British at Gloucester, mistakenly believed that Cornwallis burned his outer works before abandoning them. "Diary of the American War," p. 881. The Long Neck Redoubt (No. 2) was also abandoned at this time, although there seems to be no mention of the structure in the various diaries and journals consulted. Perhaps its close proximity to the British main works discouraged its reconnaissance by the Allies. Borresen states that the Long Neck Redoubt later served the Allies as a picket guard. "Orientation Report," p. 22.

7. D'Ancteville, "Journal of the Chesapeake Campaign," p. 2; Balch, *French in America*, 1, pp. 188, 189; Du Bourg, "Diary of a French Officer, 1781," p. 445; General John Mitchell to Major H. H. Chapman, December 13, 1805, Manuscripts Collection, box 92, item 3190, Morristown National Historical Park, Morristown, New Jersey. None of the journals or diaries adequately distinguishes which redoubt was occupied by which body of troops. D'Ancteville simply says "100 men occupying Pigeon Quarter, 50 men Penny Hill." Because the terms were interchangeable and often applied to both tracts as well as to either, the final troop disposition will probably remain unknown. A reasonable argument can be made that the larger number of soldiers went to the larger redoubt, which according to most maps, was the pentagonal structure north of Goosley Road.

8. Balch, *French in America*, 1, p. 188.

9. Deux-Ponts, *My Campaigns in America*, p. 136; *Pennsylvania Packet*, October 16, 1781, quoted in *Magazine of American History*, 6 (January, 1881): 40; Colonel St. George Tucker to Frances Tucker, October 5, 1781, in "Letters to and from St. George Tucker, October 1 through October 15,1781," ed. S. Michael Hubbell, typescript copy in the library of CNHP, Yorktown, Virginia, p. 8. Tucker left one of the best contemporary accounts by a Yorktown participant. For other accounts of the French occupation of Pigeon Hill, see St. George Tucker, "Journal kept by Col. St. George Tucker during the siege of Yorktown and Surrender of Cornwallis, Oct. 1781," photostat copy of original (in Department of Research and Record, Colonial Williamsburg Foundation, Williamsburg, Virginia) in the library of CNHP, Yorktown, Virginia, p. 7; Washington, *Diaries*, 2, pp. 262-263. The advantage to the Allies of gaining ready access to the water in York Creek has largely been overlooked by many historians.

10. Johnston, *Yorktown Campaign*, pp. 121-22; Wright, "Notes on the Siege of Yorktown," p. 238; Arthur, *End of a Revolution*, p. 120.

11. *History of the Campaigns*, p. 386.

12. Deux-Ponts, *My Campaigns in America*, p. 135; H. L. Landers, *Yorktown. The Investment of Yorktown, October, 1781* (Washington: Army War College, 1931), p. 189; Joachim Merlant, *Soldiers and Sailors of France in the American War for Independence (1776-1783)*, trans. Mary Bushnell Coleman (New York: Charles Scribner's Sons, 1920), p. 173; Davis, *Campaign that Won America*, p. 199.

13. Washington quote in Freeman, *George Washington*, 5, p. 351; Closen, *Revolutionary Journal*, p. 139.

14. Journal of Anthony Wayne, Wayne Manuscripts, Historical Society of Pennsylvania, p. 81 (hereafter cited as Wayne Journal); See also H. M. Moore, *Life and Services of Gen. Anthony Wayne* (Philadelphia: Leary, Getz and Company, 1859), p. 148; Chevalier d'Ancteville, quoted in Bonsal, *Cause of Liberty*.

15. Deux-Ponts, *My Campaigns in America*, p. 135; Hand to Jasper Yeates, October 1, 1781, Edward Hand Papers, vol. 2, item 135, New York Public Library, New York City; Pickering and Upham, *Life of Timothy Dickering*, 1, p. 302; de Fersen, "Journal of Operations, p. 439.

16. John Andreus, *History of the War with America, France, Spain, and Holland; Commencing in 1775 and Ending in 1783*, 4 vols. (London: John Fielding, 1786), 4, p. 205.

17. Ibid., p. 204.

18. "Siege of York and Gloucester, Virginia," p. 475.

19. Freeman, *George Washington*, 5, p. 351. Evidence of Allied apprehensions over the possibility of Cornwallis's trying to escape the closing jaws of the French and American armies is apparent in St. George Tucker, "Journal kept by Col. St. George Tucker," p. 7; Washington, *Writings*, 23, pp. 155-156; Washington to Weedon, September 30, 1781, Simon Gratz Autograph Collection, Historical Society of Pennsylvania; De Barneville, "War Diary," p. 272.

20. Letter dated September 30, 1781, in "Letters from the Field," *Magazine of American History*, 6 (January, 1881), p. 44. Also reproduced in Lafayette, *Memoirs, Correspondence and Manuscripts of General Lafayette*, 2 vols. (New York: Saunders and Otley, 1837), 1, p. 531; Washington to Weedon, September 30, 1781, Simon Gratz Autograph Collection, Historical Society of Pennsylvania.

21. Borresen, "Orientation Report," pp. 21-22; Whitridge, *Rochambeau*, pp. 213-14.

22. Cornwallis to Clinton, October 20, 1781, Gold Star Box, Henry Clinton Papers, William L. Clements Library.

23. The opinion is Tarleton's, cited in Hoyt, *Practical Instructions*, p. 74.

24. "Journal kept by Col. St. George Tucker," p. 7. General Weedon at Gloucester witnessed the French assault and described it in similar terms. Enclosure in Weedon to Washington, October 2, 1781, Washington Papers, vol. 185, Library of Congress.

25. Enclosure in Weedon to Washington, October 2, 1781, Washington Papers, vol. 185, Library of Congress.

26. Stephen Popp, *Popp's Journal, 1777-1783*, ed. Joseph G. Rosengarten, (from *Pennsylvania Magazine of History and Biography*; reprint ed., Philadelphia, 1902), p. 18.

27. This account of the French attack is based on data appearing in Du Bourg, "Diary of a French Officer, 1781," p. 445; La Combe, "Journal of the Siege of York," p. 2; Engineers' Journal, p. 450; Ewald, "Diary of the American War," pp. 181-83; Döhla, "Journal of Johann Conrad Döhla," p. 140; Closen, *Revolutionary Journal*, p. 140; Rochambeau, *Relation*, p. 5; Deux-Ponts, *My Campaigns in America*, p. 136; Jacob Smith, "Diary of Jacob Smith, American Born," ed. Charles W. Heathcote, in *Pennsylvania Magazine of History and Biography*, 56 (1932), p. 263; *Pennsylvania Packet*, October 9, 1781, in Frank Moore, comp., *Diary of the American Revolution, from Newspapers and Original Documents*, 2 vols. (New York: Charles Scribner, 1860), 2, p.

501. Secondary treatments appear in Johnston, *Yorktown Campaign*, p. 122; Davis, *Campaign that Won America*, pp. 199, 201-212; and Borresen, "Orientation Report," pp. 15-16.

28. James, *Journal of Rear-Admiral Bartholomew Jones*, p. 119.

29. St. George Tucker, "Journal. kept by Col. St. George Tucker," p. 7.

30. Denny, *Military Journal*, p. 41; Duncan, "Diary of Captain James Duncan," p. 747; "Itinerary of the Pennsylvania Line from Pennsylvania to South Carolina, 1781-1782," *Pennsylvania Magazine of History and Biography*, 26 (1912), p. 284; Johnston, *Yorktown Campaign*, p. 122.

31. Davis, *Campaign that Won America*, p. 200. Freeman has this incident occurring October 1. *George Washington*, 5, p. 353.

32. Riley, "Founding and Development of Yorktown," p. 284.

33. Knox to Shilds, September 30, 1781, Henry Knox Papers (CNHP). Shilds was successful in his endeavor and impressed some 13,540 board feet of pine during his assignment, but apparently contracted with Maryland citizens for the oak. All the wood was used by "the artillery and engineering departments." See Knox to Maryland Governor Thomas Lee, October 29, 1781, in ibid. The Americans seem not to have brought with them any artillery platforms with the cannon from the north, and so were forced to fashion them all before Yorktown. There is no indication in the inventories that platforms constituted part of the cargo being unloaded at Trebell's Landing. Presumably, however, the French had their own artillery platforms, sent south from Newport with de Barras.

34. There is evidence that the redoubt contemplated for the area between Pigeon Hill and the Hampton Road battery was likewise to be created from a British redan already there. Map 48F indicates such an earthwork in existence. This structure comprised, with the Hampton Road battery, what Map 48F calls "redans des Anglois convertis en redoutes contre la place par the Americains." Furthermore, a sketch map (27F) prepared by French engineers at the time of the investment shows an earthwork at this location.

35. "Journal of the Siege of York in Virginia by a Chaplain," pp. 104-5; Washington, *Writings*, 23, p. 155; Johnston, *Yorktown Campaign*, p. 126; Dumas, *Memoirs of His Own Time*, p. 64.

36. Freeman, *George Washington*, 5, p. 352.

37. Davis, *Campaign that Won America*, pp. 200-201. For Lincoln, see David B. Mattern, *Benjamin Lincoln and the American Revolution* (Columbia: University of South Carolina Press, 1996).

38. "Orderly Book kept during the Siege of Yorktown," p. 18.

39. Ibid., p. 17; Ibid., pp. 26-27.

40. Ibid., p. 18.

41. Ibid., p. 16.

42. Washington, *Writings*, 23, p. 152; Wild, "Journal of Ebenezer Wild," p. 152.

43. "Orderly Book kept during the Siege of Yorktown," p. 14; Van Cortlandt, "Autobiography," pp. 293-94; Wright, "Notes on the Siege of Yorktown," p. 239.

44. Duncan, "Diary of Captain James Duncan," p. 747; Gregory, "Diary of Mathew Gregory at Yorktown, 1781," p. 1; Washington, *Diaries*, 2, p. 263; Trumbull, "Yorktown,

Virginia," p. 335; Wayne Journal, p. 81; Samuel Shute, "Sam' Shutes Journal of the Cornwallis Expedition Commencing at Dobbs Ferry Augt 19th '81," General Revolutionary Manuscripts, Historical Society of Pennsylvania; *Rivington's Gazette*, November 24, 1781, quoting Cornwallis to Clinton, October 20, 1781, in Moore, *Diary of the American Revolution*, p. 513; Stedman, *History . . . of the American War*, 2, p. 409; Keim, *Rochambeau: A Commemoration*, p. 444; Wright, "Notes on the Siege of Yorktown," pp. 238-39; Arthur, *End of a Revolution*, p. 121.

45. Engineers' Journal, p. 450; La Combe, "Journal of the Siege of York," p. 2; Tarleton, *History of the Campaigns*, p. 386; Anais de Saint-Exupery, "The War Diary of Georges Alexander Cesar de Saint-Exupery, Lieutenant in the Regiment of Sarre-Infantry," *Legion D'Honneur*, 3 (October, 1931), p. 110; Arthur, *Sieges of Yorktown*, p. 15.

46. Maps 11 F, 15F, 16F, 17F, 19F, 26F, 28A, 29B, 31F, 33F, 41F, 48F, 49F, 61F.

47. See Maps 29B, 32F, 45F, 49F, 53F for abatis completely encircling the redoubt. Map 34F shows abatis only on the north side.

48. Engineers' Journal, p. 450.

49. "Diary of Captain James Duncan," p. 748.

50. Ibid.

51. Swartwout, "Journal of Barnardus Swartwout," p. 35.

52. Clermont-Crèvecoeur Journal, in Rice and Brown, *American Campaigns*, p. 57; Engineers' Journal, p. 450.

53. See Maps 1F, 2F, 11F, 15F, 16F, 17F, 19F, 25B, 26F, 28A, 29B, 31F, 32F, 33F, 35F, 36F, 37F, 41F, 45F, 46F, 48F, 50B, 53F, 61F, 62F. Borresen believed that both American works had abatis. "Orientation Report," p. 22.

54. Map 41F shows what appears to be a small trench leading into the southeast corner of the redoubt. The structure was built at a location Cornwallis's own chief engineer had deemed important to strengthen the British outer position. See Map 57B. As mentioned previously, there is evidence that this redoubt, too, was made from an abandoned British redan on the site. See Borresen, "Orientation Report," p. 22.

55. Closen, *Revolutionary Journal*, p. 141.

56. Nelson to Virginia delegates in Congress, October 5, 1781, in Palmer, *Calendar of Virginia State Papers*, 2, p. 527.

57. John Bell Tilden, "Extracts from the Journal of Lieutenant John Bell Tilden, Second Pennsylvania Line, 1781-1782," *Pennsylvania Magazine of History and Biography* 19 (April, 1895), p. 59. See also Gregory, "Diary of Mathew Gregory at Yorktown, 1781," p. 2; and Riley, "Founding and Development of Yorktown," pp. 285-86.

58. Washington, *Writings*, 23, p. 154; "Orderly Book kept during the Siege of Yorktown," pp. 15-16.

Chapter 7: The Lion at Bay

1. Tilden, "Extracts from the Journal of Lieutenant John Bell Tilden," p. 59.

2. Count Deux-Ponts reported that the British "fired at least 300 cannon-shots in the course of the day," October 1. *My Campaigns in America*, p. 137. Accounts of the English bombardment of October 1 are in St. George Tucker, "Journal kept by Col. St. George Tucker," p. 8; "Siege of York and Gloucester, Virginia," p. 476; Wild, "Journal of Ebenezer Wild," p. 152; Du Bourg, "Diary of a French Officer, 1781,'" p. 445; Richard Butler, "General Richard Butler's Journal of the Siege of Yorktown," *Historical Magazine*, 7 (March, 1864), p. 107; John Davis, "The Yorktown Campaign. Journal of Captain John Davis of the Pennsylvania Line," *Pennsylvania Magazine of History and Biography*, 5 (1881), p. 303; Daniel Shute, "With General Benjamin Lincoln at Yorktown. August 18, 1781-April 28, 1782. From the Journal kept by Dr. Daniel Shute of South Hingham, Massachusetts," typescript copy in the library of CNHP, Yorktown, Virginia, p. 3; Claude C. Robin, *New Travels through North America* (Philadelphia: Robert Bell, 1783), p. 56; Moore, *Life and Services of Gen. Anthony Wayne*, p. 149; and Merlant, *Soldiers and Sailors of France*, p. 173.

3. Swartwout, "Journal of Barnardus Swartwout," p. 35; Feltman, "Journal of Lieut. William Feltman," p. 316; Wright, "Notes on the Siege of Yorktown," p. 239; Freeman, *George Washington*, 5, pp. 352-353. Freeman states the general's episode with the close-flying British cannonballs occurred during this reconnaissance instead of on the previous day. Ibid.

4. Whitridge, *Rochambeau*, p. 214; George Washington Greene, *The German Element in the War of American Independence* (New York: Hurd and Houghton, 1876), pp. 71-72.

5. Tarleton, *History of the Campaigns*, pp. 386-87; Wright, "Notes on the Siege of Yorktown," pp. 238-39. The planning period was of crucial importance to the final success or failure of the siege and for that reason proceeded under the tightest security and secrecy. Even the soldiers remained uninformed as to the essential details of the planning process. Ibid., p. 240. The quote is from La Combe, "Journal of the Siege of York," p. 3.

6. This is hypothetical, but must have occurred sometime well before the opening of the trenches. Davis, "Journal of Captain John Davis," p. 303; James, *Journal*, p. 119. See also Tousard, *American Artillerist's Companion*, 1, pp. 8-9, who wrote about laying out these batteries: "By means of these prolongations the angle made by the two faces and the capital of the bastion, or any other work, is known; without these prolongations, it is a mere matter of chance if batteries are not placed in bad situations, which therefore occasion only a waste of ammunition." Ibid., p. 9.

7. Wright, "Notes on the Siege of Yorktown," p. 238; Arthur, *End of a Revolution*, p. 126. The French also established smaller depots in the arms of upper York Creek in order to maintain their posts in that vicinity. Borresen, "Orientation Report," p. 24. Closen stated that the depot sites were chosen October 3. *Revolutionary Journal*, p. 142.

8. "Journal of the Siege of York in Virginia by a Chaplain," p. 105; "Orderly Book kept during the Siege of Yorktown," p. 23; Wright, "Notes on the Siege of Yorktown," pp. 239-40; Clermont-Crèvecoeur Journal, in Rice and Brown, *American Campaigns*, p. 57.

9. "Orderly Book kept during the Siege of Yorktown," p. 25; Closen, *Revolutionary Journal*, pp. 141-42; Thacher, *Military Journal*, p. 271; Döhla, "Journal of Johann

Conrad Döhla," p. 140; Trumbull, "Yorktown, Virginia," p. 335; Washington, *Writings*, 23, p. 157; Clermont-Crèvecoeur Journal, in Rice and Brown, *American Campaigns*, p. 57; David Cobb, "Before York Town, Virginia, October 1-November 30, 1781," Proceedings of the Massachusetts Historical Society, 19 (1881-1882), p. 67; Johnston, *Yorktown Campaign*, pp. 124-25.

10. "Orderly Book kept during the Siege of Yorktown," p. 20.

11. Edward Hand to Jasper Yeates, October 1, 1781, Edward Hand Papers, vol. 2, item 135, New York Public Library; Joseph Plumb Martin, *Private Yankee Doodle: Being a Narrative of Some of the Adventures, Dangers and Sufferings of a Revolutionary Soldier*, ed. George F. Scheer (1830; reprint ed., Boston: Little, Brown and Company, 1962), p. 241; Riley, "Founding and Development of Yorktown," p. 299; Davis, *Campaign that Won America*, p. 202. On October 9, Washington issued orders against allowing his American officers to keep these blacks as servants. "Orderly Book kept during the Siege of Yorktown," pp. 77-78.

12. "Orderly Book kept during the Siege of Yorktown," pp. 20, 21.

13. Ibid., p. 22.

14. *Writings*, 23, p. 160. By October 4, however, Washington could write that "it is impossible for Cornwallis to cross his troops to Gloucester in one night for want of boats." Washington Papers, vol. 185, Library of Congress.

15. Washington, *Writings*, 23, p. 160.

16. Ibid.; General Hand opined of the possibility of Cornwallis escaping "by moving by water to the forks of York River, or crossing immediately by Gloster [sic], neither of which I think they will attempt as disgrace would in all human probability be added to the total destruction of their Army." Hand to Yeates, October 1, 1781, Edward Hand Papers, vol. 2, item 135, New York Public Library.

17. *Writings*, 23, p. 162. See also Washington to President of Congress, October 1, 1781, in ibid., p. 159. A French officer, Cromot Du Bourg, delivered Washington's requests to de Grasse via Hampton, Virginia. "Diary of a French Officer, 1781," p. 445.

18. See Weedon to Greene, November 11, 1781, in Morgan Manuscripts, vol. 1, The Siege of Yorktown and Surrender of Cornwallis, Pierpont Morgan Library; Ewald, "Diary of the American War," pp. 883-84; Bonsal, *Cause of Liberty*, p. 150.

19. Hand to Yeates, October 1, 1781, Edward Hand Papers, vol. 2, item 135, New York Public Library. There is evidence that British desertions occurred with some regularity, for frequent mention of them appears in the diaries and journals of American and French participants. Undoubtedly many of these deserters were accounted prisoners of war. British officers captured by the Americans outside the main line, however, were for some reason paroled back into Yorktown. Enlisted men were confined at Williamsburg and at Richmond. See "Return of Prisoners of War taken by the Army under the command of Major General Marquis De Lafayette," Washington Papers, vol. 185, Library of Congress.

20. Tucker to Frances Tucker, October 5, 1781, "Letters to and from St. George Tucker," p. 9. See also St. George Tucker, "Journal kept by Col. St. George Tucker," p. 8. Reference to this action also appears in Enclosure in Weedon to Washington, October 2,

1781, Washington Papers, vol. 185, Library of Congress. See also Davis, *Campaign that Won America*, p. 202.

21. Pryor to Colonel William Davies, October 2, 1781, in Palmer, *Calendar of Virginia State Papers*, 2, p. 518; Thompson, *The British Defenses of Yorktown, 1781*, p. 97. A great many diaries and journals contain mention of the several men killed by a single British shot. See Gregory, "Diary of Mathew Gregory at Yorktown, 1781," p. 2; St. George Tucker, "Journal kept by Col. St. George Tucker," p. 9; Clermont-Crèvecoeur Journal, in Rice and Brown, *American Campaigns*, p. 57; Du Bourg, "Diary of a French Officer, 1781," p. 446; Trumbull, "Yorktown, Virginia," p. 335; Shute, "With General Benjamin Lincoln," p. 3; Tilden, "Extracts from the Journal of Lieutenant John Bell Tilden," p. 59. For descriptions of the cannonade on October 2, see Feltman, "Journal of Lieut. William Feltman," pp. 316-17; Deux-Ponts, *My Campaigns in America*, p. 137; "Journal of the Siege of York in Virginia by a Chaplain, p. 105; Swartwout, "Journal of Barnardus Swartwout," p. 35; Butler, "General Richard Butler's Journal," p. 107.

22. General John Mitchell to Major H. H. Chapman, December 13, 1805, Manuscripts Collection, box 92, item 3190, Morristown National Historical Park.

23. Duncan, "Diary of Captain James Duncan," p. 748; St. George Tucker, "Journal kept by Col. St. George Tucker, p. 10; Davis, *Campaign that Won America*, p. 204.

24. Duncan, "Diary of Captain James Duncan," p. 748.

25. Feltman, "Journal of Lieut. William Feltman," p. 317.

26. Wild, "Journal of Ebenezer Wild," p. 152; Cobb, "Before York Town, Virginia," p. 68. Tielke recommended that grooved tree trunks be used to transport artillery across ditches and morasses: "Whenever the artillery may have occasion to cross a ditch, a swamp, or an old wooden bridge, two rows must be placed so as to allow the wheels to pass along the grooves." Field Engineer, 1, p. 37. Other tasks involved in transporting siege guns and wagons included cutting branches or trees and widening ruts in the road. Ibid., p. 35.

27. Knox to Board of War, October 2, 1781, Henry Knox Papers (CNHP).

28. Washington, *Diaries*, 2, p. 263; "Orderly Book kept during the Siege of Yorktown," pp. 23-24, 27-28.

29. For details of constructing these siege components, see Lochee, *Elements of Field Fortification*, pp. 143, 144, 152-53; Tousard, *American Artillerist's Companion*, 1, pp. 21-24, 507; and Tielke, *Field Engineer*, 1, pp. 207-208, 210, 215-216.

30. Martin, *Private Yankee Doodle*, pp. 218-19.

31. Vauban, *Manual of Siegecraft and Fortification*, p. 41.

32. James, Journal of Rear-Admiral Bartholomew James, p. 120.

33. Captain John Pryor to Colonel William Davies, October 2, 1781, in Palmer, *Calendar of Virginia State Papers*, 2, p. 518.

34. Ewald, "Diary of the American War," p. 884.

35. Davis, *Campaign that Won America*, p. 205; Washington Irving, *Life of George Washington*, 5 vols. (New York: G. A. Putnam and Company, 1857), 4, p. 360.

36. "Journal of the Siege of York in Virginia by a Chaplain," p. 105; Cobb, "Before York Town, Virginia," p. 68.

37. Thacher, *Military Journal*, p. 271. Freeman placed this incident on the night of October 5. *George Washington*, 5, p. 356.

38. Freeman, *George Washington*, 5, p. 356; Butler, "General Richard Butler's Journal," p. 107.

39. "Orderly Book kept during the Siege of Yorktown," p. 32; See Arthur, *End of a Revolution*, p. 127.

40. Thacher, *Military Journal*, p. 271.

41. James, *Journal of Rear-Admiral Bartholomew James*, p. 120; Ewald, "Diary of the American War," pp. 897-898; Hatch, *"York Under the Hill,"*, p. 64.

42. "Narrative of the Duke de Lauzun," *Magazine of American History*, 6 (January, 1881), pp. 52-53; Thompson, *The British Defenses of Yorktown, 1781*, p. 97; Robert A. Selig, *Hussars in Lebanon! A Connecticut town and Lauzun's Legion during the American Revolution* (Lebanon, CT.: Lebanon Historical Society, 2004).

43. "Narrative of the Duke de Lauzun," *Magazine of American History*, 6 (January, 1881), pp. 52-53; Thompson, *The British Defenses of Yorktown, 1781*, p. 97.

44. Hatch, "Gloucester Point in the Siege of Yorktown, 1781," pp. 274-275; Weedon to Washington, October 2, 1781, Washington Papers, vol. 185, Library of Congress; Thompson, *The British Defenses of Yorktown, 1781*, p. 97.

45. "Narrative of the Duke de Lauzun," *Magazine of American History*, 6 (January, 1881), p. 53; Weedon to Washington, October 2, 1781, Washington Papers, vol. 185, Library of Congress; Tarleton, *History of the Campaigns*, p. 387, wrote that some of Lauzun's troops were "armed with spears [lances]." Dr. Robert A. Selig's research on Lauzun's Legion has confirmed this to be true.

46. Ibid.; Thompson, *The British Defenses of Yorktown, 1781*, p. 97. Determining which organizations fought with Tarleton's Legion and Simcoe's Queen's Rangers at the Battle of the Hook on October 3, 1781, was not a simple task. In his memoir, Tarleton references "the 17th," which most historians and students of the battle assume was the 17th Foot, which we know fought in the siege of Yorktown. (Because the 71st Foot was also present, there also existed the possibility that Tarleton's reference to "the 17th" was a typographical error.) *History of the Campaigns*, p. 376. Hatch, "Gloucester Point in the Siege of Yorktown, 1781," p. 276, also claims the 17th Foot was at the battle and cites Tarleton, and I relied upon Tarleton's seemingly unambiguous account for my original core Bicentennial study. My editor, Theodore P. Savas, however, pointed out that Boatner, *The Encyclopedia of the American Revolution*, p. 437 (who relied upon Johnston, *Yorktown Campaign*), Selig, "The duc de Lauzun and his Légion, Rochambeau's Most Troublesome, Colorful Soldiers," pp. 59-60, and several other secondary sources place the 23rd Regiment, Royal Welsh Fusiliers at the battle instead of the 17th Foot. Because these sources seemed to directly conflict with Tarleton's recollection that it was the 17th Foot that supported him that day, I decided to research the matter more deeply in conjunction with David Riggs, Curator, CNHP, Yorktown. This issue also piqued David's curiosity because the answer was not readily forthcoming.

One of the key pieces of evidence turned on identifying a "Captain Champagne." According to Johnston, *Yorktown Campaign*, p. 129, after Tarleton was knocked from his horse, "he reformed his men under cover of Captain Champagne's infantry company."

Tarleton also refers to this officer: "he [Tarleton] dismounted forty infantry, just come up under Captain Champagne, and placed them in a thicket on his right." Apparently, identifying what regiment Captain Champagne belonged to would answer the question (17th Foot or 23rd Regiment, Royal Welsh Fusiliers).

As noted above, most historians have assumed "the 17th" was a reference to the 17th Foot. Philip R. N. Katcher, *Encyclopedia of British, Provincial, and German Army Units 1775-1783* (Harrisburg PA: Stackpole Co., 1973), p. 24, however, references a 17th Regiment *of Light Dragoons* (emphasis added). Although this organization fought mostly in the northern colonies, "one troop served with the British Legion [i.e., Tarleton] in the southern campaigns . . . and interned at Yorktown." Tarleton (p. 376) describes at least part of his order of battle this way: "part of the legion, of the 17th, and of Simcoe's dragoons." Perhaps this would have been more accurate if he had written: "part of the legion, of the 17th *Regiment of Light Dragoons* (emphasis added), and of Simcoe's dragoons." Katcher, *Encyclopedia of British, Provincial, and German Army Units 1775-1783*, makes no reference to Captain Champagne, though he only listed majors and up. And so the mystery deepened: the 17th Foot, 17th Regiment of Light Dragoons, or 23rd Regiment, Royal Welsh Fusiliers?

Robert D. Bass, *The Green Dragoon: The Lives of Banastre Tarleton and Mary Robinson* (New York: Henry Holt and Co., 1957) contains a lackluster description of the Gloucester combat, but the entries in the index for "Regiments" include "17th Regiment of Light Dragoons" and "23rd Regiment" (though no entry for the 17th Regiment of Foot!). Bass quite specifically refers to the 17th Dragoons as being with Tarleton, and on at least one occasion in February 1781, Cornwallis sent the 23rd Regiment to support Tarleton. However, a major clue is contained in Bass's description of the beginning of Tarleton's June 1781 raid to Charlottesville, Virginia: "Mounting 70 infantrymen of the 23rd Regiment under Captain Champaigne [Champagne] and choosing 180 dragoons from the Legion and the 17th Light Dragoons, before daybreak on June 3 Tarleton galloped away. . . ." *The Green Dragoon*, p. 178. Finally, a confluence of key pieces to the puzzle: Captain Champaigne (spelled differently, but associated with the 23rd Regiment, Royal Welsh Fusiliers) and the 17th Light Dragoons—a distinctly different organization from the 17th Foot, and referenced here completely separate from Captain Champagne (or Champaigne). Bass's documentation is light: he only lists books, manuscript collections, etc. for each chapter in general fashion.

Robert Selig pulled the remaining loose threads of this small mystery together by turning up a letter written by a Captain Forbes Champagne, 23rd Regiment, Royal Welsh Fusiliers, while on campaign in the southern colonies, to his brother in England, Lieutenant (Josiah) C. (Champagne) of the 31st Foot. It was dated April 17, 1781, and written in Wilmington, North Carolina. Captain Champagne commanded the grenadier company of the 23rd Regiment. The *piece de resistance* came from the pen of German soldier Johann Ewald. Ewald served in Gloucester during the siege. According to his *Diary of the American War*, p. 328, the garrison at Gloucester on or about September 20 consisted of the 23rd, 33rd, 43rd, the remainder of the 71st, etc. However, Ewald specifically states that the "remainder" of the 23rd Regiment on September 30 was across the river at York! Therefore, a portion of the 23rd Regiment was serving at Gloucester, and Captain Forbes Champagne led a grenadier company from the regiment and was specifically mentioned by Tarleton as having been in the battle.

Taken all together, it now seems clear that the organizations fighting with Tarleton and his legion at the Hook on October 3, 1781, included Simcoe's Queen's Rangers, a detachment from the 17th Light Dragoons, and Captain Forbes Champagne's company of 40 men from the 23rd Regiment, Royal Welsh Fusiliers.

47. "Narrative of the Duke de Lauzun," *Magazine of American History*, 6 (January, 1881), p. 53; Tarleton, *History of the Campaigns*, p. 387; Hatch, "Gloucester Point in the Siege of Yorktown, 1781," p. 276.

48. "Narrative of the Duke de Lauzun," p. 53.

49. Ibid.; Tarleton, *History of the Campaigns*, p. 387; Hatch, "Gloucester Point in the Siege of Yorktown, 1781," pp. 275-276.

50. "Narrative of the Duke de Lauzun," p. 53. Lauzun's killed were both hussars—Pierre Didier of the Second Squadron and Jacob Colin from the First Squadron. Jean Sscherrer of the Second Squadron was mortally shot and later died of wounds. E-mail from Dr. Robert A. Selig, December 16, 2004, regarding work he conducted based upon Lauzun's Legion muster rolls. For a history of Lauzun's Legion, organization, and route to Virginia, see Selig, *Hussars in Lebanon!* See also, Tarleton, *History of the Campaigns*, p. 387; Hatch, "Gloucester Point in the Siege of Yorktown, 1781," p. 277. Washington estimated some 600 British troops were on the field at Gloucester. Ibid. See also, Howard H. Peckham, ed., *The Toll of Independence: Engagements & Battle Casualties of the American Revolution* (Chicago: University of Chicago Press, 1974), p. 91.

51. Besides Lauzun's "Narrative," this account of the action at Gloucester on October 3 was prepared primarily from information found in the Clermont-Crèvecoeur Journal, in Rice and Brown, *American Campaigns*, pp. 57-58, Tarleton, *History of the Campaigns*, p. 387, Hatch, *Yorktown and the Siege of 1781*, p. 23, Arthur, *End of a Revolution*, pp. 122-124, Thompson, *The British Defenses of Yorktown, 1781*, pp. 97-98, Whitridge, *Rochambeau*, pp. 216-217, and Bonsal, *Cause of Liberty*, p. 151. For a contemporary account of casualties on both sides, see St. George Tucker, "Journal kept by Col. St. George Tucker," p. 9. For a highly detailed personal reminiscence of the Gloucester action, see that of Lieutenant Colonel John Francis Mercer, in Gaillard Hunt, ed., *Fragments of Revolutionary History* (1892; reprint ed., New York: Arno Press, 1970), pp. 56-60. Lauzun and Tarleton, it was later determined, had more in common than their respective leadership of the troops engaged at Gloucester. Lauzun had been, and Tarleton would be on his return to London, a lover of Mary "Perdita" Robinson, considered to be the most beautiful British actress of her day. Whitridge, *Rochambeau*, p. 218. Today, the Hook battlefield is an empty field behind a Hardee's restaurant at Hayes. Seawell's Ordinary still stands, and happens to be the finest restaurant and tavern in Gloucester County.

52. Daniel Trabue, "The Journal of Colonel Daniel Trabue," in Lillie DuPuy Harper, ed., *Colonial Men and Times* (Philadelphia: Innes and Sons,, 1916), p. 111; "Itinerary of the Pennsylvania Line," p. 284; Stryker, New Jersey Continental Line, p. 17; Arthur, *End*

of a Revolution, p. 126; Wright, "Notes on the Siege of Yorktown," p. 240; Davis, *Campaign that Won America*, p. 203.

53. Dr. Treat to Lamb, October 5, 1781, Lamb Papers, New-York Historical Society.

54. Barneville, "War Diary," p. 273.

55. "Orderly Book kept during the Siege of Yorktown," p. 30; Washington, *Writings*, 23, p. 170; Wild, "Journal of Ebenezer Wild," p. 152; Arthur, *Sieges of Yorktown*, p. 16.

56. Wayne Journal, p. 81; Deux-Ponts, *My Campaigns in America*, pp. 138-39; De Verger Journal, in Rice and Brown, *American Campaigns*, p. 139. De Verger erroneously termed the structure a "redoubt."

57. Barneville, "War Diary," p. 272; Butler, "General Richard Butler's Journal," p. 107; Duncan, "Diary of Captain James Duncan," p. 748; Swartwout, "Journal of Barnardus Swartwout," p. 35.

58. Du Bourg, "Diary of a French Officer, 1781," p. 446; Deux-Ponts, *My Campaigns in America*, pp. 138-39.

59. De Verger Journal, in Rice and Brown, *American Campaigns*, p. 139; Trumbull, "Yorktown, Virginia," p. 335.

60. Trumbull, "Yorktown, Virginia," p. 335; St. George Tucker, "Journal kept by Col. St. George Tucker," p. 9.

61. James, *Journal of Rear-Admiral Bartholomew James*, p. 120.

62. St. George Tucker, "Journal kept by Col. St. George Tucker," p. 10.

63. Ibid.; Feltman, "Journal of Lieut. William Feltman," p. 317; Butler, "General Richard Butler's Journal," p. 107.

64. Swartwout, "Journal of Barnardus Swartwout," p. 35; Du Bourg, "Diary of a French Officer, 1781," p. 446.

65. Tucker to Frances Tucker, October 5, 1781, in "Letters to and from St. George Tucker," p. 8.

66. "Itinerary of the Pennsylvania Line," p. 284; Trumbull, "Yorktown, Virginia," p. 335; Davis, *Campaign that Won America*, p. 208.

67. Gregory, "Diary of Mathew Gregory at Yorktown, 1781," p. 2; Washington, *Writings*, 23, p. 176; Cobb, "Before York Town, Virginia," p. 68; Duncan, "Diary of Captain James Duncan," p. 749.

68. "Orderly Book kept during the Siege of Yorktown," p. 40.

69. Captain Thomas Symonds to Rear Admiral Graves, October 4, 1781, Clinton Papers, William L. Clements Library; De Verger Journal, in Rice and Brown, *American Campaigns*, 1, p. 139; Thompson, *The British Defenses of Yorktown, 1781*, pp. 98-99.

70. Cobb, "Before York Town, Virginia," p. 68; Butler, "General Richard Butler's Journal," p. 108. The engagement at Eutaw Springs was indecisive, and Greene could claim victory only because he retained possession of the battleground after the British withdrew. The American loss in killed and wounded stood at about 550, and the British around 800. For his "victory" at Eutaw Springs, Congress awarded Greene its thanks, a British standard, and a gold medal. *Harper's Encyclopedia of United States History*, 2, pp. 267-268; 4, pp. 169-170.

71. With regard to Greene's victory, Tucker to Frances Tucker, October 5, 1781, in "Letters to and from St. George Tucker," p. 9.

72. See Wright, "Notes on the Siege of Yorktown," p. 231; and Vauban, *Manual of Siegecraft and Fortification*, p. 44.

73. D'Ancteville, "Journal of the Chesapeake Campaign," pp. 16-17; Closen, *Revolutionary Journal*, p. 143; Johnston, *Yorktown Campaign*, p. 131; Wright, "Notes on the Siege of Yorktown," p. 232; S. Doc. 273, p. 191; S. Doc. 318, p. 47; Arthur, *End of a Revolution*, p. 127; Hatch, "On Reconstructing Earthworks," pp. 43-44; Thomas M. Pitkin, "A Preliminary Study of American Redoubt No. 2, Yorktown Battlefield," MS, dated May 28, 1941, in the library of CNHP, Yorktown, Virginia, pp. 4-5. Just how closely the Allies adhered to European theoretical strictures can be seen by comparing the placement of the first parallel at Yorktown with this quote from Hector Straith (made in 1852):

> The distance of 600 yards is selected as suitable for the first parallel, as here there is little to fear from musketry, grape, or cannister; but when the localities of the ground require that any portion of the parallel should be advanced or retired, in order to command the ground in front, it should be done. The distance of 600 yards also is too great for sorties from the place to hope for success, and to retire without great loss.

Treatise on Fortification and Artillery, 1, p. 301.

74. Tilden, "Extracts from the Journal of Lieutenant John Bell Tilden," p. 60.

75. Shute, "With General Benjamin Lincoln," p. 4. See also Cobb, "Before York Town, Virginia," p. 68; and Duncan, "Diary of Captain James Duncan," p. 749; Wayne Journal, p. 81.

76. Washington, *Writings*, 23, p. 176.

77. *Revolutionary Journal*, p. 143.

78. *My Campaigns in America*, p. 139; The account of one of the British forward patrols the night of October 5 is in Döhla, "Journal of Johann Conrad Döhla," pp. 140-41. Inexplicably, Döhla described the sky that night as "starry." Ibid., p. 140.

79. Washington, *Writings*, 23, p. 176; Scheer and Rankin, *Rebels and Redcoats*, p. 556.

80. Quoted in Scheer and Rankin, *Rebels and Redcoats*, p. 556.

81. Colonel St. George Tucker to Frances Tucker, October 5, 1781, "Letters to and from St. George Tucker," pp. 9-10.

Chapter 8: On the Verge

1. Quoted in Merlant, *Soldiers and Sailors of France*, p. 174.

2. Cobb, "Before York Town, Virginia," p. 68; Freeman, *George Washington*, 5, p. 357.

3. Duncan, "Diary of Captain James Duncan," p. 749.

4. Feltman, "Journal of Lieut. William Feltman," p. 317; Pickering and Upham, *Life of Timothy Pickering*, 1, p. 304; Freeman, *George Washington*, 5, p. 357-358.

5. Quoted in Johnston, *Yorktown Campaign*, p. 137n.

6. Wright, "Notes on the Siege of Yorktown," p. 246; Freeman, *George Washington*, 5, p. 357. Freeman states that there were 52 articles in the *Regulations*. Ibid.; John McAuley Palmer, in *General Von Steuben* (New Haven: Yale University Press, 1937), p. 290, contends that the document was prepared under the supervision of von Steuben because "with his staff experience under Frederick the Great in the Seven Years' War, there was no officer in the whole allied army so well qualified to advise the commander in chief on the elaborate technique of fortress warfare."

7. Whitridge suggests that some American soldiers were acquainted with the vernacular of siegecraft through having read Tristram Shandy, the popular 18th-century novel by Laurence Sterne. *Rochambeau*, p. 215.

8. These articles are from "Orderly Book kept during the Siege of Yorktown," pp. 47-66, and are nearly identical editorially to those in *Orderly Book of the Siege of Yorktown, from September 26, 1781, to November 2nd, 1781* (Philadelphia: Antique Press, 1865), pp. 21-27; see also "Gist's Orderly Book of the Siege of Yorktown, Virginia, 1781," photostatic copy in the library of CNHP, Yorktown, Virginia, pp. 23-41.

9. Freeman, *George Washington*, 5, p. 357; Borresen, "Orientation Report," p. 25.

10. Diaries, 2, p. 263.

11. Gregory, "Diary of Mathew Gregory at Yorktown, 1781," p. 2; Deux-Ponts, *My Campaigns in America*, p. 139.

12. Arthur, *End of a Revolution*, p. 130. As senior officer, Lincoln took his turn at command first. Baron de Viomenil's rank (Marechal de Camp) was equivalent to a major general's in the American Army. The selection of regiments from the right of each brigade occurred because these units were customarily senior to the others and thus favored for such a "detail of honor" as the opening of the trenches. For amplification on this custom, see Wright, "Notes on the Siege of Yorktown," pp. 240-241.

13. Sanderson, "Diary of the March from the Hudson to Yorktown," in Johnston, *Yorktown Campaign*, p. 171; Oswald Tilghman, *Memoir of Lieut. Col. Tench Tilghman, Secretary and Aid to Washington* (Albany: J. Munsell, 1876), p. 104; Trumbull, "Yorktown, Virginia," pp. 335-336. Tilghman's biography is in L. G. Shreve, *Tench Tilghman: The Life and Times of Washington's Aide-de-Camp* (Centreville, Md.: Tidewater Publishers, 1982).

14. Wayne Journal, p. 81; Moore, *Life and Services of Gen. Anthony Wayne*, p. 149; Wild, "Journal of Ebenezer Wild," p. 153; Johnston, *Yorktown Campaign*, p. 131; S. Doc. 273, p. 191; Arthur, *Sieges of Yorktown*, p. 17; Arthur, *End of a Revolution*, pp. 127-130. Freeman contends the Americans paraded at 4:00 p.m., the French an hour later. *George Washington*, 5, p. 359. Most of the contemporary sources consulted state that the American assembly took place at 6:00 p.m.

15. Lamb to Governor George Clinton, October 6, 1781, in George Clinton, *Public Papers of George Clinton, First Governor of New York*, 10 vols. (Albany: Oliver A. Quayle, 1904), 4, p. 376.

16. Thompson, *The British Defenses of Yorktown, 1781*, p. 99; Davis, *Campaign that Won America*, p. 214; "Narrative of Asa Redington," p. 11.

17. Particulars of the Allied project in opening the first siege line are drawn from Thacher, *Military Journal*, pp. 272-273; Lee, *Memoirs of the War*, p. 499; Wright, "Notes on the Siege of Yorktown," p. 241; Arthur, *Sieges of Yorktown*, p. 17; Arthur, *End of a Revolution*, p. 130; See also Vauban, *Manual of Siegecraft and Fortification*, pp. 47-48.

18. *Military Journal*, p. 273.

19. Thompson, *The British Defenses of Yorktown, 1781*, p. 99. Exactly what ordnance this battery was to contain is open to dispute because the sources do not agree. Deux-Ponts claimed that it would hold eight cannon and six howitzers and mortars. *My Campaigns in America*, p. 140. D'Ancteville stated that four cannon and six howitzers were established there. "Journal of the Chesapeake Campaign," p. 17. Count de Fersen said the battery held "4 mortars, 2 howitzers and 2 pieces of 24." "Journal of Operations," p. 439.

20. St. George Tucker, "Journal kept by Col. St. George Tucker," pp. 10-11. Tucker was the only eyewitness to the siege who claimed the British fired a rocket on the night of October 6-7. Once the siege concluded, 36 signal rockets were among the captured stores. Du Bourg, "Diary of a French Officer, 1781," p. 446; "Diary of French naval operations in America," p. 192; Butler, "General Richard Butler's Journal," p. 108; Rochambeau, "War in America," in Weelen, *Rochambeau, Father and Son*, p. 231; D'Ancteville, "Journal of the Chesapeake Campaign," p. 17; U.S., Congress, Senate, *Journal of the Siege of York-Town*, by Gaspard de Gallatin, 71st Cong., 3d sess., February 17, 1931, S. Doc. 322, p. 4 (hereafter cited as S. Doc. 322); De Verger Journal, in Rice and Brown, *American Campaigns*, p. 139; Louis Antoine Thibault de Menonville, "Journal of the Siege of York," *Magazine of American History*, 7 (1881), p. 283; *"Wertgetreue Absehrift eines Tagebuehs eines markgräflischen Soldaten"*; Querenet de La Combe, quoted in Hatch, "Siege of Yorktown Opens," p. 15; Saint-Exupery, "War Diary," pp. 110-11; Johnston, *Yorktown Campaign*, p. 135; Balch, *French in America*, 1 p. 193; Freeman, *George Washington*, 5, pp. 358-359; Thomas J. Fleming, *Beat the Last Drum: The Siege of Yorktown, 1781* (New York: St. Martin's Press, 1963), p. 236; Clermont-Crèvecoeur Journal, in Rice and Brown, *American Campaigns*, p. 58.

21. Vauban urged exactly such procedure: "I . . . find it a good idea to plant a rumor that the attack will be launched on some other side. . . . I might even start a false attack there the day before the launching of the real one to draw in the strength of the enemy's guards, especially if the garrison is strong and is expected to mount a stiff resistance." *Manual of Siegecraft and Fortification*, p. 43. According to Straith, "Every endeavour is made previously to breaking ground, to deceive the garrison as to the fronts selected for attack." *Treatise on Fortification and Artillery*, 1, p. 297.

22. This was what Tielke suggested for men working in sandy soil. *Field Engineer*, 1, p. 205.

23. M. de Bousmard, *L'Essai de Fortification et de Defence des Places*, quoted in Lallemand, *Treatise on Artillery*, 2, p. 147.

24. Ibid.; Straith, *Treatise on Fortification and Artillery*, 1, p. 137; Davis, *Campaign that Won America*, p. 214.

25. Gregory, "Diary of Mathew Gregory at Yorktown, 1781," p. 3.

26. Trabue, "Journal of Colonel Daniel Trabue," in Harper, *Colonial Men and Times*, p. 111.

27. "Narrative of Asa Redington," p. 11.

28. Robin, *New Travels through North America*, p. 57.

29. Southside Historical Sites Foundation, "Archeology/Restoration/Reconstruction of the Yorktown Battlefield," p. 47.

30. "Narrative of Asa Redington," p. 12.

31. "Journal of the Siege of York in Virginia by a Chaplain," p. 106.

32. For details of the work in the American sector, see Cobb, "Before York Town, Virginia, p. 68; Duncan, "Diary of Captain James Duncan," p. 749; Tilghman, *Memoir of Lieut. Col. Tench Tilghman*, p. 104; Redington, "Narrative of Asa Redington," pp. 11-12; Nelson to Jameson, October 8, 1781, in Palmer, *Calendar of Virginia State Papers*, 2 pp. 532-533; Freeman, *George Washington*, 5, pp. 359-360.

33. La Combe, quoted in Hatch, "Siege of Yorktown Opens," p. 15.

34. Fersen, "Journal of Operations," p. 439.

35. Clermont-Crèvecoeur Journal, in Rice and Brown, *American Campaigns*, p. 58.

36. S. Doc. 322, p. 4.

37. Robin, *New Travels through North America*, p. 57.

38. Ibid., pp. 56-57. Accounts of the progress of, and events along, the French half of the parallel appear in Engineers' Journal, p. 451; S. Doc. 322, pp. 3-4; Blanchard, *Journal*, pp. 146-47; Rochambeau, *Relation*, p. 5; Barneville, "War Diary," p. 273; Closen, *Revolutionary Journal*, pp. 143-145; De Verger Journal, in Rice and Brown, *American Campaigns*, p. 139; La Combe, "Journal of the Siege of York," p. 3; Menonville, "Journal of the Siege of York," p. 283; Balch, *French in America*, 1, pp. 192-193; Wright, "Notes on the Siege of Yorktown," p. 241; Davis, *Campaign that Won America*, pp. 214-215.

39. *Diaries*, 2, p. 263.

40. Scheer and Rankin, *Rebels and Redcoats*, p. 557; Thompson, *The British Defenses of Yorktown, 1781*, pp. 100-102, citing Döhla, "The Journal of Johann Conrad Döhla"; Johnston, *Yorktown Campaign*, pp. 135-136; St. George Tucker, "Journal kept by Col. St. George Tucker," p. 10.

41. Duncan, "Diary of Captain James Duncan," pp. 749-750; Gregory, "Diary of Mathew Gregory at Yorktown, 1781."

42. Du Bourg, "Diary of a French Officer, 1781," p. 446; Shute, "With General Benjamin Lincoln," p. 4; Tilden, "Extracts from the Journal of Lieutenant John Bell Tilden," p. 60; Feltman, "Journal of Lieut. William Feltman," p. 317; Moore, *Life, and Services of Gen. Anthony Wayne*, p. 149; Washington, *Writings*, 23, p. 212; Washington, *Diaries*, 2, p. 264; "Itinerary of the Pennsylvania Line," p. 284; Engineers' Journal, p. 451; Wright, "Notes on the Siege of Yorktown," p. 242; Scheer and Rankin, *Rebels and Redcoats*, p. 557; Johnston, *Yorktown Campaign*, p. 135; "General Richard Butler's Journal," p. 108.

43. James McHenry to General Greene, October 7, 1781, in Morgan Manuscripts, vol. 2, *The Siege of Yorktown and Surrender of Cornwallis*, Pierpont Morgan Library.

44. Wright, "Notes on the Siege of Yorktown," p. 242; S. Doc. 273, pp. 191-92; Washington, *Writings*, 23, p. 197; Scheer and Rankin, *Rebels and Redcoats*, p. 557; John W. Wright, "Notes on the Continental Army," *William and Mary College Quarterly Historical Magazine*, 2d ser. 13 (April, 1933), p. 96.

45. "Siege of York and Gloucester, Virginia," p. 476; Stryker, *New Jersey Continental Line*, p. 18; Wright, "Notes on the Siege of Yorktown, p. 243. The American standards bore the expression, *"Manus Hace inimica tyrannis."* Duncan, "Diary of Captain James Duncan,'' p. 749.

46. Duncan, "Diary of Captain James Duncan," p. 749.

47. Wright, "Notes on the Siege of Yorktown," p. 243; John C. Miller, *Alexander Hamilton and the Growth of the New Nation* (New York: Harper and Row, 1959), p. 77. For Hamilton, see also, Robert A. Hendrickson, *The Rise and Fall of Alexander Hamilton* (New York: Van Nostrand Reinhold, 1981); and Richard Brookhiser, *Alexander Hamilton, American* (New York: The Free Press, 1999).

48. Duncan, "Diary of Captain James Duncan," p. 749.

49. Menonville, "Journal of the Siege of York," p. 283; "Diary of French naval operations in America," p. 192; Rochambeau, *Relation*, p. 5; Deux-Ponts, *My Campaigns in America*, p. 140; Wayne Journal, p. 81; Du Bourg, "Diary of a French Officer, 1781," p. 446; Merlant, *Soldiers and Sailors of France*, p. 174.

50. De Verger Journal, in Rice and Brown, *American Campaigns*, pp.139- 140; Engineers' Journal, p. 451; Menonville, "Journal of the Siege of York," pp. 283-284; Closen, *Revolutionary Journal*, p. 145; S. Doc. 322, p. 5; Balch, *French in America*, 1, p. 193.

51. S. Doc. 322, pp. 5-6; See also Menonville, "Journal of the Siege of York," p. 284. In some cases Gallatin's account of the number of guns and their calibers designated for particular battery units is subject to some dispute. For example, de Verger stated that in the next to the last battery described above there were four 24-pounders, and that the last mentioned battery contained, besides the cannon, two howitzers. De Verger Journal, in Rice and Brown, *American Campaigns*, p. 140.

52. There were certain drawbacks to constructing batteries in advance of the parallel, as the Americans did, instead of directly in the parallel. "If they be placed in front," wrote Lallemand, "they cannot be commenced till the night following [the opening of the trenches], and this will cause a delay of 24 hours in opening the fire, require more work, and be much more dangerous to execute. Batteries in front of the parallel have the disadvantages of masking the fire of the troops, and impeding the manoeuvres necessary to meet and repulse sorties." *Treatise on Artillery*, 2, p. 153.

53. Tilghman, *Memoir of Lieut. Col. Tench Tilghman*, pp. 104-5; Wild, "Journal of Ebenezer Wild," p. 153; Döhla, "Journal of Johann Conrad Döhla," p. 141.

54. Gregory, "Diary of Mathew Gregory at Yorktown, 1781," p. 3.

55. D'Ancteville, "Journal of the Chesapeake Campaign," p. 18.

56. Wright, "Notes on the Siege of Yorktown," pp. 234-235, 242; Fleming, *Beat the Last Drum*, p. 240.

57. *Manual of Siegecraft and Fortification*, p. 51.

58. Ibid., p. 59.

59. Lochee, *Elements of Field Fortification*, pp. 141n, 148, 149-50; Lallemand, *Treatise on Artillery*, 2, p. 154; Tousard, *American Artillerist's Companion*, 1, pp. 26-27.

60. Southside Historical Sites Foundation, "Archeology/Restoration/ Reconstruction of the Yorktown Battlefield," p. 17.

61. Tousard, *American Artillerist's Companion*, 1, pp. 30, 48; Thor Borresen, "Completion Report on American Battery No. 2, Second Parallel," MS, dated April 16, 1941, in the library of CNHP, Yorktown, Virginia, p. 79.

62. Tousard, *American Artillerist's Companion*, 1, pp. 40, 41-42, 79; Hatch, "On Reconstructing Earthworks," pp. 35, 38; Borresen, "Completion Report on American Battery No. 2," pp. 64-66; Memorandum, Borresen to Acting Park Historian, March 27, 1939, p. 5.

63. Tousard, *American Artillerist's Companion*, 1, pp. 27-28, 31, 32, 33, 40.

64. *Elements of Field Fortification*, p. 154. Lochee failed to deduct for the entrance and embrasures, but justified his method by citing the excess of materials to repair defects that were "likely to arise from accidents of different kinds." Ibid., p. 56; see also Tielke, *Field Engineer*, 1, pp. 202-203. Saucissons used to reinforce the cheeks (insides) of the embrasures were commonly 18 feet in their maximum length. Tousard, *American Artillerist's Companion*, 1, p. 39.

65. Tousard, *American Artillerist's Companion*, 1, pp. 74-75. For details of the work of the fatigue parties, etc., see pp. 25, 26, 27, 33.

66. Tousard, *American Artillerist's Companion*, 1, p. 4; Borresen, "Orientation Report," p. 30.

67. Maps 24F, 29B, 49F; Engineers' Journal, p. 451; Du Bourg, "Diary of a French Officer, 1781," p. 446. Most maps are specific concerning the presence of the four 12-pounders but appear nebulous on the matter of the number of mortars and howitzers. For example, 45F indicates six howitzers but no mortars; 15F and 41F indicate two howitzers; 17F accounts for six cannon, six howitzers, and two mortars, while Map 37F states that four howitzers were present, but no mortars. Colonel Richard Butler claimed that Battery IA held "eight 18 and 12 pounders, two 10 inch mortars, and two 8 inch howitzers." "General Richard Butler's Journal," p. 108. Such differences might account for the shifting of ordnance in accordance with need at various points on the parallel. This explanation does not seem plausible, however, when applied to this relatively isolated battery on the extreme left of the first parallel.

68. Map 24F.

69. Borresen, "Orientation Report," p. 53.

70. Maps 29B, 34F. References to these officers appear in Heitman, *Historical Register*, pp. 646, 654. Boisloger is also mentioned in Closen, *Revolutionary Journal*, p. 146.

71. Maps 1F, 2F, 6F, 7A, 11F, 18F, 19F, 28A, 29B, 30B, 32F, 33F, 34F, 35F, 37F, 50B, 61F, 62F.

72. Map 29B. The maps are not at all clear regarding the calibers of the mortars in Battery 2A. One map (34F) stated that there were three mortars present in the structure but failed to elaborate. Map 29B, of British origin, is most specific of all on the question.

73. Map 34F.

74. Maps 1F, 24F, 29B, 49F. Several maps depict this battery as having but three cannon: 15F, 16F, 17F, 34F.

75. Maps 17F, 34F; Hatch, "On Reconstructing Earthworks," p. 44.

76. Maps 24F, 29B, 35F, and 49F all show eight mortars. Maps 1F, 2F, 7A, 15F, and 17F show six mortars. Map 7A gives their calibers as being 13 inches each. Maps 19F, 34F, and 62F state that the battery had seven pieces in it. Map 48F reported the structure was occupied by six cannon. Speaking of the entire Grand French Battery, Colonel Richard Butler stated that it contained "12 32-, 24-, and 18-pounders, six 10-inch mortars, and six eight-inch howitzers." "General Richard Butler's Journal," p. 108. The presence of any 32-pounders with the Allies at Yorktown is very doubtful.

77. Maps 24F, 29B, 49F; S. Doc. 322, p. 6; De Verger Journal, in Rice and Brown, *American Campaigns*, p. 140; La Combe, "Journal of the Siege of York," p. 3; Engineers' Journal, p. 451.

78. Map 34F. Closen stated that the officer in charge of this unit was named Chanteclerc. *Revolutionary Journal*, p. 146. More details of the construction and armament of the Grand French Battery may be found in Appendix 4, "The Archaeology of the Grand French Battery Complex."

79. Maps 1F, 2F, 15F, 16F, 17F, 24F, 29B, 35F, 48F, 49F. Map 28A accounts for five cannon in Battery 5A. Map 34F states there were three pieces in the structure.

80. Ibid.

81. Details of Redoubt 6A are best represented in Maps 2F, 11F, 33F, 35F, and 37F.

82. Map 2F.

83. Maps 1F, 2F, 15F, 16F, 17F, 19F, 24F, 29B, 34F, 35F, 48F, 49F.

84. Maps 1F, 2F, 19F, 24F, 28A, 29B, 34F, 35F, 48F, 49F, 62F.

85. Maps 19F, 24F, 28A, 29B, 34F, 49F, 62F.

86. Maps 16F and 17F also show 12 cannon in Battery 8A.

87. Map 34F. Barthelemy is listed in Heitman, *Historical Register*, p. 662.

88. Maps 1F, 2F, 11F, 15F, 17F, 18F, 19F, 25B, 28A, 31F, 32F, 33F, 35F, 37F, 41F, 46F, 48F, 49F, 50B, 62F.

89. Maps 12F, 15F, 34F, 45F, 53F.

90. Map 45F.

91. Map 19F. This colored map depicts the French and American construction in much detail. French construction is red, American blue. The French line clearly extends far to the right, leading to the assumption that the French contribution to establishing the first siege line was greater than heretofore supposed.

92. Maps 11F, 17F, 28A, 33F, 35F, 37F, 48F, 50B.

93. Maps 2F, 15F, 16F, 17F, 18F, 19F, 28A, 31F, 32F, 33F, 34F, 35F, 36F, 37F, 53F, 62F.

94. See Map 19F, as mentioned in note 91.

95. Maps 24F, 49F, and 62F indicate six cannon here. Maps 1F, 2F, 7A, 15F, 16F, 17F, 19F, 28A, 34F, and 48F indicate four cannon. Maps 24F, 29B, and 49F account for seven guns (six 18-pounders; one 24-pounder) and two howitzers in this battery; Gallatin wrote that this battery held five cannon. S. Doc. 322, p. 5. Private Sanderson, evidently speaking of this structure, said that on "the night of the 7th we formd [sic] an Eight Gun

battery for 18 lbrs." "Diary of the March from the Hudson to Yorktown," in Johnston, *Yorktown Campaign*, p. 171.

96. Maps 11F, 25B, 28A, 30B, 33F, 35F, 37F, 49F, 50B.

97. Maps 1F, 2F, 15F, 17F, 41F. Map 48F shows four cannon rather than howitzers in this small battery.

98. Maps 2F, 11F, 33F, 37F.

99. Maps 29B, 35F, and 49F show two mortars were present. Map 7A, an American document, reported that the redoubt contained a battery of four 10-inch mortars.

100. Maps 29B and 49F account for the capacity figures given above. Maps 1F, 2F, and 49F also list a dozen 18-pounders, or cannon, but place no other ordnance in the battery. Maps 15F, 17F, 34F, and 41F represent 10 cannon as being in the structure. Map 28A accounts for seven cannon, two mortars, and two howitzers here, while Map 7A reports that the unit held three 18-pounders, three 24-pounders, two howitzers, and two 10-inch mortars. A British map, 50B, simply states that Battery 13A held "cannon, Howitzers and Mortars"; Gallatin, a Frenchman, reported that the American Grand Battery mounted six cannon and four howitzers. S. Doc. 322, p. 5. Colonel Richard Butler maintained that Battery 13A mounted three 24-pounders, three 18-pounders, two 10-inch mortars, and two eight-inch howitzers. "General Richard Butler's Journal," p. 108. See also Pickering and Upham, *Life of Timothy Pickering*, 1, p. 302.

101. Freeman, *George Washington*, 5, p. 361. A small section of the parallel adjacent to the left side of Redoubt 12A, along with the communications trench leading from the American depot, was excavated during the reconstruction effort of the 1930s. Early in the history of Colonial National Historical Park the superintendent's home was located on the site of Battery 13A. Pitkin, "A Preliminary Study of American Redoubt No. 2," p. 1.

102. Swartwout, "Journal of Barnardus Swartwout," p. 36.

103. *"Wertgetreue Abschrift eines Tagebuchs eines markgrälischen Soldaten."*

104. James, *Journal of Rear-Admiral Bartholomew James*, pp. 120-121. This story is almost certainly false, for the casualty lists of the 43rd Regiment do not evidence any officers killed during the siege. More likely, it was a rumor passed around the British lines and picked up by James.

105. Tilden, "Extracts from the Journal of Lieutenant John Bell Tilden," p. 61; Duncan, "Diary of Captain James Duncan," p. 750; Tilghman, *Memoir of Lieut. Col. Tench Tilghman*, p. 105; Moore, *Life and Services of Gen. Anthony Wayne*, p. 149.

106. Trabue, "Journal of Colonel Daniel Trabue," in Harper, *Colonial Men and Times*, p. 112.

107. "Orderly Book kept during the Siege of Yorktown," pp. 68, 69; Washington, *Writings*, 23, pp. 198-199; Stryker, *New Jersey Continental Line*, pp. 18-19.

108. "Orderly Book kept during the Siege of Yorktown," pp. 74, 75.

109. Ibid. , pp. 71-72; Tilden, "Extracts from the Journal of Lieutenant John Bell Tilden," p. 61; Wayne Journal, p. 81; "Itinerary of the Pennsylvania Line," p. 284; Sanderson, "Diary of the March from the Hudson to Yorktown," in Johnston, *Yorktown Campaign*, p. 171; Cobb, "Before York Town, Virginia," p. 68; Wild, "Journal of

Ebenezer Wild," p. 153; S. Doc. 273, p. 192; Riley, "Founding and Development of Yorktown," p. 289; Wright, "Notes on the Siege of Yorktown," p. 243.

110. "Orderly Book kept during the Siege of Yorktown," pp. 72-73.

111. Rochambeau, *Relation*, p. 5; Closen, *Revolutionary Journal*, p. 145; Deux-Ponts, *My Campaigns in America*, p. 140; Clermont-Crèvecoeur Journal, in Rice and Brown, *American Campaigns*, p. 58; Johnston, *Yorktown Campaign*, p. 136; Wright, "Notes on the Siege of Yorktown," p. 244; Balch, *French in America*, 1, p. 193.

112. Trumbull, "Yorktown, Virginia," p. 336.

113. Feltman, "Journal of Lieut. William Felt," p. 318. Feltman lost his bet, though whether he paid up with the silk stockings is unknown.

114. "General Richard Butler's Journal," p. 108.

115. St. George Tucker, "Journal kept by Col. St. George Tucker," p. 11; *"Wertgetreue Abschrift eines Tagebuchs eines markgräflischen Soldaten."*

116. Callahan, "Henry Knox," p. 162.

117. "Orderly Book for the 2nd Regt. of Artillery, June 10, 1781–Oct. 21, 1781," Lamb Papers, New-York Historical Society, and also quoted in Johnston, *Yorktown Campaign*, p. 137.

118. "Orderly Book for the 2nd Regt. of Artillery, June 10, 1781–Oct. 21, 1781," Lamb Papers, New-York Historical Society.

119. Ibid. In the American wing, a daily rotating duty arrangement was established for field officers commanding in the trenches. Stevens followed Lamb; Lieutenant Colonel Edward Carrington followed Stevens; and Major Sebastian Bauman followed Carrington. Arthur, *End of a Revolution*, p. 131; Johnston, *Yorktown Campaign*, p. 113.

120. Knox to Lincoln, October 8, 1781, Henry Knox Papers (microfilm), Massachusetts Historical Society, Boston, 2, p. 100 (hereafter cited as Henry Knox Papers [MHS]). Knox's expressions of the potentially limited capability of the first parallel batteries to destroy the British works coincided with the views held by siege theorist Tousard: "The fire from them [the first batteries] should be nearly perpendicular to the faces of the works attacked, and at a proper distance; that is to say, from [400] to 550 yards from the covered way: when at a greater distance the shot will often be of no effect." *American Artillerist's Companion*, 1, p. 70. Because the distance from the American sector of the parallel to the British garrison was much greater than that from the French sector, Knox's conclusions were well founded. For all intents and purposes, the French guns could expect more success than the American cannon once the Allied bombardment began. Also, the varying distance of the Allies from the British might account for the relatively light casualties sustained thus far along the first parallel, and especially along the American wing of that line.

Chapter 9: The Guns of October

1. Cobb, "Before York Town, Virginia," p. 68; Wild, "Journal of Ebenezer Wild," p. 153.

2. "Journal of Lieut. William Feltman," p. 318. Knox did not invent the process of firing mortars *en ricochet* from carriages. He probably modified the procedure to his own desires, however, and undoubtedly the particular carriage design employed at Yorktown for his mortars was based on his personal preferences and specifications. Knox had six convertible mortars variously mounted in this fashion at Yorktown. In his papers dealing with the siege, the general made reference to 10 mortars "10-inch with beds besides which six to have spare carriages to be mounted to fire as howitzes." Henry Knox Papers (MHS), 55, p. 130.

3. Popp, *Popp's Journal*, pp. 18-19; Döhla, "Journal of Johann Conrad Döhla," pp. 141-142. These two accounts by participants with the British Army are remarkably similar in their descriptions of the Allied desertions of October 9.

4. Feltman, "Journal of Lieut. William Feltman," p. 318.

5. Thompson, *The British Defenses of Yorktown, 1781*, p. 103; Popp, *Popp's Journal*, p. 18; Döhla, "Journal of Johann Conrad Döhla," p. 141. Colonel Tucker mentioned the passing of a flag from the Allies to the British sometime in the forenoon or afternoon during which the enemy cannonade continued. Tucker gives no reason for the communication. "Journal kept by Col. St. George Tucker," p. 12.

6. Rochambeau, *Relation*, p. 5; Balch, *French in America*, 1, p. 149; S. Doc. 273, p. 192; Tilden, "Extracts from the Journal of Lieutenant John Bell Tilden," p. 61.

7. Lieutenant Jacobus Swartwout, Jr., to Captain Barnardus Swartwout, October 9, 1781, Swartwout Folder, New-York Historical Society.

8. Closen, *Revolutionary Journal*, p. 146.

9. Wild, "Journal of Ebenezer Wild," p. 153.

10. "Orderly Book kept during the Siege of Yorktown," p. 82; S. Doc. 322, p. 7.

11. "Orderly Book kept during the Siege of Yorktown," p. 82. The dimensions of these materials were to match those specified in the Regulations. An earlier order of October 9 specified that the saucissons be "15 or 16 feet long each and 12 Inches diameter and well bound with withs [sic]." Ibid., p. 80.

12. *Orderly Book of the Siege of Yorktown*, p. 32.

13. "Orderly Book kept during the Siege of Yorktown," p. 80.

14. Lallemand, *Treatise on Artillery*, 2, p. 155. See also Scheer and Rankin, *Rebels and Redcoats*, p. 559.

15. Wrote Lafayette's aide-de-camp: "It was originally intended to wait until 80 pieces of cannon and mortars could be brought to operate, but a better acquaintance with circumstances has changed this plan for the number we have at present prepared; these may be about 20." James McHenry to Thomas Sim Lee, October 9, 1781, in McHenry, *Letters of James McHenry*, pp. 67-68. Cornwallis had told his soldiers that the Allies were ill-equipped to harm them greatly "and had only some field pieces." He described the French troops, traditional rivals of Britain, as "raw and unskilled in war," adding that St. Simon's soldiers especially "were nothing better than undisciplined vagabonds, collected in the West Indies, enervated by a hot climate, and would soon be conquered, were it only by the first attacks of the cold weather." Robin, *New Travels through North America*, p. 57.

16. Knox to John Jay, October 21, 1781, and Knox to John Adams, October 21, 1781, Henry Knox Papers (CNHP). See also the Knox correspondence reproduced in *Magazine of American History*, 6 (January, 1881), pp. 49-51.

17. Martin, *Private Yankee Doodle*, p. 233.

18. Clermont-Crèvecoeur Journal, Rice and Brown, *American Campaigns*, p. 59. In the case of the Grand French Battery, it has been suggested that its relatively secure position beyond the range of the enemy's small howitzers, mortars, and muskets, allowed the soldiers to work at a more leisurely pace than if they had been more dangerously exposed to the British artillery. Hatch, "On Reconstructing Earthworks," p. 33.

19. See Maps 7A, 26F, 29B, and 52A for depiction of lines of artillery fire from Structures IA and 2A. Map 29B, a British document, indicates a concentration of mortar fire from Battery 2A exclusively directed against the Fusiliers' Redoubt.

20. This account of the French artillery attack has been composed from data appearing in *"Wertgetreue Abschrift eines Tagebuchs eines markgräflischen Soldaten"*; Ewald, "Diary of the American War," p. 890; Washington, *Diaries*, 2, p. 264; Washington, *Writings*, 23, p. 212; Engineers' Journal, p. 451; *Rivington's Gazette*, November 24, 1781, in Moore, *Diary of the American Revolution*, p. 513; Döhla, "Journal of Johann Conrad Döhla," p. 142; Tilghman, *Memoir of Lieut. Col. Tench Tilghman*, p. 105; "Diary of French naval operations in America," p. 193; De Verger Journal, in Rice and Brown, *American Campaigns*, p. 140; Closen, *Revolutionary Journal*, p. 146; Menonville, "Journal of the Siege of York," p. 284; S. Doc. 322, p. 6; Johnston, *Yorktown Campaign*, p. 138; Freeman, *George Washington*, 5, p. 362; Arthur, *Sieges of Yorktown*, p. 18; and Arthur, *End of a Revolution*, p. 131. Fleming, *Beat the Last Drum*, p. 243, reports that the Americans experienced slight annoyance at Washington's decision to let the French fire first. There is at least one account that states the French under St. Simon tried to storm the Fusiliers' Redoubt but were repulsed by the British stationed there. See Broughton- Mainwaring, Historical Record of the Royal Welch Fusiliers, p. 104. That such an attack occurred at this juncture appears possible, though unlikely. Other sources make no mention of an effort to physically dislodge the defenders of the redoubt at this time.

21. At least two eyewitnesses saw Washington fire the cannon in Battery 13A. Butler, "General Richard Butler's Journal," p. 108, and Thacher, *Military Journal*, p. 274. This somewhat controversial point is further supported by the statement of Colonel Van Cortlandt, who recalled that at the time he had "heard that the gun was fired by the Commander-in-Chief, who was designedly present in the battery for the express purpose of putting the first match." Cortlandt, "Autobiography," p. 294. A somewhat romanticized version of the event appears in Callahan, "Henry Knox," p. 162.

22. Cortlandt, "Autobiography," p. 294.

23. Ibid.; Ewald, "Diary of the American War," pp. 890-91; Graham, *Memoir of General Graham*, p. 60. There is disagreement about the caliber of the gun Washington fired. Most writers presume it was a 24-pounder, the largest cannon in the Allied inventory at Yorktown. For example, see Fleming, *Beat the Last Drum*, p. 243. However, British Captain (later General) Samuel Graham reported the Americans "fired an

18-pound ball into the town as a beginning." Undoubtedly this was the shot dispatched by Washington. *Memoir of General Graham*, p. 60.

24. This according to Washington, whose figures agree substantially with other sources. See Washington, *Diaries*, 2, p. 264; Wayne Journal, p. 81; Duncan, "Diary of Captain James Duncan," p. 750; "Journal of the Siege of York in Virginia by a Chaplain," p. 106. See also the secondary accounts by Johnston, *Yorktown Campaign*, p. 138, and Arthur, *End of a Revolution*, p. 131. This battery was probably not yet filled to capacity with ordnance, and troops likely labored well into the night to bring the structure to full artillery strength.

25. Most accounts mentioned only the French battery, or batteries, at the left opposite the Fusiliers' Redoubt and the American batteries at the right as opening on October 9. Other French units, along with the remaining American battery (9A), seemingly did not open until the next day. Quite possibly, however, the four howitzers and two mortars in the American redoubts (11A and 12A) opened at this time. Frenchman Fersen spoke of "41 mouths of fire" being opened on October 9 against Cornwallis, a figure that seems excessive. Merlant, *Soldiers and Sailors of France*, p. 175. Captain Duncan noted the opening of the American battery (13A), stating that "the enemy's fire was chiefly directed against this battery, and *the others that were nearly finished*" (italics added). "Diary of Captain James Duncan," p. 750.

26. "Itinerary of the Pennsylvania Line," p. 284.

27. "Journal of Barnardus Swartwout," p. 36.

28. "Journal kept by Col. St. George Tucker," p. 12.

29. Quoted in Merlant, *Soldiers and Sailors of France*, p. 175.

30. Cited in Tousard, *American Artillerist's Companion*, 1, p. 306. Sometimes wooden rules were nailed to the platforms to insure a proper direction of fire. Ibid., p. 95.

31. Merlant, *Soldiers and Sailors of France*, p. 175; Isaac Q. Leake, *Memoir of the Life and Times of General John Lamb* (Albany: Joel Munsell, 1850), p. 278; "Siege of York and Gloucester, Virginia," p. 476; Washington, *Writings*, 23, p. 212.

32. Robin, *New Travels through North America*, p. 58. Besides the sources cited above, this account of the American and French action at 5:00 p.m. and after is drawn from Gregory, "Diary of Mathew Gregory at Yorktown, 1781," p. 3; Trumbull, "Yorktown, Virginia," p. 336; Feltman, "Journal of Lieut. William Feltman," p. 318; Moore, *Life and Services of Gen. Anthony Wayne*, p. 149; Deux-Ponts, *My Campaigns in America*, p. 140; Arthur, *Sieges of Yorktown*, p. 18, and Wright, "Notes on the Siege of Yorktown," p. 244; James, *Journal of Rear-Admiral Bartholomew Jones*, p. 121.

33. Lallemand, *Treatise on Artillery*, 2, pp. 148-149.

34. Tousard, *American Artillerist Companion*, 1, p. 130.

35. Wright, "Notes on the Siege of Yorktown," p. 233n. For use in ricochet firing, howitzers were usually pointed at angles of six, 10, or 15 degrees. Above 30 degrees the ricochet capacity of the weapon disappeared. Tousard, *American Artillerist's Companion*, 1, pp. 269-270.

36. Knox to Lincoln, October 8, 1781, Henry Knox Papers (CNHP).

37. See Maps 7A, 26F, 52A.

38. Wright, "Notes on the Siege of Yorktown," pp. 233-34n.

39. See entries in Tousard, *American Artillerist's Companion*, 1, pp. 298-304, 322-28, 330-32).

40. Döhla, "Journal of Johann Conrad Döhla," p. 142.

41. Ewald, "Diary of the American War," p. 891.

42. "General Richard Butler's Journal," p. 108.

43. Denny, *Military Journal*, p. 41.

44. "Abstract of Operations."

45. Ibid.; Swartwout, "Journal of Barnardus Swartwout," p. 36; Ewald, "Diary of the American War," p. 891; Tousard, *American Artillerist's Companion*, 1, p. 99; Freeman, *George Washington*, 5, p. 362.

46. S. Doc. 322, p. 7; La Combe, "Journal of the Siege of York," p. 4.

47. Colonel Charles Dabney to Colonel William Davies, October 10, 1781, in Palmer, *Calendar of Virginia State Papers*, 2, p. 540; Heath, *Heath's Memoirs*, p. 332; *Pennsylvania Packet*, October 23, 1781, in *Magazine of American History*, 6 (January, 1881), p. 43; Tilghman, *Memoir of Lieut. Col. Tench Tilghman*, p. 105; Clermont-Crèvecoeur Journal, in Rice and Brown, *American Campaigns*, p. 59; Duncan, "Diary of Captain James Duncan," p. 750; Washington, *Diaries*, 2, p. 264; Du Bourg, "Diary of a French Officer, 1781," p. 447; Landers, *Yorktown. The Investment of Yorktown*, p 192; Robin, in *New Travels through North America*, p. 57, stated that the Grand French Battery began firing at 7:00 a.m.

48. *My Campaigns in America*, p. 141.

49. Trumbull, "Yorktown, Virginia," p. 336; Barneville, "War Diary, p. 273.

50. Dabney to Davies, October 10, 1781, in Palmer, *Calendar of Virginia State Papers*, 2, p. 540; Du Bourg, "Diary of a French Officer, 1781," p. 447.

51. Borresen, "Orientation Report," p. 31.

52. Map 7A indicates a total of 22 cannon and mortars in the complex, but does not include the number of howitzers present. Map 2F, prepared by d'Aboville, indicates a total of 36 cannon, mortars, and howitzers in the component batteries. See also Borresen, "Orientation Report," p. 33.

53. Borresen, "Orientation Report," pp. 8-9.

54. See Appendix 4, "The Archaeology of the Grand French Battery Complex," for a detailed examination of the conclusions drawn from archaeological examination of the Grand French Battery complex.

55. Maps 7A, 52A, 26F.

56. See Hatch, "On Reconstructing Earthworks," p. 43.

57. Henry Knox Papers (MHS), 55, p. 130. This inventory is perhaps an update of one made by Knox on August 24, at which time he accounted for 23 weapons—three 24-pounders and 20 18-pounders, all iron. At this date, however, Knox stated he had 21 brass (bronze) mortars and howitzers, together with 15 brass field guns varying in caliber from 12-pounders to 6-pounders to 3-pounders, which apparently were not considered in the latter account of heavy siege armaments. The French complement, according to the August statement, numbered 20 24- and 16-pounders, along with 16 heavy mortars and howitzers. The French also had 32 field cannon and four lighter field howitzers. Based on

this August inventory, the Allies at Yorktown had access to a total of 80 pieces of siege artillery and 51 pieces of field artillery. Brooks, *Henry Knox,* pp. 154-155.

58. Swartwout, "Journal of Barnardus Swartwout," p. 36;

59. William S. Smith to Colonel Samuel B. Webb, October 10, 1781, reproduced in *Magazine of American History*, 6 (January, 1881), p 45.

60. Freeman, *George Washington*, 5, pp. 362-363; Blanchard, *Journal*, p. 148; Robin, *New Travels through North America*, p. 57.

61. Fersen, "Journal of Operations," p. 439; Merlant, *Soldiers and Sailors of France*, p. 175.

62. Robin, *New Travels through North America*, p. 57. St. George Tucker, "Journal kept by Col. St. George Tucker," pp. 12-13; Ebenezer Huntington to unknown recipient named Andrew, October 10, 1781, George Bancroft Collection, New York Public Library.

63. Döhla, "Journal of Johann Conrad Döhla," p. 141; Popp, *Popp's Journal*, p. 23.

64. Rochambeau, *Relation*, p. 5; Stevens, *System for the Discipline*, p. 196.

65. Thacher, *Military Journal*, pp. 274-275.

66. Trabue, "Journal of Colonel Daniel Trabue," in Harper, *Colonial Men and Times*, p. 112.

67. Robin, *New Travels through North America*, p. 58. Cornwallis's growing distrust of the Hessians could have stemmed from the inordinate number of desertions from the German units, and especially from the Regiment De Bose. See Popp, *Popp's Journal*, p. 19.

68. *System for the Discipline*, pp. 195, 196.

69. Graham, *Memoir of General Graham*, p. 60.

70. Rochambeau, "War in America," in Weelen, *Rochambeau, Father and Son*, p. 231; Döhla, "Journal of Johann Conrad Döhla," p. 143.

71. Döhla, "Journal of Johann Conrad Döhla," p. 143.

72. Davis, *Campaign that Won America*, p. 222.

73. Döhla, "Journal of Johann Conrad Döhla," p. 143. Several homes in the area of the beach also burned. Extract of a letter appearing in the *Pennsylvania Packet*, October 23, 1781, reproduced in *Magazine of American History*, 6 (January, 1881), p. 43; Popp, *Popp's Journal*, p. 19; *Pennsylvania Packet*, October 23, 1781, reproduced in *Magazine of American History*, 6 (January, 1881), p. 42.

74. "*Wertgetreue Abschrift eines Tagebuchs eines Markgräflischen Soldaten*"; Trabue, "Journal of Colonel Daniel Trabue," in Harper, *Colonial Men and Times*, pp. 115-16.

75. Graham, *Memoir of General Graham*, p. 60; James, *Journal of Rear-Admiral Bartholomew James*, p. 121.

76. For information on British casualties, see Döhla, "Journal of Johann Conrad Döhla," p. 143, and Popp, *Popp's Journal*, p. 19.

77. "Orderly Book kept during the Siege of Yorktown," p. 31; Gregory, "Diary of Mathew Gregory at Yorktown, 1781," p. 4; Shute, "With General Benjamin Lincoln," p. 4; S. Doc. 273, p. 192.

78. Irving, *Life of George Washington*, 4, p. 372; Johnston, *Yorktown Campaign*, p. 139; Freeman, *George Washington*, 5, p 363; Arthur, *End of a Revolution*, p. 132; Davis, *Campaign that Won America*, p. 220; Whitridge, *Rochambeau*, p. 218; Wickwire and Wickwire, *Cornwallis*, p. 377.

79. Gregory, "Diary of Mathew Gregory at Yorktown, 1781," p. 4; Tilden, "Extracts from the Journal of Lieutenant John Bell Tilden," p. 61; Pickering and Upham, *Life of Timothy Pickering*, 1, p. 304; Butler, "General Richard Butler's Journal," pp. 108-9; Fleming, *Beat the Last Drum*, pp. 245-46. Thompson, *The British Defenses of Yorktown, 1781*, pp. 87-88. Local tradition holds that Cornwallis took refuge in a shelter excavated in the cliff near the river's edge and today the site draws many visitors. Historian Benson J. Lossing described the site at about the middle of the 19th century and drew the following conclusions:

> We first descended the river bank and visited the excavation in the marl bluff, known as Cornwallis's Cave. It is square, 12-by-18 feet in size, with a narrow passage leading to a smaller circular excavation on one side. It is almost directly beneath the termination of the trench and breastworks of the British fortifications, which are yet very prominent upon the bank above. Popular tradition says that this excavation was made by order of Cornwallis, and used by him for the purpose of holding councils with his officers in a place of safety during the siege. Taking advantage of this tradition, cupidity has placed a door at the entrance, secured it by lock and key, and demands a Virginia nine piece (12-1/2 cents) entrance fee from the curious. I paid the penalty of curiosity, knowing that I was submitting to imposition, for I was assured, on the authority of an old lady who resided at Yorktown at the time of the siege, that this excavation was made by some of the people wherein to hide their valuables. A house stood directly in front of it, the foundation of which is yet there. The building made the spot still more secluded. A quarter of a mile below, Lord Cornwallis *did* have an excavation in the bank, which was lined with green baize, and used by the general for secret conferences during the siege. No traces of his council chamber are left.

Lossing, *Pictorial Field-Book of the Revolution*, 1, pp. 302-303. For a similar description, see George Washington Parke Custis, *Recollections and Private Memoirs of Washington* (New York: Derby and Jackson, 1860), p. 244.

80. Pickering and Upham, *Life of Timothy Pickering*, 1, p. 304; Butler, "General Richard Butler's Journal," p. 108; St. George Tucker, "Journal kept by Col. St. George Tucker," pp. 14-15; Fleming, *Beat the Last Drum*, p. 219; Whitridge, *Rochambeau*, p. 219. Clinton's quote in Davis, *Campaign that Won America*, p. 223. One of the couriers, Major Charles Cochrane, met a tragic end two days after his arrival. Appointed acting aide-de-camp to Cornwallis, the zealous officer undertook to fire a cannon *en ricochet* from a battery in the hornwork. As he peered across the rampart to see the effect of his shot, an Allied cannonball tore off his head. Graham, *Memoir of General Graham*, p. 60.

81. Whitridge, *Rochambeau*, p. 219.

82. Cobb, "Before York Town, Virginia," p. 68; Feltman, "Journal of Lieut. William Feltman," p. 318.

83. Washington, *Writings*, 23, p. 205. For a breakdown of materials to be provided by each unit, and for the dimensions of same, see ibid. See also "Orderly Book kept during the Siege of Yorktown," pp. 83-84.

84. De Verger Journal, in Rice and Brown, *American Campaigns*, p. 140; Menonville, "Journal of the Siege of York," p. 285; D'Ancteville, "Journal of the Chesapeake Campaign," p. 18; S. Doe. 322, p. 7; Balch, *French in America*, 1, pp. 194-95.

85. Borresen, "Orientation Report," p. 27; Blanchard, *Journal*, p. 148, mentions the lingering Allied fear that Cornwallis would try to flee Yorktown, though most likely via Gloucester and not up the Virginia peninsula along the York River.

86. Baron Closen said that the flatboats numbered 18 and that Choisy captured one barge after its occupants had fled to Gloucester. It contained a 4-pounder cannon. *Revolutionary Journal*, p. 146. Available accounts of this maneuver vary considerably. See Du Bourg, "Diary of a French Officer, 1781," p. 447; Deux-Ponts, *My Campaigns in America*, p. 141; Balch, *French in America*, 1, p. 194; Stevens, "Allies at Yorktown, 1781," p. 22; Freeman, *George Washington*, 5, p. 362; Arthur, *End of a Revolution*, p.134; Fleming, *Beat the Last Drum*, pp. 246-247. That night, a French officer noted yet another effort by the British to send soldiers across the York on barges, "but M. de Choisy had been forewarned and was on his guard." Clermont-Crèvecoeur Journal, in Rice and Brown, *American Campaigns*, p. 59.

87. D'Ancteville, "Journal of the Chesapeake Campaign," p. 19. Evidently the original plan was to open a second line October 12, or at the latest October 13. Colonel Charles Dabney to Colonel William Davies, October 10, 1781, in Palmer, *Calendar of Virginia State Papers*, 2, p. 540.

88. McHenry, *Letters of James McHenry*, p. 68.

89. Clermont-Crèvecoeur Journal, in Rice and Brown, *American Campaigns*, p. 59; Wright, "Notes on the Siege of Yorktown, p. 234; Straith, *Treatise on Fortification and Artillery*, 1, p. 138.

90. Vauban, *Manual of Siegecraft and Fortification*, p. 49; Tousard, *American Artillerist's Companion*, 1, pp. 513-514.

91. Tousard, *American Artillerist's Companion*, 1, p. 511.

92. Vauban, *Manual of Siegecraft and Fortification*, p. 49.

93. Haynes, "Siege of Yorktown," p. 8; Borresen, "Orientation Report," pp. 27, 33. The 24-pounders replaced two 12-pounders in the battery. Closen, *Revolutionary Journal*, p. 146.

94. Le Blond, *Treatise of Artillery*, p. 33.

95. Tousard, *American Artillerist's Companion*, 1, p. 100; 2, p. 253; Wright, "Notes on the Siege of Yorktown," p. 244n.

96. This account of the hot shot operation the night of October 10 incorporates data from Pickering and Upham, *Life of Timothy Pickering*, 1, pp. 302-303; Saint-Exupery, "War Diary," p. 111; Smith, "Diary of Jacob Smith," p. 263; Barneville, "War Diary," p. 273; S. Doc. 322, p. 8; Clermont-Crèvecoeur Journal, in Rice and Brown, *American*

Campaigns, pp. 58-59; Washington to de Grasse, October 11, 1781, in *Writings*, 23, pp. 208-209; Du Bourg, "Diary of a French Officer, 1781," pp. 446-447; Ewald, "Diary of the American War," p. 891; Engineers' Journal, p. 451; La Combe, "Journal of the Siege of York," p. 4; Edward Hand to Jasper Yeates, October 12, 1781, in "Edward Hand to Jasper Yeates on the Siege of Yorktown in 1781," *Bulletin of the New York Public Library*, 6 (August, 1902), p. 286, and Freeman, *George Washington*, 5, p. 365. Exactly how much of the *Charon*'s armament had been stripped from her by this time is not clear. In the 1930s, the firm of Francis Bannerman Sons, New York City, offered for sale a piece "recovered by divers at the Yorktown Centennial [in 1881] after 100 years submersion" in York River. The Bannerman company advertised that "it will take $1000 to tempt us to part with it." John D. Babington, "Known 'Yorktown' guns, siege and field, not in Colonial National Historical Park," memorandum, dated March 22, 1955, CNHP, Yorktown, Virginia, pp. 4-5.

97. Duncan, "Diary of Captain James Duncan," p. 751.

98. Custis, *Recollections and Private Memoirs of Washington*, p. 245.

99. *Mercure de France*, November 1781, quoted in Balch, *French in America*, 1, p. 194n.

100. Thacher, *Military Journal*, pp. 274-725; "Siege of York and Gloucester, Virginia," p. 476. In 1934 and 1935, underwater archeology conducted in the York River off Yorktown and Gloucester revealed several vessels sunk during the siege. Two were found close together and each measured between 60 and 80 feet long. Another, found close to the Gloucester side, could have been the wreck of the *Charon*. Salvage operations disclosed evidence of three swivel guns, plus some bar-shot, broken glass, and crockery pieces—all fire resistant items. Examiners concluded that the craft had probably been burned. Ferguson, *Salvaging Revolutionary Relics from the York River*, pp. 9, 10.

101. Feltman, "Journal of Lieut. William Feltman," p. 318; Washington, *Writings*, 23, p. 213; *Pennsylvania Packet*, October 23, 1781, reproduced in *Magazine of American History*, 6 (January, 1881), p. 42; "Abstract of Operations"; "Diary of French naval operations in America," p. 194.

102. James, *Journal of Rear-Admiral Bartholomew James*, p. 122.

103. John Graves Simcoe, *Military Journal: A History of the Operations of a Partisan Corps called the Queen's Rangers, commanded by Lieut.-col. J. G. Simcoe, during the War of the Revolution* (New York, 1844), pp. 250-51.

Chapter 10: The Earth Trembles

1. Washington to de Grasse, October 11, 1781, in *Writings*, 23, p. 209.

2. Ibid.

3. Washington, *Diaries*, 2, p. 265.

4. Washington, *Writings*, 23, p. 209.

5. S. Doc. 318, p. 49; James, *Journal of Rear-Admiral Bartholomew James*, p. 122.

6. Pickering and Upham, *Life of Timothy Pickering*, 1, p. 305.

7. Arthur, *End of a Revolution*, p. 133. Emory G. Evans, *Thomas Nelson of Yorktown: Revolutionary Virginian* (Williamsburg: Colonial Williamsburg Foundation, 1975), places the bombardment on October 9, 1781. Some doubt the bombardment took place at all.

8. For notices of the role of Allied artillery on October 11, see Barneville, "War Diary," p. 274; Washington, *Writings*, 23, p. 210; Henry Lee, *Memoirs of the War*, pp. 499-500. The artillery fire without cessation followed theoretical precepts of the time. Stated Tousard: "Always beware of the apparent tranquillity of the enemy, and do not cease to batter a work because the firing from it has discontinued. It is as essential to prevent them from making repairs, as to put a stop to their first efforts." *American Artillerist's Companion*, 1, p. 94.

9. Closen, *Revolutionary Journal*, p. 146; Tilghman, *Memoir of Lieut. Col. Tench Tilghman*, p. 105. Washington reported that "the French opened two other batteries on the left of the parallel, each consisting of three 24-pounders." *Diaries*, 2, p. 265. A French account speaks of "two new batteries of eight 24-pounders" opening on the 11th, along with "another of six mortars." "Diary of French naval operations in America," p. 194.

10. Döhla, "Journal of Johann Conrad Döhla," pp. 143-44.

11. Ibid., p. 144.

12. Cobb, "Before York Town, Virginia," p. 68; Du Bourg, "Diary of a French Officer, 1781," p. 447; S. Doc. 322, p. 8; James, *Journal of Rear Admiral Bartholomew James*, p. 123.

13. Clermont-Crèvecoeur Journal, in Rice and Brown, *American Campaigns*, p. 59.

14. Pickering and Upham, *Life of Timothy Pickering*, 1, p. 305.

15. See, for example, David Ross to Robert Crew, October 11, 1781, in Palmer, *Calendar of Virginia State Papers*, 2, pp. 544, 545.

16. "Orderly Book kept during the Siege of Yorktown," pp. 88-91.

17. Ibid., pp. 91-92.

18. Wild, "Journal of Ebenezer Wild," p. 153. Orders were given that all fascines and saucissons be firmly bound. "All that are not fit for use will be rejected at the deposit of the trenches, and the Corps in default, to make up the deficiency without loss of time." "Orderly Book kept during the Siege of Yorktown," p. 86.

19. Balch, *French in America*, 1, p. 195.

20. "Orderly Book kept during the Siege of Yorktown," p. 87; *Orderly Book of the Siege of Yorktown*, pp. 33, 34; Wild, "Journal of Ebenezer Wild," p. 153; Johnston, *Yorktown Campaign*, p. 141n; Palmer, *General Von Steuben*, p. 291-292. The conversational anecdote is based upon the story of the same facts set forth in ibid., 291. Von Steuben may have been mistaken concerning the date and Baron de Viomenil's role, because that officer did not command in the French sector on October 11.

21. Wild, "Journal of Ebenezer Wild," p. 153.

22. Wright, "Notes on the Siege of Yorktown," p. 244; Matloff, *American Military History*, p. 97; Scheer and Rankin, *Rebels and Redcoats*, p. 561.

23. Scheer and Rankin, *Rebels and Redcoats*, p. 561; Feltman, "Journal of Lieut. William Feltman," p. 319; Wright, "Notes on the Siege of Yorktown," p. 244; Arthur, *Sieges of Yorktown*, p. 19.

24. It is possible, but unlikely given the exposed location, that the American zigzag, which lay almost exactly at the center of the parallel as completed after the capture of Redoubts 9 and 10, was prepared earlier, perhaps at the time the French were preparing theirs on the left. It is also possible von Steuben's soldiers moved forward after dark through the French zigzag sap and were placed in their digging positions by the engineers. It seems reasonable, however, to presume that the advance was made over the low ground extending north from the French depot ravine and in which the American approach trench was excavated. See de Verger Journal, in Rice and Brown, *American Campaigns*, p. 141. French work began at 8:00 p.m. The inference is that the Americans started also at that time. Deux-Ponts, *My Campaigns in America*, p. 141.

25. Menonville, "Journal of the Siege of York," p. 285.

26. Straith, *Treatise on Fortification and Artillery*, 1, p. 210.

27. Lallemand, *Treatise on Artillery*, 2, p. 157.

28. "Journal of Lieut. William Feltman," p. 319.

29. Wild, "Journal of Ebenezer Wild," p. 153; S. Doc. 318, p. 49; S. Doc. 273, p. 194; Wright, "Notes on the Siege of Yorktown," p. 245; Freeman, *George Washington*, 5, p. 366.

30. Butler, "General Richard Butler's Journal," p. 109; Moore, *Life and Services of Gen. Anthony Wayne*, p. 150.

31. Swartwout, "Journal of Barnardus Swartwout," p. 36.

32. Trumbull, "Yorktown, Virginia," p. 336.

33. S. Doc. 273, p. 193; Arthur, *End of a Revolution*, p. 134.

34. Engineers' Journal, pp. 451-452; La Combe, "Journal of the Siege of York," p. 4; Closen, *Revolutionary Journal*, p. 147; S. Doc. 322, pp. 8-9.

35. "*Wergetreue Abschrift eines Tagebuchs eines markgräflischen Soldaten*"; "Diary of the American War," p. 892; "War in America," in Weelen, *Rochambeau, Father and Son*, p. 232. See also "Diary of French naval operations in America," p. 195, for an almost verbatim copy of this remark.

36. Rochambeau, Relation, p. 6.

37. D'Ancteville, "Journal of the Chesapeake Campaign," p. 19; Robin stated that the French "began to demolish our old batteries to construct new ones" the night of the 11th. *New Travels through North America*, p. 59.

38. Robin, *New Travels through North America*, p. 59; Stone, *Our French Allies*, pp. 431-432, attributed this quotation to the Chevalier de Chastellux.

39. Tarleton, *History of the Campaigns*, p. 396; Scheer and Rankin, *Rebels and Redcoats*, p. 561.

40. "Siege of York and Gloucester, Virginia," p. 476.

41. Deux-Ponts, *My Campaigns in America*, p. 142; Wright, "Notes on the Siege of Yorktown," p. 245; S. Doc. 273, p. 194.

42. S. Doc. 273, p. 141; Johnston, *Yorktown Campaign*, p. 336.

43. James, *Journal of Rear-Admiral Bartholomew James*, pp. 122-123.

44. Washington to General William Heath, October 12, 1781, in *Writings*, 23, p. 214.

45. *Diaries*, 2, p. 265.

46. Swartwout, "Journal of Barnardus Swartwout," p. 36; "Abstract of Operations"; St. George Tucker, "Journal kept by Col. St. George Tucker," p. 15; Duncan, "Diary of Captain James Duncan," p. 751; Arthur, *End of a Revolution*, p. 135.

47. "Journal of the Siege of York in Virginia by a Chaplain," p. 106; James, *Journal of Rear-Admiral Bartholomew James*, p. 123; Butler, "General Richard Butler's Journal," p. 109.

48. James, *Journal of Rear-Admiral Bartholomew James*, p. 124.

49. De Verger Journal, in Rice and Brown, *American Campaigns*, p. 141; Menonville, "Journal of the Siege of York," p. 285; S. Doc. 322, p. 9.

50. "Report of Ammunition expended in the different Batteries, the 11th F 12th Oct 1781," Henry Knox Papers (MHS), 7, p. 107.

51. Quoted in Balch, *French in America*, 1, p.197; Whitridge, *Rochambeau*, p. 220, places this incident on October 13. The episode is detailed in Dumas, *Memoirs of His Own Time*, pp. 66-67n.

52. Arthur, *Sieges of Yorktown*, pp. 19, 20.

53. Quoted in Freeman, *George Washington*, 5, p. 368.

54. Lincoln to Mrs. Lincoln, October 12, 1781, Benjamin Lincoln Papers, Massachusetts Historical Society.

55. *Orderly Book of the Siege of Yorktown*, p. 34; Feltman, "Journal of Lieut. William Feltman," p. 319; Tilden, "Extracts from the Journal of Lieutenant John Bell Tilden," p. 62; Samuel Tallmadge, *Orderly Books of the Fourth New York Regiment, 1778-1780, The Second New York Regiment, 1780-1783, by Samuel Tallmadge and others with Diaries of Samuel Tallmadge, 1780-1782 and John Barr, 1779-1782*, ed. Almon W. Lauber (Albany: University of the State of New York, 1932), p. 762; Wright, "Notes on the Siege of Yorktown," p. 245.

56. *Orderly Book of the Siege of Yorktown*, p. 37; "Orderly Book kept during the Siege of Yorktown," p. 93; Wild, "Journal of Ebenezer Wild," pp. 153-154; Gregory, "Diary of Mathew Gregory at Yorktown, 1781," p. 4; Wright, "Notes on the Siege of Yorktown," p. 245.

57. De Verger Journal, in Rice and Brown, *American Campaigns*, p. 141; Deux-Ponts, *My Campaigns in America*, p. 142; Balch, *French in America*, 1, p. 195.

58. Hand, "Edward Hand to Jasper Yeates on the Siege of Yorktown in 1781," p. 286. A slight variation of this quotation appears in Hand to Jasper Yeates, October 12, 1781, Edward Hand Papers, New York Public Library, p. 262.

59. Du Bourg, "Diary of a French Officer, 1781," p. 447; La Combe, "Journal of the Siege of York," p. 4; S. Doc. 322, p. 10; Closen, *Revolutionary Journal*, p. 148; Engineers' Journal, p. 452; Rochambeau, *Relation*, p. 6; Duncan, "Diary of Captain James Duncan," p. 751; Trumbull, "Yorktown, Virginia," p. 336; Wright, "Notes on the Siege of Yorktown," pp. 234, 245.

60. *American Artillerist's Companion*, 1, p. 77.

61. Menonville, "Journal of the Siege of York," p. 286. See also de Verger Journal, in Rice and Brown, *American Campaigns*, p. 59, which says that "a mortar battery containing 10 mortars and two 8-inch howitzers was placed in the center [of the French sector?] to deliver shells and bombs to all the enemy works." D'Ancteville mentioned

that one of the redoubts (probably 2B) had been taken over as a battery emplacement, possibly for mortars. "Journal of the Chesapeake Campaign," p. 20. This seems to have been but a temporary expedient to cover work on the other batteries. The mortars and howitzers were employed on a more sustained basis in Battery 1B.

62. Hand, "Edward Hand to Jasper Yeates on the Siege of Yorktown in 1781," p. 286.

63. Butler, "General Richard Butler's Journal," p. 109; Palmer, *Calendar of Virginia State Papers*, 2, p. 548; Arthur, *Sieges of Yorktown*, p. 20.

64. Döhla, "Journal of Johann Conrad Döhla," p. 145.

65. The contribution from each of the American artillery units of the first parallel is as follows: American Grand Battery (13A): 24 10-inch shells; 54 eight-inch shells; 36 five-1/2-inch shells; 95 24-pounder rounds; 95 18-pounder rounds. Mortar Battery (by Redoubt 12A): 95 10-inch shells; Left Battery (10A): 160 18-pounder rounds. Still on hand in Battery 13A on October 13 were 223 24-pounder cartridges, 1,012 18-pounder cartridges, 467 10-inch mortar cartridges, 31 8-inch howitzer cartridges, 200 5-1/2-inch howitzer cartridges, 140 10-inch flannel cartridges, 89 5-1/2-inch shells, 59 8-inch shells, and 129 10-inch shells, plus auxiliary supplies of 54 portfires, 3 hanks of slow match, and 200 priming tubes. Battery 10A contained 240 unfired rounds for 18-pounders. "Report of ordnance stores Expended, and on hand at the Batteries . . . from the 12 to the 13 of Octr Inst.," Henry Knox Papers (MHS), 7, p. 110.

66. Deux-Ponts, *My Campaigns in America*, p. 142; Robin, *New Travels through North America*, p. 60; Sullivan, "Documentary Study of British Redoubt No. 10," pp. 1, 7. According to Borresen, "the terrain between these two redoubts and the [second] American line did not adapt itself to the construction of batteries. Hence, the decision was made to attempt to capture both by assault." "Orientation Report," p. 40.

67. Account of Captain Stephen Olney, in Williams, *Biography of Revolutionary Heroes*, pp. 275-276.

68. Feltman, "Journal of Lieut. William Feltman," p. 320.

69. "Orderly Book kept during the Siege of Yorktown," pp. 101-102.

70. Ibid., pp. 78-79; Captain John Pryor to Governor Nelson, October 1, 1781, in Palmer, *Calendar of Virginia State Papers*, 2, p. 514; Pryor to Colonel William Davies, October 6, 1781, in ibid., p. 529.

71. "Orderly Book kept during the Siege of Yorktown," pp. 69-70; *New York Times*, October 23, 1881.

72. *Orderly Book of the Siege of Yorktown*, pp. 7-38; Washington, *Writings*, 23, p. 217.

73. "Orderly Book, Regimental Orders (2nd Artillery), Aug. 4 to Oct. 13, 1, p. 781," Lamb Papers, New-York Historical Society.

74. M. de Tarle to Governor Nelson, October , 1781, in Palmer, *Calendar of Virginia State Papers*, 2, p. 517.

75. Nelson to the Delegates in Congress from Virginia, October 5, 1781, in ibid., p. 527. See also Johnston, *Yorktown Campaign*, p. 140.

76. Colonel Charles Dabney to Colonel William Davies, October 10, 1781, in Palmer, *Calendar of Virginia State Papers*, 2, p. 540.

77. Keim, *Rochambeau: A Commemoration*, p. 447. Washington, *Writings*, 23, pp. 220-221; Stevens, "Allies at Yorktown, 1781," p. 22.

78. Hand to Jasper Yeates, October 12, 1781, in "Edward Hand to Jasper Yeates on the Siege of Yorktown in 1781," p. 286.

79. *Orderly Book of the Siege of Yorktown*, p. 37.

80. Menonville, "Journal of the Siege of York," p. 286; Closen, *Revolutionary Journal*, p. 148; De Verger Journal, in Rice and Brown, *American Campaigns*, p. 141; S. Doc. 322, p. 10; Washington, *Diaries*, , p. 266; Du Bourg, "Diary of a French Officer, 1781," p. 195.

81. Wild, "Journal of Ebenezer Wild," p. 154.

82. Barneville, "War Diary," p. 274; Menonville, "Journal of the Siege of York," p. 286. Diaries, 2, p. 266; Clermont-Crèvecoeur Journal, in Rice and Brown, *American Campaigns*, p. 59; Rochambeau, *Relation*, p. 6.

83. Clermont-Crèvecoeur Journal, in Rice and Brown, *American Campaigns*, p. 59.

84. Du Bourg, "Diary of a French Officer, 1781," p. 195.

85. "Journal of the Chesapeake Campaign," p. 19.

86. Wild, "Journal of Ebenezer Wild," p. 154; Duncan, "Diary of Captain James Duncan," p. 751.

87. Duncan, "Diary of Captain James Duncan," p. 751.

88. Ibid., p. 752; St. George Tucker, "Journal kept by Col. St. George Tucker," p. 16; Gregory, "Diary of Mathew Gregory at Yorktown, 1781," p. 4.

Chapter 11: Night of Heroes

1. Davis, "Yorktown Campaign, p. 304; "Itinerary of the Pennsylvania Line," p. 285.

2. Feltman, "Journal of Lieut. William Feltman," p. 320.

3. Washington, *Diaries*, 2, pp. 266-267.

4. St. George Tucker, "Journal kept by Col. St. George Tucker," p. 16.

5. *Orderly Book of the Siege of Yorktown*, p. 37; Duncan, of Captain James Duncan," p. 752; Butler, "General Richard Butler's Journal," p. 109.

6. "Diary of French naval operations in America," p. 196; Closen, *Revolutionary Journal*, p. 148. Other French auxiliary forces came from the Saintonge, Agenois, and Soissonois units. Balch, *French in America*, 1, p. 197.

7. Washington, *Diaries*, 2, p. 266; Cobb, "Before York Town, Virginia," p. 68; S. Doc., p. 273; Freeman, *George Washington*, 5, p. 368.

8. "Retn of stores expended at the different Batteries, on the 13th & 14th Instant," Henry Knox Papers (MHS), 7, p. 111. According to Knox, the following ammunition was expended: American Grand Battery (13A): 53 10-inch shells; 100 8-inch shells; 50 5-inch shells; 96 24-pounder rounds; 96 18-pounder rounds; Mortar Battery (by Redoubt 12A): 69 10-inch shells; Left Battery (l0A): 200 18-pounder rounds.

9. Freeman, *George Washington*, 5, p. 368.

10. Denny, *Military Journal*, p. 42; Arthur, *End of a Revolution*, p. 136. Thompson, *The British Defenses of Yorktown, 1781*, puts the number at 45; Ward, *War of the Revolution*, vol. 2, p. 892, claims 70; Ewald, "Diary of the American War," p. 897. Editor Tustin names Major James Campell as the commander inside Redoubt No. 10.

11. Gaston Marie Leonard Maussion de la Bastie to unknown recipient, November 4, 1781, in Princess Radziwill, trans., *They Knew the Washington: Letters from a French Soldier with Lafayette and from His Family in Virginia* (Indianapolis: Bobbs-Merrill Company, 1926), p. 103; Bonsal, *Cause of Liberty*, p. 154.

12. Clermont-Crèvecoeur Journal, in Rice and Brown, *American Campaigns*, p. 60; Account of Captain Stephen Olney, in Williams, *Biography of Revolutionary Heroes*, p. 276. For more on the racial make-up of the Rhode Island strike force that participated in the attack against Redoubt 10, see Sidney Kaplan and Emma Nogrady Kaplan, *The Black Presence in the Era of the American Revolution* (Amherst: University of Massachusettst, 1989), pp. 34-35, 64-65, Benjamin Quarles, *The Negro in the American Revolution* (Chapel Hill: University of North Carolina, 1961), pp. 79-82, *et. passim.*, and Lorenzo J. Greene, "Some Observations on the Black Regiment of Rhode Island in the American Revolution," *Journal of Negro History*, 27 (June, 1952), pp. 142-172.

13. Account of Captain Stephen Olney, in Williams, *Biography of Revolutionary Heroes*, p. 276. That Washington so readily acquiesced in the demands of the young officer is evidence of the commander's magnanimity. Hamilton had recently been extremely critical of his chief and Washington had good reason to refuse him his wish. The entire episode is detailed in Miller, *Alexander Hamilton and the Growth of the New Nation*, pp. 77-78.

14. Lauzun, "Narrative of the Duke de Lauzun," p. 53; Wright, "Notes on the Siege of Yorktown," p. 246; Mention of the diversionary attacks appears in Trumbull, "Yorktown, Virginia," pp. 336-337; *"Wertgetreue Abschrift eines Tagebuchs eines markgräflischen Soldaten"*; Du Bourg, "Diary of a French Officer, 1781," p. 447; Freeman, *George Washington*, 5, p. 370; Tilghman, *Memoir of Lieut. Col. Tench Tilghman*, p. 106; and St. George Tucker, "Journal kept by Col. St. George Tucker," p. 17; Menonville, "Journal of the Siege of York," p. 287. *Revolutionary Journal*, pp. 149-150; Thompson, *The British Defenses of Yorktown, 1781*, pp. 113-114, observes, "One must conclude that the attack was real, if frustrated." Ibid., p. 114.

15. Account of Captain Stephen Olney, in Williams, *Biography of Revolutionary Heroes*, p. 276.

16. Deux-Ponts claims the signal consisted of six consecutive shells fired from a battery, although some sources claim it was but one, which does not seem credible since an accidental firing could have triggered the attack. *My Campaigns in America*, p. 144.

17. Ebenezer Wild wrote that "we advanced from the battery on our right (in one column) to the redoubt on the enemys left." Journal of Ebenezer Wild," p. 154.

18. Capt. Stephen Olney, in Williams, *Biography of Revolutionary Heroes*, p. 276.

19. Ibid., pp. 276-278; Robert A. Selig, "Storming the Redoubts," *Military History Quarterly* (vol. 8, No. 1, 1995), p. 24. The espontoon Olney carried was a device similar to a half pike and about three feet long with a pointed blade. Espontoons were carried in action by colonels of the various corps, and company captains always used them. Thomas

Wilhelm, *A Military Dictionary and Gazetteer* (Philadelphia: L. R. Hamersly and Company, 1881), p. 151.

20. Account of Captain Stephen Olney, in Williams, *Biography of Revolutionary Heroes*, p. 276. Brown did not receive the first such award, however. That honor went to Sergeant Elijah Churchill, 2nd Regiment, Light Dragoons, who won the badge for meritorious service against Fort St. George and Fort Stongo on Long Island. See Theophilus F. Rodenbough, ed., *Uncle Sam's Medal of Honor, 1861-1886* (New York: G. P. Putnam's Sons, 1886), p. 405.

21. There was much discussion among the ranks of the Americans that the British prisoners had fallen to their knees in a cowardly fashion and begged Hamilton's troops not to kill them. Much was made of the kind treatment accorded the British prisoners compared to the wanton slaughter of Americans on September 6, 1781, at Fort Griswold (Groton), Connecticut, an event still fresh in the minds of the troops at Yorktown. In that affair, a lieutenant colonel of Connecticut militia surrendered his sword, only to have it run through him by enemy soldiers under General Benedict Arnold. "This Conduct [of the British prisoners at Yorktown] contrasted with English humanity displayed at Groton," penned one critic, "must stamp their Character . . . with a still deeper dye." Elias Boudinot to Lewis Pintard, October 21, 1781, Boudinot Papers, Historical Society of Pennsylvania; See also Marshall, *Life of George Washington*, 4, p. 543n. An observer of the attack against Redoubt 10 wrote: "One circumstance merits remark, that the British officers to a man threw themselves on their knees to beg for mercy, and it was generously granted them, tho' our Troops had before the attack Orders not to spare a man of them." Aedamus Burke to Arthur Middleton, October 16, 1781, in "Correspondence of Arthur Middleton," *South Carolina Historical and Genealogical Magazine*, 26 (October, 1925), p. 186. The recent and seemingly treacherous death of Colonel Scammell figured in the sense of outrage felt by some of the Americans faced with their first enemy prisoners taken in combat. Thacher, *Military Journal*, pp. 275-276; Irving, *Life of George Washington*, 4, p. 376. The inimitable Parson M. L. Weems described the taking of the redoubt with his peculiar flourish and customary unreliability: "The British called for quarters: A voice was heard, 'Remember poor Scammell!'—'Remember, gentlemen, you are Americans!' was rejoined by the commander: and instantly the points of the American bayonets were thrown up towards heaven!" *The Life of George Washington* (Philadelphia: M. Carey and Son, 1818), p. 115; Account of Captain Stephen Olney, in Williams, *Biography of Revolutionary Heroes*, p. 279. A "caul," as described by Olney, is a peritoneal fold passing from the stomach to the transverse colon, hanging like an apron in front of the intestines.

22. Hamilton's report of October 15, 1781, in Alexander Hamilton, *The Works of Alexander Hamilton*, ed. John C. Hamilton, 7 vols. (New York: Charles S. Francis and Company, 1851), pp. 270-273 (includes Hamilton's return for killed and wounded in the attack on Redoubt 10). Besides the sources cited above, this account of the American drive is prepared from data contained in Washington, *Diaries*, 2, pp. 266-267; Henry Knox Papers (MHS), 7, p. 112; St. George Tucker, "Journal kept by Col. St. George Tucker," pp. 17-18; Tilghman, *Memoirs of Lieut. Col. Tench Tilghman*, pp. 105-106; Pickering and Upham, *Life of Timothy Pickering*, 1, p. 307; Shute, "With General

Benjamin Lincoln," p. 5; Feltman, "Journal of Lieut. William Feltman," p. 320; Wild, "Journal of Ebenezer Wild," p. 154; Duncan, "Diary of Captain James Duncan," p. .752; Martin, *Private Yankee Doodle*, p. 234; Closen, *Revolutionary Journal*, p. 149; Döhla, "Journal of Johann Conrad Döhla," p. 145; Moore, *Life. and Services of Gen. Anthony Wayne*, p. 150; Freeman, *George Washington*, 5, p. 371; Arthur, *Sieges of Yorktown*, pp. 21-22; S. Doe. 273, pp. 197, 199; Sullivan, "Documentary Study of British Redoubt No. 10," pp. 3-4, 5; and Johnston, *Yorktown Campaign*, pp. 143-147; "Narrative of Asa Redington," pp. 13-14.

23. The principal criticism came from Muhlenberg's biographer and grand-nephew, Henry A. Muhlenberg, in *The Life of Major-General Peter Muhlenberg of the Revolutionary Army* (Philadelphia: Carey and Hart, 1849), p. 273. See also Broadus Mitchell, *Alexander Hamilton: Youth to Maturity, 1755-1788* (New York: The Macmillan Company, 1957), p. 258.

24. Thacher, *Military Journal*, p. 276n; Van Cortlandt, "Autobiography," p. 294; Davis, *Campaign that Won America*, p. 229. During Lafayette's visit to the United States in 1824, the citizens of Yorktown erected on the site of Redoubt 10 a triumphal arch in commemoration of the deed performed there 43 years before. Under the arch the marquis delivered a stirring address in recognition of the patriotism displayed by the troops under his command. Johnston, *Yorktown Campaign*, p. 145.

25. Georg Daniel Flohr's account is drawn from Selig, "Storming the Redoubts." The exact spot where the French command departed the trenches has been a matter of dispute. Most secondary renditions (e.g., Johnston, *Yorktown Campaign*) have avoided the question altogether except perhaps for the inclusion of maps barely suggestive of the departure of Deux-Ponts's command from a location along the first parallel. Closen seemed to suggest the French assault party could have departed either from somewhere on the first parallel or at the end of the completed part of the second. In any event, he was not clear on the issue, stating that the French "debouched in absolute silence through the communications trench almost opposite the first of the advanced redoubts." *Revolutionary Journal*, p. 148. Thor Borresen accepted the view that Deux-Ponts left the second parallel in the area of Rcdoubt 7B ("Orientation Report," p. 37), a view that is entirely plausible. Deux-Ponts himself failed to clarify the matter, reporting only that de Viomenil "ordered me at once to form my battalion, and to lead it to that part of the trenches nearest to which we ought to come out." *My Campaigns in America*, p. 143. Somewhat more certain is the journal of Gaspard de Gallatin, published in S. Doc. 322, which states on p. 11 that the French troops "issued by the right flank of the American battery of five cannon." Inasmuch as Battery 8B had not yet been completed and had yet to receive its ordnance complement, Gallatin could only have been referring to Battery 10A in the first parallel. It thus seems most likely Deux-Ponts's soldiers moved out from that point rather than from the second parallel.

26. Deux-Ponts, *My Campaigns in America*, p. 143.

27. This account of the French assault has been synthesized from data appearing in ibid., pp. 142-49, 157-61 (which contains de Viomenil's report to Rochambeau, October 14-15, 1781); Clermont-Crèvecoeur Journal, in Rice and Brown, *American Campaigns*, p. 60; Rochambeau, *Relation*, pp. 6-7; S. Doc. 322, pp. 11-13; Closen, *Revolutionary*

Journal, pp. 148-149; Du Bourg, "Diary of a French Officer, 1781," p. 447; Blanchard, *Journal,* pp. 149-150; Menonville, "Journal of the Siege of York," pp. 286-287; Dumas, *Memoirs of His Own Time*, pp. 67-68n; Aedamus Burke to Arthur Middleton, October 16, 1781, in "Correspondence of Arthur Middleton," p. 186; Balch, *French in America*, 1, pp. 197-200; Mitchell, *Alexander Hamilton*, p. 259; S. Doc. 273, pp. 198, 199; Arthur, *Sieges of Yorktown*, p. 23; Arthur, *End of a Revolution*, p. 138; Freeman, *George Washington*, 5, p. 371; and Selig, "Storming the Redoubts," pp. 22-24. Flohr may be the only eyewitness to describe a French vs. French slaughter in the redoubt; his sensational account must be weighed against other evidence and interpretations. Washington wrote that two royals (mortars) were found "in these two redoubts." *Writings*, 23, p. 230. Deux-Ponts won promotion and the title of Chevalier in the Military Order of St. Louis for his performance, while the grenadiers of Gatenois were honored by King Louis XVI, who restored the old and hallowed designation "Auvergne sans tache" to the unit in recognition of its distinction at Yorktown on October 14. Deux-Ponts, *My Campaigns in America*, pp. 156, 161-162; Johnston, *Yorktown Campaign*, p. 143. Rochambeau allowed the chasseurs and grenadiers of the Gatenois and Deux-Ponts regiments two days' additional pay for their valor in the attack. The carpenters who opened the path through the abatis received two louis d'ors each as reward. Closen, *Revolutionary Journal*, p. 150.

28. Thacher, *Military Journal*, p. 276; Stone, *Our French Allies*, 438; Arthur, *Sieges of Yorktown*, p. 24.

29. Stone, *Our French Allies*, p. 439.

30. Ibid.

31. Washington, *Diaries*, 2, p. 266.

32. Döhla, "Journal of Johann Conrad Döhla," pp. 145-146. See also Popp, *Popp's Journal*, pp. 19-20.

33. Smith, "Diary of Jacob Smith," p. 263. "Gen. Richard Butler's Journal," p. 109.

34. Barneville, "War Diary," p. 275.

35. Döhla, "Journal of Johann Conrad Döhla," p. 146.

36. James, *Journal of Rear-Admiral Bartholomew James*, p. 125.

37. Robert Andrews to John Page, October 15, 1781, in "Letters and other Papers, 1735-1829," *Virginia Magazine of History and Biography*, 23 (April, 1915), p. 182.

38. D'Ancteville, "Journal of the Chesapeake Campaign," p. 20; S. Doc. 322, pp. 12-13; De Verger Journal, in Rice and Brown, *American Campaigns*, p. 142; Menonville, "Journal of the Siege of York," p. 287; Swartwout, "Journal of Barnardus Swartwout," p. 36; Wayne Journal, p. 81; Arthur, *Sieges of Yorktown*, p. 24; Sullivan, "Documentary Study of British Redoubt No. 10," p. 4. British Redoubts 9 and 10 subsequently became Structures 9B and 10B in the Second Allied Siege Line, hence their designations as such.

39. "Journal of Lieut. William Feltman," p. 320.

40. John Burnham, "Recollections of the Revolution," *Magazine of History*, extra no. 54, pt. 2 (1917), p. 124; Denny, *Military Journal*, p. 43

41. S. Doc. 322, p. 13; De Verger Journal, in Rice and Brown, *American Campaigns*, p. 143; Menonville, "Journal of the Siege of York," p. 287; Freeman, *George Washington*, 5, pp. 371-372.

42. Hatch, "Siege of Yorktown Opens," p. 29.

43. *Writings*, 23, p. 223.

44. Ibid., p. 228; St. George Tucker, "Journal kept by Col. St. George Tucker," p. 18; Hatch, *"York Under the Hill"*, p. 63.

45. Closen, *Revolutionary Journal*, p. 150.

46. Van Cortlandt, "Autobiography," pp. 294-295.

47. Washington, *Diaries*, 2, p. 267; Van Cortlandt, "Autobiography," p. 295. Wright states that the howitzers were placed in the structures almost immediately following their capture. "Notes on the Siege of Yorktown," p. 246; Borresen reported that the conversion of the redoubts was accomplished thusly: "The earth left in the ditch and used as an approach by the British was now excavated and used to fill in the former gorge. A new entrance was cut through on the opposite side, with a ramp going down to the bottom of the ditch, which . . . connected with the second parallel." "Final Report on Redoubt No. 9, p. 78.

48. Van Cortlandt, "Autobiography," p. 295.

49. Map 7A; Borresen, "Completion Report on American Battery No. 2," pp. 7-8; Borresen, "Orientation Report," p. 41. The French Engineers' Journal, however, states that on October 15, Redoubt 10B "was occupied by a battery of guns and mortars." (p. 4); See also La Combe, "Journal of the Siege of York," p. 4.

50. Washington, *Diaries*, 2, p. 267.

51. Tilden, "Extracts from the Journal of Lieutenant John Bell Tilden," p. 62.

52. Sullivan, "Documentary Study of British Redoubt No. 10," p. 9; Borresen, "Completion Report on American Battery No. 2," p. 6.

53. Sullivan, "Documentary Study of British Redoubt No. 10," p. 14. Borresen wrote that that part of the new parallel immediately to the right (east) of Redoubt 9B was incorporated in Battery 11B when that unit was constructed October 15. That development necessitated the excavation of a new section of parallel directly behind Battery 11B. "Completion Report on American Battery No. 2," p. 11.

54. Borresen, "Completion Report on American Battery No. 2," p. 7; Engineers' Journal, p. 452.

55. St. George Tucker, "Journal kept by Col. St. George Tucker, 18; Barneville, "War Diary," p. 275.

56. Henry Knox Papers (MHS), 7, p. 113; Swartwout, "Journal of Barnardus Swartwout," p. 37; Cobb, "Before York Town, Virginia," p. 69.

57. See "Abstract of Operations."

58. Borresen, "Completion Report on American Battery No. 2," pp. 67-68; Butler, "General Richard Butler's Journal," p. 109; Deux-Ponts, *My Campaigns in America*, p. 149; Trumbull, "Yorktown, Virginia," p. 337.

59. This cryptic exchange is mentioned in Butler, "General Richard Butler's Journal," pp. 109-110, and is alluded to in Feltman, "Journal of Lieut. William Feltman," p. 321.

60. Feltman, "Journal of Lieut. William Feltman," p. 321; Wayne Journal, p. 81; *Orderly Book of the Siege of Yorktown*, p. 41.

61. Closen, *Revolutionary Journal*, p. 150; Menonville, "Journal of the Siege of York," p. 287.

62. Freeman, *George Washington*, 5, p. 372.

63. "Orderly Book kept during the Siege of Yorktown," p. 105; *Orderly Book of the Siege of Yorktown*, p. 41.

64. Tucker to Frances Tucker, October 15, 1781, in "Letters to and from St. George Tucker," pp. 19-20.

65. Henry Knox Papers (MHS), 7, p. 112. For mention of the first batteries firing on this day, see Denny, *Military Journal*, p. 43; Wild, "Journal of Ebenezer Wild," p. 154.

66. "Journal of Barnardus Swartwout," p. 37.

67. "Extracts from the Journal of Lieutenant John Bell Tilden," p. 62.

68. Shute, "With General Benjamin Lincoln," p. 6; Moore, *Life and Services of Gen. Anthony Wayne*, p. 150.

69. McHenry, Letters of James McHenry, p. 71.

70. Denny, *Military Journal*, p. 43.

71. *"Wertgetreue Abschrift eines Tagebuchs eines markgräflischen Soldaten."*

72. Ibid.; Wild, "Journal of Ebenezer Wild," p. 154; McHenry, Letters of James McHenry, pp. 71-72; Dearborn, Revolutionary War Journals, p. 220.

73. "Narrative of Asa Redington," p. 14.

74. Döhla, "Journal of Johann Conrad Döhla," p. 146.

75. Revolutionary Journal, p. 151.

76. Cornwallis to Clinton, October 15, 1781, in Chadwick, Graves Papers, p. 140.

Chapter 12: Hopes Bright and Dim

1. Properly defined, a sortie, or sally, "is when a body of troops go privately out of a besieged town, fall suddenly upon the besiegers, and destroy part of their works, nail their cannon, and do every other damage they can." Smith, *Universal Military Dictionary*, p. 234. Vauban distinguished between "sorties in force," which occurred during daylight, and "weak sorties," which took place at night and consequently required fewer men. *Manual of Siegecraft and Fortification*, p. 53. The purpose of the sortie was usually to "spike" the enemy's cannon in the battery, a process accomplished by driving a rod or nail of the proper diameter into the vent, or touchhole, of the piece, rendering it useless. A special spike of soft iron with a split tip was sometimes driven into the vent until the tip struck the bore and spread in cotter-pin-fashion. Sometimes the rammer was driven down the bore to bend, and thus lock, the pin in the vent. Usually the head of the pin was knocked off so that the nail could not be extracted and the gun put back into commission. Other methods of rendering a piece useless included ramming tiny pebbles into the vent, forcing a ball of slightly larger caliber into the bore, and, as was done at Yorktown, using the points of bayonets to stop up the vent. Le Blond, *Treatise of Artillery*, pp. 31-32; Peterson, *Round Shot and Rammers*, p. 68.

2. Graham, *Memoir of General Graham*, p. 61; Cornwallis to Clinton, October 20, 1781, in *Rivington's Gazette*, November 24, 1781, reproduced in Moore, *Diary of the American Revolution*, pp. 513-514; *"Wertgetreue Abschrift eines Tagebuchs eines markgräflischen Soldaten"*; Arthur, *Sieges of Yorktown*, p. 25; Wright, "Notes on the

Siege of Yorktown," p. 248; Arthur, *End of a Revolution*, p. 142; Bonsal, *Cause of Liberty*, p. 157. Cornwallis later drew substantial criticism for having failed to launch similar sorties long before this in order to retard Allied progress on their parallels. However, no less a critic than Henry Clinton agreed that such a course by Cornwallis would have been futile. "His Lordship was right," Clinton contended. "The others have blamed him. I think it would have been imprudent to have made Sorties upon the Enemy advancing with so much Caution." Clinton's marginalia notes in Stedman, *History . . . of the American War*, 2, p. 410.

 3.This account of the sortie is synthesized from material appearing in Closen, *Revolutionary Journal*, p. 151; Barneville, "War Diary," p. 275; Denny, *Military Journal*, p. 43; "Siege of York and Gloucester, Virginia," p. 477; Fersen, "Journal of Operations," p. 440; La Combe, "Journal of the Siege of York," p. 5; Washington, *Diaries*, 2, pp. 267-268; Washington, *Writings*, 23, pp. 228-229; Arthur, *Sieges of Yorktown*, p. 26; Freeman, *George Washington*, 5, pp. 373-374; De Verger Journal, in Rice and Brown, *American Campaigns*, 1, pp. 142-143; and Thompson, *The British Defenses of Yorktown, 1781*, p. 115. The identities of the units of the men occupying Battery 8B during the sortie, as well as the casualties sustained by each unit, are contained in "Return of Stores expended on the 15th & 16 Octr by Lt. Col. Stevens," Henry Knox Papers (MHS), 7, p. 113. See Swartwout, "Journal of Barnardus Swartwout," p. 37, for mention of the 2nd New York's presence in Battery 8B. Cornwallis to Clinton, October 20, 1781, in *Rivington's Gazette*, November 24, 1781, reproduced in Moore, *Diary of the American Revolution*, p. 514.

 4. De Verger Journal, in Rice and Brown, *American Campaigns*, p. 143.

 5. Revolutionary Journal, p. 152; Clermont-Crèvecoeur Journal, in Rice and Brown, *American Campaigns*, p. 60.

 6. Ewald, "Diary of the American War," pp. 898-899.

 7. Clermont-Crèvecoeur Journal, in Rice and Brown, *American Campaigns*, p. 60; Du Bourg, "Diary of a French Officer, 1781," pp. 447-448, stated that an officer named de Persignan (Pusignan?) commanded Redoubt 7B and was wounded and taken prisoner by the British. According to Balch, *French in America*, 1, p. 204, the commanding officer who was captured was Captain de Beurguissont of Agenois. See also Clermont-Crèvecoeur Journal, in Rice and Brown, *American Campaigns*, p. 60. The five wounded French officers were: Captain Jean Baptiste de Marin (Soissonois), First Lieutenant de Bargues (Bourbonnois), Lieutenant Marc Joseph de Colanby Houdetot (Agenois, bayonet wound in thigh), Second Lieutenant Josselin de Laumont de Castille (Agenois, two bayonet wounds in the chest), and Lieutenant de Pusignan (Persignan?, Artillery). Ibid.; Balch, *French in America*, 1, p. 204; Heitman, *Historical Register*, pp. 657, 661.

 8. Wayne Journal, p. 81; McHenry, *Letters of James McHenry*, p. 72. H. L. Landers maintained that Battery 8B did not open until the next day, October 17, a view not supported by the evidence cited here. S. Doc. 273, p. 201.

 9. Ewald, "Diary of the American War," p. 900.

 10. La Combe, "Journal of the Siege of York," p. 5; Clermont-Crèvecoeur Journal, in Rice and Brown, *American Campaigns*, pp. 60-61; S. Doc. 322, p. 14.

11. Cornwallis to Clinton, October 20, 1781, in *Rivington's Gazette*, November 24, 1781, reproduced in Moore, *Diary of the American Revolution*, p. 514.

12. Borresen, "Completion Report on American Battery No. 2," p. 61. There is the possibility that after the sortie of the morning of the 16th, the Allies, fearing a recurrence of such attacks, added palisades to the ditches surrounding their second batteries. In his "Journal of the Chesapeake Campaign," p. 21, the Chevalier d'Ancteville stated that from the 16th to the 17th, Redoubts 9B and 10B were perfected to guard against "nocturnal incursions." Likewise, he continued, "the ditches of the batteries were palisaded for the same reason." In light of the British sortie, the addition of such obstacles as palisades to the completing batteries of the second parallel seems a dangerous, though completely logical, precautionary move by the Allies.

13. Maps 1F, 16F, 34F. Map 15F indicates the zigzag as being French made. Map 45F states that this point marked the "opening of the second parallel which the French also drove to the left, and the Americans the right."

14. Southside Historical Sites Foundation, "Plan of Archaeological Excavations, Mid-Second Siege Line, Yorktown, Virginia. Preliminary Drawing" (Williamsburg, 1974).

15. Map 34F.

16. Maps IF, 7A, 15F, 16F, 17F, 19F, 28A, 34F, and 62F indicate 10 mortars. Maps 2F, 24F, 29B, 48F, and 49F indicate 12 mortars. Maps 24F and 49F report five 12-inch and seven 8-inch mortars in this battery, while American map 7A states that the unit was "designed for" 10 13-inch mortars. Most maps agree that two 8-inch howitzers were present in the work.

17. Feltman, "Journal of Lieut. William Feltman," p. 321.

18. Map 34F.

19. Ibid.

20. Maps 2F, 11F, 17F, 33F, 34F, 49F.

21. Maps 35F, 37F; Borresen, "Orientation Report," p. 35.

22. Borresen, "Orientation Report," p. 35; Maps 1F, 2F, 16F, 17F, 19F, 24F, 28A, 29B, 34F, 35F, 48F, 49F, 62F; Arthur, *Sieges of Yorktown*, p. 26.

23. Maps 2F, 11F, 28A, 33F, 34F, 35F, 37F.

24. Excavation in the road area in the 1940s, during laying of a pipeline, confirmed the location of Redoubt 4B squarely in the middle of Hampton Road. Borresen, "Orientation Report," p. 34.

25. Maps 1F, 2F, 15F, 16F, 17F, 19F, 24F, 28A, 29B, 34F, 35F, 48F, 49F, 62F.

26. Maps 24F, 29B, 49F.

27. "Journal of Lieut. William Feltman," p. 321. Feltman and other Americans frequently described the French guns as 18-pounders, when they were actually the standard 16-pounders.

28. Ibid.; "This was not an unusual practice in a second parallel," explained Borresen, "which was so close to the enemy that their shots could be very damaging and it was necessary for the artillery commander to place his guns for immediate firing in order to protect himself." "Completion Report on American Battery No. 2," pp. 4-5.

29. Map 34F.

30. Maps 1F, 2F, 15F, 16F, 17F, 24F, 28A, 29B, 35F, 48F, 49F. Map 34F shows five cannon here.

31. Borresen, "Orientation Report," p. 37.

32. Map 34F.

33. Southside Historical Sites Foundation, "Plan of Archaeological Excavations."

34. See the color scheme of Map 19F.

35. Maps 2F, 11F, 19F, 33F, 34F, 35F, 37F, 49F; Borresen, "Orientation Report," p. 37.

36. Southside Historical Sites Foundation, "Plan of Archaeological Excavations."

37. Maps 1F, 2F, 15F, 16F, 17F, 24F, 29B, 35F, 48F, 49F, 62F. Maps 7A and 34F indicate but four guns here; See Walter S. Flickinger, "Report on the Excavation of American Gun Battery known as No. 4, in Advance of the 2nd Parallel, including Additional Supplementary Data," MS, dated April 11, 1938, in the library of CNHP, Yorktown, Virginia, pp. 2-3.

38. See Map 7A.

39. Borresen, "Orientation Report," p. 37.

40. Borresen, "Report on American Guns and Carriages," p. 56; Southside Historical Sites Foundation, "Plan of Archaeological Excavations." Borresen found six recesses at the foot of the epaulement of Battery 8B, indicating that six gun platforms were employed in the structure. "Memorandum to the Historical Division," dated March 31, 1938, in the library of CNHP, Yorktown, Virginia.

41. Even so, the apparent depth of this sunken battery was so great as to dictate against naval ordnance unless the floor of the earthwork was considerably raised. Borresen, "Memorandum to the Historical Division," March 31, 1938.

42. Maps 1F, 2F, 6F, 7A, 11F, 15F, 16F, 17F, 18F, 19F, 24F, 25B, 26F, 28A, 30B, 31F, 34F, 35F, 37F, 41F, 45F, 46F, 48F, 49F, 50B, 53F, 57B, 59B, 62F.

43. Maps 32F, 33F.

44. Borresen, "Final Report on Redoubt No. 9," pp. 77-78.

45. The decision to reconstruct Redoubt 9B to its British form was made by Superintendent Floyd B. Flickinger. Essentially, this meant that the gorge cut through by the Allies on the night of October 14 was not reconstructed. Ibid., pp. 72, 74. See also the preface and pp. 37, 40, 59, 60-61, 65, 71, 75-76, of ibid., for highlights of the excavation and reconstruction (then called "restoration") of Redoubt 9.

46. Maps 24F, 29B, 49F.

47. Maps 33F, 34F, 53F, 57B.

48. Maps 1F, 2F, 6F, 7A, 11F, 15F, 16F, 17F, 19F, 24F, 25B, 26F, 27F, 28A, 29B, 30B, 31F, 32F, 35F, 37F, 41F, 45F, 48F, 49F, 50B, 62F. Participant renderings of the French and American attacks on the evening of the 14th mention the presence of palisades at both Redoubts 9 and 10.

49. See, generally, Chapter 2: "The Lion Comes to Yorktown."

50. Within these limits, however, there is disagreement. A British map, 29B, states, for example, that the battery contained a dozen 18-pounders, three 24-pounders, and eight mortars, while two French maps (24F and 49F) showed but six mortars. Map 15F stated

that there were 12 cannon, four mortars, and two howitzers in the structure. Map 34F said that it held nine cannon. See also Maps 1F, 2F, 16F, 17F, 28A, 35F, 48F.

51. Map 7A.

52. "Journal of Lieut. William Feltman," p. 321.

53. Borresen, "Completion Report on American Battery No. 2," pp. 33-35, 68, 69-71, 87. The archeological evidence confirmed the account by Feltman. Ibid., p. 62.

54. Ibid., pp. 67-68. The width of the gun platforms (three sleepers each) was about nine feet, considerably narrower than the 10 to 12 feet recommended in the siegecraft manuals of the period. Ibid., pp. 66. Borresen had earlier suggested that garrison carriages, which were much narrower than siege carriages, could have been used in Battery 11B and would have alleviated the spacing problem. "Report on American Guns and Carriages," pp. 54-55. Borresen's later view was expressed after completion of the archeological work and represents a revision of his earlier estimate.

55. Borresen, "Completion Report on American Battery No. 2," p. 69.

56. Ibid., pp. 80, 82.

57. Maps 15F, 16F, 17F, and 41F show the lines of the intended drive against the Fusiliers's Redoubt. Work on this plan was curtailed October 17 with the suspension of fire from both sides. See Closen, *Revolutionary Journal*, pp. 152-53; La Combe, "Journal of the Siege of York," p. 5; and Engineers' Journal, p. 452.

58. *Orderly Book of the Siege of Yorktown*, p. 41; Shute, "With General Benjamin Lincoln," p. 5.

59. Engineer's Journal, p. 452; Du Bourg, "Diary of a French Officer, 1781," p. 448; Fersen, "Journal of Operations," p. 440; La Combe, "Journal of the Siege of York," p. 5; Cobb, "Before York Town, Virginia," p. 69; Butler, "General Richard Butler's Journal," p. 110.

60. Trumbull, "Yorktown, Virginia," p. 337.

61. "Orderly Book kept during the Siege of Yorktown, pp. 110-111; *Orderly Book of the Siege of Yorktown*, p. 43.

62. *Orderly Book of the Siege of Yorktown*, pp. 42-43; "Orderly Book kept during the Siege of Yorktown," p. 110.

63. Menonville, "Journal of the Siege of York," p. 288; De Verger Journal, in Rice and Brown, *American Campaigns*, p. 143; Closen, *Revolutionary Journal*, p. 152.

64. Closen, *Revolutionary Journal*, p. 152; Rochambeau, *Relation*, 7; "Diary of French naval operations in America," p. 198.

65. Knox and Alexander episode quoted from Scheer and Rankin, *Rebels and Redcoats*, p. 565. Asa Redington reported on a similar (and perhaps the same) incident:

> One afternoon one of the British shells struck six feet from where I was sitting, took a whirl in the ground and rolled out on the surface, with the fuse spurting out wild-fire. We all, including Gen. Knox, threw ourselves flat on the ground, watched the fire spitting from the shell, and dreaded its explosion. In a few seconds it burst and wholly disappeared without injuring a single person, although a soldier beside me had his canteen

knocked from his side. General Knox picked himself up, shook off the dirt from his fat sides, and laughed heartily.

"Narrative of Asa Redington," p. 14.

66. The rough outline of this proposal is presented in Washington to de Grasse, October 16, 1781, in *Writings*, 23, pp. 225-226. See also Washington to Colonel Timothy Pickering, October 14, 1781, ibid., p. 222.

67. Denny, *Military Journal*, p. 43; Tilghman, *Memoir of Lieut. Col. Tench Tilghman*, p. 106; Du Bourg, "Diary of a French Officer, 1781," p. 448; Shute, "With General Benjamin Lincoln," p. 5. Although d'Ancteville stated that "as early as nine o'clock in the morning of the 16th we unmasked a great part of our new batteries," he probably was speaking of the units mounted in the French sector rather than of the second parallel as a whole. "Journal of the Chesapeake Campaign," p. 21. Washington wrote that "about 4 o'clock this afternoon the French opened two Batteries of 2 23s. and four 16s. each. 3 pieces from the American grand battery were also opened, the others not being ready." *Diaries*, 2, p. 268. Washington seems to have been in error regarding the calibers of the French weapons employed, for there were no 23-pounders in service among the Allies at Yorktown.

68. Redington, "Narrative of Asa Redington," p. 15. According to Muller, *Treatise Containing the Elementary Part of Fortification*, p. 212, "Breach, is an opening made in a wall or rampart, with cannon or mines, sufficiently wide for a body of troops to enter the works, and drive the besieged out of it."

69. "Journal of the Chesapeake Campaign," p. 22.

70. Lamb, *Journal of Occurrences*, p. 378; Andreus, *History of the War with America*, 4, p. 208.

71. Henry Knox Papers (MHS), 7, p. 113; Heitman, *Historical Register*, p. 411.

72. The latter alternative (striking north out of Gloucester) was neither as feasible nor as attractive as heading directly toward Clinton. As Cornwallis later explained,

> Being without baggage, I should have gained the upper country by rapid marches, mounting my infantry, by collecting horses on the way, and leaving my intended route doubtful, until I was opposite to the fords of the great rivers; I then intended to have turned off to the northward, expecting that the enemy would principally take their measures to prevent my escape to the southward. The success of this attempt would, no doubt, have been precarious.

> *An Answer to That Part of the Narrative of Lieutenant-General Sir Henry Clinton*, p. xiv.

The man Cornwallis intended to leave behind in Yorktown, Lieutenant Colonel Henry Johnson (1748-1835), had been defeated and captured at Stony Point, New York on July 15, 1779. Embarrassed, he requested his own court-martial to wipe the stain away from his military record. After he was exchanged, Johnson's wish was granted and he was tried in New York City in January 1781. Although the court members found fault with his conduct, he was also cited for his bravery (along with his men) and received as a result only a reprimand.

73. One account states that "the second division had actually embarked" when the storm arose. Irving, *Life of George Washington*, 4, p. 380; "Diary of the American War," p. 900; Thompson, *The British Defenses of Yorktown, 1781*, p. 117, makes the same claim. The bulk of contemporary sources, however, indicates otherwise.

74. This account is based principally on material contained in Cornwallis to Clinton, October 20, 1781, published in *Rivington's Gazette*, November 24, 1781, and reproduced in Moore, *Diary of the American Revolution*, pp. 514-515; Ewald, "Diary of the American War," p. 900; Stedman, *History . . . of the American War*, 2, pp. 411-412; Nickerson, "Yorktown, 1781," p. 89; and Arthur, *End of a Revolution*, p. 144.

75. Henry Knox Papers (MHS), 7, p. 115.

Chapter 13: Britain Against the Sky

1. Burgoyne's surrender was celebrated in Peekskill, New York, by officers of the 3rd Massachusetts Brigade. "The recollection of the glorious victory which was completed on that day, and the prospect of events equally glorious, animated every breast with the most pleasing sensations, and diffused a lively joy on every countenance." *New York Packet*, October 25, 1781, reproduced in Moore, *Diary of the American Revolution*, pp. 505-506; "Journal of the Siege of York in Virginia by a Chaplain," p. 107.

2. The details of Clinton's plans for relief appear concisely in Arthur, *End of a Revolution*, pp. 114-116. A longer firsthand explanation can be found in Henry Clinton, *The American Rebellion: Sir Henry Clinton's Narrative of His Campaigns, 1775-1782, with an Appendix of Original Documents*, ed. William B. Willcox (Hamden, Connecticut: Archon Books, 1971), the last part of which contains Clinton's "Narrative" of operations in the campaign of 1781.

3. Clinton's marginalia notes in Stedman, *History . . . of the American War*, 2, p. 412.

4. Irving, *Life of George Washington*, 4, p. 357.

5. Henry Clinton Papers, vol. October 29-November 6, 1781, William L. Clements Library. Irving described a more simplified system: "if all went well at Yorktown his lordship was to make three separate columns of smoke; and four, should he still possess the post at Gloucester Point." *Life of George Washington*, 4, p. 357. On September 29, Cornwallis wrote Clinton that he "must depend more on the Sound of our Cannon than the Signal of Smokes for information. However I will attempt it on the Gloucester Side." Cornwallis to Clinton, September 29, 1781, Henry Clinton Papers, William L. Clements Library.

6. Andreus, *History of the War with America*, 4, p. 208; Arthur, *Sieges of Yorktown*, p. 28; Burne, "Cornwallis at Yorktown," p. 76.

7. "Journal of the Siege of York in Virginia by a Chaplain," p. 107; General Thomas Nelson, Jr. to George Webb, October 17, 1781, in Nelson, *Letters*, p. 53; Barneville, "War

Diary," p. 275; James Thatcher, *A Military Journal During the American Revolutionary War, From 1775 to 1783* (Boston, 1827), p. 277; Stryker, *New Jersey Continental Line*, p. 23; Clermont-Crèvecoeur Journal, in Rice and Brown, *American Campaigns*, p. 61; Freeman, *George Washington*, 5, pp. 375-376.

8. *Diaries*, 2, p. 268.

9. Henry Knox Papers (MHS), 7, pp. 108, 115.

10. Popp, *Popp's Journal*, p. 20; Cornwallis to Clinton, October 20, 1781; See also Maps 1F, 7A, 17F, 26F, 29B, and 52A for lines of fire from the second parallel batteries.

11. *Orderly Book of the Siege of Yorktown*, p. 42.

12. Closen, *Revolutionary Journal*, p. 152.

13. Gregory, "Diary of Mathew Gregory at Yorktown, 1781," p. 5; and Washington, *Diaries*, 2, p. 268; "Siege of York and Gloucester, Virginia," p. 477; S. Doc. 322, p. 15; Barneville, "War Diary," p. 276 (4:00 p.m..); Clermont-Crèvecoeur Journal, in Rice and Brown, *American Campaigns*, p. 61 (3:00 p.m.); and Closen, *Revolutionary Journal*, p. 152 (1:00 p.m.).

14. "Chamade, is when a town besieged wants to capitulate, or to make some proposals to the besiegers. In that case one or more drums mount the rampart, and beat what the military call a Chamade." Smith, *Universal Military Dictionary*, p. 232.

15. Denny, *Military Journal*, p. 44; Philip Van Cortland to unknown recipient, October 17, 1781, James S. Schoff Collection, William L. Clements Library; S. Doc. 322, p. 15; Bonsal, *Cause of Liberty*, p. 158; Whitridge, *Rochambeau*, p. 224.

16. Cornwallis to Washington, October 17, 1781, copy in Cornwallis to Clinton, October 20, 1781, Henry Clinton Papers, William L. Clements Library. The full texts of this and ensuing communications between Cornwallis and Washington are presented in Appendix 2.

17. As one might expect, there is much disagreement regarding the actual period of time granted for the intermission. Apparently there occurred brief suspensions during the day as notes were exchanged, but the two-hour cessation did not start until late in the afternoon. This evidently was successively extended through the night and following day. See "Siege of York and Gloucester, Virginia," p. 477; Washington, *Diaries*, 2, pp. 268-269; Cornwallis to Washington, 4:30 p.m., Oct. 17, 1781; Closen, *Revolutionary Journal*, pp. 152-153; Swartwout, "Journal of Barnardus Swartwout," p. 37; and Gregory, "Diary of Mathew Gregory at Yorktown, 1781," p. 5. Barneville wrote that Cornwallis "was given only two hours and [was] told that if he did not surrender all the batteries would be opened and the assault would follow." "War Diary," p. 276. With the cessation, the French dispensed with their preparations against the Fusiliers' Redoubt. Engineers' Journal, p. 452; La Combe, "Journal of the Siege of York," p. 5; Closen, *Revolutionary Journal*, p. 153. Menonville mentioned the "second flag" coming out of Yorktown about 3:00 p.m. "with proposals which caused a cessation of hostilities on both sides." "Journal of the Siege of York," p. 288.

18. Washington, *Diaries*, 2, p. 269. Believing the end was indeed near, Washington sent an invitation to Admiral de Grasse so that he could be present for the surrender, should he so desire. Thompson, *The British Defenses of Yorktown, 1781*, p 120.

19. *"Wertgetreue Abschrift eines Tagebuchs eines markgräflischen Soldaten."*

20. Jonathan Trumbull, October 17, 1781, George Weedon Papers, Allyn K. Ford Collection, Minnesota Historical Society, St. Paul. Quoted in Lydia Lucas, "Yorktown Campaign is Featured in Allyn K. Ford Collection," *Minnesota History*, 44 (Summer, 1975), p. 225.

21. Memo dated October 24, 1781, aboard *London at Sea*, in Chadwick, Graves Papers, p. 142.

22. Captain Thomas Symonds to Rear Admiral Graves, October 20, 1781, in Chadwick, *Graves Papers*, p. 151; *"Wertgetreue Abschrift eines Tagebuchs eines markgrälischen Soldaten"*; Fleming, *Beat the Last Drum*, p. 314.

23. Ibid., p. 315; St. George Tucker, "Journal kept by Col. St. George Tucker," pp. 21-22.

24. Washington, *Diaries*, 2, pp. 268-269; Gregory, "Diary of Mathew Gregory at Yorktown, 1781," p. 5. By coincidence, Lord Cornwallis was also Constable of the Tower of London, in which Laurens's father was incarcerated. Thacher, *Military Journal*, p. 288n. The Moore house was owned in fee by Governor (General) Thomas Nelson, although Mrs. Moore held a life interest in the structure. Lossing, *Pictorial Field-Book of the Revolution*, 2, p. 324.

25. Denny, *Military Journal*, p. 44; Davis, *Campaign that Won America*, pp. 260-261; Arthur, *End of a Revolution*, p. 149.

26. Davis, *Campaign that Won America*, p. 261.

27. *Orderly Book of the Siege of Yorktown*, p. 44; Closen, *Revolutionary Journal*, p. 153; Greene, *German Element in the War of American Independence*, p. 72; Wright, "Notes on the Continental Army," p. 96; Arthur, *End of a Revolution*, p. 155.

28. Feltman's breakdown of ordnance for the respective batteries follows: Battery 1B: one 8-inch howitzer, eight 13-inch mortars, and two royals, all of brass; Battery 3B: six 24-pounders, brass; Battery 5B: four 18-pounders and two 24-pounders, brass; Battery 6B: four 18-pounders and two 24-pounders, brass; Battery 8B: four 18-pounders, iron; Redoubt 9B: two 10-inch mortars and two royals; Battery 11B: 10 18-pounders (some of these were apparently 24-pounders), three 10-inch mortars, one 8-inch howitzer, and two royals; Redoubt 10B: one iron 18-pounder, two howitzers, two mortars, and two royals. Feltman did not include the ordnance mounted in the French batteries 1A and 2A at the far left opposite the Fusiliers' Redoubt. "Journal of Lieut. William Feltman," p. 321.

29. Washington, *Diaries*, 2, p. 268.

30. Patton, "Campaign of the Allies," p. 264. "The most honourable and ordinary terms of capitulation are, for the garrison to march out at the breach with arms and baggage, drums beating, colours flying, matches lighted, with some pieces of artillery, waggons, and convoys for their baggage, and for the sick and wounded etc." Smith, *Universal Military Dictionary*, p. 232.

31. Fleming, *Beat the Last Drum*, p. 322.

32. Whitridge, *Rochambeau*, pp. 225-226.

33. Agniel, *Late Affair*, p. 133; Arthur, *End of a Revolution*, p. 151. Suspecting the worst, some Loyalists, along with blacks and other refugees, were already fleeing

Yorktown in whatever small boats were available. Memo dated October 24, 1781, aboard *London at Sea*, in Chadwick, *Graves Papers*, p. 141; Hatch, *"York Under the Hill,"* p. 64.

34. Washington, *Diaries*, 2, p. 268; Thompson, *The British Defenses of Yorktown, 1781*, p 121.

35. Hamilton to wife, October 18, 1781, George Bancroft Collection, New York Public Library.

36. Thacher, *Military Journal*, p. 289; Edward Burke to Arthur Middleton, October 16 (when letter was begun), 1781, "Correspondence of Arthur Middleton," p. 186; Davis, *Campaign that Won America*, pp. 263-264.

37. Laurens to Lieutenant Colonel Dundas, October 19, 1781, Morgan Manuscripts, vol. 1, The Siege of Yorktown and Surrender of Cornwallis, Pierpont Morgan Library. As evidence of the great technical detail accorded preparation of the Articles of Capitulation, Laurens requested his British counterpart "to erase the word *light* in the article relative to the possession of the works—that the clause may express American Infantry instead of American Light Infantry." Ibid. A complete text of the "Articles of Capitulation" appears in Appendix 3.

38. Washington, *Diaries*, 2, p. 269.

39. Cornwallis to Clinton, October 20, 1781, containing copies of the Articles of Capitulation, Henry Clinton Papers, William L. Clements Library; De Grasse was suffering from an attack of asthma, and could not attend the ceremony. Closen, *Revolutionary Journal*, p. 152.

40. Denny, *Military Journal*, p. 44. Exactly what the flag looked like that Lieutenant Denny was carrying and von Steuben actually planted is open to speculation. "Journal of Johann Conrad Döhla," pp. 145-146.

41. Colonel Richard Butler to Brigadier General William Irvine, October 22, 1781, William Irvine Papers, vol. 5, Historical Society of Pennsylvania; Closen, *Revolutionary Journal*, p. 153; *New York Journal*, November 12, 1781, reproduced in Moore, *Diary of the American Revolution*, p. 508; Johnston, *Yorktown Campaign*, p. 155; Arthur, *End of a Revolution*, p. 151.

42. Cornwallis's message to his troops is taken from Thompson, *The British Defenses of Yorktown, 1781*, pp. 67-68.

43. The relative positions of the French and American troops as they lined Hampton Road has long been in doubt. There exists, however, good documentary evidence for placing the Americans east and the French west of the highway. A soldier of a Pennsylvania regiment just landed on October 19 recalled: "[T]he British Army marched out and grounded their arms in front of our line. Our whole army drew up for them to march through. The French on *their* [the British] right and the Americans on *their* left" (italics added). William McDowell, "Journal of Lieut. William McDowell, of the First Penn'a Regiment, In the Southern Campaign. 1781-1782," in William H. Egle, ed., *Journals and Diaries of the War of the Revolution* (Harrisburg: E. K. Meyers, 1893), p. 303. According to a German soldier who participated in the ceremony, "the French stood by our marching out on our right . . .[while] on the left stood the . . . American regular troops, after them the Virginia militia." Second Lieutenant Jakob Ernst Kling to unknown recipient, November 4, 1781, Hessisches Staatsarchiv, Marburg/Lahn, Germany,

translated by John Luzader. Yet another participant, this one a French soldier, noted, "the Americans [were] on the right and the French on the left" of Hampton Road, doubtless as he faced Yorktown. "Abstract of Operations." French officer Barneville similarly reported that the American Army stood "in line on the right and the French army on the left." "War Diary," p. 276; see also Thacher, *Military Journal*, p. 289. Furthermore, it would have been eminently logical for the French and American forces to retain the relative positions they had occupied throughout the siege. The one known extant diagram of the surrender ceremony places the Americans east, and the French west, of Hampton Road. See Map 56A ([Ezra Stiles], "Surrendery Oct. 19, 1781," Yale University Library, New Haven, Connecticut). Artist John Trumbull, who visited Yorktown ten years later to gather data for a painting of the surrender, learned that "the American troops were drawn up on the right of the road *leading into York* [emphasis added]. . . . The French troops on the opposite side of the road facing them." *Autobiography, Reminiscences and Letters of John Trumbull, from 1756 to 1841* (New York: Wiley and Putnam, 1841), p. 424; "Abstract of Operations"; Burke to Arthur Middleton, October 16 (when letter was begun), 1781, "Correspondence of Arthur Middleton," p. 186. On the reverse of his painting, Trumbull observed that the view depicted was that "seen from the point at which the British Army enter'd between the two lines of the Allied troops of America & France at the Surrender in 81.—distance from the advanc'd [British horn]work, 270 yards." MSS, box 1, item 14, Fordham University Library, Bronx, New York.

44. Arthur, *End of a Revolution*, p. 153; Scheer and Rankin, *Rebels and Redcoats*, p. 570; Döhla, "Journal of Johann Conrad Döhla," p. 57.

45. Scheer and Rankin, *Rebels and Redcoats*, p. 570; Arthur, *End of a Revolution*, pp. 152-153; William T. Partridge, Jr., "The Battleflags at Yorktown," *St. Nicholas*, 62 (October, 1935), p. 11.

46. Letter dated October 21, 1781, in the *New Jersey Gazette*, November 7, 1781, reproduced in Moore, *Diary of the American Revolution*, p. 508; Map 56A; Trumbull, *Autobiography*, p. 424; Thompson, *The British Defenses of Yorktown, 1781*, p. 124.

47. Ibid.; "Orders of General Lord Cornwallis. Head-Quarter. 19th October 1781," in *"Wertgetreue Abschrift eines Tagebuchs eines markgräflischen Soldaten"*; Barneville, "War Diary," p. 276; Johnston, *Yorktown Campaign*, p. 177. Lieutenant Jakob Ernst Kling in a letter to unknown recipient, November 4, 1781; Letter from Johann Radler to his mother in Mainbernheim, December 1781, Historischer Verein, Mittelfranken, Germany, translated by John Luzader; Knox to John Adams, October 21, 1781, Henry Knox Papers (CNHP); Closen, *Revolutionary Journal*, p. 153; "Journal of Barnardus Swartwout," p. 38.

48. Davis stated that "about 3500 troops had come out to surrender; as many more waited in Yorktown, mostly the sick and wounded." *Campaign that Won America*, p. 267.

49. North, *Military Uniforms*, pp. 24-26. For specific dress of the various British and Hessian units, see Mollo and McGregor, *Uniforms of the American Revolution*, passim; Thacher, *Military Journal*, p. 289. Cornwallis was doubtless sick at heart from his capitulation but, conceivably, he could have been ill from the same fever that afflicted many of his troops throughout the siege. Both Rochambeau and Lafayette, on several

occasions during the Yorktown operations, had been indisposed with fever. Whitridge, *Rochambeau*, pp. 226-227.

50. Quoted from Johnston, *Yorktown Campaign*, p. 167.

51. Barneville, "War Diary," p. 276; Döhla said that the muskets were shouldered. "Journal of Johann Conrad Döhla," p. 56. There is little doubt that the British musicians played a march as the army advanced down Hampton Road. The very fact that the Articles stipulated against their playing a French or American march implied as much. For specific references to what was played, see "Journal of Barnardus Swartwout," p. 38; *Military Journal*, p. 44; "Abstract of Operations"; Edward Hand to Jasper Yeates, October 19, 1781, Edward Hand Papers, vol. 2, item 139, New York Public Library; Thacher, *Military Journal*, p. 289; Lieutenant Jakob Ernst Kling to unknown recipient, November 4, 1781; Letter from Johann Radler to his mother in Mainbernheim, December 1781; "Journal of Johann Conrad Döhla," p. 150. Edward Burke letter, October 16 (when letter was begun), 1781, "Correspondence of Arthur Middleton," p. 187; Asa Redington, "Narrative of Asa Redington," p. 15; Thomas J. Fleming, *Beat the Last Drum*, p. 357n; Alexander Garden, *Anecdotes of the American Revolution*; John R. Alden, *A History of the American Revolution* (New York: Alfred A. Knopf, 1972), p. 474. As of the date of publication, the Colonial Music Institute offered an enlightening examination of this interesting issue online at http://www.colonialmusic.org/Resource/Schrader.htm. For another exhaustive treatment of this subject written by the same author, see http://www.findarticles.com/p/articles/mi_m2298/is_2_16/ai_53552767/print. As he insightfully noted, Thompson, in *The British Defenses of Yorktown, 1781*, p. 126, observed: "What is amazing is that no witness mentioned a single bagpipe playing. Three of the regiments were Scottish! That instrument must definitely have been prohibited."

52. O'Hara told Washington that Cornwallis was sick and could not be present. Blanchard, *Journal*, pp. 151-52; Thacher, *Military Journal*, p. 289; Commodore Richard Taylor, cited in Davis, *Campaign that Won America*, p. 264; Whitridge, *Rochambeau*, pp. 226-227.

53. This description of the sword ceremony is based on the account of Count Mathieu Dumas, in Scheer and Rankin, *Rebels and Redcoats*, pp. 571-572; Thacher, *Military Journal*, p. 289; Blanchard, *Journal*, p. 152; Commodore Richard Taylor's account in Davis, *Campaign that Won America*, p. 264; the account of Lieutenant Colonel Henry Lee, in Johnston, *Yorktown Campaign*, p. 176; Letter dated October 21, 1781, in the *New Jersey Gazette*, November 7, 1781, reproduced in Moore, *Diary of the American Revolution*, p. 508; and the *New York Journal*, November 12, 1781, reproduced in ibid. Freeman, *George Washington*, 5, pp. 388-389, is not convinced O'Hara was intentionally trying to slight or avoid Washington, and thinks he probably made a mistake. Freeman also calls into question Washington's purposed response as recorded by Dumas, and whether a sword was offered at all at this time.

54. "Description of the Surrender by Colonel Fontaine, Virginia Militia, dated October 26, 1781," in Johnston, *Yorktown Campaign*, p. 177; Lieutenant Jakob Ernst Kling to unknown recipient, November 4, 1781.

55. Feltman, "Journal of Lieut. William Feltman," p. 322; McDowell, "Journal of Lieut. William McDowell," in Egle, *Journals and Diaries*, p. 303.

56. Thacher, *Military Journal*, p. 289; account of Lee reproduced in Johnston, *Yorktown Campaign*, p. 167.

57. Edward Burke to Arthur Middleton, October 16 (when letter was begun), 1781, "Correspondence of Arthur Middleton," p. 187.

58. Letter dated October 21, 1781, in the *New Jersey Gazette*, November 7, 1781, reproduced in Moore, *Diary of the American Revolution*, p. 508.

59. Jakob Ernst Kling to unknown recipient, November 4, 1781. One story, perhaps apocryphal, described how the British kept their eyes turned to the French, as if to ignore American participation in the victory. When this occurred, Lafayette snapped an order to an American band, which suddenly broke into a loud rendition of "Yankee Doodle." The British jerked their heads to the left in surprise and by this ploy the vanquished visually acknowledged their subjugation by United States soldiers. Fleming, *Beat the Last Drum*, pp. 328-329.

60. See "Historic Base Map, "Yorktown Battlefield," Colonial National Historical Park, Virginia," in Hatch and Greene, *Developed Sites and Colonial Rural Fences*, p. 82. The ground today called "Surrender Field" does not conform exactly to that indicated by the historical base map cited above, which if correct, places the site slightly north of the vestiges of a Confederate redoubt situated on the terrain. See map, Department of the Interior, U.S. Geological Survey, "Colonial National Monument, Yorktown Battlefield, Virginia," 1931. The discrepancy can possibly be explained by the confusion engendered by local residents over the years as to the exact location of the surrender. As early as 1848 this was apparent, as Benson Lossing recounted:

> We next visited the places designated by tradition as the spot where the British laid down their arms. In a field, not more than half a mile southward of the British entrenchments, three tulip poplars were pointed out for many years as indices of the exact place of surrender. The old trees are now gone, but three small ones supply their places. This on the east side of the Hampton road. In Trumbull's picture of the *Surrender*, the house of Governor Nelson is seen. Trumbull visited Yorktown for the purpose of sketching the ground, in 1791, and doubtless had the true location pointed out to him. From the field where the tulip poplars are, however, the house can not be seen, but from a large field on the west side of the Hampton road, sloping in the direction of the 'Pigeon Quarter,' and about a mile from the British lines (the distance mentioned in history), the house may be plainly seen. It is the opinion of Mr. [William] Nelson and other intelligent gentlemen at Yorktown, that the large field . . . is the locality where the captive soldiers laid down their arms.

Lossing, *Pictorial Field-Book of the Revolution*, 2, p. 324. Quite possibly the presence of private holdings along the eastern side of Hampton Road contributed to influence the development of the present surrender site by the National Park Service. See, for example, the map, "Yorktown Battlefield," following p. 55 in Robert L. Steenhagen et. al., *A Master Plan for Colonial National Historical Park* (Washington: National Park Service, 1971).

61. These French cavalrymen probably belonged to the Volunteers of St. Simon and were mounted after their arrival in Virginia from the West Indies. It is extremely doubtful that these troops belonged to Lauzun's Legion, which had been sent overland directly to Gloucester before the siege began and which remained there until after the surrender.

62. The ensign was an 18-year-old named Wilson, supposedly the youngest commissioned officer then in the Continental Army. Lossing, *Pictorial Field-Book of the Revolution*, 2, pp. 318, 320; "Narrative of Asa Redington," p. 15. Robert Arthur believed that the color ceremony followed the grounding of arms. *End of a Revolution*, pp. 154-55.

63. Swartwout, "Journal of Barnardus Swartwout," p. 38; Döhla, "Journal of Johann Conrad Döhla," p. 58; "Abstract of Operations"; Closen, *Revolutionary Journal*, p. 153; Barneville, "War Diary," p. 276; Lieutenant Jakob Ernst Kling to unknown recipient, November 4, 1781; Letter from soldier Johann Radler to his mother in Mainbernheim, December 1781; Fleming, *Beat the Last Drum*, pp. 332-333.

64. Closen, *Revolutionary Journal*, p. 153.

65. Döhla, "Journal of Johann Conrad Döhla," p. 57; Thacher, *Military Journal*, p. 290; Arthur, *End of a Revolution*, p. 154.

66. Blanchard, *Journal*, p. 152.

67. Map 56A.

68. Letter from soldier Johann Radler to his mother in Mainbernheim, December 1781; Lieutenant Jakob Ernst Kling to unknown recipient, November 4, 1781.

69. Barneville, "War Diary," p. 276; Swartwout, "Journal of Barnardus Swartwout," p. 38.

70. Swartwout, "Journal of Barnardus Swartwout," p. 38.

71. Thompson, *The British Defenses of Yorktown, 1781*, p. 128; Washington to Choisy, October 19, 1781, in *Writings*, 23, pp. 240-241.

72. Choisy to Washington, 2:00 p.m., October 19, 1781, Simon Gratz Autograph Collection, Historical Society of Pennsylvania.

73. "Account of the Surrender by Lieutenant-colonel Harry Lee," in Johnston, *Yorktown Campaign*, p. 177; Arthur, *End of a Revolution*, p. 155.

74. "Account of the Surrender by Lieutenant-colonel [sic] Harry Lee," in Johnston, *Yorktown Campaign*, p. 177; Fleming, *Beat the Last Drum*, p. 332; Arthur, *End of a Revolution*, p. 156.

75. *Military Journal*, p. 44.

76. Ibid., pp. 44-45.

77. Ibid., p. 45.

78. Ibid.

79. Davis, *Campaign that Won America*, pp. 268-69.

80. Gaston Marie Leonard Maussion de la Bastie to his mother, November 5, 1781, in Radziwill, *They Knew the Washingtons*, p. 108.

Chapter 14: Broken Sword

1. "Orderly Book kept during the Siege of Yorktown," pp. 119-120.

2. Henry Knox Papers (CNHP).

3. Lafayette to M. de Vergennes, October 20, 1781, in Lafayette, *Memoirs, Correspondence and Manuscripts*, 1, p. 444.

4. Ibid., p. 445.

5. Nelson to Virginia delegates, October 20, 1781, in Palmer, *Calendar of Virginia State Papers*, 2, p. 558.

6. *New York Packet*, November 15, 1781, reproduced in Moore, *Diary of the American Revolution*, pp. 511-512.

7. Excerpt of Lieutenant Soret de Boisbrunet's diary, in Warrington Dawson, "A New Record of the Sieges of Yorktown and Pensacola," *Legion D'Honneur*, 4 (1933-34), p. 85.

8. Arthur, *End of a Revolution*, pp. 156-157.

9. For an example of this elocution, heavily laden with religious overtones, see Israel Evans, *A Discourse Delivered Near York in Virginia, on the Memorable Occasion of the Surrender of the British Army to the Allied Forces of America and France* (Philadelphia: Francis Bailey, 1782).

10. See Cornwallis to Clinton, October 20, 1781, in *Rivington's Gazette*, November 24, 1781, reproduced in Moore, *Diary of the American Revolution*, pp. 512-516.

11. Symonds to Graves, October 20, 1781, in Chadwick, *Graves Papers*, p. 151.

12. Nelson to Cornwallis, October 20, 1781, in Nelson, *Letters*, p. 55.

13. Carl Leopold Baurmeister, *Revolution in America: Confidential Letters and Journals 1776-1784 of Adjutant General Major Baurmeister of the Hessian Forces*, trans. Bernhard A. Uhlendorf (New Brunswick, New Jersey: Rutgers University Press, 1957), p. 475.

14. Swartwout, "Journal of Barnardus Swartwout," p. 38; Hatch, "*York Under the Hill*," p. 65.

15. The figures provided are drawn from Arthur, *End of a Revolution*, p. 159. Freeman, *George Washington*, 5, p. 515, stated that the Americans lost 125 and the French 253 in killed and wounded. The former figure is approximate and includes militia losses which, though not exactly known, were calculated proportionately from knowledge of the Continentals' own rate of loss. Freeman cites Du Bourg as authority for the French casualties. Washington noted only the number of losses sustained by the Americans and the French through the assault on Redoubts 9 and 10. *Diaries*, 2, p. 267. For other accounts of the Allied casualties at Yorktown see La Combe, "Journal of the Siege of York," p. 5, who said that about 90 Frenchmen were killed or died from wounds and about 180 received wounds and survived. According to La Combe, "the losses of Americans is still less important, since they did not take part in the 30 September attack to the left side [Fusiliers' Redoubt] and they found little resistance from the redoubts they took during the night 14-15." Ibid. Baron Closen gave yet higher estimates for the Allied dead and wounded. *Revolutionary Journal*, p. 154. Because most accounts of casualties

do not include those men who died from their wounds, the actual number of killed was probably considerably higher than indicated. Arthur, *End of a Revolution*, p. 159. See also Peckham, *Toll of Independence*, p. 92. For names of many of the Allied dead see Appendices N, O, and P, in Schuyler Otis Bland, comp., ed., *The Yorktown Sesquicentennial: Proceedings of the United States Yorktown Sesquicentennial Commission in Connection with the Celebration of the Siege of Yorktown, 1781* (Washington: United States Government Printing Office, 1932), pp. 376-82.

16. Washington, *Diaries*, 2, p. 270n.

17. Arthur, *End of a Revolution*, pp. 158-159. Johnston includes an unofficial statement that the number of sick and otherwise unfit for service in both the French and American armies numbered 1,430. *Yorktown Campaign*, p. 158. As late as October 16, Dr. Thacher observed a propensity toward sickness, especially on the part of the New England troops: "The prevalent diseases are intermittent and remittent fevers, which are very prevalent in this climate during the autumnal months." *Military Journal*, p. 286. The records are such that no exact number will ever be ascertained with certainty.

18. "Return of the Killed, Wounded and Missing from 28th September to 19th October 1781," Henry Clinton Papers, William L. Clements Library; Arthur, *End of a Revolution*, p. 160. For a discussion of the problems of enumerating British casualties in relation to total British Army strength, see Freeman, *George Washington*, 5, p. 515. See also "Loss of Prisoners at York," Bamberg Manuscripts, collection C5, number 160, Bamberg State Archives, Bamberg, Germany, translated by James D. Mote, pp. 21-23. While the number of killed by the German account appears inordinately high, it does agree with the number provided in the return included in Colonel George Reid to Colonel Daniel Reynolds, dated sometime after October 19, 1781, Miscellaneous Collection, William L. Clements Library. A breakdown of losses incurred among the Hessian units is given in Baurmeister, *Revolution in America*, p. 475.

19. Johnston, *Yorktown Campaign*, p. 158.

20. Arthur, *End of a Revolution*, p. 160. These figures are based on a general return of prisoners dated October 27, 1781. A return dated October 19, 1781, gave 7,249 as the total surrendered, though this did not include the 840 seamen. "State of the Army in Virginia under the Command of Lieut. Gen. Earl Cornwallis," Henry Clinton Papers, William L. Clements Library; See also the return for the preceding day in ibid., also contained in Cornwallis, *Answer to That Part of the Narrative of Lieutenant-General Sir Henry Clinton*, Appendix XXI following p. 237. Washington reported to Congress that 7,247 British troops, plus 840 sailors, were surrendered. Johnston, *Yorktown Campaign*, p. 158. Unofficial returns, which provide a fairly detailed breakdown of the force surrendered, are given in Colonel George Reid to Colonel Daniel Reynolds, dated sometime after October 19, 1781, Miscellaneous Collection, William L. Clements Library; and in "A List of Captures Taken at the Surrender of Lord Cornwallis at York the 17th [sic] October 1781," Lenoir Family Papers, Southern Historical Collection, University of North Carolina Library, Chapel Hill.

21. Swartwout, "Journal of Barnardus Swartwout," p. 38; Brigadier General Edward Hand to Lieutenant Colonel Jeremiah Olney, October 24, 1781, Papers of Major General Edward Hand, Historical Society of Pennsylvania, 2, p. 21.

22. Fersen, "Journal of Operations," p. 440.

23. Arthur, *End of a Revolution*, p. 160. Few of these standards can today be located. Only four can be accounted for, all German (two at West Point, one at the Smithsonian, and one at the CNHP, Yorktown, Virginia). The others may have burned in Washington, D. C., during the fire there in 1814. Thompson, *The British Defenses of Yorktown, 1781*, p 135. Counting both undamaged vessels and those sunk or otherwise ruined, the French could claim four ships of war, one fire ship, 29 transports, four craft directly in the service of the British Army, at least six privately owned craft, and many small boats and other vessels beyond salvage. The names of the various craft are given in "Return of Vessels Taken or Destroyed in York River Virginia 19 Octo," Papers of Major General Edward Hand, Historical Society of Pennsylvania. Closen wrote that of 63 British ships, 32 were sunk. Six of the remaining vessels were armed. *Revolutionary Journal*, p. 154.

24. *New York Journal*, November 12, 1781, reproduced in Moore, *Diary of the American Revolution*, p. 509; Fersen, "Journal of Operations," p. 440; Johnston, *Yorktown Campaign*, p. 158; Freeman, *George Washington*, 5, pp. 515-516.

25. The halbert was "a weapon borne up to the close of the 18th century by all sergeants of foot, artillery, and marines . . . in the various regiments of the English army. It consisted of a strong wooden shaft about 6 feet in length, surmounted by an instrument much resembling a bill-hook, constructed alike for cutting and thrusting, with a crosspiece of steel, less sharp, for the purpose of pushing; one end of this cross-piece was turned down as a hook for use in tearing down works against which an attack was made." Wilhelm, *Military Dictionary and Gazetteer*, p. 212.

26. "An acct of Stores taken from the Enemy which were brought to the Magazine Near the Park of Artillery October 19th 1781," Henry Knox Papers (MHS), 7, p. 130.

27. "Return of Ordnance and Military Stores, taken at York and Gloucester in Virginia by the Surrender of the British Army Oct. 19, 1781," Henry Knox Papers (CNHP). See also an apparently earlier return in Henry Knox Papers (MHS), 7, p. 129, which gives the total number of cannon and mortars as 214. A German account of the ordnance surrendered substantially confirms that given by Knox. Its only discrepancy is in the total number of cannon, which is 10 less than that indicated by Knox. "Loss of Prisoners at York," Bamberg Manuscripts, collection CS, number 160, pp. 21-23. An amusette was a swivel-mounted musket so large it was often considered a light field cannon. It was invented by Marshal Maurice de Saxe. Harold L. Peterson, *Book of the Continental Soldier* (Harrisburg: The Stackpole Company, 1968), pp. 54-55.

28. Captain John Pryor to Colonel William Davies, April 18, 1782, in Palmer, *Calendar of Virginia State Papers*, 3, p. 132.

29. "Notes," *Magazine of American History*, 7 (July, 1881), p. 65.

30. Knox to Colonel John Lamb, November 2, 1781, Henry Knox Papers (CNHP). Today, there are 10 authenticated "Yorktown" pieces at the battlefield park. The ordnance taken from the British were customarily inscribed "Surrendered at the Capitulation of Yorktown," which makes identification of these pieces relatively easy. Determination of the authenticity of Allied artillery is somewhat more difficult since these weapons were not always so marked. Seven of the Yorktown pieces were acquired by transfer from Fort Monroe, Virginia, in 1937. Two others, both 12-pounders and

including the so-called "Lafayette" cannon, were transferred to the park from the Watervliet Arsenal, Troy, New York, by sanction of the War Department in 1938. Other Revolutionary War pieces exhibited at Yorktown but that played no role in the 1781 siege were transferred in the 1930s from the Army War College, the Norfolk Navy Yard, and the national military parks at Gettysburg, Pennsylvania, and Petersburg, Virginia. Still others came to the park by virtue of underwater salvage operations in the York River. Other extant examples of Yorktown vintage artillery have been tentatively located at Fort McNair, Virginia; the College of William and Mary in Williamsburg; the old State and War Building in Washington; and in Albany, New York. Babington, "Known 'Yorktown' guns," pp. 1-4. Two more authentic Yorktown 12-pounders, one British and one French, took part in ceremonies marking the centennial of the siege in 1881. The cannon belonged to the "Chatham Light Artillery" unit of Chatham, Georgia, and were said to have been presented to the unit in 1791 by George Washington. Descriptions of these pieces are detailed in the *New York Times*, October 20, 1881; and in "Replies," *Magazine of American History*, 7 (October, 1881), p. 299. For information on the food supplies, see Thompson, *The British Defenses of Yorktown, 1781*, p 136.

31. "Shott & Shells expended by the Allied Army at the Siege of York in Virginia, from the 9th to the 17th of October inclusive," Henry Knox Papers (MHS), 7, p. 48.

32. Closen, *Revolutionary Journal*, p. 155; Trabue, "Journal of Colonel Daniel Trabue," in Harper, *Colonial Men and Times*, p. 116; De Verger Journal, in Rice and Brown, *American Campaigns*, 1, p. 151; Robin, *New Travels through North America*, p. 65.

33. Ibid.

34. See Hatch, "*York Under the Hill,*", pp. 67, 155-174.

35. Scheer and Rankin, *Rebels and Redcoats*, p. 573.

36. Washington, *Writings*, pp. 275-276.

37. Pitkin, "A Preliminary Study of American Redoubt No. 2," p. 8; Borresen, "Memorandum for the Regional Supervisor of Historic Sites," p. 2.

38. Denny, *Military Journal*, p. 45; Gregory, "Diary of Mathew Gregory at Yorktown, 1781," p. 6.

39. "Orderly Book kept during the Siege of Yorktown," pp. 117-118; *Orderly Book of the Siege of Yorktown*, p. 45.

40. Hatch, "Siege of Yorktown Opens," p. 30; Closen, *Revolutionary Journal*, p. 160; Swartwout, "Journal of Barnardus Swartwout," p. 38.

41. Swartwout, "Journal of Barnardus Swartwout," p. 38. 42. Washington, *Writings*, 23, p. 263.

43. "Itinerary of the Pennsylvania Line," p. 285.

44. Washington, *Writings*, 23, pp. 264, 270, 275-276; Stryker, *New Jersey Continental Line*, p. 26.

45. Gregory, "Diary of Mathew Gregory at Yorktown, 1781," p. 6; Swartwout, "Journal of Barnardus Swartwout," p. 38; Borresen, "Final Report on Redoubt No. 9," p. 52.

46. Hatch, *Yorktown's Main Street*, p. 121; Borresen, "Final Report on Redoubt No. 9," pp. 52-53.

47. *Journals of the Council of the State of Virginia*, 3, pp. 171, 204; Donald O. Dewey, ed., ". . . to level the works at York . . . A Letter of David Jameson," *Virginia Magazine of History and Biography*, 71 (April, 1963), pp. 150-151n. In a related dispute, some Yorktown citizens resented the practice by militia stationed in the village of burning palisades from the earthworks as fuel. Major Alexander Dick of the Virginia State Regiment appealed the matter to the Council of State, which upheld the practice. *Journals of the Council of the State of Virginia*, 3, p. 182.

48. Dewey, ". . . to level the works at York," p. 151. 49. Ibid., pp. 151, 152.

50. Ibid., p. 152.

51. *Yorktown Campaign*, p. 139n. During an 1848 visit, Benson J. Lossing noted that "in the fields farther south, crossing the Hampton road, and extending almost to the old Jamestown road along which the American division of the allied armies approached Yorktown, might be seen a ridge, the remains of the second parallel." *Pictorial Field-Book of the Revolution*, 2, p. 323.

52. Of the six earthworks still discernible in 1934, only one was originally erected by the Allies: the pentagonal redoubt constructed by the French to guard the Gatenois Regiment against possible British incursions along Ballard Creek. See C. L. Coston to Flickinger, memo dated May 22, 1934, CNHP, Yorktown, Virginia.

53. Washington, *Diaries*, 2, pp. 269-270.

54. Baurmeister, *Revolution in America*, p. 475; Arthur, *End of a Revolution*, p. 160.

55. Broughton-Mainwaring, *Historical Record of the Royal Welch Fusiliers*, p. 105; Baurmeister, *Revolution in America*, p. 475; Bonsal, *Cause of Liberty*, p. 159.

56. Rochambeau experienced difficulty getting these funds reimbursed, as evidenced in his letter to Sir Henry Clinton dated December 9, 1781. "Headquarters Papers of the British Army in America," Great Britain, Historical Manuscripts Commission, *Report on American Manuscripts in the Royal Institution of Great Britain*, 4 vols. (Dublin: John Falconer, 1906), 2, p. 362. (Photostatic copies in the archives of the Colonial Williamsburg Foundation, Williamsburg, Virginia.).

57. Bonsal, *Cause of Liberty*, p. 159. Implications of the differences relative to the disposition of Loyalist prisoners are contained in a letter from General Nelson to Cornwallis, October 21, 1781, in Nelson, *Letters*, p. 56.

58. "British and Hessian Officers who Served in America," Thomas T. Myers Collection, item 1620, New York Public Library.

59. Baurmeister, *Revolution in America*, p. 475; Smelser, *Winning of Independence*, p. 328.

60. Wayne Manuscripts, 14, p. 90, Historical Society of Pennsylvania; Thompson, *The British Defenses of Yorktown, 1781*, p 140.

61. Lt. Jakob E. Kling to unknown recipient, November 4, 1781; Gen. Nelson to Commissary at Fredericksburg, October 21, 1781, in Nelson, *Letters*, p. 58; Nelson to Governor Thomas Sim Lee, October 21, 1781, in ibid., pp. 57-58; Johnston, *Yorktown Campaign*, p. 157; Arthur, *End of a Revolution*, p. 160; Edward C. Bruce, "The Yorktown Prisoners and Their Custodian," *Potters's American Monthly*, 18 (May, 1882), p. 556.

62. Clermont-Crèvecoeur Journal, in Rice and Brown, *American Campaigns*, 1, p. 64; Thompson, *The British Defenses of Yorktown, 1781*, p 140.

63. Arthur, *End of a Revolution*, pp. 141-42, 156; Willcox, *Portrait of a General*, pp. 439-40; Bonsal, *Cause of Liberty*, pp. 161-62; Whitridge, *Rochambeau*, p. 225. Clinton to Gloucester, October 29, 1781, Clinton's Letters to Gloucester, 1778-1789. The British squadron was additionally delayed in leaving New York by the visit of Prince William at Clinton's headquarters. Smelser, *Winning of Independence*, p. 326.

Chapter 15: Endings, Beginnings

1. Arthur, *End of a Revolution*, p. 158; Patton, "Campaign of the Allies," pp. 265-266.

2. Arthur, *End of a Revolution*, pp. 160-61.

3. Ibid., p. 161; Johnston, *Yorktown Campaign*, p. 158; Heitman, *Historical Register*, p. 667; Samuel F. Scott, *From Yorktown To Valmy: The Transformation of the French Army in an Age of Revolution* (Niwot CO: University Press of Colorado, 1998), p. 94. Most earlier interpretations (including my own) have the French leaving Yorktown in the spring of 1782. Scott's research, ibid., however, is corroborated with the research and opinion of David F. Riggs, Yorktown Curator, Colonial National Historical Park. Therefore, I have chosen to use that date.

4. Tilghman's ride to Philadelphia is recounted in Bonsal, *Cause of Liberty*, pp. 164-165. An account of the presentation ceremony is in *Freeman's Journal*, November 7, 1781, and quoted in ibid., p. 166; see also Smelser, *Winning of Independence*, p. 328.

5. *New Jersey Journal*, January 9, 1782, reproduced in Moore, Diary *of the American Revolution*, p. 527.

6. November 12, 1781, reproduced in ibid., p. 510.

7. Reprinted in *New York Packet*, November 22, 1781, reproduced in ibid., p 521.

8. Nathan Fiske, *An Oration Delivered at Brookfield, November 14, 1781, in Celebration of the Capture of Lord Cornwallis and his Whole Army at York-Town and Gloucester, in Virginia* (Boston: Thomas and John Fleet, 1781), p. 6.

9. The visit of the Indians to Yorktown occurred in November 1781. *Journals of the Council of the State of Virginia*, 2, p. 400.

10. Captain William Pierce, Jr., to Greene, December 11, 1781, Morgan Manuscripts, vol. 2, The Siege of Yorktown and Surrender of Cornwallis, Pierpont Morgan Library.

11. Clinton, *Narrative*, p. 36.

12. Randolph G. Adams, *A View of Cornwallis's Surrender at Yorktown*, reprinted from *American Historical Review*, 39 (October, 1931). p. 49; Willcox, *British Road to Yorktown*, p. 3; Arthur, *End of a Revolution*, p. 163; A vindication for Clinton appears in *A Brief Review of the Campaign in North America, in the Year 1781, Intended to Justify the Conduct and opinions of Sir Henry Clinton, K. B., and to Place the Character and Proceedings of Earl Cornwallis in a Fair Light* (Nova Scotia: Printed for the Author, 1789). The author of this publication is unknown. The copy examined is in the William L. Clements Library and bears a handwritten note on its title page: "Never published at Sir Henry Clintons request."

13. Willcox, *British Road to Yorktown*, pp. 3, pp. 34-35.

14. Ibid., p. 3; Arthur, *End of a Revolution*, p. 163; Adams, *A View of Cornwallis's Surrender*, p. 49.

15. Smelser, *Winning of Independence*, p. 330. Peckham, *Toll of Independence*, pp. 92-93, 126, 130.

16. Claude Halstead Van Tyne, "The Results of Yorktown," in Edward Creasy, *The 15 Decisive Battles of the World from Marathon to Waterloo*, rev. ed. (New York: Harper and Brothers Publishers, 1908), p. 426.

17. Quoted in Johnston, *Yorktown Campaign*, p. 161.

18. Ibid.

Appendix 4: The Archaeology of the Grand French Battery

1. Borresen, "Orientation Report," p. 64.

2. B. Floyd Flickinger, "Press Release," dated April 16, 1935, in the library of CNHP, Yorktown, Virginia; Bingham Duncan and Fred G. Farthing, memorandum, "French Battery Reconstruction," dated January 25, 1935, in the library of CNHP, Yorktown, Virginia, p. 1.

3. Southside Historical Sites Foundation, "Archaeology/Restoration/Reconstruction of the Yorktown Battlefield," p. 47; "Restoration [sic] of French Battery, York-Hampton Road," MS, dated October 24, 1935, in the library of CNHP, Yorktown, Virginia, p. 3; The use of the principal siege trench as an avenue for transporting ordnance is affirmed by the discovery during excavation of chains and wedges used in moving the pieces. Flickinger, "Press Release," p. 3.

4. Borresen, "Orientation Report," pp. 32, 33. One memo states that fraises were used. Bingham Duncan and C. L. Coston, "A French Battery of the Siege of Yorktown: 1781," dated August 9, 1934, in the library of CNHP, Yorktown, Virginia, p. 1.

5. Duncan and Coston, "A French Battery of the Siege of Yorktown: 1781," p. 1.

6. Ibid.

7. Flickinger, "Press Release," p. 1.

8. Hatch, "On Reconstructing Earthworks," pp. 41, 42.

9. "Restoration of French Battery," p. 4.

10. Ibid., pp. 12-13; Hatch, "On Reconstructing Earthworks," pp. 40, 41, 42.

11. Flickinger, "Press Release," p. 3; "Restoration of French Battery," pp. 4-5; Another view held that this piece was mortar. See Bingham Duncan, Fred G. Farthing, and Thor Borresen, memorandum, "French Battery Reconstruction," dated March 13, 1935, in the library of CNHP, Yorktown, Virginia, p. 1; and Hatch, "On Reconstructing Earthworks," p. 42.

12. Hatch, "On Reconstructing Earthworks," p. 42; Borresen, "Completion Report on American Battery No. 2," p. 67.

13. "Restoration of French Battery," p. 6. Map 7A confirms these angles of fire.

14. "Restoration of French Battery," p. 6.

15. Ibid., p. 8.

16. Ibid., p. 9.

17. Ibid.

18. Ibid., p. 10.

19. Ibid.

20. Ibid., pp. 7-8.

21. A traverse was reconstructed at this point "after considerable discussion. No evidence could be found to show that one existed [in 1781] but conventional practice at the time was to construct traverses between different sections of a battery." Ibid., p. 8.

22. Duncan, Farthing, and Borresen, "French Battery Reconstruction," p. 1; "Restoration of French Battery," pp. 10-11.

23. "Restoration of French Battery," p. 11; Borresen, "Completion Report on American Battery No. 2," p. 82; Hatch, "On Reconstructing Earthworks," p. 41.

24. Borresen, "Completion Report on American Battery No. 2," p. 79; "Restoration of French Battery," pp. 11-12.

25. "Restoration of French Battery," p. 11; Flickinger, "Press Release," p. 3.

26. The idea of reproducing the platforms in concrete is credited to Project Foreman Frank L. Glenn. A. E. Booth, "Report on Use of Concrete for Permanent Restoration Work on Fortifications," MS, dated April 21, 1936, CNHP, Yorktown, Virginia, p. 1.

27. Southside Historical Sites Foundation, "Archaeology/Restoration/ Reconstruction of the Yorktown Battlefield," pp. 15, 43-44.

28. Ibid., p. 44.

29. Ibid., pp. 46-47.

30. Ibid., pp. 15-16, 45-46; Borresen, "Orientation Report," pp. 32, 34.

31. Hatch, "On Reconstructing Earthworks," p. 44.

32. "Journal of the Siege of York in Virginia by a Chaplain," p. 106. The figures given in regard to the particular ordnance in Battery 10A vary somewhat, probably because a great many changes occurred during its use. See, for example, Moore, *Life and Services of Gen. Anthony Wayne*, p. 149; Washington, *Diaries*, 2, p. 264; and Washington, *Writings*, 23, p. 212. See also, for further disparities, Johnston, *Yorktown Campaign*, p. 139; S. Doc. 273, p. 193; and Arthur, *End of a Revolution*, p. 132.

33. Wright, "Notes on the Siege of Yorktown, p. 244.

34. Henry Knox Papers (MHS), 7, p. 104.

35. Tilghman, *Memoir of Lieut. Col. Tench Tilghman*, p. 105; Moore, *Life and Services of Gen. Anthony Wayne*, p. 149; Washington, *Diaries*, 2, p. 264; Washington, *Writings*, 23, p. 212.

36. Henry Knox Papers (MHS), 7, p. 104.

37. Borresen, "Final Report on Redoubt No. 9," p. 56.

38. Pitkin, "A Preliminary Study of American Redoubt No. 2," pp. 8-9, 11-12, 13; Borresen, "Orientation Report," p. 38.

39. Maps 1F, 2F, 15F, 17F, 41F, 48F. None of the American maps checked indicated the presence of such a battery. See also Pitkin, "A Preliminary Study of American Redoubt No. 2," p. 8n. One contemporary mentioned an "American bomb battery ... of four 10-inch mortars." Duncan, "Diary of Captain James Duncan," p. 750. This reference

possibly confused the mortar unit of two pieces opened in Redoubt 12A and the four howitzers or cannon in 11A.

40. "Return of Stores expended at the grand Battery, on the 9th and 10th Instant," Henry Knox Papers (MHS), 7, p. 105.

41. Ibid. , p. 104.

Appendix 5: The Artillery at Yorktown

1. Manucy, *Artillery Through the Ages*, pp. 54-55.

2. Ibid., pp. 52-53; Tousard, *American Artillerist's Companion*, 1, pp. 131-132. Before the start of the Southern campaign, the Americans requested a traveling and a garrison carriage for each of their 18- and 24-pounders. Consequently, most of their guns probably had both types of carriages at Yorktown.

3. Manucy, *Artillery Through the Ages*, p. 51.

4. Peterson, *Round Shot and Rammers*, p. 45.

5. Manucy, *Artillery Through the Ages*, p. 46; Tousard, *American Artillerist's Companion*, 1, p. 131.

6. Peterson, *Round Shot and Rammers*, p. 51. The French livre equaled 1.1 pound English weight.

7. Ibid., p. 48.

8. Ibid.

9. Ibid., p. 54. At least one source specifically refers to Gribeauval artillery being present at Yorktown in 1781. French writer de Cugnac, who authored studies on Napoleon's campaigns, noted that "the French artillery has the pieces of the Gribeauval system," and that "the artillery of Gribeauval was excellent and marked a great improvement on the previous artillery systems." *Yorktown (1781). Trois mois d'operations combinees sur terre et sur mer dans une guerre de coalition* (Nancy-Paris-Strasbourg: Imprimerie Berger-Levrault, 1932), pp. 36, 36n.

10. Peterson, *Round Shot and Rammers*, p. 60; Manucy, *Artillery Through the Ages*, pp. 49-50.

11. Manucy, *Artillery Through the Ages*, pp. 50, 53; Thor Borreson, "Report on American Guns and Carriages," MS, December 1939, CNHP, Yorktown, Virginia, p. 58.

12. John Muller, *A Treatise of Artillery* (London: John Millan, 1757), pp. 260-261.

13. Manucy, *Artillery Through the Ages*, p. 55.

14. Peterson, *Round Shot and Rammers*, p. 60.

15. Le Blond, *Treatise of Artillery*, p. 28.

16. Ibid. The usual rate of fire from artillery pieces during a siege was nine rounds an hour, per gun. Tousard, *American Artillerist's Companion*, 1, p. 100.

17. Manucy, *Artillery Through the Ages*, p. 23.

18. Tousard, *American Artillerist's Companion*, 1, p. 130.

19. Ibid., pp. 340, 345; Manucy, *Artillery Through the Ages*, p. 25. Sometimes the cartridges caused problems by building up residue to such an extent that it blocked the vent opening of the piece and had to be removed with a wormer or wad hook. Sometimes

it smoldered even after the bore had been sponged, which threatened to prematurely ignite the next charge. Artillerymen preferred flannel cartridges over paper ones. Peterson, *Round Shot and Rammers*, pp. 63-64.

20. Tousard, *American Artillerist's Companion*, 1, pp. 345-346; Peterson, *Round Shot and Rammers*, p. 63.

21. Le Blond, *Treatise of Artillery*, p. 20.

22. Manucy, *Artillery Through the Ages*, p. 53.

23. Tielke, *Field Engineer*, 1, p. 227.

24. Lochée, *Elements of Field Fortification*, p. 9n.

25. Tousard, *American Artillerist's Companion*, 1, p. 100.

26. Tielke, *Field Engineer*, 1, pp. 228-229; Muller, *Treatise Containing the Elementary Part of Fortification*, p. 218.

27. Muller, *Treatise Containing the Elementary Part of Fortification*, pp. 229-230; Tielke, *Field Engineer*, 1, pp. 228-229n; Tousard, *American Artillerist's Companion*, 1, pp. 9-10, 100.

28. Le Blond, *Treatise of Artillery*, p. 23.

29. *Field Engineer*, 1, p. 229n.

30. Ibid., pp. 229-230.

31. Peterson, *Round Shot and Rammers*, p. 64.

32. William Stevens, *A System for the Discipline of the Artillery of the United States of America; or, the Young Artillerists' Pocket Companion* (Albany: Websters and Skinners, 1815), p. 44.

33. Manucy, *Artillery Through the Ages*, pp. 55, 75.

34. Ibid., p. 73; Tousard, *American Artillerist's Companion*, 1, p. 390.

35. Tousard, *American Artillerist's Companion*, p. 394.

36. Ibid., pp. 272, 391; Manucy, *Artillery Through the Ages*, p. 74.

37. Manucy, *Artillery Through the Ages*, p. 73; Tousard, *American Artillerist's Companion*, 1, p. 391.

38. Tousard, *American Artillerist's Companion*, pp. 366-367; Manucy, *Artillery Through the Ages*, p. 26.

39. Tousard, *American Artillerist's Companion*, 1, p. 386, 393; Peterson, *Round Shot and Rammers*, p. 64.

40. Peterson, *Round Shot and Rammers*, p. 64. When slow match ignited cartridges when priming powder was used, a priming wire penetrated the cartridge prior to discharge. Tousard, *American Artillerist's Companion*, 1, p. 393.

41. Tousard, *American Artillerist's Companion*, p. 392; Manucy, *Artillery Through the Ages*, p. 73.

42. Peterson, *Round Shot and Rammers*, p. 66.

43. Ibid.

44. Ibid.

45. Stevens, *System for the Discipline*, pp. 62-64.

46. Tousard, *American Artillerist's Companion*, 1, pp. 298-304.

47. Ibid., p. 219.

48. Ibid., pp. 220, 221n; Wright, "Notes on the Siege of Yorktown," p. 247n.

49. Manucy, *Artillery Through the Ages*, p. 60; Peterson, *Round Shot and Rammers*, p. 41. There also existed 2-1/4- and 3-1/2-inch mortars, apparently designed exclusively for shooting hand grenades. Ibid.

50. Tousard, *American Artillerist's Companion*, 1, pp. 254-255, 325n; Muller, *A Treatise of Artillery*, p. 191; Manucy, *Artillery Through the Ages*, pp. 58-59.

51. Stevens, *System for the Discipline*, p. 196; Tousard wrote: "The method of firing en ricochet out of mortars was first tried in 1723 at the artillery school at Strasburg, [France] and with success. At the battle of Rosback, in 1757, the king of Prussia had several six-inch mortars made with trunnions and mounted on traveling carriages, which fired obliquely on the enemy's lines, and amongst their horse, loaded with eight ounces of powder, and at an elevation of one degree and 15 minutes, which did great execution." *American Artillerist's Companion*, 1, p. 2n.

52. Stevens, *System for the Discipline*, p. 196.

53. Tousard, *American Artillerist's Companion*, 1, p. 260.

54. Ibid., pp. 220, 255-56.

55. Ibid., p. 96.

56. Ibid., p. 395; Le Blond, *Treatise of Artillery*, p. 50.

57. Tousard, *American Artillerist's Companion*, 1, p. 395.

58. Peterson, *Round Shot and Rammers*, p. 63.

59. Tousard, *American Artillerist's Companion*, 1, pp. 261-62, 394, 395.

60. Stevens, *System for the Discipline*, p. 237.

61. Tousard, *American Artillerist's Companion*, 1, p. 220.

62. Ibid., pp. 95, 262, 263-64, 395.

63. Ibid., p. 256; Wright, "Notes on the Siege of Yorktown," pp. 246-247.

64. Tousard, *American Artillerist's Companion*, 1, p. 256.

65. Ibid., 1, p. 101; Stevens, *System for the Discipline*, p. 196.

66. *Treatise of Artillery*, p. 39.

67. From Tousard, *American Artillerist's Companion*, 1, p. 322-328. For details of movement consequent with each command, see ibid.

68. Manucy, *Artillery Through the Ages*, p. 56; Peterson, *Round Shot and Rammers*, p. 36.

69. Stevens, *System for the Discipline*, p. 195

70. Peterson, *Round Shot and Rammers*, p. 36; Wright, "Notes on the Siege of Yorktown," p. 247n; Tousard, *American Artillerist's Companion*, 1, p. 269. Technically, the calibers for howitzers were 8.52 inches and 6.53 inches. Ibid., p. 261.

71. Tousard, *American Artillerist's Companion*, 1, p. 272.

72. Ibid., pp. 264, 272.

73. Muller, *Treatise Containing the Elementary Part of Fortification*, 222-23; Lochee, *Elements of Field Fortification*, p. 22n.

74. Le Blond, *Treatise of Artillery*, p. 123.

75. Stevens, *System for the Discipline*, pp. 86, 97. For information on signaling artillery by drum beat, see ibid., pp. 95-96.

Bibliography

MANUSCRIPT COLLECTIONS

Ann Arbor. University of Michigan. William L. Clements Library.

Henry Clinton Papers.
James S. Schoff Collection.
Miscellaneous Collection.
Nathanael Greene Papers.

Ansbach, Germany. Historical Society for Middle Frankonia. Ansbach State Library.

"Wertgetreue Abschrift eines Tagebuchs eines markgräflischen Soldaten / uber / den Aufenthalt in Amerika." Translated by John Luzader.

Bamberg, Germany. Bamberg State Archives.

"Loss of Prisoners at York." Translated by James D. Mote.

Boston. Massachusetts Historical Society.

Benjamin Lincoln Papers.
Henry Knox Papers.

Bronx. Fordham University Library.

Manuscript Collections.

Chapel Hill. University of North Carolina Library.

Southern Historical Collection. Lenoir Family Papers.

Denver. National Park Service. Denver Service Center.

Ewald, Johann. "Diary of the American War." Translated and edited by Joseph
P. Tustin (1979). Unpublished manuscript furnished by Joseph P. Tustin.

Tustin, Joseph P. Letter to Erwin N. Thompson, December 9, 1974.

Fort Belvoir, Virginia. Engineers Museum

Querenet de La Combe, "Journal of the Siege of York in Virginia in October
1781." Translated copy of original.

Marburg/Lahn, Germany. Hessisches Staatsarchiv.

Letter from 2d Lt. Jakob Ernst Kling to unknown recipient, November 4, 1781.
Translated by John Luzader.

Mittelfranken, Germany. Historischer Verein.

Letter from soldier Johann Radler to his mother in Mainbernheim, December
1781. Translated by John Luzader.

Morristown, New Jersey. Morristown National Historical Park Library.

Manuscripts Collection.

New-York Historical Society.

John Lamb Papers.
Swartwout Folder.
"The Journal of Barnardus Swartwout Junr during the American Revolution
from Nov. 1777 to June 1783—as Copied and corrected by himself in 1834."

New York Public Library.

Edward Hand Papers.
George Bancroft Collection.
Thomas A. Emmet Collection.
Thomas T. Myers Collection.

Pierpont Morgan Library.

The Siege of Yorktown and Surrender of Cornwallis. Collected by J. Pierpont Morgan, 1908. 2 vols. Manuscripts.
Yorktown Documents.

Philadelphia. Historical Society of Pennsylvania.

Boudinot Papers.
General Revolutionary Manuscripts.
Papers of Major General Edward Hand.
Simon Gratz Autograph Collection.
Wayne Manuscripts.
William Irvine Papers.

Washington, D.C. Library of Congress, Manuscript Division

Edward Hand Papers.
George Washington Papers.

Williamsburg. College of William and Mary. Department of Anthropology. Southside Historical Sites Foundation.

"Archaeology/Restoration/Reconstruction of the Yorktown Battlefield, Colonial National Historical Park,Virginia: Preliminary Thoughts and Recommendations." Mimeographed report dated September 27, 1974.

"Plan of Archaeological Excavations, Mid-Second Siege Line, Yorktown, Virginia. Preliminary Drawing." 1974.

Williamsburg. Archives of Colonial Williamsburg Foundation.

"Headquarters Papers of the British Army in America." *Report on American Manuscripts in the Royal Institution of Great Britain.* 4 vols. Dublin: John Falconer, 1906. Photostatic copies.

Yorktown. Colonial National Historical Park.

Berthier Papers. "Abstract of the Operations of the Campaign of the combined French and American Army 1781." Copy translated by Laura Feller.

John D. Babington. "Known 'Yorktown' guns, siege and field, not in Colonial National Historical Park." Memorandum dated March 22, 1955.

A. E. Booth. "Fusileers Redoubt." Unpublished manuscript dated November 4, 1936.

____. "Report on Use of Concrete for Permanent Restoration Work on Fortifications." Unpublished manuscript dated April 21, 1936.

Thor Borresen. "Completion Report on American Battery No. 2, Second Parallel." Unpublished manuscript dated April 16, 1941.

____. "Drawings Illustrating Field Fortifications of Revolutionary War Period." Unpublished manuscript dated April 1942.

____. "Final Report on Redoubt No. 9, Second Parallel." Unpublished manuscript dated December, 23, 1938.

____. "Memorandum for the Regional Supervisor of Historic Sites," dated April 5, 1940.

____. "Memorandum to the Acting Park Historian, Subject: Bridges," dated March 27, 1939.

____. "Memorandum to the Historical Division," dated March 31, 1938.

____. "Orientation Report on the Yorktown Battlefield Area Containing the Fortifications, Encampment Areas, Headquarter Sites and Artillery Parks Constructed by the British, French and American Armies in the Year 1781." Unpublished manuscript dated February 21, 1940.

____. "Report on American Guns and Carriages." Unpublished manuscript dated December 1939.

____. "Report on the Proposed Reconstruction of a Pigeon Hill Redoubt." Unpublished manuscript dated October 27, 1939.

____. "Report on the Stone Mortar placed in the Grand French Battery." Unpublished manuscript dated May 16, 1938.

Dupleix de Cadignan, "Journal of Chevalier Dupleix de Cadignan." Warrington Dawson Papers.

Rock L. Comstock, Jr. "The French Artillery Park at Yorktown: A Report and Exhibit Plan." Unpublished manuscript dated January 13, 1957.

C. L. Coston. "Memorandum to Mr. Flickinger," dated May 22, 1934.

Chevalier d'Ancteville. "Journal of the Chesapeake Campaign." Translated by Thomas M. Pitkin. Copy dated March 1941.

"Diary of French naval operations in America, January 5, 1779-September 2, 1782." Translated typescript copy.

Johann Conrad Doehla. "The Journal of Johann Conrad Doehla, 1777-1785." Translated by Robert J. Tilden. Typescript copy dated September 1941.

Bingham Duncan: "Notes on Auxiliary Siege Materials." Memorandum to Mr. Cox dated March 23, 1934.

Bingham Duncan and C. L. Coston. "A French Battery of the Siege of Yorktown: 1781." Memorandum to Mr. Flickinger dated August 9, 1934.

Bingham Duncan and Fred G. Farthing. "French Battery Reconstruction." Memorandum to Mr. Flickinger dated January 25, 1935.

Bingham Duncan, Fred G. Farthing, and Thor Borresen. "French Battery Reconstruction." Memorandum to Mr. Flickinger dated March 13, 1935.

"Extracts from the Lamb Papers Relating to the Yorktown Campaign." Transcribed copy.

Floyd B. Flickinger. "Press Release." Manuscript dated April 16, 1935.

Walter S. Flickinger. "Report on the Excavation of American Gun Battery known as No. 4, in Advance of the 2nd Parallel, including Additional Supplementary Data." Unpublished manuscript dated April 11, 1938.

"Gist's Orderly Book of the Siege of Yorktown, Virginia, 1781." Photostatic copy.

Mathew Gregory. "Diary of Mathew Gregory at Yorktown, 1781." Penciled notes by G. E. Hubbard. Typescript copy.

Charles E. Hatch, Jr. "On Reconstructing Earthworks (with Application to the Grand French Battery)." Typescript copy signed by S. Michael Hubbell, March 3, 1964.

____. "The Siege of Yorktown Opens." Unpublished, undated manuscript.

Henry Knox Papers. Photostatic copies.

Robert R. Madden. "Memorandum to Files, through Superintendent," dated July 17, 1972.

"Orderly Book kept during the Siege of Yorktown, Va. Sep. 26-Nov. 2, 1781." Photostatic copy.

Thomas M. Pitkin. "A Preliminary Study of American Redoubt No. 2, Yorktown Battlefield." Unpublished manuscript dated May 28, 1941.

Asa Redington. "Narrative of Asa Redington." Typescript copy from an unidentified source.

"Restoration of French Battery, York-Hampton Road [Grand French Battery]." Unpublished manuscript dated October 24, 1935.

Edward M. Riley. "The History of the Founding and Development of Yorktown, Virginia, 1691-1781." Unpublished manuscript dated March 20, 1942.

Daniel Shute. "With General Benjamin Lincoln at Yorktown. August 18, 1781—April 28, 1782. From the Journal kept by Dr. Daniel Shute of South Hingham, Massachusetts." Typescript copy.

James R. Sullivan. "A Documentary Study of British Redoubt No. 10 in the Yorktown Battlefield in Colonial National Historical Park." Unpublished manuscript dated November 1952.

St. George Tucker. "Journal kept by Col. St. George Tucker during the siege of Yorktown and Surrender of Cornwallis, Oct. 1781." Photostatic copy.

_____. "Letters to and from St. George Tucker, October 1 through October 15, 1781." Edited by S. Michael Hubbell. Typescript copy.

HISTORICAL MAPS

1F. Aboville, Francois Marie de. "Plan du siege d'York en Virginie par l'armee alliee d'Amerique et de France sous les ordres des Genaux. Washington et Cte. de Rochambeau Contre l'Armee Angloise commandee par le lord Cornwallis en Octobre 1781." Colonial Williamsburg Foundation.

2F. _____. "Plan du Siege d'York en Virginie par l'armee alliee d'Amerique et de france, sous les Ordres des Gaux. Washington & Comte de Rochambeau, contre l'Armee Angloise Commandee par Lord Cornwallis, en Octobre 1781." John Carter Brown Library.

3A. "A Draught of York and its Environs." Henry Knox Papers. Massachusetts Historical Society.

4B. "A Plan of the Entrance of Chesapeak Bay, with James and York Rivers; wherein are shewn the Respective Positions (in the beginning of October) 1. of the British Army Commanded by Lord Cornwallis at Gloucester and York in Virginia; 2. of the American and French Forces under General Washington, 3. and of the French Fleet under Count de Grasse. Published by William Faden, London, 1781. Map Division. Library of Congress.

5AB. "A sketch map of York and Gloucester peninsula, July 20, 1781." Colonial Williamsburg Foundation.

6F. "Attaque de la ville d'York en Virginie prise le 19 fibre 1781 par les armees combinees de France et d'Amerique." Henry Clinton Papers. William L. Clements Library.

7A. Bauman, Sebastian. "To His Excellency Gen. Washington Commander in Chief of the Armies of the United States of America This Plan of the investment of York and Gloucester. . . ." Map Division. Library of Congress.

8F. Berthier, Louis Alexandre. Map of the Encampment of the French and American Armies at Archer's Hope, 25 September 1781. Berthier Papers. Princeton University.

9F. ____. Map of the Encampment of the French and American Armies outside Williamsburg, 26 September 1781. Berthier Papers. Princeton University.

10F. ____. "Plan d'York Town pour Servir a l'Establissement de Quartier d'hyver du Regiment de Soissonnois; et des Grenadiers et Chasseurs de St. Onge le 12 8bre 1781." Berthier Papers. Princeton University.

11F. Berthier, L.-A. and C.-L. "Plan figure a vue du Siege d'Yor Map Division. Library of Congress.

12F. "Carte de la campagne de la division aux ordres du Mis. de St. Simon en Virginie depuis le 2. 7bre. 1781, jusqu'a l'redition d'York le 19. 8bre. meme annee." Ayer Collection. The Newberry Library.

13F. "Carte de la Partie de la Virginie ou l'Armee Combinee de France F des Etats-Unis de l'Amerique a fait prissonniere l'Armee Anglaise commandee par Lord Cornwallis le 19 Octbre. 1781. Avec le Plan de 1'Attaque d'York-town & de Glocester." Map Division. Library of Congress.

14F. "Carte des environs de Williamsburg en Virginie ou les Armees Francoise et Americaine ont campe's en Septembre 1781. Armee de Rochambeau, 1782." Map Division. Library of Congress.

15F. "Carte des Environs de York en Virginie avec les attaques et la position des Armees Francoise et Americaine devant cette place en 1781." Henry Clinton Papers. William L. Clements Library.

16F. "Carte des environs de York en Virginie avec les attaques a la position des armees francaise et americaine devant cette place." Henry Clinton Papers. William L. Clements Library.

17F. "Carte des Environs d'York avec les attaques a la position des Armees francaise et Americain devant cette place." Map Division. Library of Congress.

18F. "Carte des Environs d'York en Virginie avec les attaques et la position des Armees francoise et Americaine pendant la Siege en 8bre 1781." Map Division. Library of Congress.

19F. "Carte des Environs d'York en Virginie avec les attaques et la position des armees francaise et americaine pendant le Siege En 8bre 1781." Map Department. William L. Clements Library.

20B. Chesapeake Bay, with Place names. Henry Clinton Papers. William L. Clements Library.

21B. Confluence of the James River, York River and Chesapeake Bay. (Rough sketch.) Henry Clinton Papers. William L. Clements Library.

22B. Delaware Bay and Chesapeake. Henry Clinton Papers. William L. Clements Library.

23A. DeWitt, Simeon. "No. 124, U. From Allen's Ordinary through Williamsburgh to York." Erskine-DeWitt manuscript map. New York Historical Society.

24F. DuBourg. "Plan du Siege d'York par L'Armee combinee, commandee par les Generaux Washington et Cte. de Rochambeau en 1781." Map Department. William L. Clements Library.

25B. Fage, Captain. "A Plan of the Posts of York and Gloucester in the Province of Virginia, Established by His Majesty's Army under the Command of Lieut General Earl Cornwallis. . . ." Includes overlay entitled "The Position of the Army between the Ravines on the 28th and 29th of Sept. 1781." Mariners Museum. Newport News, Virginia.

26F. French Engineers. "Plan de l'Armee de Cornwallis, attaquee et faitte Prisoniere dans Yorktown, le 19 8bre par l'Armee Combine Francaise et Americaine. Dessine sur les Lieux par les Ingeniers de l'Armee a Paris. Chez Le Rouge, Xbre, 1781." Map Division. Library of Congress.

27F. ____. "Plan des ouvrages faits a York town en Virginie." Map Division. Library of Congress.

28A. Gouvion, Jean-Baptiste. "Plan of the Attacks of york in Virginia by the Allied Armies of America and France Commanded by his Excellency General Washington his Excellency the Count Rochambeau Commanding the French Army." Map Division. National Archives.

29B. Hayman, John. Map of the Siege of Yorktown. Map Division. Library of Congress.

30B. Hills, Jonathan. "A Plan of York Town and Gloucester, in the Province of Virginia, Shewing the Works constructed for the Defence of those Posts by the British Army, under the Command of Lt. Genl. Earl Cornwallis, together with the Attacks and Operations of the American and French Forces, Commanded by Genl. Washington and Count Rochambeau, to whom the said Posts were Surrendered on the 17th October 1781." Map Division. National Archives.

31F. LaCombe, Querneal de. "Carte des Environs D'York en Virginie avec les Attaques et la Position des Armees Francoise et Americaine pendent la Siege de 8bre 1781." Map Division. Library of Congress.

32F. LaCombe, Querenet de. "Carte des Environs d'York en Virginie avec les attaques et la position des Armees Francoise et Americaine pendant la Siege en 8bre. 1781." Map Division. Library of Congress.

33F .____. "Plan d'York en Virginie avec les attaques et les campmens de l'armee combinee de France et d'Amerique. Siege d'York, 1781." Map Division. Library of Congress.

34F. "Plan d'York en Virginie avec les attaques faites par les Armees Francoise et Americaine en 8bre 1781." Map Division. Library of Congress. A nearly identical map is in the Engineers Museum, Fort Belvoir, Virginia.

35F. "Reconnaissance Des Ouvrages de la Ville d'York, avec le Trace des attaques dirigees contre eux." Map Division. Library of Congress.

36F. "Reconnaissance des Ouvrages de la Ville d'York avec le Trace des attaques diriges contre eux.'" Map Division. Library of Congress.

37F. ____. "Siege d'York 1781." Map Division. Library of Congress.

38B. Locke, John Hartwell. Map of the Siege of Yorktown. Yale University Library.

39B. "Map and Chart of those Parts of the Bay of Chesapeak York and James Rivers which are at present The Seat of War." Colonial Williamsburg Foundation.

40F. "Notes sur les environs de York." Map Division. Library of Congress.

41F. Opterre, Henri Crublier d'. "Carte des Environs d'York avec les attaques et la position des Armees Francaise et Americaine devant cette place." Paul Mellon Collection. Upperville, Virginia.

42F. "Virginie. Embouchure de la Baye de Chesapeake a Environs de Williamsburg, York, Hampton, Et Portsmouth." Paul Mellon Collection. Upperville, Virginia.

43F. Perron, Joachim du. "Environs de Glocester." Princeton University Library.

44F. "Expedition de Chesapeack." Princeton University Library.

45F. "Plan des postes d'York et Glocester pris sur les Anglais au mois d'octobre 1781." Shrady Papers. Princeton University Library.

46F. "Plan de Siege d'York, en Virginie par l'Armee alliee d'Amerique et de france sous les Ordres des Gaux. Washington et Cte. de Rochambeau, contre l'Armee Anglaise Commandee par Lord Cornwalis [sic] en Octobre 1781." Map Division. Library of Congress.

47F. "Plan du debarquement et de la Marche de la division Commandee par le Mr de St. Simon, sa reunion avec le Corps du Mr. de la Fayette, et cette de l'Armee combinee de Washington et de Rochambeau, et le Siege d'Yorck, 1781." Map Division. Library of Congress.

48F. "Plan du siege d'York fait par l'armee combinee de Amerique et de France sous les ordres du General Washington." Map Division. Library of Congress.

49F. "Plan'du siege d'York par l'armee combinee commandee par les Generaux Washington et Cte. de Rochambeau." Henry Clinton Papers. William L. Clements Library.

50B. "Plan of York Town and Gloucester in Virginia Shewing the Works constructed for the Defence of those Posts by the Rt. Honble. Lieut. General Earl Cornwallis with the Attacks of the Combined Army of French and Rebels under the Command of the Generals Count de Rochambeaud [sic] and Washington which Capitulated October 1781." Map Division. Library of Congress.

51B. "Position of the Troops under Earl Cornwallis, on the 28 and 29th September 1781; when the Enemy first appeared." Henry Clinton Papers. William L. Clements Library.

52A. Renault, Jn. F. "Plan of York Town in Virginia and adjacent Country.Exhibiting the Operations of the American, French & English Armies during the Siege of that Place in Oct. 1781. Drawn by Jn. F. Renault. With a Crow-Pen and presented to the Marquis de Lafayette." Map Division. Library of Congress.

53F. "Siege d'Yorck 1781 19 8bre 1781." Map Division.Library of Congress.

54F. "Siege d'York." Map Division. Library of Congress.

55A. Stiles, Ezra. "Approach & Position of our Works Oct. 17, 1781." Yale University Library.

56A. "Surrendery Oct. 19,1781." Yale University Library.

57B. Sutherland, Alexander. "Sketch of the posts of York Town and Gloucester Point shewing the French and Rebel attacks upon the former in October, 1781." Henry Clinton Papers. William L. Clements Library.

58B. ____. The British' Works at Yorktown and Gloucester. Henry Clinton Papers. William L. Clements Library.

59B. Tarleton, Banastre. "Plan of the Siege of York Town in Virginia." Record Group 77. National Archives.

60B. Williamsburg and the slip of land between York and James Rivers from thence to Hampton. Henry Clinton Papers. William L. Clements Library.

61F. Yorktown Area. Map Division. Library of Congress.

62F. "York en Virginie Octobre 1781." Map Division. Library of Congress.

63B. Yorktown, Virginia and the surrounding area. Simcoe Papers. William L. Clements Library.

GOVERNMENT DOCUMENTS

U.S Department of the Interior. U.S. Geological Survey. "Colonial National Monument, Yorktown Battlefield, Virginia." Map, 1931.

U.S Senate. *Journal of the Siege of York-Town*. By Gaspard de Gallatin. 71st Cong., 3d sess., February 17, 1931, S. Doc. 322.

____. *The Story of the Campaign and Siege of Yorktown*. 71st Cong., 3d sess., February 17, 1931, S. Doc. 318.

____. *The Virginia Campaign and the Blockade and Siege of Yorktown, 1781*. By Colonel H. L. Landers. 71st Cong., 3d sess., February 7, 1931, S. Doc. 273.

ARTICLES AND NEWSPAPERS

Atkinson, C. T. "British Forces in North America, 1774-1781: Their Distribution and Strength." *Journal of the Society for Army Historical Research* 16 (Part 1); 19 (Part 2); 20 (Part 3).

Barneville, Brisout de. "War Diary, May, 1780-October, 1781." *French-American Review* 3 (October-December, 1950): 217-78. Typescript copy of pp. 269-78, translated by Herbert Olsen, in the library of Colonial National Historical Park.

Bruce, Edward C. "The Yorktown Prisoners and Their Custodian." *Potter's American Monthly* 18 (May, 1882): 555-58.

Burne, A. H. "Cornwallis at Yorktown." *Journal of the Society for Army Historical Research* 17 (Summer, 1938): 71-76.

Burnham, John. "Recollections of the Revolution." *Magazine of History*, extra number 54, part 2 (1917): 119-33.

Butler, Richard. "General Richard Butler's Journal of the Siege of Yorktown." *Historical Magazine* 8 (March, 1864): 102-12.

Callahan, North. "Henry Knox, General Washington's General." *New-York Historical Society Quarterly* 44 (April, 1960): 151-66.

Cobb, David. "Before York Town, Virginia, October 1-November 30, 1781." *Proceedings of the Massachusetts Historical Society* 19 (1881-1882): 67-73.

Davis, John. "The Yorktown Campaign. Journal of Captain John Davis of the Pennsylvania Line." *Pennsylvania Magazine of History and Biography* 5 (1881): 290-305.

Dawson, Warrington. "A New Record of the Sieges of Yorktown and Pensacola." *Legion D'Honneur* 4 (1933-1934): 80-86.

_____. "The Chevalier D'Ancteville and His Journal of 'The Chesapeake Campaign.'" *Legion D'Honneur* 3 (October, 1931): 83-96.

Dewey, Donald O. ". . . to level the works at York . . .: A Letter of David Jameson." *Virginia Magazine of History and Biography* 71 (April, 1963): 150-52.

Du Bourg, Cromot. "Diary of a French Officer, 1781." *Magazine of American History* 4 (June, 1880): 441-49.

Duncan, James. "Diary of Captain James Duncan, of Colonel Moses Hazen's Regiment, in the Yorktown Campaign, 1781." *Pennsylvania Archives*, 2d ser. 15 (1890): 743-52.

Engineers. "Journal of the Siege of York in Virginia." *Magazine of American History* 4 (June, 1880): 449-52.

Feltman, William. "The Journal of Lieut. William Feltman, of the First Pennsylvania Regiment, from May 26, 1781 to April 25, 1782, embracing the Siege of Yorktown and the Southern Campaign." *Pennsylvania Historical Society Collections* 1 (May, 1853): 303-48.

Fersen, Axel de. "Journal of Operations." *Magazine of American History* 3 (July, 1879): 437-45.

Fitzpatrick, J.C. "George Washington," in Dumas Malone (ed.), *Dictionary of American Biography* (New York: Charles Scribner's Sons, 1936; 1964-), 10: 509-27

Gardner, Asa Bird, arr. "Disposition and Order of Battle of the Allied Armies on the March from Williamsburgh, to the Siege of York." *Magazine of American History* 7 (October, 1881): 267-69.

Greene, Lorenzo J. "Some Observations on the Black Regiment of Rhode Island in the American Revolution," *Journal of Negro History*, 27 (1952), pp. 142-172.

Guerlac, Henry. "Vauban: The Impact of Science on War," in Edward Mead Earle, ed., *Makers of Modern Strategy: Military Thought from Machiavelli to Hitler*. Princeton: Princeton University Press, 1941.

Hand, Edward. "Edward Hand to Jasper Yeates on the Siege of Yorktown in 1781." *Bulletin of the New York Public Library* 6 (August, 1902): 286.

Handley, Augustus E., trans. "Comments After Yorktown by a French Newspaper." *Mississippi Valley Historical Review* 25 (1931): 76-79.

Hatch, Charles E., Jr. "Gloucester Point in the Siege of Yorktown, 1781." *William and Mary College Quarterly Historical Magazine*, 2d ser. 20 (April, 1940): 265-84.

Haynes, Edward C. "The Siege of Yorktown." *Chautauquan* 15 (April; 1892): 1-10.

"'Itinerary of the Pennsylvania Line from Pennsylvania to South Carolina, 1781-1782." *Pennsylvania Magazine of History and Biography* 36 (1912): 273-92.

Johnson, C. S. "The Surrender of Cornwallis." *Harper's New Monthly Magazine* 63 (August, 1881): 323-45.

"Journal of the Siege of York in Virginia by a Chaplain of the American Army." *Collections of the Massachusetts Historical Society* 9 (1804): 102-8.

Lauzun, Armand Louis de Goutant. "Narrative of the Duke de Lauzun." *Magazine of American History* 6 (January, 1881): 51-53.

"Letters and other Papers, 1735-1829." *Virginia Magazine of History and Biography* 23 (April, 1915): 182.

Lucas, Lydia. "Yorktown Campaign is Featured in Allyn K. Ford Collection." *Minnesota History* 44 (Summer, 1975).

Menonville, Louis Antoine Thibault. "Journal of the Siege of York." *Magazine of American History* 7 (October, 1881): 283-88.

Middleton, Arthur. "Correspondence of Arthur Middleton." *South Carolina Historical and Genealogical Magazine* 26 (October, 1925): 186-89.

Newspaper Accounts. *Magazine of American History* 6 (January, 1881). "Yorktown Number."

Newton, A. P. "Forgotten Deeds of the Empire: Surrender at Yorktown and its Lessons." *Saturday Review* 161 (February 29, 1936): 285.

New York Times. 1881.

Nickerson, Hoffman. "Yorktown, 1781." *American Mercury* 24 (September, 1931): 79-89.

Orderly Book. "A Gap in History Filled." October 16, 1881; "The March from Dobbs Ferry as shown by an Orderly Book." *New York Times*. October 23, 1881.

Partridge, William T., Jr. "The Battleflags at Yorktown." *St. Nicholas* 62 (October, 1935): 11, 40.

Patton, Jacob Harris. "The Campaign of the Allies: The Surrender of Lord Charles Cornwallis." *Magazine of American History* 7 (October, 1881): 241—66.

Raymond, Richard D., and Loreen Finkelstein. "George Washington's Field Tents: The Challenge of Preserving and Interpreting a National Treasure in the 21st Century." CRM. Vol. 23 (No. 3, 2000), 3-5.

Rochambeau, Donatien Marie Joseph de Vernier, Viscount de. "The War in America: An Unpublished Journal (1780-1783)," in Jean-Edmond Weelen, *Rochambeau, Father and Son: A Life of the Marechal de Rochambeau*. Translated by Lawrence Lee. New York: Henry Holt and Company, 1936.

Saint-Exupery, Anais de. "The War Diary of Georges Alexander Cesar de Saint-Exupery, Lieutenant in the Regiment of Sarre-Infantry." *Legion D'Honneur* 3 (October, 1931): 107-13.

Sanderson, Reuben. "Diary of the March from the Hudson to Yorktown, and Return, by Lieutenant Reuben Sanderson, Fifth Connecticut Continental Line, on Duty with Scammell's Light Infantry Corps," in Henry P. Johnston, *The Yorktown Campaign and the Surrender of Cornwallis*. New York: Harper and Brothers, 1881.

Selig, Robert. "Storming the Redoubts." *Military History Quarterly*, Vol. 8, no. 1 (1995), 18-27.

_____. "The duc de Lauzun and his Légion, Rochambeau's Most Troublesome, Colorful Soldiers." *Colonial Williamsburg: The Journal of the Colonial Williamsburg Foundation*. Vol. 21, No. 6 (December/January 2000), 59-60.

_____. "Deux-Ponts Germans. Unsung Heroes of the American Revolution." *German Life*. Vol. 2, No. 2 (August/September 1995), 50-53.

_____. "François Joseph Paul Comte de Grasse, the Battle off the Virginia Capes, and the American Victory at Yorktown," *Colonial Williamsburg. The Journal of the Colonial Williamsburg Foundation*. Vol. 21, No. 5 (October/November 1999), pp. 26-32.

Shafroth, John F. "The Strategy of the Yorktown Campaign, 1781." *United States Naval Institute Proceedings* 57 (June, 1931), 721-736.

"Siege of York and Gloucester, Virginia." *American Museum* (June, 1787), pp. 475-77.

Smith, Jacob. "Diary of Jacob Smith, American Born." Edited by Charles W. Heathcote. *Pennsylvania Magazine of History and Biography* 56 (July, 1932) : 260-64.

Stevens, John Austin. "The Allies at Yorktown, 1781." *Magazine of American History* 6 (January, 1881): 17-26.

"The Bauman Map of the Siege of Yorktown." *Yale University Library Gazette* 21 (October, 1946): 14-17.

Tilden, John Bell. "Extracts from the Journal of Lieutenant John Bell Tilden, Second Pennsylvania Line, 1781-1782." *Pennsylvania Magazine of History and Biography* 19 (April, 1895): 51-63; (July, 1895): 208-33.

Trabue, Daniel. "Colonel Daniel Trabue's Description of the Siege of Yorktown," in Lillie DuPuy Harper, ed., *Colonial Men and Times*. Philadelphia: Innes and Sons, 1916.

Trumbull, Jonathan. "Yorktown, Virginia, Aug. 12-Nov. 5, 1781." *Proceedings of the Massachusetts Historical Society* 14 (1875-1876): 331-38.

Urwin, Gregory J. W., "Cornwallis and the Slaves of Virginia: A New Look at the Yorktown Campaign," *International Commission of Military History Proceedings, Norfolk Virginia, 2002*. Ed. by John A. Lynn (Wheaton, Ill.: The Cantigny First Division Foundation, 2003): 172-92.

Van Cortlandt, Philip. "Autobiography of Philip Van Cortlandt, Brigadier General in the Continental Army." *Magazine of American History* 2 (May, 1878): 278-98.

Van Tyne, Claude Halstead. "The Results of Yorktown," in Edward Creasy, *The Fifteen Decisive Battles of the World from Marathon to Waterloo*. rev. ed. New York: Harper and Brothers, Publishers, 1908.

Wild, Ebenezer. "Journal of Ebenezer Wild." *Proceedings of the Massachusetts Historical Society*, 2d ser. 6 (1890-1891): 79-160.

Willcox, William B., and Wyatt, Frederick. "Sir Henry Clinton: A Psychological Exploration in History." *William and Mary College Quarterly Historical Magazine* 16 (January, 1959): 3-26.

Wright, John W. "Notes on the Continental Army." *William and Mary College Quarterly Historical Magazine*, 2d ser. 13 (April, 1933): 63-97.

_____. "Notes on the Siege of Yorktown in 1781 with Special Reference to the Conduct of a Siege in the Eighteenth Century." *William and Mary College Quarterly Historical Magazine*, 2d ser. 12 (October, 1932): 229-49.

BOOKS (PRIMARY AND SECONDARY)

A Brief Review of the Campaign in North-America, in the Year 1781; Intended to Justify the Conduct and Opinions of Sir Henry Clinton, K. B., and to Place the Character and Proceedings of Earl Cornwallis in a Fair Light. Nova Scotia: Privately printed, 1789.

Adams, Randolph G. *A View of Cornwallis's Surrender at Yorktown*. Reprint from *American Historical Review* 37 (October, 1931).

Agniel, Lucien. *The Late Affair has Almost Broke My Heart*. Riverside, Connecticut: The Chatham Press, Inc., 1972.

Alden, John R. *A History of the American Revolution*. New York: Alfred A. Knopf, 1972.

Andreus, John. *History of the War with America, France, Spain, and Holland; Commencing in 1775 and Ending in 1783*. 4 vols. London: John Fielding, 1786.

Arthur, Robert. *The End of a Revolution*. New York: Vantage Press, 1965.

_____. *The Sieges of Yorktown, 1781 and 1862*. Fort Monroe, Virginia: The Coast Artillery School, 1927.

Babits, Lawrence E. *A Devil of a Whipping: The Battle of Cowpens*. Chapel Hill: Universityof North Carolina Press, 1998.

Bailyn, Bernard. *The Ideological Origins of the American Revolution*. Cambridge, Mass.:Harvard University Press, 1967.

_____. *To Begin the World Anew: The Genius and Ambiguities of the American Founders*. New York: Alfred A. Knopf, 2003.

Balch, Thomas. *The French in America during the War of Independence of the United States, 1777-1783*. 2 vols. Philadelphia: Porter and Coates, 1891.

Bancroft, Aaron. *Life of George Washington, Commander in Chief of The American Army through the Revolutionary War, and the First President of the United States*. London: John Stockdale, 1808.

Bass, Robert D. *The Green Dragoon: The Lives of Banastre Tarleton and Mary Robinson*. New York: Henry Holt and Co., 1957.

Baurmeister, Carl Leopold. *Revolution in America: Confidential Letters and Journals 1776-1784 of Adj. Gen. Major Baurmeister of the Hessian Forces*. Translated by Bernhard A. Uhlendorf. New Brunswick, New Jersey: Rutgers University Press, 1957.

Belfield, Eversley. *Defy and Endure: Great Sieges of Modern History*. New York: Crowell-Collier Press, 1967.

Berg, Fred Anderson. *Encyclopedia of Continental Army Units*. Harrisburg: Stackpole Books, 1972.

Blanchard, Claude. *The Journal of Claude Blanchard, Commissary of the French Auxiliary Army Sent to the United States During the American Revolution, 1780-1783*. Translated by William Duane. Edited by Thomas Balch. Albany, 1879.

Bland, Schuyler Otis, comp., ed. *The Yorktown Sesquicentennial: Proceedings of The United States Yorktown Sesquicentennial Commission in Connection with the Celebration of the Siege of Yorktown, 1781*. Washington: United States Government Printing Office, 1932.

Boatner, Mark Mayo, III, comp. *The Encyclopedia of the American Revolution*. New York: David McKay, 1966.

Bonsal, Stephen. *The Cause of Liberty*. London: Michael Joseph Limited, 1947.

Brialmont, Alexis H. *Hasty Intrenchments*. Translated by Charles A. Empson. London: Henry S. King and Company, 1872.

Brookhiser, Richard. *Alexander Hamilton: American*. NY: The Free Press, 1999.

Brooks, Noah. *Henry Knox, A Soldier of the Revolution*. New York: G. Putnam's Sons, 1900.

Broughton-Mainwaring, Rowland, comp. *Historical Record of the Royal Welch Fusiliers Late the Twenty-third Regiment, or, Royal Welsh Fusiliers (The Prince of Wales's Own Royal Regiment of Welsh Fuziliers)*. London: Hatchards, Piccadilly, 1889.

Buchanan, John. *American Revolution in the Carolinas*. New York: John Wiley and Sons, 1997.

Buchser, John J. *Yorktown, Cradle of the Republic*. Hampton, Virginia: Houston Printing and Publishing House, 1937.

Carp, E. Wayne. *To Starve the Army at Pleasure: Continental Army Administration and American Political Culture*. Chapel Hill: University of North Carolina Press, 1984.

Chadwick, French Ensor, comp. *The Graves Papers and Other Documents Relating to the Naval Operations of the Yorktown Campaign, July to October, 1781*. New York: The Naval History Society, 1916. Reprint. New York: Arno Press, 1968.

Clairac, M. le Chevalier de. *The Field Engineer of M. le Chevalier de Clairac*. Translated by John Muller. London, 1760.

Clinton, George. *Public Papers of George Clinton, First Governor of New York*. 10 vols. Albany: Oliver A. Quayle, 1904.

Clinton, Henry. *Observations on Mr. Stedman's History of the American War*. London: John Debrett, 1794.

_____. *Observations on Some Parts of the Answer of Earl Cornwallis to Sir Henry Clinton's Narrative*. London: John Debrett, 1783.

_____. *The American Rebellion: Sir Henry Clinton's Narrative of His Campaigns, 1775-1782, with an Appendix of Original Documents*. Edited by William B. Willcox. Hamden, Connecticut: Archon Books, 1971.

_____. *The Narrative of Lieutenant-General Sir Henry Clinton, K.B., Relative to His Conduct during Part of His Command of the King's Troops in North America: Particularly to That which Respects the Unfortunate Issue of the Campaign in 1781*. London: John Debrett, 1785.

Clos, Jean Henri. *The Glory of Yorktown*. Yorktown: The Yorktown Historical Society, 1924.

Closen, Ludwig. *The Revolutionary Journal of Baron Ludwig Von Closen, 1780-1783*. Translated and edited by Evelyn M. Acomb. Chapel Hill: University of North Carolina Press, 1958.

Cornwallis, Earl. *An Answer to That Part of the Narrative of Lieutenant-General Sir Henry Clinton, K.B., which Relates to the Conduct of Lieutenant-General Earl Cornwallis, during the Campaign in North America, in the Year 1781*. London: John Debrett, 1783.

Cugnac, General de. *Yorktown (1781). Trois mois d'operations combinees sur terre et sur mer dans une guerre de Coalition*. Nancy-Paris-Strasbourg: Imprimerie Berger-Levrault, 1932.

Custis, George Washington Parke. *Recollections and Private Memoirs of Washington*. New York: Derby and Jackson, 1860.

Davis, Burke. *The Campaign that Won America: The Story of Yorktown*. New York: The Dial Press, 1970.

Dearborn, Henry. *Revolutionary War Journals of Henry Dearborn, 1775-1783*. Edited by Lloyd A. Brown and Howard H. Peckham. Chicago: The Caxton Club, 1939.

Denny, Ebenezer. *Military Journal of Major Ebenezer Denny, An Officer in the Revolutionary and Indian Wars*. Philadelphia: J. B. Lippincott and Company, 1859.

Deux-Ponts, William de. *My Campaigns in America: A Journal Kept By Count William de Deux-Ponts, 1780-81*. Translated and annotated by Samuel Abbott Green. Boston: J. K. Wiggin and William Parsons Lunt, 1868.

Dumas, Mathieu. *Memoirs of His Own Time*. London: Richard Bentley, 1839.

Duncan, Louis C. *Medical Men in the American Revolution, 1775-1783*. Carlisle Barracks, Pennsylvania: Medical Field Service School, 1931. Reprint. Augustus M. Kelley, Publishers, 1970.

Dupuy, Trevor N., Johnson, Curt, and Bongard, David L., comps., eds. *The Harper Encyclopedia of Military Biography*. New York: Harper Collins Publishers, Inc., 1992.

Egle, William H., ed. *Journals and Diaries of the War of the Revolution*. Harrisburg: E. K. Meyers, 1893.

Evans, Emory G. *Thomas Nelson of Yorktown: Revolutionary Virginian*. Williamsburg: The Colonial Williamsburg Foundation, 1975.

Evans, Israel. *A Discourse Delivered Near York in Virginia, on the Memorable Occasion of the Surrender of the British Army to the Allied Forces of America and France*. Philadelphia: Francis Bailey, 1782.

Ferguson, Homer L. *Salvaging Revolutionary Relics from the York River*. Reprinted from *William and Mary College Quarterly Historical Magazine*, 2d ser. 14 (July, 1939).

Ferling, John E. *Setting the World Ablaze: Washington, Adams, Jefferson and the American Revolution*. New York: Oxford University Press, 2000.

Fiske, Nathan. *An Oration Delivered at Brookfield, Nov. 14, 1781, in Celebration of the Capture of Lord Cornwallis and his Whole Army at York-Town and Gloucester, in Virginia*. Boston: Thomas and John Fleet, 1781.

Fleming, Thomas J. *Beat the Last Drum: The Siege of Yorktown, 1781*. New York: St. Martin's Press, 1963.

Freeman, Douglas Southall. *George Washington: A Biography*. 6 vols. New York: Charles Scribner's Sons, 1952.

Garden, Alexander. *Anecdotes of the American Revolution*. Charleston, 1828.

Gardiner, Robert, ed. *Navies and the American Revolution, 1775-1783*. Anapolis, Md.: Naval Institute Press, 1996.

Graham, James J., ed. *Memoir of General Graham with Notices of the Campaigns in which He was Engaged from 1779 to 1801*. Edinburgh: R. and R. Clark, 1862.

Greene, George Washington. *The German Element in the War of American Independence*. New York: Hurd and Houghton, 1876.

Hamilton, Alexander. *The Works of Alexander Hamilton*. Edited by John C. Hamilton. 2 vols. New York: Charles S. Francis and Company, 1851.

Harper's Encyclopaedia of United States History, From 458 A.D. to 1902. 10 vols. New York: Harper and Brothers, Publishers, 1902.

Hatch, Charles E., Jr. *Yorktown and the Siege of 1781*. Washington: United States Government Printing Office, 1957.

_____. *Historic Resource Study, Yorktown's Main Street (From Secretary Nelson's to the Windmill) and Military Entrenchments Close In and Around the Town of York, Colonial National Historical Park, Virginia*. Denver: National Park Service, 1974.

_____. *Historic Resource Study, "York Under The Hill," Yorktown's Waterfront, Colonial National Historical Park, Virginia.* Denver: National Park Service, 1973.

_____, and Greene, Jerome A. *Historic Structure Report, Combined Study Developed Sites and Colonial Rural Fences, Yorktown Battlefield, Colonial National Historical Park, Virginia.* Denver: National Park Service, 1975.

_____, and Pitkin, Thomas M., eds. *Yorktown, Climax of the Revolution.* Washington: National Park Service, 1941.

Hatch, Louis Clinton. *The Administration of the American Revolutionary Army.* New York: Longmans, Green, and Company, 1904.

Heath, William. *Heath's Memoirs of the American War.* 1798. Reprint. New York: A. Wessels Company, 1904.

Heitman, Francis B. *Historical Register of Officers of the Continental Army during the War of the Revolution, April, 1775, to December, 1783.* rev. ed. Washington: The Rare Book Shop Publishing Company, Inc., 1914.

Hendrickson, Robert A. *The Rise and Fall of Alexander Hamilton.* New York: Van Nostrand Reinhold, 1981.

Higginbotham, Don. *The War of American Independence: Military Attitudes, Policies, and Practice, 1763-1789.* New York: The Macmillan Company, 1971.

_____, and Nebenzahl, Kenneth. *Atlas of the American Revolution.* Chicago: Rand McNally and Company, 1974.

Hoyt, Epaphras. *Practical Instructions for Military Officers.* Greenfield, Massachusetts: John Denio, 1811. Reprint. Greenwood Press, Publishers, 1971.

Hunt, Gaillard, ed. *Fragments of Revolutionary History.* 1892. Reprint. New York: Arno Press, 1970.

Idzerda, Stanley J. (ed.), *Lafayette in the Age of the American Revolution: Selected Letters and Papers, 1776-1790.* 5 vols.; Ithaca, N.Y.: Cornell U. Press, 1977-83, vol. 4.

Irving, Washington. *Life of George Washington.* 5 vols. New York: G P. Putnam and Company, 1857.

James, Bartholomew. *Journal of Rear-Admiral Bartholomew James, 1752-1828.* John Knox Laughton, ed. London: Publications of the Naval Records Society, 1896.

Johnston, Henry P. *The Yorktown Campaign and the Surrender of Cornwallis.* New York: Harper and Brothers, 1881.

Kaplan, Sidney and Kaplan, Emma. *The Black Presence in the Era of the American Revolution Revolution* (U of MA Press: Amherst, 1989).

Katcher, Philip R. N. *Encyclopedia of British, Provincial, and German Army Units 1775-1783* (Harrisburg PA: Stackpole Co., 1973).

Keim, DeB. Randolph. *Rochambeau. A Commemoration by the Congress of the United States of America of the Services of the French Auxiliary Forces in the War of Independence.* Washington: United States Government Printing Office, 1907.

Kemp, Alan. *American Soldiers of the Revolution.* London: Almark Publishing Company, Ltd., 1972.

Ketchum, Richard M. *The World of George Washington.* New York: American Heritage Press, 1974.

Kidder, Frederic. *History of the First New Hampshire Regiment in the War of the Revolution.* Albany: Joel Munsell, 1868.

Lafayette, Marie Jean Paul Roch Yves Gilbert Motier, Marquis de. Memoirs, *Correspondence and Manuscripts of General Lafayette*. 2 vols. New York: Saunders and Otley, 1837.

Lallemand, H. *A Treatise on Artillery*. 2 vols. New York: C. S. Van Winkle, 1820.

Lamb, Roger. *An Original and Authentic Journal of Occurrences During the Late American War, from its Commencement to the Year 1783*. Dublin: Wilkinson and Courtney, 1809.

Landers, H. L. *Yorktown. The Investment of Yorktown, October; 1781*. Washington: Army War College, 1931.

Landman, I. *The Field Engineer's Vade-mecum*. London: W. and C. Spilsbury, 1802.

Leake, Isaac Q. *Memoir of the Life and Times of General John Lamb*. Albany: Joel Munsell, 1850.

Le Blond, Guillaume. *A Treatise of Artillery*. Translated from the French. London: E. Cave, 1746.

_____. *Elemens de Fortification*. Paris: Charles-Antoine Jombert, 1764.

Lee, Henry. *Memoirs of the War in the Southern Department of the United States*. rev. ed. New York: University Publishing Company, 1870.

Lee, Henry, Jr. *The Campaign of 1781 in the Carolinas*. Philadelphia, 1824. Reprint. Quadrangle Books, Inc., 1962.

Lendy, A. F. *Treatise on Fortification*. London: W. Mitchell, Military Bookseller, 1862.

Linn, John Blair, and Egle, William H., eds. *Pennsylvania in the War of the Revolution, Battalions and Line, 1775-1783*. Harrisburg: Lane S. Hart, State Printer, 1880

Lochée, Lewis. *Elements of Field Fortification*. London: T. Cadell, 1783.

Lossing, Benson J. *Pictorial Field-Book of the Revolution*. 2 vols. New York: Harper and Brothers, Publishers, 1855.

Mackenzie, Roderick. *Strictures on Lt. Col. Tarleton's History "of the Campaigns of 1780 and 1781, in the Southern Provinces of North America."* London: R. Faulder, 1787.

Mackesy, Piers. *The War for America, 1775-1783*. Cambridge, Massachusetts: Harvard University Press, 1965.

Mahan, Alfred Thayer. *The Influence of Sea Power Upon History, 1660-1783*. Boston: Little, Brown, and Company, 1908.

Malo, Servan. *The Men of Yorktown. Uniforms and Flags Drawn After Official Documents*. Paris: Georges Bertrand, 1918.

Manucy, Albert. *Artillery Through the Ages: A Short Illustrated History of Cannon, Emphasizing Types Used in America*. Washington: United States Government Printing Office, 1949.

Marshall, John. *The Life of George Washington, Commander in Chief of the American Forces . . . and First President of the United States*. 5 vols. London: Richard Phillips, 1805.

Martin, Joseph Plumb. *Private Yankee Doodle Being a Narrative of Some of the Adventures, Dangers and Sufferings of a Revolutionary Soldier*. Hallowell, Maine, 1830. Reprint. Edited by George F. Scheer. Boston: Little, Brown, and Company, 1962.

Matloff, Maurice., ed. *American Military History*. Washington: Office of the Chief of Military History, 1969.

Mattern, David B. *Benjamin Lincoln and the American Revolution*. Columbia: University of South Carolina Press, 1996.

McHenry, James. *A Sidelight on History, Being the Letters of James McHenry, Aide-de-Camp of the Marquis de Lafayette to Thomas Sim Lee, Governor of Maryland, Written during the Yorktown Campaign, 1781*. N. p.: Privately printed, 1931.

Merlant, Joachim. *Soldiers and Sailors of France in the American War for Independence (1776-1783)*. Translated by Mary Bushnell Coleman. New York: Charles Scribner's Sons, 1920.

Miller, John C. *Alexander Hamilton and the Growth of the New Nation*. New York: Harper and Row, Publishers, 1959.

Mitchell, Broadus. *Alexander Hamilton: Youth to Maturity, 1755-1788*. New York: The Macmillan Company, 1957.

Mollo, John, and McGregor, Malcolm. *Uniforms of the American Revolution*. New York: Macmillan Publishing Company, Inc., 1975.

Moore, Frank, comp. *Diary of the American Revolution, from Newpapers and Original Documents*. 2 vols. New York: Charles Scribner, 1860.

Moore, H. N. *Life and Services of Gen. Anthony Wayne*. Philadelphia: Leary, Getz and Company, 1859.

Muhlenberg, Henry A. *The Life of Major-General Peter Muhlenberg of the Revolutionary Army*. Philadelphia: Carey and Hart, 1849.

Muller, John. *A Treatise Containing the Elementary Part of Fortification, Regular and Irregular*. London: J. Nourse, 1746. Reprint. Museum Restoration Service, 1968.

_____. *A Treatise of Artillery*. London: John Millan, 1757.

Nelson, Thomas, Jr. *Letters of Thomas Nelson, Jr., Governor of Virginia*. Richmond: Virginia Historical Society, 1874.

North, Rene. *Military Uniforms, 1686-1918*. New York: Grosset and Dunlap, Publishers, 1970.

Orderly Book of the Siege of Yorktown, from September 26th, 1781, to November 2nd, 1781. Philadelphia: Antique Press, 1865.

Palmer, John McAuley. *General Von Steuben*. New Haven: Yale University Press, 1937.

Palmer, William P., ed. *Calendar of Virginia State Papers and Other Manuscripts, from January 1, 1782, to December 31, 1784*. 11 vols. Richmond: Virginia State Library, 1883.

Pancake, John S. *This Destructive War: The British Campaign in the Carolinas, 1780-1782*. Tuscaloosa: University of Alabama Press, 1992.

Peckham, Howard H., ed. *The Toll of Independence: Engagements & Battle Casualties of the American Revolution*. Chicago: University of Chicago Press, 1974.

_____. *The War for Independence: A Military History*. Chicago: University of Chicago Press, 1958.

Peterson, Harold L. *Round Shot and Ramners*. Harrisburg: Stackpole Books, 1969.

_____. *The Book of the Continental Soldier*. Harrisburg: Stackpole Company, 1968.

Pickering, Octavius, and Upham, C. W. *The Life of Timothy Pickering*. 4 vols. Boston: Little, Brown, and Company, 1867-1873.

Pitkin, Thomas M., et al. *A Bibliography of the Virginia Campaign and Siege of Yorktown,1781*. Yorktown: Colonial National Historical Park, 1941.

Popp, Stephen. *Popp's Journal, 1777-1783*. Edited by Joseph G. Rosengarten. Reprint from *Pennsylvania Magazine of History and Biography*. Philadelphia, 1902.

Quarles, Benjamin. *The Negro in the American Revolution* (U of NC Press, Williamsburg, VA 1961).

Radziwill, Princess, trans. *They Knew the Washingtons: Letters from a French Soldier with Lafayette and from His Family in Virginia*. Indianapolis: The Bobbs-Merrill Company, 1926.

Reps, John W. *Tidewater Towns: City Planning in Colonial Virginia and Maryland*. Williamsburg: Colonial Williamsburg Foundation, 1972.

Rice, Howard C., Jr., and Brown, Anne S. K., eds. *The American Campaigns of Rochambeau's Army, 1780, 1781, 1782, 1783*. 2 vols. Princeton and Providence: Princeton and Brown University Presses, 1972.

Robin, Claude C. *New Travels through North America*. Philadelphia: Robert Bell, 1783.

Rochambeau, Jean Baptiste Donatien, Count de. *Relation, ou Journal des Operations*. Colophon: A Philadelphie De l'Imprimerie de Guillaume Hampton, 1781. Facsimile: Americana Series; *Photostat Reproductions by the Massachusetts Historical Society*, No. 225. Boston, 1929.

Rodenbaugh, Theophilus F., ed. *Uncle Sam's Medal of Honor, 1861-1886*. New York: G. P. Putnam's Sons, 1886.

Royster, Charles. *A Revolutionary People at War: The Continental Army and American Character, 1775-1783*. New York: Norton Publishers, 1981.

Savas, Theodore P., and Dameron, J. David. *A Guide to the Battles of the American Revolution*. Savas Beatie, 2005. (Manuscript to be published in 2005)

Scheer, George F., and Rankin, Hugh . *Rebels and Redcoats*. New York: The New American Library, 1957.

Scott, Samuel F. *From Yorktown To Valmy: The Transformation of the French Army in an Age of Revolution*. Niwot CO: University Press of Colorado, 1998.

Selig, Robert A. *Hussars in Lebanon! A Connecticut town and Lauzun's Legion during the American Revolution* (Lebanon, CT, 2004).

Shreve, L.G. *Tench Tilghman: The Life and Times of Washington's Aide-de-Camp*. Centreville, Md.: Tidewater Publishers, 1982.

Simcoe, John Graves. *Military Journal: A History of the Operations of a Partisan Corps called The Queen's Rangers, commanded by Lieut.-col. J. G. Simcoe, during the War of the Revolution*. New York, 1844.

Smelser, Marshall. *The Winning of Independence*. New York: New Viewpoints, 1973.

Smith, George. *An Universal Military Dictionary: A Copious Explanation of the Technical Terms etc. Used in the Equipment, Machinery, Movements, and Military Operations of an Army*. London: J. Millan, 1779.

Spiller, Roger J., Dawson, Joseph G. III, and Williams, T. Harry. *Dictionary of American Military Biography*. 3 vols. Westport, Conn.: Greenwood Press, 1984.

Stedman, Charles. *The History of the Origin, Progress, and Termination of the American War*. 2 vols. London: Printed for the Author, 1794.

Steenhagen, Robert L., et al. *A Master Plan for Colonial National Historical Park.* Washington: National Park Service, 1971.

Steuben, Friedrick Wilhelm Ludolf Gerhard Augustin Von. *Regulations for the Order and Discipline of the Troops of the United States.* Philadelphia: Styner and Cist, 1779.

Stevens, William. *A System for the Discipline of the Artillery of the United States of America; or, The Young Artillerists' Pocket Companion.* Albany: Websters and Skinners, 1815.

Stille, Charles J. *Major-General Anthony Wayne and the Pennsylvania Line in the Continental Army.* Philadelphia: J. B. Lippincott Company, 1893.

Stone, Edwin Martin. *Our French Allies.* Providence: Providence Press Company, 1884.

Straith, Hector. *Treatise on Fortification and Artillery.* 2 vols. London: William H. Allen and Company, 1852.

Strykcr, William S. *New Jersey Continental Line in the Virginia Campaign of 1781.* Trenton: John L. Murphy, 1882.

Tallmadge, Samuel. *Orderly Books of the Fourth New York Regiment, 1778-1780, The Second New York Regiment, 1780-1783, by Samuel Tallmadge and others with Diaries of Samuel Tallmadge, 1780-1782 and John Barr, 1779-1782.* Edited by Almon W. Lauber. Albany: University of the State of New York, 1932.

Tarleton, Banastre. *A History of the Campaigns of 1780 and 1781, in the Southern Provinces of North America.* Dublin: Colles, Exshaw, White, H. Whitestone, Burton, Byrne, Moore, Jones, and Dornin, 1787.

Thacher, James. *A Military Journal during the American Revolutionary War, from 1775 to 1783.* Boston: Cottons and Barnard, 1827.

Thayer, Theodore. *Yorktown: Campaign of Strategic Options.* Philadelphia: J. B. Lippincott Company, 1975.

Thompson, Erwin N. *Historic Resource Study, The British Defenses of Yorktown, 1781, Colonial National Historical Park, Virginia.* Denver: National Park Service, 1976.

Tielke, J. G. *The Field Engineer; or Instructions Upon Every Branch of Field Fortification.* Translated by Edwin Hewgill. 2 vols. London: J. Walter, 1789.

Tilghman, Oswald. *Memoir of Lieut. Col. Tench Tilghman, Secretary and Aid to Washington.* Albany: J. Munsell, 1876.

Tousard, Louis de. *American Artillerist's Companion, or Elements of Artillery.* 3 vols. Philadelphia: C. and A. Conrad and Company, 1809. Reprint. Greenwood Press, Publishers, 1969.

Treacy, M. F. *Prelude to Yorktown: The Southern Campaign of Nathanael Greene, 1780-1781.* Chapel Hill: University of North Carolina Press, 1963.

Trumbull, John. *Autobiography, Reminiscences and Letters of John Trumbull, from 1756 to 1841.* New York: Wiley and Putnam, 1841.

Vauban, Sebastien LePrestre de. *A Manual of Siegecraft and Fortification.* London, 1740. Reprint. Translated by George A. Rothrock. Ann Arbor: University of Michigan Press, 1968.

Verner, Coolie. *Maps of the Yorktown Campaign 1780-1781. A Preliminary Checklist of Printed and Manuscript Maps Prior to 1800.* London: The Map Collectors' Circle, 1965.

Virginia Council of State. *Journals of the Council of the State of Virginia*. Edited by H. R. McIlwaine. 4 vols. Richmond: Virginia State Library, 1932.

Washington, George. *The Diaries of George Washington, 1748-1799*. Edited by John C. Fitzpatrick. 4 vols. Boston and New York: Houghton Mifflin Company, 1925.

_____. *The Writings of George Washington, from the Original Manuscript Sources, 1745-1799*. Edited by John C. Fitzpatrick. 39 vols. Washington: United States Government Printing Office, 1937.

Webster, Noah. *1781 Yorktown. Letter from Noah Webster to George Washington, and from George Washington to Noah Webster*. Brooklyn: Privately printed, 1881.

Weems, M. L. *The Life of George Washington*. Philadelphia: M. Carey and Son, 1818.

Weigley, Russell F. *History of the United States Army*. New York: The Macmillan Company, 1967.

Weincek, Henry. *An Imperfect God: George Washington, His Slaves, and the Creation of America*. New York: Farrar, Straus, and Giroux, 2003.

Whitridge, Arnold. *Rochambeau*. New York: The Macmillan Company, 1965.

Wickwire, Franklin, and Wickwire, Mary. *Cornwallis: The American Adventure*. Boston:Houghton Mifflin Company, 1970.

_____. *Cornwallis: The Imperial Years*. Chapel Hill: University of North Carolina Press, 1980.

Wilbur, C. Keith. *Picture Book of the Continental Soldier*. Harrisburg: Stackpole Books, 1969.

Wilhelm, Thomas. *A Military Dictionary and Gazetteer*. Philadelphia: L. R. Hamersly and Company, 1881.

Willcox, William B. *Portrait of a General: Sir Henry Clinton in the War of Independence*. New York: Alfred A. Knopf, 1962.

_____. *The British Road to Yorktown: A Study in Divided Command*. Reprinted from *American Historical Review* 52 (October, 1946).

Williams, Catherine R. *Biography of Revolutionary Heroes: Containing the Life of Brigadier Gen. William Barton, and Also, of Captain Stephen Olney*. Providence: Published by the Author, 1839.

Winsor, Justin, ed. *The American Revolution: A Narrative, Critical and Bibliographical History*. Reprint. New York: Bicentennial Sons of Liberty Publication, 1972.

Wood, Gordon S. *The American Revolution: A History*. New York: Random House, 2002.

Wright, Robert K., Jr. *The Continental Army*. Washington, D.C.: Center for Military History, 1983.

Yule, Henry. *Fortification for Officers of the Army and Students of Military History*. London: William Blackwood and Sons, 1851.

Index